The Organization
of American States

The Organization of American States

O. CARLOS STOETZER

Second Edition

PRAEGER

Westport, Connecticut
London

Copyright Acknowledgments

The author and publisher gratefully acknowledge the following for permission to reproduce copyrighted materials:

The Organization of American States, Department of General Legal Services (General Secretariat)

The Organization of American States, Department of Legal Affairs

Oceana Publications

Duke University Press, for permission to quote from M. Margaret Ball. *The OAS in Transition.* Copyright © 1969, Duke University Press, Durham, North Carolina. Reprinted by permission of the publisher.

Library of Congress Cataloging-in-Publication Data

Stoetzer, O. Carlos.
   [Panamerika, Idee und Wirklichkeit. English]
   The Organization of American States / O. Carlos Stoetzer.—2nd
ed.
     p. cm.
   Includes bibliographical references and index.
   ISBN 0–275–93633–3 (alk. paper)
   1. Organization of American States—History. 2. Pan-Americanism—
History. I. Title.
KDZ1134.S7613 1993
341.24'5—dc20   92–1752

British Library Cataloguing in Publication Data is available.

Copyright © 1993 by O. Carlos Stoetzer

Library of Congress Catalog Card Number: 92–1752
ISBN 0–275–93633–3

First published in 1993

Praeger Publishers, 88 Post Road West, Westport, CT 06881
An imprint of Greenwood Publishing Group, Inc.

Printed in the United States of America

The paper used in this book complies with the
Permanent Paper Standard issued by the National
Information Standards Organization (Z39.48–1984).

10 9 8 7 6 5 4 3 2 1

Contents

Preface to the First American Edition (1965)   vii

Preface to the Second Edition   ix

Acknowledgments   xi

Abbreviations   xiii

1. Basis and Background: Simón Bolívar and the Different Interpretations of His Vision of American Union   1

2. The Pan American Movement from the Union of American Republics to the Organization of American States: The First Four Phases (1889–1890 through 1948)   13

3. The Strengthened Inter-American System: The Establishment of the OAS   31

4. The OAS (1948 through 1967–1970): The Inter-American Conference, the Meeting of Consultation of Ministers of Foreign Affairs, and the Council of the OAS   39

5. The OAS (1948 through 1967–1970): The Pan American Union   67

6. The OAS (1948 through 1967–1970): The Specialized Conferences and Specialized Organizations, Agencies, and Commissions   97

 7. The Road toward the Revision of the Charter   135

 8. The Revised Charter and the New Structure of the OAS   149

 9. The Last Two Decades and the Protocol of Cartagena de
    Indias (1970–1991)   199

10. Related Organizations: Latin America and the Caribbean
    Connection   229

11. The OAS and International Law, Human Rights, and
    Democracy   241

12. The OAS and Peace and Security   265

13. The Balance Sheet and the Future   293

    Appendixes   303

    Notes   399

    Bibliography   409

    Index   417

Preface to the First American Edition (1965)

This work was originally published in German in May, 1964, as the second volume of a series of the recently established Institute of Ibero-American Studies of Hamburg. It was intended as an introduction to a field about which German-speaking Europeans had heard a great deal in recent years but with which few were acquainted. The need for such an introductory book on the OAS was further enhanced by the traditionally close ties between Europe and Latin America and the increasing collaboration of the OAS with Europe and the European intergovernmental organizations.

Although there exist several specialized books on the OAS in this country, it was found that there was a definite need for an introductory work especially geared to students of Latin American affairs and of international organizations and politics. This book does not lay claim to being exhaustively detailed; it is intended as a concise and comprehensive account of the structure and activities of the OAS. Its publication coincides with the seventy-fifth anniversary of the founding of the Pan American Union.

The present book, although a translation of the German volume, has been brought up to date to include references to the latest Meeting of Consultation of Ministers of Foreign Affairs, held in Washington, D.C., in July, 1964; to the special Inter-American Conference, held in Washington, D.C., in December, 1964; and to a new inter-American institution, the Inter-American Committee on the Alliance for Progress (ICAP), which became affiliated with the Inter-American Economic and Social Council after the original version was published in Hamburg in May, 1964. Several other minor changes and additions have also been made.

For the sake of clarity, the United States is always referred to by that name and not "America," a term that might be misinterpreted, since Latin

Americans rightly also consider themselves Americans. With regard to the other members of the OAS, I have used the term "Spanish America" for the eighteen Spanish-speaking nations south of the border, "Hispanic America" for these eighteen republics and Brazil, and "Latin America" for the totality of the twenty independent republics (including Haiti).

Preface to the Second Edition

The first edition of the book was published in 1965, at a time when international cooperation on both the world scene and the regional level was riding high, perhaps being best symbolized by John F. Kennedy's idealism and optimism. In the Americas this was best reflected by the Alliance for Progress, which was launched in Punta del Este, Uruguay, in 1961.

Twenty-five years have since elapsed: years that have seen major political, social, and economic changes in the Americas. These changes have affected the relations between the United States and the various Latin American and Caribbean countries. As the latter achieved independence, they became members of the Organization of American States (OAS), changing the character of what had been, until then, a regional intergovernmental association in which the United States cooperated with twenty Latin American republics.

Also gone are the days of the Good Neighbor and the Fair Neighbor policies, and the Alliance for Progress no longer captures the imagination of the hemisphere. The new realities of the last third of the twentieth century are reflected in major structural transformations within the inter-American system. After 1970 the OAS was governed by the Protocol of Amendment to the charter of the organization, the Protocol of Buenos Aires of 1967, and since 1988 it has been governed by the new revision of the charter, the Protocol of Cartagena de Indias of 1985. Both represent adjustments of the organization to these new realities as they have made themselves felt.

Despite numerous upheavals, reflecting the revolutionary character of the period, and a general decline of the organization in the last few decades (highlighted by the war in the South Atlantic, U.S. interventions in Central America, and especially the U.S. invasion of Panama), the OAS has been able to survive and to face optimistically and with renewed energy the even more difficult realities of the 1990s. The entrance of Canada as a member and a new awareness by the United States that its "power politics"—trying to impose its will and intervene whenever it sees fit—have limitations and that the OAS can serve a useful task after all all have combined to give the OAS a sense of renewal as the twentieth century draws to a close.

It is this background that justifies a second edition, which has been revised and enlarged and incorporates the major changes that have occurred in the last twenty-five years within the inter-American system. This new, updated edition thus reflects the increasing importance of the OAS as it enters the last decade of the twentieth century and at a time when international debt and illegal drugs, democracy and human rights, international trade, and the economic and political integration of Latin America and the Caribbean represent new challenges. Finally, this publication will coincide with the fifth centennial of Columbus's discovery of America, "The Encounter of Two Worlds," when both North and South America, together with the Iberian countries, will join in celebrating this historic event.

Acknowledgments

I wish to thank Celso Rodríguez, editor of the *Inter-American Review of Bibliography*, Department of Cultural Affairs of the Organization of American States in Washington, D.C., for his enthusiastic encouragement and many valuable suggestions in carrying out this new study on the OAS. I also wish to express my deep appreciation to the Columbus Memorial Library for its kindness in providing me with the records of the many Meetings of Consultation of Ministers of Foreign Affairs and for the records of the General Assembly annual sessions, as well as special sessions, of the last twenty years. I also want to thank Edgar Maya, Director of the Office of Public Relations, and Clarita Altamar, of the Office of Council and Conferences Services of the General Secretariat of the OAS, for their generosity in providing me with important information and documents necessary for the manuscript. Finally, I would like to express my gratitude to the Director of Research Services of Fordham University, Nancy McCarthy, as well as to her Administrative Assistant, Laura Ebert, for the financial help that allowed me to travel to the headquarters of the OAS in 1990 and 1991.

Abbreviations

AALAPSO	*Afro-Asian-Latin American Peoples' Organization*
ADELA	Atlantic Community Development Group for Latin America
AIESEC	*Association Internationale des Etudiants en Sciences Economiques et Commerciales* (International Association of Students in the Economic and Commercial Sciences)
AIFLD	American Institute for Free Labor Development (U.S.)
ALADI	*Asociación Latinoamericana de Integración* (Latin American Association for Integration)
ALALC	*Asociación Latinoamericana de Libre Comercio* (Latin American Free Trade Association, LAFTA)
APRA	*Alianza Popular Revolucionaria Americana* (Peru) (American Popular Revolutionary Alliance)
ASEP	*Acuerdo Sudamericano de Esencias Psicotropicales* (South American Accord on Narcotic Drugs and Psychotropic Substances)
BID	*Banco Interamericano de Desarrollo* (Inter-American Development Bank, IDB)
CAC	*Comité de Acción Cultural* (Cultural Action Committee)
CACM	Central American Common Market (*Mercado Común Centroamericano*, MCCA)
CARICOM	Caribbean Community
CARIFTA	Caribbean Free Trade Association

CCD	*Comité Consultivo de Defensa* (Advisory Defense Committee)
CEC	*Cuenta Especial de Cultura* (Special Cultural Account)
CECAL	*Comité Européen de Coopération avec l'Amérique Latine* (European Committee for Cooperation with Latin America)
CECE	*Comisión Especial para Estudiar la Formulación de Nuevas Medidas de Cooperación Económica (Comisión de los 21)* (Special Committee to Study the Formulation of New Measures of Economic Cooperation [Committee of the 21])
CECLA	*Comisión Especial de Coordinación Latinoamericana* (Special Committee on Latin American Coordination, SLAC)
CECON	*Comisión Especial de Consulta y Negociación* (Special Commission for Consultation and Negotiation)
CECS	*Comisión Especial de Consulta sobre Seguridad* (Special Consultative Committee on Security, SCCS)
CEIFI	*Comisión Especial para una Institución Financiera Interamericana* (Special Committee for an Inter-American Financial Institution)
CEMLA	*Centro de Estudios Monetarios Latinoamericanos* (Center of Latin American Monetary Studies)
CENDES	*Centro de Desarrollo de la Universidad Central de Venezuela* (Development Center of the Central University of Venezuela)
CEPAL	*Comisión Económica para la América Latina* (UN) (Economic Commission for Latin America, ECLA)
CEPCIECC	*Comisión Ejecutiva Permanente del Consejo Interamericano para la Educación, la Ciencia y la Cultura* (Permanent Executive Commission of the Inter-American Council for Education, Science and Culture)
CEPCIES	*Comisión Ejecutiva Permanente del Consejo Interamericano Económico y Social* (Permanent Executive Commission of the Inter-American Economic and Social Council)
CEPERN	*Centro Panamericano de Entrenamiento para la Evaluación de Recursos Naturales* (Pan American Training Center for the Evaluation of Natural Resources)
CERA	*Comisión Especial de Expertos para el Estudio de las Necesidades Financieras que Plantea la Ejecución de Planes de Reforma Agraria* (Special Commission of Experts for the Study of the Financial Needs for the Execution of Agrarian Reform Plans)
CIAP	*Comité Interamericano de la Alianza para el Progreso* (Inter-American Committee of the Alliance for Progress, ICAP)
CIAT	*Centro Interamericano de Administradores Tributarios* (Inter-American Center for Tax Administrators)

CIC   *Consejo Interamericano Cultural*
(Inter-American Cultural Council, ICC)

CICAD   *Comisión Interamericana para el Control del Abuso de Drogas*
(Inter-American Drug Abuse Control Commission)

CICYP   *Consejo Interamericano de Comercio y Produccion*
(Inter-American Council of Commerce and Production)

CICYT   *Comité Interamericano de Ciencia y Tecnología*
(Inter-American Committee for Science and Technology)

CID   *Comité Interamericano de Desarrollo*
(Inter-American Committee on Development)

CIDEC   *Comité Interamericano de Cultura*
(Inter-American Cultural Committee)

CIDEM   *Consejo Interamericano de Música*
(Inter-American Music Council, IMC)

CIDH   *Comisión Interamericana de Derechos Humanos*
(Inter-American Commission on Human Rights, IACHR)

CIDIP   *Conferencia Interamericana de Derecho Internacional Privado*
(Inter-American Conference on Private International Law)

CIE   *Centre International de l'Enfance*
(International Childhood Centre)

CIE   *Comité Interamericano de Educación*
(Inter-American Educational Committee)

CIECC   *Consejo Interamericano para la Educación, la Ciencia y la Cultura*
(Inter-American Council for Education, Science and Culture)

CIEF   *Centro Interamericano de Enseñanza de Estadística Económica y Financiera*
(Inter-American Teaching Center for Economic and Financial Statistics)

CIEN   *Comisión Interamericana de Energía Nuclear*
(Inter-American Nuclear Energy Commission, IANEC)

CIENES   *Centro Interamericano de Enseñanza de Estadística*
(Inter-American Statistical Teaching Center)

CIER   *Centro Interamericano de Educación Rural*
(Inter-American Center for Rural Education)

CIES   *Consejo Interamericano Económico y Social*
(Inter-American Economic and Social Council, IA-ECOSOC)

CIESPAL   *Centro Internacional de Estudios Superiores de Periodismo para América Latina*
(International Center for Advanced Studies in Journalism for Latin America)

CIET   *Centro Interamericano de Estudios Tributarios*
(Inter-American Center for Tax Studies)

CIJ	*Consejo Interamericano de Jurisconsultos* (Inter-American Council of Jurists, IACJ)
CIM	*Comisión Interamericana de Mujeres* (Inter-American Commission of Women, IACW)
CIME	*Comité Intergubernamental para las Migraciones Europeas* (UN) (Intergovernmental Committee for European Migration, ICEM)
CINVA	*Centro Interamericano de Vivienda y Planeamiento* (Inter-American Center for Housing and Planning)
CIP	*Comisión Interamericana de Paz* (Inter-American Peace Committee, IAPC)
CIRA	*Centro de Adiestramiento en Reforma Agraria* (Inter-American Agrarian Reform Center)
CIRP	*Comité Interamericano de Representantes de los Presidentes* (Inter-American Committee of Representatives of the Presidents)
CITEL	*Comisión Interamericana de Telecommunicaciones* (Inter-American Telecommunications Commission)
CJI	*Comité Jurídico Interamericano* (Inter-American Juridical Committee, IAJC)
CMP	*Cuenta Mar de Plata* (Mar de Plata Account)
COAS	Council of the Organization of American States
COEA	*Consejo de la Organización de los Estados Americanos* (Council of the Organization of American States, COAS)
COINS	*Comisión de Mejoramiento de las Estadísticas Nacionales* (Commission for the Improvement of National Statistics)
COPACA	*Comité Directivo Permanente de los Congresos Panamericanos* (Permanent Executive Committee of the Pan American Congresses)
COTPAL	*Comité Técnico Permanente sobre Asuntos Laborales* (Permanent Technical Committee on Labor Matters)
CPD	*Comité Consultivo de Emergencia para la Defensa Política* (Emergency Advisory Committee for Political Defense)
CPP	*Comisión de Programa y Presupuesto* (OEA) (Committee of Program and Budget, PBC) (OAS)
CREFAL	*Centro Regional de Educación Fundamental para América Latina* (UNESCO-OAS) (Regional Center on Basic Education for Latin America)
EC	European Community
ECCM	Eastern Caribbean Common Market
ECLA	Economic Commission for Latin America (UN)
EEC	European Economic Community
EFTA	European Free Trade Association
EIAP	*Escuela Interamericana de Administración Pública* (Inter-American School of Public Administration)

ELN	*Ejército de Liberación Nacional* (Argentina) (Army of National Liberation)
EURATOM	European Atomic Energy Commission
FAO	Food and Agriculture Organization (UN)
FEAC	*Comité Consultivo Económico Financiero Interamericano* (Inter-American Financial and Economic Advisory Committee)
FEAD	*Fondo Especial de Asistencia para el Desarrollo* (Special Development Assistance Fund, SDAF)
FEDECAME	*Federación Cafetalera de América* (American Coffee Federation)
FEMCIECC	*Fondo Especial Multilateral del Consejo Interamericano para la Educación, la Ciencia y la Cultura* (Special Multilateral Fund of the Inter-American Council for Education, Science and Culture)
FONDEM	*Fondo Interamericano de Emergencia* (Inter-American Fund for Emergency Situations)
GARS	General Assembly—Regular Session
GASS	General Assembly—Special Session
GATT	General Agreement on Tariffs and Trade
GS	General Secretariat
IACHR	Inter-American Commission on Human Rights
IACI	Inter-American Children's Institute
IACJ	Inter-American Council of Jurists
IACW	Inter-American Commission of Women
IADB	Inter-American Defense Board
IA-ECOSOC	Inter-American Economic and Social Council
IAIAS	Inter-American Institute of Agricultural Sciences; now Inter-American Institute for Cooperation on Agriculture (IICA)
IAII	Inter-American Indian Institute
IAJC	Inter-American Juridical Committee
IANEC	Inter-American Nuclear Energy Commission
IAPC	Inter-American Peace Committee
IAS	Inter-American System
IASI	Inter-American Statistical Institute
IBRD	International Bank for Reconstruction and Development (UN)
ICA	International Cooperation Administration (U.S.)
ICAP	Inter-American Committee of the Alliance for Progress
ICAS	International Conference of American States
ICC	Inter-American Cultural Council
ICEM	Intergovernmental Committee for European Migration (UN)

ICETEX	*Instituto Colombiano de Estudios Técnicos en el Exterior* (Colombian Institute for Technical Studies Abroad)
ICNND	Interdepartmental Committee of Nutrition for National Defense (U.S.)
ICT	*Instituto de Crédito Territorial* (Colombia) (Territorial Credit Institute)
IDB	Inter-American Development Bank
IDC	Inter-American Defense College
IICA	*Instituto Interamericano de Ciencias Agrícolas;* now Institute Interamericano de Cooperación Agrícola (Inter-American Institute of Agricultural Sciences [IAIAS]; now called Inter-American Institute for Cooperation in Agriculture)
IIE	*Instituto Interamericano de Estadística* (Inter-American Statistical Institute, IASI)
III	*Instituto Indigenista Interamericano* (Inter-American Indian Institute, IAII)
IIN	*Instituto Interamericano del Niño* (Inter-American Children's Institute, IACI)
ILAFA	Latin American Iron and Steel Institute
ILO	International Labor Organization (UN)
ILPES	*Instituto Latinoamericano de Planificación Económica y Social* (Latin American Institute for Economic and Social Planning)
IMC	Inter-American Music Council
INCAP	*Instituto de Nutrición de Centroamérica y Panamá* (Institute of Nutrition of Central America and Panama)
IPGH	*Instituto Panamericano de Geografía e Historia* (Pan American Institute of Geography and History, PAIGH)
ISAP	Inter-American Center for Training in Public Administration
JCT	*Junta de Cooperación Técnica* (PCT de la OEA) (Board of Technical Cooperation, Technical Cooperation Program of the OAS)
JID	*Junta Interamericana de Defensa* (Inter-American Defense Board, IADB)
LAFTA	Latin American Free Trade Association
MCCA	*Mercado Común Centroamericano* (Central American Common Market, CACM)
MCMFA	Meeting of Consultation of Ministers of Foreign Affairs (*Reunion de Consulta de Ministros de Relaciones Exteriores*)
NAACP	National Association for the Advancement of Colored Peoples (U.S.)
NAFSA	National Association for Foreign Student Advisors (U.S.)
NAFTA	North American Free Trade Agreement

NGO	Nongovernmental organizations
OAS	Organization of American States (*Organización de los Estados Americanos*, OEA)
OC	Organ of Consultation (*Organo de Consulta*)
ODECA	*Organización de los Estados Centroamericanos* (Organization of Central American States)
OEA	*Organización de los Estados Americanos* (Organization of American States, OAS)
OECD	Organization for Economic Cooperation and Development
OEEC	Organization for European Economic Cooperation (predecessor of OECD)
OICE	*Organización Interamericana de Cooperación Económica* (Inter-American Organization for Economic Cooperation)
OLAS	Organization of Latin American Solidarity
OMS	*Organización Mundial de la Salud* (World Health Organization, WHO [UN])
OPANAL	*Organización para la Prohibición de Armas Nucleares en América Latina* (Organization for the Prohibition of Atomic Weapons in Latin America)
OPS	*Organización Panamericana de la Salud* (Pan American Health Organization, PAHO)
ORIT	*Organización Regional Interamericana de Trabajadores* (Inter-American Regional Workers' Organization)
OSP	*Oficina Sanitaria Panamericana* (Pan American Sanitary Bureau, PASB)
PAHO	Pan American Health Organization
PAIGH	Pan American Institute of Geography and History
PASB	Pan American Sanitary Bureau
PAU	Pan American Union
PBC	Program and Budget Committee (PAU)
PC	Permanent Council (OAS) *Consejo Permanente* (OEA)
PCT	*Programa de Cooperación Técnica* (OEA) (Program of Technical Cooperation, PTC [OAS])
PIAPUR	*Programa Interamericano de Planeamiento Urbano y Regional* (Inter-American Program for Urban and Regional Planning)
PICSA	*Programa Interamericano para el Adiestramiento de Postgraduados en Ciencias Sociales Aplicadas* (Inter-American Program for the Training of Postgraduate Students in Applied Social Sciences)

PICSES	*Programa Interamericano de Estudios Superiores de Ciencias Sociales en la Región del Caribe* (Inter-American Program of Higher Learning in the Social Sciences in the Caribbean Area)
PIEB	*Programa Interamericano de Estadisticas Basicas* (Inter-American Program of Basic Statistics)
POC	Provisional Organ of Consultation (OAS) (*Organo Provisional de Consulta*) (OAS)
PRDC	*Programa Regional de Desarrollo Cultural* (Regional Program of Cultural Development)
PRI	*Partido Revolucionario Institucional* (Mex.) (Institutional Revolutionary Party)
PTCP	Permanent Technical Committee on Ports
RAE	*Reunión Anual Especial* (CIES) (Special Annual Meeting, IA-ECOSOC)
RIT	*Red Interamericana de Telecomunicaciones*
ROCAP	Regional Office for Central America and Panama
SCCS	Special Consultative Committee on Security
SDAF	Special Development Assistance Fund
SELA	*Sistema Económico Latinoamericano* (Latin American Economic System)
SIECA	*Secretaría Permanente del Tratado de Integración Económica Centroamericana* (Permanent Secretariat of the Central American Common Market)
SLAC	Special Committee on Latin American Coordination
SUBCECE	*Subcomisión de la CECE* (OEA) (Subcommittee of CECE [OAS])
UNCTAD	United Nations Conference on Trade and Development
UNESCO	United Nations Educational, Scientific and Cultural Organization
UNIA	Universal Negro Improvement Association (U.S.)
UNIAPAC	*Union Internationale Chrétienne des Dirigeants d'Entreprise* (International Union of Christian Employers)
UNICEF	United Nations Children's Fund
WAY	World Assembly of Youth
WHO	World Health Organization (UN)

1

Basis and Background: Simón Bolívar and the Different Interpretations of His Vision of American Union

The Organization of American States (OAS) is a phenomenon of the twentieth century. The oldest international organization of a regional character, it represents the institutional expression of the inter-American system, which, in turn, is the organizational form taken by the Pan American cooperative effort. Pan-Americanism generally means the expression of the political, cultural, social, and economic solidarity of the American states; in other words, it includes the Spanish-, Portuguese-, English-, French-, and Dutch-speaking republics of the American continent. The inter-American system hence represents the political system in which the Pan American movement is institutionalized as the OAS.

When the Pan-American movement was launched in the years 1889–1890, its membership included nineteen countries: Argentina, Bolivia, Brazil, Chile, Colombia, Costa Rica, the Dominican Republic, Ecuador, El Salvador, Guatemala, Haiti, Honduras, Mexico, Nicaragua, Paraguay, Peru, the United States of America, Uruguay, and Venezuela. In 1948, when the OAS was established, its membership covered two more nations: Cuba and Panama. Finally, in 1990, after one hundred years of activities and achievements, the OAS has a membership of thirty-three countries: Antigua and Barbuda, Argentina, Bahamas, Barbados, Bolivia, Brazil, Canada, Chile, Colombia, Costa Rica, Cuba, Dominica, Dominican Republic, Ecuador, El Salvador, Grenada, Guatemala, Haiti, Honduras, Jamaica, Mexico, Nicaragua, Panama, Paraguay, Peru, St. Kitts and Nevis, Saint Lucia, Saint Vincent and the Grenadines, Suriname, Trinidad and Tobago, the United States, Uruguay, and Venezuela. Belize and Guyana joined in 1991.

The OAS has deep roots that go back to the nineteenth century. Generally speaking, Simón Bolívar, Latin America's supreme hero, is credited with its intellectual creation, but we should distinguish here between various different experiences. First, there was the movement for a purely Spanish-American union, a kind of reconstruction of the old Spanish Empire in America, without Spain or a Spanish king, and based on a federal system. This, strictly speaking, is rooted in Bolívar's political vision of the 1820s.

A second, though different, approach was the truly Pan American movement, the inter-American system, which covered all areas of the American continent. This approach was entirely the instrument of U.S. policy as it evolved in the late nineteenth century to lead and dominate the rest of the continent, even though such a policy is no longer viable.

The difference between the two concepts was well established by Indalecio Liévana Aguirre in his *Bolivarismo y Monroísmo.*[1] The former is linked to Bolívar, the *Pacificador de Colombia* and *Libertador de Venezuela*, while the latter is connected to the policies initiated in 1889 by U.S. Secretary of State James G. Blaine with the First International Conference of American States (ICAS) in Washington, which later, in 1948, resulted in the establishment of the OAS.

There is also a third approach, which represents an extension of the purely Spanish-American feelings of the nineteenth century with the ultimate aim of establishing a united Latin America, including the Caribbean, to be outside the influence and sphere of both the United States and the OAS. This movement for Latin American unity has gained momentum in the past decades ever since the United States chose to abandon the Good Neighbor policy of 1933–1945 and to treat Latin America with increasingly complacent neglect, a sad policy manifested in the Malvinas/Falklands case of 1982 (when the United States should have done everything possible to avoid a war between Argentina and Great Britain and under no circumstances should have joined the British in siding against Latin America), and topped with the U.S. invasion of Panama in 1989. This trend is also the result of Latin America's diminishing role in world affairs, it being recognized that only a united Latin America will be able to face the power of such giants as the United States, Japan, and the European Community.

The Colombian José María Torres Caicedo (1830–1889), who served the governments of Mexico, El Salvador, Uruguay, Venezuela, and Colombia in their European embassies, launched the term "Latin America" in 1856 in his poem *"Las dos Américas."* Extremely critical of North American policies in Central America and the Caribbean, he appealed for a Latin American union to protect against the intrusions of the United States. The concept found expression in his work *Unión Latino-Americana: Pensamiento de Bolívar para formar una Liga America; su origen y sus desarrollos* (1865).[2]

Torres was also highly critical of William Walker's adventures in Nicaragua. Walker (1824–1860), from Nashville, Tennessee, and known by his admirers as the "grey-eyed man of destiny," was a fascinating adventurer who in 1853 invaded the Mexican states of Lower California and Sonora proclaiming both as an independent state with himself as president. Two years later, with a group of some fifty supporters, he landed on the Nicaraguan coast, took sides in the political upheavals in Central America by joining the liberal cause, and became president of Nicaragua. When the United States recognized his government in 1856 it sent shivers through Latin America, which then convoked a special congress (Continental Congress of Santiago, 1856) to deal with the problem. When Walker collided with Vanderbilt interests in Central America, his luck vanished; Juan Rafael Mora Porras, conservative president of Costa Rica, then led a coalition that succeeded in defeating him (May 1, 1857). Walker's attempt to launch a second invasion of Nicaragua as well as subsequent landings in 1858 and 1859 failed. In 1860 he made his way back to Central America, this time attempting a revolt in Honduras that failed when the British captured him. Turned over to Honduran authorities, he was promptly executed.

The Walker episode was seen in Latin America as one more sign of U.S. Manifest Destiny, especially coming so soon after the Mexican war of 1846–1847. To this must be added the Bidlack-Mallarino Treaty between the United States and New Granada of 1846 guaranteeing the United States the right of transit across Panama and representing the legal basis for the construction of the Panama Railroad in 1850–1853; the Hise-Silva Treaty of 1847 between the United States and Nicaragua, which provided for U.S. rights in Nicaragua and which, although never ratified, clearly showed the increasing U.S. involvement in the area; the Nicaraguan concessions of 1849 to Cornelius Vanderbilt for a future isthmian canal; and the Clayton-Bulwer Treaty of 1850 between the U.S. and Great Britain, which provided for joint control of a future transisthmian canal. Finally, these realities also included U.S. attempts to acquire Cuba, an almost permanent fixation since the acquisition of the Floridas in 1819; Franklin Pierce's offer to Spain to buy the island for $130 million in 1853; and the Ostende Manifesto of that same year announcing U.S. intentions either to buy Cuba or to take it with or without the consent of Spain. These events all signaled the growing U.S. interests in the area, with its menacing implications.

As a practical realization, the idea of a Latin American union found expression almost a century later in the *Asociación Latinoamericana de Libre Comercio* (ALALC)— the Latin American Free Trade Association (LAFTA)—which was founded in Montevideo, Uruguay, in 1960. It lasted until 1980 when, at the Nineteenth Extraordinary Conference of ALALC, on June 16–27, 1980, in Acapulco, Mexico, a new agency was set up, the *Asociación Latinoamericana de Desarrollo e Integración* (ALADI)—Latin American Association for Development and Integration—which then replaced the ALALC.

Another example of a purely Latin American approach is the *Comisión Especial de Coordinación Latinoamericana* (CECLA)—Special Coordinating Commission for Latin America—a joint UN–OAS organization that, in 1969, approved a Latin American Consensus (in Viña del Mar, Chile) by which a common Latin American policy was established in regard to the United States, and in 1970, through the Declaration of Buenos Aires, established a common policy toward the European Community.

The *Organización para la Prohibición de Armas Nucleares en América Latina* (OPANAL)—Organization for the Prohibition of Atomic Weapons in Latin America—which was founded in 1967 through the Treaty of Tlaltelolco, represents another tool for Latin American unity. Finally, the same goal is reflected in the *Sistema Económico Latinoamericano* (SELA)—the Latin American Economic System—which was founded in 1975 and represents an impressive unity of some twenty-five Latin American and Caribbean countries.

Moreover, a wide variety of political and economic subdivisions was created. In some cases they were set up as a first step toward Latin American economic and political integration, such as:

the *Grupo Andino* (1969)—Bolivia, Chile, Colombia, Ecuador, and Peru;

the *Cuenca del Río de la Plata* (1970s)—Argentina, Bolivia, Brazil, Paraguay, and Uruguay;

the *Organización de los Estados Centroamericanos* (ODECA, 1951)—Costa Rica, El Salvador, Guatemala, Honduras, and Nicaragua;

the *Mercado Común Centroamericano* (MCCA, 1960)—Costa Rica, El Salvador, Guatemala, Honduras, and Nicaragua;

the *Contadora* group (1983–1986)—Mexico, Colombia, Panama, and Venezuela, established to deal with the situation in Central America; and

the *Cartagena* group (mid-1980s)—Mexico and the ten South American countries, established in an attempt to set up a joint front in regard to the debt problem.

All these groupings, including also the Caribbean movements (the West Indian Federation, CARIFTA, and CARICOM), aimed at a common Latin American and Caribbean policy and also represented a critical stance toward both the United States and the OAS.

On the other hand, there is no question that in the larger context, and despite their conceptual differences, all these regional approaches could be associated with Bolívar's federalist ideas and their first realization in the Congress of Panama of 1826.

THE FORERUNNERS OF THE PRESENT OAS

An early attempt to establish a Spanish-American union, a kind of forerunner to Bolívar's plans, was the famous Memorandum of 1783, written by the count of Aranda, King Charles III of Spain's first secretary until 1792, in which, with prophetic insight in regard to a possible emancipation of

Spanish-America and the dangers of an expanding United States, he proposed to the king the establishment of three independent Spanish-American kingdoms (New Spain, Peru, and *Tierra Firme*), each headed by the three *infantes* (the sons of the royal family) and linked to Spain only dynastically—a proposal that, in a slightly different manner, was also made by Manuel Godoy, the Prince of Peace, Spain's powerful minister from 1792 until his fall in 1808, in 1804. Neither plan was accepted by the Spanish Crown.

As the Spanish-American Revolution took its course, there were many plans for union. In Venezuela it was Francisco de Miranda who, in an ill-fated expedition, attempted in 1806 to free Spanish America and establish an independent nation covering the four old viceroyalties of the Spanish Empire in America. Juan José Castelli and José de San Martín in the River Plate area had similar concepts, as did Bernardo Monteagudo in Upper Peru and Martínez de Rozas and Juan Egaña in Chile. A similar view was expressed by José Cecilio del Valle of Central America. All these individuals embraced, in principle at least, the idea of a united Spanish America once independence had been won.

Another Americanist whose ideas and achievements not only molded his own country but also attempted to establish a union through an American international law was Juan Bautisti Alberdi (1810–1884). He went deeper into the subject matter of an American union, and in his *Memoria sobre la conveniencia y Objetos de un Congreso General Americano* (1844) he conceived of an American international law that enumerated some of the principles that would have to be incorporated into any such union:

Settlement of the territorial boundaries among the American nations,

Protection of commerce,

Founding of a hemisphere-wide bank and public credit,

Construction of international roads,

Extradition of criminals, except persons accused of political crimes,

Arms limitations,

Establishment of a tribunal of international peace,

Determination of American international law,

Prevention and regulation of war,

Promotion of land settlement programs, and

Construction of a trans-Andean railroad.[3]

Increasingly, however, the concept of an independent Spanish America, in its totality, seemed impossible to realize; thus, ideas that were more modest in scope and limited to a smaller area (usually within the borders of a former vice-royalty), were expressed. Thus, in 1811, the Paraguayans Mariano Antonio Molas and Gaspar Rodríguez de Francia expressed support for a confederation of the United Provinces of the River Plate, provided autonomy of the component parts was assured; the previously mentioned Egaña called in the same year for a "Sovereign Diet of South America" that would unite Buenos Aires, Chile, and Peru. Similar concepts were aired at the time by Manuel Belgrano and Bernardino Rivadavia in Buenos Aires for a kingdom uniting the River Plate, Chile, and Peru; Juan Martín de Pueyrredón also had a similar plan for a United Kingdom of Buenos Aires and Chile; and Bernardo O'Higgins, with his Pacific Confederation, as well as San Martín and Bolívar, held similar views in regard to setting up some kind of an Andean federation linked to the River Plate. The establishment of Greater Colombia in 1819 by Bolívar became the first real application of these dreams, and was the only one that, for a short time, survived.

THE PAN AMERICAN MOVEMENT: THE SPANISH-AMERICAN PHASE (1826–1865)

This first phase began with the Congress of Panama. It was convoked by Bolívar, who was far ahead of his time when he elaborated an alliance of reciprocal assistance: an early application of the principle of collective security. This congress represents not only Bolívar's highest political achievement but also the birth of the Pan American movement. It covered the nineteenth century and encompassed a series of attempts at a purely Spanish-American solidarity. It lasted until 1865 and would continue in a different manner when the United States launched its version of the Pan American movement—the inter-American system—the forerunner of the OAS.

Congress of Panama (1826)

After Bolívar's victory at Junín (August 6, 1824) and Antonio José de Sucre's triumph at Ayacucho (December 9, 1824), the Spanish Empire in America began to crumble and the Spanish-American Revolution reached its final goal. It was in those years, between 1822 and 1826, that Bolívar made final plans to convoke the newly born states to a historic congress in Panama. This concept did not fall from the sky in 1825—it had been mentioned earlier in Bolívar's *Carta de Jamaica* of September 6, 1815. In this letter Bolívar reviewed the situation in every region of the Spanish-American realm and looked to the future. The situation in Spanish America resembled that of the Roman Empire when it dissolved and opened the way to new political systems.[4] It was also here that Bolívar imagined that Panama might become the seat of a great Spanish-American federation, just as Corinth had been for the Greeks.

In the year 1822, Vice President Francisco de Paula Santander of Greater Colombia proceeded with Bolívar's plans by signing treaties of union, league, and perpetual confederation with Peru and Chile (1822) and with Buenos

Aires and Mexico (1823). These treaties established a loose confederation in peace and war and called for a common attitude toward foreign powers. Two days before the historic battle of Ayacucho, Bolívar, as head of the Peruvian government, invited the independent governments of Colombia, Mexico, River Plate, Chile, and Guatemala—Central America had seceded from Mexico—to send delegates to Panama so that the assembly of plenipotentiaries could discuss the great problems that the newly free states had to face. This assembly would counsel the governments in regard to all questions of common concern, establish direct contact with all federated states, and thus be a true interpreter of public treaties in case difficulties arose; finally, it would also act as an instrument for conciliation and for the peaceful settlement of disputes.[5]

The historic meeting of the Congress of Panama took place, indeed, in the year 1826, the same year Bolívar proclaimed the famous constitution including a lifetime presidency for himself in imitation of Napoleonic precedents. Actually, the Congress and the constitution went hand in hand and have to be seen as a whole. The Bolivarian or Bolivian Constitution was supposed to furnish the foundation of Bolívar's Federation of the Andes, since the various components of the federation would have the same constitutional document and he would be at its head.

This federation would be the centerpiece of Bolívar's larger league of free nations or confederation. It would cover six or seven federated areas, and the Bolivian Constitution would be the instrument to unite and strengthen the entire structure. From this basis, all other Spanish-American countries would join: Mexico and Central America, Chile, and Argentina. The United States and Haiti were alien elements, as was Brazil, which at that time was not viewed by Bolívar with sympathy. Not only was Brazil a monarchy, but it was also an extended arm of the Holy Alliance in the western hemisphere through family ties to the Austrian court. The Holy Alliance comprised the eastern powers of Austria, Prussia, and Russia and was set up in 1814 to maintain the Allied victory over Napoleonic France and to combat the ideas of the French Revolution—that is, nationalism, liberalism, and republicanism—and Brazil, whether as kingdom (1815) or as empire (1822), persistently attempted to thwart the establishment of republics around its borders and encouraged the establishment of monarchical regimes.

By the time the Congress of Panama met, many things had changed. Only four countries sent representatives to Panama: Greater Colombia, Peru, Mexico, and Central America. Neither Chile nor Argentina accepted the invitation; the former was too involved in domestic problems, while the latter was engaged in a war with Brazil. Bolivia and Paraguay, for different reasons, also declined to attend, and Cuba and Puerto Rico remained in Spanish hands. Great Britain, the Netherlands, and the United States had also been invited, but Britain reacted with much coolness, although it did send an observer, as did the Netherlands. The United States acted with utmost circumspection: It sent two delegates, but one died en route from Bogotá and the other arrived too late, a symbolic prelude to the future relationship with Latin America of that northern neighbor.

This hesitancy already contained the seeds of the distrust that has colored the relationship between the great country to the north and the many Latin American states to the south. However, no one familiar with the history of both regions will be surprised. The colonization of the United States followed a totally different course from that of the Hispanic area of influence. In the north, a political entity that bore the stamp of Puritanism was formed from groups of European origin, without the remnants of the primitive population, while the heritage left by the Hispanic peoples, notably Spain, to the young nations in the south was basically different. The Spanish and Portuguese empires, unlike the Anglo-Saxon countries, which had a parliamentary tradition, rested on a hierarchical order that, in harmony with the historic traditions of the Iberian Peninsula, attempted to assimilate the native populations into its national life. However, no total national integration of the original population (a goal toward which an able colonial government worked) took place. The internal weaknesses resulting from this, as well as the political troubles and growing pains of the nineteenth century, led to the rise of a multitude of states in the south that were internally weak and had no feeling of interrelationship. Spanish-American or Hispanic-American solidarity existed only in theory; in practice, the young states looked to Europe, each going its own way almost without intercommunication, as had been the case in the centuries of Spanish and Portuguese rule.

On this basis, the immediate practical application of the ideas of Pan-American cooperation, or of only a purely Spanish-American cooperative effort, proved to be impossible at that early stage. Thus, Bolívar failed with the idealistic Pan American dreams that he had tried to implement through the Congress of Panama. The Pan American endeavors have only very tardily, and after several fruitless attempts, become actualities. The past failures, however, can be understood only in light of the relationship between the Anglo-Saxon north and the Latin American south, with the latter's many unbalanced elements and Iberian heritage.

The Congress of Panama, which had started its activities on June 22, 1826, signed a Treaty of Union, League, and Perpetual Confederation on July 15, 1826. The four participating countries also signed two more treaties: a convention for common defense and a military agreement for its application. Then they adjourned to Tacubaya, near Mexico City, where these treaties were to be ratified.

The object of the Perpetual Treaty was to protect the sovereignty and the integrity of each of the signatory states against any attempt by foreign powers to interfere in the territories of the confederation. It was a defensive alliance in which an attack on one was interpreted as an attack on all members of this league of free nations. The four states assumed full responsibility to help by all means at their disposal if they were attacked. It thus represented the first modern attempts at collective security. The citizens of the confederated states also enjoyed full rights in the respective countries of the league. Moreover, the relations of the contracting parties were based on full equality, and in the case that disputes arose between them, the league would solve them through the General Assembly (which was supposed to meet every two years in Tacubaya), thus amounting to the first modern attempt at arbitration. Finally, racial discrimination and slavery were eliminated wherever they were still in existence.

The Congress of Panama and its continuation in Tacubaya were failures in that none of the treaties signed were ever ratified. However, the main point is not so much the failure but the seed that Bolívar had planted. The main reason for nonratification was indeed the different political situation in 1826 as compared with 1822: Any threat by the Holy Alliance had evaporated in the meantime.

First Congress of Lima, the "American Congress" (1848)

The Congress of Panama of 1826 was repeated several times during the nineteenth century. Thus, in 1847–1848, the five countries of Bolivia, Chile, Ecuador, New Granada, and Peru met in the First Congress of Lima, which was also called the "American Congress." The background was a possible Spanish reconquest of the Andean states of South America. Three treaties were signed, the most important of which was the Treaty of Lima (February 8, 1848), which again set up a confederation of the signatory nations. There were also treaties on commerce and navigation. However, none of these treaties was ever ratified, and again the immediate reason was similar to that of 1826: The dangers of 1847 had dissipated by the time the different delegates sat down to discuss the necessary measures.

Continental Congress of Santiago (1856)

Three countries attended this Spanish-American assembly: Chile, Peru, and Ecuador. The background in this case consisted of the activities of William Walker and the resulting threat of U.S. imperialism. Linked in the first place to the liberal-conservative ideological struggle in Central America, the episode was also connected to the rivalry between Britain and the United States over a possible future interoceanic route. The Tennessean Walker even became president of Nicaragua, and his actions were never discouraged by U.S. authorities. On September 15, 1856, the three countries signed a Treaty of Mutual Assistance—Union and Confederation, which stated that in case one or more of the contracting parties was attacked by the United States, all would unite against the aggressor. Again, the congress was an example of collective security like its predecessors, and again the treaty was never ratified, since the threat evaporated.

However, the above agreement was further amplified by the Treaty of Washington (Draft Alliance) of the same year. This treaty was signed on November 9, 1856, by the diplomatic representatives in the United States of New Granada, Guatemala, El Salvador, Mexico, Peru, Costa Rica, and Venezuela.

Second Congress of Lima (1865)

The last of these purely Spanish-American meetings was the Second Congress of Lima (1864–1865), which was attended by Bolivia, Colombia, Chile, Ecuador, Guatemala, Peru, and Venezuela. The background of this assembly was the French intervention in Mexico and the Spanish return to Santo Domingo. The congress met in 1864 to discuss the possible responses to these events and signed the Treaty of Union and Alliance. The participants wanted to avoid a repetition of the events that had been provoked earlier by General Juan José Flores in 1847. (Bolívar's death in 1830 had led to the collapse of Greater Colombia, his creation of 1819; Quito, Colombia, and Venezuela went their own ways. In Quito, now called Ecuador, the Venezuelan Flores, one of Bolívar's aides, was appointed first president of the country by a constitutional convention in Riobamba. For fifteen years, off and on, Flores dominated Ecuador but in 1845 lost out to intrigue abroad for a comeback that actually never materialized.) The Treaty again recommended arbitration in case of disputes that the contracting parties were unable to solve among themselves. The Congress also signed two more treaties, one on commerce, and the other on postal matters. Again, the treaties were not ratified.

Spanish-American solidarity became increasingly difficult to achieve in view of growing internal problems and such international wars as the War of the Triple Alliance (1865–1870), with Argentina, Brazil, and Uruguay against Paraguay, and the Pacific War (1879–1883), with Chile against Bolivia and Peru. However, a fascinating continuation of the attempt to achieve some kind of solidarity or uniformity was undertaken on the juridical level. Thus, a Congress of Jurists was held in Lima (1877–1879), as well as the first South American Congress of Private International Law in Montevideo (1888–1889). Both conferences had in mind some kind of codification of legal principles to be applicable to the continent, but the United States, which had been invited, refused to join on the basis that its legal system had different roots and thus could not be harmonized with that of Latin America.

The Juridical Congress of Lima (1877–1879)

This congress, which was joined by representatives from Argentina, Bolivia, Chile, Costa Rica, Ecuador, Peru, and Venezuela, and later by delegates from Guatemala and Uruguay, adopted a treaty that aimed at establishing uniform rules for the settlement of disputes regarding civil matters and the legal capacity of individuals; goods situated in the country, contracts signed in a foreign country and those signed by foreigners in the country; succession; the competence of national courts over juridical acts performed outside the territory and over acts by foreigners who did not reside therein; national jurisdiction over crimes committed in a foreign country and over crimes of falsification that were harmful to other states; the execution of sentences and other jurisdictional acts; and the legalization of letters rogatory and other instruments from a foreign country.[6]

The First South American Congress on Private International Law, Montevideo (1888–1889)

This congress was held on the initiative of Argentina and Uruguay. It was attended by these two countries as well as Bolivia, Brazil, Chile, Paraguay, and Peru. The result of the congress was the signature of eight treaties and one protocol, as follows: Treaty on Procedural Law, treaties on Literary and Artistic Copyright, Treaty on Patents of Invention, treaties on Merchants' and Manufacturers' Trademarks, Treaty on International Penal Law, and Treaty on International Civil Law, and an additional protocol stating the general rules for the application of the laws of any contracting state in the territory of the others.[7]

As F. V. García Amador, a former secretary general of the Inter-American Institute of International Legal Studies and an authority on international law and inter-American legislation, stated, "This was the first serious effort in the Americas to codify private international law."[8] It is true that the treaty adopted by the Congress of Jurists in Lima did not enter into force, in view of the fact that only one country ratified it, but the treaties of Montevideo were ratified and are actually in effect in most of the signatory states.[9] It is also worthwhile to note that many of the above-mentioned subject matters were also discussed in the early Pan American Conferences. Finally, the Treaty on International Penal Law incorporated a chapter on diplomatic asylum for political refugees that represented the earliest codified manifestation of this Latin American tradition, a tradition that has survived to this day and remains part and parcel of Latin American legal history and diplomacy.[10]

The Second Congress of Lima ended a chapter of purely Spanish-American attempts at union and solidarity. A prime example was the Congress of Panama of 1826, which had aimed at a federation or league of free nations. These attempts were sporadic and ad hoc: Treaties were signed as a demonstration of the desire for union and confederation, but the process dissipated as soon as the particular perceived threat had vanished. Deeper commitment and broader engagements would gradually arise in a later period. The two juridical congresses belong to an entirely different area, although they too aimed at bringing together the region: in this case, Latin American countries, since the Montevideo Congress went beyond Spanish America and included Brazil.

2

The Pan American Movement from the Union of American Republics to the Organization of American States: The First Four Phases (1889–1890 through 1948)

THE FIRST PHASE: 1889–1890 THROUGH 1920

The inter-American system began in earnest in 1889 when it was initiated by the United States. This Pan American movement, which gradually developed into the inter-American system and the Organization of American States, cannot be directly associated with Bolívar and the Congress of Panama. The Pan American movement, which was begun in 1889 with U.S. Secretary of State James G. Blaine, did not represent a continuation of the earlier dreams and endeavors of Bolívar and thus has no connection with the Spanish-American attempts at union and confederation prior to 1889. In an *indirect* way, however, the Pan American movement of the United States was connected to the Congress of Panama in that it revived on an extended basis the concept of a closer union of all countries in the Western Hemisphere.

The United States, was ending its period of reconstruction, which followed the Civil War, and was expanding into the Caribbean and Pacific. One of its goals was an increase in economic relations with its neighbors to the south. Thus was launched the Pan American movement that, uniquely, was not based on a treaty but rather developed organically from one conference to the next.

Although when speaking of the modern Pan American movement we mean the events of the entire period beginning in 1889–1890, the movement passed through several different phases. The first phase (1889–1920) covered the first four International Conferences of American States: Washington, D.C., 1889–1890; Mexico, 1902; Rio de Janeiro, 1906; and Buenos Aires, 1910. They dealt essentially with matters of trade, communications, and peace; international legal questions; procedures for arbitration of disputes;

and forcible collection of debts, including consideration of the Drago Doctrine (which stated that public debt cannot be used as a pretext for intervention) and the Calvo Clause (foreigners should not receive additional extralegal protection by appealing to their respective diplomatic representations). Both the Drago Doctrine (named after Argentine jurist Luis María Drago, 1859–1921) and the Calvo Clause (named after Argentine diplomat Carlos Calvo, 1822–1906) represented Latin American answers to some aspects of the distorted Monroe Doctrine, the "Roosevelt Corollary" and "Dollar Diplomacy."

For those readers who are unfamiliar with the Monroe Doctrine and its subsequent corollaries, we offer the following explanation: The original meaning of President James Monroe's message to Congress of December 2, 1823, written by Secretary of State John Quincy Adams, was simply a declaration addressed to the European nations making up the Holy Alliance, which stated that "we could not view any interposition for the purpose of oppressing them (the newly independent Latin American nations), or controlling in any other manner their destiny, by any European power in any other light than as the manifestation of an unfriendly disposition towards the United States." The same declaration stated later that "the American continents, . . . are henceforth not to be considered subject to future colonization by any European powers." In return, the United States would not interfere with the existing colonies of the European powers and would not become involved in intracontinental European wars. At that time, the warning to Europe was mere bluff since the only power that could stop the Holy Alliance was the British Royal Navy.

In 1845 President James K. Polk, in referring to French activities in Texas and British aims in Oregon and California, restated the Monroe declaration, which by then had become a permanent principle of U.S. foreign policy and was upgraded to the Monroe Doctrine. Already President Polk added the "Polk corollary" when he wrote: "Should any portion of them (the people of this continent), constituting an independent state, propose to unite themselves with our Confederacy, this will be a question for them and us to determine without any foreign interposition." Thus began the distortion of the Monroe Doctrine for purposes of U.S. intervention in Latin America, which had nothing to do with the original meaning of 1823. This distortion reached its high points with the "Roosevelt Corollary" and "Dollar Diplomacy." The former, known as the Roosevelt Corollary to the Monroe Doctrine, refers to a statement made by President Theodore Roosevelt in 1904 that in case a Latin American republic failed to respect its obligations, the United States would intervene in order to prevent a European intervention. It was then applied in the Dominican Republic, Haiti, and Nicaragua. "Dollar Diplomacy," used particularly under the administration of President William H. Taft (1909–1913), meant the employment of U.S. dollars to advance the political goals of the United States; it was successfully applied in Nicaragua, invoking the Monroe Doctrine, but failed in Guatemala and Honduras. Obviously, Latin America never accepted the Monroe Doctrine with or without distortions.

In 1928, Under Secretary of State J. Reuben Clark undertook a study of the Monroe Doctrine. His subsequent Clark Memorandum officially repudiated the many distortions of the doctrine since its inception, and was a prelude to the later "Good Neighbor policy," which was a return to the original meaning of 1823.

The First International Conference of American States, Washington, D.C. (1889–1890)

Seventeen countries accepted the invitation of the United States and attended this first inter-American gathering. The Dominican Republic was absent, and neither Cuba nor Panama had gained independence. The conference established the Commercial Bureau of the American Republics, based in Washington, D.C. Its functions included the collection of economic data and other information relating to production, trade, and customs laws. The date of this resolution was April 14, 1890, which was adopted forty years later as Pan American Day.

This first conference laid the foundation for economic cooperation among the member states; it also took the first steps in the direction of arbitration procedures for the peaceful settlement of disputes that might arise among its members. The conference also aired the idea of an inter-American bank, which, however, did not prosper at the time: It would take an additional seventy years before such an organization would be adopted with different goals and within a different structure.

The Second International Conference of American States, Mexico City (1902)

It was more than a decade before the next inter-American gathering took place. The conference changed the name of its headquarters to the International Bureau of the American Republics, since "Commercial Bureau" did not sound appropriate for an intergovernmental agency. The conference participants also decided that the International Bureau should be directed by a governing board with representatives of all member states accredited to the U.S. government and whose chairman would be the U.S. secretary of state. At the same time, the bureau's director was retained for the effective operation of the secretariat, although these functions were now much enlarged.

The conference passed a variety of resolutions that clearly showed how the inter-American system was moving ahead: Treaties and conventions that were signed on pecuniary claims; extradition and protection against anarchism—the latter had become an element of subversion in several Latin American countries and would only be replaced by Marxism after World War I; practice of learned professions; elaboration of codes on both public and private international law; copyrights, trademarks and patents; and exchange of official, scientific, literary, and industrial publications. Finally, the conference also dealt with the rights of aliens and with compulsory arbitration. The latter obviously reflected an echo of the famous First Hague Peace Conference of 1899.

The Third International Conference of American States, Rio de Janeiro (1906)

Two additional countries attended this conference: Cuba and Panama. The conference again dealt with many of the subjects that had been the focus of attention earlier. Thus, a Convention of Pecuniary Claims was adopted since the earlier one was due to expire in 1907; a single convention on patents, including trademarks as well as literary and artistic copyrights, replaced the earlier agreements on these matters. A Convention on Naturalized Citizens who take up residence in their country of origin was also adopted. Finally, codification of public and private international law was again on the agenda.

The Fourth International Conference of American States, Buenos Aires (1910)

After Mexico and Brazil it was the turn of the Argentine Republic to hold the next conference in the inter-American system, since it ranked as the most important country in Latin America. The centennial celebrations of the May Revolution in Argentina provided an excellent opportunity for the Fourth International Conference. It was an important conference, which changed the name of the organization to Union of American Republics, while the bureau received the name Pan American Union. Again, the latter was given more power. The governing board remained the highest authority and the Pan American Union was led by a director whose official title was now director general. He was appointed by the governing board, as was a new position, the assistant director, whose functions included those of secretary of the board.

The fourth conference also made an attempt to put the inter-American system on a permanent basis, but the concept did not prosper. It would reappear in 1928, at the Sixth International Conference of American States, but it would again be defeated. Only in 1948 would the inter-American system be based on a treaty.

The year 1910 is also important in that it closed the first phase in inter-American activities. No further conference would be held until 1923, although World War I should have provided ample opportunities for discussion and involvement. Woodrow Wilson had proposed his famous Pan American Peace Pact at a time when Argentina, Brazil, and Chile formed a loose understanding (the "ABC countries"), which was inspired by the Brazilian foreign minister, Lauro Muller. The peace pact mutually guaranteed political independence, territorial integrity, and a republican form of government. It also stated that the contracting parties agreed to acquire complete control of the manufacture and sale of munitions of war.[1] Despite its Pan American record, Argentina's ambassador to the United States, Rómulo S. Naón, provided the Argentine signature to the pact; however, Wilson's Pan American Peace Pact did not prosper due to Chile's reluctance to join. Actually, U.S. ambassador to Argentina, Frederic Jessup Stimson, was inclined to blame the U.S. Department of State itself for the fate of the treaty.[2]

The political disagreements between the United States and Latin America increased after World War I, when "Wilsonianism," President Woodrow Wilson's idealism, which was opposed to the big stick policy of the preceding U.S. administrations and was aimed at better relations with Latin America, failed. Wilson had become involved with the Victoriano Huerta regime in Mexico over the Tampico incident that then led to the U.S. occupation of Veracruz, and in 1916 he ordered General Pershing to lead an expedition into Mexico to capture Pancho Villa "dead or alive." Despite his idealism, Wilson openly intervened in the domestic affairs of the Dominican Republic, Haiti, and Central America (Costa Rica, 1917). No wonder that Latin America then joined the newly founded League of Nations, believing primarily that the league would provide protection from further North American aggression. Argentina soon became disillusioned when the United States pressured for incorporation into the covenant of the league of "such regional understandings as the Monroe Doctrine," which Latin America had never accepted and which, in the mind of Argentina's president Hipólito Yrigoyen, was tantamount to the pursuit of exclusively national policies. Argentina then attacked the notion as incompatible with true Pan Americanism and contrary to the ideals of the new international organization.[3] The fact that the United States ultimately did not join the League of Nations was a further disappointment for Latin America, which now encouraged the continuation of the inter-American system as the only avenue for the improvement of relations between the powerful North and the weaker South.

Still, despite the fact that this first phase ran parallel to the implementation of aggressive North American policies (the Spanish American War, Panama, interventions in Haiti and the Dominican Republic, and interference in Mexico and Central America), the Pan American movement grew with the establishment of several inter-American specialized agencies, such as the Pan American Sanitary Bureau in Washington, D.C. (1902), the International Law Commission (1915, the predecessor of the Inter-American Council of Jurists), and the Inter-American High Commission (1915, forerunner of the Inter-American Economic and Social Council).

There is an additional reason why 1910 was a significant date in inter-American relations. Shortly before the inauguration of the fourth conference, the new Pan American building was formally unveiled. Known as the House of the Americas, it became the headquarters of the Pan American movement and the inter-American system, and a true landmark in the Washington, D.C., landscape. This beautiful and imposing building was built on land donated by the U.S. government, with the majority of the funds coming from Andrew Carnegie, supplemented by other Latin American financial contributions.

THE SECOND PHASE: 1920–1930

The second phase of the inter-American system occurred during the turbulent 1920s. Two inter-American conferences were held: the Fifth International Conference of American States in Santiago de Chile (1923) and the Sixth International Conference of American States in Havana (1928). In both cases the Latin Americans expressed their opposition to U.S. domination and encroachment. Both international conferences represented inter-American assemblies at which Latin America was determined to reduce U.S. dominance of the inter-American system. This also included discussion of possible modifications of the Monroe Doctrine, the original meaning of which had increasingly been distorted from a diplomatic tool for the defense of the hemisphere to a unilateral instrument for U.S. intervention and domination south of the Mexican border.

The Fifth International Conference of American States, Santiago de Chile (1923)

This was the first conference of the Pan American movement after World War I, a different situation altogether if compared with the decades prior to the war. Originally, the conference was to be held in 1915, but the war and the different viewpoints in its regard led to its postponement.

This fifth conference was one of the most important to be held so far. It confirmed the existence of the Union of American Republics, and of the Pan American Union as its permanent seat. The fifth conference determined that the chairman of the governing board of the Pan American Union was to be elected by the members of the board of the Union of American Republics. In practice, nothing really changed, since, for reasons of courtesy and political realism, the U.S. secretary of state continued to be the chairman. However, the principle was established that this right of chairmanship was dependent on a majority decision and not some divine right of the strongest power. The conference also made the significant determination that any American state, by the mere fact of geography, had the right to membership in the Union of American Republics, and, therefore, to a voice and a vote in the organization. Until that time, if a Latin American state had no diplomatic relations with the United States, it could no longer be represented on the governing board of the Pan American Union. The decision of Santiago separated the functions of a Latin American delegate to the United States from those of the governing board of the Pan American Union, and thus eliminated an awkward situation.

Finally, the conference approved the famous Treaty to Avoid or Prevent Conflicts between American States, also known as the Gondra Treaty after its Paraguayan author, Manuel Gondra. At the time, the Gondra Treaty represented a high point in the peaceful settlement of national conflicts. Other issues that were dealt with in the fifth conference referred to conventions on the publicity of customs documents and the protection of commercial, agricultural, and industrial trademarks and commercial brands, as well as on the uniformity of nomenclature for the classification of merchandise.

The Sixth International Conference of American States, Havana (1928)

Again, as in Buenos Aires in 1910, the sixth conference dealt with the problem of giving the inter-American system a solid legal foundation based on a treaty or convention. A convention to this effect was circulated but never approved, since it was not ratified by all the members; only sixteen states did so. Hence, the inter-American system continued on its flexible basis as launched in 1889–1890.

The sixth conference was quite prolific. Some ten conventions were signed regarding such subject matters as asylum; consular agents and diplomatic officials; aliens; maritime neutrality; commercial aviation; copyright for literary and artistic works (thus revising the earlier convention of the Fourth International Conference of Buenos Aires in 1910); and private international law (the famous Sánchez de Bustamante Code, which was named for the Cuban lawyer and legal expert Antonio Sánchez de Bustamante y Sirvén who had elaborated a detailed and complete code of private international law for application in all member states. It was approved by this conference, although with reservations to some topics by a variety of countries.) Another highlight was the Convention on Duties and Rights of States in the Event of Civil Strife, which was designed to prevent the use of any American territory for revolutionary activity against another American country.

Again, despite the nadir that U.S.–Latin American relations had reached in the 1920s, the period was very positive for the expansion and deepening of the inter-American system. The first of the series of specialized inter-American conferences was inaugurated as follows:

The Extraordinary International American Conference of American States on Conciliation and Arbitration, Washington, D.C. (1928–1929)

This special conference produced two treaties: a General Convention on Inter-American Conciliation and a General Treaty of Inter-American Arbitration. Both agreements dealt in depth with their respective subject matters.

Finally, the inter-American system was also able to expand on various other levels. Thus, the Inter-American Child Institute was set up in Montevideo (1927); the Inter-American Commission of Women was established in Washington, D.C. (1928); and the Pan American Institute of Geography and History was inaugurated in Mexico City (1929).

THE THIRD PHASE: THE GOOD NEIGHBOR POLICY, 1933–1942

During the fateful 1930s, a new stage occurred: the Good Neighbor policy of the United States and its positive impact on the inter-American system. The United States had already made changes in its relations with its neighbors to the south, exemplified by Ambassador Dwight W. Morrow, who in 1927 inaugurated an improved relationship with Mexico. It was also the time of J. Reuben Clark, Jr.'s, "Memorandum on the Monroe Doctrine," which was published in 1928. "One of the epochal documents in American diplomatic history," it called for a return to the original meaning of the Monroe Doctrine, although it did not disavow the right of intervention.[4] These political changes prepared the ground for Franklin D. Roosevelt's Good Neighbor policy, that was launched immediately after he became the new president of the United States. This policy was to mark the most positive period in U.S.–Latin American relations and has in reality never been surpassed; on the contrary, soon after World War II the United States abandoned this policy and returned to the harmful aggression that has been seen since then, with the exceptions of the Kennedy and Carter administrations. On a bilateral basis, the Good Neighbor policy of President Roosevelt meant that the United States withdrew its troops from Haiti ahead of time, failed to intervene to protect U.S. interests in the oil nationalizations of Mexico and Bolivia, invalidated the Platt Amendment, which justified U.S. intervention in Cuba, renegotiated the Panama Treaty, and attempted, though unsuccessfully, to eliminate U.S. discrimination against Argentine beef— the infamous beef quarantine of 1927 for alleged contamination by hoof-and-mouth disease, which represented a disguised tariff measure and justified Argentine complaints. On a multilateral basis, a series of inter-American conferences were held that gave new impetus to the Pan American movement and united the hemisphere as never before or since in regard to threats from other continents.

The Seventh International Conference of American States, Montevideo (1933)

This conference symbolized the opening of the Good Neighbor policy on a multilateral level. It dealt with a vast array of issues, such as questions of nationality, citizenship of women, extradition, political asylum, and the teaching of history. The conference also passed resolutions on good offices and mediation; commercial, economic, and tariff policies; commercial arbitration and tourism; codification of international law; agricultural and industrial use of international rivers; agrarian reform; and improvement of the conditions of the working classes.

However, the most important results of the Seventh Conference were the Additional Protocol to the General Convention of Inter-American Conciliation of 1929 and the Convention on Rights and Duties of States. With this convention the United States explicitly recognized that it had no right to intervention (nonintervention had been a battle cry of all the Latin American countries ever since the Pan American movement was launched). Thus, Article 4 stated: "States are legally equal, enjoy equal rights and have equal capacity to exercise them. The rights of each one does not depend on the power of which it disposes in order to assure its exercise but on the simple fact of its existence as a person of International Law"; Article 5: "The fundamental rights of the States are not susceptible to be affected in any form;" and, especially significant, Article 8: "No State has the right to intervene in the internal as well as external affairs of another."[5] Latin Americans were impressed with such an acknowledgment by the United States in a written legal document. It did not mean that henceforth the United States would no longer use its power to influence policies to its advantage, but it did mean that it would abstain—as it did—from the more crude and outrageous forms of intervention it had used so often in the past; it was also a recognition that the United States did not have a God-given right to "put things straight" in Latin America every time it saw fit.

The Inter-American Conference for the Consolidation of Peace, Buenos Aires (1936)

This special inter-American gathering was held in order to make the final arrangements for a peace to the Chaco War between Bolivia and Paraguay. This conflict, begun in 1928, dragged on intermittently until 1935, and is linked to Bolivia's landlocked situation. Bolivia had lost its coastal areas in the Pacific War (1879–1883); it then attempted, unsuccessfully, to find an outlet to the Atlantic through the Amazon Jungle via the Madeira-Mamoré railroad in 1903. This failure led to Bolivian attempts to find a solution via the River Plate. The Chaco region had received attention already, in 1852, but all attempts at a peaceful arrangement then between Bolivia and Paraguay failed. The inevitable then took place in 1928. Neither the inter-American system nor the League of Nations were able to settle the matter. Fighting continued and led to full-fledged war in the northern part of the Chaco (Chaco Boreal). By 1935 the Paraguayan army had overrun most Bolivian positions. Both sides being exhausted, they were then willing to negotiate; 70,000 square miles were given to Paraguay and 30,000 square miles to Bolivia. Furthermore, Bolivia would be entitled to use the Paraguay River as an outlet to the South Atlantic and the Paraguayan port of Puerto Casado became a free port. The inter-American conference of 1936 thus signed the Convention for the Maintenance, Preservation and Reestablishment of Peace and an additional protocol relative to nonintervention (dear to the Latin Americans), to make sure that the United States had not changed its policy since 1933. Many other problems were also discussed that went beyond the Chaco War and the issue of nonintervention.

It was obvious that the threats to peace in Europe (such as the Italian invasion of Ethiopia, the Spanish Civil War, and Japanese aggression in China) were the object of much discussion, even if countries like Argentina were reluctant to embrace the viewpoint of the U.S. Department of State. It was obvious that the United States aimed at getting Latin America on its side for the coming global challenge; on the other hand, many Latin American countries did not want to be involved but wished to maintain neutrality. President Roosevelt, who had proposed the conference, also appeared personally, which added to its brilliance and success. This extraordinary meeting produced a variety of conventions on such varied subjects as the prevention of controversies; good offices and mediation; fulfillment of existing treaties between American states (since Argentina had only ratified a few); the Pan-American Highway; promotion of cultural relations; interchange of publications; facilities for artistic exhibitions and for educational and publicity films; and peaceful orientation of public instruction. However, the most significant result of this conference was the Consultative Pact or Convention for the Maintenance, Preservation and Reestablishment of Peace, which made it obligatory to consult in case of actions outside the hemisphere that would affect or disturb the peace in the Americas. It was not an obligation to take any action or to act in a uniform manner, but the conference did establish the principle of obligatory consultation. The Consultative Pact, thus, amounted to a continentalization of the Monroe Doctrine. It did not mean that the United States had given up the Monroe Doctrine, but it did mean that its policies would be carried out in a more subtle manner. The substance of U.S. actions had not changed, but the form had, and Latin Americans appreciated this new policy; indeed, it was enough to satisfy the Latin American point of view. Even if, in the long run, the Good Neighbor policy was simply a tool of expediency, it was still quite successful, as can be gauged from the very productive and positive years of 1933 through 1942, when U.S.–Latin American relations were at their very best. There is no question that Montevideo (1933) and Buenos Aires (1936) rank among the most successful conferences of the inter-American system.

The Eighth International Conference of American States, Lima (1938)

Five years after Montevideo, and two years after the extraordinary conference in Buenos Aires, the inter-American system held its next regular meeting. In the meantime, the international situation had darkened and dangerous clouds had gathered: the Anschluss (the union of Germany and Austria) had occurred, as well as the Munich Conference and the dismemberment of Czechoslovakia. The conference's main task was to apply the principles of consultation that were adopted in 1936 in Buenos Aires. It thus issued the Declaration of Lima, which reaffirmed continental solidarity and the intent of the American republics to collaborate in the maintenance of the principles on which this solidarity was grounded. The declaration also proclaimed the common concern of all member states and their determination to make their solidarity effective. Finally, it set up a new institution: the Meeting of Consultation of Foreign Ministers of the American Republics, to be held whenever a common concern called for an immediate and high-level consultation.

During World War II, no new conference was held, either regular or extraordinary, but instead, the first three Meetings of Consultation took place in order to discuss and decide on measures that the situation warranted.

The First Meeting of Consultation of Foreign Ministers of the American Republics, Panama (1939)

This meeting of American foreign ministers was held after the war broke out between Germany and Poland in September 1939. This first Meeting of Consultation approved a General Declaration of Neutrality of the American Republics and the Declaration of Panama, which unilaterally set up a zone of neutrality on both the Pacific and the Atlantic, from the U.S.-Canadian borders to the southern tip of the continent, in which hostile acts by the belligerents were not to take place. Needless to say, the belligerents paid scant attention to this declaration, as seen in the naval engagement of the River Plate in December 1939.

The Second Meeting of Consultation of Foreign Ministers of the American Republics, Havana (1940)

This meeting took place after Germany had overrun the Netherlands, Belgium, and France. Both the Netherlands and France held territories in the Western Hemisphere, and it was feared (though it proved to be a ground-less concern) that the Axis powers would seize control of the French and Netherlands Antilles. The Second Meeting of Consultation reaffirmed con-tinental solidarity, reciprocal assistance, and collective security, and issued the Act of Havana Concerning the Provisional Administration of European Colonies and Possessions in the Americas, which represented a Latin Amer-ican blank check to the United States to temporarily occupy and administer these colonial areas in the case that they were either seized by the Axis powers or were in danger of changing their nationality or being bartered away. Since neither occupation nor a change of sovereignty ever took place, or was even intended, the Act of Havana was never put into effect. The act, nonetheless showed how much the relationship between the United States and Latin America had improved: It would have been inconceivable only a few years earlier that Latin America as a unit would have given the green light to the United States to occupy foreign areas in the Caribbean or South America (such as Suriname and French Guiana).

The Third Meeting of Consultation of Foreign Ministers of American Republics, Rio de Janeiro (1942)

This third meeting took place in Rio de Janeiro in early 1942, shortly after Japan had attacked the United States at Pearl Harbor (on December 7, 1941). The meeting was no doubt the high point in U.S. policy in Latin America and of the inter-American system as a whole. The conference rec-ommended—if this had not already happened—breaking off diplomatic re-lations with Japan, Germany, Italy, and their allies, and it also resolved that all commercial and financial relations with the Tripartite powers be halted. The Meeting of Consultation purposely did not decide on such actions but simply made recommendations in order to soothe the more recalcitrant countries, such as Argentina and Chile. As a matter of fact, the latter did not break relations with the Tripartite powers until much later in the war.

With the year 1942 ended the third phase of the inter-American system. Unhappily, after the United States had obtained what it wanted, it gradually, after 1942, turned its back on the Good Neighbor policy. Still, it was in this third phase that another technical agency was incorporated into the inter-American system. Thus, in 1940, the Inter-American Indian Institute (IAII), a technical agency, saw the light of day in Mexico City. Indian problems had already been dealt with, in the Seventh International Conference of American States in Montevideo (1933): Resolution XVIII requested the Pan American Union to hold a conference on such matters in the Mexican capital. It took some time before this could materialize; however, finally a conference on Indian affairs held in Pátzcuaro in 1940 led to the establishment of the IAII.

THE FOURTH PHASE: 1942-1948

The idea that the Good Neighbor policy was a permanent trend in U. S. policies toward Latin America soon revealed itself as erroneous. As the war progressed, the United States, which had always been practical and pragmatic in its approach, was now considering a different orientation. Since January 1, 1942, when the Declaration of the United Nations had been proclaimed, it was becoming clear that a new international organization of a global character would emerge after the war. After the end of World War I, Woodrow Wilson had launched the League of Nations, but the United States had not joined it; it now recognized this failure and would not repeat it after the end of World War II. A major effort was thus initiated, as early as 1942, to make sure that the future United Nations would be built on solid ground and taking into account all the experiences of the defunct league. As the war dragged on, increasing numbers of discussions were held on the future global intergovernmental organization. Thus the Dumbarton Oaks Proposals—an Allied conference that took place in the Georgetown section of Washington, D.C. from August 21 through October 7, 1944, and that was attended by Undersecretary of state Edward Stettinius, Sir Alexander Cadogan of Britain, and Andrei Gromyko of the Soviet Union—dealt with such questions as the seat of the future world organization and the composition and powers of the Security Council (whether or not it would have veto power) and others, and it became apparent that the United States was willing to sacrifice the inter-American system since in many ways the United Nations would duplicate its efforts and because the interests of the United States would, in any case, no longer be limited to the Western Hemisphere but instead would cover the entire globe. The fact that the Pan American movement had a historic record of half a century and was, indeed, a very positive element in U.S. foreign policy was now forgotten. Ironically, moreover, while many in the United States felt that the inter-American system could now be ignored, Latin Americans who, in the earlier stages, had been lukewarm to the idea of strengthening the organization through a treaty and other reforms, now came to believe that their interests definitely required a much stronger and better fortified inter-American system. This became particularly important when certain information was leaked from the Dumbarton Oaks Proposals that clearly showed that the future United Nations could intervene in Latin America through its Security Council. This piece of news was especially galling because it had taken almost fifty years to convince the United States to publicly acknowledge that it had no divine right to intervention; now it seemed that the United Nations would be able to intervene through the back door. This is the background of a strong Latin American offensive that arose to change this North American course of action and also explains the significant decisions that were taken in the next years when the war seemed to come to an end and the post–World War II era was to begin.

This fourth phase covers, first of all, an important inter-American conference that decided to strengthen the organization and thus not to scuttle it; once that point had been decided on, it followed logically that the next moves had to encompass the changes with which the organization was to be fortified. This would be done after the war had ended, in two other inter-American conferences which would lead, respectively, to the Rio Treaty and the formation of the Organization of American States (OAS).

The Inter-American Conference on Problems of War and Peace, Chapultepec, Mexico (1945)

This represented the first high-level inter-American assembly to discuss the future. Three basic areas were the focus of attention: Argentina, the economic issues of the inter-American system, and its future. The Argentine question was quickly solved. Argentina, together with Chile, had not severed relations with the Tripartite powers in 1942. Chile did so in 1943, and Argentina froze relations in 1944. However, that was only the tip of the iceberg. Ever since the launching of the Pan American movement, which was supposed to make the United States the leader of the hemisphere, Argentina had looked to Europe, never really warming up to the new regionalism of the United States. Instead, it continued to maintain ties with Europe, especially Spain, France, and Italy in the cultural field and Britain and Germany in the commercial sphere. This basic attitude did not mean hostility toward Washington; it was simply a fact of life directed by differing economic interests and national affinities.

The new Pan American policies of the United States, together with its growing international power, were not only reflected in its Latin American and Pan American orientation but became especially apparent with the Spanish-American War and the beginning of what was called the imperialist age of the United States. On the other hand, Argentina's variant European outlook, its growing trade, which already rivaled that of the United States, and its own international policies, which collided with U.S. doctrine, no doubt showed a widening gap. The United States wanted hegemony over Latin America and thus found Argentina to be an obstacle and a nuisance; Argentina, in return, wanted to lead Latin America, and in many ways it succeeded. The United States extolled regionalism while Argentina responded with universalism; Washington proclaimed Pan Americanism while Buenos Aires in return preferred Latin Americanism. Argentina's record in the Pan American movement of the twentieth century remained rather negative: Of some eighty-seven inter-American conventions, it only ratified seven,[6] a situation further compounded by an almost total lack of economic relations between the United States and Argentina. It was only prior to

World War I that U.S. investments began to reach Argentina and trade between the two countries increased, although it was only a small percentage compared to Argentina's trade with Britain, Germany, and other European countries.

In World War I Argentina remained neutral, and in the 1920s and 1930s, Argentine products were burdened with United States tariffs (as set by the Fordney Tariff Act of 1922 and the Smoot-Hawley Tariff Act of 1930). This changed when the Good Neighbor policy publicly condemned the use of sanitary regulations as a disguised tariff measure against Argentina. Although Argentina was never really convinced of Washington's change of heart, it did applaud U.S. actions at the conferences in Montevideo (Seventh International Conference, 1933) and Buenos Aires (Inter-American Conference for the Consolidation of Peace, 1936). Moreover, President Roosevelt's visit to the country was an extraordinary success, with a popular welcome that was overwhelming. Still, during World War II Argentina clung to the same policies as in World War I, which increased tensions with the United States since the latter wanted a united Pan American front. Despite the fact that Argentina was generally cooperative in its inter-American relations, it was not willing to go as far as to relinquish its historic role of neutrality, especially after the United States increased pressure and coercion. In view of the Argentine belief that it was an extension of Europe in the South Atlantic, this would be to go against its own national character.

In any case, after 1943, relations between the two countries deteriorated further. For Argentina, neutrality was simply a question of national dignity, but whatever it did to please the U.S. government, it was never enough, and thus, the South American nation was never in a position to redeem itself. By 1944 Argentina had broken off relations with Japan and Germany, but to the United States, this did not seem enough. Thus, the country was excluded—illegally—from the Chapultepec Conference, where it was forced to rely on its Latin American friends. Indeed, the Argentine question was thus quickly solved: Argentina would declare war on Japan and Germany, and, in return, it would be "readmitted" to the Pan American family, with the United States also formally endorsing Argentine membership in the future United Nations as a founding member.

Another problem dealt with economic matters. Latin America had greatly helped the Allied cause, and it was concerned that the increased volume of economic relations that had developed during the war would not suddenly cease when peace was reestablished. The Mexican Conference thus was intended to make sure that the United States would take into consideration the Latin American point of view and not walk away from its economic and social responsibilities. This economic problem was a simple quid pro quo: Latin America expected economic understanding after the end of the war. The result was the Declaration of Mexico which reaffirmed certain principles governing the relations of the American community; it thus included the

Economic Charter of the Americas along with other resolutions of an economic nature. The conference also dealt with the inter-American peace system and the international protection of human rights.

However, the main focus was the future of the inter-American system. At the conference, the Latin American point of view of strengthening the inter-American system won out with the help of many North Americans, especially U.S. Senator Arthur Vandenberg. The result was the famous Act of Chapultepec. This was Resolution VIII, on "Reciprocal Assistance and American Solidarity." It was to be in effect only during the war, and thus would be provisional until it was later incorporated in a treaty or convention. Together with Resolution IX, the Mexican conference signaled the direction in which the inter-American system would go and thus laid the basis for the two important inter-American conferences of 1947 and 1948.

Another important issue to be solved was the future relationship of the inter-American system with the soon-to-be-established United Nations. Now that it had been decided to strengthen the inter-American system, it was vital to know what its role was to be in regard to the new world organization. The problem was solved to the satisfaction of both the regional and the global institutions with Article 51 of the UN Charter (Chapter VIII, "Regional Arrangements") in the sense that the regional organization had the inherent right of individual and collective self-defense. Regional action was thus legitimate with respect to the pacific settlement of disputes as well as to collective security: Such action would plainly be compatible with the principles of the UN Charter. Thus, the United Nations would only intervene in the Americas if and when the inter-American system had exhausted its possibilities. In any event, the regional organization held priority rights; that is, in case of a conflict or controversy the inter-American system would handle the matter first, and only when it did not succeed would the United Nations step in.

This was the last great inter-American gathering before the United Nations was founded in San Francisco on April 25, 1945, and before the war ended in both Europe and the Far East. In Mexico, the inter-American system had achieved a great victory that would soon find expression in the next years. Not only had the Pan American movement succeeded in blocking all efforts to eliminate it from the political scene, it had succeeded in turning a possible defeat into victory: The new post–World War II system would be altogether different. It would be stronger and better fortified, and the Latin American position within it would be considerably improved.

The Inter-American Conference for the Maintenance of Continental Peace and Security, Rio de Janeiro [Quitandinha] (1947)

This inter-American gathering was the first follow-up to the special Mexico City Conference of 1945. The Rio de Janeiro, or Quitandinha, Conference dealt with a single object: the strengthening of inter-American peace and security in light of the new international situation as it had evolved in the two years since 1945. It thus carried out Resolution VIII—the Act of Chapultepec—of the Mexico City Conference.

The result of the conference was the Inter-American Treaty of Reciprocal Assistance, known as the Rio Treaty, which later became the model for the North Atlantic Treaty Organization (NATO). It was in this respect the first of the many military agreements that the United States promoted to meet the new communist threat, including as well the Central and Southeast Asia treaty organizations (CENTO and SEATO). Past experiences were taken into account in the elaboration of the Rio Treaty in order not to infringe on the sovereign rights of its members; this contributed to its success. As a matter of fact, the Rio Treaty, which is still the basic instrument for collective security in the inter-American system and has survived for more than four decades, is clear evidence of its quality and of the successful growth of the inter-American system in such important matters. Its flexible character has allowed it to be applied with great frequency since its adoption.

The Rio Treaty became the first solid pillar on which the new, renovated inter-American organization was built. The next regular conference would provide another pillar for the strengthened inter-American system; it was held just one year later.

The Ninth International Conference of American States, Bogotá (1948)

Just as Resolution VIII of the Mexico City Conference of 1945 had resulted in the Rio Treaty, the other decision, Resolution IX, of that same conference referred to the reorganization, consolidation, and strengthening of the inter-American system. In other words, the decision taken in Mexico City meant that the inter-American system would now be built on a treaty.

The Bogotá Conference represented the high point in a development that had begun in 1889–1890 with the Union of American Republics, and which, over a period of almost sixty years, had gained an enormous amount of experience in inter-American cooperation on all levels—political, legal, cultural, economic, and social. Six decades of experience in the field of inter-American multilateral relations helped to shape the mold for the necessary structure that would enable the new organization to meet inter-American problems with renewed strength and confidence.

The conference, which had been well prepared since 1945 for the impending structural changes, adopted the Charter of the Organization of American States (OAS). The charter thus put the inter-American system on a treaty basis that incorporated the most important principles and subject matters that so far had guided the Pan American movement and that were to continue. Essentially, nothing really new was introduced: It was simply a codification of the principles and institutions that, over a long period, had been part of the system, and at the same time the organization was modernized in order to face the new world situation as it was reflected after World War II. There is also no question that the establishment of the United Nations with its own charter was in many ways a significant influence.

The result of the ninth conference was, first of all, the Charter with its eighteen chapters and 112 articles. Technically, the charter only went into force on December 31, 1951, after Colombia had deposited the fourteenth instrument of ratification, resulting in a two-thirds majority. However, immediately after the Conference of Bogotá in 1948, the organization functioned provisionally as if the charter was already legally binding on all member states, in accordance with Resolution XL of the ninth conference.

Other important decisions that were taken at Bogotá included the American Treaty on Pacific Settlement (Pact of Bogotá), which codified the respective procedures that had been adopted in earlier treaties, and the Economic Agreement of Bogotá, which also represented a follow-up of the Mexico City Conference of 1945, and as such meant the beginning of a rather painful and disappointing dialogue between the United States and Latin America in regard to economic problems. In 1945 Latin America had voiced the wish that its economic problems be taken into account by the United States as a matter of equity and justice and resulting from its cooperation during World War II. The economic dialogue would be dragged from conference to conference with no substantial solution until the 1960s. The Economic Agreement of Bogotá would thus remain dead in the water, as with so many other similar resolutions on economic and social matters.

Other important decisions taken at the ninth conference covered the Inter-American Convention on the Granting of Political Rights to Women (the right to vote and to hold public office) and the Inter-American Convention on the Granting of Civil Rights to Women. Others included the American Declaration of the Rights and Duties of Man, the Inter-American Charter of Social Guarantees, and the Organic Statute of the Inter-American Commission of Women. Finally, the ninth conference also dealt with the problems of the preservation and defense of democracy in America, colonies and occupied territories on the continent, and the exercise of the right of legation: all in all, some fifty resolutions.

With the Bogotá Conference of 1948, a historic era of some sixty years in inter-American relations ended and a new period, to be guided by the Charter of the OAS, began. The Union of American Republics had become the Organization of American States.

This fourth phase also added a new technical agency: In 1944, the Inter-American Institute of Agricultural Sciences was established in Turrialba, Costa Rica. For a long time it would remain only partially representative, since only those countries interested in tropical agriculture actually joined it. Only when the purpose of the institute was expanded to cover other types of agriculture did the countries of the Southern Cone become members.

3

The Strengthened Inter-American System: The Establishment of the OAS

The new inter-American system, as it resulted from the two postwar conferences (Rio de Janeiro, 1947, and Bogotá, 1948), led to the establishment of the Organization of American States. The new organization, which had been built on the past experience of some sixty years, rested now on two pillars: the Rio Treaty of 1947, for peace and security, and the Charter of the OAS concerning the reorganization, consolidation, and strengthening of the inter-American system. A third legal instrument was the Pact of Bogotá, also of 1948, although it has not yet been ratified by a majority. Nonetheless, it plays an important role since many of its provisions have indirectly served as guideposts.

Furthermore, the juridical basis of the OAS, as it was set up in 1948, is supplemented by several inter-American treaties as well as by the many statutes and regulations of its councils, committees and commissions, organs, and institutions. These not only concern the relations between the different member states but also serve as a guide for the administrative structure of the organization.

ORGANIZATIONAL NAME CHANGE

The Ninth International Conference of American States in Bogotá gave the new structure of the inter-American system the name "Organization of American States." This new designation was suggested by the name of the United Nations. "Organization" seemed more sober, detached, and thus more juridical than either "Union of American Republics" or "Pan American Union," both of which had a more idealistic ring. Moreover, the adoption of the new name was intended to prevent any possible political misunderstanding connected with the Pan American Union. The word "States" was included in order to open the door for possible membership by Canada. The permanent offices of the OAS also received a new name: instead of "Pan American Union," it was now called "General Secretariat."

MODERNIZATION OF THE INTER-AMERICAN SYSTEM

The OAS can be understood properly only if one takes into account its historical evolution. Neither the Rio Treaty, nor the Charter, nor the Pact of Bogotá laid down totally new principles, spelled out new aims, or established new institutions. Rather, these documents are a concentration and codification of the work so far accomplished, and they offer a new formulation and modernization of the inter-American system and its different institutions. In the course of the reorganization, the various official and nongovernmental organizations that had previously belonged to the inter-American system (in the course of time, there were approximately sixty of them) were now put under the new overall organization of the OAS. It was as part of this process that the old Pan American Union (PAU) became the General Secretariat of the OAS.

THE CHARTER

The most important pillar on which the OAS rests is the Charter. Signed in May 1948 by all American republics at the Ninth International Conference of American States (at that time, twenty-one), it became fully operative by January 1952 after a majority of two-thirds of the signatory powers had deposited their instruments of ratification at the General Secretariat (Article 109). The twenty-first country, Argentina, ratified the Charter in April 1956, about six months after the fall of Juan Domingo Perón, who had been elected twice to the Argentine presidency (1946, 1952) but was ousted in a military coup in 1955. As stated earlier, between 1948 and the time the Charter was ratified by its fourteenth member, Colombia, in December 1951, the organization gradually began operating according to its new structure. As Article 109 stated:

Art. 109.—The present Charter shall enter into force among the ratifying States when two-thirds of the signatory States have deposited their ratifications. It shall enter into force with respect to the remaining States in the order in which they deposit their ratifications.

The charter is divided into two distinct parts: the first deals with the organization's nature and purposes; its principles; fundamental rights and duties of states, pacific settlement of disputes, and collective security; and economic, social, and cultural standards, and the second, with the structure of the OAS. Some of the subjects in the first part are treated in greater length and depth in the Pact of Bogotá (peaceful settlement of disputes), the Rio Treaty (collective security), various resolutions of earlier Pan American conferences, and special treaties, agreements, or conventions. Thus, the conventions of 1928 and 1933 dealt extensively with fundamental rights and duties of states; they were included in the Charter solely as a matter of principle.

Nature and Purposes

The first chapter of the Charter deals with the nature and purposes of the organization. Thus, Article 1 states that the OAS is an international organization that the American States have developed

to achieve an order of peace and justice, to promote [the states'] solidarity, to strengthen their collaboration, and to defend their sovereignty, their territorial integrity and their independence. Within the United Nations, the Organization of American States is a regional agency.

In Article 4, the Charter proclaims the following five essential purposes "in order to put into practice the principles on which the OAS is founded and to fulfill its regional obligations under the Charter of the United Nations":

a. To strengthen the peace and security of the continent;
b. To prevent possible causes of difficulties and to ensure the pacific settlement of disputes that may arise among the Member States;
c. To provide for common action on the part of those States in the event of aggression;
d. To seek the solution of political, juridical and economic problems that may arise among them; and
e. To promote, by cooperative action, their economic, social and cultural development.

Principles

Article 5 deals with the principles that guide the organization and on which the OAS is based. It enumerates twelve principles that the American States here reaffirm. Among the most important are the following:

a. International law is the standard of conduct of States in their reciprocal relations;
b. International order consists essentially of respect for the personality, sovereignty and independence of States, and the faithful fulfillment of obligations derived from treaties and other sources of international law;
c. Good faith shall govern the relations between States;

d. The solidarity of the American States and the high aims which are sought through [the OAS] require the political organization of those States on the basis of the effective exercise of representative democracy;

e. The American States condemn war of aggression; victory does not give rights;

f. An act of aggression against one American State is an act of aggression against all the other American States;

[(g) through (i) are not listed here];

j. The American States proclaim the fundamental rights of the individual without distinction as to race, nationality, creed or sex;

k. The spiritual unity of the continent is based on respect for the cultural values of the American countries and requires their close cooperation for the high purposes of civilization;

[(l) is not listed here].

The principles on which the OAS is based have Western liberal-democratic and Spanish-medieval roots, but they show American traits. Some have their origin in the work of Francisco de Vitoria, the founder of modern international law. Others show a synthesis, namely that of the Puritan North American tradition with the characteristic Hispanic-American idealism, as in the case of the condemnation of wars of aggression, which is reminiscent of the Kellogg-Briand Pact of Paris (1928), and the very Argentine doctrine that "victory does not give rights." The OAS Charter clearly indicates that international law is the standard of conduct of states in their reciprocal relations, that good faith shall govern the relations between the states, and that the solidarity of the American states and the aims that are sought through it require a political realization of these purposes on the basis of the effective exercise of representative democracy. It also affirms that the American states condemn war of aggression and that victory does not give rights, that an act of aggression against one American state represents an act of aggression against all the others, that the controversies that may arise between the member states shall be settled by peaceful means through the existing inter-American procedures, and that social justice and social security are the basis of a lasting peace.

Fundamental Rights and Duties of States, Pacific Settlement of Disputes, and Collective Security

In its next three chapters, the Charter deals with the fundamental rights and duties of states, pacific settlement of disputes, and collective security. Again, the Charter makes it clear that states, whether small or big, powerful or weak, enjoy equal rights and have equal duties. Moreover, Article 15 explicitly states a goal that Latin American countries had been seeking for a very long time:

Art. 15.—No State or group of States has the right to intervene, directly or indirectly, for any reason whatever, in the internal or external affairs of any other State. The foregoing principle prohibits not only armed force but also any other form of inter-ference or attempted threat against the personality of the State or against its political, economic and cultural elements.

Equally clear are the next two articles. Article 16 states explicitly that no state "may use or encourage the use of coercive measures of an economic or political character" in order to pursue selfish aims, and Article 17 says that "the territory of a State is inviolable; it may not be the object, even temporarily, of military occupation or of other measures of force taken by another State, directly or indirectly, on any grounds whatever."

In regard to the pacific settlement of disputes (Articles 20–23), the Charter reaffirms that all international disputes "that may arise between American States shall be submitted to the peaceful procedures set forth in this Charter" before being referred to the Security Council of the United Nations, and it lists the different methods for such pacific settlement: direct negotiation, good offices, mediation, investigation and conciliation, judicial settlement, arbitration, "and those which the parties to the dispute may especially agree upon at any time."

Finally, concerning collective security, the member states reaffirm in Article 24 that aggression by a state "against the territorial integrity or the inviolability of the territory or against the sovereignty or political inde-pendence of an American state shall be considered an act of aggression against the other American States."

Standards

The first part of the Charter ends with the economic, social, and cultural standards (Articles 26–31). The social standards refer to social legislation that member states shall enact for the benefit of all, without distinction as to race, nationality, sex, creed, or social condition, in order to have them attain material well-being and grow spiritually. Economic cooperation is also stressed as essential to the common welfare and prosperity of all peoples of the continent. Furthermore, the Charter proclaims the fundamental rights of the individual, the spiritual unity of the continent, which is based on the respect for the cultural values of each of the American countries, and the goals toward which the education of the peoples should be geared, namely justice, freedom, and peace. The cultural standards deal with the explicit right of each human being to education (particularly elementary education, which shall be accessible to all), and to the free cultural interchange among the member states.

It is evident that, in many instances, the enumeration of principles, stan-dards, and purposes reflects an ideal that is not readily realizable. This becomes particularly apparent in the operation of two principles that are fundamental to the inter-American system yet at times contradict each other: the principles of the effective exercise of representative democracy and nonintervention. Concerning the former, Latin America is much at fault; while in regard to the second, the United States is at fault, intervening even today whenever it feels its interests are at stake. Many of the ideals expressed in the charter are typical expressions of the Hispanic idealization of a program without regard to the possibility of its realization.

This tendency runs throughout all Hispanic-American history. It was found during the Spanish colonial period with the progressive *Recopilación de las Leyes de los Reynos de Indias* and in the nineteenth century with the region's idealistic constitutions. It was true of Bolívar's Constitution of 1826, which has been called a poem rather than a legal document. Moreover, the Alliance for Progress, as well as the hundreds of resolutions, acts, and declarations of the OAS, also reflect that same spirit, which was brilliantly captured by Miguel de Cervantes and which, despite the passage of centuries, has been preserved with tenacity in the Hispanic-American republics. In this respect it makes no difference whether the Hispanic-American republics are basically Indian (e.g., Guatemala, Ecuador, Peru, and Bolivia), have a mestizo character (e.g., Mexico, Nicaragua, Honduras, El Salvador, Chile, Venezuela, Colombia, and Paraguay), are white (e.g., Argentina, Uruguay, and Costa Rica), or have strong black elements: Essentially, their culture is marked by Hispanic traits.

Furthermore, this tendency of idealization is also linked to a historic laxity in the enforcement of laws that began with the Spanish conquest (as well as the Portuguese penetration of Brazil)—a direct result of the Spanish policy of assimilation that was in keeping with the philosophy of the Spanish monarchs to respect rights of the vanquished, as long as doing so did not contradict the interests of the Crown.[1] It resulted in Indian legislation and in a divorce between law and reality—between the legal situation (the situation as it ought to be) and the situation as it really was (the social reality)—a situation symbolized by the formula *Se acata, pero no se cumple*. With this formula, a viceroy, who did not like a certain law or thought it was not applicable, had the right to publish the law with the fascinating little notice that "the law was followed but did not need to be enforced (or obeyed)."[2]

Structure

The second part of the Charter refers to the structure of the OAS. Chapter IX, Article 32, enumerates the various bodies in the order of importance:

a. The Inter-American Conference (Articles 33–38);

b. The Meeting of Consultation of Ministers of Foreign Affairs (Articles 39–47);

c. The Council of the OAS, to which are attached three technical bodies (Articles 48–77);

d. The Pan American Union (Articles 78–92);

e. The Inter-American Specialized Conferences (Articles 93–94); and

f. The Inter-American Specialized Organizations (Articles 95–101), of which there are six.

The first three groups are the highest bodies of the OAS. They form, so to speak, the political elite, from which emanate the directives and assignments to the lower bodies, such as, for instance, the technical organs of the Council of the Organization or the Pan American Union, now called General Secretariat. These three bodies make all decisions, be they political, military, legal, administrative, economic, social, technical, or cultural.

In addition, there are several technical institutions of a special status, all of which have their permanent seat in Washington, D.C. They include the Special Consultative Committee on Security (SCCS), the Inter-American Statistical Institute (IASI), the Inter-American Commission on Human Rights (IACHR), the Inter-American Defense Board (IADB), the Inter-American Nuclear Energy Commission (IANEC), and the Inter-American Peace Committee (IAPC).

Electoral System: No Veto Right

The OAS Charter does not require that decisions be reached unanimously. Hence, unlike the UN Security Council, there is no veto right; therefore, there is no veto abuse. The reason for this provision is simple: It is inherent in the nature of the organization, in which twenty weak Latin American states face a strong neighbor. The veto right would never be accepted by the Latin Americans; had they had enough political influence in 1945, it would not even have been accepted in the United Nations. The democratic principle of the equality of nations (one country, one vote), as it guides the General Assembly of the United Nations, corresponds also to Latin American nationalism, which is the successor of Hispanic regionalism and local patriotism. Ordinary decisions are made by simple majority (i.e., by eleven out of twenty-one votes). However, in the higher bodies, and on important decisions, a two-thirds majority is required.

This Charter was valid from 1948–1951 to 1970, when it was superseded by the Protocol of Amendments to the Charter, signed on February 27, 1967, at the Third Special International Conference of American States in Buenos Aires (it went into effect on February 27, 1970, after ratification of more than the mandatory two-third's majority had been achieved). The original charter guided the OAS through one of the most important periods of the inter-American system, but by the 1960s it had become clear that, for a variety of reasons, it had to be changed and updated again in order to reflect a rapidly moving world.

4

The OAS (1948 through 1967–1970): The Inter-American Conference, the Meeting of Consultation of Ministers of Foreign Affairs, and the Council of the OAS

THE INTER-AMERICAN CONFERENCE

In accordance with Article 32, the first three bodies of the OAS hold the highest rank, and among these the Inter-American Conference tops the list. The Inter-American Conference, the highest authority of the organization, is divided into regular and special conferences. It determines the policy of the organization as well as the structure and authority of its bodies. Moreover, it is empowered to deal with any matter concerning the American republics.

The Regular Inter-American Conference

The Inter-American Conference is a sizable assembly of the American member states and is composed of large delegations of prominent citizens. The agenda and the regulations of the Inter-American Conference are prepared in advance by the Council of the OAS and are submitted to the various governments before the conference is convened. The agenda usually comprises political, juridical, social, economic, and cultural problems that have been worked on for months, and sometimes years, in committees and subcommittees. When they are deemed suitable, they are submitted to the governments, which then determine if they can be presented to the Inter-American Conference. The numerous resolutions, declarations, and acts that are accepted by the Inter-American Conference become the directives and assignments for the lower bodies. Unfortunately, many of these resolutions tend to disappear in the deep recesses of the General Secretariat, where they gather dust.

The Inter-American Conference meets every five years. It was institutionalized through the charter after functioning in an irregular manner, and with only some Spanish-American countries as participants, during the nineteenth century. It has met regularly at intervals of approximately five years since the establishment of the inter-American system (1889–1890). The most important of these conferences were those of Washington, D.C. (1889–1890), Santiago (1923), Montevideo (1933), and Bogotá (1948). Until the Ninth International Conference of American States, the largest capitals had been chosen as conference hosts. Few other large capitals remained by 1948, so that in the future Caracas, Quito, La Paz, and Guatemala would have been the next choices. Actually, the Tenth International Conference of American States was indeed held in Caracas, and the eleventh was supposed to take place in Quito.

The Tenth International Conference of American States, Caracas (1954)

This Tenth International Conference was actually the last of the original conferences of the inter-American system. Two important problems came under discussion: the communist danger in Latin America and the possibility of large-scale U.S. economic aid. The conference also decided on the so-called Declaration of Solidarity for the Preservation of the Political Integrity of the Americas against the Intervention of International Communism. This Declaration, which was urged by U.S. Secretary of State John Foster Dulles, stated that control of the political institutions of any American state by international communism would constitute a menace to all and would call for a Meeting of Consultation of Ministers of Foreign Affairs to consider the steps necessary to deal with such a situation. The reason for this declaration was the "communist" danger in Guatemala. The OAS was split: While the United States, in the middle of its anticommunist crusade, saw in the government of Jacobo Arbenz Guzmán a communist threat to its interests in Guatemala—a prelude of things to come in Central America in the 1980s— Latin America held a different view, seeing in the policies of the Guatemalan regime a necessity for social reform. The Declaration remained ineffective in practice, not only in this case, but particularly in the case of Cuba that was to be seen later. The Declaration was reminiscent of the famous Protocol of Troppau (1820), signed by the three Holy Alliance powers, which was a statement of collective security against revolution that read:

States belonging to the European alliance, which have undergone in their internal structure an alteration brought about by revolt, whose consequences may be dangerous to other states, cease automatically to be members of the alliance. [If such states] cause neighboring states to feel an immediate danger, and if action by the Great Powers can be effective and beneficial, the Great Powers will take steps to bring the disturbed area back into the European system, first of all by friendly representations, and secondly by force if force becomes necessary to this end.[1]

The tenth conference was characterized by a tenacious U.S. display of so-called Pan American unity in the form of requesting the Latin Americans for concerted action against communist subversion while at the same time showing no great concern for Latin American economic and social troubles. It was to become a landmark in the erosion of U.S.–Latin American relations and, hence, of the Pan American movement, since similar manifestations of "partnership" were to occur in the future.

The Eleventh International Conference of American States, Quito (1959)

The Eleventh Conference was scheduled to meet in Quito in 1959, but it was never convened. The internal situations of Ecuador and Peru, and the political instability and uncertainty that the two countries faced, was one factor in the postponement; however, the general erosion of the Pan American movement also was responsible. No one desired a repetition of the sad display of disunity that had characterized the Tenth Conference in Caracas. Thus, the Eleventh Conference was never held, and many subjects that were to be discussed in the Quito Conference were simply handled by the special economic and political conferences of the OAS of the late 1950s and early 1960s.

In 1963, the OAS resolved to convoke the Quito Conference on April 1, 1964, but then it was decided to postpone it indefinitely. In its stead, a Meeting of Consultation was held in Washington in July 1964, at which Cuba was again discussed.

The Special Inter-American Conference

In extraordinary circumstances, special Inter-American Conferences can be convened. Four such special, unnumbered conferences have been held. Thus, in 1928–1929, such a conference met in Washington, D.C., in order to discuss the question of the procedure of conciliation and arbitration of disputes among the American states. The special Inter-American Conference for the Consolidation of Peace (1936), which met to settle the Chaco War, dealt with the question of collective security and thus also with the problems of neutrality and inter-American solidarity and cooperation. Moreover, it strengthened the principle of nonintervention by adopting an Additional Protocol, and it proclaimed a new and interesting principle: obligatory consultation, the mechanism of which was elaborated at the Eighth International Conference of American States (Lima). The Meeting of Consultation, which had already been put into practice three times during World War II, was then institutionalized by the Charter. The special Inter-American Conference on Problems of War and Peace (Chapultepec, 1945) met to discuss postwar problems in general as well as the forthcoming conference of the United Nations in San Francisco, the Argentine question, and the preparatory works for a military pact of assistance, which was taken up two years later in the special Inter-American Conference for the Maintenance of Continental Peace and Security in Rio de Janeiro (1947).

The special Inter-American Conference can be convoked only when two-thirds of the American governments agree that special problems justify and require a conference on the highest level; in other words, when problems arise that cannot be postponed until the next regular Inter-American Conference. With the Eleventh International Conference of American States continuously being postponed, and with some serious problems to be resolved, a series of special Inter-American conferences were held, which in some cases were actually stopgap measures until the Charter could be revised. Since more than one special conference was held, the organization began to number them, as in the case of the regular Inter-American Conferences, although this did not include the four that had already taken place between 1928–1929 and 1947.

The First Special Inter-American Conference of American States, Washington, D.C. (1964)

The background of this meeting was the independence of Jamaica and of Trinidad and Tobago, the first two countries to become independent in the Commonwealth Caribbean. It was not only the fact that a whole avalanche of new mini-states would soon become independent and thus apply for membership in the OAS, but also the realization that with this new membership, the traditional inter-American system was finished. For over seventy years, the inter-American system, both before and after the establishment of the OAS, represented an intergovernmental agency in which a majority of Latin American countries (especially the eighteen Spanish-speaking nations, despite their political and economic weaknesses), held a dominant role in regard to the powerful United States. The new reality was a serious development that was more than a matter of adding new members and possibly changing voting patterns. It was the question of whether, in the future, an independent Caribbean, comprising the English-speaking area and Dutch-speaking Suriname, would represent a revolutionary element; in other words, whether, in the last analysis, it would side with Latin America on basic issues or whether, in view of its different culture, it would follow the lead of the United States. In the latter case, the traditional Latin American role would be seriously challenged—it would upset the entire organization. There were also other questions that concerned Guatemala and Venezuela in particular.

The first special conference was held in December 1964 in Washington, D.C., to draft procedures for the admission of such new members, thus remedying an omission in the charter, which did not provide for this. The conference thus confronted the issue, although it was only the beginning of a new relationship that gradually would be solved in the sense that Latin

America and the Caribbean would essentially join forces and share a perspective on problems of political democracy, collective security, nonintervention, and so forth.

Participants at the First Special Inter-American Conference of American States signed the Act of Washington setting forth procedures for admitting new members. Since membership was an important issue, it required a two-third's majority. At the same time, the Act of Washington excluded territories that were subject to claim by an American state (Guyana in regard to Venezuela, and Belize/British Honduras in regard to Guatemala). At that time, both Venezuela and Guatemala hoped that their territorial claims to most parts of Guyana (in the case of Venezuela) and to the totality of Belize/British Honduras (in the case of Guatemala) would eventually be solved to their full satisfaction. This did not happen, and both countries, in the course of the past few decades, have relaxed their opposition to the membership of Guyana and Belize. As a matter of fact, both Guyana and Belize became full members of the OAS on January 8, 1991.

The Second Special Inter-American Conference of American States, Rio de Janeiro (1965)

The background of this special inter-American meeting was a growing malaise in the OAS. No doubt, the inter-American system had served its purpose, and the modernization and streamlining of the organization in 1948 was a very positive development. However, the nations of the world, including those of the Western Hemisphere, had evolved very quickly, and many changes that had been incorporated in the OAS when it was established in 1948 no longer seemed adequate. Problems had accumulated, as had criticism. The 1950s were still productive years, but already in 1954, Secretary General Alberto Lleras Camargo resigned at the Tenth International Conference of American States in Caracas because he was unhappy about the way in which the organization was moving, that is, lack of funds and an increase in bureaucracy with no tangible positive results. Moreover, the powers of a secretary general of the OAS were much weaker than those of the Secretary General of the United Nations; his hands were tied since many governments, such as Mexico, did not want a stronger OAS. His criticism was a symptom of a much larger issue that obviously also involved U.S.–Latin American relations, which were fast deteriorating following the U.S. abandonment of the Good Neighbor policy. The direct U.S. intervention, in 1954, in Guatemala through a Central Intelligency Agency–led invasion only showed that the old ghosts of marine landings were quite alive.

A growing movement for new changes in the OAS, for a new modernization, and again for a new strengthening of the political, juridical, and institutional aspects of the Inter-American system thus took place, resulting in another special inter-American Conference to deal specifically with this issue.

The Second Special Inter-American Conference acknowledged the need to reform the charter and began the difficult task of readjusting the inter-American system to the new realities of the 1960s. Although the system had been strengthened in 1948, there was clearly room for improvement, and thus the agenda was sufficiently broad to incorporate any question of mutual interest. The conference, which was based on a nine-point memorandum submitted by then Secretary General José Antonio Mora Otero, was scheduled for May 1965 but had to be postponed in view of the landing of U.S. marines in the Dominican Republic and took place in November of that year. Besides recognizing the urgent need for reforming the charter and providing instructions to proceed in that direction, the conference also dealt with the Inter-American Commission on Human Rights, whose powers were broadened significantly, especially in Art. 9bis of its statute.[2]

The Third Special Inter-American Conference of American States, Buenos Aires (1967)

This conference continued the work that was begun in the first special conference and intensified in the second. It produced the Protocol of Amendment to the Charter of the OAS (known as the Protocol of Buenos Aires), which entered into effect three years later.

The protocol introduced substantial changes into the charter. Suffice it to mention the elimination of the Inter-American Conferences, both regular and special, and their replacement by yearly meetings of the General Assembly. No special Inter-American Conferences were held after the third.

THE MEETING OF CONSULTATION OF MINISTERS OF FOREIGN AFFAIRS

As stated earlier, the Meetings of Consultation were established at the Eighth International Conference of American States in Lima in 1938. During World War II, three consecutive Meetings of Consultation of this special inter-American conference proved its validity. (These meetings are held whenever urgent problems arise jointly concerning member states.) A request for such a meeting can be addressed by any member state to the Council of the OAS, which then decides on the appropriateness and the necessity of such a conference. The agenda and the regulations of the Meeting of Consultation are prepared by the Council of the OAS and submitted to the member governments in advance.

The Rio Treaty stipulates that in the case of an act of aggression committed against an American state or within the geographic security zone (Article 4, which established a security zone from the North Pole to the South Pole and included the Atlantic and Pacific oceans but excluded the Hawaiian Islands), a Meeting of Consultation must be called immediately. Simultaneously, the chairman of the Council of the OAS convokes the Council of the Organization, which then meets provisionally as the Organ of Consultation. In the case of an act of aggression, the Organ of Consultation is assisted by an Advisory Defense Committee, which is composed of the highest military personnel of the American states and convened under the same circumstances as the provisional Organ of Consultation. However, to date, this committee has never met. If the problem can be solved by the council acting provisionally as an Organ of Consultation, a Meeting of Consultation does not take place; however, if the crisis deepens, a Meeting of Consultation of Foreign Ministers is a foregone conclusion. After World War II, many more Meetings of Consultation were held, as follows:

The Fourth Meeting of Consultation of Ministers of Foreign Affairs, Washington, D.C. (1951)

The background of this Meeting of Consultation was the communist takeover of China and the North Korean invasion of South Korea in June 1950. The agenda of the meeting included political and military cooperation for the defense of the hemisphere, the strengthening of internal security, and emergency economic measures. The meeting produced some thirty resolutions, including the Declaration of Washington, which reaffirmed inter-American solidarity and recognized the threat of international communism. It declared its firm support of the United Nations and recommended measures to increase the defense capabilities of the hemisphere in order to safeguard peace and security.

On the other hand, many delegates felt that the danger of international communism could best be prevented by raising standards of living; thus, Resolution X stated that underdevelopment created a friendly environment for alien ideologies. In a way, the question of economic measures was a continuation of the U.S.–Latin American debate on economic cooperation that was begun at the Mexico City Conference of 1945.

The Fifth Meeting of Consultation of Ministers of Foreign Affairs, Santiago de Chile (1959)

The background of this famous meeting was the extraordinary increase in revolutionary activity, especially in the Caribbean, and the resulting conviction that simple solutions were no longer possible. The Fifth Meeting of Santiago strengthened the powers of the Inter-American Peace Committee, though subject to rescission. However, the centerpiece of the fifth meeting was the Declaration on the Principles of Representative Democracy and Human Rights. It was believed that the underlying cause of the political turmoil, which in one instance had led to the downfall of the Fulgencio Batista y Zaldívar regime in Cuba and the seizure of power by Fidel Castro on the island, was the lack of representative democracy and human rights, and that if both could be instilled the source of so much social and political trouble could be overcome. Though the proclamation of the declaration was a welcome demonstration of both idealism and realism, it should have been evident that simple proclamations do not solve problems and that the issues were much broader than representative democracy and human rights. Thus, despite the fact that the Inter-American Peace Committee was being kept quite busy, the solution sought at Santiago remained an illusion. Very soon, two more Meetings of Consultation had to be convened because of increased tensions in the Caribbean.

The Sixth and Seventh Meetings of Consultation of Ministers of Foreign Affairs, San José, Costa Rica (1960)

The Sixth Meeting of Consultation was convoked in San José, Costa Rica, as a result of a Venezuelan protest and request for such a meeting, which accused the regime of Rafael Leónidas Trujillo Molina, president of the Dominican Republic, of plotting against the life of President Rómulo Betancourt of Venezuela. The OAS decided to send an investigating committee, which reported on August 17, 1960, to the Meeting of Consultation in San José that the Venezuelan charges were valid. The sixth meeting thus found the Dominican Republic guilty on all counts, proceeded to condemn it, and decreed the breaking off of diplomatic relations with that nation as well as imposing economic sanctions, beginning with the immediate suspension of arms and implements of war of every kind. Sanctions would be discontinued only when a two-thirds majority had agreed that the government of the Dominican Republic had ceased to be a danger to the peace and security of the hemisphere.

As a result of this damaging indictment, the OAS recommended that the economic sanctions be widened to include petroleum and petroleum products, trucks, and truck parts—an extension which was voted favorably by the Council of the OAS on January 4, 1961.[3] It was due to the sanctions that the regime of Trujillo collapsed in the same year. After the resignation and assassination of Trujillo in that same year, the Council of the OAS lifted the sanctions on the grounds that the Dominican Republic no longer presented a threat to peace and security.[4]

The Seventh Meeting of Consultation followed immediately after the sixth in the same city. This time, the focus was on Cuba. It would be the first of the many inter-American gatherings on the Castro Revolution. It was called on the request of Peru at a time when that revolution signaled a radicalization and a deterioration of relations between the United States and Cuba. Moreover, Castro was now exporting his revolution, with his partisans landing in Panama, Nicaragua, and Haiti. We should also bear in mind that at the time, the Cuban Revolution was highly popular all over Latin America and governments were not much inclined to listen to the usual U.S. position on the protection of its citizens' lives and properties. At the same time, it was quite popular to move against the increasingly criticized Trujillo regime in the Dominican Republic. This explains the result of the two Meetings of Consultation that were held in San José in 1960.

A first decision in regard to the two issues was not to deal with Trujillo and Castro in the same meeting. This is why two Meetings of Consultation were held in the same capital. Actually, the first week dealt with the relatively easier case of Trujillo, while the second week represented a continuation of the Sixth Meeting of Consultation but was called the seventh meeting and dealt with a much more difficult problem. As in the case of Guatemala, which had come to the fore at the regular Tenth International Conference of American States in Caracas in 1954, the United States argued that communism and Soviet assistance threatened the hemisphere with international communism. The case of Guatemala had shown clearly that a Latin American country that was bent on social and economic reforms had to collide with the interests of the United States, particularly in the countries of the Caribbean and Central America, and that real protection could only come from the Soviet bloc—neither Latin America nor Europe would be willing or able to extend prolonged aid. Furthermore, Latin America saw the Cuban problem differently, as part of the usual principle of the legitimate exercise of self-determination, and was in favor of nonintervention as outlined in the fundamental rights and duties of states set forth by the OAS. Latin America also viewed the Cuban situation as a bilateral problem concerning only the United States and Cuba. Hence, Latin Americans were not prepared to accept the U.S. point of view, which was presented, in this case, by U.S. Secretary of State Christian Herter.

The result of the debates on the issue was the Declaration of San José, the intention of which was to solve the problems between Washington, and Havana peacefully and not to take drastic measures against Castro. The Cuban delegation walked out of the sessions with the argument that the OAS offered no protection against the United States. In any case, the Declaration of San José condemned intervention, or the threat of intervention, by extracontinental powers in the affairs of an American state on the grounds that it endangered American solidarity and security, and it rejected the attempts of the Sino-Soviet powers to make use of the political, economic, or social situation of any American state. At the same time, the meeting reaffirmed the principle of nonintervention by any American state in the internal or external affairs of the other American states and reiterated that each state had the right to develop its cultural, political, and economic life freely and naturally, respecting the rights of the individual and the principles of universal morality. No American state might intervene for the purpose of imposing on another its ideologies or its political, economic, or social principles. Finally, the Declaration of San José reaffirmed the incompatibility of the inter-American system with any form of totalitarianism, proclaimed the duty of all members of the OAS to submit to the discipline of the inter-American system, stated that all controversies should be resolved by the instruments of the regional system, and reaffirmed its faith in the seventy-year-old organization.

The result of these two meetings was not fully satisfactory and was much influenced by the relative popularity of the two protagonists. On the one hand, an economic boycott was voted against the rightist Trujillo regime, while on the other hand Latin America refused to take common action against Castro's Cuba, although it had approved joint action against Trujillo a week earlier, at the Sixth Meeting of Consultation. The measures taken at the sixth and seventh Meetings of Consultation were soon to prove themselves Pyrrhic victories because they watered down the principle of collective security (in the case of Cuba) and transgressed against the principle of nonintervention (in the case of the Dominican Republic). This situation would only be corrected at the next—the eighth—Meeting of Consultation. In the meantime, the Cuban problem, far from vanishing, would increase tensions and lead to the ill-fated Bay of Pigs invasion, and as a result, U.S. prestige deteriorated further.

The Eighth Meeting of Consultation of Ministers of Foreign Affairs, Punta del Este, Uruguay (1962)

This meeting dealt again with the Cuban problem, which had not been solved at either the fifth or seventh Meetings of Consultation, or through the political portions (representative democracy, political stability, and social justice) of the Alliance for Progress. It was held at a time of lowered U.S. prestige. Both Colombia and Peru argued for a meeting to deal with what was perceived as an increasing threat to the stability of the Latin American countries. Peru had started the ball rolling by requesting a Meeting of Consultation with the aim at looking at the increasing Cuban-Soviet ties. This request was referred to the General Committee of the OAS, which in time gave the task to the Inter-American Peace Committee under Resolution IV of the Fifth Meeting of Consultation. Then, Colombia requested a meeting, invoking the Rio Treaty since peace and security were threatened. Although most other Latin American countries were not very happy in dealing with Cuba in a new Meeting of Consultation, such a gathering was finally held in Punta del Este in early 1962. Since it was isolated and had only one main road leading to it, Punta del Este seemed the perfect place for such a conference. It was certainly more secure than Montevideo.

Whatever the specific quarrel between Cuba and the United States, it was agreed that Cuban ties to the Sino-Soviet bloc were incompatible with the principles and nature of the inter-American system. By now, the Cuban crisis with its revolutionary challenge had become the most important issue in inter-American as well as U.S.–Latin American relations.

The Eighth Meeting of Consultation did not provide a model for a unified hemisphere. The members of the OAS were much divided in regard to the continued Cuban crisis. Those who insisted on punishment were the United States, the Dominican Republic, Colombia, Venezuela, Paraguay, Peru, and the Central American nations.[5] Argentina, Bolivia, Brazil, Chile, Ecuador, and Mexico opposed sanctions, while Uruguay and Haiti were undecided. Some members did not believe in any Cuban threat to the hemisphere, and others questioned the legality of suspending Cuba from the organization. Thus, Argentina opposed both communism and intervention into Cuban affairs; Bolivia stood on self-determination and nonintervention; Brazil opposed OAS intervention into the internal affairs of member countries for any reason; Chile questioned the legal basis of the meeting, even while it agreed that communism was incompatible with the inter-American system and that Cuba had "placed itself on the periphery of the latter"[6]; Mexico argued that the meeting had not been properly called and thus lacked a legal basis; and Haiti wished to remain neutral, opting for both non-intervention and self-determination.[7]

Eight resolutions were passed. Resolution I dealt with the communist offensive in America which established the legal basis against Cuba, while the others spelled out the measures to be taken. Resolution II established a "Special Consultative Committee on Security against the Subversive Actions of International Communism," similar to the one set up during World War II; the motion passed almost unanimously, with only Bolivia abstaining and Cuba voting against it. Resolution IV dealt with the holding of free elections, and Resolution V with the Alliance for Progress. The last three resolutions, VI–VIII, were the most important ones, and are described below.

Resolution VI

While reaffirming the desirability of strengthening the inter-American system on the basis of respect for human rights and support of representative democracy, the eighth meeting resolved:

1. That adherence by any member of the Organization of American States to Marxism-Leninism is incompatible with the inter-American system and the alignment of such a government with the communist bloc breaks the unity and solidarity of the hemisphere.
2. That the present Government of Cuba, which has officially identified itself as a Marxist-Leninist government, is incompatible with the principles and objectives of the inter-American system.
3. That this incompatibility excludes the present Government of Cuba from participation in the inter-American system.
4. That the Council of the Organization of American States and the other organs and organizations of the inter-American system adopt without delay the measures necessary to carry out this resolution.[8]

This resolution excluded Cuba from the OAS, but since this was legally questionable, the Meeting of Consultation decided to use a legal nicety: "the present Government of Cuba." After all, at the Fifth International Conference of American States in Santiago de Chile (in 1923), in its twelfth session (on May 1), the resolution on the Organization of the Pan American Union (number 45) stated explicitly that "the representation of the Governments in International Conferences and in the Pan American Union is by their own right."[9]

The voting in regard to this problem at the eighth meeting was quite revealing. While on the first two points there was unanimity (twenty votes in favor; Cuba opposed), the tricky third point hardly passed. Only Haiti's last-minute change of mind through U.S. pressure enabled approval of the resolution for the exclusion of "the present Government of Cuba." Six countries abstained: Argentina, Bolivia, Brazil, Chile, Ecuador, and Mexico; Cuba voted against. In the past there had been another exclusion, although only at one meeting—the Inter-American Conference on Problems of War and Peace in Mexico City, 1945, when Argentina was refused attendance by the United States. This also had been legally questionable, and was thus an unfortunate precedent in the minds of many delegates.

Resolution VII

Here Cuba was excluded from the Inter-American Defense Board. The resolution seemed logical and thus was passed unanimously (with Cuba voting against the resolution).

Resolution VIII

This resolution dealt with sanctions, and therefore again many difficulties arose. Arms traffic with Cuba was forbidden, and the Council of the OAS was instructed to extend this prohibition to commercial goods as well. The vote on the entire resolution was sixteen in favor, Cuba voting against, and four abstentions (Argentina, Bolivia, Brazil, and Mexico).

The Eighth Meeting of Consultation did not achieve the sort of broad collective action that it had set as a goal for itself. Cuba protested its exclusion from the entire inter-American system—it even appealed to the United Nations, and the OAS gave the appearance of disarray. It is thus correct to assert that, in the long run, the eighth meeting was to be judged as possibly more prejudicial than useful to the Pan American movement and the inter-American system. It certainly did not deter Cuba from exporting revolution, nor did it immunize Latin American government against it, since the latter firmly believed that Cuba's form of government was solely a Cuban affair and not for others to decide. Moreover, these same governments did not believe that Castro's Cuba and its relations with the Soviet Union represented a threat to them. However, those who had to face Castro-backed guerrilla movements took a diferent view (e.g., Central America and Venezuela), and no doubt, the missile crisis of October 1962, which arose in the same year, convinced many skeptics that not everything emanating from Havana was as peaceful as was earlier believed.

The Cuban Missile Crisis

The Cuban Missile Crisis of 1962, which followed soon after the Eighth Meeting of Consultation, was a U.S.–Soviet affair, and thus did not lead to a new Meeting of Consultation. The United States informed the OAS on October 22, 1962, about the unacceptable stationing of foreign nuclear missiles on Cuban soil and requested a meeting. The Council of the OAS then constituted itself provisionally as an Organ of Consultation, although it never called for a Meeting of Consultation. One reason was simply that the crisis was moving too fast and was too sensitive. In reality, it was being dealt with on a purely bilateral basis. The Council of the OAS, acting provisionally as an Organ of Consultation, accepted U.S. evidence of nuclear weapons in Cuba and resolved to call for the immediate dismantling and withdrawal from Cuba of all missiles and other weapons with any offensive capability. Moreover, it recommended to all member states, on the basis of Articles 6 and 8 of the Rio Treaty, that they take all necessary steps, including the use of force. The Organ of Consultation thus gave the United States full backing. Though it did not provide for collective action, it made it possible for other member states, in case of need, to cooperate with the United States.

The Ninth Meeting of Consultation of Ministers of Foreign Affairs, Washington, D.C. (1964)

The request for the ninth meeting came from Venezuela, which requested consideration of the case of the Dominican Republic during the Sixth Meeting of Consultation in 1960. Venezuela accused the Cuban government of complicity in the terrorization of Venezuelan political life. On the basis of the Venezuelan accusation, the Council of the OAS convoked the Organ of Consultation (with the council acting provisionally as such), which then resolved to convoke the Ninth Meeting of Consultation after its Investigating Committee had proved the charge that was brought by Venezuela. The Ninth Meeting of Consultation decided on further sanctions against the present government of Cuba.

The meeting, basing itself on Articles 6 and 8 of the Rio Treaty, then asserted the following:

a. That the governments of the American states not maintain diplomatic or consular relations with the Government of Cuba;

b. That the governments of the American states suspend all their trade, whether direct or indirect, with Cuba, except in foodstuffs, medicines, and medical equipment that may be sent to Cuba for humanitarian reasons; and

c. That the governments of the American states suspend all sea transportation between their countries and Cuba, except for such transportation as may be necessary for reasons of a humanitarian nature.[10]

These measures were adopted with the abstention of Bolivia, Chile, Mexico, and Uruguay, states that, at the time, still maintained relations with Cuba. In contrast with their actions at Punta del Este (eighth meeting), several countries—Argentina, Brazil, and Ecuador—now voted in favor of positive action against Cuba, since in the meantime their governments had changed. Following the end of the conference, three of the abstaining countries—Bolivia, Chile, and Uruguay—broke off relations with Cuba and hence followed the mandate of the Ninth Meeting of Consultation. That left Mexico as the only country to maintain relations with Havana, and indeed, Mexico never broke off relations. The sanctions adopted at the Ninth Meeting of Consultation in 1964 were binding on all member states and could be lifted only by a two-thirds vote of the Council of the OAS at a time when the Cuban threat to peace and security would be judged to have ceased to exist.

The Tenth Meeting of Consultation of Ministers of Foreign Affairs, Washington, D.C. (1965–1970)

The background of this meeting was the landing of U.S. marines in the Dominican Republic in order to forestall the possibility of another Cuban-type revolutionary government. We should not forget that Castro continued to export revolution despite many setbacks. In the Dominican Republic, the collapse of the Trujillo regime as a result of the sanctions imposed by the Sixth Meeting of Consultation (1960), and Trujillo's assassination a year later, led to a period of turmoil. In 1962, Juan Bosch, an old opponent of Trujillo, had won the elections, thus becoming the first democratically elected president to take office after three decades of Trujillo's tyranny. However, Bosch attempted to introduce changes into the country too quickly, and therefore, after only seven months, was overthrown by armed forces representing not only landholders and businesspersons but other sectors of society as well. The military was not able to pacify the country and three years later was challenged by a revolutionary movement which quickly was able to take control of an important small part of the capital city, Santo Domingo. It was the aim of this revolutionary group to bring Bosch back to power.

It was at this stage that the United States, not wanting a repetition of the Castro experience in Cuba (and thus for purely domestic reasons), landed the marines. As usual, the reasons for the invasion (in this case, as given by the Lyndon Johnson administration), was the protection of American lives. Soon afterwards, and again following the usual pattern, this pretext was modified, as in the case of Grenada, in 1983, in the form of an invasion intended to prevent a communist takeover.

At the request of Chile, dated May 1, 1965, the Council of the OAS called for a Meeting of Consultation which then became the tenth meeting. In this case, Articles 39 and 42 of the Charter of the OAS were invoked in order to call for the gathering. Before the meeting took place, the council appealed for a cease-fire.

For Latin Americans, the overt U.S. invasion was a very serious problem, and thus again represented a setback in inter-American relations. It was a much more serious question than the Central Intelligence Agency–financed and–led invasion of Guatemala in 1954. Most Latin American governments considered the U.S. intervention totally unjustified; they were also unhappy about the council having invoked the charter instead of the Rio Treaty.

Actually, the Tenth Meeting of Consultation was divided into two parts: the First Period of Sessions, May 1–June 2, 1965, and the Second Period of Sessions, August 9–November 2, 1965. In the First Period of Sessions, the Tenth Meeting of Consultation decided on the establishment of a Special Committee—Argentina, Brazil, Colombia, Guatemala, and Panama—which had instructions to go to Santo Domingo and reestablish peace and normalcy. This resolution passed with sixteen votes in favor, one against, and four abstentions. The United States had a hard time convincing Latin America that its marines were in the Dominican Republic only for a short time in order to protect foreign nationals; it would have been less of a problem had there existed an inter-American force for such eventualities. Most Latin American countries felt that such a force might be useful but by the same token felt that the Meeting of Consultation, instead of establishing such an inter-American force under the auspices of the OAS, should first of all condemn the United States for its violation of inter-American principles.

A great deal of diplomacy, both official and unofficial, took place in order to convert the U.S. invasion force into an inter-American force. The final vote on the establishment of the inter-American force in the Third Plenary of May 6, 1965, was fourteen in favor, five opposed (Mexico, Uruguay, Ecuador, Chile, and Peru), and one abstention (Venezuela). The text that set up the inter-American force read as follows:

1. To request governments of member states that are willing and capable of doing so to make contingents of their land, naval, air or police forces available to the Organization of American States, within their capabilities and to the extent they can do so, to form an inter-American force that will operate under the authority of this Tenth Meeting of Consultation.

2. That this Force will have as its sole purpose, in a spirit of democratic impartiality, that of cooperating in the restoration of normal conditions in the Dominican Republic, in maintaining the security of its inhabitants and the inviolability of human rights, and in the establishment of an atmosphere of peace and conciliation that will permit the functioning of democratic institutions.

3. To request the commanders of the military contingents that make up this Force to work out directly among themselves and with a committee of this Meeting the technical measures necessary to establish a Unified Command of the Organization of American States for the coordinated and effective action of the Inter-American Force. In the composition of this Force, an effort will be made to see that the national contingents shall be progressively equalized.

4. That at such time as the Unified Command of the Organization of American States shall have determined that the Inter-American Force is adequate for carrying out the purposes set forth in the resolution adopted by this Meeting on May 1, 1965, the full responsibility of fulfilling these purposes shall be assumed by that Force.

5. That the withdrawal of the Inter-American Force from the Dominican Republic shall be determined by this Meeting of Consultation.

6. To continue in session in order to keep the situation under review, to receive the report and recommendations of the Special Committee, and in the light thereof to take the necessary steps to facilitate the prompt restoration of democratic order in the Dominican Republic.

7. To inform the Security Council of the United Nations of the text of this resolution.[11]

The following countries offered troops: Brazil, Costa Rica, El Salvador, Honduras, Nicaragua, Paraguay, and the United States. Since no major country had volunteered, the United States was indeed lucky in striking a diplomatic deal with Brazil, whose armed forces had just staged a coup against the leftist regime of João Goulart in 1964 and were eager to be fully accepted. With Brazil furnishing over a thousand troops to the whole inter-American force, the latter looked better internationally. A Brazilian commander with a U.S. deputy commander took over after a few weeks.

This multilateral force superseded the U.S. invasion force and was to be withdrawn as soon as normalcy returned to the Dominican Republic. It should be emphasized that the establishment of the inter-American force was, strictly speaking, an ad hoc matter conducted exclusively for this case. It was obvious that the idea of a permanent inter-American force would come up, and the United States was very much interested in such a body. However, the concept of a permanent "inter-American fire brigade," to be unleashed every time a problem arose in Latin America, never really prospered; it was known that countries like Chile, Ecuador, Mexico, and Peru were against the establishment of such a permanent force, while others, like Argentina and Venezuela, were lukewarm.[12]

The special committee submitted two reports to the tenth meeting. In the first report, the special committee stated that the different parties in the civil strife had been brought together, that agreement had been reached for a cease-fire, that a security zone had been established, and that refugees were being evacuated. These gains were consolidated in the Act of Santo Domingo, which was signed on May 5, 1965, by the military junta and the "Constitutional Government," together with the members of the special committee, whose signature was a guarantee of its compliance and execution.[13] Now that the first phase of the special committee was terminated, it focused on the next steps to be taken: supervising the cease-fire, organizing humanitarian aid, and planning for the new force.[14]

The second report was submitted to the tenth meeting on May 19. It reported progress in regard to the evacuation of the refugees and the extension of the neutral zone, which now included the French embassy in Santo Domingo. On May 21, 1965, the tenth meeting terminated the special committee and asked the secretary general of the OAS—who was still in Santo Domingo—to see to it that the Act of Santo Domingo was being complied with and that OAS work in the Dominican Republic was coordinated with that of the United Nations, since there had been much friction between the two organizations in handling the crisis.[15]

On June 2, 1965, the tenth meeting created a new ad hoc committee to continue the work of the earlier special committee. It was able to bring together the two factions in the Dominican Republic, Héctor García Godoy, as provisional president, and Eduardo Real Barreras, as vice president, of the Republic. On August 9, the committee submitted to both parties the draft of an Act of Dominican Reconciliation, which was accepted and led to García Godoy becoming provisional president.[16]

Gradually, the political problem was solved. On September 3, 1965, the provisional government was set up with elections to be followed on June 1, 1966. On June 24, 1966, in view of normalcy having returned to the country, the tenth meeting decided to withdraw the Inter-American Force.

The U.S. landing in the Dominican Republic in 1965 and the subsequent establishment of an inter-American force was no doubt a happy ending to a very turbulent beginning. The United States was also lucky in the sense that representative democracy became consolidated in the Dominican Republic through the presidencies of its favored candidate, Joaquín Balaguer. Much of the credit to the lucky outcome at the tenth meeting went to U.S. diplomat Ellsworth Bunker and to the OAS; the former had launched the idea of a permanent inter-American force (which, as stated earlier, did not prosper and was thus not included in the future amendments to the charter).

Margaret Ball summarized it well when she said that the tenth meeting "was somewhat confusing."[17] She continued:

The Dominicans were fighting each other, which was presumably a domestic matter unless outside elements were really behind the civil conflict. The United States intervened militarily both to protect foreign nationals, including its own, and to prevent what it thought might well be another Cuba. The United States was anxious to see itself replaced by an inter-American force, in which it succeeded. The object of the Inter-American Force was not to compel an American withdrawal but both to end the unilateral activity and to assist in creating a climate in which the Dominicans, with the assistance of an OAS committee, might agree on a solution of their political problems. The Meeting which sent in the Force was acting, not under the Rio Treaty, which permits the collective use of force, but under the Charter, which prohibits either individual or collective intervention, armed or otherwise. Defense was at issue, however, no matter how one looked at the situation. From the standpoint of the United States, it was a matter of defense against an outside Communist threat, among other things; from the standpoint of most of Latin America, it was defense against the United States in the only feasible way—which, oddly enough, was by the establishment of a force not to fight the United States or a Dominican fraction but to take over from the United States the self-imposed task of defending the hemisphere against potential outside aggression. Whichever way one looks at it, the affair served to illustrate the fact that in an electronic era, military defense and political defense are perforce inextricably intertwined.[18]

Although the Tenth Meeting finished its work in 1966, it was kept open until 1970, when it finally was declared ended.

The Eleventh Meeting of Consultation of Ministers of Foreign Affairs—First Session, Washington, D.C., January 24– February 1, 1967; Second Session, Buenos Aires, February 5– 25, 1967; Third Session, Punta del Este, Uruguay, April 8–14, 1967

The background of this meeting was to prepare the groundwork for a projected assembly of American chiefs of state which was supposed to strengthen the faltering Alliance for Progress. At issue was also the increasingly important goal of Latin American economic integration and the role of the United States in this historic movement.

Thus, the agenda of the Eleventh Meeting of Consultation was quite impressive, ranging from Latin American integration and industrial development; to multinational action for infrastructure projects; to measures to improve international trade relations and conditions in Latin America; to modernization of rural life and increases of agricultural productivity (principally of food); to educational, technological and scientific development, and intensification of health programs; to elimination of unnecessary military expenditures.

The meeting (in three sessions held in different places) decided on the strengthening and consolidation of the Alliance for Progress. It also affirmed that attendance at meetings of the permanent organ of the OAS, or at conferences and meetings provided for in the charter in accordance with the multilateral nature of those organs, did not depend on any member state's bilateral relations with the government of the host country. It further decided on intensification of inter-American cooperation in order to accelerate the economic and social development of Latin America, and it reaffirmed the principles of the Charter of Punta del Este.

As one of the aims of the eleventh meeting, this conference led to the historic Meeting of American Chiefs of State, in Punta del Este, which also included for the first time the prime minister of Trinidad and Tobago and was held on April 12–14, 1967. The meeting reaffirmed the principles of the Alliance for Progress and took steps to accelerate the process. In the far distance was the goal of the establishment of a future Latin American common market.

Two points should be raised here. In the first place, the Eleventh Meeting of Consultation was held simultaneously with the Third Special Inter-American Conference, which approved the Protocol of Amendments to the Charter (the Protocol of Buenos Aires). This entered into effect in 1970 and led to the contemporary OAS structure. Though it was strange that these meetings were held simultaneously, by far the more questionable issue was the use of a Meeting of Consultation (a very serious step that always concerned the threat to peace and security) for the purpose of preparing a summit meeting. Whatever the seriousness of an economic situation may be, it does not warrant the use of such a high-level body—which was established for very specific reasons—for the promotion of the Alliance for Progress and for laying the groundwork for an inter-American gathering of chiefs of state.

The Twelveth Meeting of Consultation of Ministers of Foreign Affairs, Washington, D.C., June 19–September 24, 1968

The background of this Meeting of Consultation was the continuation of Cuban subversive activities in Venezuela; the request for the meeting came from the Venezuelan government. Subversive activities had increased in Venezuela as a result of a further falling out between the Cuban and Venezuelan governments and, of the increased revolutionary activities in that country following the Tricontinental Conference—the Afro-Asian-Latin American Peoples' Solidarity Conference, which was held in Havana in early 1966. This led to the establishment of the Organization of Latin American Solidarity (OLAS), which in turn aimed at ranging the Third World against the West and its positions all over the globe. The tripartite conference had also decided that political activity had to be closely linked to military action. Venezuela, in view of its great value to the United States (due to its oil deposits) was obviously the target of the revolutionaries, in addition to the more personal hostility betwen the Cuban and Venezuelan leaders. Furthermore, OLAS was coordinating these activities with others in Bolivia, where Ernesto (Ché) Guevara was to link up with the Argentine Ejército de Liberación Nacional (ELN).

The meeting decided to appoint a committee to investigate the charges on the spot and report to both the OAS and the Security Council of the United Nations (Resolution I). It also set up a committee of eight members to report on the above-mentioned Afro-Asian-Latin American Peoples' Solidarity Conference (Resolution II), and it condemned Cuba for repeated violations of aggression and intervention in Venezuela, Bolivia, and other

American states; it also requested governments that were not members of the OAS to restrict commercial and financial operations with Cuba, and those who supported the Afro–Asian–Latin American Peoples' Organization (AALAPSO) to withdraw their support. Moreover, the twelfth meeting also recommended steps to coordinate surveillance, security, and intelligence (Resolution III). Finally, it recommended that OAS members take this matter to the UN Security Council and urged the Latin American group at the United Nations to cooperate in the execution of this resolution (Resolution IV.

The Thirteenth Meeting of Consultation of Ministers of Foreign Affairs, Washington, D.C.—First Session, July 26, 1969–July 30, 1969; Second Phase of Activities, August 1969–November 17, 1980

Following the pattern of the tenth and eleventh Meetings of Consultation, the thirteenth also had several sessions. The background for the meeting was a Honduran request in regard to the war between that country and El Salvador, the so-called Soccer War. El Salvador had increasing demographic problems, and increasing numbers of its citizens had moved into Honduras where, in the areas close to the frontier, there developed large Salvadorean communities. It was this situation that led to war. The Thirteenth Meeting of Consultation, in its first session, ordered the immediate withdrawal of Salvadorean troops from Honduran territory and instructed the committee, which was established by the Council of the OAS acting provisionally as Organ of Consultation, to monitor the withdrawal (Resolution I). It also instructed the committee to monitor the faithful observance of the guarantees given by Honduras and El Salvador "to ensure respect for the lives, personal safety, and property of the nationals of each of these countries residing in the other." It also requested the Inter-American Commission on Human Rights to cooperate with the committee and urged both parties to bring to justice all those violating human rights. Moreover, it recommended that a census be taken of the nationals of each country residing in the other for the study of migration purposes, it requested international agencies to cooperate, and it appealed to OAS members to provide help (funds, food, medicine, services; Resolution II).

The second phase of activities dealt with the reestablishment of friendly relations between the two countries: peace and treaties, free transit, diplomatic and consular relations, boundary questions, the Central American Common Market, claims and differences, human rights, and the family.

The Thirteenth Meeting of Consultation, which was the last meeting before the Protocol of Amendments to the Charter went into effect in 1970, held a total of twenty-one plenary sessions. It was only officially declared closed in 1980.

THE INFORMAL MEETING OF MINISTERS OF FOREIGN AFFAIRS

A new kind of meeting of ministers of foreign affairs is the so-called Informal Meeting of Ministers of Foreign Affairs. Unlike the Inter-American Conference and the Meeting of Consultation of American Foreign Ministers, this is an informal meeting of ministers of foreign affairs in which important questions that are the concern of all member states are discussed informally and acted on quickly. The reasons for such informal meetings may vary. In any case, this kind of meeting, which invariably is quite brief, has never been institutionalized. It was first introduced in September 1959, when Operation Pan America—a joint effort to cope with the rising economic and social problems in Latin America based on proposals launched by Brazilian president Juscelino Kubitschek Oliveira in 1958—was taken up. Another example of this type of meeting took place in Washington, D.C., on October 2–3, 1962, when the Cuban Missile Crisis was the urgent topic of discussion. Finally, another such informal meeting of ministers of foreign affairs was held in May 1965 in Washington, D.C., to review the Dominican crisis, which had arisen with the landing of U.S. marines in Santo Domingo and led to the convocation of the Tenth MCFMA.

THE COUNCIL OF THE OAS

The Council of the OAS is the third highest organ of the organization, in accordance with the charter. Until 1967 (i.e., before Barbados and Trinidad and Tobago joined the OAS), the council was composed of twenty-one representatives of the American republics, all of whom had the rank of ambassador. In some instances, Latin American ambassadors accredited to the White House serve on the Council of the OAS. The reasons for this dual role are financial as well as political or administrative. In addition to the ambassador, each delegation comprises one or more alternate members as well as the usual diplomatic and administrative officials. In November of each year, the Council of the OAS elects its chair and vice chair, who preside over the council for one year.

Regular, Special, and Protocol Meetings

The Council of the OAS is scheduled to meet regularly the first and third Wednesday of each month, though already by the early 1950s this rule had been broken. Numerous special meetings have been called in order to take up urgent matters; starting in the 1950s, the Council of the OAS has often met weekly or even more often. Besides holding regular and special meetings, the Council also acts as the Provisional Organ of Consultation if one or more governments makes such a request based on the Rio Treaty or the charter. Finally, the council also meets in protocol sessions. To give an idea of the work load of the Council of the OAS, in 1962, it held twelve regular and nineteen special meetings. Furthermore, four meetings of the Council of the OAS took place as meetings of the Provisional Organ of Consultation, and ten sessions were protocol meetings (e.g., in honor of the presidents of Brazil, Colombia, Ecuador, Chile, Honduras, and Panama).

Functions and Authority

The Council of the OAS is empowered to deal with any matter referred to it by the Inter-American Conference or the Meeting of Consultation of Ministers of Foreign Affairs, and it is responsible for the functioning of the Pan American Union. The council elects the secretary general and the assistant secretary general; moreover, it can submit proposals to the governments and to the Inter-American Conference for the establishment or the fusion and abolition of specialized organizations as well as matters regarding their financing and maintenance.

After prior discussion, the council can submit recommendations to the governments, the Inter-American Conference, the specialized conferences, and the specialized organizations with regard to their activities. Furthermore, it can enter into special agreements with other inter-American organizations and can strengthen cooperation with these organizations as well as with the United Nations and other international institutions. For the establishment of the various technical and administrative departments within the PAU, the secretary general must obtain authorization from the Council of the OAS. Finally, the Council of the OAS draws up the formula for determining the quota each government is to pay for the maintenance of the PAU. Until the 1980s, when the Reagan administration adopted a negative policy toward all international intergovernmental organizations (including the OAS), this formula, in accordance with the system of the United Nations, was based on population figures and per capita income, but no member state (e.g., the United States) pays more than 66 percent of the total sum. The annual program and budget are established by the Council of the OAS by a two-thirds majority.

The Council of the OAS has its own regulations. Its meetings are held in the building of the PAU. Until the late 1950s they were held in the so-called Council Room, but in view of the necessity for more space, a special council room was built on the ground floor that has repeatedly been enlarged in order to adjust to larger delegations, permanent observer country representatives, and the media. An exception to the rule was the historic council session of July 18–22, 1956, in Panama City, in honor of the Bolivarian Congress of Panama in 1826, which was followed by the first Conference of American Presidents and Chiefs of State.

The Technical Organs of the Council of the OAS

The Council of the OAS established three technical subdivisions: the Inter-American Economic and Social Council (Washington, D.C.), the Inter-American Council of Jurists (Rio de Janeiro), and the Inter-American Cultural Council (Mexico City). Their functions and authority are laid down in the charter (Articles 57–77) and in their respective statutes and regulations. These three groups were to assist the Council of the OAS, as well as the various governments, in a technical capacity, answering requests and furnishing expert opinions on demand. The statutes of these specialized groups must be approved by the Council of the OAS after prior consultation with the governments and discussion with the respective groups themselves.

The Inter-American Economic and Social Council (IA–ECOSOC) was reorganized in 1961, after years of debate. In accordance with Article 11 of its statutes, it was to hold two regular, successive annual meetings of short duration. The first of these annual sessions was to be a meeting of experts, while the subsequent meeting was to take place on a ministerial level to discuss and vote on proposals of the experts. The Inter-American Economic and Social Council could also meet, in accordance with Article 14 of its statutes, outside its permanent seat.

For a long time, IA-ECOSOC was the only technical organ of the Council of the OAS, which did not have a smaller working unit of a permanent character, such as the Inter-American Committee for Cultural Action (for the Inter-American Cultural Council) or the Inter-American Juridical Committee (for the Inter-American Council of Jurists). This evident lack in the structure of the organization was remedied in 1963, when the second ministerial-level meeting of IA-ECOSOC (in São Paulo, Brazil) established the Inter-American Committee on the Alliance for Progress (ICAP).

The ICAP came into being after two and a half years of Alliance for Progress activities, which many people considered a time of trial and experience. In São Paulo, against the background of a faltering Alliance for Progress, it was agreed to establish ICAP as a special and permanent committee of IA-ECOSOC in order to carry out policies of the Alliance for Progress, the Council of the OAS, and IA-ECOSOC. As drafted by the meeting of experts that preceded the main ministerial conference, the proposal, which had received the support of the United States, called for "representing, coordinating, and promoting multilaterally the implementation of the Alliance for Progress." The ICAP grew out of proposals made by former Presidents Lleras of Colombia and Kubitschek of Brazil in their respective reports submitted to the São Paulo meeting to adapt the inter-American system to the needed dynamism of the Alliance for Progress and aiming at the latter's "Latinization" or "multilateralization."

The functions of the new ICAP were of a coordinating type. ICAP was to continuously scrutinize the development programs, make annual estimates of the internal and external resources needed for development, prepare and present proposals for the allocation of public funds, coordinate activities for promoting integration and external trade, and review budget questions coming within the sphere of IA-ECOSOC. ICAP, with headquarters in Washington, D.C., consisted of a president and seven regional representatives, including one from the United States and one from Central America. The first ICAP team was elected in January 1964. ICAP also linked several other inter-American and international institutions to the OAS: the secretary general of the OAS, the coordinator of the "Nine Wise Men" (the Panel of Nine established in the Alliance for Progress, experts who were to evaluate national development plans in accordance with the Charter of Punta del Este), and the director of ECLA were all advisors to ICAP. While the president was elected for three years (1964–1967) and could be reelected once, the other six Latin American members would serve two-year terms, beginning in 1965. The United States had a permanent representative. In this context, the Declaration of Bogotá (August 16, 1966) is important. Proclaimed by the presidents of Colombia, Chile, and Venezuela and the representatives of Ecuador and Peru at their Andean Group meeting, it was later accepted by ICAP at the latter's Ninth Meeting in Bogota, October 1–6, 1966.

The Inter-American Council of Jurists was the advisory organ in the field of law. It was charged with promoting the development and codification of international public and private law, and, if possible, it was to coordinate the legislation of the various American republics. The Inter-American Council of Jurists held meetings only when the Council of the OAS convoked it, but it was represented by the Inter-American Juridical Committee, which has its seat in Rio de Janeiro.

The purpose of the Inter-American Cultural Council was the promotion of educational, cultural, and scientific relations among the American states. To this end, it carried on a variety of activities as enumerated in Article 74 of the charter. The permanent commission of the Inter-American Cultural Council is the Inter-American Committee for Cultural Action, the seat of which is in Mexico City. This committee is composed of five members, which are chosen at each Inter-American Conference by the Inter-American Cultural Council from a list submitted by member countries. The Committee for Cultural Action prepares the work that is assigned to it by the Inter-American Cultural Council.

Finally, the Council of the OAS has a large number of regular and special commissions and special committees, which, on average, holds about a total of 200 sessions a year.

Historical Development of the Council of the OAS

The Council of the OAS, as it was established in 1948, carried on the activities that, before that year, had been handled by the International Bureau of American Republics (1901–1910) and the governing board of the

PAU (1910–1948). From 1889 to 1923, the chairmanship of the governing board was reserved for the U.S. secretary of state. At any rate, this was the case in 1889–1890 at the First International Conference of American States. Later, it was expressly stated: in 1902 at the Second International Conference of American States in Mexico City, when the Commercial Bureau of American Republics was renamed the International Bureau of American Republics.

The historic development of the Council of the OAS is illuminating. Originally, the Commercial Bureau of American Republics was under the direction of the U.S. department of state; it was also from here that the director of the Commercial Bureau was appointed. As early as 1896, the first step was taken toward the establishment of the board, when a permanent executive committee with representatives of five member states (of which the U.S. secretary of state was chair ex officio) was established. Then, in 1902, the governing board of the International Bureau of American Republics, the forerunner of the present Council of the OAS, was established. In accordance with the resolution of 1902, the governing board was an assembly of Latin American representatives who were accredited to the U.S. government; it met under the chairmanship of the U.S. secretary of state. It is evident that both these provisions limited the flexibility of the Latin American delegations. A change of these provisions was made in 1923, at the Fifth International Conference of American States in Santiago, when it was decided that the two chairs of the governing board of the PAU were to be elected by the board members. As stated earlier, in practice the old system remained in place for the next quarter century on the basis of courtesy toward the host country and political realism.

Santiago also solved another problem of long standing (which was also mentioned earlier): Until 1923, a state that did not maintain diplomatic relations with the United States found itself in a strange situation since it could not be represented in the governing board. The fifth conference decided that every American government, no matter whether it maintained diplomatic relations with other American governments, had the right to a voice and a vote at an Inter-American Conference and in the PAU. (At that time, Mexico did not maintain diplomatic relations with the United States.)

Now, a further step had been taken in the endeavors to separate the affairs of the PAU from those of the White House. In 1962, the Santiago decision was brought up in connection with the decision in Punta del Este to exclude Cuba from the OAS, an act which, juridically, was improper. The dilemma was solved by excluding "the present Government of Cuba."

When the council of the OAS replaced the former governing board of the PAU (Bogotá, 1948), it actually took over the provision of Santiago with regard to the chairship (Article 49 of the charter), but it was now really carried out. The changes from PAU to OAS, and from governing board to council, were also echoed in the election of the two chairs: Thus, a greater

Latin American voice became evident in a changing world. It is true that the U.S. secretary of state, who until 1948 had demonstrated genuine interest through personal participation and who was always at hand, from then on did not appear in the PAU except on April 14, the high point of the annual Pan American Week. Obviously, the global responsibilities of the United States after World War II had much to do with the change. Before World War II, the U.S. secretary of state had been able to devote himself more energetically to Pan American affairs.

A further consequence of this electoral provision was that the U.S. delegation to the OAS was often not composed of major political figures, which became evident in the council. In the early 1960s, this issue was also raised in the media in discussions of U.S. foreign policy, especially in regard to inter-American relations and the OAS. It was said that the value of the OAS as an element of stabilization of Latin America was related to the capabilities and the prestige of the U.S. ambassador to the organization. It seemed obvious that if the United States decreased its interest by not appointing important people to the post of U.S. ambassador to the OAS, Latin America would do likewise as a matter of dignity.

So-Called Political Functions

Some important problems of the Council of the OAS as it functioned between 1948 and 1967–1970 concerned the so-called political functions. These functions, which are very vague, had, in the course of time, been exercised partially and in a restricted manner by the governing board of the PAU, but the Latin Americans had never been prepared openly to acknowledge this authority, either to the governing board or to the PAU as such. Indeed, after the Second International Conference of American States, the board became a purely administrative organ of the PAU, and in Havana (1928), the representatives of the American republics decided that neither the governing board nor the PAU as such should ever exercise political functions. Despite this resolution, an opposite tendency set in slowly but constantly, and the governing board increasingly came to exercise political functions, which then were recognized in the Conference of Chapultepec (Mexico City) in 1945. It was here that the governing board received authority that it had never had before, namely, to take action on any matter affecting the solidarity and general welfare of the American republics.

This new spirit was implemented in the provision of the Rio Treaty, which stated that the governing board of the PAU should function, in case of crisis, as the Provisional Organ of Consultation until the Meeting of Consultation of Ministers of Foreign Affairs. It was to function, at the same time, as the liaison office between the inter-American system and the United Nations with regard to questions of peace and security (Articles 12 and 15 of the Rio Treaty). It is justified to maintain, therefore, that Chapultepec and Rio de

Janeiro can be regarded as the high points of Pan Americanism. However, in Bogotá, a reaction set in: The broad powers explicitly granted to the governing board (now Council of the OAS) in Chapultepec were again withdrawn. Article 50 of the charter clearly states that the new Council of the OAS can take cognizance of only those matters with which it is entrusted by the Inter-American Conference or the Meeting of Consultation of Ministers of Foreign Affairs.

The Council of the OAS—The Most Important Body of the Organization, 1948–1970

However, despite all this, the Council of the OAS, because it met permanently, was probably the most important body in the period 1948 to 1967–1970, even though formally it was not the highest. It was the executive committee of the inter-American system and determined the rules for the three technical bodies. It was in permanent and constant contact with inter-American affairs and maintained contact with other inter-American organizations, whereas the two highest organs met only every five years or at irregular intervals and for the deliberation of very specific matters.

The council reflected not only the weaknesses of the organization but also the fragmentation and disunity of the twenty-one republics. This was particularly apparent when the Council of the OAS met as the Provisional Organ of Consultation in application of the Rio Treaty. Bitter and heated debates resulted, which served neither the organization nor the inter-American system; nor did they contribute to forging a united front. However, a cure for this problem was not easy to find since the council (as the entire organization) simply mirrored the sad state of affairs between the United States and Latin America. The Protocol of Amendments of 1967 attempted to solve some of the problems that arose in the period 1948–1967, and it decided to downgrade the importance of the Council of the OAS, which, after 1967–1970, would no longer play the role that it had under the original charter.

5

The OAS (1948 through 1967–1970): The Pan American Union

The Pan American Union was the name adopted in 1910 for the secretariat of the Union of American Republics. The name was maintained in 1948, although Article 78 of the charter clarified it when it stated: "The Pan American Union is the central and permanent Organ of the Organization of American States and the General Secretariat of the Organization." Generally speaking, the seat of the OAS was still referred to as PAU after 1948, but Latin Americans wanted to eradicate any romantic notion that might be linked to the name, gradually downgrading PAU until the Protocol of Amendments of 1967 totally eliminated any reference to the old title. From 1910 on the name on the main building in Washington had the inscription *UNION OF AMERICAN REPUBLICS*, later it became *PAN AMERICAN UNION*, and finally, as a sign of the changing times, in the 1960s it came to read *ORGANIZATION OF AMERICAN STATES*.

PURPOSES AND STRUCTURE

In accordance with Article 78 of the charter, the PAU was to exercise all those powers that the charter and other inter-American treaties and agreements entrusted to it. The PAU thus represented more than would appear at first glance; perhaps this situation was best illustrated by the PAU's extraordinary expansion from the historic site of 1910 to the more modern white building of 1948, which became its immediate addition, and its many annexes of recent decades.

The main function of the PAU as General Secretariat of the OAS was the promotion—under the guidance of the council of the organization—of economic, social, political, and cultural relations among its member states. For this purpose, the PAU was divided into numerous departments and divisions. By the early 1960s it had ten technical departments and three service offices that ranked on the same level as the departments. The economic field comprised four technical departments under the assistant secretary for economic and social affairs: Economic Affairs, Social Affairs, Statistics, and Technical Cooperation. Four other technical departments were placed under the position of assistant secretary for cultural, scientific, and information affairs: Cultural Affairs, Scientific Affairs, Public Information, and Education. Finally, the other two departments—Legal Affairs and Administrative Affairs— were directly under the secretary general, as were the three service offices: Office of Council and Conferences Secretariat Services, Financial Services, and Publications. All departments and service offices were headed by directors and had separate divisions and sections.

As the organization grew, so too did the PAU as General Secretariat. Increasing numbers of requests were being made to the General Secretariat, not only by the Council of the OAS and its technical organs but also by the highest organs of the organization and by the governments of the member states. This was particularly true in the economic field, once the Alliance for Progress was launched in 1961, also leading to the reorganization of IA-ECOSOC. Actually, the Alliance for Progress was a real watershed since its creation in 1961 had extraordinary consequences on the entire structure of the PAU. The assistance that the PAU gave to the various governments covered almost any subject matter, whether economic development, promotion of exports, urban planning, training in tax systems, or programs in the areas of education, public health, and agrarian reform.

In addition to these spheres, the PAU also had another, very special field of activity, which was specified in Article 83 of the charter. According to this provision, the PAU was responsible ex officio for issuing invitations to member states to the Inter-American Conference, the Meeting of Consultation of Ministers of Foreign Affairs, and the specialized conferences. Besides these functions, Article 83 of the Charter listed other functions as follows:

a. [not listed here];

b. Advise the Council and its organs in the preparation of programs and regulations of the Inter-American Conference, the Meeting of Consultation of Ministers of Foreign Affairs, and the Specialized Conferences;

c. Place, to the extent of its ability, at the disposal of the Government of the country where a conference is to be held, the technical help and personnel which such Government may request;

d. Serve as custodian of the documents and archives of the Inter-American Conference, of the Meeting of Consultation of Ministers of Foreign Affairs, and, insofar as possible, of the Specialized Conferences;

e. Serve as depository of the instruments of ratification of inter-American agreements;

f. Perform the functions entrusted to it by the Inter-American Conference, and the Meeting of Consultation of Ministers of Foreign Affairs;

g. Submit to the Council an annual report on the activities of the Organization;

h. Submit to the Inter-American Conference a report on the work accomplished by the Organs of the Organization since the previous Conference.

It might be added that the annual report of the secretary general covered not only the activities of the PAU but also those of all the organs of the organization, just as the secretarial services not only covered the Council of the OAS but also the Inter-American Conference, the Meetings of Consultation, and the specialized conferences. The PAU also had secretarial responsibilities in regard to several specialized organizations, agencies, and commissions. Some of these agencies, like the Inter-American Statistical Institute and the Inter-American Commission of Women, were physically located in the PAU and thus were linked particularly closely.

Finally, we should not forget the duties of liaison with other organizations (especially the United Nations and all its specialized agencies) and the PAU's responsibility to furnish information to all those who requested it. This last function was very much emphasized and was given a much needed priority as a result of the launching of the Alliance for Progress. Public information on the OAS had been a particularly sore point in the United States, where the media seldom showed an interest in Latin American affairs in general or the inter-American system in particular. The resolution that the ministerial-level IA-ECOSOC meeting passed in 1961 in Punta del Este, Uruguay, attempted to address this issue directly. It called on the Department of Public Information of the PAU to give high priority to the dissemination of news in regard to the Organization of American States and the Alliance for Progress. Thus, Resolution E—"Public Opinion and the Alliance for Progress"—stated as follows:

WHEREAS:

The Alliance for Progress pursues the noble aims of establishing social justice and guaranteeing the system of representative democracy in Latin America, by accelerating economic development in the Hemisphere; . . .

In order to reach its objectives it is essential that public opinion be fully informed of the causes that have brought about this movement, of the goals it seeks, and of its successive achievements. . . .

[We RESOLVE]:

1. To recommend that the Council of the Organization of American States study the possibility of convoking, as soon as possible, a Special Meeting on Information Media, for the purpose of promoting the most appropriate action for informing public opinion on these development plans and mobilizing it in their favor.

2. To bring to the attention of the Council of the Organization of American States the necessity for having the Department of Public Information of the Organization give preferential attention to the dissemination of information on the efforts to be undertaken and, with the collaboration of the Inter-American Development Bank and the United Nations Economic Commission for Latin America, prepare a program whose main objectives would be:

   a. To promote the creation or development of information media, for cultural and educational purposes, in those regions of the Americas where they do not exist, or where they are insufficient, using the native languages where necessary, and particularly encouraging the activity of national information agencies;

   b. To promote the distribution and circulation among member countries of all documents and other information materials that tend to emphasize the urgency of complying with the objectives of the Alliance for Progress; to publicize its democratic ideals and achievements; and to obtain increasing support from the peoples of the Hemisphere for its program, particularly by strengthening the information services of regional offices of the inter-American organizations; and

   c. To spread, among the peoples of the Americas, knowledge of each other and of the solutions they are finding to their problems, within the spirit of Operation Pan America and of the Alliance for Progress, promoting the exchange of persons at all social levels, especially of students and urban and rural workers.

3. To recommend that news agencies, the press, radio and television companies, and foundations direct and intensify their efforts toward ending the present ignorance on the part of the peoples of the Americas of each other and of the conditions prevailing in their countries.

4. To bring to the attention of governments and educators the need for educational centers to contribute to the dissemination of knowledge of the social and economic development inspired by the Alliance for Progress, and to provide those centers with adequate material for doing so.

5. To suggest to the Organization of American States and the governments of the member countries that they promote the holding of conferences, seminars, and round tables to report on and discuss the main economic and social problems of the Hemisphere and their possible solution within the framework of the Alliance for Progress.

6. To call upon the public opinion of the Hemisphere, and especially the trade unions, labor organizations, and student associations to become aware of the social implications of the Alliance for Progress and to take an active part in the dissemination of information on its objectives and in the discussion and execution of its programs.

HISTORICAL DEVELOPMENT OF THE PAU, 1890–1948

Like the OAS, the permanent secretariat also has expanded over the years. It began in 1890 in a rather modest way, as the Commercial Bureau of the

American Republics, with the simple purpose of collecting commercial statistics and publishing information on consular and customs matters in the
Latin American countries. However, with each successive conference, its
field of activity grew—a fact expressed by the change of its name, in 1902,
to the International Bureau of American Republics. That same year, the
bureau was authorized to publish booklets and maps, as well as other geo-
graphical documents. Four years later, it was entrusted with educational
matters, and in 1910, when it was given the name Pan American Union,
the Fourth International Conference of American States (Buenos Aires) authorized it to execute all resolutions of the Inter-American Conferences.
That important decision pointed the way to the future work of the PAU.
With this growth in scope, its internal administration, influence, and experience increased as well. While the PAU as the permanent secretariat
continued to grow, the activities of the organization—its conferences, specialized organizations, ad hoc councils, commissions and committees—also
increased. This was also the period in which major internal changes were
made, as in 1923, at the Fifth International Conference of American States
(Santiago de Chile), with regard to the governing board of the PAU, the
forerunner of future Council of the OAS. Moreover, in the next twenty-five
years, the PAU grew to the position that it held when the OAS was established in 1948, successfully tackling economic, social, and cultural matters.

MODERNIZATION OF THE PAU, 1948–1958

A major reorganization took place in 1948, in the course of which the
entire organization was overhauled and modernized. The Charter of Bogotá
created the main lines of the administrative mechanism of the PAU until
passage of the Protocol of Buenos Aires.

At the same time, an increasing internationalization and Latin Americanization of the PAU took place. Although U.S. influence was naturally overwhelming, the Department of Cultural Affairs had become a purely Latin
American sphere (famous Latin American philosophers, historians, and journalists, such as Jorge Basadre, Alceo Amoroso Lima, Juan Marín, and Erico
Verissimo, were all directors of the department after 1948), and a similar
process took place at the very top, with the position of the secretary general.
In the meantime, growth continued at a rapid pace, especially because of
the urgency of economic and social questions. At Bogotá, the term of office
of the secretary general was extended to ten years. Before 1948, there had
been eight directors, all U.S. nationals. The best known and the most outstanding was Leo Stanton Rowe, who, for a quarter century, had directed
the PAU in a most distinguished manner.

When, in 1948, Alberto Lleras Camargo and William Manger were elected
as secretary general and assistant secretary general, it was the first time that
a Latin American was at the top with a U.S. national at his side. The choices

were sound and avoided giving the impression that the PAU was primarily a U.S. institution or a kind of "U.S. Ministry of Colonies." In fact there was already at that time much less U.S. influence on the PAU than was thought outside Washington, D.C., and the Latin American character of the PAU has increased with every successive year. This manner of filling the two highest positions was borrowed from U.S. political life, in which the president and the vice president are also selected from different parts of the union, and also from countries like Lebanon and Cyprus (before the former was destroyed and the latter partially occupied by Turkey). When the secretary general of the OAS was given an elective term of ten years, it was not realized that such a long period had drawbacks. On the one hand, this was not favorable, since a prominent Latin American politician could not really afford to keep out of the political life of his or her country that long, but on the other hand, this long tenure did make for a certain continuity. The Protocol of Buenos Aires would come with the right solution: a five-year term with the possibility of reelection.

THE REORGANIZATION OF 1958–1960

In 1958–1960, after the election of Secretary General José Antonio Mora, a reorganization of the PAU took place, which continued for several years. Obviously the growth of the organization since 1945 had been too rapid to be systematic and organic. Thus, the secretariat often had become overstaffed, with a resultant loss of efficiency. Criticisms directed toward the organizational structure were perhaps more justified than those that concentrated on the people in leadership positions. It was argued that the OAS was, in fact, directed by two heads and that the assistant secretary general as secretary of the Council of the OAS and chief of that secretariat wielded much greater power than provided for by the charter. It was overlooked that the secretariat of the council of the OAS must have greater latitude in order to carry out its important role. Rules for it could not be laid down systematically as for other departments, nor should it be compared with them.

A report submitted by a firm of management consultants failed to take into account the fact that an international intergovernmental organization simply cannot be operated like a business, and this shortcoming brought about a deterioration of operations. The Department of Administrative Affairs was broken up, the secretary general was surrounded by a "general staff," and the secretariat of the Council of the OAS lost its autonomy. Since then, however, these changes have been modified. The Department of Administrative Affairs reappeared, the "general staff" was limited to its real functions (i.e., advisory), and the secretary of the Council of the OAS has again been given much greater autonomy.

One objection raised during this reorganization was that the low salaries paid by the PAU—in comparison with the United Nations and its agencies—made it impossible to recruit first-rate people. Thus, in order to attract prominent personalities, two new posts were created: assistant secretary for economic and social affairs and assistant secretary for cultural, scientific, and information affairs. New departments were established, sometimes—as was also the case with the specialized organizations—for technical reasons, but also for purely personal ones. There were also political motives, the role of experience, and the changes in emphasis to be addressed. As a result, there was the danger of a "superbureaucratization" and of almost uncontrollable budget growth. Member states had to be careful lest they could not carry the financial burden in those cases in which the organization did not prove to be efficient in its activity, economic in its work, and responsible in its attitude.

THE STAFF, THE BUDGET, AND FINANCIAL RESOURCES

Until the establishment of the OAS in 1948, the staff of the old PAU was rather modest. It could be said without exaggeration that the PAU under Rowe was operated like a family establishment. Thus, in 1928, it had some 61 staff members; between 1945 and 1948, the staff numbered from 150 to 175, most of whom were U.S. citizens.[1] In the course of time, this figure grew even more. The increased demands of the member states on the organization found expression in an unusually rapid rise of both personnel and budget. Thus, by 1966, there were 715 regular employees, with some 201 employed under contract, in addition to some 287 employed in connection with the Special Development Assistance Fund. The grand total by that year was thus 1,203.[2]

The more the OAS followed the model of the United Nations, the more it came to distinguish between regular employees of the General Secretariat and those employed with the Special Development Assistance Fund; it also distinguished between persons of international or local character. In addition, over the years, the staff began to show a real inter-American character, as seen in the period 1953–1959, when the number of staff jumped from 361 to 489.[3]

If we look briefly at the budget, the sum to maintain the Commercial Bureau of the American Republics of 1890 was $36,000. Over the next fifty years, the budget increased, reflecting the expansion of the organization, but this rise was rather modest. Suddenly, however, it jumped with the establishment of the OAS.

The strengthening of the bureaucracy and the budget was the trademark of the period 1948–1970, especially during the tenure of Secretary General Mora. Immediately after World War II, the OAS annual budget amounted to roughly $2 million; in 1954, it was $3 million; in 1959, $7 million; and by

1965, it was around $15.8 million. This sum did not include the $2 million for the Program of Technical Cooperation, the $6 million of the Special Fund for the Alliance for Progress, the $3 million for the Special Fund of the so-called Darien Gap (the parts of the Pan-American Highway between Panama and Colombia, which were not ready at that time), nor the $7 million of the Retirement and Pensions Fund. At the end of the 1950s and early 1960s, the PAU began to have increasing difficulties obtaining the quotas of the different states—a problem that had also begun to trouble the United Nations. Thus, on December 31, 1962, the debt had reached the significant sum of $9 million.

In defense of the increase in budget and personnel, one should bear in mind that it has been the practice at the various inter-American conferences for delegates to pass one resolution after another, without due regard to the financial implications and the actual working capabilities of the PAU or the specialized organizations. Only in the early 1960s, as a measure of self-defense, did the PAU send a budget officer to such conferences, in order to brief delegates of the financial implications of proposals.

The PAU always had a Finance Committee that screened the budget that the secretary general had to submit to the Council of the OAS. As part of the internal reorganization of 1958–1960, this committee was then changed to the Committee of Program and Budget in order to balance the programs with the corresponding expenditures. The budget of the secretary general (which usually was amended, here and there, according to instructions from the various governments) included also the budgets for the IACW, the IACI, and the IADB.

The basic financial resource for the maintenance of the OAS was the contribution of the member states, although there were other revenues available arising from grants from foundations, and minor ones from the sale of publications. The scale of these contributions was determined by the Council of the OAS and followed essentially the system developed by the United Nations (i.e., individual state contributions were based on a percentage of population and per capita income). In the United Nations, the largest contributor was limited to 33 percent, while in the OAS it was 66 percent. This meant, of course, that the United States bore the heaviest financial burden, but had it not been for this rule, the burden would have been even higher. There is no comparison, in this case, between the United Nations and the Organization of American States, since in the former, there is a variety of wealthy member states, whereas in the latter, the United States is over-whelmingly the richest country. The 66 percent standard came under fire in the last decade when the Reagan administration objected to this rule.

Once the PAU had assessed the quota that member state had to pay, the respective amount of the contribution was sent to the member state and it was supposed that the quotas would be received by the beginning of each fiscal year (i.e., in July), in line with the fiscal year of the United States. However, with increasing regularity many quotas were not received each year, thus illustrating not only the financial plight of many Latin American countries but also the overall situation of the OAS. Although this financial situation was already quite serious in the 1960s, it became a real crisis in the next decades, particularly when the Reagan administration initiated an unfriendly policy of nonpayment of its full contributions, thus showing an embarrassing hostility for all international organizations, not only the OAS.

Already in the 1950s and 1960s, the PAU had to face this reality with the Working Capital Fund, that is, with funds that were really available, and had to reduce expenditures as it did in the 1960s. The annual report of the secretary general showed this awkward situation, and Margaret Ball commented correctly that both the PAU and the Council of the OAS "made herculean efforts to improve the situation, even to publishing data on outstanding contributions from time to time."[4] The financial crisis became so urgent that the council, in a famous resolution of November 13, 1953, requested the secretary general to make a study of the feasibility of paying the quotas, either totally or partially, in local currencies. At the Tenth International Conference of American States (Caracas, 1954), Brazil proposed such a solution, but nothing ever came of it.

THE EXECUTIVE OFFICE

The original structure of the PAU in 1948 and in the following years included an executive office comprised only of the secretary general and the assistant secretary general. The Secretarial Services of the Council were directly linked to the assistant secretary general, and there existed the various departments: Administrative Affairs, Legal Affairs, Economic and Social Affairs, Cultural Affairs, Statistics, and Public Information.

The modernization that took place after 1948 and continued with the reorganizations of 1958–1960 and later years changed the earlier, modest picture. Thus, the PAU looked differently during the 1960s, even if it maintained the basic structure given in 1948. The revisions and expansions signified not only the latest trends in emphasizing particular topics such as technical cooperation or scientific affairs or very powerful trends of a more personal nature, but also the rapidly changing realities. Thus, in the 1960s the Executive Office consisted not only of the offices of the secretary general and assistant secretary general but included also the Protocol Office and the PAU offices in the member states.

As part of the reorganization of 1958–1960, the Executive Office was directly linked to the Departments of Administrative Affairs and Legal Affairs. It could also count on an Advisory Group, the aforementioned "general staff" under the direction of Angel Palerm, which aided the secretary general in all matters relating to the administration of the PAU; however, in 1962, its powers were curtailed and it was transferred to the Department of Administrative Affairs.

At the time of the signature of the Protocol of Amendments in 1967, the structure of the PAU consisted of nine "substantive departments": Legal Affairs, Economic Affairs, Social Affairs, Statistics, Technical Cooperation, Cultural Affairs, Educational Affairs, Scientific Affairs, and Information and Public Affairs. There were also three "auxiliary" offices: Council and Conference Secretarial Services, Financial Services, and Publication Services. Finally, two new top positions had been created in the early 1960s: the assistant secretary for economic and social affairs and the assistant secretary for cultural, scientific and information affairs; the former was responsible for the Departments of Economic Affairs, Social Affairs, Statistics, and Technical Cooperation; the latter, for the Departments of Cultural Affairs, Educational Affairs, Scientific Affairs, and Information and Public Affairs.

The Secretary General and the Assistant Secretary General

At the head of the PAU was placed a secretary general and an assistant secretary general, both elected by the council of the organization for a ten-year period. The secretary general could not be reelected, nor could he or she have the same citizenship as his or her predecessor. The secretary general directed and represented the PAU. In all assemblies and meetings—the Inter-American Conference, the Meeting of Consultation of Ministers of Foreign Affairs, the specialized conferences, and the sessions of the Council of the OAS and its subsidiary bodies—the secretary general was entitled to speak but did not have voting rights. The assistant secretary general had advisory functions and represented the secretary general in the latter's absence. The assistant secretary general, who could be reelected, also served as the secretary of the Council of the OAS.

Weak Position of the Secretary General

There exists a fundamental difference between the systems of the United Nations and the OAS. The highest position of each organization, the secretary generalship, is similar in form, but in reality, the degree of authority that each is granted is quite different. The secretary general of the United Nations has much greater freedom to maneuver and more authority than the secretary general of the OAS. Actually, the founding fathers of the United Nations, looking back to the experience of the League of Nations, where the secretary general also had a rather weak position, drastically changed this situation and gave the secretary general of the United Nations a position of greater strength with more flexibility and freedom of action. That is not the case with the OAS, and this touches on a central problem, which also helps explain some aspects of the crisis undergone by the OAS in the 1950s and

1960s. Some critics of the OAS in those years argued that an improvement of the organization could only come about with a stronger council and secretary general. It was perceived as a crisis of leadership, and it was expected that leadership could only come from the two institutions that were seen as the most important for that role: the Council of the OAS and the secretary general. However, in reality, the Latin American governments were careful not to give authority to the PAU or the secretary general. Since the organization grew bigger with every Inter-American Conference and the PAU dealt with ever greater technical and political activity—especially in the period from 1923 (Santiago de Chile) to 1947 (Rio de Janeiro), many observers believed that further development would continue in this way, particularly since the new OAS was supposed to follow the United Nations closely as regards the leadership role of the top posts, institutional structure, and technical programs. Furthermore, since it was presumed that the new top position in the OAS of 1948 would no longer be filled with a citizen of the United States but rather would be "Latin-Americanized," there was even more reason to believe that the role of secretary general would be made stronger. Hispanic civilization being rather contradictory (the duke of Wellington during the Peninsular War was supposed to have said that two and two never make four in Spain), the results in this case also were predictable. Latin Americans want a strong government (and only respect a government that is strong), but at the same time, they distrust strong government. Latin America's presidential system takes into account this psychological element: Presidents have a strong position, but cannot be reelected immediately.

Latin American individualism and the Hispanic tradition lead the Latin Americans to distrust strong executive powers. Furthermore, these governments were afraid to endow the OAS (i.e., the secretary general) either implicitly or explicitly with great authority. They thought this could turn a loose intergovernmental organization into a strong, centralized authority with supranational powers, and that this authority might then be used for collective intervention. This fact accounted for the weaknesses of the inter-American system as well as the weak position of the secretary general.

Just as the Latin Americans wanted to keep their states and the OAS politically independent of the United Nations, they were not at all willing to grant greater authority to the secretary general of the OAS. When, in 1948, Lleras became the first secretary general of the OAS, it was generally thought that he would have much greater authority than the previous directors of the PAU. Moreover, it was believed that he would turn the ramified inter-American system into a strong, tightly knit organization. That was also the hope of the new secretary general. He wanted, among other things, to use the annual report as an instrument for disseminating his opinions on various problems, and thus, to orient the organization (a matter-of-fact procedure in the United Nations). However, when Lleras tried this procedure, he was criticized by some members of the council. As a result, the annual reports became nothing but an enumeration of the work done, and whenever the secretary general availed himself of his right to speak, he confined himself principally to praising Pan Americanism and the inter-American system. The disappointment for Lleras was such that, in 1954, at the Tenth International Conference of American States, he resigned from the OAS.

At that time he made the famous "Caracas statement," announcing his resignation: "The Organization is neither good nor bad; it can be nothing else than what the governments which are members of the Organization want it to be." It is also quite evident that, ever since that incident, no secretary general has dared to act against the will of the council, even when both sides—the Council of the OAS and the secretary general—needed more powers as well as a much greater sense of responsibility and more initiative and flexibility.

This fear of vesting too much authority in the general secretariat explained other factors as well such as the great numbers of committees, working groups, and councils whose norms were often drafted in vague terms and which overlapped in their functions and were restricted in their activities.

The only situation in which a secretary general of the OAS was given larger powers was in the exceptional case of the Dominican crisis of 1965, when U.S. military intervention in the Dominican Republic became the subject of the Tenth MCFMA. In view of its seriousness and urgency, the Council of the OAS authorized the secretary general, José Antonio Mora Otero, to travel to Santo Domingo and directly cooperate in the solution of that issue. It was an interesting precedent which, however, so far has remained the exception.

Before the OAS was established, the United States furnished the directors general. The best known was Leo Stanton Rowe, who died in an automobile accident in 1946, after having served the Union of American Republics and the PAU for over twenty-five years. With his death and the establishment of the OAS a new era dawned, as it did also in regard to the two highest positions in the PAU. In the period from 1948 to 1970 (i.e., under the original charter of the OAS), the following officials were elected: After the period of Lleras, former President of Colombia (1948–1954), followed Carlos Dávila, former President of Chile, to finish the term of his Colombian predecessor (August 1, 1954–1958); however, he died on October 19, 1955. The Uruguayan ambassador to Washington, José Antonio Mora, was then elected to complete the term of Dávila, and in 1957 was elected to the ten-year term of his own which expired in 1968. It was under Lleras that the OAS took a new path in 1948, and it was in the ten years of Mora's term that the organization had to face increasing tensions that signaled a new era: that of the revised charter. At the end of his term, Mora was succeeded by Galo Plaza Lasso, former president of Ecuador, who witnessed the transition of the OAS with the Protocol of Amendments of 1967 (which came into effect in 1970).

While Latin Americans were able, with the reorganization of the inter-American system in 1948, to secure the position of the secretary general, the assistant secretary general was reserved to the United States, at least during this period. As stated earlier, this official was also elected for ten years, but he or she could be succeeded by someone of the same nationality, and in case the office of secretary general was vacant, the assistant secretary general was authorized to serve as secretary general for some ninety days.

Prior to the new changes of the OAS with the Protocol of Buenos Aires, two outstanding U.S. nationals served as assistant secretary general. William Manger had been a former counselor of the PAU and had a vast experience in inter-American affairs; in 1948 he was elected assistant secretary general and served in this capacity until 1958. He was followed by William Sanders, former chief of the Juridical Division of the PAU, who was elected in November 1957 to serve for ten years (until 1968).

The assistant secretary general, besides aiding and advising the secretary general in his functions over the PAU, was also the secretary of the council, and for some time (1948 to 1956), he or she also filled the position of acting secretary of the Inter-American Institute of Agricultural Sciences, since the latter's board of directors was in Washington, D.C., and not Costa Rica.

In 1968, in the course of amending the charter and as part of the policy of giving Latin America a greater influence in the OAS, the office of assistant secretary general was opened to aspirants from all the nations. Miguel Rafael Urquía of El Salvador was then elected for the ten-year term beginning in 1968. Hence, by 1968, both top positions in the PAU (or general secretariat) had been Latin-Americanized. However, this arrangement would again change in the future.

The Protocol Office

Like any government or intergovernmental agency of importance, the OAS also established a Protocol Office. This was necessary in view of the many visits from foreign dignitaries and other ceremonial activities.

The PAU Offices Abroad: In Member States

The idea of establishing national offices of the PAU was not really original. Already at the Third International Conference of American States in Rio de Janeiro, 1906, such a concept was being aired as support for the new organization of the Union of American Republics. However, nothing came of it at that time or later when, on several occasions, the same idea surfaced.

It was only in 1953, on the initiative of Brazil, that the concept was resurrected, and this time the Council of the OAS quickly approved it.

The first such offices were created in 1954 in Rio de Janeiro, Santiago de Chile, and Lima. In the following years, PAU offices were set up in other countries, and by 1960 they operated in all member states except Cuba. In 1961 a regional office was also established in Miami.

Originally the functions were modest (dissemination of information about the OAS and the inter-American system), but in due course, these national offices expanded their operations and their functions would be included in official agreements between the OAS and the various host countries. Their duties, as stated by the secretary general in his report for the five years 1954–1959, covered the following items:

1. promoting knowledge and understanding of the OAS, its organs, and the member states by intensifying the distribution and circulation of Pan American Union publications;
2. maintaining liaison with national organizations, international and inter-American agencies, nongovernmental organizations, and private individuals so as to interest them in, and obtain their support for, the work of the Organization;
3. promoting the organization of Commissions on Cooperation with the OAS and serving as executive secretariats of such commissions;
4. intensifying at the national level the dissemination of information on the OAS and its programs, through the press, radio, and television;
5. undertaking various administrative functions and serving the OAS representatives, on specific request of the Secretary General;
6. organizing lectures and courses on inter-American cooperation in universities and institutions of higher learning; and
7. promoting and planning the observance of Pan American Day and Week celebrations on a national basis, in accordance with the General Secretariat's program.[5]

These duties were later amplified in an agreement with Bolivia (1959) in which cooperation with various programs, such as technical cooperation, professorship, and scholarship programs, was included. Of particular importance was the new function of the PAU Office in La Paz, which was to serve "as secretariat to the national committee on the Alliance for Progress in Bolivia."[6]

By 1964–1965, the functions of the PAU offices in member states were further expanded. These new duties covered representation of the secretary general in the host country, aid of secretarial services for OAS missions to official meetings, processing of fellowship applications, and handling of payments for field operations of the PAU.[7]

The PAU Offices Abroad: In Europe and at UN Headquarters

The first initiative to establish some official link with Europe, in view of the extraordinary importance of the newly established European Common

Market, was launched in 1958 at the Second Meeting of the Special Committee to Study the Formulation of New Measures of Economic Cooperation (CECE), also called the Committee of 21, in Bogotá, which resulted in the Act of Bogotá. A close link with the new Europe which was developing was of great interest to such countries as Argentina, Brazil, and Uruguay. It was in this meeting that Uruguayan ambassador Carlos Clulow, launched such an idea, which amounted to heresy at that time. The concept prospered, and in 1962 the Council of the OAS approved it. The first office of the OAS was located in Paris, in 1963, as that was where the Organization for Economic Cooperation and Development (OECD) was located; in 1964 the office was transferred to Geneva because also located there were the UN European headquarters and several of its agencies, the World Health Organization (WHO), and the International Labor Organization (ILO). A year later, the council adopted guidelines for this office, stressing its function as a liaison with the European Economic Community, OECD, the European Free Trade Association (EFTA), the General Agreement of Tariffs and Trade (GATT), the UN headquarters in Europe, and the International Law Commission, among others.

These guidelines were amplified in the sense that the office was supposed to advise OAS members in regard to the above-mentioned international organizations. Moreover, at their conferences and meetings,.the office was to represent the OAS and work with these organizations as well as with European governments in joint projects of mutual interest. It would also arrange for the training of Latin Americans in Europe and for the contracting of European experts for Latin American projects in the realm of economic development. The European office was to submit reports of its activities in Europe to the Council of the OAS. In view of the interest of the South American countries, the first officials of the European Office were Daniel Rodríguez Larreta (Uruguay) and Raúl C. Migone (Argentina).

A similar arrangement was also made with the United Nations. The idea of a personal representative of the OAS at the United Nations was aired by the secretary general in the years 1965–1966, and by 1967 the council had resolved to set up such an office in New York.[8]

The Department of Administrative Affairs

In its new robes, the reorganized Department of Administrative Affairs, (established in 1962 as part of the reorganization undertaken in the years 1958–1960), became more important than in previous years and also covered more areas. Besides personnel and budget matters, general services, and internal audit, it now also dealt with organization and methods, and with planning.

The Department of Legal Affairs

The Department of Legal Affairs, which dealt with various legal questions, put its legal knowledge as well as its secretariat at the disposal of the organization. It has given secretarial aid to the Inter-American Commission on Human Rights, the Inter-American Peace Committee, and the Special Consultative Committee on Security. In the early 1960s, it participated in special missions to the Dominican Republic and Costa Rica. It also sent a delegation to the First Meeting on Representative Democracy, in the Dominican Republic (December, 1962). The department was furthermore known for its sizeable collection of publications, among which at that time the Treaty Series, the Constitutions Series, and the Legal Series (statements of the laws of various countries) deserve special mention.

The department was headed by a director who, at the same time, was also the executive secretary of the Inter-American Council of Jurists. Moreover, the secretariat of the Council of Jurists and the Inter-American Juridical Committee have also been attached to the department. Two separate branches covered the legal responsibilities of the department: the General Legal Division and the Codification Division. The former was responsible for treaty registration and deposit of ratifications of multilateral treaties, and the latter, for codification. Finally, the department has also, when requested, provided legal opinions or studies on a great number of topics, either of a political nature, like possible amendments to the charter, or legal questions regarding the many problems concerning nations such as Cuba, the Dominican Republic, Honduras, and Nicaragua, or economic issues, such as the legal aspects of economic integration.

THE TECHNICAL FIELDS OF ACTIVITY OF THE PAU: THE ASSISTANT SECRETARY FOR ECONOMIC AND SOCIAL AFFAIRS

This office covered four areas: Economic Affairs, Social Affairs, Statistics, and Technical Cooperation. Together they embraced an activity that, after 1961—the year of the Alliance for Progress—registered an extraordinary growth and which, in turn, resulted in the establishment of this umbrella office with overall responsibility for the above four areas. The creation of this top position was the result of the reorganization of 1958–1960 and the new emphasis on the solution of economic and social problems.

Before 1961 there existed a single Department of Economic and Social Affairs whose director was also the executive secretary of IA–ECOSOC. The Alliance for Progress reformed IA–ECOSOC. That organization's executive secretary now became the assistant secretary for economic and social affairs; at the same time, the other two departments—Statistics and Technical Cooperation—were also put under the supervision of this umbrella office. The reason for this new arrangement was simply to help in the promotion and success of the Alliance for Progress, and to coordinate and streamline the four areas for economic and social advancement. In 1966, a further step was taken: the new Technical Unit for Latin American Economic Integration was set up in order to establish close relationships with ICAP, LAFTA, and CACM.

The Department of Economic Affairs

In 1962, the department published its annual report on the economic and social situation in Latin America, which served as a basis for the talks on development aid at the First Annual Meeting of the new IA–ECOSOC (Mexico City). These annual reports superseded those published earlier by ECLA and appeared now in collaboration with ECLA and IDB in a joint publication according to the ad hoc agreement OAS-IDB-ECLA.

The department sent several missions to Latin America, all of which were connected with development aid; thus, in 1962, a mission went to Panama (advising on the drafting of the development program), to Honduras (advising on a paper and cellulose production project), and to the Dominican Republic (advising on investment and planning for development aid).

In the field of more specialized tasks, the department dealt with planning and programming. These activities were carried out in 1962 in three sectors: (1) active participation at meetings (Assembly of Planning Experts and Planning Officials in Santiago de Chile, 1962; First Annual Meeting of IA-ECOSOC in Mexico City, 1962; First Meeting of the Special Committee for Planning and Program Formulation in Buenos Aires, 1963; as well as the Planning Seminar in Guatemala, 1962); (2) technical assistance for the elaboration and drafting of development programs of the member states and similar programs for the Dominican Republic, Ecuador, Guatemala, Honduras, Panama, and Peru; and (3) collaboration in an advisory capacity on the national development programs for Bolivia, Colombia, and Mexico submitted to the approval of the "Nine Wise Men," the panel set up by the IA-ECOSOC meeting in Punta del Este.

The department has also been active in the field of industrial programming, and in 1962, it published a report entitled *El desarrollo industrial y el financiamiento del sector privado*. Also, in 1962, special missions were sent to Haiti, Honduras, and Ecuador to study natural resources. These missions were often undertaken in cooperation with ECLA and the IDB.

In the field of technology and productivity, several projects were carried out, and courses and meetings were held. This was a type of activity in which the department had been active for years. In 1962, it was able, in cooperation with ECLA, UNESCO, ILO, ICEM, FAO, and OECD, as well as several governments and universities, to establish several courses, hold meetings on human resources, and publish a work entitled *Institutos de investigación tecnológica—Informe preliminar.*

In the late 1950s and early 1960s the department became increasingly concerned with questions of international economics. These problems naturally dealt mainly with commodities, the economic integration of Latin America (the Latin American Free Trade Association and the Central American Common Market), and the European Common Market.

The problems of transportation, agrarian policy, and development, as well as public administration and finance, were other areas on which the department focused its attention. Several meetings and conferences were held within this framework during the early 1960s.

In the field of tourism, much was done in the late 1950s and early 1960s in regard to promoting and easing travel restrictions. This found expression also in publications such as the earlier *Travel in . . . Series, Motoring in Mexico,* and *Chronology of the Pan American Highway.*

The Department of Social Affairs

As in the case of economics, social affairs received a boost. The activities of the department were also closely connected with IA-ECOSOC, ICAP and the panel of experts or the "Nine Wise Men." The autonomous Department of Social Affairs dealt with problems of public housing, municipal and regional planning, social planning and programming, municipal and rural development, cooperatives, labor relations, social insurance, community development, social welfare, and training. Meetings, special courses (in 1962 alone, five courses in the social field were arranged), assemblies, research, and advisory and information work were conducted.

In the field of public housing, a number of interesting publications deserve mention, such as *Guía de investigaciones para el planeamiento de la vivienda dentro de la alianza para el progreso* (1962), as an example of the work on this subject. The department also published a report on the various types of Latin American cities. Moreover, in the late 1950s and early 1960s, the department gave technical assistance in this area to several governments (e.g., Bolivia, Chile, Ecuador, and Honduras), as well as to the University of Santo Domingo. In 1963, a book was published entitled *Housing in Peru,* the first of a new series on the complex housing situation in Latin America. This first volume was part of an experimental program within the Alliance for Progress.

The Inter-American Center for Housing and Planning (CINVA), established in Bogotá in 1952, also fell within this framework. This center, which was incorporated directly into the PAU on January 1, 1959, had three goals: education, research, and documentation. It cooperated with the Colombian government (through the ICT) and was assisted in its work by Yale University.

The main purpose of CINVA was higher education in the field of housing, an activity that the institute carried out by means of apprenticeships and special training courses. The apprenticeships on housing dealt not only with construction theory but also with social anthropology, construction, methods of research, self-help in housing, statistics, financing, administration, and drafting. In December 1962, CINVA held its tenth course, in which 38 students participated. By 1965, CINVA had trained and specialized 258 experts.

Several of the CINVA meetings in the field of housing were of great interest, for example, the Technical Assembly on the Formation of Capital for Housing in the Latin American Economy, which met in May 1963 in Los Angeles, California. This meeting was carried out by the OAS in conjunction with the research program for real estate questions of the University of Los Angeles and with observers, of various banks, such as IDB and housing credit institutions. Another meeting, the Latin American Seminar on Housing Statistics and Housing Programs, took place in Copenhagen in September 1962.

Still another field of activity was social planning and the formulation of programs. These activities also included seminars, studies, opinions, technical assistance, advisory services, and information work, which were carried out on the basis of the Charter of Punta del Este and resolutions of the Latin American Seminar on Planning (Santiago de Chile, 1962). In that same year, special missions were sent to Central America, Haiti, Paraguay, and Uruguay.

Municipal development, which in Latin America has been characterized by unhealthy, chaotic growth, also fell within the scope of the department. The main works in this field aimed at the elaboration of knowledge necessary to keep municipal development within bounds and to find solutions for problems of municipal development. In the middle of 1962, studies concerning social structure were carried out in six Brazilian cities. These resulted in the publication of two works: *Brazilian Careers and Social Structure, with Implications for Planning and Actions Programs* and *Brazilian Careers and Social Structure: A Case History and Model.*

Other works that were more concerned with informative and advisory aspects, dealt with the establishment of fellowships for sociology and economic policy. They were also concerned with aiding U.S. and European students traveling to Latin America, so that they could conduct research, teach, and cooperate in development plans. Round-table talks in this area in 1962 concerned studies about the lower social strata in Brazil, the social organization in Central America, a study of LAFTA, and a work on the political and economic elite in various Latin American countries. In this field in 1962, the special attention of the department was given to the Seminar on Social Structure, Social Strata and Mobility (with reference to Latin America) that took place in Rio de Janeiro.

The department was also very active in the field of rural development. The rural situation, as it existed at that time, was not likely to promote the development of Latin America, for agriculture and the population which was linked to it had been neglected for too long. Work in this field consisted of research on structural changes. For this purpose, material on the social rural development in Latin America has been collected and evaluated. A list of all studies in this field was compiled and was always being supplemented. Furthermore, a study has been made in four Latin American countries regarding the relationship of agrarian reform and the socio-economic situation. These problems have also been touched upon in research carried out by the department using as comparisons Israel, Italy, and Greece, and the documents that were published in the *Revista interamericana de ciencias sociales*. Also in this field, the department participated in several meetings, such as the Seventh Regional Conference of FAO for Latin America (Rio de Janeiro, 1962), the Regional Seminar of UNESCO for Social Research and Rural Problems in Mexico, Central America, and the Caribbean Area (Mexico City, 1962), and others that were organized in Washington, D.C.

In the field of cooperatives (a concern of the OAS since World War II), the department was particularly active in disseminating knowledge on cooperatives in Latin America. There can be no doubt that under the aegis of the Alliance for Progress, this area was strengthened further, especially in view of its large role in agrarian reform. Great progress had been made in regard to cooperative housing, consumption, transportation, electric power, and public health, and the department has issued several publications on these topics. A second edition of the *Manual de organización y administración de empresas cooperativas* and the *Manual de educación cooperativa* appeared in the early 1960s. Some studies on the cooperative movement in Brazil, Chile, and Costa Rica were to be published later, under the title *La experiencia cooperativa como método de desarrollo de regiones y comunidades*.

The department also participated in a seminar on rural cooperatives, organized in 1962 by the German Foundation for Development Aid in Bonn. The following three documents were prepared for the seminar by the Department: *El cooperativismo agrario en América Latina*, *La educación cooperativa en América Latina*, and *El movimiento cooperativo en América Latina*.

Finally, an Organization of American Cooperatives, with headquarters in Montevideo, was being organized and would delve further into this important subject matter. The department has participated in its establishment and would cooperate to the fullest with this new institution. Another institution for which plans have been made is the Inter-American Institute for the Financing of Cooperatives.

The subject of labor relations has been taken up by the Department of

Social Affairs, whose purpose was to stimulate a greater sense of responsibility on the part of employees and their associations and to explain to them their important role in development plans. A further purpose was to demonstrate clearly to all concerned, including the governments, the necessity of having employees collaborate in development plans, and furthermore, of creating the necessary machinery for achieving a practical implementation of the principles of consultation and participation in this field.

In view of the practical difficulties in the field of labor relations in Latin America (which have attracted great attention, especially within the framework of the Alliance for Progress), the department set up study groups, elaborated opinions, strengthened technical assistance, participated in meetings, and furnished advisory services and information. Another organization in this field, the International Group of Labor Leaders (1962), had examined the role of labor organizations in the Alliance for Progress. This study group, consisting of experts from Colombia, Denmark, the Federal Republic of Germany, Israel, Italy, and the United States, visited various Latin American countries. The conclusions supported by their study were accepted by IA-ECOSOC in its Resolution no. 10, "Popular Support of the Programs of the Alliance for Progress." The aim of this resolution was the creation of a greater awareness and activity in this field.

In the field of technical assistance to labor organizations, a number of seminars and apprenticeships were set up in the early 1960s especially for labor leaders. An orientation training course was carried out in Colombia. Two institutes were established, and the department assisted with the preparatory work of the *Instituto de Relaciones Laborales* within the National University of Bogotá, which was aided by the School of Labor and Industrial Relations of the State of New York on the basis of a procedure developed with a similar institution within the University of Chile. The department also worked in close cooperation with the American Institute for Free Labor Development (AIFLD) and the International Institute for Trade Union Studies in Geneva.

Finally, there were many advisory and information services and numerous meetings, the most important of which has been the Inter-American Conference of Ministers of Labor, held in Bogotá in May 1963, where the role of the Latin American Ministries of Labor in the economic and social development policy of Latin America was established.

Social security was another area on which the department had concentrated its attention. Although all Latin American countries did have extensive social insurance, implementation and execution was not as efficient as the statistics would have us believe. The department had therefore ordered investigations and studies in this field (resulting in the booklet *Síntesis de la seguridad social*).

The subject of community development and social welfare also received much attention since the formation of the Alliance for Progress. The goal was quite clear: to achieve results in the Latin American republics by work that would also contribute toward a success of the Alliance for Progress. Among the studies that deserve attention was the report entitled *Algunos aspectos de la situación de las escuelas de servicio social en América Latina*, which was prepared for the Eleventh Congress of the International Association of Schools of Social Service (Belo Horizonte, Brazil, 1962). Here also technical assistance was much in evidence, especially in regard to Program no. 8 of the PTC of the OAS (Inter-American Program for the Training of Personnel for the Development of Indigenous Communities). Several countries received advice and information in this field.

The Department of Social Affairs participated in a number of meetings in the field of community development and social welfare, among them the Fifth Conference of the International Union for the Education of the Public in Questions of Health (Philadelphia, 1962); the Eighth Regular Assembly of the Inter-Institutional Committee of CREFAL (Mexico, 1962), which was held with representatives of FAO, ILO, UNESCO, WHO, and the United Nations; the Eleventh Congress of the International Association of Schools of Social Service (Belo Horizonte, Brazil, 1962); and the Eleventh International Conference for Social Service (Quitandinha, Brazil).

The Department of Social Affairs also dealt with training in the field of the social sciences. In this area it participated during 1962 in five projects of the PTC of the OAS (Mexico City, São Paulo, Lima, Río Piedras, Guatemala, and La Paz). Furthermore, it assisted CINVA, the Inter-American Program of Higher Learning of the Social Sciences in the Caribbean Area (PICSES), and the Inter-American Program for Urban and Regional Planning (PIAPUR).

The Inter-American Program for the Training of Postgraduates in the Field of Applied Social Sciences (PICSA) was started in 1959. It enrolled its fourth class, comprising eighteen scholarship students from fourteen countries, in 1962. The subjects covered by PICSA were social anthropology, problems of industrialization, methods of research, applied anthropology, and social planning. The classes of the two-year curriculum were held in Mexico City at the Escuela Nacional de Antropología e Historia; they also met in other parts of the country. In 1962, thirty-three scholarships were awarded.

The PICSES training program was also begun in 1959, on the basis of an agreement between the president of the University of Puerto Rico (Río Piedras) and the secretary general of the OAS. This course lasted from sixteen to twenty-four months. In 1962, twenty-three students received specialized training under this program.

PIAPUR was established in 1961 in the Planning Institute of Lima and was administered by the department. Here the basis was an agreement between the OAS and the Universidad Nacional de Ingeniería. PIAPUR was to receive assistance from Yale University for a period of six years. Through

PIAPUR, the Planning Institute was put on a solid footing and even expanded, so that it was able to set up a postgraduate training program in the field of social planning. The first group of students finished its studies in 1962, and a second group of forty began in April 1963.

The development of indigenous communities was at that time the most recent activity of the department. This was a mutual enterprise of the OAS and the Inter-American Indian Institute (IAII), and in this program two courses of one year each were offered in both Guatemala and Bolivia.

Other courses given by the department covered the fields of social welfare and business administration. In the field of social welfare, the Inter-American Course of Administration of Programs of Social Welfare was set up in 1958 and ended in 1961. It was, however, expected that an Argentine university might adopt the course, so that it would not be permanently discontinued. Another project, dealing with training in business administration, had been carried out since 1959 at the School for Business Administration of the Getulio Vargas Foundation (São Paulo).

The Department of Statistics

Statistics became even more important after the launching of the Alliance for Progress, and this found an echo in the department, which was also closely linked to IA–ECOSOC and ICAP. The Department of Statistics worked in cooperation with the Inter-American Statistical Institute (IASI), which also had its headquarters in the PAU. The department provided the secretariat for IASI. However, IASI's work was geared more toward a long-range view and was not limited in its scope, while the department tackled only immediate problems assigned to it by the Council of the OAS and requested by the units of the PAU. Institute and department worked hand in hand; interestingly enough, Canada was a full member of the institute.

The statistical work became known through the program entitled "Censo de América" as well as through special demographic, social, and scientific statistics. The publication of specialized studies, such as *Características da estructura demográfica dos paises americanos, La situación de la vivienda: análisis estadístico-censal de los resultados obtenidos bajo el programa del Censo de las Américas de 1950* (compiled with the cooperation of the United Nations, ECLA, and Denmark), *Indices de precios al consumidor (costo de la vida) de las naciones americanas* (a quarterly magazine), and *La estructura agropecuaria de las naciones americanas* should also be mentioned here. The review *Estadística* and the very well-known and useful series entitled *América en cifras* not only disseminated important information on America but also made the institute and the department better known. Of course, both units also dealt with organization of statistics (the Inter-American Program of Basic Statistics) and with statistical science. Reference should also be made here to the Inter-American Center for Teaching in the Field of

Statistics (CIENES), which was established in Santiago de Chile in 1962 on the basis of an agreement between IASI, OAS, and the Chilean government.

The Department of Technical Cooperation

This department, which grew tremendously, particularly since the introduction of development aid, consisted of six technical services: Program for Technical Cooperation (PTC) of the OAS; Scholarship and Fellowship Program; Special Scholarships; Advisory Services; Information, Coordination and Promotion Services for the Exchange of Persons; and the Leo S. Rowe Memorial Fund. The further growth was obviously the result of the Alliance for Progress and the goals it wanted to achieve.

The program for technical cooperation had been in existence since 1951. During 1962, it was engaged in carrying out twelve projects, of which three were new, the costs of which amounted to more than $2 million.[9]

Another large sector of this department was concerned with the scholarship and fellowship program set up in 1957 on the basis of Recommendation no. 22 of the Inter-American Committee of Personal Representatives of the Presidents (CIRP). The recommendation was implemented in 1958 by the PAU, after the respective decision was passed by the Council of the OAS. Operations began on July 1, 1958, with a budget of $1.2 million. In those years the program operated on an annual budget of $1.5 million. Of the 682 scholarships granted in 1962, some were awarded to U.S. students. The fellowship program was approved by the Council of the OAS in March 1962 and began operations that same year.

Of particular interest were the scholarships granted by non-American governments. Thus, in the first years of its operation, three nations made these available to the OAS: Spain, Italy, and Israel. In 1962, twenty-six scholarships for Italy (Istituto di Studi per lo Sviluppo Economico, Naples; Istituto Agronomico per l'Oltremare, Florence) as well as about twenty-six for Spain (Escuela Técnica Superior de Ingenieros de Montes, Madrid; Instituto de Estudios Agrosociales, Madrid) had been granted. Other agreements for such scholarships were at that time being negotiated with the Federal Republic of Germany, France, Switzerland, Belgium, England, Denmark, Sweden, Norway, Netherlands, Finland, and Republic of China.

Another field of activity of this department was the advisory service carried out through two programs: the program of direct technical assistance and the missions for the elaboration of programs of the Alliance for Progress.

The program of direct technical assistance was created in order to assist the member states in the solution of problems they could not solve because of the lack of technical personnel. The standards for this direct service of technical assistance were approved by the Council of the OAS in 1959. Since its inception, this program had proved its value. This evaluation was corroborated by the very good impression it has been able to make on the various governments. The program achieved good results largely because of its flexibility. The required experts could be chosen either from the OAS, the member states, or from outside the OAS and the continent. Since the beginning of the program, until 1962, 106 missions had been sent. By 1964, some seventeen missions were either working or had been approved, and others were being studied. In 1962, the member states addressed thirty-one requests for technical assistance to the department, and that same year the following services were rendered:

Argentina: Study of the possibility of using electronic material for the collection of statistical data; evaluation of human resources.

Brazil: Study of coffee economics; rural sociology and economy; mining; advisory activities in regard to the rural electrification project of Itacurubá-Rodelas.

Colombia: Training of technical personnel for the national steelworks (Paz del Río); population census.

Costa Rica: Cartographic, statistical, and tabulation works; social services.

Chile: Agricultural cooperatives.

Ecuador: Population, housing, and livestock census; tourist promotion.

Guatemala: Minimum wage; national education plan; income tax.

Honduras: Agriculture; land tenure.

Panama: Evaluation of the results of the first industrial trade and service census.

Dominican Republic: Electoral, penal, and sociological matters; revision of the curriculum of the engineering, chemistry, and pharmacy faculties.

Uruguay: Customs nomenclature.

Central America: Coordination of teaching in the basic sciences at the five Central American universities and evaluation of the faculties of chemistry of the universities of El Salvador and Costa Rica in order to determine which of them should become the home of the Central American School of Industrial Chemistry.

Another matter referred to missions for the elaboration of programs of the Alliance for Progress, which was regulated by an agreement between the OAS and the United States dated November 29, 1961. In accordance with this agreement, the full responsibility of these missions of technical assistance for the economic-social development of Latin America was transferred to the OAS. For this activity, $6 million was put at its disposal, of which $3.5 million was used for the financing of these missions. Generally speaking, the missions covered the following activities: assistance in the establishment or strengthening of national planning boards, assistance in the elaboration or in the improvement of national development plans, elaboration or improvement of national plans in the socioeconomic field, and preparation of special projects for purposes of investment.

In view of the new goals within the framework of the Alliance for Progress, the department demonstrated an intensified activity in the field of information, coordination, and promotion in regard to the exchange programs. Several universities—Grinnell College and Loyola University (Chicago) in the United States, and Universidad Católica de Lima—had such agreements with Latin America. Within this framework, contact was also established with the Peace Corps and with such organizations as the International Association of Students in the Economic and Commercial Sciences (AIESEC), and the Center of Latin American Monetary Studies (CEMLA).

Publications such as the *Boletín intercambio de personas, becas y préstamos de la Organización de los Estados Americanos y sus Organismos Especializados para estudios en el extranjero* and the *Encuesta anual sobre el intercambio interamericano de personas* (1960–1961) gave an impressive picture of these important fields of activity. Finally, the numerous conferences and assemblies that were often held bear mention, such as the Inter-American Seminar on Educational Matters (Bogotá, 1962), in cooperation with the Colombian Institute for Technical Studies Abroad (ICETEX), the Annual Assembly of the National Association of Foreign Students Advisors (NAFSA), the First Annual Assembly on the Alliance for Progress (Miami, Florida), and the Tenth International Student Conference (Quebec, Canada).

The funds for the extraordinary number of programs managed by the department came in part from the general secretariat, in part from a Special Development Assistance Fund established in 1963–64, and in part from non-American governments.[10]

THE ASSISTANT SECRETARY FOR EDUCATION, SCIENCE AND CULTURE

This office was originally created in 1962 and approved by the Council of the OAS as "Assistant Secretary for Cultural, Scientific and Informational Affairs," and thus coordinated the activities of the respective departments. From 1964 to 1966 it also covered the newly created Department of Education. Then, in 1966, the Department of Information and Public Affairs was put directly under the secretary general and the title of the overall office was changed to "assistant secretary for education, science and culture." Though this office was at first not given the weight as the assistant secretary for economic and social affairs, it gradually reached the same level of importance, and its four areas were grouped together to form a coherent unit, streamlined and coordinated in order to better face the realities of the fourth quarter of the century.

The Department of Cultural Affairs

Originally this department was divided into several divisions dealing with philosophy and letters, visual arts, music and education. In 1964, the educational part was taken out and elevated to a separate department. In general terms, the Department of Cultural Affairs has promoted the literature, arts and music of the Americas through publications, liaison, exchange, festivals, and exhibitions.

The Department of Cultural Affairs issued several series of publications, including one on intellectual currents in America comprising about twenty-five publications in the early 1960s. Since 1958, it has published the *Diccionario de la literatura latinoamericana*; by the early 1960s, sections of this work on Argentina, Bolivia, Ecuador, and Central America appeared. Also of note was the joint work with UNESCO regarding the publication of Latin American classical works, such as the *Travels* by Domingo Faustino Sarmiento, the *Royal Commentaries* of the Inca Garcilaso de la Vega, and the *Antología de los cronistas de las culturas precolombinas*. In the program of publication of basic bibliographies, a monograph entitled *English Translations of Latin American Literature* has been in preparation since 1962. Finally, there was the excellent *Inter-American Review of Bibliography*, which has appeared quarterly since 1951 under the scholarly editorship of Maury A. Bromsen. Requests for information, talks, conferences, meetings, and collaboration with U.S., Latin American, and international institutions and organizations such as the Instituto Caro y Cuervo (Bogotá), the University of Puerto Rico (Río Piedras), the Inter-American Committee for Cultural Action (Mexico City), round out the activities.

Every month, the Department of Cultural Affairs of the PAU organized art exhibitions in which a new Latin American artist was presented to the U.S. public. In 1962, pictures from these exhibitions sold for a total of approximately $27,500. Besides these exhibitions, there was a permanent collection of Latin American art, as well as many traveling art expositions. A total of 1,514 slides, works of graphic art, and films were distributed in 1962. Finally, there was the Division of Music, which organized concerts, musical festivals, and competitions; it also granted scholarships. Publications of the division comprised the *Inter-American Music Bulletin* and *A Guide to Latin American Music*, by Gilbert Chase. The division furthermore acted as the general secretariat of the Inter-American Council of Music (CIDEM) and provided the necessary secretarial services.

A special field of activity in this sphere was the Columbus Memorial Library in the PAU. Its collections totaled approximately 200,000 volumes, and, apart from the Library of Congress, it was the library of greatest significance in the area of Latin American studies and the inter-American field. Not only was it open to the public, but it also promoted activities affecting libraries and bibliographic work. It furthermore endeavored to make accessible to young people and adults a great number of books at low prices by way of a special program, the People's Book.

Finally, the Division of Cultural Relations published the magazine *Américas*, the official organ of the OAS. It has been published since the late 1940s and went back to the initiative of the first secretary general, Lleras. *Américas* was the successor to the excellent *Pan American Union Bulletin*, which was published before the establishment of the OAS, in 1948. For years, *Américas* floundered, since it attempted to address itself to everybody and hence appealed to no one. At first, it was published by the Division for General Publications of the Department of Public Information, but in the early 1960s, when a major effort was made to improve it, it was put under the direction of the Division of Cultural Relations of the Department of Cultural Affairs. Since then, the artistic and literary contents have improved, and the publication paid greater attention to the economic and social problems of Latin America and to the great cultural contributions of that part of the world.

The Department of Educational Affairs

Until 1964, as stated above, educational matters were dealt with as a division in the Department of Cultural Affairs, but the new emphasis resulting from the Alliance for Progress led to an independent Department of Educational Affairs. Its activities were especially emphasized in the Alliance for Progress, and thus, the new department concentrated on helping the various governments to cope with and improve their educational programs. The department endeavored to assist the member states on problems of education and to further international cooperation in this field. The department had research, editing, and information functions. It also administered the Inter-American Center of Rural Education (CIER) in Rubio, Venezuela, and (with UNESCO) the Regional Center of Fundamental Education for Latin America (CREFAL) in Pátzcuaro, Mexico.

On the basis of recommendations of a Special Committee, which looked into the educational activities of the PAU (Washington, D.C., PAU, 1958), the department began to concentrate on research. Its quarterly magazine, *La educación*, published the results of this research (e.g., "Corrientes de la escuela primaria en América Latina" and "El texto escolar para la escuela primaria de América"). Besides *La educación*, the department also published several information bulletins, monographs, and comparative social studies, such as *Una comparación entre las actitudes personales y sociales de adolescentes de Buenos Aires y Chicago*. Among the other publications of the department were *Organization and Structure of Latin American Universities, La televisión educativa, Study in Latin America*, and *Teaching Opportunities in Latin America for U.S. Citizens*.

The department also has organized technical conferences. In the early 1960s two of these were especially important: The Third Inter-American Assembly of Ministers of Education (Bogotá, 1963) and the Conference on Education and Economic and Social Development in Latin America (Santiago de Chile, 1962), which dealt with the Alliance for Progress.

Seminars, meetings, and technical assemblies rounded out the work of this department. Finally, it published the collection—comprising thirty-five titles—entitled *Biblioteca popular latinoamericana*. This series was designed especially to assist barely literate adults and to give them a basic knowledge in the most important fields.

The Department of Scientific Affairs

This department also grew originally from a Division of Scientific Development within the Department of Cultural Affairs. Like so many other changes, it owed its new independent status as a department to the Alliance for Progress. Beginning in 1962, when its establishment was approved by the Council of the OAS, it endeavored to promote the natural sciences throughout Latin America on the high-school and university level, which included nuclear science, radio isotopes and science information. It organized special classes, summer courses, meetings, and the exchange of scientists. Furthermore, it dealt with the exchange, elaboration, and publication of scientific information, as well as with the promotion of regional centers for scientific documentation, the collection of bibliographic works, and the promotion of scientific and technical publications.

The department established contact with a number of universities in the United States so that students of mathematics, chemistry, physics, and biology might attend summer courses that it organized. Latin American universities, as well, participated in the department's program. Special meetings were held in 1962 in Brazil, Mexico, and Peru. The department also sponsored an Exchange of Students Program supported financially by the Natural Science Foundation of the United States.

Finally, the department acted as the secretariat of the Inter-American Nuclear Energy Commission (IANEC), which held its Fourth Assembly in Mexico City, in 1962. The director of the department acted as the executive secretary of the IANEC. In this capacity, the department also cooperated with EURATOM and the International Agency for Atomic Energy in Vienna.

Among the department's most important publications was the magazine *Ciencia interamericana*.

The Department of Information and Public Affairs

Also as a result of the Alliance for Progress, this Department was boosted in order to intensify an information campaign about the inter-American system and the activities of the OAS for a better understanding and rapprochement between the American peoples. This campaign was geared not only to Latin America, but especially toward the United States where the misconceptions and misunderstandings, prejudices and distortions about Latin American realities continued to be a serious handicap for a better relationship between the United States and its neighbors to the South.

This department consisted of the Divisions for General Information, Radio and Television, Press, and General Publications. Under the Division for General Information, a permanent program of lectures, meetings, round tables, and courses was carried out in order to disseminate knowledge about the OAS and the member states among the general public. This program also sought to establish and deepen contacts with universities and colleges in the United States; educational offices and boards; women's clubs; and professional, labor, religious, and youth groups. A special activity highlighting its work was the Pan American Week, observed annually in April, using materials that the department distributed.

The Radio and Television Division grew tremendously in the 1950s and 1960s. Station WRUL (Boston) broadcast daily on shortwave transmission—forty-five minutes in Spanish, thirty minutes in Portuguese to Brazil, and forty-five minutes in French to Haiti. *La Voz de la OEA* (The Voice of the OAS) was linked to the entire continent; it broadcast through approximately 270 affiliated stations and transmitted a short summary of the current activities of the OAS. "Pan American Party," which was broadcast for more than twelve years by the American Broadcasting Corporation, and the weekly program "Pan American Rhapsody," were known to many U.S. radio listeners. In the case of important events in Washington or Latin America, transmissions were made directly from the spot. The concerts which were held in the PAU fell into this category, and they were rebroadcast by about forty Latin American radio stations.

The Press Division provided information on events in the OAS. The leading information media were the *Carta aérea*, the *Boletín de noticias*, and *Alliance Newsletters*. The department also offered fellowships to journalists to attend courses at the International Center for Advanced Studies in Journalism for Latin America (CIESPAL) in Quito. An important innovation took place in the years 1965–1966: the department began to publish the *OAS Chronicle*, which replaced the earlier *Annals of the Organization of American States*. The new publication contained official information about OAS activities.

The Division for General Publications published the *Serie de las Repúblicas Americanas* and the *Commodity Series*.[11] On the subject of the Alliance for Progress, publications included *The New World Will Be a Better World* (in three languages), *The Alliance for Progress—What You Should Know about It*, and *The Inter-American Milestones of 1961*; a publication about the OAS and the inter-American system in general was *The Inter-American System* (in three languages).[12]

6

The OAS (1948 through 1967–1970): The Specialized Conferences and Specialized Organizations, Agencies, and Commissions

THE SPECIALIZED CONFERENCES

The inter-American system also included the so-called Specialized Conferences (different from the Special Conference), which met when purely technical matters were under discussion, or when special aspects of inter-American cooperation were to be dealt with. Specialized Conferences were to be held when the Inter-American Conference or the Meeting of Consultation of Ministers of Foreign Affairs called for such meetings, when the Council of the OAS considered them necessary, or when treaties or agreements required them. This should not be interpreted to mean that Specialized Conferences were only held since the charter came into effect in 1951. On the contrary, Specialized Conferences had already been held since the beginning of the inter-American system; some had been convoked by the regular Inter-American Conference, others were held in view of some action by other bodies of the inter-American system. Thus, the Second International Conference of American States called for the convocation of a Pan American sanitary conference, a railroad conference, and a geographic conference. The Third International Conference of American States in Rio de Janeiro (1906) recommended the convocation of an international coffee conference, and the Fourth International Conference of American States (1910) congratulated the Argentine government for holding the first International American Scientific Congress, sponsored by the Argentine Scientific Society.[1]

The more the inter-American system advanced, the more it branched out into a variety of technical fields of mutual interest. Thus, at the time of the Ninth International Conference of American States there had been Specialized Conferences that had dealt with many different technical subjects on a periodic basis, and had established a well-deserved legitimacy that could not be ignored. Hence, the charter codified this experience and included the Specialized Conferences in Articles 93 and 94.

The Bogotá Conference of 1948 created in the charter three technical organs—IA–ECOSOC, Council of Jurists, and Cultural Council—and thus the problem arose as to which of the many technical conferences would be considered specialized. It was obvious that the three above-mentioned technical bodies of the OAS council would slow down the increasing number of technical meetings, but they continued to spread. The Council of the OAS, thus, was forced to come to a decision, which it did on April 21, 1949, when it made a distinction between "specialized meetings" and "other meetings" and adopted standards in order to clarify the matter. Thus, to qualify as a Specialized Conference, it had to include four elements: to be governmental, technical, of common interest, and open to participation by all the member states.[2] The Council of the OAS, at that meeting and later, declared the following technical meetings to fall into the above distinction:

Assemblies of the Inter-American Commission of Women

Conferences on Agriculture

General Assemblies of the Pan American Institute of Geography and History and the Pan American Consultations on Cartography, Geography and History held under the Institute's auspices

Inter-American Congresses of Public Health

Inter-American Economic Conferences

Inter-American Indian Conferences

Inter-American Meetings of Ministers of Education

Inter-American Port and Harbor Conferences

Inter-American Specialized Conference on Conservation of Natural Resources

Inter-American Statistical Congresses

Inter-American Telecommunications Conferences

Inter-American Travel Congresses

Meeting of Copyright Experts of the American Republics

Pan American Child Congresses

Pan American Highway Congresses

Pan American Sanitary Conferences.[3]

However, despite this classification of 1949, problems popped up because the charter had not given the Council of the OAS an exclusive right to regulate them, and the further proliferation of these technical meetings eluded a final solution, so that the "Standards for the Exercise of Authority of the Council With Regard to the Specialized Conferences" was referred to the Tenth International Conference of American States in Caracas. This conference was unable to come up with a final solution and turned the issue back to the council which, in 1962, adopted a *Report on Standards for Inter-American Conferences.*[4] These standards defined the Specialized Conferences as "intergovernmental, technical, and of common interest," and as meeting the following criteria:

a. All delegations [must] represent their respective governments and vote in their name;

b. They [must] have as their object to deal with special matters or to develop determined aspects of inter-American cooperation;

c. They [must] deal with matters that are of general interest to the American community, and they are open to the participation of all the states member of the Organization, in conformity with the provisions of Chapter IV.[5]

The standards also defined who could vote and limited the observers, such as "inter-American specialized organizations" and "inter-governmental regional agencies of the Americas"; "the United Nations and its specialized agencies"; "international or national organizations . . . parties to agreements or arrangements establishing cooperative relations with the council of the organization, its organs, or the organization sponsoring the conference"; "and non-member governments indicating a desire to attend, provided the OAS Council had approved the invitation."[6]

Later, an important new provision was added to these standards in the sense that any proposed activity should specify the financial implications in order to avoid financial irresponsibility or abuse.[7]

The Specialized Conferences were one of the most interesting activities of the OAS. Only in the five-year period between 1954 and 1959 some seventeen such Specialized Conferences took place:

Fifth Inter-American Tourist Congress (Panama: June 12–19, 1954);

Sixth Pan American Highway Congress (Caracas: July 11–23, 1954);

Fourteenth Pan American Health Conference (Santiago de Chile: October 7–22, 1954);

Third Inter-American Indian Congress (La Paz: August 2–12, 1954);

Third Inter-American Statistical Conference (Quitandinha: June 9–23, 1955);

Tenth Pan American Children's Conference (Panama: February 6–12, 1955);

Specialized Inter-American Conference on the "Preservation of Natural Resources: Continental Shelf and Waters" (Santo Domingo: March 15–28, 1956);

First Inter-American Harbor Conference (San José: April 25–May 3, 1956);

Sixth Inter-American Tourist Congress (San José: April 14–21, 1956);

Seventh Pan American Highway Congress (Panama: August 1–10, 1957);

Second Inter-American Assembly of Ministers of Education (Lima: May 3–9, 1956);

Economic Conference of the OAS (Buenos Aires: August 15–September 4, 1957);

Seventh Inter-American Tourist Congress (Montevideo: December 9–17, 1958);

Fifteenth Pan American Health Conference (San Juan, Puerto Rico: September 21–October 3, 1958);

Eleventh Pan American Children's Conference (Bogotá: November–December 1959);

Fourth Inter-American Indian Congress (Guatemala: May 16–27, 1959);

Commemorative Meeting of the Presidents of the American Republics (Panama: July 21–22, 1956).

In the early 1960s, there was the Eighth Inter-American Tourist Congress (Guadalajara, Mexico: September 19–28, 1962), the Inter-American Conference of Ministers of Labor regarding the Alliance for Progress (Bogotá: May 5–11, 1963), the Ninth Pan American Highway Congress (Washington, D.C.: May 6–18, 1963), and the Second Inter-American Harbor Conference (Mar del Plata, Argentina: May 29–June 8, 1963).

An interesting aspect of the Specialized Conferences was recorded by García Amador when he stated that meetings of this kind offered the advantage to study all angles of a given problem, so that practical and suitable solutions could be found.[8] One such conference dealing with the Law of the Sea prepared the formula that was later adopted by the International Law Commission and the First Conference on the Law of the Sea (Geneva, 1958), in regard to the juridical aspects of the continental shelf and submarine areas.[9]

Thus, in conclusion, very fruitful work was done in the field of specialized conferences, especially in view of the fact that here technical matters, rather than purely political problems, were treated, and hence tension and friction were rare.

THE SPECIALIZED ORGANIZATIONS

The Charter of the OAS established six specialized organizations and six special agencies and commissions. They were directly linked to the Specialized Conferences and indirectly to the Council of the OAS. In accordance with the Charter of the OAS, the Specialized Organizations belonged to the organs of the OAS, and Article 95 of the charter defined them as "intergovernmental organizations established by multilateral agreements and having specific functions with respect to technical matters of common interest to the American States." For this purpose, the Council of the OAS had certain specific duties, which were enumerated in Article 53 of the charter. These organizations, in accordance with Article 97 of the charter, enjoyed the fullest technical autonomy, although they naturally had to take into account the recommendations of the Council of the OAS.

Long before the Charter of the OAS was adopted by the organization there existed numerous inter-American organizations, some of which were official, others semi-official, and others private. Thus, at the time of the Ninth International Conference of American States in Bogotá, the latter requested a study to be made by the new Council of the OAS in order to determine which of these many agencies would meet the requirements to be included as a Specialized Organization of the inter-American system. The new Council of the OAS then proceeded to study and enumerate those requirements, as follows:

a. It should be intergovernmental, that is, an official entity made up of governments;
b. it should be established by multilateral agreement, in other words, by agreement between governments;
c. it should have a specific function;
d. that function should be of a technical nature; and
e. its field of activities should be of common interest to the American states.[10]

As a result of these findings, the Council of the OAS then would sign an agreement in order to establish the kind of relationship that should exist between the Specialized Organization and the OAS. Once the conditions of these procedures have been met, the respective specialized organization was recognized as such and was covered by Articles 53 and 95–101 of the charter, i.e.,

a. It enjoys the fullest technical autonomy but it is to take into account the recommendations of the council, in conformity with the provisions of the charter;
b. its relations with the organization are determined by means of the aforesaid agreement with the council;
c. it submits periodic reports to the council on the progress of its work and on its annual budget and expenses;
d. it should establish cooperative relations with world agencies of the same character, in order to coordinate their activities;
e. it should preserve its identity and status as an integral part of the Organization of American States, even when it performs regional functions of international agencies; and
f. its geographic location should be determined after taking the interests of all the American states into account.[11]

As stated before, the Charter of the OAS distinguished between Specialized Organizations and special agencies and commissions. Among the first group were the Pan American Health Organization (PAHO), the Inter-American Children's Institute (IACI), the Inter-American Commission of Women (IACW), the Pan American Institute of Geography and History (PAIGH), the Inter-American Institute of Agricultural Sciences (IAIAS), and the Inter-American Indian Institute (III).

The Pan American Health Organization (PAHO) (Washington, D.C., 1902)

The Pan American Health Organization—Organización Panamericana de la Salud (OPS)—and its secretariat, the Pan American Sanitary Bureau, were founded in 1902 as a result of the Second International Conference of American States (Mexico City). It was then called the International Sanitary Bureau and became the oldest international health agency. In 1923, the Fifth International Conference of American States changed the name to Pan American Sanitary Bureau, and the International Sanitary Conferences became the Pan American Sanitary Conferences. In 1958, at the Fifteenth Pan American Sanitary Conference in San Juan, Puerto Rico, the organization received the name under which it is known today: Pan American Health Organization; the name "Pan American Sanitary Bureau," however, was retained for its central office in Washington.

In its long history since 1902 the organization's goal was to coordinate the endeavors of all American republics in the field of health—"to fight disease, prolong life and encourage the physical and mental improvement of their peoples."[12] After World War II the organization was the cause of a serious crisis since it seemed that external powers were attempting to interfere in the inter-American system. The International Health Conference of 1946, while drafting the constitution for the future World Health Organization (WHO), the successor to the League Health Organization, unilaterally decided that the Pan American Sanitary Bureau should act as the regional agency of WHO in the Americas.[13] The fact that an international body had made such a decision without consultation upset the Union of American Republics to the extent that the then governing board studied the matter in depth in that same year and came to the conclusion that international organizations could only establish such relationships with inter-American agencies provided the latter maintained their identity and position as an integral part of the inter-American system, even when exercising regional functions for an international organization.[14] The report of the governing board of 1946 served as a precedent for future cases and established the principle that a specialized organization of the inter-American system could serve in a dual capacity—regional and international—as long as its status as an agency of the inter-American system was not impaired. The dual role of the Pan American Sanitary Bureau was later recognized in 1949 when the latter signed an agreement with WHO. In its capacity as regional office of WHO in America, it also included Canada, as well as the United Kingdom, France and the Netherlands, as spokesmen for their respective American territories.

PAHO was based on four constitutional documents: its own constitution; its agreement with the OAS, which extended it the status of a specialized organization of the inter-American system; the WHO constitution; and the 1949 agreement between the Pan American Health Organization and WHO.[15]

The older PAHO, in its Pan American Sanitary Conferences, functioned between 1902 and 1920 under its original statutes; these were reorganized in 1920. Then, in 1924, it followed the Pan American Sanitary Code of Havana, amended with the additional Protocols of 1927 and 1952. Finally, in 1947, PAHO adopted a new version, which again was revised in 1961.

According to its statutes, the Pan American Sanitary Conference, meeting every four years, was the highest body that determined PAHO policy and was the forum for technical discussion. These technical discussions were guided by special rules adopted in 1958.[16] The meetings of the Sanitary Conference, with few exceptions, represented simultaneous meetings of the Regional Committee of WHO. These meetings took place at its headquarters, although they could also be held in member countries. The conference elected its own officers: a president and two vice presidents.

Next to the Sanitary Conference was the directing council, which performed the functions delegated to it by the conference, acting in its name between conferences and executing the decisions taken by the sanitary conference. It met annually and consisted of one public health specialist representing each member state; the director of PAHO and the director general of WHO, or his representative, participated ex officio and without vote.

There was also an executive committee, composed of seven members, representing seven member states and chosen by the sanitary conference or the directing council for three years with advisory and administrative duties. The executive committee had at least two meetings a year and elected its chairman and vice-chairman. The secretary of the committee was the director of the Sanitary Bureau.

Finally, the Pan American Sanitary Bureau (PASB) was PAHO's central office and secretariat. It was headed by a director chosen by majority vote of the Pan American Sanitary Conference for four years, although he could be reelected indefinitely.[17]

PAHO's work was quite vast: It operated through the Washington, D.C., headquarters and six zonal offices:

Washington Headquarters: United States, Puerto Rico, U.S. Virgin Islands, Canada.

Field Headquarters in El Paso, Texas: coordinated much along the U.S.-Mexico border.

Zone I (Caracas): Venezuela, French Guyana and French Antilles, Netherlands Antilles (parts), and Commonwealth Caribbean.

Zone II (Mexico City): Mexico, Cuba, Dominican Republic, and Haiti.

Zone III (Guatemala): Central America.

Zone IV (Lima): Bolivia, Colombia, Ecuador, and Peru.

Zone V (Rio de Janeiro): Brazil.

Zone VI (Buenos Aires): Argentina, Paraguay, Uruguay, and Chile.[18]

Between 1954 and 1959, PAHO spent more than $25 million to achieve its goal: to fight malaria, smallpox, yellow fever, leprosy, hoof-and-mouth disease, and other contagious diseases. The work of this specialized organization also focused on the instruction and training of technical and professional personnel, the strengthening of national health offices, research, health planning, and health economy. In the area of planning and economy, PAHO had a special agreement with the Development Center of the Central University of Venezuela (CENDES).

PAHO's importance and its growing activities were reflected in its budgets. Whereas in 1958 it amounted to some $8.6 million, the figure for 1965 increased to $17.3 million, thus following the general trend of the OAS itself.[19]

The Inter-American Children's Institute (IACI) (Montevideo, 1927)

The second inter-American Specialized Organization owed its existence to the initiative of an Uruguayan pediatrician, Luis Morquio, who proposed such an institute at the Second Pan American Child Congress, and later became its first director. The Fourth Pan American Child Congress, held in Santiago de Chile in 1924, did indeed follow up on this initiative, and thus it was set up as the American International Institute for the Protection of Childhood. It grew slowly, and not all the members of the inter-American system participated in it. In 1949, the institute was recognized as a Specialized Organization within the framework of the OAS, and in 1957, when its statutes were revised at the 38th Meeting in Lima, it adopted the present name—in Spanish, Instituto Interamericano del Niño. Five years later, the agreement of 1949 was amended for the purpose of clearing up financial questions since the institute had developed financial problems.

As part of the new agreement, the Office of the Institute functioned administratively as part of the general secretariat of the OAS. Hence, its activities and expenditures were part of the program and budget of the PAU, although it always maintained its technical autonomy. Its situation was thus different from the Pan American Health Organization and similar to the Inter-American Commission of Women.

In order that the 1957 statutes could be adapted to the new agreement of 1962, the institute elaborated a new draft at the 43rd Meeting in Montevideo, which, once submitted to the Council of the OAS, was approved in 1963. In accordance with these statutes the institute had as its purpose and goal the promotion of all matters relating to childhood: maternity, childhood, adolescence, and family. The institute was thus mainly a center for social work; research; and inquiry, information, and documentation services that dealt with the well-being of children, young people, and the family. The institute endeavored to keep in close contact with all Specialized Organizations of the OAS, as well as with WHO, FAO, UNESCO, UNICEF, and also with CIE and ICNND.

The institute consisted of three organs: a directing council, the Child Congress, and a central office in Montevideo. The directing council was the highest authority, and all American governments were represented in it. This body directed policy and nominated the candidates for the directorship. Between 1954 and 1956 it met twice a year; since 1957, it has met annually. The Child Congress took place every four years to discuss any matter that the governments or the directing council had put on the agenda. Finally, the central office, located in Uruguay's capital, was headed by a director general who, together with other members of the staff, was appointed by the secretary general of the OAS.

The institute organized seminars on child and youth protection, infantile paralysis, and child nutrition. It was also active in other social fields designed to strengthen the family and mobilized general public interest in youth. Statistical work and comparative legal research in the same field completed the activities of the Institute. Among its periodic publications were the *Boletín*, a quarterly which was a source of information in this field for more than thirty years, and the *Noticiario*, a monthly magazine.

The Inter-American Commission of Women (IACW)
(Washington, D.C., 1928)

This Specialized Organization was established by resolution of the Sixth International Conference of American States, meeting in Havana in 1928. Prior to its establishment women did not have equal rights anywhere on the continent, and it was in these inter-American conferences that women were given the floor to explain their positions, their ambitions, and their goals. The Inter-American Commission of Women (Comisión interamericana de Mujeres) was thus set up, with headquarters in Washington, D.C., since Latin American countries lagged behind concerning this subject. We should bear in mind that even in the United States and Europe, women's rights had only recently been granted (United Kingdom, 1918; United States, 1919). Initially, the commission had only seven members, but eventually all governments would be represented by female delegates. The first Conference of the Inter-American Commission of Women was held in Havana in 1930.

With every Inter-American Conference the commission succeeded in imposing its status and prestige, attempting to conform to the ideals proclaimed by the Fifth International Conference of American States in Santiago de

Chile, in 1923, for equality of rights between men and women. At the Eighth International Conference of American States in Lima in 1938, the commission was made an advisory institution of the inter-American system and governments were urged to join if they had not yet done so. The PAU was instructed to appoint the two top officers of the commission and to draft "Organic Statutes" to be approved by the next Inter-American Conference. Indeed, after several drafts, the Ninth International Conference of American States approved these Organic Statutes, submitted by the governing board in 1946, and the Inter-American Commission of Women was then recognized as a permanent institution. In 1953, the Council of the OAS made it a Specialized Organization when it signed an agreement with the IACW. Finally, the Tenth International Conference of American States in Caracas, in 1954, recognized this arrangement when it amended the statutes of the IACW. The permanent secretariat of the commission had its seat in Washington, D.C., in the PAU building, and its expenses were covered by the budget of the PAU.

The commission worked for the civil, political, economic, and social rights of women. It was to study the problems of women, to propose solutions, and to demand that the governments carried out resolutions adopted at inter-American conferences, international congresses, or their own assemblies. Furthermore, IACW was at the disposal of the OAS as an advisory organ for all matters related to women, and it submitted reports to the Inter-American Conference, the Council of the OAS, and the governments regarding its work and the position of women on the civil, political, economic, and social level.

IACW carried out its work through representatives sent by every American country—one representative for each state. The chair and the vice chair were elected from among them, but neither could be reelected. There were also an executive committee, a permanent secretariat, and the annual and special meetings, called assemblies.

The executive committee, consisting of the delegates of four countries, were chosen by absolute majority on a rotation basis for two years; the election took place at the same time when the chair and the vice chair were elected. The executive committee exercised its functions at the seat of the IACW. For 1963–1965, this executive committee was composed of the representatives of the Dominican Republic (chair), Costa Rica (vice chair), Panama, Chile, and the United States.

The assemblies were supposed to meet once a year but rarely did. The assembly determined the policy of the IACW and was convoked by the secretary general of the OAS upon request of the chair.

The commission aired its views through a number of publications: the *News Bulletin*, the *Noticias* (also in English), and *Enlace*; it also published several of its reports to the UN Commission of Women and a variety of special studies for inter-American Conferences.

IACW has been very successful. When it was established in 1928, women had political rights only in the United States. By the 1960s, women enjoyed such political rights in all member states. In Colombia, this became a reality in 1954, and in Honduras, Nicaragua, and Peru, in 1955. In 1956, women could exercise these rights for the first time in Bolivia, Honduras, and Peru, and in 1957 in Colombia, Haiti, and Nicaragua. Two conventions have also been ratified by the mid-1960s: the Inter-American Convention for the Conferring of Political Rights on Women and the Inter-American Convention for the Conferring of Civil Rights on Women.

IACW has also been successful in the economic field: Several conventions of the ILO regarding equal working opportunities for women (Convention No. 100 of ILO) were ratified by most American states.

IACW continued its fight, but since 1957, the fight has no longer been for the rights of women but rather for the improvement of their situation, so that they might have the chance of playing a role in the civic life of America that is in keeping with their newly acquired status. To support its activities, IACW set up cooperative committees in most of the American countries which were thought of as liaison offices between IACW and the national women's associations. Finally, IACW tried to enlist women for the Alliance for Progress.

The Pan American Institute of Geography and History (PAIGH) (Mexico City, 1928)

The same year that saw the establishment of the IACW was also the year of the Pan American Institute of Geography and History—the Instituto Panamericano de Geografía e Historia. It was also set up by a resolution of the Sixth International Conference of American States in Havana, in 1928. The Mexican government offered a site in its capital, which was gladly accepted. The first statutes of the new institution were adopted in 1929, and prior to World War II it held two general assemblies. At the Fourth General Assembly in Caracas (1946), these statutes were amended; in 1949, through a special agreement with the OAS, it became a Specialized Organization of the inter-American system.

At its Fifth General Assembly in Mexico City, in 1960, the directing council of the institute worked on revised statutes, which were then submitted to the Council of the OAS, as required by Article V of the agreement between the two organizations. The council gave its assent, and subsequently they were also approved by the Seventh General Assembly in Buenos Aires.

PAIGH was composed of several organs: the general assembly, the directing council, the national sections, the general secretariat, and the institute's three commissions: cartography, geography, and history. There were also other committees and working groups. Moreover, it administered the Pan American Training Center for the Evaluation of Natural Resources (CE-

PERN), which had its seat in Rio de Janeiro and which belonged to the PTC of the OAS.

The general assembly was the highest organ of PAIGH. It was composed of the representatives of the various governments and comprised all American governments including Canada, although Cuba was excluded since 1962. It has been an accepted principle that whenever a general assembly met, which was every four years, the technical commissions met concurrently with it.

The next organ was the directing council, which replaced the former executive committee and comprised a president, vice president, alternate vice president, and a secretary general, all of whom were elected by the general assembly for a period of four years until the next assembly. They were in charge between general assemblies and met once a year.

The national sections, formerly called national departments, were made up of the various national representatives on the three technical commissions; in fact, they were the nucleus of the institute; they were the ones that encouraged the research which was to be done within the various countries.

The general secretariat, located in Mexico City, was headed by the institute's general secretary, whose numerous tasks covered the implementation of resolutions from the general assemblies, preparation for the forthcoming assemblies, liaison, and research. It had a fine reference library with books, periodicals, and maps.

The three technical commissions were commissions on cartography, geography, and history. Each had its own committees, which were quite numerous. In 1966, twenty-eight committees were active at that time and some 450 experts were engaged in one or another aspect of these technical commissions.[20] The Commission of Cartography was set up in 1942 and had its seat in Buenos Aires, in line with the policy of the inter-American system to decentralize and have every region participate to the fullest. Some twenty-five years later, this same commission had permanent committees on Geodesy, Gravimetry and Earth Tides; Topographic Maps and Aerophotogrammetry; Aeronautical Charts; Hydrography; Special Maps; and Survey of Urban and Rural Areas.[21] Among the many activities, we should mention at least the journals, the *Atlas de América*, and the collection of data for a seismo-techtonic map of the continent. In order to get a better idea of the work that was silently done by this commission, we quote from a 1966 report:

The tremendous increase, in both quality and quantity, in basic cartography carried out since the Commission on Cartography was organized in 1941 is one of the clearest, most tangible achievements of the American nations through the Institute to date. Since this Commission was established, a surprising increase can be noted in the production of various kinds of basic maps and charts that are essential to the discovery and development of resources and that also contribute to national and international security. This increase in production has been accompanied by an actual improvement in the quality of the work and in the adoption of uniform standards. The basic geodetic control carried out by different countries similarly follows a system of uniformity in the procedures used and the accuracy of results.[22]

The Commission on Geography was created by the Fourth General Assembly, in 1946, and had its seat in Rio de Janeiro. Its committees were just as numerous as the one on cartography (e.g., Regional Geography, Basic Natural Resources, Urban Geography, Geography Applied to Development Programs, Teaching and Texts, and Geographic Terms).[23] Its main interest was mineral, plant, animal, and human resources, and thus it covered a wide range of specialties such as woods, classification and utilization of soil, climatology, fauna, geology, hydrology, meteorology, mineralogy, oceanography and fishery, population studies, land settlement, and economics.[24]

The third commission was on history, and its seat was in Caracas, Venezuela. It had committees on "Anthropology, on Archives, on the Teaching of History and on Textbooks, on Bibliography, on History of Ideas, on the Origins of the Emancipation movement, and on Folklore."[25] Its publication, the *Revista de Historia de América* is well known all over the world.

The institute has, in the course of its existence, published hundreds of geographic and historical works; it has done many excellent research studies and attracted a great number of eminent American scientists who at one time or another have been working with the institute for years and were connected with it in various capacities.[26]

The Inter-American Indian Institute (IAII) (Mexico City, 1940)

This fifth Specialized Organization saw the light of day as the result of the endeavors of those countries that have an Indian population and wanted to focus on Indian problems and their solutions. Thus, already at the Seventh International Conference of American States in Montevideo, in 1933, Resolution XVIII instructed the PAU to convene a special conference on Indian problems in Mexico City. This proposed conference was to report to the Eighth International Conference of American States. For a variety of reasons the First Inter-American Conference of Experts on Indian Life in the Americas could only be held in 1940 when it met in Pátzcuaro, Mexico, with all countries, except Haiti and Paraguay, attending. It should be noted that the Eighth International Conference of American States had recommended the establishment of an Indian Institute.

It was this First Inter-American Indian Congress that then put into practice the idea of the Inter-American Indian Institute—Instituto indigenista interamericano. A convention was then drafted in the same year and soon ratified by seventeen American countries: Argentina, Bolivia, Brazil, Colombia, Costa Rica, Chile, Ecuador, El Salvador, Guatemala, Honduras, Mexico, Nicaragua, Panama, Paraguay, Peru, Venezuela, and the United States.

It took a while before the Inter-American Indian Institute received full accreditation as a Specialized Organization of the OAS. It was in 1953 that an agreement between the institute and the OAS was signed which stipulated, among other things, reciprocity in meetings and in the exchange of documents, that annual reports be sent to IA–ECOSOC, and that both the budget and the statement of its quota to each member state be forwarded to the council.

As with some other Specialized Organizations of the inter-American system, membership was not automatic. Thus, in this case, for a long time membership was restricted to the seventeen nations that had signed and ratified the convention. Only later did the remainder join.

The institute had three organs: the Inter-American Indian Conference, the Institute, and the National Indian Institutes. The conference was also here the highest policy-determining body. Its tasks related to all aspects of Indian life, especially the socioeconomic development of the Indian community.

The institute, located in Mexico City, was to perform its task as a standing committee of the Inter-American Indian Conference; it was responsible for the implementation of resolutions of these conferences, direct research and liaison, and promotion of the education of Indians. The institute had three organs: a board of directors, in which all member states of the IAII were represented; an executive committee, which consisted of five members; and a director, whom the board elected for a period of six years.

The director of the institute acted as the secretary of the executive committee, which, in turn, was controlled by the board of directors. The governing board was the highest organ of the institute. It met twice a year, chose the executive committee, designated the institute's director, approved the plans of the executive committee, decided the financial basis of the institute, and had the authority to convene meetings. Finally, the director of the institute was also the secretary of the board.

Of all the specialized organizations, this was by far the smallest unit and the most modest. However, its tasks were thereby not diminished.

The goal of the institute was to promote and coordinate social and economic development programs on behalf of the American Indians. Furthermore, the institute granted several training scholarships and reported through its publications on the work accomplished. Finally, the institute also functioned as the Permanent Committee of the Inter-American Indian Congresses.

The institute dealt with the problems of the Indians in Central America (Seminar, 1955), and with the diffusion of the special Indian legislation in Argentina, Chile, Colombia, Costa Rica, Ecuador, Guatemala, Honduras and Mexico. Other countries—Bolivia, Brazil, Nicaragua, Panama, Peru, the United States, and Venezuela—also collected and published their legislation in this field. A manual on the Indian population and several projects on the status of Indian women had been developed by the institute. One of its special undertakings, begun in 1960, was a project for developing Indian village communities in Mexico. This project was considered a training center for Latin American scholarship grantees (scholarship program of the OAS, students of CREFAL, etc.). Here scholarship grantees also acquainted themselves with what Mexico was doing in the fields of economics, agriculture, public health, and administration.

The institute became known for its publications in the field of American Indian affairs. These included the periodical *América indígena*, the *Anuario indigenista* (1962), and the *Bibliografía antropológica* (1962). Exhibitions and conferences were also among its activities. When the Thirty-fifth International Congress of Americanists was held in Mexico City in 1962 the Institute acted as the general secretariat.

The expansion plans for the Institute, within the framework of the Alliance for Progress, provided for a department on the development problems of Indian village communities and a publications department that would make available handbooks on the social, economic, public health, and educational problems of these village communities.

The Inter-American Institute of Agricultural Sciences (IAIAS) (Turrialba/San José, 1944)

This Specialized Organization was the last of the six accredited as such by the OAS, and, as with the IAII, for a long time its membership did not extend to all member states of the inter-American system. The history of this institute is quite interesting and goes back to the Fifth International Conference of American States in Santiago de Chile, in 1923, which recommended the establishment of an inter-American agency dealing with agriculture and industry. The matter was later taken up by the Sixth International Conference of American States in Havana, in 1928, which decided to study the establishment of an "Inter-American Board of Agricultural Defense," to be based on a convention; at the same time, it decided to set up a permanent commission in the PAU concerning agriculture.[27]

Not much happened in the 1930s in regard to the agricultural initiative of the 1920s, but suddenly the United States became interested in the subject matter. Thus, in 1939, the Interdepartmental Committee on Cooperation with the American Republics followed in the footsteps of the Sixth International Conference of American States: it recommended the creation of such an agricultural agency. A year later, the Eighth American Scientific Congress also endorsed the idea and proposed the establishment of an Inter-American Institute of Tropical Agriculture to serve as a training center for rubber production. The congress then approached the PAU whose governing board now also got into gear and recommended an "Inter-American Commission on Agriculture." This commission then reported back in 1942 recommending the establishment of an institution with some by-laws and a certificate of incorporation in the District of Columbia. The governing board of the PAU accepted this proposal, and at the same time Turrialba, Costa Rica, was chosen as the site of the future institution with a director and a secretary. All these arrangements had to be confirmed by the member governments before giving it final approval.[28] The next step was a draft convention, which was approved by the governing board in 1943 and then submitted to the governments in 1944.

The institute thus came into existence under the laws of the District of Columbia before a convention was signed. Still, by 1944, the idea that had been launched as far back as 1923 had finally succeeded, although the difficulties involved in maintenance and expansion were great. By the end of World War II, only seven governments—Costa Rica, Nicaragua, United States, Honduras, Dominican Republic, El Salvador, and Guatemala—had ratified the convention, and the budget was extremely meagre ($168,728) and was mostly paid by the United States.[29]

The institute, which was thus established in Turrialba as the Inter-American Institute of Agricultural Sciences (Instituto Interamericano de Ciencias Agrícolas) in 1944, in accordance with the Convention on the Inter-American Institute of Agricultural Sciences, was created for the development of agriculture through research, teaching, and dissemination of theoretical and practical information. Until the 1960s, only fifteen American states were members of the institute; Argentina, Bolivia, Brazil, Paraguay, Peru, and Uruguay did not join because they maintained that the institute dealt only with tropical agriculture. The administrative structure was not designed in a manner that would give the Institute the necessary support; its highest body, the board of directors was in Washington, D.C., but the institute itself had its seat in Costa Rica. The board of directors was composed of representatives of those member countries of the Council of the OAS that belonged to the institute (i.e., that had ratified the convention on the institute). It was obvious that those ambassadors in the Council of the OAS who made up the fifteen-member board of directors of the IAIAS had little concern with agricultural problems. In addition to the board, there was a technical advisory council, but it did not facilitate the functioning of the system. Moreover, the assessment system for the maintenance of the institute ($1.00 per 1,000 inhabitants, or $1.25, as per a later resolution) was outdated. When the institute was founded, only 25 percent of its funds were contributed by the fifteen states; more than 50 percent came from other sources (ICA, the U.S. Atomic Energy Commission, the PTC of the OAS, the Inter-American Cocoa Agency, the Rockefeller and Kellogg foundations, and the Inter-American Association for Economic and Cultural Development).

The change in the quota system was essential and was discussed in the next decade, but it was the Commemorative Meeting of American Presidents in Panama, 1956, that started the ball rolling. As one of its first measures for the CIRP (Recommendation no. 1, 1956), the board of directors of IAIAS passed a Protocol of Amendment to the Convention on the IAIAS (December 1, 1958), which was to enable the institute to do justice to the increasing demands made on it. The lack of interest of the American states in the institute that existed until the 1950s was the result of the prevalent attitude toward agriculture after World War II, when industrialization became a fashionable slogan, too often to the detriment of agriculture. It took some time before the Protocol of Amendment of December 1, 1958, was signed and ratified by all states. It was first signed and ratified by the states that had not yet joined. With Brazil's incorporation into the IAIAS on March 25, 1964, all the OAS member states now belonged to the Institute; the Chilean government, however, had still to deposit the instruments of ratification.

In accordance with the Protocol of Amendment, the board of directors was no longer composed of diplomatic representatives but of agricultural experts who were subordinate to their respective ministries of agriculture. The technical advisory council was eliminated and no longer figured in the Protocol. The assessment system for the maintenance of the institute was adapted to the system of the OAS. At the time of this structural reform, San José became the seat of the institute.

The institute was set up as follows: a head office with several departments; three regional offices (Guatemala, Lima, and Montevideo); official representatives of the institute in countries in which there were working groups of institute technicians or in which there was no official agency of the institute; five research and teaching centers for agriculturists (a main center financed by the institute in Turrialba, Costa Rica; a center in La Estanzuela, Uruguay, which was dependent on the regional office of the Southern Zone of Argentina, Uruguay, and Paraguay and was administered by the Agricultural Research Institute of the Uruguayan Government; a third center at the Agricultural University La Molina, Peru, which was dependent on the regional office of the Andean Zone; and two more centers located in Bogotá and Mexico City); and the "technical groups," with purely regional goals, which explored the possibilities in the research and teaching institutions of the member states.

After a thorough reform of its program by the Ford and the Rockefeller foundations, the institute under its director, Ralph Lee, set up a list of priorities for the implementation of its programs: (1) the training of specialists and research as well as coordination of all agricultural studies in Latin America; (2) advising governments on strengthening public institutions connected with agriculture; (3) the development of agricultural contacts; and (4) the creation of dynamic relations to the governments, the national institutions, and the public in general. These goals also found clear expression in the budget, which, in 1962, concentrated on the following fields: rural development; strengthening of the institutions; agricultural use of top soil in the tropical, Andean, arid, and temperate zones; a regional cooperative program for the temperate zone; and agricultural associations.

The institute dealt with technical assistance through courses, seminars, special classes in the field of agricultural credits (in cooperation with CEMLA, FAO, ECLA, CREFAL, as well as with various banks and other institutions), agrarian reform (in cooperation with the IDB, PAU, FAO, and several national institutions), and rural development (with the assistance of the Rockefeller-sponsored American International Association).

In 1962, the Tropical Research and Teaching Center for Graduates in Turrialba trained 161 students. Intensive research was always in progress, especially about cocoa, coffee, and livestock production.

Also in 1962, the institute organized nine international assemblies; seventy-nine seminars were held in Turrialba alone. Since its establishment in 1944, by the mid-1960s the institute had trained more than 10,000 professionals in its various centers, in national and international short courses and through in-service training. It is evident that the emphasis that the institute was now giving to such activities as agrarian reform and agricultural credit was essential to the Alliance for Progress.

The many publications of the institute included the periodical *Turrialba* and the *Suplemento Bibliográfico*. The annual *Informe técnico* was significant because the institute's research findings were summarized in it.

Finally, the institute had been entrusted with the important Project no. 39 of the PTC of the OAS on Technical Assistance for the Improvement of Agriculture and Rural Life. Moreover, the institute was still the only institution in Latin America using atomic energy for research purposes.

IAIAS expanded constantly since 1944, for the American states came to realize that agriculture was one of the most important areas requiring generous assistance. The fact that the Special Fund of the United Nations was willing to put the sum of $4.5 million at the disposal of the institute was symbolic of a new spirit. This spirit also found expression in other ways, such as the transfer of a large United Fruit ranch ("La Lola," Costa Rica) to the institute, and the establishment of an agricultural development zone in San Lorenzo, Paraguay, on the basis of an agreement with the Paraguayan government.

THE SPECIAL AGENCIES AND COMMISSIONS

Another group of six organizations that belonged to the OAS but that were juridically of a different nature, were the Special Agencies and Commissions, which included the Inter-American Commission on Human Rights (IACHR), the Inter-American Peace Committee (IAPC), the Inter-American Defense Board (IADB), the Inter-American Statistical Institute (IASI), the Inter-American Nuclear Energy Commission (IANEC), and the Special Consultative Committee on Security (SCCS). They were all located in Washington, D.C., some of them within the PAU itself, and all of them had similar, though not identical, relationships with the OAS.

The Inter-American Commission on Human Rights (IACHR)

The subject matter of human rights was more recent. World War I had produced the October Revolution and the Soviet Union, while World War II had resulted in a synthesis between capitalism and socialism with an ever-increasing tendency toward democracy. It also resulted in the internationalization of the whole issue of human rights. After traveling from Ancient Greece and Rome through the Middle Ages, with an increasing acceleration from the Renaissance and the Enlightenment, human rights succeeded in being incorporated into contemporary philosophy. On a national level, Constitutional Law was proof of this trend; on an international level, whether regional or global, human rights were also part of Positive Law. Finally, these human rights were no longer restricted to the purely political rights but covered the experiences of the past and of our own present situation, so that in our times they covered political, economic, social, and cultural aspects.

In the latest phase of their evolution, human rights were incorporated in the United Nations in 1945 and in contemporary international law. Obviously, as in other areas, the United Nations influenced the regional level. Even before the United Nations incorporated human rights in its global system, however, the inter-American system, in its Eighth International Conference of American States (1938) adopted resolutions on human rights, women, and laborers, and in its Chapultepec Conference of 1945 already proclaimed the obligation to observe the standards to be incorporated in a future "Declaration of the International Rights and Duties of Men," which it requested the Inter-American Juridical Committee to prepare.

The Ninth International Conference of American States, which met in Bogotá in 1948 and established the OAS, dealt extensively with human rights. First of all, as a follow-up of the Inter-American Conference on Problems of War and Peace (Chapultepec) of 1945, the Bogotá Conference came up with the mentioned "American Declaration of the Rights and Duties of Man" and then went a step further: It proposed the setting up of the Inter-American Court, to guarantee human rights and humanity's basic freedoms, and again the Juridical Committee in Rio de Janeiro was instructed to prepare the necessary draft. The concept of the Inter-American Court did not prosper, but the issue of such a court would come up repeatedly—at the Inter-American Council of Jurists' Conferences of 1950 and 1953; at the Tenth International Conference of American States in Caracas (1954), where Uruguay proposed a Commission on Human Rights; and often at the heart of the organization, in the Council of the OAS. The tenth conference thus strengthened the concept of human rights but approved neither a Human Rights Commission nor a Human Rights Court.

The Charter of the OAS fully recognized the problem and not only included human rights but also cited its close link to representative democracy, individual liberty, and social justice. Thus, the preamble of the charter stated that

the true significance of American solidarity and good neighborliness can only mean the consolidation on this continent, within the framework of democratic institutions, of a system of individual liberty and social justice based on respect for the essential rights of man.[30]

Human rights were thus an intrinsic part of the inter-American system, long before the Inter-American Commission on Human Rights (Comisión interamericana de derechos humanos) was established in 1959. Hernán Montealegre listed the incorporation of human rights in the inter-American system under four aspects:

1. Acceptance of the principle of the compulsive legal character of their enforcement by the member states;
2. Impropriety to invoke the reservation of domestic jurisdiction;
3. The links which are established in the inter-American system between the violations of human rights and both regional and international peace; and
4. The connection which the inter-American system has set up between human rights and representative democracy.[31]

As the result of the heightened tensions in the Caribbean, which had also spread to South America by the late 1950s, the Fifth Meeting of Consultation of Ministers of Foreign Affairs was convoked and met in Santiago de Chile. It was here in 1959 that the Inter-American Commission on Human Rights was created; it was also here that the Inter-American Peace Committee was given extensive powers. Resolution VIII (Human Rights) repeated the aforementioned paragraph of the preamble of the Charter of the OAS and referred specifically to the link between human rights and representative democracy, and between the lack of such human rights and tyranny and oppression. It called attention to the "American Declaration of the Rights and Duties of Man" and to both the Universal and the European Declarations on the same subject. It then decided, in Part I, to request from the Inter-American Council of Jurists a draft convention on human rights, which, once accomplished, should be referred to the Council of the OAS, and likewise, a draft convention for an inter-American court for the protection of human rights, with both of these draft conventions to be submitted to the Eleventh International Conference of American States—which, however, never took place.

In Part II, the Fifth Meeting of Consultation resolved:

To create an Inter-American Commission on Human Rights, composed of seven members elected, as individuals, by the Council of the Organization of American States from panels of three names presented by the governments. The Commission, which shall be organized by the Council of the Organization and have the specific functions that the Council assigns to it, shall be charged with furthering respect for such rights.[32]

In September 1959, the Council of the OAS began to set up the Inter-American Commission on Human Rights. The draft statutes recommended by the special committee that dealt with the subject were finally approved with some reservations, and in June 1960, the IACHR's seven members were elected by the Council of the OAS. In October, it was formally installed. As such, IACHR was then incorporated into the inter-American system.

The statutes of the new agency severely limited its authority. At that time it could not do much in practice, since it was only allowed to call attention to certain conditions and could not directly intervene in any one case. The possibility that individuals could request intervention and action by the commission was thoroughly studied and debated, but the governments shied away from giving the commission such wide powers, since it obviously could lead to violations of the principle of nonintervention. IACHR's functions and powers were listed in Articles 9 and 10 of its statutes, which stated as follows:

[Art. 9.]

a. To develop an awareness of human rights among the peoples of America;

b. To make recommendations to the Governments of the member states in general, if it considers such action advisable, for the adoption of progressive measures in favor of human rights within the framework of their domestic legislation and in accordance with constitutional precepts, appropriate measures to further the faithful observance of those rights;

c. To prepare such studies or reports as it considers advisable in the performance of its duties;

d. To urge the Governments of the member states to supply it with information on the measures adopted by them in matters of human rights;

e. To serve the Organization of American States as an advisory body in respect of human rights.[33]

[Art. 10.]

In performing its assignment, the commission shall act in accordance with the pertinent provisions of the charter of the organization and bear in mind particularly that, in conformity with the American Declaration of the Rights and Duties of Man, the rights of each man are limited by the rights of others, by the security of all, and by just demands of the general welfare and the advancement of democracy.[34]

It may be worthwhile, in this context, to quote former ambassador of the United States to the OAS, John C. Dreier:

In a reversal of usual roles, the leadership of the nonintervention forces on this issue passed from the more familiar hands of Mexico to those of the United States. Mexico joined several other Latin American countries in favoring the delegation of authority to the Commission to review and take limited action on certain kinds of complaints by individual persons against governments. The United States opposed this authority on both legal and political grounds. It maintained that such authority to intervene in the internal affairs of member states could only be given to an OAS organ by means of a treaty, which the statute was not intended to be; and furthermore, that any attempt to investigate complaints of violations of human rights in member states was unwise in the absence of any inter-American or international agreement as to the precise nature of the rights that were to be protected. This uncertainty, it was held, would make of the commission a scene of political maneuverings and contribute more to the creation of inter-American tensions than to the protection of human rights.

These views of the United States, ultimately backed by some of the larger South American countries, prevailed.[35]

It was with these limited powers that the commission began its work which seemed to be relegated solely to recommendations. Very soon both governments and the Council of the OAS realized that IACHR became a laughingstock if it did not obtain more powers. Even a modest amendment, submitted in November 1960, which simply would have authorized the commission to hear complaints and make recommendations, had to be studied by the Council of the OAS, where it died.

The Eighth Meeting of Consultation of Ministers of Foreign Affairs gave the commission an opportunity to change the statutes. In the meantime the political situation in the Caribbean and South America had deteriorated even more and the Cuban Revolution was the subject of yet another Meeting of Consultation. It was here that the meeting decided to recommend to the Council of the OAS that the IACHR's statutes be revised so that it could play a greater role in the pursuit of the protection of human rights. The council dragged its feet, and two years later, in 1964, decided "to defer the study of the draft amendments to the statute of the Inter-American Commission on Human Rights."[36] At the same time other inter-American bodies were considering the elaboration of a Convention on Human Rights, which would include measures for enforcement and thus, somehow, the problem would be solved in a different manner.[37]

It was the Second Special Inter-American Conference, in 1965, which somehow solved the problem. This Second Conference was part of the process to amend the charter of the OAS, although it dealt specifically with the Alliance for Progress, and strangely enough, as the preparatory instrument for a Meeting of American Chiefs of State. It was here that the commission requested from the meeting that it be strengthened, especially since it believed that a Convention on Human Rights would take some time before it would be really effective. The Special Inter-American Conference accepted the views of the commission, particularly since the latter's wishes were rather modest: It only wanted to be empowered to request information from, and to make recommendations to, the appropriate government, in case of violations of human rights, and, if the respective government failed to act on the recommendations, it would have the right to publish its report on the case.[38] It was not entirely a new solution, since already in 1960 such an amendment had been submitted to the Council of the OAS.[39]

Resolution XXII of the Second Special Inter-American Conference permitted the commission to consider communication and other data, to request additional information from the appropriate governments, and to make recommendations. It also instructed the commission to exhaust all domestic juridical channels before taking up any case. Moreover, the resolution stated that it considered the Statutes of 1960 thus amended, and in its Thirteenth Period of Sessions, the IACHR incorporated these amendments into its original statutes.[40]

Margaret Ball commented on this happy outcome as follows:

With the adoption of these amendments, the commission received the powers which it had so long been denied and which represented a minimum of authority if it were to be truly effective. . . . Intervention or no intervention, an inter-American body had been given formal authority to make recommendations with respect to an area which the nineteenth-century world had considered well within the domestic jurisdiction of every sovereign state. That the Commission was now in a position to make a formal contribution to the defense of democracy as well as to the protection of individual rights went without saying. Yet it should not be overlooked that the formal amendment of the Statute in large measure simply recognized procedures which the Commission had already adopted by virtue of its own exceedingly liberal interpretation of its basic instrument.[41]

The IACHR became, so to speak, the vedette of the 1960s. It consisted of seven members elected by the Council of the OAS, submitted from a list of three persons by each of the American governments. They could be reelected and were supposed to represent all American nations not their own. There was a chair and a vice chair, elected for a two-year period by absolute majority. At the Fourteenth Period of Sessions, IACHR suggested that the tenure of the two high officers be limited to two terms (i.e., four years). Until 1965, its secretariat was the Division of Codification of the PAU, but after 1966, with its increased prestige, it set up its own secretariat, even though its budget was still included in that of the PAU.

The seat of the commission was Washington, D.C., but it could meet wherever it wished, if sanctioned by the respective government. The commission was to meet for eight weeks each year, but was at liberty to have two periods of sessions if it decided to do so. All decisions of the IACHR required an absolute majority.

The IACHR was supposed to watch over the observance and respect of human rights by investigating alleged violations of human rights in the American countries. In order to develop an awareness of the issues at stake, the commission prepared studies and reports, undertook research for distribution to official institutions, educational centers, civic associations, unions, and others. It also organized lectures, seminars, and exchange of information to foment interest in the study of human rights at the academic and professional levels.[42]

In the years before the Protocol of Amendments to the Charter of the OAS became effective, IACHR got involved in the human rights issue in the Dominican Republic (1960–1965), Cuba (1960–1965), Haiti (1963–1964), Ecuador (1964), Guatemala (1963), Honduras (1963), Nicaragua (1962), and Paraguay (1960s). In most cases the respective governments cooperated and allowed the commission to visit their countries in order to see for themselves that the complaints were false; some cooperated better than others, though the exception was Cuba.[43]

The Inter-American Peace Committee (IAPC)

The Inter-American Peace Committee (Comisión interamericana de paz) is a fascinating institution within the inter-American system, which especially illustrated the flexibility of the OAS. Like the Meeting of Consultation it was created for the maintenance of peace and security. It was established in 1940 at the Second Meeting of Consultation of Ministers of Foreign Affairs in Havana at the request of Haiti. The Havana meeting approved Resolution XIV, which recommended to the governing board of the PAU to set up such a committee with five members in order to keep a watch on any possible dispute among member states, and thus to prevent such a dispute from developing into a more serious crisis. The Resolution, however, had not answered the question, whether the committee could act only with the consent of the parties. Thus, more and more countries came forward— including Argentina, Dominican Republic, Honduras, Peru, and Venezuela—and formulated reservations. Still, by the end of 1940, the governing board asked Argentina, Brazil, Cuba, Mexico and the United States to proceed with the appointment of their respective representation, but only Cuba complied. Thus, the committee, which did not even have a name at that time, remained inactive until the year the OAS was established.

The inter-American system almost forgot about this committee, since it was not mentioned in any of the basic constitutional documents, but suddenly, through a Dominican request, the Council of the OAS reactivated the committee, which then received the name "Inter-American Committee on Methods for the Peaceful Solution of Conflicts." The Dominican Republic had a problem with Cuba, which prompted them to request the aid of this committee, and thus reactivate it. The Dominican request became, thus, the first case given to the committee, which for eight years had been kept inactive. The Dominican action also forced the OAS to look into the entire problem if it wanted the committee to play a significant role. The fact that the committee was able to solve the Dominican-Cuban issue as well as another case in 1949 involving Haiti and the Dominican Republic, meant that it represented a valuable asset for solving disputes that were not too serious but that at the same time were more than a political nuisance. The way was thus cleared for the committee to build a stronger and more solid basis.

Thus, in 1950, the committee approved its statutes, but the governments now challenged them and listed three reasons for doing so: (1) Since the Ninth International Conference of American States had ignored the committee, and the Pact of Bogotá had been signed, the committee had thus been replaced; (2) the committee should only act with the consent of all parties to a dispute; and (3) the Resolution of 1940 had made no provision as regards membership, and thus the committee was unrepresentative.[44] This challenge prompted the Council of the OAS to request a legal opinion from the Inter-American Juridical Committee and to have the matter decided at the next Tenth International Conference of American States. Indeed, the Caracas meeting of 1954 took up the matter with the result of stepping on a hornet's nest. It was either the question that the committee lacked proper legal foundation (Chile, Peru), that it had exceeded its powers (Uruguay), or that it had been inactive for too long and now resurrected for situations which both the charter and the Pact of Bogotá had intentionally eliminated (Mexico). The committee was saved by the United States, which proposed that the committee continue its work as it had done until then, that is, before it had approved its own statutes in 1950, but that the Council of the OAS should revise the statutes of the committee, which then would be submitted to the governments. This U.S. proposal passed as Resolution CII.[45]

Two years later, in 1956, the council accepted the revised statutes under which the committee began to operate in that year. According to these statutes, it was the purpose of the committee to be concerned constantly with the preservation of peace of states between which a controversy had broken out, with the understanding, however, that procedures decided upon between both states were to be respected. The Inter-American Peace Committee, as it was then called, could intervene only when one or the other state drawn into the conflict agreed to it and when no other procedure of a similar kind for a solution was pending. Under the Statutes of 1956, the IAPC consisted of five delegates designated by the governments of five OAS members and selected by the Council of the OAS. They were always representatives in the council. The term was for five years on a rotating basis with one country being replaced by another; the chairship was for a year.

The significant difference between the Statutes of 1950 and those of 1956 was that the former allowed activation of the Committee by any member of the OAS, whether or not it was a party to a dispute, and that it could even suggest procedures of settlement without the assent of the quarreling parties, whereas the latter meant that the committee could only act if a party to a dispute requested it.[46] It was a pity that the governments acted in that way, thus again condemning the IAPC to inactivity. It was a fact that the committee had solved some nine cases so far, that the financial angle of its activities was relatively slight, and that its interventions had not caused any upheavals.[47] However, the governments thought differently and resented the powers and liberties of the committee. The result was that in the next three years, 1956–1959, the IAPC played no role. On the other hand, we should bear in mind that the situation in the Caribbean had significantly deteriorated and it was doubtful that under these circumstances the committee could be as valuable as before.

The committee's history was a very significant one. As long as no great restraints were imposed, it was able to demonstrate an impressive flexibility, and the five ambassadors composing the committee—in 1963–1964, Venezuela, Colombia, United States, Dominican Republic, and Argentina were its members—under the chairmanship of the respective president, worked most fruitfully, since they possessed much freedom of movement. When, in 1956, statutes limiting its autonomy and flexibility were imposed on the committee, it could no longer function as it had in the past.

When the Fifth Meeting of Consultation of Ministers of Foreign Affairs met in Santiago de Chile, 1959, it was exactly the increase of tensions in the Caribbean that prompted the governments, among other things, to take another look at the IAPC. The result in Santiago was a reversal. The committee received extensive powers subject to rescission that annulled the restrictions of 1956. The IAPC was supposed to possess these powers until the Eleventh International Conference of American States—which, however, was never convened.

Under the new rules, the IAPC had to obtain the express consent of any country in which it was to work, and the next—the Eleventh International Conference—was to decide whether the new powers were to be confirmed for a longer period. The issue of the IAPC's powers did not terminate there. On the basis of new revisions demanded by Ecuador, the Council of the OAS requested the Inter-American Juridical Committee for an opinion; the latter then stated that the question whether the committee be allowed to operate in any country, or simply on request, was not a legal but a political question.

The above-mentioned Eleventh International Conference of American States was continuously postponed, a fact that kept the commission in limbo, even though it continued to settle several more cases. As a matter of fact, the committee had worked on some fourteen cases between 1948 and 1960; between 1961 and 1964, it became involved in another four.

In the meantime, an avalanche of reforms and revisions were aired to modernize once more the entire OAS. This would, obviously, also affect the IAPC. However, even under the best of conditions, the IAPC would hardly have been able to settle the much more difficult issues arising from the Cuban Revolution. As a matter of fact, these had to be solved by several Meetings of Consultation. Furthermore, much of the work that might have been shifted to the IAPC was now entrusted to the new IACHR, which had been set up at the Fifth Meeting of Consultation as a consequence of the heightened tensions in the Caribbean and South America.

The topic of the IAPC came to the fore again when the revision of the Charter was in full swing. Thus, the Second Special Inter-American Conference of 1965 proposed a new revision of the IAPC's statutes, which meant essentially a return to the situation of 1950, that is, before the passage of the more rigid statutes of 1956. The new statutes would mean that any country could again request the intervention of the IAPC, whether or not it was a party to a dispute. However, since neither this Second Special Inter-American Conference nor the Council of the OAS were able to solve the riddle, it was then decided that the special committee created to revise the Charter of the OAS for consideration by the Third Special Inter-American Conference (1967) take up this matter. It was this special committee that then proposed that in the amendments to the charter, "the functions of watching for threats to the peace be transferred to the future Permanent Council."[48]

The Inter-American Defense Board (IADB)

The Inter-American Defense Board (Junta interamericana de defensa) was established on the basis of Resolution XXXIX of the Third Meeting of Consultation of Ministers of Foreign Affairs in Rio de Janeiro in 1942. It was created at a time of war when interest in such an important agency was at a high point. As the war was coming to a close and peace was reestablished, the entire matter began to change, in a similar way as Bolívar's proposal of 1822 received less approval four years later in 1826, when the Panama Congress really met. Thus, when plans were drawn up after the Chapultepec Conference of 1945 for the reorganization and strengthening of the inter-American system, it was presumed that the IADB would be incorporated into the structure of the charter of the OAS, alongside the Economic and Social Council, the Council of Jurists and the Cultural Council, as the fourth technical organ of the Council of the OAS. Such an arrangement was proposed in 1948, but had to be discarded because several Latin American countries, led by Mexico, did not agree to such a procedure. It was an attitude similar to the later idea of John Foster Dulles, when NATO proposed in 1957 that a closer link be established between the OAS and NATO. Even though those who were opposed to the incorporation of the IADB as a fourth technical council did not fully win, they succeeded in neutralizing the issue. The deliberations on the subject at the Ninth International Conference of American States in Bogotá in 1948 resulted in the incorporation of the IADB in the inter-American system as a special agency. The compromise worked out in Bogotá also provided for a nonpermanent Advisory Defense Committee to assist the Meeting of Consultation. As such it was incorporated into the charter. But the strange surprise was that while the IADB survived as a special agency, and even expanded its activities, the Advisory Defense Committee never came into being, although in theory it remained on the books as linked to the Meetings of Consultation.

The IADB had its own offices, which were quite far away from the seat of the OAS. It survived the early debates despite its downgrading in 1948 and its continued ambiguities. The problem arose again at the time when the amendments to the charter were being discussed. Thus, in 1965, the Act of Rio de Janeiro, of the Second Special Inter-American Conference, with which instructions were given to elaborate the possible amendments to be considered in the next Special Inter-American Conference, the IADB was not opposed. The United States then proposed that Articles 44–47 of the charter of the OAS be revised so as to make the IADB permanent, but these ideas did not prosper. Later, in the discussions in the Council of the OAS, it became evident that the member states wanted to leave things as they had been since IADB's inception. However, when the Third Special Inter-American Conference met in Buenos Aires, in 1967, the Argentine delegation submitted amendments to the same articles that would have resulted in the Advisory Defense Committee to be a permanent body. The Argentine proposal was then put to a vote and defeated in the following manner: In favor: six (Nicaragua, El Salvador, Honduras, Argentina, Brazil, and Paraguay); against: eleven (Venezuela, Ecuador, Dominican Republic, Costa Rica, Uruguay, Haiti, Mexico, Chile, Guatemala, Peru, and Colombia); and abstaining: three (United States, Panama, and Bolivia).[49]

The IADB, as an independent inter-American and intergovernmental agency, was always in a strange situation—it was part of the OAS and yet it was not really. Already in 1950, two years after the OAS had been established, the Council of the OAS decided that the IADB was not a Specialized Organization, but at the same time and despite its technical independence, the budget was always submitted to the Program and Budget Committee of the PAU. The 1950 decision of the council stated that the IADB had a specific character that entitled it to act in preparation of collective self-defense against aggression.

While this ambiguous situation kept the relationship between the IADB and the OAS on an even keel, in the 1960s there developed two problems. In 1961, there arose again the question of financial autonomy in view of the OAS proposing cuts in the IADB budget; the board stated then that it was independent and not subject to control by the OAS, and that until this case the mentioned PBC of the PAU had not asked for cuts. It seemed to be the usual controversy between civilians and armed forces, this time on the level of the OAS. In any case, the board was unable to convince the PAU that its point of view was right, and that was the situation all along after 1961. A different question arose when the Council of the OAS had to consider the board's request for an Inter-American Defense College. This question led to a legal tangle with the result that the Council of the OAS approved the establishment of the Inter-American Defense College because it felt it could not legally prevent the IADB from going ahead with this project.[50] Thus, in 1962, on the occasion of its twentieth anniversary, the IADB set up a new institution: the Inter-American Defense College.

The ambiguity was not clarified by this last issue. The Annual Report of the secretary general of the OAS for fiscal year 1964–1965 dealt with the problem, and in it the secretary general reiterated that the IADB was an intergovernmental agency, established by the Third Meeting of Consultation, that it functioned independently but within the inter-American system, and was financed with the financial resources of the PAU.[51]

The various member states of the OAS were represented in the IADB by their respective officers from the armed forces of the American countries. There was a chairman, a council of delegates, staff and secretariat, which since 1962 also maintained the Defense College. The chairman was the most important official of the board, and the Council of Delegates the highest organ, which thus determined policy. The staff comprised officers from the three branches—army, navy, and air force—and dealt with technical questions. Obviously, the United States has always been very interested in the IADB and has over the decades furnished a great deal of the equipment. There is also no question that the close relationship between the armed forces of all American countries in the IADB developed into a kind of camaraderie that could influence the political role of the military.

Besides purely military matters, training courses, and liaison and inspection trips, the IADB tried to achieve uniformity in its field. During 1961, it thus attempted to standardize maps, technical dictionaries, landing signals for the control of air traffic, and many other matters within its scope. The IADB also undertook special studies concerning the establishment of an Inter-American Force, bases for the defense of the continent, as well as the role of the armed forces in economic and social development, communications, within the inter-American system, and such special issues as guerrilla warfare.[52]

The Defense College, which was located at Fort McNair in Washington, D.C., with facilities offered by the United States, served as an academic institution offering a variety of courses with the idea of preparing the armed forces for the challenge of modern times. Thus, not only technical courses but also political, economic and social issues were offered.

Finally, it should be noted that the IADB did not have formal links with the United Nations or NATO, which was in line with the Latin American point of view. An exception was the cooperation of the IADB with the Central American Defense Council since 1965.[53]

The Inter-American Statistical Institute (IASI)

Although the PAU established its own Department of Statistics, the subject matter seemed important enough to go a step further and set up an institute. The Inter-American Statistical Institute (Instituto interamericano de estadística) attained almost a position as a Specialized Organization but never achieved it. Still, it enjoyed a special relationship that puts it almost at the same level as the Specialized Organizations, a kind of in-between position. The relationship between the new institute and the OAS was established in 1950, when an agreement was signed between the two organizations, which in 1955 underwent a revision.

The original agreement stipulated that the institute was set up within the PAU and that the Department of Statistics would function as its secretariat. Thus the activities of the one and the other were included in those of the PAU and were supervised by IA-ECOSOC.

IASI's membership, like that of PAIGH, included Canada from the very beginning of its existence, but also extended to individuals, institutions, and ex officio members. Individual membership was divided into "constituent" and "associate," while institutional members could be "governmental," "affiliated," and "sponsoring"; ex officio were members who either occupied certain statistical offices or were related to statistics in national or international agencies in the same field. The goal of the institute was to promote and disseminate statistical data, official or unofficial, in the Americas.

The institute had the usual organs: a general assembly, an executive committee, a general secretariat, and both technical committees and working groups. The general assembly, which met from two to four years, was the highest policy-shaping body and served also as a platform for technical discussions. The executive committee consisted of a president and four vice-presidents of the institute, who were elected by the general assembly. The functions of the executive committee included the responsibility for IASI's work and activities, and advice for the department. In view of the close relationship between the institute and the OAS, it was obvious that the Department of Statistics became the secretariat of the institute. Thus, also, the secretary general of the institute was at the same time the director of the department, and was appointed by the secretary general of the OAS in agreement with IASI's executive committee.

The Inter-American Nuclear Energy Commission (IANEC)

This important commission was established as a result of the recommendations that were adopted by the Inter-American Committee of Representatives of the Presidents (CIRP), which in turn had been set up by the American presidents and chiefs of state at their famous meeting in Panama, in July 1956. IANEC (Comisión interamericana de energía nuclear) was thus established in 1957 with its Statutes approved by the Council of the OAS two years later.

The statutes gave the commission the same technical autonomy as the specialized organizations, but like IASI and other special agencies and commissions of the OAS, it never achieved the status of a specialized organization. Its basic goals were research and training at a time when nuclear energy became a significant new source of power, when nations were developing their own nuclear programs, and when Europe had set up EURATOM and joined it to the other two European organizations (European Coal and Steel Community, European Common Market) to make up the European Community (EC). IANEC, obviously, from its inception, cooperated with similar national and international bodies, especially the United Nations Atomic Energy Agency in Vienna, Austria. As with other special agencies, the OAS–PAU provided secretarial services to IANEC, which was housed in the PAU itself, and thus was in a similar position as the IACW and IASI.

The Special Consultative Committee on Security (SCCS)

This special commission, in Spanish, the Comisión especial de consulta sobre seguridad, was established in accordance with Resolution II of the Eighth Meeting of Consultation of Ministers of Foreign Affairs and represented an echo of the Consultative Emergency Committee on Political Defense set up in 1941 during World War II. Its task was to be a kind of watchdog for the political defense of the continent, warning against any kind of aggression, subversion, or infiltration that might be considered a threat to peace and security. Its target was the increasing communist menace.

The committee was convoked on March 8, 1962, and the seven candidates for this new organization were chosen on March 21, 1962, in a secret election. A year later, on April 23, 1963, the Council of the OAS approved its statutes.

This new inter-American intergovernmental organization began its activities immediately after having chosen its membership, and already on May 2, 1962, it reported back to the Council of the OAS about its preliminary work, devoting some five chapters to a discussion of the methods of international communism and counterdefense possibilities.[54] In the same year, the committee was requested by the Dominican government to aid in defending itself against the new revolutionary government of Cuba. A final report on this situation (issued in September 1962) was, however, of a confidential nature. In this respect, SCCS also undertook a study of the First Afro–Asian–Latin American Solidarity Conference (October, 1966). The committee was quite busy at the time when the Cuban problem raised so many tensions all over Latin America. Indeed, SCCS held some seven regular meetings alone in 1966, with others to be held in the following years. Margaret Ball stated it clearly when she said:

Meanwhile it had at long last been realized that as far as the battle of ideologies was concerned, positive as well as negative action was required. The American republics had been slow in getting around to the thought of positive support for democracy—other than in terms according to which improvement of living standards was a good defense against Communism—but get to it they finally did.[55]

THE INTER-AMERICAN DEVELOPMENT BANK (IDB)

The concept of the establishment of an inter-American bank was not new. It was already proposed in earlier inter-American conferences. Thus, in the First International Conference of American States in Washington, D.C., 1889–1890; in the Second International Conference of American States in Mexico City, 1902; and again, in the Third International Conference of American States in Rio de Janeiro, in 1906, the idea of a bank was launched. The PAU itself tried to advance the concept in 1911, but for a variety of reasons got nowhere. At that time the idea for such a banking institution was essentially for the promotion of trade; later the purpose was wider and covered all kinds of economic cooperation.

After World War I, the concept was resurrected in the 1930s. Thus, both the Seventh and Eighth International Conferences of American States, in Montevideo in 1933 and Lima in 1938, as well as the special Conference for the Consolidation of Peace in Buenos Aires (in 1936), took up the topic, but again without much success. During World War II the subject seemed again to be of importance. The First Meeting of Consultation of Ministers of Foreign Affairs in Panama, in 1939, created the Inter-American Financial and Economic Advisory Committee (FEAC), which, among other things, was instructed to study the feasibility of establishing an inter-American financial institution. Latin America had always been interested in the matter, but the United States was cautious and lukewarm. Thus, when the topic was again raised in 1942 at the Third Meeting of Consultation of Ministers of Foreign Affairs in Rio de Janeiro, those countries that so far had not ratified the convention, especially the United States, were urged to do so, but no progress could be registered.

The idea did not come up at the Chapultepec meeting of 1945, but the Ninth International Conference of American States in Bogotá, in 1948, in view of the purpose of reorganizing and modernizing the inter-American system, again took up the matter of an inter-American banking institution. The issue was sidetracked in the sense that the new IA–ECOSOC was requested to study the subject matter and submit a report on the issue to the next inter-American Conference. It took quite some time before IA–ECOSOC resolved the problem: It did so in its Extraordinary Meeting at Ministerial Level, November–December 1954, and strongly recommended the establishment of such a bank. Again, however, the project did not prosper due to U.S. resistance.

Several factors should be borne in mind in connection with this famous issue: In the first place, IA-ECOSOC had gradually lost prestige after having been created, in accordance with the charter of the OAS, as a technical organ of the Council of the OAS. In a way, this was a logical development based on a vicious circle: With IA–ECOSOC being perceived as simply a debating society, major interest in Latin America had shifted to the United Nations Economic Commission for Latin America (ECLA) in Santiago de Chile. At that time, all Latin American governments looked to ECLA for inspiration and solution of their increasing economic problems. ECLA, under the direction of Raúl Prebisch, preached development and integration. On the other hand, the United States distrusted populist governments, of which there were a number in Latin America, and saw no need for the establishment of an inter-American financial institution to carry out ECLA's goals when there were already two global institutions of the United Nations that could very well take care of the financial needs: the International Bank for Reconstruction and Development (IBRD, founded 1946), and the International Monetary Fund (IMF, founded 1947), as well as a later organization, the International Finance Corporation (IFC, founded 1956). In the view of the United States, the Inter-American Bank would be an unnecessary duplication of efforts. The Latin Americans countered that the world organizations were controlled by the United States and the Europeans and thus their chances were minimal for a solution of their problems. What they wanted was an inter-American bank in which their wishes would be respected and that, thus, to some extent would be controlled by them. Finally, the United States, for obvious reasons, preferred to negotiate on a purely bilateral basis and avoided dealing with the problem on a multilateral basis where it would have to confront a united Latin American continent.

The problem of the bank and of the more general issue of U.S.–Latin American economic relations was dragged from one conference to the other, from Chapultepec (1945) to Bogotá (1948) and Caracas (1954), without any solution in sight. Thus, the Latin American request for an inter-American economic conference was always postponed *ad calendas Grecas*. What shook both the economic dialogue and the issue of the inter-American Bank was the highest inter-American meeting so far: the inter-American Meeting of Presidents and Chiefs of State in Panama, in 1956. The result of this famous meeting was the establishment of CIRP, which in turn decided on a list of recommendations.

In 1957, the United States finally gave the green light for holding the long-awaited Economic Conference of the OAS in Buenos Aires, a project dear to the Latin American heart since 1948, in which they would jointly confront the United States. The conference was duly held in 1957 but ended in a fiasco when the United States did not give Latin America the massive investments, both public and private, that were needed to improve the infrastructure and thus the general economic and social situation. Its total failure, however, prompted Brazilian president Juscelino Kubitschek Oliveira to begin a correspondence with President Dwight D. Eisenhower pointing out that the failure of the conference in Buenos Aires was no reason to ignore the growing economic problems. This exchange of letters (of 1958) launched President Kubitschek's Operation Pan America. It was this initiative that, in 1959, led to the establishment of two committees at the OAS headquarters in Washington: CECE and CEIFI. The former, also called the Committee of the 21, held three meetings (Washington, D.C., 1958; Buenos Aires, 1959; and Bogotá, 1960), which led to the inauguration of the Alliance for Progress; the latter led to the creation of the IDB in 1960, when the United States reversed its opposition and changed to a more positive course.

Originally the idea was to incorporate the new bank into the closer OAS system (i.e., as a Specialized Organization or a Special Agency). However, for a variety of reasons, at a time when the OAS came more and more under fire and with increasing criticism, the governments decided to opt for a different solution: to organize the bank outside the established structure of the OAS. Hence, the IDB, which began its operations on January 1, 1960, was, in latu senso, part of the inter-American system but not, strictly speaking, of the OAS. Thus, it did not figure in the official chart of the OAS, although originally, for a short time (in 1959–60), it did. The decision that was made at that time was based primarily on the idea of giving the new institution the greatest possible flexibility and independence of action and not to allow a financial institution to be at the whims of politics. Also, it seemed awkward that an institution with such enormous resources would be under the control of a parent organization that had much less.

The IDB started with a capital of $850 million, divided in 84,000 shares of $10,000 each. Of this sum, $400 million was to be paid in actual capital and the remainder of $450 million in so-called callable capital—that is, capital subject to recall. Besides this basic financial foundation for "hard" loans, the bank also created a Fund for Special Operations, amounting to $150 million, to be used for "soft" loans. ("Hard" loans meant loans in hard currencies [dollars, deutschmarks, swiss franks, etc.], while "soft" loans referred to local currencies.)

The bank's funds were contributed by all the American countries, although the highest contributions came from the United States, Argentina, Brazil, Mexico and Venezuela, and from the beginning of its operations, it requested and obtained the participation of nonmembers: Canada, the nations of Europe, and Japan.

The IDB became the most successful single institution in the inter-American system and with every year it increased its capital and its impact. Already by 1965, the Fund for Special Operations was increased to $900 million; in 1967, it grew by another $1.2 billion, so that at the end of that year it had reached the sum of $2,321,430,000.

The Social Program Trust Fund, administered by the bank on behalf of the United States, had an initial total of $394 million based on a U.S. grant; in 1964, it was increased to $525 million. An agreement between the IDB and the United States stipulated the use of this fund for "soft" loans for the following purposes:

a. land settlement and improved land use, including access and feeder roads, assistance to agricultural credit institutions, assistance to supervised credit and agricultural extension, and development of storage and marketing facilities, provided that the resources of the Fund shall not be used for the purchase of agricultural land;
b. housing for low income groups, through assistance to self-help housing and to institutions providing long-term housing finance and engaged in mobilizing domestic resources for this purpose;
c. community water supply and sanitation facilities;
d. such supplementary financing of facilities for advance education and training related to economic and social development as may be agreed upon from time to time between the United States and the Administrator.[56]

Another fund was created in 1966 in view of increased interest in Latin American economic integration: the Preinvestment Fund for Latin American Integration.

The bank's structure included a board of governors, a board of executive directors, a president, and a vice president for the Fund for Special Operations. The board of governors consisted of a governor and his alternate for each member state. The governors were appointed by the respective governments for a period of five years. The chair of the board was elected by the board at its regular annual meeting, but a majority of two-thirds was required. The board of governors determined the policy which the smaller group, the board of executive directors then implemented, except for some twelve powers, as follows, in accordance with Article 8, Section 1.2, of the IDB's agreement:

i. Admit new members and determine the conditions of their admission;

ii. Increase or decrease the authorized capital stock of the Bank and contributions to the Fund;

iii. Elect the President of the Bank and determine his remuneration;

iv. Suspend a member, pursuant to Article IX, Section 2;

v. Determine the remuneration of the executive directors and their alternates;

vi. Hear and decide any appeals from interpretations of this Agreement given by the Board of Executive Directors;

vii. Authorize the conclusion of general agreements for cooperation with other international organizations;

viii. Approve, after reviewing the auditors' report, the general balance sheet and the statement of profit and loss of the institution;

ix. Determine the reserves and the distribution of the net profits of the Bank and of the Fund;

x. Select outside auditors to certify to the general balance sheet and the statement of profit and loss of the institution;

xi. Amend this Agreement; and

xii. Decide to terminate the operations of the Bank and to distribute its assets.[57]

The Board of Executive Directors consisted of seven members, one of whom had to be from the United States, with the other six chosen from outside its membership by the remaining members of the board of governors. Their term of office was three years, and they could be reelected. They were responsible for the organization and the operation of the bank and for whatever other powers were delegated to it by the board of governors.

The most important fact about the IDB was that the United States, although wielding overwhelming powers, was limited in the exercise of this power. In both bodies, in the board of governors and in the board of executive directors, decisions were made by absolute majority. In the board of governors, each country had 135 votes plus an additional vote for every share of stock it held in the bank. In the board of executive directors, the appointed director cast the votes of the state he or she represented, while each of the other six members cast the votes of all states that contributed to their election. The Latin American states held over 50 percent of the total shares and an even larger percentage of the basic country vote where an absolute majority of voting power was required; thus, they could outvote the United States, which held less than 50 percent. Loans from ordinary capital for which an absolute majority was required could not be vetoed by the United States; in other areas, like the Fund for Special Operations, its power did give it a veto.[58]

The bank's president was elected by the board of governors. An absolute majority was required for this election. The term of office was five years but the president could be reelected. The president recommended the vice president, and the board of executive directors appointed that person. The vice president replaced the president in the latter's absence but had no vote at meetings, unless substituting for the president.

The bank divided its operations into two categories: Ordinary and Special Operations. The former referred to those activities that were financed from the bank's ordinary capital while the latter were those financed by the Fund for Special Operations. All loans made in connection with ordinary operations, had to be repaid in the currency in which they were handled (i.e., essentially in "hard" currencies), whereas the Special Operations dealt with "soft" loans.

Finally, all decisions in the Fund for Special Operations were by a two-thirds majority, unless otherwise provided. In its lending policies, the bank was guided by two basic principles: The IDB gave priority to such programs that, in its opinion, would make a definite contribution to the economic growth of the member countries, and the bank's loans were designed to supplement, not replace, national capital.[59] The various resources of the bank in 1967 included ordinary capital resources and the IDB Fund for Special Operations, as well as the IDB loans by sources of funds, and a number of approved loans.

From the very beginning, the bank supported Latin American economic integration. Thus, from 1960 onward, the bank worked closely with the Preparatory Committee of the Latin American Free Trade Association (LAFTA) and also helped the Central American Bank for Economic Integration. By the mid-1960s, the bank had developed a number of projects geared toward economic integration of Latin America, and it gave financial help to LAFTA's weakest members. It also gave financial assistance to two Latin American multilateral institutions: the Latin American Institute for Economic and Social Planning (ILPES) and the Latin American Iron and Steel Institute (ILAFA).

The bank's development in the 1960s has been both positive and constructive. While the OAS was experiencing a true challenge and was moving toward a different structure with the Protocol of Amendments in 1967, the IDB continued to be extremely successful, not only in its first decade but throughout its thirty years of existence. The bank by itself gave hope that international organizations could provide positive solutions to improve not only standards of living, but also, implicitly, peace and security. Furthermore, the bank was an example of a generous and wise U.S. policy that showed the world that the nation could, at least in the case of the IDB, voluntarily restrict its overwhelming economic power for the benefit of its weaker neighbors to the south and thus avoid a unilateral dictation of its policies.

7

The Road toward the Revision of the Charter

THE BACKGROUND: THE CRISIS OF THE 1950s

When the OAS began on its path in 1948, it did so with extraordinary optimism and vitality. After all, the organization had not only been saved as such in 1945, but it had been revitalized and strengthened through the Rio Treaty, the charter, and the Pact of Bogotá. The new OAS had become more Latinized than ever before. Thus, after 1948 the OAS plunged into an ever-increasing number of activities with energy and zeal. The late 1940s and the early 1950s represented a significant new start for an organization that had had a long tradition with a practical experience of some sixty years. However, by the mid-1950s a malaise had set in in view of mounting dissatisfaction from the Latin Americans, the United States, and the OAS itself on a variety of issues. There is no doubt that since the 1950s the OAS entered an ever-increasing state of crisis. The reasons were not merely to be found in the human and administrative factors; they were much more profound. They were connected with the relationship of the United States to Latin America as well as with increasing economic and social problems that already plagued Latin America at that time. These problems were closely linked to U.S.–Latin American relations and in the 1950s began to draw Latin America into the orbit of the East-West conflict.

The crisis of the OAS did not express itself only financially, even though several member states had been unable to meet their financial obligations to the organization. It was also a crisis of confidence that, above all, involved political-juridical, economic, and social problems, it was also related to the leadership.

Political–Juridical Weaknesses

If, to begin with, we ask ourselves how well the organization had solved the problems of peace and security on the American continent in the almost two decades of its existence, the answer is not satisfactory, despite all the inter-American institutions and treaties.

Provisions of the Rio Treaty were to apply in the settlement of conflicts arising from outside acts of aggression on the American zone of security. The Pact of Bogotá made provisions for conflicts arising within the American security zone; these provisions were based on some seventy years of experience. However, since the Bogotá Pact had not been ratified, the Rio Treaty had had to serve in all pertinent cases. Since 1948, Article 6 of the Rio Treaty has been applied in more than ten cases involving supposed acts of aggression or threats to peace and security on the American continent. However, all the cases of those years in which settlements were applied— with the exception of the complaints of Venezuela against the Dominican Republic (Seventh Meeting of Consultation, San José, 1960) and against Cuba (Ninth Meeting of Consultation, Washington, D.C., 1964)—were settled by negotiation and similar means that were more in line with the Bogotá Pact. In other words, the Rio Treaty, which is primarily a treaty of mutual assistance and collective security, was applied in situations for which it was not originally intended.

Despite the many years of experience in the realm of arbitration and similar procedures, no unanimity could be achieved on this issue after the signing of the Bogotá Pact, and it was doubtful that this problem could be solved in the near future. Hence, the Rio Treaty would continue to be applied in the solution of inter-American controversies. It has been said that this use of the treaty was a positive one, because the document had been ratified by all member states and because the machinery for its application could be set in motion much more easily than the Bogotá Pact. In the long run, however, the application of a treaty for purposes not originally foreseen is rather prejudicial since it can encroach on its efficacy.

In the year 1960 this purely objective application was buttressed by political and opportunistic applications that however, appear rather dubious and that, in the long run, tended to heighten the crisis. A classic example was provided in the Caribbean area after the Castro Revolution. In 1959, Panama, Haiti and Nicaragua were attacked by irregular Castro forces, and, although there could be no doubt that Cuba was guilty of an act of aggression, the OAS acted as if Castro's Cuba had nothing to do with the matter. The reason was obvious: The Cuban regime was then quite popular in Latin America and in certain sectors of the United States, and because of this purely emotional factor, several Latin American governments did not wish to face the facts. Hence, the decisions made at the Fifth Meeting of Consultation (Santiago de Chile, 1959) were just as unsatisfactory as those made a year later at the Sixth and Seventh Meetings of Consultation. At the Sixth Meeting of Consultation (San José, 1960), sanctions were applied against the unpopular Trujillo regime. William Manger delved into this problem in detail in his *Pan America in Crisis*. He pointed out that in the application of the Rio Treaty in the case of Venezuela against the Dominican Republic, "it is difficult to avoid the conclusion . . . [that] it was used to punish rather than to restrain, and that sanctions were imposed for national rather than international purposes." The former assistant secretary general of the OAS stated further that "this is hardly the way to build an institution on firm and durable foundations."[1] It is clear that pragmatic motivations apparently were more important here than the principles embodied in the charter.

There could be no doubt that the ability of the OAS to maintain peace and security had diminished since 1948 if we look at the situation from the vantage point of the mid-1960s. This reflected the weakness of the various governments, which frequently did not dare to fight energetically for established laws and principles. An exception was the courageous act of Chile's President Jorge Alessandri, in August 1964, when, despite the unpopularity of the measure, he broke off relations with Cuba, in accordance with the mandate of the Ninth Meeting of Consultation. Thus, it seemed that only in extreme situations, such as the Cuban missile crisis in October 1962, could one expect the OAS to take a strong stand. This problem of weakness was not only related to the Latin American fear of granting an international organization special powers. It went much deeper; it was, as Walter Lippmann pointed out in *The Public Philosophy* (and at that time emphasized anew), a symptom of the crisis of authority in the world, which began locally and extended to the state and international organizations. Hence, as long as the United States and the nations of Latin America did not take a firmer stand but rather followed a policy that considered the exigencies of the moment before law and principles, the OAS would not succeed in gaining respect.

There were also other reasons. The Tenth International Conference of American States (Caracas, 1954) had shown the division between the United States and Latin America, especially in the Guatemala case and in economic matters. These problems did not blow over but rather became worse in the following years, so that the Eleventh International Conference of American States, which was to be held in 1959, was postponed time and again and finally canceled in 1964. This cancelation was obviously a symptom of the situation.

The extraordinary changes in the world, with Latin America no longer isolated from world events and instead being drawn into the Cold War, with its traditional markets overseas being threatened by the new political and economic orientation in Western Europe, required a more thorough, and quicker, reaction. Thus, the traditional inter-American conferences every five years no longer seemed to be justified in a world that was moving ever faster. Thus, the idea of following the United Nations, which held annual meetings in its General Assembly, seemed to be a better solution. That was definitely one issue that could easily be incorporated into the system. Problems would no longer wait for five years or be dealt with by special conferences. Thus, a radical overhaul of this issue was required.

Another issue was unhappiness about the term of the secretary general, whose ten years in office seemed too long and, it was felt, could be halved with the possibility of reelection.

There was also much criticism of the Council of the OAS—on the grounds that it wielded too much power, although other voices believed that the salvation of the organization could only come from the organ that was in daily and permanent contact with the organization, and especially the PAU. By this they meant further strengthening the council and the secretariat, and expecting a greater display of leadership and statesmanship. A similar belief was also directed toward some of the technical organs.

Other critics voiced the opinion that the headquarters of the organization should be removed from the United States, but these same voices never really came up with a specific solution. Actually, such a move would have been a grave error in judgment since the special relationship between the United States and Latin America, and the political and economic realities of the world, made Washington the best place for the seat of the organization to be located. Any other place for the headquarters of the OAS in Latin America would cause jealousy and friction. Likewise, it was pointed out that the organization should decentralize further, but in this respect, also, the criticism of those years was not justified, since the organization had done so in the past as the Union of American Republics, and was continuing this policy after 1948. In any case, whether true or alleged, the urgency of the problems, compounded by the crisis of the Eleventh International Conference of American States, showed that the movement for revision of the charter was gaining momentum.

Economic and Social Problems

To the sphere of political–juridical issues were now added economic and social problems at a time when Latin America was focusing on their urgent solution. Until the mid-1950s, these economic and social problems were not felt as much since Latin America was still in relatively good shape in view of the economics of World War II. However, this situation was changing very quickly and, as stated earlier, the new Europe that was emerging, with its European Common Market, was changing traditional trade relations. We should also bear in mind that the organization, since its inception, had been focusing on certain items that at the time required attention. Thus, in the years 1889–1890 to 1914, the emphasis had been on such subject matters as copyright, patents, trademarks, arbitration. Then, in the 1920s–1940s, the organization shifted to peace and security, with the highlight being the strengthening of the inter-American system through the Rio Treaty and the Charter of the OAS. Now in the 1950s a new trend became visible and was now pursued with extraordinary zeal and devotion: economic and social affairs. Thus, the solution of the increasing economic and social problems became the most important issues that had to be tackled in depth and with urgency, but unfortunately, the organization was not prepared for this shift and was found wanting, particularly in the technical organs.

The economic and social sphere of activity of the OAS and of the former PAU had always been quite weak. Before the 1950s, the juridical–political work of the OAS may be said to have shown positive results, but in the field of economic and social questions, nothing happened for a long time. The first attempts to deal with economic and social issues were made in 1945 (Chapultepec) and 1948 (Bogotá), but they led nowhere. The Economic Conference of the OAS, planned since 1945, did not meet until 1957 in Buenos Aires, and it was a failure. By then, a new political wind was blowing, and it was expected that quick solutions would be found. The General Economic Pact of Bogotá (1948) also remained a dream: it never became operative and was ratified by only three states: Costa Rica (1948), Honduras (1950), and Panama (1951). Likewise, IA-ECOSOC was a disappointment. Until its reorganization in 1961 (an event linked to the launching of the Alliance for Progress), IA-ECOSOC was rather ineffectual. It was composed of representatives of the member states of the OAS, most of whom had no specialized knowledge. Moreover, how could the participating governments have made great strides in IA–ECOSOC? Their eyes were focused on ECLA where, under the leadership of Raúl Prebisch, the theoretical foundation for a solution of the economic problems of Latin America was being created. This explains the situation of IA–ECOSOC that, until 1961, operated almost in a vacuum, in spite of the fact that it was holding continuous sessions.

A first truly practical approach to the economic problems was made at the historic Commemorative Meeting of the Presidents in Panama (1956), after the Tenth International Conference of American States (Caracas, 1954) had come no closer to a solution of Latin America's economic problems. The Panama meeting decided to establish the Inter-American Committee of Representatives of the Presidents (CIRP), which was to submit important recommendations (1957). Despite the fact that the Economic Conference of the OAS, held that same year, represented a Latin American setback, Brazilian President Juscelino Kubitschek Oliveira tackled the problem and called for the above-mentioned Operation Pan America. This initiative, based on an exchange of letters with U.S. President Dwight D. Eisenhower, suggested a bold new approach—a new hemispheric plan for united and common action—to solve economic and social problems before the rising flood against the United States did any real damage. It resulted in the formation of two committees, the earlier mentioned CEIFI and CECE. CEIFI led to the establishment of the IDB, and CECE ultimately, via the Act of Bogotá (1960), led to the reorganization of IA–ECOSOC and the Alliance for Progress.

It would be irresponsible to maintain that neither economic nor social problems had been tackled or that nothing had been achieved between 1945 and 1965. However, in view of the magnitude of Latin America's economic problems, the achievements were only a drop in the bucket. Moreover, these achievements must be viewed in relation to the massive aid given by the United States to Europe and Japan after World War II. One can then understand Latin American dissatisfaction with a policy that seemed to take Latin America more and more for granted. Actually, despite the Alliance for Progress, this basic situation did not change over the next twenty-five years. The economic and social problems have, for many years, been generally linked to the development policy, especially the stabilization and the strengthening of existing economies, the diversification of products for export, industrialization, and other related questions, such as agrarian reform and social change. It was obvious that two of the goals that in 1961 served as a foundation for the Alliance for Progress—economic development and social improvement—posed new tasks to the OAS and created problems that, by the mid-1960s, the OAS had not been able to solve. Had it seen the urgency of these problems and had the United States come around earlier by paying more attention to Latin America, treating Latin American nations as equals and not with arrogance or neglect, and helping them economically, then the picture may have been more promising in the mid-1960s and expensive consequences such as the Cuban Revolution could have been avoided. On the other hand, Latin Americans had to do their part and rid themselves of antiquated and excessive socialistic and nationalistic tendencies as well as their penchant to follow fashionable intellectual trends. Most experts were in agreement with the need for economic development and social change (for example, industrialization and agrarian reform), but too frequently in those decades Latin Americans continued to follow slogans and apply them in a facile way. In other words, just as industrialization after 1945 was too often achieved only to the detriment of agriculture, agrarian reform could not be simply a measure of expropriating land from the wealthy and turning it over to the landless peasants, since such a measure would neither solve the problem of greater agricultural productivity, which was essential for Latin American development, nor provide the needed agricultural modernization.

The economic problems demonstrated more clearly than all others the role of the United States in the organization. Only reluctantly did the United States engage in an economic dialogue; when it finally did enter into such a discussion, it did so quite late in the game and only as a result of unpleasant political facts: the reaction to then Vice President Richard Nixon's 1958 visit to Latin America and Castro's Revolution. Since the OAS was very much linked to the Alliance for Progress, and since the expectations of the latter had not been fulfilled by 1965, the crisis in the OAS turned into another unpleasant political fact. The failures in the economic and social sectors had the obvious result that Latin Americans united in the OAS, leading to an almost constant confrontation with the United States, whose role was obviously of the highest importance.

Hence, the economic and social problems further sharpened the crisis of the OAS. One of the options to improve the possibilities of solving these problems was to attract a greater European participation, at a time when Europe, after having been rebuilt, was able to offer investments for the benefit of both the OAS and the West in general. OAS interest in Europe was demonstrated by the OAS secretary general's visit to western Europe in 1961 and by the establishment of OAS offices in Paris and Brussels in 1962. In turn, European interest in Latin America had increased as early as the 1960s, along with Europe's growing economic and political importance, which was shown at that time by the visits of Latin American states-persons to western Europe and visits of the heads of state of Italy, the Netherlands, West Germany, and France to Latin America. However, perhaps the single greatest development in the sphere of economics was the Atlantic Community Development Group for Latin America (ADELA), the new investment concern formed by fifty-four major U.S., European, and Japanese firms for the financing of economic development plans in Latin America. This was in line with the new orientation of the Alliance for Progress, which, in 1963, decided to give private enterprise a greater role.

THE INSTRUMENTS AND THE WORK OF REVISION

Latin America's crisis in the socioeconomic and political spheres—the crisis of the OAS—demanded a greater sense of responsibility and a steady pursuit of aims and goals. Expressed in more concrete terms, it meant that the highest permanent bodies of the OAS, including the general secretariat, had to become more conscious of the great tasks, goals, and leadership needed, for the internal crisis could only be solved from the top. On the other hand, however, it must be added that such a mastering of the crisis depended ultimately on the cooperation of the member states. Since even some chiefs of state had warned in the mid-1960s that the OAS would be finished if it could not show positive achievements, those states should have set the example. The successful handling of all these elements thus would determine whether the OAS would master the crisis and solve the problems in the spirit of the 1930s and 1940s. The fact that the Alliance for Progress almost came to a standstill and that the 1963 meeting of IA-ECOSOC in São Paulo was not successful merely underscored the seriousness of the situation. The reorganization of the Alliance for Progress that President Lyndon Johnson had undertaken was supposed to benefit the OAS, but it was quite evident that more than a mere reform was needed.

Among the presidential voices that called for a thorough OAS reform was Eduardo Frei Montalva, Chile's new president in 1964, who stressed the need for overhauling the organization by calling for a "more dynamic and constructive approach of the organization to ease political tensions in Latin America, a revitalization of the inter-American system, and a high-level review of the Alliance for Progress activities in order to increase Latin American responsibility in their execution" (press report). On September 6, 1964, after his election, he commented that "the Organization of American States no longer has any real vitality. The moment is approaching for a decision whether to put it in line with a rapidly changing world and with the goals of the Alliance for Progress, or to let it become a coffin of outmoded ideas" (press report). He announced that after assuming office, on November 4, 1964, he would call for specific steps in that direction.

Confronted with the harsh facts, the organization itself became aware of the crisis it was facing. As a result of mounting dissatisfaction, on October 15, 1964, the secretary general of the OAS called for a special meeting to deal with this crisis, particularly since the Eleventh International Conference of American States never became a reality. The secretary general called for, among other things, a strengthening of the bases of pacific settlement; a greater role for the council; a major emphasis on human rights, basic freedoms, and representative democracy; and furtherance of Latin American economic integration. There were other problems besides the crisis of the OAS that also had to be taken care of, such as the growing number of applications for membership in the OAS by the newly independent Commonwealth Caribbean countries. Thus, a series of special Inter-American Conferences were held that took care of these questions between 1964 and 1967.

The First Special Inter-American Conference (Washington, D.C., December 16–18, 1964)

This conference dealt with the increasing problem of Commonwealth Caribbean applications to membership in the OAS once independence had been achieved. The subject matter—the norms that should govern the admission of new members—had many angles since, in the first place, it had not been foreseen that the European colonies in the Caribbean would become independent and request membership in the OAS. Second, some Latin American countries had historic claims, totally or partially, to some areas of these states (e.g., Guatemala: British Honduras/Belize; and Venezuela: the Esequibo area of Guyana); and third, there was the fact that the Commonwealth Caribbean countries would entirely modify the organization as it was set up at the end of the nineteenth century. There had been a great deal of disagreement in the OAS committee that had discussed these issues prior to the conference. These disagreements were not resolved then and came up again during the conference. At the time of the discussion, Jamaica and also Trinidad and Tobago had applied for membership, but it was only a matter of time before the rest of the Commonwealth Caribbean and the Dutch area would also apply. Over the objections of a minority, represented by Guatemala, Nicaragua, Panama, Chile, and El Salvador—which wanted a protocol that would settle the question by interpretation without changing the charter—the conference adopted the aforementioned Act of Washington. This act determined in its first paragraph that any state applying for membership should address the respective application to the secretary general of the OAS and declare its willingness to sign and ratify the Charter of the OAS and its acceptance of all obligations, especially those concerning collective security (Articles 24 and 25 of the charter). The other sensitive issue was established in the third paragraph, which stated that the Council of the OAS should not take any action in those cases where an American state had a territorial claim toward the state that was applying for membership unless that claim had been solved by some form of pacific settlement.

The Act of Washington settled the matter of the norms for admission for the time being, since neither Jamaica nor Trinidad and Tobago posed any problem. However, since the movement to reform the charter was now accelerating, no action on new admissions were acted on. Thus, the Act of Washington proved to be a temporary solution since the Third Special Inter-American Conference would reopen the question and introduce an amendment into the revised charter that dealt with membership.

The Second Special Inter-American Conference (Rio de Janeiro, November 17–30, 1965)

In regard to the main problem (the crisis of the OAS), and after the secretary general had issued his call for a special Inter-American Conference to discuss basic reforms to the charter on October 15, 1964, the Council of the OAS decided on November 4, 1964, following a request of Brazil, Guatemala, and Uruguay, to hold such a Special Inter-American Conference in order to strengthen the inter-American system. This meeting, the Second Special Inter-American Conference, was to be held in Rio de Janeiro in May 1965. It was hoped that it would give the inter-American system much needed reorganization and stimulation, so that, strengthened and revitalized, it would be able to face the pressing Latin American problems. However, the meeting was then postponed to August, 1965, in view of the Dominican crisis of 1965, which had almost given the kiss of death to the OAS, since the organization was bypassed. The issue became even more confused with the involvement of the United Nations. The solution of the Dominican crisis made it possible to hold this Special Inter-American Conference but it had to be postponed again, from August until November 17–30, 1965.

Prepared by a Preparatory Committee, the Second Special Inter-American

Conference dealt with a vast variety of problems ranging from structural change, economic and social development, and pacific settlement, to the Inter-American Peace Committee, protection of human rights, representative democracy, and international waterways.[2] The Preparatory Committee, which initially had seven members, dealt at first with only some of these topics, but as it proceeded further it covered all of them, which, in turn, resulted in all members of the council being represented. Although this Second Special Inter-American Conference was also supposed to deal with the revision of the charter, the ever-increasing extension of topics to be discussed by the Preparatory Committee gave it an entirely new dimension. The Second Special Inter-American Conference thus became the most important meeting for the revision of the charter: its most important topics were revision of the charter, pacific settlement and security, economic assistance to Latin America, and economic integration of the region.

The basis for this reform was a draft submitted by Argentina, Bolivia, Brazil, Chile, the United States, Haiti, Mexico, Peru, and Uruguay, which was called the Act of Rio de Janeiro. It reaffirmed the nature and purpose, as well as the principles and standards, of the organization as contained in Part I of the original charter, and ordered the convocation of a Third Special Inter-American Conference, to be held in 1966 in Buenos Aires for the final approval of all the proposed amendments, which would be prepared by a Special Committee in which all members of the OAS—with the exclusion of Cuba—would be represented. The Special Committee was to meet in Panama and then report back to the council, and after receiving the governments' comments, the council would proceed to convoke this Third Special Inter-American Conference as scheduled.

The Special Committee was to include a set of new "additional standards for inter-American cooperation in the economic, social, and cultural fields" and received guidelines for the general direction of the revised charter.[3] These guidelines included the proposed changes: elimination of the Inter-American Conference and its replacement by a General Assembly to meet annually; retention of the Meeting of Consultation and the general secretariat—the old PAU; and a shortening of the terms of office of both secretary general and assistant secretary general to five years with the possibility of reelection for another five years. The Council of the OAS would be downgraded and put on the same level as IA-ECOSOC and the new IA Educational, Scientific and Cultural Council, and all three were subordinated to the general assembly. The Inter-American Juridical Committee would be retained but its Council of Jurists might be dissolved as it was; finally, the Act of Washington concerning membership in the organization would be incorporated.

Other important subjects covered pacific settlement (Resolution XIII) and security. In regard to the former, it was a fact that the Pact of Bogotá had never been ratified by all members, not even a majority—only ten had done so. Therefore, the nations that so far had not ratified were now urged to do so. The IAPC's special powers were rescinded. As far as security was concerned, the U.S. concept of an Inter-American Force never had a chance and thus was dropped from the agenda of the Third Special Inter-American Conference. The Chileans opposed it from the very beginning, and the Colombians wanted instead a new and strengthened declaration of nonintervention.[4] On the other hand, the Latin Americans were willing to make it more difficult for de facto governments to receive international recognition. Thus, Resolution XXVI ("Informal Procedure on the Recognition of De Facto Governments") stated that "the overthrow of a government and its replacement by a de facto government could be dangerous to the peace and solidarity of the hemisphere," and recommended that the members of the OAS discuss the matter informally before recognition was given to governments that came to power by force.[5]

Besides the subjects of peace and security, the other main topic was economics. Resolution II, The Economic and Social Act of Rio de Janeiro, was based on the need to continue the Alliance for Progress beyond 1970 and to incorporate into the economic and social fields of the inter-American system, in a legally binding way, "principles of mutual security, solidarity, cooperation and assistance" in regard to economic matters; what could be defined, on one side, as defense against economic aggression, and on the other, as mutual cooperation and assistance.[6]

Despite the Alliance for Progress, economic and social affairs had not been satisfactory to Latin Americans. In the 1960s, Latin America felt more disillusioned than ever in this respect, especially since the problems had increased, and it was a fact that the United States continued to pay little attention to these growing issues. Thus, the resolution was intended to strengthen the provisions of economic and social standards and to put into the revised charter legal obligations that so far had simply been passed as resolutions, or, expressed differently, Latin America wanted to make economic and social matters just as legally binding as peace, security, and political matters.[7]

The work on the revised charter began with the Second Special Inter-American Conference and continued by the Special Committee that met in Panama, February 25–April 1, 1966. On the basis of its work, the Special Committee produced a preliminary draft proposal that incorporated all the above matters. It eliminated the IA Council of Jurists but kept the IA Juridical Committee, which was now upgraded. For the United States, however, some of the economic and social standards were unacceptable, especially in view of their obligatory nature; on the other hand, for many countries, including the United States, the draft proposal did not solve the problem of pacific settlement. Thus, a new revision set in on both issues: It modified the obligation concerning economic assistance and enlarged the earlier rather vague social obligations, which were the results of decisions taken by the Fourth Special Meeting of IA-ECOSOC, to which this matter had been referred. Thus, the stage was set for the final special conference that, although postponed, was finally held in Buenos Aires.

The Third Special Inter-American Conference (Buenos Aires, February 11–27, 1967)

The work and final results of this last special inter-American conference was based on the preliminary draft proposal, the council's observations on the proposal, the drafts on the economic and social standards decided on by the Fourth Special Ministerial Level of IA-ECOSOC (proposals that the governments themselves submitted to the conference), and government proposals submitted before the conference actually met. In general terms, the Third Special Inter-American Conference accepted the work done and made a few substantial changes. Thus, it did not grant the Inter-American Juridical Committee the rank of an organ like the three councils but rather acknowledged it "as an advisory body on juridical matters" and incorporated the IACHR, at the same level, into the close system of the OAS with a higher ranking than the "Other Entities" (now reduced to four).

The Third Special Inter-American Conference accepted the General Assembly as the highest organ, thus eliminating the International Conference of American States, but for good measure added a new article (Article 138 of the revised charter, reminiscent of the famous Resolution of Santiago de Chile, 1923), stating that attendance at any organization meeting was not to "depend on the bilateral relations between the Governments of any Member State and the Government of the host country." The conference also ratified the new proposed status of the three councils, although the Council of the OAS, which had been downgraded in the proposals, was now somewhat more enhanced as a Permanent Council; the suggested terms of chair and vice chair were changed from the proposed two-month period to six months. In addition, the Inter-American Juridical Committee was enlarged from nine to eleven members.[8]

In line with the proposals, the secretariat was given greater autonomy, and the conference lessened further United States influence by deciding that neither secretary general nor assistant secretary general could be re-elected more than once and that neither could be succeeded by the same nationality. On the other hand, the conference rejected the idea of changing the seat of the OAS, although the traditional method of decentralizing the organization would continue.

Finally, following the experience and the model of the original charter of 1948, the Third Special Inter-American Conference adopted a system by which the revised charter would go into force when the instruments of ratification had been deposited by a two-third's majority; thereafter, the amended charter would be valid for each subsequent ratifier as of the date of the deposit of ratification. At the same time, the conference appealed to the governments to ratify the protocol, which contained the amendments as soon as possible; to the IA-ECOSOC, IA Cultural Council, ICAP, and the Committee for Cultural Action to "adapt their functioning to the spirit of the Protocol of Amendments"; and to the general secretariat, to take into consideration the respective changes for the forthcoming program budgets of the OAS.[9]

The Protocol of Amendments, signed in 1967 as the Protocol of Buenos Aires, came into force in 1970, and with it a new chapter (the most recent period) of the organization began.

8

The Revised Charter and the New Structure of the OAS

NEW STANDARDS

In accordance with the Protocol of Amendments (the Protocol of Buenos Aires of 1967, which came into force in 1970), the Organization of American States received a new structure with which it continued to pursue its objectives of peace and security; pacific settlement of disputes; common action against aggression from any quarter; solution of political, juridical, social, and economic problems; and cooperation with the member states' social, economic, and cultural development. The new structure did not change the original tripartite division of the charter but introduced substantial modifications in all of them.

The Protocol of Buenos Aires kept the nature and purposes (Articles 1 and 2) as well as the principles (Article 3) intact, but introduced a set of provisions in regard to membership (Chapter III, Articles 4–8), which incorporated the previously mentioned Act of Washington. It also did not change the original provisions regarding the fundamental rights and duties of states (Articles 9–22), pacific settlement of disputes (Articles 23–26), and collective security (Articles 27–28).

However, when it came to the different standards (economic, social, and cultural), the protocol did introduce major changes. Thus, first of all, the Economic Standards (Chapter VII, Articles 29–42) were vastly amplified. Article 29 stated that, inspired by the principles of inter-American solidarity and cooperation, the member states pledged themselves "to a united effort to ensure social justice in the Hemisphere and dynamic and balanced economic development for their peoples, as conditions essential to peace and security." In Article 30, the member states pledged themselves "to mobilize their own national human and material resources," recognizing the importance of an efficient domestic structure for their economic and social development and for assuring effective inter-American cooperation. In Article 31, the member states listed an entire set of norms that echoed the Alliance for Progress, as follows:

a) Substantial and self-sustained increase in the per capita national product;

b) Equitable distribution of national income;

c) Adequate and equitable systems of taxation;

d) Modernization of rural life and reforms leading to equitable and efficient land-tenure systems, increased agricultural productivity, expanded use of undeveloped land, diversification of production; and improved processing and marketing systems for agricultural products; and the strengthening and expansion of facilities to attain these ends;

e) Accelerated and diversified industrialization, especially of capital and intermediate goods;

f) Stability in the domestic price levels compatible with sustained economic development and the attainment of social justice;

g) Fair wages, employment opportunities, and acceptable working conditions for all;

h) Rapid eradication of illiteracy and expansion of educational opportunities for all;

i) Protection of man's potential through the extension and application of modern medical science;

j) Proper nutrition, especially through the acceleration of national efforts to increase the production and availability of food;

k) Adequate housing for all sectors of the population;

l) Urban conditions that offer the opportunity for a healthful, productive, and full life;

m) Promotion of private initiative and investment in harmony with action in the public sector; and

n) Expansion and diversification of exports.

The next article, Article 32, stated the need for cooperation and solidarity in order to achieve the goals sustained in the preceding provision. Article 33 then amplified these goals, and the member states agreed that

the resources made available from time to time by each, . . . should be provided under flexible conditions and in support of the national and multinational programs and efforts undertaken to meet the needs of the assisted country, giving special attention to the relatively less developed countries.

The member states further declared that for these purposes they would seek "financial and technical cooperation from resources outside the Hemisphere and from international institutions."

In the next two articles, the member states declared that "they should make every effort to avoid policies, actions, or measures that have serious adverse effects on the economic or social development of another Member State" (Article 34) and that they agreed to join together in seeking solutions whenever urgent or critical problems arose that might endanger the economic development or stability of a member state affected by conditions that could not be remedied through its own efforts (Article 35).

The member states also pledged to help each other in regard to science and technology through the exchange and utilization of scientific and technical knowledge (Article 36). In the next provision (Article 37) the member states spelled out the close interrelationship between foreign trade and economic and social development and pledged to adhere to the following standards:

a) Reduction or elimination, by importing countries, of tariff and nontariff barriers that affect the exports of the Members of the Organization, except when such barriers are applied in order to diversify the economic structure, to speed up the development of the less-developed Member States or to intensify their process of economic integration, or when they are related to national security or to the needs for economic balance;

b) Maintenance of continuity in their economic and social development by means of:

   i. Improved conditions for trade in basic commodities through international agreements, where appropriate; orderly marketing procedures that avoid the disruption of markets; and other measures designed to promote the expansion of markets, and to obtain dependable incomes for producers, adequate and dependable supplies for consumers, and stable prices that are both remunerative to producers and fair to consumers.

   ii. Improved international financial cooperation and the adoption of other means for lessening the adverse impact of sharp fluctuations in export earnings experienced by the countries exporting basic commodities; and

   iii. Diversification of exports and expansion of export opportunities for manufactured and semi-manufactured products from the developing countries by promoting and strengthening national and multinational institutions and arrangements established for these purposes.

In Article 38 the member states reaffirmed the principle that when the more developed countries have granted concessions in international trade agreements that benefit lesser developed nations, they should not expect reciprocity of treatment. Finally, Articles 39–42 dealt with the economic integration of Latin America. Thus, in Article 39, the member states pledged to promote the improvement or coordination of transportation and communications as necessary by-products for the acceleration of their economic development and integration. In Article 40, the member states acknowledged the necessity of integration of the developing countries of the hemisphere and pledged to orient their efforts toward acceleration of the process of integration with a view of establishing in the future a Latin American common market; in Article 41, the member states declared that "in order to strengthen and accelerate integration in all its aspects"; they also agreed to give adequate priority to the preparation and execution of multinational projects and to their financing, as well as to encourage economic and financial institutions of the inter-American system and "to continue giving their broadest support to regional integration institutions and programs." Article 42 stated that technical and financial cooperation for the promotion of regional economic integration should be based on the principle of "harmonious, balanced, and efficient development," with particular emphasis on the relatively less-developed countries.

The Social Standards (Articles 43–44), which in the original charter had two articles, were also considerably extended in its Chapter VIII. Article 43 took over the first two provisions of the old Article 29 (a and b) but added seven new ones in which new rights and obligations were expressed, such as:

c) Employers and workers, both rural and urban, have the right to associate themselves freely for the defense and promotion of their interests, including the right to collective bargaining and the workers' right to strike, and recognition of the juridical personality of associations and the protection of their freedom and independence, all in accordance with applicable laws;

d) Fair and efficient systems and procedures for consultation and collaboration among the sectors of production, with due regard for safeguarding the interests of the entire society;

e) The operation of systems of public administration, banking and credit, enterprise, and distribution and sales, in such a way, in harmony with the private sector, as to meet the requirements and interests of the community;

f) The incorporation and increasing participation of the marginal sectors of the population, in both rural and urban areas, in the economic, social, civic, cultural, and political life of the nation, in order to achieve the full integration of the national community, acceleration of the process of social mobility, and the consolidation of the democratic system. The encouragement of all efforts of popular promotion and cooperation that have as their purpose the development and progress of the community;

g) Recognition of the importance of the contribution of organizations such as labor unions, cooperatives, and cultural, professional, business, neighborhood, and community associations to the life of the society and to the development process;

h) Development of an efficient social security policy; and

i) Adequate provision for all persons to have due legal aid in order to secure their rights.

Moreover, in Article 44, the protocol linked the economic integration of Latin America to the necessity of harmonizing "the social legislation of the developing countries, especially in the labor and social security fields, so that the rights of the workers . . . [can] be equally protected."

Finally, the Cultural Standards of the original charter were enlarged and were now called Educational, Scientific and Cultural Standards (Chapter IX, Articles 45–50). Again codifying concepts from the Alliance for Progress, the new six articles incorporated a new emphasis on these topics. Thus, Article 45 states that the member states will give primary importance to the encouragement of education, science, and culture, both in order to improve the moral and material wellbeing of the individual and "as a foundation for democracy, social justice and progress." In Article 46 the member states proclaimed that they would cooperate with one another in order "to meet their educational needs, to promote scientific research, and to encourage technological progress." They also stated that they considered themselves "individually and jointly bound to preserve and enrich the cultural heritage of the American peoples."

Article 47 stated that the member states "will exert the greatest efforts, . . . to ensure the effective exercise of the right to education" for elementary, middle-level and higher education, while Article 48 dealt with the elimination of illiteracy so that the benefits of culture could be available to all segments of the population. The development of science and technology and of cooperation in these fields was the subject of Article 49. Finally, Article 50 dealt with the promotion of cultural exchange "as an effective means of consolidating inter-American understanding"; moreover, the member states recognized that regional integration programs should be strengthened through education, science, and culture.

THE NEW GENERAL ASSEMBLY, THE MEETING OF CONSULTATION, AND THE NEW COUNCILS

Part 2 of the charter, in its revised form according to the Protocol of Buenos Aires, underwent the greatest modifications by far. Article 51 enumerated the organs of the organization with which the OAS planned to accomplish its goals. Thus, the article lists the following organs in their hierarchical order:

1. The General Assembly;
2. The Meeting of Consultation of Ministers of Foreign Affairs;
3. The Councils;
4. The Inter-American Juridical Committee;
5. The Inter-American Commission on Human Rights;
6. The General Secretariat;
7. The Specialized Conferences; and
8. The Specialized Organizations.

The article left the door open in the sense that other entities, agencies and subsidiary organs could in the future be established, such as the Inter-American Court of Human Rights.

The General Assembly (Articles 52–58)

The General Assembly is now the highest policy-making organ. It meets regularly every year, although it can also meet in special sessions if a required majority of two-thirds of the member states is obtained and if such a special meeting does not cover topics that are within the jurisdiction of the Meetings of Consultation. The General Assembly thus deals with all problems that may arise in a particular year except those pertaining to a Meeting of Consultation. It can meet at the headquarters in Washington or in any of the member states.

As the highest policy-making organ of the organization, it has a variety of powers in addition "to such others as are assigned to it by the Charter" (Article 52), as follows: It decides the general action and policy of the OAS, determines the structure and functions of its organs, and considers any matter concerning relations among the American states; it establishes measures for coordinating the activities of the organs, agencies and entities of the organization among themselves and with those of other institutions of the inter-American system; and it coordinates cooperation with all UN organizations. Moreover, it promotes collaboration with other international organizations whose purposes are similar to those of the OAS; it approves the program budget of the OAS and determines the quotas of the member states; it considers the annual and special reports submitted to it by the organs, agencies, and entities of the inter-American system; it adopts the general standards for the governance of the general secretariat; and it adopts its own rules of procedure in accordance with the charter and other inter-American treaties.

The General Assembly also establishes the bases for fixing the quota that each member state is to contribute. Article 53 states that "decisions on budgetary matters require the approval of two-thirds of the Member States." In the General Assembly, all member states have the right to be represented, and each state has the right to one vote. All decisions at the General Assembly are adopted by "the affirmative vote of an absolute majority of the Member States, except in those cases which require a two-thirds vote as provided in the Charter or as may be provided by the General Assembly in its rules of procedure" (Article 57).

The Protocol of Amendments also incorporated into the revised charter the provision that the General Assembly would have a Preparatory Committee, composed of the representatives of all member states, to:

a) Prepare the draft agenda of each session of the General Assembly;

b) Review the proposed program-budget and the draft resolution on quotas, and present to the General Assembly a report thereon containing the recommendations it considers appropriate; and

c) Carry out such other functions as the General Assembly may assign to it.

The General Assembly thus replaces what used to be the International Conference of American States which met every five years. In view of the dynamics of world realities, the new structure, with the General Assembly as its supreme organ, is no doubt an improvement over the original charter of 1948. During the year 1970, when the General Assembly replaced the International Conference of American States, it held three sessions during the course of seven months in order to put the new mechanism that was provided for in the revised charter into operation.

So far, between 1970 and 1990, the General Assembly has held twenty regular and fourteen special sessions. The list of these General Assembly meetings with the most important problems of their respective agendas follows:

The Regular Sessions

First Regular Session (San José, Costa Rica; April 14–23, 1971). The first regular session met under the terms of the revised charter. It dealt with the partial renewal of CIECC and the strengthening of its special multilateral fund; the brain drain from Latin America; the financial status of the OAS; the possibility of establishing a youth office within the organization; an administrative tribunal; permanent observers to the OAS; trade expansion; norms regarding relations of cooperation between the OAS and the United Nation and among the specialized organizations of both; and the strengthening of the inter-American system of peace.

Second Regular Session (Washington, D.C.; April 11–21, 1972). This session dealt with the convocation of several specialized conferences of the OAS; revision of the regulations of the General Assembly; the strengthening of the principles of nonintervention and self-determination; the strengthening of the cultural heritage of America as a means of strengthening regional integration; and the activities of the fishing sector within the inter-American system.

Third Regular Session (Washington, D.C.; April 4–15, 1973). The third regular session dealt with a study of a draft legal instrument regarding the definition of cases where the principle of nonintervention was violated; study of a draft convention on extradition; regulations of the Pan American Highway congresses and the Inter-American Tourist congresses; consideration of new financing sources for development; revision of the retirement plan; principles regarding relations among American states; transnational corporations; and application of Article 34 of the charter. The session created a special committee for the purpose of restructuring the inter-American system so that it might respond adequately to changing hemisphere and world conditions.

The session has also become famous for the proclamation of the American Convention on Human Rights (the Pact of San José de Costa Rica).

Fourth Regular Session (Atlanta, Georgia; April 19–May 1, 1974). A variety of important issues were discussed in this session, such as norms of the consultative system of CECON; difficulties in the balance of payments of member states; cultural policy; revision of Article 39 of the charter and of the statutes of the administrative tribunal; cooperation policy with countries not members of the OAS; information regarding the constitutional evolution of nonautonomous territories located on the American continent and belonging to non-American states; and revision of the norms covering the system of representation of the member states in the permanent executive commissions of IA-ECOSOC and CIECC.

Fifth Regular Session (Washington, D.C.; May 8–19, 1975). This session dealt with several subject matters related to legal and political affairs and economic and social matters as well as in the field of education, science, culture, administration, and the budget. The session decided positively on the admission of Grenada.

Sixth Regular Session (Santiago de Chile; June 4–18, 1976). The session signed the Convention for the Protection of Flora, Fauna and the Natural Scenic Beauties of America. It also dealt with the restructuring of the inter-American system; financial help to countries that have no outlet to the sea— Study of a special fund; draft convention on extradition; transnational corporations; means to promote the respect of human rights and to facilitate cooperation among member states; changes to the statutes of the permanent Council of the OAS; and financial reports on the organization.

Seventh Regular Session (St. George's, Grenada; June 14–22, 1977). A variety of issues were treated in this session, including revision of Article 44 of the regulations of the General Assembly; inter-American Indian action; resolutions on the increase of dues of the Permanent Council; and relations between the General Secretariat, and the Pan American Development Foundation.

Eighth Regular Session (Washington, D.C.; June 21–July 1, 1978). This session was one of the more important meetings. First of all, a Deposit of the Panama Treaties on Permanent Neutrality and Functioning of the Canal took place. The session also continued with the process of reform to the charter contained in Resolutions AG/RES. 178 (V-O/75) and AG/RES. 225 (VI-O/76); inter-American Indian action; the fight against cancer; consolidation of cultural activities in the Caribbean subregion; export development; transnational corporations; simplification of the process of revision; discussion and approval of the OAS program budget; and annual reports of IAJC, IACHR, and others. The session also decided the seat of the Court of Human Rights (San José, Costa Rica). It should also be mentioned that it was in this year that the American Convention on Human Rights, which established the Inter-American Court of Human Rights, entered into force.

Ninth Regular Session (La Paz, Bolivia; October 22–31, 1979). The ninth session dealt with meat exports to the United States; canal dues; continuation of the functioning of the Inter-American Center of Capacitation in Business Administration (CICAP) in 1980; and exclusion of Ecuador and Venezuela from the General System of Preferences of the U.S. Law of International Trade. It also issued the Resolution of La Paz, concerning "The First Decade of Regional Progress on Education, Science, and Culture." Old Guatemala (Antigua), Sucre, and Potosí were declared American monuments. Finally, the ninth regular session issued the Declaration of La Paz (concerning Bolivian access to the Pacific Ocean), signed the Statutes of the Inter-American Court of Human Rights, and proclaimed the Caribbean as a zone of peace.

We should also bear in mind that in this year the Panama Canal Treaty and the Treaty Concerning the Permanent Neutrality of the Canal and Operation of the Panama Canal entered into force. Finally, the Commonwealth of Dominica and Saint Lucia became members of the OAS.

Tenth Regular Session (Washington, D.C.; November 19–27, 1980). A number of important issues were dealt with in this session. These included a Regional Fund for Economic Cooperation; collective economic security; the economic and social situation of Latin America and the Caribbean; restrictions of the imports of maritime products from Latin America to the United States—the case regarding Ecuador; promotion of cooperative action in the field of energy by Venezuela, Trinidad and Tobago, and Mexico; Bolivian maritime problems; recognition of the International Committee of the Red Cross; and Belize—its right to independence and the endorsement of Res. 35/20 of the United Nations on the Belize problem. The session also issued the Declaration of Bogotá of CIECC (CIECC–459/80) of the Eleventh Ordinary Session of CIECC and accepted the Draft Convention which Defines Torture as an International Crime. Also in this year the peace treaty between El Salvador and Honduras was deposited at OAS headquarters.

Eleventh Regular Session (Castries, Saint Lucia; December 2–11, 1981). This session discussed or decided on several issues. It admitted Saint Vincent and the Grenadines as well as Antigua and Barbuda to the organization, and it dealt with the revision of Article 42 of the regulations of the General Assembly; development problems of small countries; embargoes imposed by the United States against tuna fish from countries of the area; transit through the Panama Canal; Canada's admission to the Inter-American Telecommunications Commission (CITEL); debts accumulated in the Inter-American Fund for Emergency Situations (FONDEM); restrictions of national offices, and the annual reports of IAJC and IACHR.

Finally, we should also mention that the Inter-American Convention on Extradition was approved in this year.

Twelfth Regular Session (Washington, D.C.; November 15–21, 1982). A variety of issues were dealt with in this session, including the strengthening of CIECC and of the Regional Program of Cultural Development (PRDC);

creation of women's offices; suppression of the Under-Secretariat of Cooperation and Development; Resolution on the Malvinas; dues and transit through the canal; the tuna fish embargo; and the trade in textiles.

In this year the Commonwealth of the Bahamas was admitted as a full member to the OAS.

Thirteenth Regular Session (Washington, D.C.; November 14–18, 1983). This session delved into an impressive agenda. It dealt with international trade arbitration, the U.S. general system of trade preferences, and the fifth centennial of Columbus's discovery of America. It issued the Declaration on the Strengthening of Inter-American Relations in the Field of Finance and Trade and approved the Draft Inter-American Convention on Immunities of Jurisdiction of the States. It also approved resolutions on human displacements in the region; the Malvinas; the convenience of creating a mechanism of inspection of weapons and military hardware in America; the end of mandates of transnational corporations; and peace overtures in Central America. It issued the Inter-American Declaration on the Rights of the Family and approved resolutions on procedures for the peaceful settlement of controversies; greater emphasis on the participation of women in the problem of integration and development; integration of women through education; use of local currencies for the Multilateral Fund of Support to the Five-Year Plan of the Inter-American Indian Action; and a report on the Bolivian maritime problem.

We should also remember that in this year the Specialized Conference on External Financing was held, which unanimously approved the Bases for Understanding. These bases established principles that would make it possible to reverse the trend toward crises of economic and social development.

Fourteenth Regular Session (Brasilia; November 12–17, 1984). The fourteenth session also had an impressive agenda. It dealt with the annual reports of various inter-American specialized organizations; the meeting of the national liaison offices; convocation of a specialized conference on drug abuse; the Malvinas; Bolivia's outlet to the sea; peace in Central America; evaluation of the Decade on Women; international financial organizations; U.S. Law on Tariffs and Trade and the U.S. Preferential System; strengthening and diffusing public international law on the American continent; twenty-five years of IACHR; and a declaration of satisfaction on the Beagle Channel. The highpoint of the session was the Declaration of Brasilia. Through it, the member states reiterated their willingness to join efforts in the continuing task of bringing about conditions of well-being and integral development that would ensure for their peoples a life of freedom and dignity. It thus emphasized the strict observance of the charter and the advance of democracy; it reaffirmed regional integration and the will to link efforts of general welfare and development to a free and dignified life of all peoples of America.

It was in this year that Saint Christopher and Nevis became a member of the organization.

Fifteenth Regular Session (Cartagena de Indias, Colombia; December 5–9, 1985). This session dealt with the annual reports of CIECC, the Pan American Development Fund, IAJC, IACHR and the Inter-American Court of Human Rights, the Board of External Auditors, IA–ECOSOC, and of the organs, agencies, and entities of the organization. It also covered the Draft Inter-American Convention on the Jurisdictional Immunity of States; the cooperative program between the Office of the United Nations High Commissioner for Refugees and the General Secretariat and the status of the work relating to the serious problem of the massive displacement of persons in the hemisphere; constitutional evolution of the nonautonomous territories in the American hemisphere and other territories in the Americas having ties with countries outside the hemisphere; historical records of the OAS; geographic distribution of the staff of the general secretariat; and personnel costs. The conference dealt with compliance with Resolution AG/RES. 705 (XIV-O/84) on Evaluation of the Decade of Women; inventory of the cultural heritage of the Americas; preservation, enhancement, and utilization of the monuments and the historical and artistic heritage of the Greater Caribbean; extension of the Five-Year Inter-American Indian Action Plan; contributions in national currencies to the multilateral fund to support the Five-Year Inter-American Indian Action Plan; Inter-American Year of the Quincentennial of the Discovery of America: "Encounter of Two Worlds"; and the question of the Malvinas Islands. There were discussions of the report on the maritime problem of Bolivia; site for the Inter-American Specialized Conference on Drug Trafficking; special session of the general assembly on inter-American cooperation for development; limitation of conventional weapons; communication of the Contadora Group (Colombia, Venezuela, Mexico, and Panama) with regard to efforts on behalf of peace in Central America; convocation of the Fourth Inter-American Specialized Conference on Private International Law (CIDIP-IV); international solidarity with the people and government of Colombia; strengthening of the inter-American system; legal status of asylees, refugees, and displaced persons in the American hemisphere; condemnation of terrorist methods and practices; some priority guidelines for 1986; Draft Additional Protocol to the American Convention on Human Rights (Pact of San José); and reaffirmation of the principle of nonintervention. Additional topics included a tribute to Andrés Aguilar, Chairman of the Inter-American Commission on Human Rights; Inter-American Convention to Prevent and Punish Torture; Panama Canal tolls; proposed plan for the integrated development of the hemisphere; imports of copper by the United States; general standards to govern the operations of the General Secretariat; bases of financing of the program budget of the organization and that of the organization biennium (1986–1987); 1986 quotas; and contributions to the voluntary funds.[1]

Sixteenth Regular Session (Guatemala; November 11–15, 1986). This session dealt with private investments; dues for the Panama Canal; the fight against absolute poverty; annual reports of several inter-American specialized organizations and of the various councils of the organization; Inter-American Action Program against Drug Trafficking; Malvinas; Bolivia's outlet to the sea; limitation of conventional armaments; study of the new American Treaty of Pacific Settlement; draft of the Inter-American Convention of Judicial Assistance on Criminal Matters; solidarity and support to the people and government of El Salvador; Inter-American Financial Fund for Haiti; OAS priorities; oil tax; and financing of the Inter-American Action Program of Rio de Janeiro.

The sixteenth regular session also issued the Declaration of Guatemala ("Alliance of the Americas Against Drug Trafficking") and established the Inter-American Drug Abuse Control Commission.

Seventeenth Regular Session (Washington, D.C.; November 9–14, 1987). Again, a great variety of topics were discussed and resolutions passed. As usual, many annual reports were approved: those of the Inter-American Institute for Cooperation on Agriculture, Pan American Health Organization, IA-ECOSOC, Inter-American Children's Institute, Inter-American Indian Institute, Inter-American Nuclear Energy Commission, Pan American Institute of Geography and History, CIECC, Inter-American Commission of Women, IAJC, IACHR, and the Inter-American Court of Human Rights. Other subject matters included Amendment of Articles 3 and 33 of the CITEL Organization Plan; U.S. Trade Bills; copper exports to the U.S. market; horizontal cooperation; the fight against extreme poverty; development problems of the small states of the Caribbean subregion and Suriname; Panama Canal tolls; a single statute that would replace the statutes of the three accounts of FEMCIECC (regular account, CEC [Special Cultural Account], and CMP [Mar de Plata Account]; evaluation of the Resolution of Maracay (decided on February 28, 1968, by CIECC at its meeting in Maracay, Venezuela, this resolution meant the launching of new regional programs for development in education, science, and technology); the educational and social development of the states of the Central American isthmus; report on the procedure for establishing firm and lasting peace in Central America; communication from the foreign ministers of the Contadora Group and the Support Group on their peace negotiations in Central America; the question of the Malvinas Islands; and Report on the Maritime Problem of Bolivia. There was a special session of the General Assembly on Inter-American Cooperation for Development; presentation of annual reports on the drug traffic problem in the Americas; report of the Ninth Inter-American Conference of Ministers of Agriculture; draft new American Treaty on Pacific Settlement; limitation of conventional weapons; compliance with the Mandate on Possible Steps to Strengthen the Chairmanship of the Permanent Council; cooperation between the Organization of American States and the United Nations; ratification of the Protocol of Cartagena; report on the implementation of resolution AG/RES. 850 (XVI-O/86), "Support for the Activities Commemorating the Quincentennial of the Discovery of America: Encounter of Two Worlds"; draft Inter-American Convention on Judicial Assistance in Penal Matters; draft additional protocol to the American Convention on Human Rights; standards on reservations to Inter-American multilateral treaties and rules for the general secretariat as depositary of treaties; additional protocol to the American Convention on Human Rights to Abolish the Death Penalty; the situation of the Central American refugees and regional efforts to resolve their problems; specialized technical meeting of CEPCIES on Inter-American Policy for Cooperation on Sugar; and a variety of resolutions on financial and budgetary items. Perhaps the most outstanding item of this session was the encouragement given by the General Assembly to the five Central American presidents in signing the "Procedure for Establishing a Firm and Lasting Peace in Central America."[2]

Eighteenth Regular Session (San Salvador, El Salvador; November 14– 19, 1988). As in other sessions, this session also dealt with the usual annual reports of the various councils and specialized organizations. It again dealt with such items as copper exports to the United States; U.S. trade policy; Panama Canal tolls, report on the maritime problem of Bolivia; the question of the Malvinas Islands; strengthening of the OAS; cooperation between the OAS and the United Nations; and the usual financial and budgetary items. Among other resolutions were the following: OAS participation in the war on the illicit use and production of narcotic drugs and psychotropic substances, and traffic therein; additional protocol to the American Convention on Human Rights in the area of economic, social and cultural rights (Protocol of San Salvador); social investments program for the development of the Central American countries; "Trifinio Plan" (development of the border area of Guatemala, El Salvador, and Honduras); uniform statute for FEMCIECC and its accounts; evaluation of the Resolution of Maracay; activities commemorating the Quintcentennial of Columbus's discovery of America: "Encounter of Two Worlds"; establishment of the Secretariat for Special Political Affairs as a technical-administrative unit of the general secretariat; first biennial report on compliance with AG/RES. 829 (XVI-O/86)—Full and Equal Participation of Women by the Year 2000; meeting of ministers on the illicit use of narcotic drugs and psychotropic substances, and traffic therein; and communication from the foreign ministers of the Contadora Group and the Support Group on their peace negotiations in Central America. There was also a report on the procedure for establishing firm and lasting peace in Central America; clandestine arms traffic and its effect on the peace and security of the hemisphere; agreement on privileges and immunities and headquarters agreement; additional protocol to the American Convention on Human Rights to Abolish the Death Penalty; draft American Convention on Extradition and Preventive Measures in Drug Trafficking; draft declaration on Extradition and Preventive Measures in Drug Trafficking; study of the reasons why more states are not parties to the American Treaty on

Pacific Settlement (Pact of Bogotá); creation of an inter-American system for nature conservation; Central American refugees and regional efforts to resolve their problems; tribute to the people and president of El Salvador; and solidarity with and support for the peoples and governments of Jamaica and Nicaragua.[3]

Nineteenth Regular Session (Washington, D.C.; November 13–18, 1989). Again this session dealt with the usual annual reports of the councils and the specialized organizations. Perhaps the most important item was the admission of Canada as a member of the Organization of American States; after all, the organization had waited precisely one hundred years for this to happen. Other subject matters were as follows: request from the government of Belize to accredit a permanent observer to the Organization of American States; the situation in El Salvador; Panama Canal tolls; regional conference on poverty in Latin America and the Caribbean; seminar on the strengthening of trade; election of members of the Inter-American committees; Inter-American Quintcentennial fund; activities commemorating the Quintcentennial of Columbus's discovery of America: "Encounter of Two Worlds"; and strengthening of the fellowships and training programs of the organization. There was also an evaluation of the Resolution of Maracay; uniform statute for FEMCIECC and its accounts; regulation of the obligation of the member states of the organization to pay their assessments; declaration on the topic, "The Question of the Malvinas Islands"; program of action for the strengthening of the OAS; strengthening of the OAS in international trade; strengthening of the OAS in the field of information; report on the maritime problem of Bolivia; the Panamanian crisis in the international context (discussed in detail later); human rights and democracy—electoral monitoring; integration and development of inter-American law; Report on the procedure for establishing firm and lasting peace in Central America; the problem of the illicit use and production of narcotic drugs and psychotropic substances, and traffic therein; permanent observer status for the European communities in the Organization of American States; summit meeting of heads of state and of government; participation of the Organization of American States in the International Decade for the Eradication of Colonialism and the status of colonial territories in the American hemisphere; revision of the statutes, rules of procedure, and other instruments governing the organs, agencies, and entities of the organization; tribute to the French Republic on the occasion of the bicentennial of the French Revolution; solidarity with and support for the people and governments of Antigua and Barbuda, Dominica, and St. Kitts and Nevis. Also discussed were an additional protocol to the American Convention on Human Rights to Abolish the Death Penalty; draft Inter-American Convention on the Forced Disappearance of Persons; agreement on privileges and immunities and headquarters agreement; creation of an inter-American system for nature conservation; revision of the statutes of the Permanent Council; congratulations to the Inter-American Juridical Committee on its fiftieth anniversary; Central American refugees and the International Conference on Central American Refugees; thirtieth anniversary of the creation of the Inter-American Commission on Human Rights; and recommendations of the Fourth Inter-American Specialized Conference on Private International Law (CIDIP-IV) to the General Assembly. There were also the usual financial and budgetary resolutions.[4]

Twentieth Regular Session (Asunción, Paraguay; June 4–8, 1990). This session commemorated the first hundred years of the inter-American system and the twentieth regular meeting of the General Assembly. The agenda covered forty-seven items, mostly devoted to political–juridical problems and budgetary issues. More important were the issues that were discussed informally: external debt and human rights, Latin American integration, drug trafficking, U.S. interventionist policies, the possibility of a Cuban return to the OAS, the search for peace in Central America, the Bolivian claim to an outlet to the sea against Chile, arising from its lost Pacific War (1879–1883), and the Malvinas issue.

One of the major problems to be aired in depth was Latin American integration, which was now more urgent than ever in view of the growing economic and political power of the European Community, the reincorporation of Eastern Europe into Western Europe, the increasing impact of Japan and the Asian rim (South Korea, Hong Kong, Taiwan, and Singapore), and especially the rise of the North American Free Trade Area (NAFTA) involving the United States and Canada (and possibly also Mexico), which put the South American continent on notice. Six Latin American presidents (of Argentina, Bolivia, Brazil, Paraguay, Suriname, and Uruguay) called on Latin America to integrate, with Uruguayan President Luis Lacalle proving to be the most critical in regard to U.S. policies in Latin America.

The Twentieth Regular Meeting of the General Assembly also proclaimed the Centennial Declaration (*Declaración del Centenario*), expressing therein the firm will to consolidate democracy, defend freedom, maintain peace and security, and respect human rights. In the document, which was signed by the six presidents and open to signature and ratification by all other member states, the presidents stated:

1. Their decision to give the highest political priority to the process of regional integration, since only through an effective and quick execution of its strategy could the economic conditions be created that are necessary to secure the well-being of their peoples.

2. Their determination to respect the sovereignty and territorial integrity of the States, with strict observance of the principles of nonintervention, of nonapplication of threats or the use of force in international relations, and of the solution of all conflicts through pacific means.

3. Their decision to adopt adequate means for the solution to the political and

financial crisis of external debt, thus allowing countries to reach and maintain appropriate levels of economic growth.

4. Their resolution to undertake jointly actions that affect the legitimate needs of their peoples in regard to the promotion and financing necessary for development, especially in science and technology.

5. Their firm determination to carry out, in a concerted manner, those actions that are necessary for the prevention of the unwarranted use of drugs and psychotropical substances and to combat their illicit traffic, as they were convinced that the struggle against drugs requires the establishment of a common front.

6. Their vehement rejection of terrorism in any form and their decision to take all measures that are deemed necessary to combat the clandestine traffic in weapons, munitions, and explosives.

7. Their will to coordinate actions for the protection, promotion, and conservation of the environment.

8. Their determination to engage the active presence of their nations in the establishment of a more just and democratic international order.

9. Their conviction that all these objectives require, in order to be reached, the action of the OAS, the strengthening of which constitutes an obligation to all the member states.[5]

Twenty-First Regular Session (Santiago de Chile; June 2–8, 1991). Thirty-four countries attended this historic meeting, although Cuba had still not returned to the fold. The agenda of this meeting included the Bush administration's new program for Latin America. Called the "Enterprise for the Americas" initiative, it was an effort to reduce debt, liberalize trade, and boost investments in Latin America. It also included the current commercial and multilateral negotiations of GATT, the consolidation of democracy, and the procedures for establishing a durable and lasting peace in Central America. There were also problems under discussion related to drug abuse and drug trafficking, as well as questions related to violations of human rights and the environment.

Perhaps the most outstanding result of this session was the resolution that required an emergency meeting of the organization—a Meeting of Consultation—in the event of a military coup in any member State. Given the present zeitgeist, such a meeting would almost certainly have the result of a collective condemnation of the new government and a basis (should a two-thirds majority be obtained) for economic sanctions, as had happened earlier in such isolated cases as Rafael Trujillo's Dominican Republic (1960), Fidel Castro's Cuba (1962), and Anastasio Somoza's Nicaragua (1979). However, the difference between those cases and the new Resolution of Santiago de Chile is the simple fact that in the above cases, the measures adopted were quite extraordinary and exceptional, whereas now the OAS had approved a general and uniform rule. The original proposal came from the presidents of the five Andean countries of Bolivia, Peru, Ecuador, Colombia, and Venezuela, who had in mind a much tougher proposition, but in view of the feelings of Mexico and other criticisms it was watered down, as is usually the case in such matters. Mexico, whose extreme rejection of any kind of intervention was traditional and well known, in view of its own history, again had made its position clear at the time of the ratification of the new Protocol of Cartagena de Indias, when it stated:

1. The second paragraph of Article 1 of the Protocol specifically establishes that the Organization of American States has no implicit or residual powers, rejects the legal possibility of extensive interpretations of its governing precepts, and subordinates the Organization itself to the principle set forth in Article 18 of the Charter whereby no State or group of States has the right to intervene, directly or indirectly, for any reason whatever, in the internal or external affairs of any other State.

2. Article 3 e) introduces political pluralism into the Charter as the guiding principle of inter-American co-existence and stresses the inalienable right of every State to choose, without external interference, the political, economic and social organization best suited to it; establishes the obligation of the American States to cooperate fully among themselves, independent of their political, economic and social systems; and aspires to a plural and democratic Organization composed of all the American States.[6]

The new resolution is obviously a milestone in the history of the OAS, although it does not mean that the organization will intervene in such possible cases in the future. All the resolution says is that in case of a military coup, a Meeting of Consultation shall take place, and the merits of the case will determine what the OAS will then do. After all, the old contradiction between representative democracy as a necessity for all member states and the principle of nonintervention (which in the last decades has been legally strengthened, not weakened) has not been eliminated, even though at the time of the resolution, all governments in the hemisphere except Cuba could qualify as representative democracies—quite a record. The resolution has only shown that Latin America is concerned about the problem and that the OAS is attempting to strengthen the present democratic trend of the past decade, even though people know only too well that democracy is not yet based—if it ever can be—on a solid foundation in view of the social and educational inequalities and the rampant poverty in many parts of the region, which have only increased. In any case, it does signal a new trend that is worth watching.

The Special Sessions

First Special Session (Washington, D.C.; June 25–July 8, 1970). This Special Session of the General Assembly approved regulations of the General Assembly and the statutes of the Permanent Council of the OAS, IA-ECOSOC, and CIECC.

Second Special Session (Washington, D.C.; August 24–25, 1970). This session decided on the filling of vacancies of the IAJC.

Third Special Session (Washington, D.C.; January 25–February 2, 1971). Prior to the meeting, the General Assembly had instructed the Permanent Council of the OAS to study international terrorism. The result was the Convention to Prevent and Punish Acts of Terrorism Taking the Form of Crimes against Persons and Related Extortion that Are of International Significance.

Fourth Special Session (Washington, D.C.; February 22, 1977). This special session accepted the admission of Suriname to the OAS.

Fifth Special Session (Washington, D.C.; November 20–28, 1977). This special Session decided on the program budget for the General Assembly and other inter-American organs for 1978. It did likewise for the executive secretary for economic and social affairs, the executive secretary for education, science and culture, and the under secretary of administration and common services of administration.

Sixth Special Session (Washington, D.C.; December 12–15, 1977). This special session took up several important items. It decided on streamlining the OAS program budget, methods of financing the new OAS building, contributions to the financing of the OAS; promotion of exports, and restructuring of the national offices for greater efficiency.

Seventh Special Session (Washington, D.C.; May 22, 1979). This session admitted Dominica and Saint Lucia to the OAS. It also approved the procedures for the election of members of IACHR, and for the election of the seven judges to the Inter-American Court of Human Rights.

Eighth Special Session (Washington, D.C.; February 17, 1982). This session decided on the filling of new vacancies of the IAJC. It also approved the order of precedence of OAS delegations and permanent observers.

Ninth Special Session (Washington, D.C.; March 3, 1982). This special session decided on the admission of the Bahamas to the OAS.

Tenth Special Session (Washington, D.C.; March 12, 1984). This session approved a new order of precedence for OAS delegations and permanent observers. It also dealt with the filling of vacancies for both the secretary general and the assistant secretary general. The candidates were João Clemente Baena Soares (Brazil) and, for assistant secretary general, Valerie Theodore McComie (Barbados). Baena Soares won, but McComie failed.

Eleventh Special Session (Washington, D.C.; March 12, 1984). This session approved the admission of St. Christopher and Nevis. It also established a new order of precedence for OAS delegations and permanent observers.

Twelfth Special Session (Washington, D.C.; July 6, 1984). This session was requested by Peru for filling a vacancy in the IAJC.

Thirteenth Special Session (Washington, D.C.; July 19, 1985). This meeting was requested by Mexico for filling a vacancy in the IAJC.

Fourteenth Special Session (Cartagena de Indias, Colombia; December

5, *1985*). This special session approved the new Protocol of Amendments, the Protocol of Cartagena de Indias, subject to ratification by the Member States.

Fifteenth Special Session (Washington, D.C., January 8, 1991). This Special Session was convoked in order to approve and welcome two new members that until then, in view of the Act of Washington, had been barred from membership. Belize and Guyana thus entered the OAS, leaving the organization with thirty-five member states.

The Meeting of Consultation of Ministers of Foreign Affairs (Articles 59–67)

This important organ of the organization has not changed in substance or in form. The Meeting of Consultation continues, as established in the Eighth International Conference of American States (Lima, 1938). It was incorporated in the original charter under Articles 39–47 and is now in the revised charter under Articles 59–67. The changes introduced in the new articles are slight: What used to be the Council of the Organization is now referred to as the Permanent Council, and Article 82 (formerly Article 47) replaced the International "Conference" of American States with "General Assembly."

The Meeting of Consultation thus has the same requirements for being convoked: either under the Charter of the OAS or under the Rio Treaty. Any member state can call for such a Meeting of Consultation "to consider problems of an urgent nature and of common interest to the American States" (Article 59), or to serve as an organ of consultation in cases of armed attack or other threats to international peace and security (Rio Treaty). In either case, the request must be addressed by the governments to the Permanent Council of the organization, which then decides by absolute majority vote—that is, a majority of the body, whether voting or not—if such a meeting is to be held. In the case of a dispute between two or more American states, the parties directly involved are obviously excluded from all voting.

Should an attack take place within the territory of an American state or within the geographic security area of the Western Hemisphere, a Meeting of Consultation must be convened without delay. Until such a Meeting of Consultation can be assembled, the Permanent Council is empowered to act as a provisional organ of consultation and to take the necessary measures. In all these matters, there is no change from the original provisions in the Charter of 1948, and this is also true of the Advisory Defense Committee, which was incorporated into the revised version without any modification whatsoever.

There had been thirteen Meetings of Consultation until 1969 (i.e., between 1939 and 1970 and under the original charter). After 1970 and under the revised charter, the following Meetings of Consultation took place.

The Fourteenth Meeting of Consultation of Ministers of Foreign Affairs, Washington, D.C.; January 30–31, 1971

This Meeting of Consultation was requested by Ecuador in regard to "Coercive Measures Affecting the Sovereignty of States and Their Economic and Social Development." The background of this Ecuadorean request was the seizure by Ecuador of foreign fishing boats, mostly under the U.S. flag. Ecuador tried the owners in Ecuadorean courts and levied heavy fines on foreign fishing boats that were discovered fishing within the 200 mile radius that Ecuador and other Latin American countries had unilaterally set up for the protection of their fishing wealth. The Ecuadorean request thus dealt with a dispute between Ecuador and the United States regarding territorial waters: Ecuador having proclaimed its territorial waters covering 200 miles from the coastline while the United States, at that time at least, recognized only 12 miles. As the dispute became more acrid, the United States retaliated by suspending sales of military equipment to Ecuador. In this conflict with its mighty northern neighbor, Ecuador was supported by Chile and Peru, which had proclaimed the same extension of their territorial waters to 200 miles and had the same problem with Washington, D.C. The Meeting of Consultation urged the parties to avoid aggravating their differences, to use negotiations for a solution, and to observe the principles of the Charter of the OAS.

The Fourteenth Meeting of Consultation, which started in 1971, has as yet not officially been ended. However, in the meantime, the United States not only acknowledged the existence of such extended territorial waters (for the protection of fishing, though not for other acts of sovereignty), and thus also the justice of the Ecuadorean claim, but extended its own territorial waters to this distance for similar purposes.

The Fifteenth Meeting of Consultation of Ministers of Foreign Affairs, Quito, Ecuador; November 8–12, 1974

Several Latin American countries—Colombia, Costa Rica and Venezuela—requested the Meeting of Consultation in order to readmit Cuba into the inter-American family. The reasoning behind the request was, in the first place, the perception of many Latin American countries there was no longer a Cuban threat, and second, their belief that made little sense that while the West was opening up to the East in political, economic, and cultural matters, Cuba continued to be isolated. Thus, the request, which also implied a criticism of U.S. policies, meant discontinuing the application of Resolution I of the Ninth Meeting of Consultation (Washington, D.C., 1964). The meeting was duly held but did not succeed in eliminating, multilaterally, the isolation of Cuba. Thus, the member states were still bound by the decisions of the Ninth Meeting of Consultation. In the General Committee, prior to the Meeting of Consultation, the draft resolution proposed by Colombia, Costa Rica, and Venezuela, to discontinue the measures taken against Cuba in 1964, had the following results: Twelve governments voted in favor (Argentina, Colombia, Costa Rica, Dominican Republic, Ecuador, El Salvador, Honduras, Mexico, Panama, Peru, Trinidad and Tobago, and Venezuela), three countries voted against (Chile, Paraguay, and Uruguay), and six abstained (Bolivia, Brazil, Guatemala, Haiti, Nicaragua, and United States). The proposal, thus, had not obtained the required two-thirds majority, a situation that did not change during the Meeting of Consultation.

The Sixteenth Meeting of Consultation of Ministers of Foreign Affairs, San José, Costa Rica; July 29, 1975

In a way, this Meeting of Consultation was a follow-up of the previous Meeting of Consultation, which had not produced the results that the majority of Latin American nations had expected. The same parties pressed for a new meeting (which did meet in San José, Costa Rica) in order to establish "Freedom of Action of the States Parties to the Inter-American Treaty of Reciprocal Assistance to normalize or conduct their relations with the Government of Cuba at the level and in the manner each State deems advisable."[7] This time, the proposal carried in the sense that sixteen states voted in favor of this draft resolution in the General Committee prior to the Meeting of Consultation: Argentina, Bolivia, Colombia, Costa Rica, the Dominican Republic, Ecuador, El Salvador, Guatemala, Haiti, Honduras, Mexico, Panama, Peru, Trinidad and Tobago, the United States, and Venezuela; three continued to oppose it: Chile, Paraguay, and Uruguay; and two abstained: Brazil and Nicaragua. The decision of the Meeting of Consultation reaffirmed the principle of nonintervention and left "the States Parties to the Rio Treaty free to normalize or conduct their relations with the Republic of Cuba at the level and in the manner that each State deems advisable, in accordance with each one's national policy and interests."[8] The result, then, was the end of Cuban isolation from most of Latin America, although the United States did maintain its present Cuban policy, and especially in the following years under both the Reagan and Bush administrations.

The Seventeenth Meeting of Consultation of Ministers of Foreign Affairs, Washington, D.C. First Session, September 21–23, 1978; Second Session, June 23, 1979

The increasing tensions in Central America, such as the revolutionary activity of the Sandinistas against the Somoza regime in Nicaragua, as well as other such revolutionary turmoil in Central America, prompted Costa Rica and Nicaragua to request a Meeting of Consultation to call the attention of the inter-American community to these incidents in Central America. (The Somoza regime began in 1934 with Anastasio Somoza García. This was the year César Augusto Sandino, who lead guerrilla resistance groups in the late 1920s and early 1930s, was murdered in Managua. Following the assassination, Anastasio Somoza ruled the country, although not always as president. Reelected in 1951, he was assassinated in 1956 in León. His two sons, Luis and Anastasio, continued the family domination of the country until challenged in the late 1970s by the Sandinistas, a leftist revolutionary movement that took Sandino as its model. Although in many ways the Somoza regime was positive, especially under the father and son Luis, by the late 1970s, when the younger Anastasio was running the country's affairs, the regime used oppressive measures against any challenge to its rule.) In the first session (September 21–23, 1978), the governments that were directly involved were urged by the Meeting of Consultation to refrain from aggravating the present situation. After closely watching the situation, a second session took place on June 23, 1979, in which "the inhuman conduct of the dictatorial regime governing Nicaragua" was attacked, and which led the Seventeenth Meeting of Consultation to issue a declaration in which it was stated that the Somoza regime be replaced by one that represented the free will of the people, with "holding of free elections as soon as possible," so that "a truly democratic government that guarantees peace, freedom and justice" be set up. In the voting (in which Trinidad and Tobago did not participate), the following countries voted in favor of the resolution: Argentina, Barbados, Bolivia, Brazil, Colombia, Costa Rica, the Dominican Republic, Ecuador, Grenada, Haiti, Jamaica, Mexico, Panama, Peru, Suriname, the United States, and Venezuela (seventeen). Against the resolution were Nicaragua and Paraguay (two), with five abstentions: Guatemala, El Salvador, Honduras, Chile, and Uruguay.

Soon after this resolution had passed, which for all practical purposes ended this Seventeenth Meeting of Consultation, the Somoza regime collapsed leading to a new tragedy in the volatile history of Nicaragua: the Sandinista regime and the increasingly hostile policy by the United States to dislodge it from power.

The Eighteenth Meeting of Consultation of Ministers of Foreign Affairs, Washington, D.C.; December 30, 1978

This Meeting of Consultation dealt again with the explosive situation in Nicaragua and its immediate neighbors. The Meeting of Consultation was requested by Costa Rica and concerned a serious threat to its sovereignty and territorial integrity. While the seventeenth Meeting of Consultation had dealt with the domestic upheavals in Nicaragua and their repercussions all over Central America, the eighteenth Meeting of Consultation referred to Nicaraguan violations of Costa Rican sovereignty.

This eighteenth Meeting of Consultation was not its final and formal convocation. The Permanent Council, acting as a provisional organ of consultation, reaffirmed the principles proscribing the threat and use of force in international relations (Article 1 of the Rio Treaty; Article 21 of the revised charter of the OAS; and Article 2, paragraph 4 of the UN Charter), and requested Nicaragua to refrain from any further threat against Costa Rica.

The Nineteenth Meeting of Consultation of Ministers of Foreign Affairs, Washington, D.C.; February 2–4, 1981

The background for this Meeting of Consultation was a request by Ecuador relating to military operations allegedly initiated by Peru in the El Condor mountain range. The Meeting of Consultation, which met for two days in Washington, D.C., urged both Ecuador and Peru to demobilize and disperse their forces. It also took note of the four guarantors of 1942 (Argentina, Brazil, Chile, and the United States, which guaranteed the Ecuadorean–Peruvian borders as set up that year) and decided to send a team to the border area to monitor observance of the cease-fire.

The Twentieth Meeting of Consultation of Ministers of Foreign Affairs, Washington, D.C.; April 26–28, 1982, and May 27, 1982

The background of this historic meeting was the South Atlantic conflict between Argentina and the United Kingdom. It dealt with the Argentine invasion of the Malvinas/Falkland Islands on April 2, 1982. This dispute betwen Argentina and the United Kingdom goes back to the year 1833 when the British landed in the islands and occupied them by force, thus usurping Argentine rights of sovereignty that were inherited from Spain (the *Ius Uti Possidetis, Ita Possedeatis*—"As you held territory in 1810, so you shall keep it as your property"). This was affirmed by Argentine military occupation in 1820, followed in 1829 by the appointment of the first Argentine governor, Luis Vernet. After protesting for over a century and a half and negotiating for some twenty years with the British, who had no intention of relinquishing the islands (although the British Foreign Office agreed that sooner or later the Malvinas would have to be turned over to the government in Buenos Aires), Argentina lost patience and invaded the "lost sister." The Argentine position was not to hold the islands by this fait accompli but to strengthen its hand in the diplomatic game with London, with the ultimate aim of reincorporating the Malvinas and their dependencies into the national patrimony. The Argentines did not expect the violent British reaction and requested the Meeting of Consultation in order to invoke the Rio Treaty.

The Meeting of Consultation had a first session on April 26–27, 1982, in which the government of the United Kingdom was urged to cease hostilities within the security zone of the Rio Treaty and likewise, the government of Argentina not to exacerbate the situation. The Meeting of Consultation also urged the parties to agree to a truce "taking into account the rights of sovereignty of the Republic of Argentina over the Malvinas Islands and the interests of the Islanders (Kelpers)." It also deplored the coercive measures of the European Community and other states, which constituted a serious precedent not covered by Resolution 502 (1982) of the United Nations Security Council and were incompatible with the Charter of the OAS and with GATT (Resolution I).

The voting record on this resolution represented a historic manifestation of Latin American solidarity against a neo-colonialist approach. Seventeen countries voted
::%s:one against, with four abstentions: Colombia, Chile, Trinidad and Tobago, and the United States. It should be noted that Cuba, favorable to the Argentine and Latin American point of view, was not represented in this Meeting of Consultation, and that outside the OAS, SELA had passed a unanimous resolution favoring Argentina and condemning both the European Community and the United States for violating GATT principles. Finally, it should also be noted that in that session, the following Caribbean states acted as observers: Antigua and Barbuda, Bahamas, Barbados, Grenada, Jamaica, and Suriname.

A second session of the same twentieth Meeting of Consultation was held in Washington, D.C. on May 27, 1982, at a time when the Argentine position on the islands was fast eroding and the British were in the final stages of their reoccupation. Here a second resolution was passed that condemned the United Kingdom, deplored British actions frustrating peace efforts, and demanded Britain to cease immediately all hostilities. It also requested the United States and the European Community to immediately drop all sanctions against Argentina. Finally, the meeting asked all member states of the OAS to apply the Rio Treaty and help Argentina. The meeting considered all coercive measures against Argentina, including the British blockade of the Argentine coast, a violation of international law. This resolution of the second session had the same voting results as the first (i.e., seventeen Latin American countries voted in favor and none against it, with four abstentions: Colombia, Chile, Trinidad and Tobago, and United States).

Although from an idealistic point of view, the two sessions of the twentieth Meeting of Consultation represented a resounding victory for the union and solidarity of Latin America and a sad exhibition of U.S. policy in regard to Latin America, the practical side was a failure. British Prime Minister Margaret Thatcher had not the slightest intention to undo a historic violation of Argentina's rights and return the islands, and the United States showed its usual disdain and contempt for Latin America. For once there had arisen a case in which the United States could have shown a greater sensitivity, a concern for justice, and thus an identification with the Latin American point of view; instead, it showed clearly that it preferred Great Britain and its usurpation, since indirectly, through the United Kingdom, the United States also wanted to control the South Atlantic and the future shape of the Antarctic. In other words, when it came to the bottom line, the United States would stand against Latin America, just as 150 years before it had helped create the situation in which British power simply took the islands. Moreover, the Monroe Doctrine, to which Argentina then appealed, was, in Washington's view, not applicable. The meeting thus represented, in symbolic and practical terms, a milestone in the unhappy relationship between the United States and Latin America—with the United States always expecting, voluntarily or by elbow twisting, to have Latin American support when its own interests were at stake, but hardly willing to do likewise when Latin American interests were involved. The Twentieth Meeting of Consultation has so far officially not been declared ended.

The Twenty-First Meeting of Consultation of Ministers of Foreign Affairs, Washington, D.C.; May 17, 1989, December 20, 21, and 22, 1989, and January 8, 1990

This Meeting of Consultation dealt with the recent Panamanian crisis involving General Manuel Noriega, the successor to strongman Omar Torrijos. The story dates to the military seizure of power in 1968 that put Omar Torrijos, leader of the Panamanian Revolution, in the saddle until 1981 when he died mysteriously in a small plane crash. Panamanian reality was such that, despite civilian presidents, the real power was with Omar Torrijos and his National Guard. It was Torrijos who had successfully negotiated the two Panama Canal Treaties with the United States that were signed in 1978 with President Jimmy Carter. It was also Torrijos who had sponsored Manuel Noriega's career; eventually the latter would emerge as Panama's commander of what are now called the Defense Forces in the aftermath of Torrijos' death, again despite civilian presidents, like Nicolás Ardito-Barletta of Torrijos's Revolutionary Democratic Party. Ardito-Barletta elected in 1984, but needed the aid of an Electoral Tribunal to decide that he had been the victor.

By 1980 the United States had evidence that Noriega was gun-smuggling illegal exports to the tune of $2 million from Miami to Panama for final destination in El Salvador and Nicaragua, but a possible arrest, on one of the visits of Noriega to the United States, was blocked because he was Washington's man in Panama. He was useful in many ways, especially for the U.S. Central Intelligence Agency in Langley, Virginia; under the Reagan Administration he was even put on the payroll. Noriega served all sides: the United States, and Castro's Cuba, and the Sandinistas in Nicaragua. Noriega obviously knew about the Iran-Contra affair, and even had the Panamanian Congress pass a law in 1987 that allowed U.S. narcotic agents access to Panamanian bank accounts suspected of laundering drug money. It was, however, evident that, while helping the Drug Enforcement Agency, he was himself trading in drugs, arms, and illicit money.

Parallel to the Noriega case, U.S.–Panamanian relations soured with the Reagan Administration's goal of undoing or watering down the Panama Canal treaties negotiated in 1978. By 1984 Panama complained when the Panama Canal Commission (five U.S. and four Panamanian members) granted special privileges to U.S. employees and operators of the canal; Panama then accused the United States of violating the spirit and the letter of the treaties. Since the United States could not control Panama's strongman, the latter increasingly became a U.S. target. Drug trafficking was thus only one part of the U.S.–Panamanian story as it unfolded in the 1980s and reached a climax with the U.S. invasion in December 1989.

On February 4, 1988, Noriega was indicted by Miami and Tampa grand juries for drug crimes. The crisis heated up when Noriega forced the ouster of President Delvalle, although the United States continued to recognize Delvalle. When the contradictory policies of the Reagan and Bush administrations were abandoned in favor of a tough policy—economic sanctions, freezing of Panamanian assets, and suspension of U.S. trade preferences of nearly $100 million—the U.S.–Panamanian crisis increasingly became a Latin American concern. To save face, Noriega called elections; when he lost them (May 7, 1989), he declared them invalid and made it clear he would not accept an offer to step down and reside abroad. The result was more violence and upheaval. The crisis deepened, with an increasing possibility of U.S. intervention to topple Noriega. The government of Venezuela then requested a Meeting of Consultation, which began its first session on May 17, 1989.

In this first session, the Meeting of Consultation urged all authorities and political forces in Panama to abstain from taking any measure or executing any action that might aggravate the situation. Ecuador, Guatemala, and Trinidad and Tobago were appointed to negotiate a national accord for a quick transfer of political power through democratic means.

This first session, however, did not lead to a peaceful solution. Instead, the situation led to U.S. intervention, which was well prepared in advance and cynically called "Operation Just Cause." In the best traditions of nineteenth-century imperialism, U.S. forces, to the tune of 26,000 troops, intervened in Panama with great loss of life and property to Panamanians, violation of the Nicaraguan embassy in Panama City, and much arm twisting by the Vatican for the release of Noriega who had found diplomatic asylum at the Papal Nunciature. Eventually, Noriega left the sanctuary of the Vatican and surrendered to U.S. authorities. The victor in the earlier Panamanian elections was officially installed as president of Panama on a U.S. military base in Panama. It was a unique case in history where a superpower used excessive military operations to kidnap a foreign chief of state under the pretense of drug trafficking and brought him to trial in the United States for alleged drug abuses and violations of human rights. To top this, a president of Panama was then installed by U.S. authorities. Needless to say, the Panama affair marked another low in U.S.–Latin American relations.

A second session of the twenty-first Meeting of Consultation took place on December 20, 21, and 22, 1989, and on January 8, 1990, in Washington. In the December meeting, the United States was condemned for the invasion of Panama with twenty votes in favor of the resolution, one against (the

United States), and six abstentions. In the January meeting, the United States was condemned for the violation of the premises of the Nicaraguan Embassy in Panama City by U.S. troops and thus the violation of two important conventions (Havana 1928 and Vienna 1961); nineteen countries voted in favor and none against, and there were seven abstentions. The twenty-first Meeting of Consultation, like the preceding one, has not been officially declared ended.

The New Councils

Chapter XIII of the new charter deals with the common provision of the three different councils (Articles 68–77), and thereafter, each council is dealt with separately (Chapters XIV–XVI). These three councils—the Permanent Council of the Organization, the IA–ECOSOC, and the Inter-American Council for Education, Science and Culture—are directly responsible to the General Assembly, and each has the authority granted it by the charter and other inter-American instruments, as well as the functions assigned it by the General Assembly or the Meeting of Consultation. In all councils, the member states have the right to voice and vote, and, with the restrictions imposed by the charter and other inter-American instruments, the power to make recommendations in matters within their authority.

Within their respective authority, the councils may present to the General Assembly "studies and proposals, drafts of international instruments, and proposals on the holding of Specialized Conferences, on the creation, modification or elimination of Specialized Organizations and other inter-American agencies, as well as on the coordination of their activities."[9] The councils may also present drafts and proposals as well as drafts of international instruments to the Specialized Organizations. In urgent cases, the councils may also convoke Specialized Conferences, in matters of their competence, after consultation with the member governments and without having to resort to the provisions of Article 128 regarding Specialized Conferences. They shall also render such specialized services as requested by the governments.

In Article 74 the councils were given the power to require from the other councils, as well as from subsidiary agencies, such information and advisory services as needed within their respective spheres of interest. They can also request such services from other inter-American agencies. With the approval of the General Assembly, the councils may establish subsidiary organs and agencies that they deem necessary for the better performance of their duties. These subsidiary organs or agencies may be established provisionally when the General Assembly is not in session. Finally, the councils have the authority to hold meetings in any member state, when advisable, and with the prior consent of the respective government; moreover, they have their own statutes that must be approved by the General Assembly, and their own rules of procedure.

The Permanent Council of the OAS (Chapter XIV, Articles 78–92)

The Permanent Council of the OAS replaced the old Council of the OAS. In the original charter the old council held a centralized position above its three subsidiary Councils—IA–ECOSOC, the IA Council of Jurists, and the IA Council for Education, Science, and Culture. Now the Permanent Council of the Organization ranks on the same level as the IA-ECOSOC and the IA Council for Education, Science and Culture; the IA Council of Jurists has totally disappeared. Furthermore, while the original council was downgraded, the Protocol of Buenos Aires returned some of the old council's authority but still ranked it on the same level as the other two councils; furthermore, its functions were restricted. Basically, the new Permanent Council has two functions: one is in the area of pacific settlement and the other incorporates much of the old council's authority. Thus, many of the old provisions were incorporated in the revised version: Article 78 is similar to the old Article 48, although the new provision no longer mentions that "the appointment may be given to the diplomatic representative accredited to the Government of the country in which the Council has its seat," for the simple reason that in view of the work load and other facts, the member states have no longer linked the two diplomatic positions to both the White House and the OAS.

The offices of chair and vice chair are now for six months instead of the previous one-year term (Article 79). Articles 80 and 81 remained unchanged (old Articles 51 and 52).

In the first category are the powers of the Permanent Council regarding the peaceful settlement of disputes. Article 82 states that the Permanent Council shall keep vigilance over the maintenance of friendly relations among the member states and thus assist in the peaceful settlement of any disputes in accordance with provisions outlined in the next eight articles (Articles 83–90), making these functions the most important aspect of the new organ. In Article 83 the revised charter maintains the establishment of an Inter-American Committee on Peaceful Settlement—the old Inter-American Peace Committee—as a subsidiary organ of the Permanent Council, the Statutes of which to be prepared by the council and approved by the General Assembly. In Article 84 the parties to a dispute may resort to this subsidiary organ, and if the parties so wish, the Chair of the Permanent Council "shall refer the dispute to the Inter-American Committee on Peaceful Settlement." In Article 85 the Permanent Council is "given the authority, either through the Committee or by any other means," to assert the facts, and may do so in the territory of any of the parties "with the consent of the governments concerned." Article 86 states that in case none of the procedures mentioned in Article 23 are followed, the parties to a dispute may appeal to the Inter-American Committee on Peaceful Settlement. In such a case, the Permanent Council shall refer the issue to the committee, which then shall decide whether it is competent, and, if so, shall then offer its services to the party or parties. In the exercise of its duties, the committee may carry out the necessary investigation in the respective territory provided it has the consent of the government concerned. If one of the parties should refuse the offer, the committee shall limit itself to informing the Permanent Council "without prejudice to its taking steps to restore relations between the parties, if they were interrupted, or to reestablish harmony between them" (Article 87). After submitting a report, the Inter-American Committee on Peaceful Settlement is empowered to make suggestions in line with the previous Article 87, and if one of the parties continues to refuse cooperation, the Permanent Council shall then limit itself to reporting to the General Assembly (Article 88). Finally, in the exercise of these functions, the Permanent Council shall decide by an affirmative vote of two-thirds of its members, "excluding the parties to the dispute, except for such decisions as the rules of procedure provide shall be adopted by a simple majority" (Article 89), and in this field of peaceful settlement, the Permanent Council and the subsidiary organ shall always act in accordance with the provisions of the charter and the principles and standards of international law, including the existing treaties in force between the parties (Articles 89–90).

The second category follows essentially the powers of the old council of the OAS, though these have been somewhat restricted. These are listed in Article 91 as follows:

a) Carry out those decisions of the General Assembly or of the Meeting of Consultation of Ministers of Foreign Affairs the implementation of which has not been assigned to any other body;

b) Watch over the observance of the standards governing the operation of the General Secretariat and, when the General Assembly is not in session, adopt provisions of a regulatory nature that enable the General Secretariat to carry out its administrative functions;

c) Act as the Preparatory Committee of the General Assembly, in accordance with the terms of Article 58 of the Charter, unless the General Assembly should decide otherwise;

d) Prepare, at the request of the Member States and with the cooperation of the appropriate organs of the Organization, draft agreements to promote and facilitate cooperation between the Organization of American States and the United Nations or between the Organization and other American agencies of recognized international standing. These draft agreements shall be submitted to the General Assembly for approval;

e) Submit recommendations to the General Assembly with regard to the functioning of the Organization and the coordination of its subsidiary organs, agencies, and committees;

f) Present to the General Assembly any observations it may have regarding the reports of the Inter-American Juridical Committee and the Inter-American Commission on Human Rights; and

g) Perform the other functions assigned to it in the Charter.

Finally, Article 92 states that the Permanent Council and the General Secretariat "shall have the same seat."

The Inter-American Economic and Social Council (Chapter XV, Articles 93–98)

The IA-ECOSOC had been substantially upgraded with the Alliance for Progress of 1961 and its own internal changes, which, by 1967 had made it a very different institution from that of the 1950s. In a similar manner as other councils, IA-ECOSOC is composed "of one principal representative of the highest rank" of each member state, to be specially appointed by the respective government (Article 93). The purpose of IA–ECOSOC, as stated in Article 94, "is to promote cooperation among the American countries in order to attain accelerated economic and social development, in accordance with the standards set forth in Chapters VII and VIII," and in order to achieve these goals, which are different from those listed in the old Article 64, Article 95 lists them, as follows:

a) Recommend programs and courses of action and periodically study and evaluate the efforts undertaken by the Member States;

b) Promote and coordinate all economic and social activities of the Organization;

c) Coordinate its activities with those of the other councils of the Organization;

d) Establish cooperative relations with the corresponding organs of the United Nations and with other national and international agencies, especially with regard to coordination of inter-American technical assistance programs; and

e) Promote the solution of the cases contemplated in Article 35 of the charter, establishing the appropriate procedure.

IA-ECOSOC is to hold at least one meeting each year at the ministerial level. It also meets when convoked by the higher organs—the General Assembly or the Meeting of Consultation—"at its own initiative, or for the cases contemplated in Article 35 of the Charter" (Article 96). IA-ECOSOC still has its subsidiary organ, a Permanent Executive Committee composed of a chair and no less than seven members, who are elected by the council for terms to be established in the council statutes. As long as the Alliance for Progress lasts, the Permanent Executive Committee is to be the old CIAP (Article 97). Finally, in Article 98, the Permanent Executive Committee is instructed to perform the tasks assigned to it by IA-ECOSOC, in accordance with the general standards established by the council.

The Inter-American Council for Education, Science and Culture, Chapter XVI, Articles 99–104)

This new council replaced the old Inter-American Council for Education, Science, and Culture and was thus very much upgraded, including its area of competence. In the first place, it like the Permanent Council and IA-ECOSOC, is composed of "one principal representative of the highest rank, especially appointed by the respective government" (Article 99). The purpose of the council is to promote

friendly relations and mutual understanding between the peoples of the Americas through educational, scientific, and cultural cooperation and exchange between Member States, in order to raise the cultural level of the peoples, reaffirm their dignity as individuals, prepare them as fully for the tasks of progress, and strengthen the devotion to peace, democracy, and social justice that has characterized their evolution. (Article 100)

The long Article 101 inumerates in fourteen points how this council shall accomplish its objectives. These include coordination of all types of cultural activities, adoption of the pertinent measures as stated in the respective standards incorporated in Chapter IX, improvement of education at all levels, integration of all population sectors, encouragement of scientific and technological research, exchange programs, promotion of education for the understanding of the common values and destiny of the American peoples, and stimulation of intellectual and cultural creativity. They also included support of cooperative relations with the corresponding organs of the United Nations and with other national and international bodies, strengthening the civic conscience for the effective exercise of democracy and for the observance of the rights and duties of man, intensification of procedures that tend to intensify the integration of the hemisphere by means of programs in education, science, and culture, and periodic evaluation of the efforts made by the member states in the fields of education, science, and culture. Finally, as with the other two councils, this body is also to meet at least once a year at the ministerial level (Article 102); it also has a Permanent Executive Committee—the old Inter-American Cultural Committee—composed of a chair and no less than seven other members, who are elected by the council for terms to be established in the statutes of the council (Article 103). This committee is to perform the tasks "assigned to it by the IA-Council for Education, Science and Culture, in accordance with the general standards established by the Council" (Article 104).

THE INTER-AMERICAN JURIDICAL COMMITTEE AND THE INTER-AMERICAN COMMISSION ON HUMAN RIGHTS (CHAPTERS XVII AND XVIII, ARTICLES 105–111 AND 112)

As a result of the amendments adopted in 1967, the Inter-American Juridical Committee was upgraded, while the Inter-American Council of Jurists was terminated. The Inter-American Juridical Committee took over some of the functions of the old Inter-American Council of Jurists, but now it serves the entire organization and not, as before, its higher authority, the Inter-American Council of Jurists. As stated in Article 105,

The purpose of the Inter-American Juridical Committee is to serve the Organization as an advisory body on juridical matters; to promote the progressive development and the codification of international law; and to study juridical problems related to the integration of the developing countries of the Hemisphere.

As far as possible, it is to aim at uniformity. It is to undertake studies and any work assigned to it by the higher organs, and on its own initiative it can undertake any study it considers advisable and hold specialized juridical conferences (Article 106). Formerly composed of nine members, it now has eleven, who are elected by the General Assembly for a period of four years from panels of three candidates presented by the member states. In the election, as in other cases, a system shall be used that takes into account partial replacement of membership, and, as far as possible, an equitable geographic representation. No two members of the committee may be from the same state (Article 107).

The committee represents all member states and has the broadest autonomy (Article 108); it shall have cooperative relations with universities and other teaching centers as well as national and international entities that are devoted to study, teaching, and research (Article 109). As in other cases, the Inter-American Juridical Committee drafts its own statutes, which have to be approved by the General Assembly, and it can establish its own rules of procedure (Article 110). Finally, its seat is in Rio de Janeiro, but for special occasions it may meet at any place after consultation with the respective member state (Article 111).

The Inter-American Commission on Human Rights was also upgraded in the revised charter as a symbol of the changes affecting the organization in the late 1950s and 1960s. In line with the Protocol of Amendments, the IACHR is no longer just a special commission but has become a subsidiary organ of the General Assembly. The revised charter now includes the IACHR, even though it only dedicates a chapter (XVIII) with only one article (Article 112) to it. According to the latter, the IACHR's purpose is "to promote the observance and protection of human rights and to serve as a consultative organ of the Organization on these matters." It states further that an Inter-American Convention on Human Rights shall determine its "structure, competence and procedure," as well as those of other organs responsible for these matters.

THE GENERAL SECRETARIAT (CHAPTER XIX, ARTICLES 113–127)

The General Secretariat now definitely replaced the old Pan American Union (Chapter XIII, Articles 78–92 of the original charter). Although the new provisions follow the older ones in general terms, the new General Secretariat was given greater autonomy from the Permanent Council. Thus, a notable change is reflected in the revised charter: The old Pan American Union was much more subservient to the old OAS Council than the new General Secretariat is to the new Permanent Council. The General Secretariat "is the central and permanent organ of the Organization" and performs the tasks assigned to it in the charter, in other inter-American treaties and agreements, and by the General Assembly, the Meeting of Consultation, or the councils (Article 113).

The secretary general's term is now five years, and he or she may be reelected only once and cannot be succeeded by someone of the same nationality. The assistant secretary general shall assume the office of secretary general when the latter has become vacant until the time when the General Assembly elects the new secretary general (Article 114). The secretary general directs the General Secretariat and is responsible to the General Assembly for the proper fulfillment of the obligations and functions of the General Secretariat (Article 115). As head of the organization, the secretary general participates with voice but without vote in all meetings of the organization (Article 116). The secretary general "shall promote economic, social, juridical, educational, scientific and cultural relations among all the Member States of the Organization, in keeping with the actions and policies decided upon by the General Assembly and with the pertinent decisions of the Councils (Article 117)."

In Article 118, the revised charter enumerates the new functions of the General Secretariat, which, among other things, include transmissions of notices of meetings of the General Assembly, Meetings of Consultation, the Councils, and of Specialized Conferences; advice on the preparation of agendas of meetings; preparation of the proposed annual program budget of the organization—subject to review by the General Assembly's Preparatory Committee and approval by the General Assembly itself; and provision of secretariat services for the organs of the OAS and for the normal custodian functions. The General Secretariat also has to submit an annual report to the General Assembly on the activities of the organization and its financial status, and, finally, it has the duty to establish cooperative relations with the Specialized Organizations as well as with national and international organizations in line with decisions reached by the General Assembly and the Councils.

Articles 119–124 deal with the powers of the secretary general and the assistant secretary general. The secretary general is entitled to set up the necessary offices of the General Secretariat to accomplish the secretariat's purposes, and also determines the number of officers and employees, appoints them, and regulates their obligations and their remuneration.

Both secretary general and assistant secretary general are elected by the General Assembly for five years, and, in the event that the office of assistant secretary general becomes vacant, the General Assembly shall elect a substitute to hold that office until a new assistant secretary general is elected. As in the old OAS Council, the assistant secretary general is the secretary of the Permanent Council and serves the secretary general as an advisory officer and as a delegate in all matters entrusted to him or her by the secretary general.

During the absence or disability of the secretary general, the assistant secretary general performs the latter's duties. Moreover, both of these high positions must be filled by different nationalities. Both officials can be removed by the General Assembly through a two-thirds majority "whenever the proper functioning of the Organization so demands." The secretary general is also empowered to appoint, with the approval of the respective council, the executive secretary for economic and social affairs and the executive secretary for education, science and culture. Article 124 states that "in the performance of their duties the Secretary General and the personnel of the Secretariat shall not seek or receive instructions from any Government or from any authority outside the Organization" and shall also "refrain from any action that may be incompatible with their position as international officers responsible only to the Organization."

In the last three provisions (Articles 125–127), the new charter more or less follows the old provisions (Articles 90–92 of the 1948 Charter) when it says that "the Member States pledge themselves to respect the exclusively international character of the responsibility of the Secretary General and the personnel of the General Secretariat, and not to seek to influence them in the discharge of their duties" (Article 125). In the selection of the personnel, the first consideration is to be given to efficiency, competence, and integrity, and to "the necessity of obtaining as wide a geographic representation as possible." Finally, Washington, D.C., was retained as the seat of the organization.

THE SPECIALIZED CONFERENCES, THE SPECIALIZED ORGANIZATIONS, AND OTHER ENTITIES (CHAPTERS XX AND XXI, ARTICLES 128–129 AND 130–136)

These three instruments were kept in the revised charter with some modifications. The Specialized Conferences (Articles 128–129) may be held when either the General Assembly or the Meeting of Consultation so decides; they may also be convoked on their own initiative or at the request of one of the councils or Specialized Organizations. As far as the agenda and the rules of procedure are concerned, both are prepared by the respective councils or Specialized Organizations and shall be submitted to the governments for consideration.

The Specialized Organizations (Articles 130–136), numbering six, were kept intact as in the original charter. They are the Pan American Institute of Geography and History (PAIGH), Inter-American Children's Institute (IACI), Inter-American Indian Institute (IAII), Inter-American Institute for Cooperation in Agriculture (IICA), Inter-American Commission of Women (IACW), and Pan American Health Organization (PAHO). The new provisions also introduced modifications, and generally speaking, they were upgraded. Article 130 defines them without change from the old charter (Article 95) as "intergovernmental organizations established by multilateral agreements and having specific functions with respect to technical matters of common interest to the American States." The General Secretariat is to maintain a register of these Specialized Organizations (Article 131), and they shall enjoy full technical autonomy, although they shall take into account the recommendations of the General Assembly and the councils (Article 132). Moreover, the Specialized Organizations shall transmit their annual reports to the General Assembly detailing their accomplishments with their annual budgets and expenses (Article 133).

As in the original charter, the relations between the OAS and the Specialized Organizations "shall be defined by means of agreements concluded between each organization and the Secretary General, with the authorization of the General Assembly" (Article 134). The Specialized Organizations shall establish cooperative agreements with world agencies of the same character in order to coordinate their activities, and in concluding such agreements, "the Inter-American Specialized Organizations shall preserve their identity and their status as integral parts of the Organization of American States, even when they perform regional functions of international agencies" (Article 135). This is a reference to the past experience of the PAU with WHO and PASB (now PAHO). Finally, in Article 136, it is stated that in determining the seat of a Specialized Organization, consideration is to be given "to the interest of all the Member States and to the desirability of selecting the seats of these organizations on the basis of a geographic representation as equitable as possible."

In regard to other entities, the Protocol of Buenos Aires replaced the original "Special Agencies and Commissions" with "Other Entities." In the first place, the original six were now reduced to four: the Inter-American Defense Board (IADB), the Inter-American Statistical Institute (IASI), the Inter-American Nuclear Energy Commission (IANEC), and the Special Consultative Committee on Security (SCCS), an arrangement that would not last intact but would later on undergo new modifications.

What used to be the Inter-American Peace Committee (IAPC) became the above-mentioned Inter-American Committee on Peaceful Settlement, upgraded to the Executive Committee of the Permanent Council of the Organization in cases in which a peaceful settlement was to be arranged through this channel; in other words, the old IAPC, which had gone through incredible upheavals since its inception, has been upgraded through a slightly different name and thus taken out of the old structure where it had been one of the six "Special Agencies and Commissions." The other special agency or commission was IACHR, which also was upgraded. Together with the Inter-American Juridical Committee, it achieved a rank slightly below the Meeting of Consultation, the Specialized Conferences, and the Specialized Organizations. These four other entities remained in the same position as in the old Charter of the OAS; hence, they were not upgraded as were the Specialized Organizations.

THE UNITED NATIONS, MISCELLANEOUS PROVISIONS, RATIFICATION AND ENTRY INTO FORCE, AND TRANSITORY PROVISIONS. RESERVATIONS AND DECLARATIONS (CHAPTERS XXII-XXIII, ARTICLES 137–150)

The revised charter kept intact its original requirement (Article 102) that "none of the provisions of this Charter shall be construed as impairing the rights and obligations of the Member States under the Charter of the United Nations" (Article 137), but under "Miscellaneous Provisions" it introduced a new rule stating that attendance at any meeting of the organization "shall not depend on the bilateral relations between the Government of any Member State and the Government of the host country" (Article 138), which is reminiscent of the famous decision taken at the Fifth International Conference of American States in Santiago de Chile in 1923. The other provisions (Articles 139–142) are no different from the original Articles 103–106, though Article 143 was expanded in scope to state that the OAS "does not allow any restriction based on race, creed, or sex, with respect to eligibility to participate in the activities of the Organization and to hold positions therein." Finally, in regard to "Ratification and Entry into Force," the revised charter adopted the old provisions (Articles 108–112), the only change being the use of the term "General Secretariat" instead of "Pan American Union" (Articles 114, 146, and 148) and "General Assembly" instead of "Inter-American Conference" (Article 147).

The Protocol of Buenos Aires introduced into the revised charter Chapter XXV—"Transitory Provisions" (Articles 149–150)—which stated that ICAP would act as the Permanent Executive Committee of IA-ECOSOC "as long as the Alliance for Progress is in operation" (Article 149), and "until the Inter-American Convention on Human Rights (referred to in Chapter XVIII) enters into force, the present IACHR shall keep vigilance over the observance of human rights" (Article 150).

Finally, the revised charter of the organization contains the reservations of three Member States, whereas the old charter contained no reservations at all. Thus, Guatemala declared that none of the stipulations of the revised charter "may be considered as an impediment to Guatemala's assertion of its rights" over Belize. Peru stated that "the principles of Inter-American solidarity and cooperation and essentially those set forth in the preamble and declarations of the Act of Chapultepec constitute standards for the mutual relations between American States and juridical bases of the Inter-American system"; and the United States declared that none of the revised charter's provisions

shall be considered as enlarging the powers of the Federal Government of the United States of limiting the powers of several states of the Federal Union with respect to any matters recognized under the Constitution as being within the reserved powers of the several states.

At the time of signing the protocol, several member states made the following declarations. Thus, Ecuador signaled its unhappiness that the new Permanent Council of the Organization had not been given sufficient powers "to aid the Member States effectively in the peaceful settlement of their disputes." In the view of the Ecuadorean government,

none of its provisions in any way limits the right of the Member States to take their disputes, whatever their nature and the subject they deal with, to the Organization, so that it may assist the parties and recommend the suitable procedures for peaceful settlement thereof.

Panama, which had an increasingly severe dispute with the United States in regard to the Panama Canal and the Canal Zone, declared in writing at the time of signing the protocol,

that it [did] so in the understanding that none of its provisions limits or in any way impedes the right of Panama to bring before the Organization any conflict or dispute that may have arisen with another Member State to which a just solution has not been given within a reasonable period after applying, without positive results, any of the procedures for peaceful settlement set forth in Article 24 of the present Charter.

Finally, last but not least, Argentina declared its unhappiness that the revised charter did not contain, "in addition to the organic, economic, social, and cultural standards, the essential provisions that would make the security system of the Hemisphere effective." It thus reiterated the conviction that the amendments introduced in the revised charter did not duly cover the requirements of the organization.

NEW CHANGES IN THE 1970s AND 1980s

After the revised Charter of the OAS came into force in 1970, several new modifications were introduced in the organization, again modernizing the OAS and updating its structure. A new link of the General Assembly was set up with a new institution: the Inter-American Court of Human Rights, which had been inaugurated in 1979. Three administrative agencies, which existed before with different names and in a weaker position, were now given more authority: the Board of External Auditors, the Administrative Tribunal, and the Advisory Committee on Administrative and Budgetary Matters. "Other Entities" were now reduced to two: the Inter-American Nuclear Energy Commission (IANEC) and a new organization, the Inter-American Drug Abuse Control Commission (CICAD). The Inter-American Defense Board (IADB) was upgraded; no longer a part of "Other Entities," it became directly linked to the General Assembly.

There were other changes in the General Secretariat. For example, the Office of the Secretary General was now aided in its tasks by an Advisory Group and a Cabinet besides the Office of the Assistant Secretary General.

Directly linked to the Office of the Secretary General are six divisions: the Secretariat of IACHR, the Secretariat of CICAD, the Offices of the General Secretariat in the Member States, the Inspector General, Public Information, and Protocol.

In the Office of the Assistant Secretary General there is a direct link to five divisions: the Secretariat to the General Assembly, the Meeting of Consultation, the Permanent Council, and Conferences; the Permanent Secretariat of the Inter-American Commission of Women; the Permanent Secretariat of the Inter-American Children's Institute; the Museum of Modern Art of Latin America, and the Columbus Memorial Library.

Under the Secretary General's Office are the four undersecretaries and their respective departments, as follows:

1. The Executive Secretary for Economic and Social Affairs:
   a. Department of Economic Affairs;
   b. Department of Social Affairs; and
   c. Department of Regional Development.
2. The Executive Secretary for Education, Science and Culture:
   a. Department of Educational Affairs.
   b. Department of Scientific and Technological Affairs;
   c. Department of Cultural Affairs; and
   d. Department of Fellowships and Training.
3. The Secretariat for Legal Affairs
   a. Department of Development and Codification of International Law.
   b. Department of General Legal Services; and
   c. Department of Legal Publications and Informatics.

The Secretariat of Legal Affairs also contains the Secretariat of the Administrative Tribunal and the Secretariat of the Inter-American Juridical Committee.
4. The Secretariat for Management is divided into two offices (a–b) and four departments (c–f):
   a. Office of the Treasurer;
   b. Printing;
   c. Department of Human Resources;
   d. Department of Program-Budget;
   e. Department of Material Resources; and
   f. Department of Management Systems.

Most of these departments and offices existed before but were now upgraded
and strengthened in order to streamline the administration and guarantee
greater efficiency.

The OAS also established two new institutions that were not ready by the
time the Protocol of Buenos Aires went into effect in 1970: the Inter-
American Court of Human Rights, set up in 1979, and the Inter-American
Drug Abuse Control Commission (CICAD), established in 1986. Each reflects the interest of the OAS in a very important, and delicate, subject
matter.

The Inter-American Court of Human Rights

Although pressure had increased for the establishment of an Inter-
American Court of Human Rights, especially after the inauguration of
IACHR, many obstacles had to be surmounted. Thus, despite the fact that
the court was highly desired by many, it was only in 1979 that it saw the
light of day. Its establishment for the protection and enforcement of human
rights is closely linked to the question of human rights in general and the
IACHR in particular.

The question of human rights began to be discussed within the inter-
American system at the Inter-American Conference for the Consolidation
of Peace in Buenos Aires, in 1936, when a Chilean proposal was submitted
that would recognize the right of every individual to life, liberty, and the
free exercise of religion, the practice of which did not conflict with public
order; it also stated that every country should grant protection of these rights
to everyone within its territory without distinctions based on race, sex,
nationality, or religion. The conference rejected the proposal, which was
obviously ahead of its time. However (as stated earlier), the same question
was discussed at the Eighth International Conference of American States in
Lima in 1938 and at the Chapultepec Conference of 1945. Here the delegations of Cuba, Mexico, and Uruguay presented projects on human rights
that the conference considered in its Resolution XL requesting the Inter-
American Juridical Committee to prepare a draft Declaration of the International Rights and Duties of Man.

The Ninth International Conference of American States in Bogotá (in 1948) dealt extensively with human rights at a time when this topic had received increased attention. The Ninth International Conference decided to incorporate human rights into the charter—Article 5(j)—and to proclaim the American Declaration of the Rights and Duties of Man which included both political and social rights (Resolution XXX). However, as could be expected, the proclamation of these rights, in Chapter 1, and of the attendant duties, in Chapter 2, were highly idealistic and difficult to implement. They were thus rather ideals to be followed in good faith than political and social facts. For example, Chapter 1 listed the following rights:

to life, liberty, personal security; to equality before the law; to freedom of religious worship; to freedom of opinion and expression; to protection of reputation, private and family life; to found a family; to protection during pregnancy and to special protection as children; to freedom of movement; to inviolability of dwelling; to inviolability of correspondence; to health and well-being; to education; to participation in the national culture; to work and a fair salary; to leisure; to social security; to civil rights; to a fair trial; to nationality; to political rights; of assembly; of association; to property; of petition; to protection from arbitrary arrest; to due process; and to asylum.[10]

Chapter 2 enumerated the following duties:

to society; duties toward children and parents; duty to accept education; duty to vote; duty to render civil and military service; duty to cooperate in social security and welfare programs; duty to pay taxes; duty to work; and duty "to refrain from taking part in political activities that, according to law, are reserved exclusively to the citizens of the State in which he is an alien."[11]

However, the most important question was how to implement these rights and duties. It was here that the Inter-American Court of Human Rights became a goal. At that time (1948), however, it was concluded that it was premature for such a court. The Inter-American Juridical Committee decided then not to work on the draft and reported this decision to the First Meeting of the Inter-American Council of Jurists (1950).

In the Fourth Meeting of Consultation of Ministers of Foreign Affairs (Washington, D.C., 1951), the question of implementation came up again in regard to the Declaration and to Resolution XXXII—"The Preservation and Defense of Democracy in America." Nothing substantial happened and the question was postponed for the Tenth International Conference of American States in Caracas, 1954, to resolve. It was Mexico that prevailed here with a draft on human rights that would affect neither national sovereignty nor nonintervention. The result was Resolution XXVII, which recommended to the governments to incorporate human rights in their respective legislations, disseminate the knowledge of human rights in order to create a strong civic conscience, and include them in school programs. The PAU was requested to collect information on human rights and to make comparative studies. In other resolutions of the same conference—Resolutions XXVIII, XXIX, and XXX—the governments expressed their intention to support free labor unions, asked the Council of the OAS to study the possibility of creating an Inter-American Court of Human Rights, and paid tribute to those countries that had extended suffrage to illiterates. The question of the court, however, remained difficult: It was passed with only a slight margin: 11–2–7.

In May 1954, the OAS Council sent the court proposal to the Inter-American Juridical Committee pursuant to Resolution XXIX of the Tenth Inter-American Conference. Now, however, another roadblock appeared: The Political–Juridical Committee agreed with the Inter-American Juridical Committee that before the question of a court could be decided there should first be a decision on a Convention on Human Rights. Thus, no further action was taken, and a council resolution referred the matter to the Eleventh International Conference of American States in Quito. Since that conference was never held, the matter simply was thus left up in the air until 1965.

The Fifth Meeting of Consultation of Ministers of Foreign Affairs (Santiago de Chile, 1959) dramatically changed the situation: It revived the issue in view of the increased tensions in the Caribbean and in South America. In the meantime, on a global level, the Europeans had created the Council of Europe (1950) and had come up with the European Convention on Human Rights. They also had set up the European Coal and Steel Community, which merged with the European Common Market and Euratom in 1957. Initially, each had its own commission or high authority, council, parliament, and court—(later reduced to one each of these organs for the three institutions) for the integration of Western Europe. Thus, in Santiago, as a result of a synthesis of drafts submitted by several countries (Brazil, Colombia, Chile, Ecuador, El Salvador, Uruguay, and Venezuela), Resolution VIII requested from the Inter-American Juridical Committee or the Inter-American Council of Jurists the preparation of a draft Convention on Human Rights and on the "creation of an Inter-American Court for the Protection of Human Rights and of other organizations appropriate for the protection and observance of those rights." The Resolution also created the Inter-American Commission on Human Rights (IACHR, mentioned earlier).

While the draft Convention on Human Rights was being prepared by the Inter-American Council of Jurists in its fourth meeting, the Council of the OAS set up IACHR on September 10, 1959. The 1959 draft Convention on Human Rights is divided into six parts. Part I of the convention distinguishes between civil and political rights (Chapter I), and among economic, social, and cultural rights (Chapter II). Chapter I thus includes such essential rights as freedom of thought, reply to libel and defamation, marriage and family. Political rights, included participation in public affairs, universal suffrage, and access to public service. An exception is Article 19, dealing with the suspension of rights in time of crisis. Chapter II includes such rights as the right to employment, healthy working and living conditions, reasonable working hours, protection of the family, free education, and private property. Article 33 (1), states that no provisions of this convention "shall be interpreted as granting to any state, group, or person, any right to engage in activities or to perform acts aimed at the destruction of the rights and freedoms recognized in this Convention."[12]

Part II refers to the enforcement agencies: the Inter-American Commission for the Protection of Human Rights and an Inter-American Court of Human Rights. Part III covers the terms, methods of selection, and size of the commission, along with its organization and procedures. Part IV deals with the Inter-American Court of Human Rights, which is to have an equal number of judges to the parties to the convention, but with no more than nine judges sitting in any one case. The court would have nine-year terms that would overlap. It may only act when the commission has failed in its endeavors. Under the convention, either governments, acting on their own or on behalf of an individual, or the commission may refer cases to the Court.

Finally, the general provisions of Part V deal with information to be supplied by the commission, allocation of expenses for both the commission and the court, and diplomatic immunities. The last part, Part VI, on "Special Clauses," states that the convention goes into effect after seven ratifications, and thereafter for each ratifying state as its ratification is deposited. The convention could be terminated and amended; in the former case, after five years on one year's notice, and in the latter, by a special conference if requested by one-third of the parties.

At the time of the Council of Jurists' approval of the draft convention, there were reservations by Argentina, the United States, and Mexico. The Argentine reservations referred to Part II (Organs); the United States declared that individual rights were a matter of the states, not the federal government, and Mexico explained its abstention, since in its view the draft convention had not been sufficiently studied because it restricted domestic jurisdiction and compromised the international responsibilities of the state.[13]

The entire subject did not stop there but rather continued to be a troublesome topic. The Eleventh International Conference of American States was supposed to approve the draft convention; since it was never held, the document went instead to the Second Special Inter-American Conference (Rio de Janeiro, November 17–30, 1965), which decided to refer it to the Council of the OAS, together with drafts from Chile and Uruguay. Within a year, the OAS Council was to receive the opinions of the IACHR and other organizations, and to amend the draft if advisable.

On January 11, 1966, the Council of the OAS referred Resolution XXIV to its Juridical–Political Committee; a few months later, IACHR decided to send the Chile and Uruguay draft conventions to the governments. Then, in May 1966, the OAS Council sent the three drafts to the IACHR and requested a report on the subject, as required by Resolution XXIV. Finally, in October 1966, the commission began its detailed study, and, as Margaret Ball commented, it was evident by that time that "the Convention would have greater responsibility for the draft Convention than would the Organization's legal bodies."[14]

The concept of an Inter-American Court of Human Rights continued to receive wide attention despite the many difficulties it encountered. When the American Convention on Human Rights, which established the Inter-American Court of Human Rights, went into force in 1978, the way was opened for the Court to function. It was finally established in 1979, through the Pact of San José. The court is an autonomous judicial institution whose purpose is to apply and interpret the American Convention on Human Rights of 1959. It is composed of seven jurists and its headquarters is in San José, Costa Rica.

There is a history behind the selection of Costa Rica as the seat of the Inter-American Court of Human Rights. In 1902 a Tribunal of Central American Arbitration was established in San José as a consequence of the Corinto Pact, which was drawn up to settle Central American disputes. The initiative had come from Nicaragua's strongman, José Santos Zelaya, who had ruled the country since 1893. The tribunal, however, was not successful in settling the many Central American conflicts. Central America, although aiming once more at unification, had little stability: Revolutionaries tried to unseat Guatemala's president, Manuel Estrada Cabrera (1898–1920), who was friendly to the United States; El Salvador supported the revolutionaries, as did Honduras, with the result that a war erupted between Guatemala and El Salvador. It was then that the United States became involved, since its interests in the area and in the Caribbean had increased following the Spanish American War of 1898. When its attempts at a peaceful solution failed, and as skirmishes increased in the area, the United States, with the friendly co-operation of Mexico's Porfirio Díaz (1876–1911), arranged the *Marblehead* meetings off the coast of El Salvador (1906). Both Díaz and Theodore Roosevelt were empowered by the Central Americans who, with the exception of Zelaya, attended these meetings, to arbitrate the disputes and settle them in a spirit of justice and equity. Zelaya opposed the *Marblehead* talks on the grounds that they were an illegal and unjustified intervention in Central American affairs; we should bear in mind that his ultimate goal was the formation of a Union of Central America under his leadership. In compliance with the *Marblehead* talks, a Central American conference took place in San José, Costa Rica (1906), which confirmed the Corinto Pact, reestablished the Tribunal of Central American Arbitration, and took additional steps toward some kind of union.[15] However, further trouble arose, with Nicaragua and Honduras on one side and Costa Rica, El Salvador, and Guatemala on the other. A Washington, D.C., conference on Central American Peace was held in 1907 whose key was the establishment of a Central American Court, "the most remarkable judicial organ in the world."[16] A treaty and some six conventions were signed and quickly ratified, so that they became the law of the land in Central America in 1908.[17] It was indeed remarkable that the Central Americans could sign and ratify these accords so quickly and thus make the Central American Court of Arbitration a successful institution. Although it was not the first of its kind, since the Hague Court of Arbitration had been in existence since 1899, it seemed to lead the way to more successful ventures regarding peace and security in Central America.

Many of the court's recommendations were an echo of some of the concepts launched by American delegations at the Second Hague Conference in 1907, but the idea of the court was more originally Central American. On May 25, 1908, the Central American Court of Justice, to be constituted for a ten-year period, was declared officially in existence in Cartago, Costa Rica.

The Court, despite mounting difficulties, was able to rule on ten cases. However, in two failures (1908 and 1912), the precedent was set that a nation or faction could disregard the court with impunity if it had the support of the United States. After Zelaya boycotted both the Marblehead talks (1906) and the Washington Conference (1907), the United States decided that it was time to get tough. Moreover, the Mexican Revolution of 1910 and the overthrow of Díaz a year later weakened the court. It was further diminished in its power by increasing U.S. involvement in Nicaragua, which was justified on the grounds of the Nicaraguan debt problem and Zelaya's nationalist resistance, which had also been a reason for opting in favor of Panama as a site for a transisthmian canal. By 1909, a revolution broke out that quickly led to Zelaya's downfall when the United States wasted no time in recognizing the revolution's leader, Juan Estrada, as head of the new Nicaraguan government. To prevent further turmoil, the dissatisfied Nicaraguans, led by General Emiliano Chamorro, requested U.S. military intervention in order to halt the violence in the country, and President William H. Taft obliged by sending in the marines. They would remain in Nicaragua between 1909 and 1925 and then between 1926 and 1933. Chamorro was rewarded with an ambassadorship in Washington, where a series of agreements led to the Bryan-Chamorro Treaty of 1916. Basically, this treaty meant that Nicaragua accepted the status of a U.S. protectorate, giving the United States exclusive and perpetual rights over a transisthmian canal in the San Juan river and Lake Nicaragua, a ninety-nine-years' lease to the Caribbean Corn Islands, and a naval base in the Gulf of Fonseca in the Pacific; in return Nicaragua received $3 million. Although the treaty was never ratified by the U.S. Senate, the United States acted as if there was indeed a protectorate over Nicaragua. Needless to say, the treaty was attacked by Costa Rica, El Salvador, and Honduras. When the United States refused to abide by the decisions of the Central American Court, even declining to appear before the Permanent Tribunal at The Hague, the end of the Court was in sight.

The Central American Court of Justice died in 1917 at the hands of the United States but nonetheless remained as an ideal that continued to inspire not only Central Americans but many other people as well.[18]

The Inter-American Drug Abuse Control Commission (CICAD)

In view of the increased threat posed by drugs, with their illegal production, illicit traffic, and unlawful consumption, which affect all humanity and threaten society in every country, the organization began to discuss this problem in the 1980s and to take the necessary measures to unite the thirty-one member states in a common effort. On the suggestion of the Permanent Council, the Fourteenth Regular Session of the General Assembly in 1984 decided on Resolution 699, which declared drug trafficking a crime and convoked an Inter-American Specialized Conference on Drug Trafficking. Brazil offered to host the conference, which was then held in Rio de Janeiro in April 1986.

The Conference decided unanimously on the Program of Action of Rio. The "Inter-American Program of Action of Rio de Janeiro against the Illicit Use and Production of Narcotic Drugs and Psychotropic Substances and Traffic Therein," adopted April 24, 1986, was approved in November of the same year by the OAS General Assembly in Guatemala, when CICAD was also set up in order to implement it. Furthermore, at that General Assembly the Inter-American Alliance to Combat Illicit Drug Trafficking was launched.

The Inter-American Action Program is based on the following principles and objectives:

1. The main goal of socioeconomic development is to improve standards of living and the quality of life; therefore, policies that reduce the demand for drugs, prevent drug abuse, and combat unlawful trafficking in drugs are essential for development.

2. Socioeconomic development cannot flourish in an environment lacking conditions that promote personal dignity, democracy, and state security.

3. There is an interrelationship between the prevention of drug abuse, the well-being of the individual, and socioeconomic development. The Program of Action reflects recognition by the inter-American community of the importance of that interrelationship.

4. Socioeconomic development must include a reduction in the demand for drugs, the prevention of drug abuse, and the combat of unlawful trafficking, and such policies must be consistent with human rights, individual rights and liberties, respect for traditions and customs of national or regional groups, and environmental protection.

5. Recommendations made under the Action Program must take into account "the imperative need for respect for the sovereignty of nations in determining their

policies to reduce the demand for drugs, prevent drug abuse, and combat drug trafficking."

6. Drug trafficking is a global phenomenon that threatens all peoples and states.

7. Bilateral and multilateral cooperation is, therefore, a necessity and should be carried out free of pressures of any kind.[19]

The objectives of the Action Program are not only to increase the cooperation between the various member states but also to strengthen their capacity to fight back, to reduce the demand for drugs, and to prevent drug abuse. The exchange of information, training of specialized personnel, and mutual assistance are all part of the new OAS program.

After stating its principles and objectives, the Inter-American Specialized Conference on Traffic in Narcotic Drugs recommended certain actions to achieve its goals, which were listed in four chapters. In chapter I it listed actions to prevent the improper demand for and abuse of narcotic drugs and psychotropic substances, such as the carrying out of epidemiological and other relevant studies to identify the causes and prevalence of drug abuse; the promotion of studies to increase knowledge of the most appropriate ways of making society aware of the causes and effects of drug abuse; the promotion of programs for the treatment and rehabilitation of drug addicts, as well as the promotion of primary prevention campaigns through education, social welfare, and health departments; and the establishment of mechanisms in the appropriate government agencies for supervising and controlling the production, marketing, and use of legal drugs, among others. In chapter II the conference recommended actions to combat the unlawful production and supplying of narcotic drugs and psychotropic substances, such as development and expansion of mechanisms for an exchange of information on the structures of illegal marketing with the study and possible approval of draft legislation to prosecute unlawful drug trafficking, to forfeit assets derived from or used to facilitate drug trafficking, and to treat as a punishable offense the acquisition, possession, use, or so-called laundering of assets that are known to be the proceeds of unlawful drug trafficking. It also recommended the establishment of rigid controls for the manufacture, importation, exportation, transport, and marketing of solvents, precursors, and chemical products essential for narcotic drugs, as well as the establishment of judicial, police, and customs cooperation mechanisms among member states; the substitution of illegal crops and the eradication of such illegal crops—as defined by each state—from which narcotic drugs and psychotropic substances may be extracted; and research in order to develop biological methods for the eradication of illegal crops, among others.

In chapter III the conference recommended general measures to combat the illicit use and production of narcotic drugs and psychotropic substances and traffic therein, such as the establishment of central agencies at the national level that are charged with the elaboration of national plans, policies, and programs. Finally, in chapter IV, in order to help the member states to implement the actions detailed in those three chapters, the conference recommended to the General Assembly of the OAS the establishment of an Inter-American Drug Control Commission (CICAD). Moreover, it recommended to the Inter-American Juridical Committee, that it conduct the necessary juridical research to help the member states on four levels: to adopt bilateral or multilateral instruments against drug abuse and unlawful trafficking in drugs, such as extradition procedures and cooperation among a variety of authorities, and compatible national laws; to the General Secretariat of the OAS that it establish a data bank on drug abuse and unlawful trafficking in drugs, set up training centers and a documentation center, and increase coordination and cooperation between the OAS member states, the respective UN agencies, the South American Accord on Narcotic Drugs and Psychotropic Substances (Acuerdo Sudamericano de Estupefacientes Psicotropicales, or ASEP), the Caribbean Community, and other subregional entities. It also asked the secretariat to propose draft statutues and regulations of CICAD and to prepare an annual report on the drug problem to be submitted to the member states; moreover, it asked that body to submit to the Sixteenth Regular Session of the General Assembly of the OAS a study on financing mechanisms. Finally, the conference also urged the closest cooperation with other specialized organizations (such as IAII, IACI, IACW, IICA, and PAHO).[20]

As a consequence of the decisions of the Inter-American Specialized Conference on Trafficking in Narcotic Drugs, the Sixteenth Regular Session of the General Assembly established CICAD which, since its inception, has been one of the two "Other Entities." CICAD is thus the youngest of the agencies created by the OAS. Its first meeting was in 1987, and in that same year the members of CICAD were elected for a three-year term. Originally it was made up of eleven of the thirty-one member states, but in the 1988 General Assembly the membership was increased to twenty in view of the great interest. So far, the following states are members: Antigua and Barbuda, Argentina, the Bahamas, Bolivia, Brazil, Chile, Colombia, Guatemala, Jamaica, Mexico, Nicaragua, Panama, Paraguay, Peru, the United States, Uruguay, and Venezuela.

CICAD has a secretariat of twelve and an administrative budget of under $1 million a year; however, even though the Action Program of Rio covered all the fields in the fight against drugs, the available funds were not sufficient to cover all these areas. This, in turn, forced CICAD, which was already at the very beginning of its operations, to concentrate on selected priority targets. The annual budget of $1 million hardly covers the needs since already in 1989 the approved plans of action were running as high as three times that amount and called for additional professional resources. Hence, fund-raising has already become one of CICAD's main preoccupations.[21]

To support the many actions throughout the hemisphere, CICAD has developed the Inter-American Information Center for the use of the member states and private organizations. The center is also organizing an Inter-American Network of regional, subregional, and national information centers, for which CICAD could serve as clearinghouse. Moreover, there is a plan to standardize data collection in the hemisphere, since without some standardization, a data bank would not be able to provide the necessary services. There are also Inter-American Training Centers, and, as the executive secretary of CICAD stated, his institution does not wish to duplicate efforts of organizations such as the United Nations Fund for Drug Abuse Control and the U.S. government's program to reduce drug crop production in Latin America through crop substitution and income diversification projects.[22]

CICAD identified two critical problem areas: first, demand reduction, and second, improving the capability of governments to act effectively against the illegal drug syndicates. In view of the above-mentioned shortage of funds, CICAD established five priority lines of action: legal development, education for prevention, community action efforts, Inter-American Information System, and Inter-American Statistical Systems. Its accomplishments in the few years since its inauguration have been many. Thus, in legal development, it has supported national legislation on critical problems, including money laundering, asset seizure, controls on drug precursors, regulation of legal production, and extradition; it has also harmonized national legislation among member states, trained law enforcement officials, and enhanced the effectiveness of the judicial process. In prevention education, CICAD has helped to set up national programs of all participating countries that have adopted the proposed strategy and planning, either partially or totally; it has been instrumental in creating the Argentina–Uruguay Binational Prevention Program and has helped the incorporation of drug abuse prevention programs into the Caribbean Regional Drug Abuse Abatement Programme, which was approved by the Ministers of Education of CARICOM. In community mobilization, it sponsored the First Latin American Workshop on Narcotics Public Awareness, in Santo Domingo, January 1989; it has also developed training manuals and materials on social marketing. Moreover, it prepared videos in English and Spanish of television spots used in various member countries, and it has detailed media programs prepared by each participating country. It has also sponsored the training of community leaders in the English-speaking Caribbean and parents from slum areas in Peru, the development by an Argentine nonprofit organization of a program to extend a regional network of nongovernmental organizations (NGOs) and training centers for their staff, and a multicountry project to support NGO efforts to deal with the exploding drug problem among abandoned street children in South America.

Finally, the Inter-American Information System that CICAD set up consists of the Inter-American Documentation Center and the Inter-American

Data Bank, both located at CICAD headquarters in Washington, D.C. The Documentation Center is a clearinghouse for drug abuse prevention materials, while the Data Bank collects raw data and statistics on all aspects of drug trafficking and abuse in the OAS Member States. Both the Inter-American Documentation Center and the Inter-American Data Bank represent important links to CICAD's goals.

9

The Last Two Decades and the Protocol
of Cartagena de Indias (1970–1991)

POLITICAL PROBLEMS

Infused with new vigor and enthusiasm, the OAS had plunged ahead in 1948 when the Rio Treaty and the charter modernized the inter-American system and Latin America had obtained a greater role in the organization. The inter-American system thus had adjusted at the time to the new international reality of the postwar era. Very soon, however, this new energy dissipated in view of a variety of reasons, and of these, the gradual dismantling of the Good Neighbor policy and the new global role of the United States were by far the most important ones. There were also the increasing Latin American economic and financial woes, some a consequence of the new world realities and others self-imposed by erroneous socialist policies, which, by the mid-1950s, became ever more difficult to solve. The speed with which the entire world was changing had to lead to new adjustments of the inter-American system. The member states realized then that the Charter of 1948 had not provided the adequate tools in order to meet the challenge of the age. Thus, the Inter-American Conference, which had met every five years, could no longer provide the answer as it had since the inception of the Pan American movement, and this was just one of many issues. Moreover, problems that seemed to have been solved for good, like nonintervention, surfaced again, and others, like the new revolutionary activities and subversion, as a result both of increasingly deteriorating social and economic conditions and ideological conflicts, required new forceful approaches. The result of this mounting dissatisfaction was the Protocol of Buenos Aires of 1967, which went into effect in 1970.

The revised charter was supposed to give the OAS a new lease on life, and indeed, in a new and complex period, it created a new organization with new energy that attempted to regain lost ground and achieve the goals that the new international order required. The new realities of the 1970s and 1980s demanded even more leadership and imagination, and the Latin American governments, at least, expected a major role from the organization at a time when the world was changing from a bipolar situation to a variety of major political and economic centers of power that in the meantime, had arisen and spread with increasing dynamism. Besides the United States and Canada, these included Western Europe, the Soviet bloc, China, the Middle East, and, last but not least, Japan. Unfortunately, the role of the OAS was made more difficult in the decades of the 1970s and 1980s since it also reflected the weakening status of Latin America, and it was no secret that it had decreased relative to the rest of the world. It was fashionable at the time to speak of the centers of power and of the periphery, and Latin America was certainly a part of the periphery, a situation that was echoed in the organization and was compounded by the United States, which had switched over the years from the Good Neighbor policy to that of Fair Neighbor, from benign neglect to the policies of the cold shoulder. Thus, the OAS struggled along, but despite its many achievements, it could not, under the circumstances, reach all its goals. After all, the organization reflected not only Latin American and Caribbean realities but also the relationship between the United States and its weaker neighbors to the South.

The 1970s and 1980s, the years of presidents Richard Nixon, Gerald Ford, Jimmy Carter, Ronald Reagan, and George Bush, saw in Latin America the continuation of several military governments that had come to power for basically two interrelated reasons: to solve the increasingly worsening economic and social situation and to combat alien ideologies and subversion. This was the case with Argentina (1966–1973; 1976–1983), Brazil (1964–1985), Chile (1973–1989), Peru (1968–1980), and Uruguay (1973–1984), with some remnants like Nicaragua (1936–1979) and Paraguay (1954–1989). Major events in the 1970s included the two Panama Canal treaties. These were due largely to President Carter's sensitivity to Latin American wishes, since it was he who was willing to give up outdated U.S. "rights" to both the Canal Zone and the Panama Canal, something President Reagan wanted under all circumstances to undo, as did President Bush to some extent through his attack on Panama in December 1989. The treaties were thereby not invalidated, but U.S. influence in the country was restored. The other major event was the Nicaraguan Revolution ending the long dictatorship of the Somozas in that country but then unleashing a horrible civil war, which was paid for and managed by the United States in order to control Central America. However, instead, the influence of the United States in the entire hemisphere decreased with its Central American policies, the South Atlantic war, and other misguided policies, a fact that was obviously visible in the OAS.

In the 1950s and 1960s, the OAS had to face the increasing turmoil in the Caribbean and in Central America, which increasingly swept over South America as well, eventually leading to U.S. intervention in Guatemala (1954), where the leftist regime of Jacobo Arbenz was forced out in 1954, and later to the Cuban Revolution, with its extraordinary consequences. It also led to the illfated Bay of Pigs disaster (1960) and the Cuban Missile Crisis of 1962, and to the new U.S. intervention, this time with military force, in the Dominican Republic shortly after the fall and assassination of Rafael Trujillo in 1965. The OAS could not stop U.S. interventions but tried to soften the blow. Its answer at that time was a greater emphasis on representative democracy and human rights.

Although the situation in both Guatemala and the Dominican Republic returned to relative normal—in the latter case, due mostly to the elder statesman and distinguished former vice president Joaquín Balaguer the Cuban situation kept the OAS quite busy. The OAS had played a small role in the Guatemalan case in 1954, and likewise in regard to the early stages of the Cuban Revolution. This changed with the Cuban Missile Crisis, when the OAS gave full support to the U.S. government in its most serious confrontation with both Cuba and the Soviet Union. In the later case of the Dominican Republic, the OAS became increasingly involved. It was in a kind of competition with the United Nations, but, angered by this new U.S. intervention, it refused to accept an Inter-American Force as suggested by Washington.

On the other hand, the Cuban question would be on the agenda of several Meetings of Consultation in the 1960s, but the policy of isolating the Castro regime was unrealistic and did not prosper. As late as 1968, the Twelfth Meeting of Consultation dealt with Cuban subversive activities, after having addressed the same problem in 1961, 1962, 1964, and 1967, although gradually Latin America changed its attitude, realizing that, first of all, the Cuban problem was more a U.S.-Cuban affair than one affecting the entire hemisphere, and second, that the policy of isolating Cuba was a failure and inconsistant with other U.S. policies. This explains the attempt in the 1970s to change course. The Fifteenth Meeting of Consultation attempted to discontinue the measures taken against Cuba in 1964. The respective resolution did not obtain the necessary two-thirds majority, and thus the situation remained unchanged for another year. In 1975, through the Sixteenth Meeting of Consultation it was resolved that every country had the freedom to decide on resumption of relations with Cuba in accordance with each country's national policies and interests. The problem thus vanished from the agenda of future OAS gatherings.

With the 1970s the OAS began a new life centered on the regular annual sessions of the General Assembly and basically in line with the tradition of the United Nations. The organization had to deal with several important inter-American issues and thus continued its activities to further the cause of peace and security in the hemisphere. It was engaged in all minor and major inter-American conflicts and confrontations, even though there were cases where it was helpless and could do little or nothing. Obviously, in some cases it did better than in others.

The "Soccer War" between Honduras and El Salvador, 1969

The OAS played a major role in this conflict, proving instrumental in the withdrawal of Salvadorean troops from Honduras and in the reestablishment of peace among the two neighbors. The conflict was the subject of the Thirteenth Meeting of Consultation (1969–1980). There were two phases, both in 1969, and some twenty-one plenary sessions. Still, the conflict dragged on, but in 1976, through an agreement signed at the General Secretariat of the OAS in Washington, D.C., between El Salvador and Honduras, both countries accepted the good offices of a mediator for the purpose of reestablishing peace and friendly relations. Peace was finally achieved on November 17, 1980, the year this Thirteenth Meeting of Consultation was formally closed.[1]

The Dispute between Ecuador and the United States Concerning Fishing Jurisdiction and the Extent of Territorial Seas, 1971

In 1971 the OAS delved into a very complex question for which the Fourteenth Meeting of Consultation was convoked: the dispute between Ecuador and the United States concerning the claim of Ecuador to have fishing jurisdiction over an area of up to 200 miles from its shores. Latin American countries, particularly Chile and Peru, sided with Ecuador. Although the case was never officially closed, it was basically resolved in favor of the right of states to proclaim an extension of their territorial seas for the protection of what they considered to be their fishing resources.

The Argentine–Chilean Issue of the Beagle Channel, 1971– 1972 through 1985

The OAS was not involved in this serious case since the issue never resulted in an armed confrontation, although at one point it came very close (1981–1982). Thus, the issue of the Beagle Channel was handled outside the sphere of the OAS and through papal mediation (Cardenal Saporé) with the contribution of ideas of the Uruguayan political scientist Bernardo Quagliotti de Bellis. Although an old problem, it was finally solved under Argentine President Raúl Alfonsín in an Argentine–Chilean accord of the year 1984. The accord recognized the Chilean claim to the three islands of Picton, Lennox, and Nueva but restated the accepted bioceanic principle of "Argentina in the Atlantic, Chile in the Pacific"; in other words, leaving the sea for the Argentines and the islands for the Chileans.[2] The Papal Arbitration Award of 1984 took into consideration preceding treaties, especially the Border Treaty of 1881 and the Additional and Explanatory Protocol of 1893 (consolidated in the *Pactos de Mayo* of 1902), as well as the British Arbitral Award of 1971, which was denounced by Argentina the next year. The case was thus totally outside the OAS.

The Nicaraguan Revolution and the Fall of the Somoza Regime, 1978

Just as in the case of the earlier political changes in the Dominican Republic, the decline of the Somoza regime also led to turmoil and civil war. Two Meetings of Consultation (the Seventeenth and the Eighteenth) dealt with the revolutionary activities in Nicaragua, where the Somoza regime was eventually toppled, and with the confrontation between Costa Rica and Nicaragua. The OAS played an important role and essentially helped in the collapse of the dictatorial regime in Nicaragua.[3]

The Peruvian-Ecuadorian Confrontation in the El Condor Mountain Range, 1981

This represented a relatively minor issue between the two countries, which was the subject of the Nineteenth Meeting of Consultation (1981), relating to some military operations in the border area of El Condor. Given the historic problems between the two countries, especially after Ecuador lost its Amazonian area in 1942, the military operations in the El Condor mountain range could become serious. The OAS successfully solved the crisis through its intervention in 1981.

The War of the South Atlantic (the War of the Malvinas/ Falklands), 1982

The OAS tried its best in this very serious confrontation but was unable to force a peaceful solution when the British prime minister did not want one and instead ordered the destruction of the Argentine cruiser *General Belgrano*, although it was not in the war zone and at the same moment Peruvian President Fernando Belaúnde Terry was submitting a new peace plan. The serious problem of the War of the South Atlantic was the subject of the Twentieth Meeting of Consultation (Washington, D.C., 1982), where Argentina received almost unanimous support from the member states and the United States remained isolated (it abstained from the voting) in view of the incredible switch from neutrality to open support for the British, which violated both the spirit and the letter of all inter-American agreements. Furthermore, the OAS called for negotiations between the parties after the end of the War of the South Atlantic. The islands had been Spanish until 1811, and Spanish sovereignty was not only recognized by the British Crown in the Nootka Sound Convention of 1790 but exercised through thirty-two Spanish governors (1773–1811).[4] Argentina inherited the islands in accordance with international law—the *ius Uti Possidetis, Ita Possideatis* ("As you held territory in 1810, so you shall keep it as your property")—and occupied them in 1820 through a New England Yankee in the service of the United Provinces of South America, Colonel David Jewett.[5]

In 1829, a civil and military authority was established by Luis Vernet; this was the first such Argentine combined authority. The British illegally seized the islands in 1833, however, and Argentina could do nothing except protest.[6] The United States looked the other way when Argentina attempted to invoke the Monroe Doctrine. In 1982, the Argentines tried to recover the islands in a military invasion because their patience had run thin after some twenty years of negotiations. The attempt failed, especially when Britain was aided by the United States. Right after the end of the war, with its seventy-four days of Argentine occupation of the islands, the OAS, in the Twelfth Regular Session of the General Assembly, called again for negotiations to solve the issue. As Wayne S. Smith said recently, the solution of the problem "will require a political settlement satisfactory to all sides, the islanders included."[7] This call for negotiations was repeated in all the following regular sessions of the General Assembly: the Thirteenth (1983), the Fourteenth (1984), the Fifteenth (1985), the Sixteenth (1986), the Seventeenth (1987), the Eighteenth (1988), the Nineteenth (1989), and the Twentieth (1990).

Bolivian Maritime Problems, 1979

This issue is one of the oldest Latin American problems that is still awaiting a satisfactory solution. The Bolivian claim for an outlet to the sea is justified and legitimate. The OAS not only issued the Declaration of La Paz (1979) at the Ninth Regular Session of the General Assembly—exactly one hundred years after the Pacific War (1879–1883), which led to the loss of the Bolivian territories on the Pacific Ocean in 1883—but it also repeated a call for a solution of this long overdue issue, just as in the case of the Malvinas. It thus appealed for a solution of the Bolivian maritime problems at the Tenth Regular Session of the General Assembly, and again pointed to the problem at the Fourteenth Regular Session of the General Assembly in 1984. It reiterated the necessity to solve this question in the next regular sessions, from the Fifteenth (1985) to the Twentieth (1990).

Central America and the Nicaraguan Civil War, 1985–1990

It was obvious that the OAS would also try to intervene in the Central American crisis of the 1980s and find a peaceful settlement, but here solutions were difficult to come by. In its endeavors, the organization was handicapped and basically derailed by the obstinate U.S. policy that saw in the Sandinista revolution a communist cancer that had to be radically extirpated. Moreover, this fundamental rule also applied to any other revolutionary activity in other parts of Central America (e.g., El Salvador or Guatemala). When the Latin Americans, who interpreted events in Central America differently and saw them not as a Soviet-inspired and -aided foreign intervention but as a purely social and economic problem rooted in Central American conditions, they tried to find a Latin American solution through the Contadora Group (Panama, Colombia, Venezuela, and Mexico) and the Contadora Support Group (Argentina, Brazil, Peru, and Uruguay). The OAS cooperated and gave the effort its full support, but this was in vain, since the United States insisted on war and victory via the Contras, a mercenary group organized and paid by the U.S. government.

At the Fifteenth Regular Session of the General Assembly (meeting in Cartagena de Indias, 1985), the OAS took notice of a communication of the Contadora Group with regard to efforts on behalf of peace in Central America. In the next regular session of the General Assembly, the Sixteenth, the OAS issued a statement of solidarity and support to the People and Government of El Salvador; at the seventeenth regular session, 1987, it again took notice of a communication of the Foreign Ministers of the Contadora Group and the Contadora Support Group on their peace negotiations in Central America. The Contadora Support Group had been set up by the aforementioned countries in order to give the negotiations of the Contadora Group more weight and to signal Washington that this was a Latin American affair aiming at a Latin American solution of a Latin American problem. However, this did not change matters at all. At the same meeting, the OAS also dealt with the increasingly sad problem of refugees in its resolution on the situation of the Central American refugees and regional efforts to resolve their problems. The most outspoken attempt by the OAS to aid the peace endeavors against U.S. wishes was the public applause that this regular session of the General Assembly gave to the five Central American presidents in signing the "Procedures for Establishing a Firm and Lasting Peace in Central America."

In 1988, at the Eighteenth Regular Session of the General Assembly, the OAS again received a report from the Contadora Group and publicly took note of it, issuing two resolutions: one, the communication from the foreign ministers of the Contadora Group and the Support Group in their peace negotiations in Central America; and the other, the "Report on the Procedures for Establishing a Firm and Lasting Peace in Central America." The OAS pursued its peace policies again at the Nineteenth Regular Session of the General Assembly when it took up a new report on the procedures for establishing a firm and lasting peace in Central America. Finally, at the centennial commemorative Twentieth Regular Session of the General Assembly in Asunción, Paraguay, in 1990, the OAS again delved into the search for peace in Central America. It was obvious that any solution that was contrary to the wishes of the Reagan and Bush administrations would not work, but the problems were somehow solved in a different way, through the elections of 1990 in Nicaragua which, to the surprise of most people, ended the Sandinista regime in Nicaragua. To some extent they were also solved in El Salvador through the electoral victories of the rightist party, ARENA—the National Republican Alliance. In the 1980s the United States had backed the Christian Democrat José Napoleón Duarte who won the presidency in 1984 with great expectations, which, however, were not fulfilled. The civil war thus continued with ever more ferocity, and Salvadorean society became increasingly polarized: on the one side was the extreme rightist party ARENA under Roberto d'Aubuisson; on the other was the leftist guerrillas FLNFM (the Farabundo Martí National Liberation Front) under Guillermo Ungo and Rubén Zamora, with Duarte's Christian Democrats squeezed in the middle. Duarte's retreat on human rights and his personal woes (his daughter Inés was kidnapped by the FLNFM, his negotiation for her release, and his cancer), compounded by increasing corruption in government, finally resulted in ARENA's victory in the elections of March 19, 1989, with their new leader Alfredo Cristiani. The collapse of Communism in the Soviet Union and Eastern Europe and the fall of the Berlin Wall also contributed to ARENA's victory. With the victory, U.S. policy in El Salvador collapsed, as it did in Nicaragua a year later. Thus, the United States was forced to recognize both elections, but there were differences: In El Salvador, the guerrillas had been weakened by world events; in Nicaragua, the Sandinistas remained a powerful opposition.

THE NEW LEADERSHIP

It was within this framework of changing times that the OAS continued its activities during the last two decades. In the period of the original charter, three Latin American secretaries general had followed each other: Alberto Lleras Camargo, former president of Colombia (1948–1954); Carlos Dávila, former president of Chile (1954–1955); and José Antonio Mora Otero, former Uruguayan Ambassador to the United States (1956–1966). In those years, the assistant secretaries general came from the United States: William Manger (1948–1958) and William Sanders (1958–1968).

With the decade beginning in 1970, this picture changed and the role of assistant secretary general was reserved to the smaller countries of Central America and the Caribbean. Understandably, with the loss for the United States of the highest position in the organization, while at the same time it was required to pay the highest quota, another reason for disregarding the OAS arose.

With the decades of the 1970s and 1980s new individuals and new countries came to the top of the organization as secretary general: Galo Plaza Lasso, former president of Ecuador (1968–1975); Alejandro Orfila, former ambassador of Argentina to Japan and to the United States (1975–1984); and after 1984, João Clemente Baena Soares, from Brazil. The position of assistant secretary general was given first to Miguel Rafael Urquía from El Salvador (1968–1978), then to another Central American, Jorge Luis Zelaya Coronado, and then to Val T. McComie from Barbados. It is now Christopher R. Thomas from Trinidad and Tobago.

Just as the Meetings of Consultation give us a good overview of the most urgent political problems that the OAS faced in these twenty years, the annual reports of the secretary general as well as the proceedings of the regular and special sessions of the General Assembly obviously tell us the extraordinary variety of activities in which the organization was engaged. There were the usual problems with which the General Assembly had to cope in its annual sessions, such as convocations of Specialized Conferences; renewal of vacant positions in the various Specialized Agencies and Commissions; approval of the program budget of the OAS, as well as that of the various Specialized Agencies and Commissions; revision of the regulations and statutes of some agencies, including those of the General Assembly (1972) and the Permanent Council (1976); the strengthening of the inter-American system and the principles of nonintervention and self-determination (1977); and difficulties in collecting the payments of member states (1971). Moreover, there were numerous other important subject matters that drew the attention of the organization and their top officials.

OBSERVER COUNTRIES AND NEW MEMBERS

Two important facts emerged in these two decades. One was the new phenomenon of accepting observers from countries that were not members of the organization. This question was first raised in the First Regular Session of the General Assembly in San José, Costa Rica, which also dealt with the brain drain from Latin America and the possibility of establishing a youth office within the OAS, and decided to emphasize the activities of CIECC. The first such observers were then accepted in 1972 (from Belgium, Canada, France, the Federal Republic of Germany, Guyana, Israel, Italy, the Netherlands, and Spain). In the meantime, Canada and Guyana became full members of the OAS in 1989 and 1991, respectively, and hence, their respective observer status lapsed. Today, the organization counts some twenty-four permanent observer countries, a definite demonstration (if one is needed) of the growing importance of the OAS outside the Western Hemisphere.

The other important development was the admission of new members, which arose as the colonial areas of Britain and the Netherlands in the Caribbean achieved independence. In some cases this was a thorny issue, since several Latin American states either totally or partially claimed territory of these new nations. The Act of Washington of 1964 took care of the latter issue, or so it was thought, since it closed the door to membership in the organization to Belize and Guyana. However, this prescription would eventually be overruled in the later Protocol of Cartagena de Indias.

The admission of new members of the Caribbean was a revolution in itself. Since 1889–1890, the Pan American movement and the inter-American system signified a more-or-less homogeneous relationship: it was a club of some eighteen Spanish-speaking republics, one Portuguese-speaking nation, and one French-speaking country all facing the "Colossus of the North"; in other words, the Organization of American States and its forerunner, the Union of American Republics, have traditionally provided a meeting ground for the twenty Latin American republics to find solutions to common problems with the powerful United States. Although weak in comparison to the United States, the Latin American bloc represented a continental majority, with an impact that was quite formidable. For some eighty years this group of nations, despite its ups and downs, and the numerous and predictable U.S. interventions, had grown into a kind of family that now seemed to be threatened by what looked like a real explosion of little Caribbean islands of different cultural and racial background and with political and economic ties outside the hemisphere. No doubt, the Commonwealth Caribbean as well as other Caribbean areas, should they become independent, had a right to become members of the organization, since geography could not be denied. However, what would happen if, in a few years, some eighteen Commonwealth Caribbean countries became full members of the OAS? Full membership did not mean only signing and ratifying the charter, but also being part of the Rio Treaty, and again it must be pointed out that the OAS does not have the veto and would never accept it. As stated earlier, decisions in the inter-American system are by simple majority, except in important questions where a two-thirds majority is required. Unlike the Security Council of the United Nations, the OAS has never had the veto; thus no one country can block decisions as in the world organization. In other words, with so many small Caribbean countries of different cultural backgrounds, decisions could be influenced, if not managed, by bigger and mightier countries. This thought weighed particularly heavy in regard to the Rio Treaty.

If the Latin American point of view had been one of increasing apprehension, especially in view of the voting power that can be manipulated by outside influences, at the same time, over the years, the governments of the region have drawn certain conclusions and thus have come up with positive solutions. The Latin Americans realized that a simple exclusion was neither morally right nor politically sound. Thus, exclusion of non-Hispanic Caribbean areas was neither envisioned nor practiced. This was already seen with clarity in such a Latin American private organization as SOLAR—the Sociedad Latinoamericana de Estudios Sobre America Latina y El Caribe, the professional parallel organization to the Latin American Studies Association in the United States, in which the Caribbean is fully represented.

The Commonwealth Caribbean problem that arose in the 1960s thus contained two fundamental issues: one, the admission of non-Hispanic countries, in view of their different background, their link to extracontinental organizations, and their sheer number, would change the character of the Organization of American States, and two, the issue would be compounded by territories that, as stated earlier, were wholly or partially claimed by several Latin American countries. Furthermore, the conflict of the South Atlantic in 1982 showed clearly what many observers had feared earlier: In 1982 the only Caribbean country that had ratified the Rio Treaty was Trinidad and Tobago, and it abstained, as did the United States, Chile, and Colombia in the famous Resolution of that year (Twentieth Meeting of Consultation). The Latin Americans opted for a variety of solutions: one, if possible, to strengthen the OAS, and two, also in view of other reasons, to set up their own Latin American organizations, such as the Contadora Group, the Contadora Support Group, and the Cartagena Group, the last of which was intended to deal jointly with the huge debt problem.

The Charter of the OAS of 1948 had made no provisions for new members because none was foreseen within the old areas of the Spanish and Portuguese empires except in case of secession, and the Act of Washington of 1964, later incorporated into the Protocol of Buenos Aires (which revised the original charter) took care of the matter as it was seen at the time. It was a practical solution that would deny access to Belize and Guyana. Thus, Barbados as well as Trinidad and Tobago became members in 1967, followed in 1969 by Jamaica. Others then followed: Grenada in 1975; Suriname in 1977; the Commonwealth of Dominica and St. Lucia, both in 1979; St. Vincent and the Grenadines as well as Antigua and Barbuda in 1981; the Commonwealth of the Bahamas in 1982; and St. Christopher and Nevis in 1984.

It would be interesting to hear also the Caribbean point of view, and nobody would be more qualified to represent it than the present assistant secretary general of the OAS, Val T. McComie, whose *patria chica* (country in a smaller context) is Barbados and whose *patria grande* (country in a larger context) is the Caribbean, the Commonwealth Caribbean. In a very important speech to the Center of Colombian Studies and the Economic Society of the Friends of the Country (in October 1985 in Bogotá, just before the General Assembly of the OAS was to meet in Cartagena de Indias, Colombia, in December 1985, to deal with the new revisions to the charter), he discussed in depth the problems of the traditional OAS and the new Caribbean members.[8] He mentioned two fundamental difficulties that the early Commonwealth Caribbean nations, such as Barbados and Trinidad and Tobago in 1967 and Jamaica in 1969, already faced in the OAS in the 1960s. The first problem was the geographic, demographic, and economic size, which was a real challenge to the entire system as it had been conceived and put into practice since 1889–1890. In theory, the legal equality of states prevails, but the reality was quite different. The second problem was more subtle, since the Latin Americans wanted the Commonwealth Caribbean to define itself as Latin American, while the new Caribbean members wanted to reassert their independence. The assistant secretary general quite bluntly stated that it was a problem that so far had not been solved and was not related solely to those areas that are now independent but are claimed, in part or wholly, by some Latin American countries. The Commonwealth Caribbean still perceives the Organization of American States as a club that is exclusively for Latin Americans, the United States, and, possibly in the future, Canada. The Act of Washington had made that abundantly clear. The Commonwealth Caribbean did not like Article 8, which was incorporated in the Protocol of Buenos Aires of 1967 and reflected the Act of Washington of 1964. It stated that neither recommendation nor decision would be taken in regard to a request for membership by any political entity whose territory was subject, prior to December 1964, to a controversy or claim with an extracontinental state and one or more states of the Organization of American States as long as that conflict has not been settled. In his speech, McCowie mentioned that no international organization, except the Organization for the Prohibition of Nuclear Weapons in Latin America (OPANAL), had such a provision and that there was no reason for it. In the case of OPANAL, "it approaches the absurd."[9] He reiterated the Caribbean point of view that the Caribbean nations were opposed to Article 8 of the protocol since it represented a discrimination. What the Caribbean nations wanted was simply the elimination of Article 8, which then would put the OAS on the same level as the United Nations. Article 8 put the organization in opposition to the universal system. In sum, the Caribbean nations wanted the same degree of trust that they have in the United Nations where, immediately after independence, they were received as full members, while, for example, neither Guyana nor Belize were members of the OAS.

Ambassador McCowie mentioned in his speech the ideals and goals of the Caribbean, which are basically those of all other members of the organization: respect for law and human rights. He found it rather contradictory that the Protocol of Buenos Aires cited all kinds of economic, social, educational, scientific, and cultural norms but omitted those referring to human rights and obligations. He also delved into the two basic principles of the Organization of American States: representative democracy—which he wanted strengthened, defining it as ideological pluralism, and of nonintervention—which he interpreted as a necessary corollary of the inviolability of the fundamental rights of the state. The latter represented the basis needed so that the civilized coexistence between nations could be assured. Intervention into the domestic affairs of another state, including the application of sanctions, however, should be acceptable to the members of the Organization of American States in such cases where the intervention is carried out to reestablish the respect for human rights and where these rights had been violated and democracy had been interrupted or threatened. It is obvious that this attack on the principle of nonintervention, as it has been understood in Latin America (or at least a certain weakening of it), would be totally unacceptable to the region as a whole; moreover, it was quite obvious that he was speaking as a Bajan (i.e., a native of Barbados), since Barbados has, unquestionably, the deepest English tradition, with local assemblies that have been in place since the early seventeenth century. (After all, the "Little England" of the Caribbean was molded in British tradition, and, following the example first introduced in Virginia [1619], Barbados, as a Crown colony, was the first English colony in the Caribbean to be given the right to a legislative assembly in which the planters [obviously not the black slaves] could make their voices heard; thus Barbados demonstrated a historical legacy of representative government as it was known in the Caribbean in the seventeenth century.) Obviously, he had in mind the invasion of Grenada to restore democracy.

Finally, the assistant secretary general also dealt with the maintenance of peace, a very special desire for small and vulnerable nations like the new Caribbean states that are located in a strategically important region of the world. Hence, the Caribbean nations wanted the charter, in its revised form of 1985, to contain provisions for disarmament, and in general to stop the arms race, instead devoting more energies to the development of both Latin America and the Caribbean. Linked to the maintenance of peace were two further principles: the pacific settlement of controversies and collective security. He also called for a strengthening of the Pact of Bogotá.

In sum, the Caribbean nations, as seen through the eyes of the Caribbean assistant secretary general of the Organization of American States, called for policies that would eliminate past obstacles between Latin America and the Caribbean area. Among them, he listed the following:

1. The absence of hemispheric strategies to promote closer links and better understanding between the peoples of Latin America and the Caribbean—this lack of communication being a most serious factor in making cooperation difficult;

2. The consequences of the political, economic, and military links with extracontinental peoples and states;

3. The implications for the hemisphere of a nuclear power, particularly in view of the increasing demand for a nuclear disarmament in both regional and global spheres;

4. Finally, new standards for international economic relations must be worked out, since those established after World War II are obsolete and no longer realistic.[10]

The ambassador appealed for a new approach between Latin America and the Caribbean nations within the Organization of American States. The Caribbean nations had become members of the OAS in order to strengthen their interests; they believe that organizations are not static and that renewal or reorganization implies more than the revision of its fundamental instruments. Besides, as Ambassador McCowie stated, the fundamental interests of the Caribbean coincide with those of many Latin American nations and aim at achieving new attitudes and new behaviors that go far beyond the mere changes of the legal instruments and the administrative alterations that may be agreed upon. In other words, the Commonwealth Caribbean believes in the same principles that for so long have maintained the Organization of American States and its inter-American system: supremacy of law, in opposition to private or national interests, which furthers the wish for peace and security of all American nations; the promotion of a constructive and all-encompassing solidarity on behalf of the maintenance and defense of basic principles that define the system; and the rise of a spirit of full membership in the organization that would help as a basis for cooperation and harmony.

With the entry into force of the new revised Charter of the OAS, the Protocol of Cartagena de Indias of 1985, the door was also opened to Belize and Guyana, two countries whose membership was objected to by Guatemala and Venezuela, respectively. Article 8 states that membership in the OAS be confined "to independent States of the Hemisphere that were members of the United Nations as of December 10, 1985." This opened the door to Belize and Guyana, both of which became full members in 1991. It was the final (and right) solution, but it does close the door to the Falkland Islands should the British choose to give that region independence in the future.

In the meantime, and due to the changing world situation, those dire predictions of the 1960s and 1970s did not come true. On the contrary, the Caribbean countries, even though of a different background, found increasingly common ground with Latin America and thus narrowed the gap between them. On such issues as representative democracy, nonintervention, self-determination, the drug problem and the debt issue, and human rights, there is universal agreement, so that instead of divisiveness we encounter more of a common front.

A different membership was that held by Canada. The country was invited to join at the inception of the Pan American movement in 1889–1890, and although it had become independent in 1867, it remained very much aloof of the inter-American system. Since 1910, when today's General Secretariat building, the old Pan American Union palace, was inaugurated, there was also a chair with the name "Canada" and the Canadian coat-of-arms to be used in the old council room, but this did not happen; it caught a lot of dust before it was rediscovered in the basement. Neither World War I nor World War II changed the situation: Canada was still too attached to the British Empire, and, since 1931, to the British Commonwealth of Nations. To make it easier for Canada to join, the Union of American Republics changed its name to Organization of American States, thus explicitly stating that monarchies were not excluded.

It was true that Canada was a full member of the Inter-American Statistical Institute (IASI), which worked closely with the Department of Statistics in the old Pan American Union (the latter was IASI's headquarters), but apparently, Canadian membership in IASI was an isolated case. In 1981, however, the Eleventh Regular Session of the General Assembly, meeting in Castries, St. Lucia, approved Canada's admission to the Inter-American Telecommunications Commission (CITEL), a significant fact that foreshadowed Canada's possible membership in the OAS in the near future.

It took a long time for Canada to join, since it seemed to find more pain than pleasure in doing so; as Canada's role in the world and the hemisphere grew, however, it finally took the plunge. Everybody was happy, since the United States, Latin America, and the Caribbean, even though they all may have had different reasons, applauded the Canadian action. No doubt, it was a historic event that demonstrated anew the importance and vitality of the organization. With the entry of Canada, Belize, and Guyana in the years 1989 and 1991, the OAS reached the significant number of thirty-five member countries.

NEW INSTITUTIONS, TREATIES AND CONVENTIONS, AND DECLARATIONS

During these two decades, the OAS was also active on other fronts. Thus, as far as new institutions were concerned, we should mention the Inter-American Court of Human Rights (1978) and the Inter-American Drug Abuse Control Commission (1986), both referred to earlier. The latter commission signaled a new activity of utmost interest to the United States but increasingly also to the rest of the member states. In regard to the seat of the new Inter-American Court, the General Assembly, in its Eighth Regular Session decided on San José, Costa Rica, in view of a historic precedent: the Central American Court of Justice (1908–1918). The establishment of the Administrative Tribunal within the General Secretariat by the General Assembly's first regular session in 1971 was another achievement in improving the working conditions of the staff within a framework of greater fairness and justice. The creation of Womens' Offices within the General Secretariat by the Twelfth Regular Session of the General Assembly in 1982 signaled a more active feminist policy and thus put into action more feminist goals while at the same time suppressing the Office of Under-Secretariat of Cooperation and Development, which was eliminated by executive order and absorbed by other sections of the General Secretariat. Finally, the OAS also created an Inter-American System for Nature Conservation in 1988 at the eighteenth regular session, dealing with a subject that had been aired and studied earlier.

The last twenty years saw a variety of important conventions. In the first place, in the decade of the 1970s there was the Convention to Prevent and Punish Acts of Terrorism Taking the Form of Crimes against Persons and

Related Extortion that Are of International Significance (1971), which was signed at the Third Special Session of the General Assembly in that year. We also witnessed the signature of the American Convention on Human Rights (1973), the Pact of San José de Costa Rica, which entered into force five years later (and with it the above-mentioned Inter-American Court of Human Rights, since the latter was part of the convention). Furthermore, studies were made that resulted in a draft Legal Instrument Regarding the Definition of Cases Where the Principle of Non-Intervention Was Violated (1973) and in a draft convention on Extradition (1973, 1976) and Principles Regarding Relations among American States (1973), again signaling the deep concern of Latin America in regard to the ever-present threat of new interventions or infringements on national sovereignty by the mighty neighbor to the north. It might be mentioned here that, for the United States, the entire framework of U.S.–Latin American relations, and its role in the OAS has always been basically political, whereas Latin Americans see this relationship in terms of law and legal instruments as their defensive armor, always attempting to perfect this legal protection and adjust it to changing times. Finally, it should also be clear that the various treaties or conventions, as well as institutions and declarations, echo the concerns and issues of the contemporary scene. The above draft on extradition resulted in 1981 in the Inter-American Convention on Extradition, which was signed at the Eleventh Regular Session of the General Assembly in Castries, St. Lucia. Another important legal instrument of a different nature was the Convention for the Protection of Flora, Fauna and the Natural Scenic Beauties of America (1976), which was signed at the Sixth Regular Session of the General Assembly in Santiago de Chile, thus signaling a new trend: an awareness of the environment, which the organization took up now in earnest. Finally, at the Eighth Regular Session a historic event took place: the deposit of the two Panama treaties—on Permanent Neutrality and on Functioning of the Canal (Washington, D.C., 1978).

In the 1980s there was, first of all, the draft Convention which Defines Torture as an International Crime, which was approved in 1980 at the Tenth Regular Session of the General Assembly (Washington, D.C.). In 1983, at the Thirteenth Regular Session of the General Assembly, the OAS studied a draft Inter-American Convention on the Jurisdictional Immunity of States that was later approved at the Fifteenth Regular Session of the General Assembly in Cartagena de Indias in 1985. At the Seventeenth Regular Session of the General Assembly (1987), the OAS approved a draft New American Treaty on Pacific Settlement. This was supposed to replace the older American Treaty on Pacific Settlement (Pact of Bogotá) of 1948, which never became effective since a majority of states would not ratify. This new treaty will thus solve a long-standing problem, provided that it is ratified in due course.

Three other drafts were also approved by this regular session of the General Assembly in 1987: a draft Inter-American Convention on Judicial Assistance in Penal Matters, a draft Additional Protocol to the American Convention on Human Rights, and an Additional Protocol to the American Convention on Human Rights to Abolish the Death Penalty. Finally, in 1988, at the Eighteenth Regular Session of the General Assembly, held in San Salvador, the OAS approved the latter additional protocol and yet another Additional Protocol to the American Convention on Human Rights in the Area of Economic, Social and Cultural Rights, which was incorporated in the Protocol of San Salvador.

Many statements and declarations of the OAS in these last twenty years emphasize particular problems, issues, and goals. Thus, first of all, at the Ninth Regular Session of the General Assembly in 1979, in La Paz, Bolivia, we have the Resolution of La Paz, an evaluation of the First Decade of Regional Programs in Education, Science and Culture, and the Declaration of La Paz in regard to the legitimate Bolivian claim to an outlet to the sea that the country had lost in the Pacific War (1879–1883) and that it tried unsuccessfully to resolve by different means and in different directions, such as the Bolivian-Brazilian Agreement on the Acre Territory, in which it lost, the ill-fated Madeira-Mamoré railroad (1903), and the Chaco War (1928–1936). Also in 1979, the OAS declared the Caribbean a Zone of Peace, at the same time that the Panama Canal treaties entered into force.

In 1980, at the Tenth Regular Session of the General Assembly, the OAS proclaimed the Declaration of Bogotá of CIECC (CIECC 459/80), of the latter's Eleventh Ordinary Session, and accepted the Draft Convention Defining Torture as an International Crime.

At the Thirteenth Regular Session of the General Assembly (1983), the OAS issued the Declaration on Strengthening the Inter-American Relations in the Field of Finance and Trade and also the Inter-American Declaration on the Rights of the Family.

At the Fourteenth Regular Session of the General Assembly in Brasilia (1984), the OAS proclaimed the Declaration of Brasilia, which reiterated the member states' willingness to join efforts in developing conditions of well-being within a framework of freedom and dignity. Finally, at the Sixteenth Regular Session of the General Assembly, held in Guatemala in 1986, the OAS issued the Declaration of Guatemala—"an Alliance of the Americas against Drug Trafficking"—and established the aforementioned new inter-American agency, the Inter-American Drug Abuse Control Commission (CICAD). Finally, in 1989, at the Nineteenth Regular Session of the General Assembly, the OAS issued a declaration on the topic, "The Question of the Malvinas Islands."

THE NEW REVISION OF THE CHARTER: THE PROTOCOL OF CARTAGENA DE INDIAS

Perhaps the most important event in the 1980s besides the political and military events in the South Atlantic (1982), Caribbean (Grenada, 1983),

Central America (1983–1990), and Panama (1989) was the new revision of the OAS Charter. Already in 1973 at the Third Regular Session of the General Assembly in Washington, D.C., a special committee was set up to take a new look at the revised charter of 1967 since several governments had been dissatisfied with the Protocol of Buenos Aires, particularly Argentina, which at the time of signature reiterated

its firm conviction that the amendments introduced in the Charter of the OAS do not duly cover the requirements of the Organization, inasmuch as its basic instrument should contain, in addition to the organic, economic, social, and cultural standards, the essential provision that would make the security system of the Hemisphere effective.[11]

The "provision" referred, obviously, to the ineffectual manner in which the OAS had faced the many violations of the principle of nonintervention in the latest cases of U.S. interventions in Guatemala and the Dominican Republic as well as the subversive activities emanating from revolutionary Cuba.

The special committee was entrusted with the task "of restructuring the inter-American system so that it might respond more adequately to changing hemisphere and world conditions."[12] Eventually, this would lead to a new revision of the charter, the Protocol of Cartagena de Indias of 1985, which entered into force in 1988. The Fourth Regular Session of the General Assembly in 1974 took up the revision of Article 39 (cultural policy) and the Sixth Regular Session of the General Assembly, in Santiago de Chile in 1976, continued the debates on the restructuring of the inter-American system, at the same time delving into the problem of how to promote further the respect for human rights and how to facilitate cooperation among the member states. Then, at the Seventh Regular Session, the revision of Article 44 was taken up, and at the Fourteenth Special Session of the General Assembly, held in Cartagena de Indias, 1985, the new legal instrument, called the Protocol of Cartagena de Indias, was approved on December 5, 1985, subject to ratification of the member states. The changes, additions, and eliminations that together represent the new charter are not as deep and substantial as those of the Protocol of Buenos Aires of 1967 in regard to the original Charter of 1948, but nonetheless, in some areas they did introduce a different document.

The new charter follows the original pattern of division into three parts. It introduced the following changes:

Part One: Chapters I-VII

Chapter I

Article 1. The new Protocol introduced a second paragraph that read:

The Organization of American States has no powers other than those expressly conferred upon it by this Charter, none of whose provisions authorize it to intervene in matters that are within the internal jurisdiction of the Member States.

This echoed a new concern of Latin America in regard to intervention into the internal affairs of its member states and fear that the powerful nations might manipulate the organization for their own interests.

Article 2 (a–g). Two new subdivisions were incorporated that again showed new trends and new adjustments to a changing world. They proclaimed the following essential purposes:

b. To promote and consolidate representative democracy, with the respect for the principle of nonintervention;

and the new subdivision (g) read:

g. To achieve an effective limitation of conventional weapons that will make it possible to devote the largest amount of resources to the economic and social development of the Member States.

Chapter II

Article 3 (a–m). An additional subdivision (e) was introduced as follows:

e. Every State has the right to choose, without external interference, its political, economic, and social system and to organize itself in the way best suited to it, and has the duty to abstain from intervening in the affairs of another State. Subject to the foregoing, the American States shall cooperate fully among themselves, independently of the nature of their political, economic and social systems.

The former subdivision (e) now became (f), and so on.

Chapter III

While Articles 4, 5, 6, and 7 remained unchanged, the new charter now contains a new article, as follows:

Article 8. "Membership in the Organization shall be confined to independent States of the Hemisphere that were members of the United Nations as of December 10, 1985, and the nonautonomous territories mentioned in document OEA/Ser. P, AG/doc.1939/85. of November 5, 1985, when they become independent." This famous and controversial article opened the door to Belize and Guyana but closes it if, in the future, the Malvinas/Falklands should become independent, a remote possibility in view of the few inhabitants of the British colony. The new text replaced the older text of the Protocol of Buenos Aires.

Chapter IV

Here Articles 9–22 remained unchanged.

Chapter V

The old Article 23 was replaced by a new text with two paragraphs as follows:

Article 23. "International disputes between Member States shall be submitted to the peaceful procedures set forth in this Chapter.

This provision shall not be interpreted as an impairment of the rights and obligations of the Member States under Articles 34 and 35 of the Charter of the United Nations." All other articles (Articles 24–26) remained as in the old text of the Protocol of Buenos Aires.

Chapter VI

There were no major changes in Articles 27 and 28, except that in Article 28, the text "in furtherance of the principles of [hemispheric] solidarity or collective self-defense" was modified as follows: "in furtherance of the principles of continental solidarity or collective self-defense."

Chapter VII

In the first place, this chapter consolidated the older Chapters VII, VIII, and IX, and thus, the older subtitles, "Economic Standards," "Social Standards," and "Cultural Standards" disappeared. There is now only one chapter, VII, with the subtitle "Integral Development." The new Articles 29, 30, 31, and 32 read as follows:

Article 29.

The Member States, inspired by the principles of inter-American solidarity and cooperation, pledge themselves to a united effort to ensure international social justice in their relations and integral development for their peoples, as conditions essential to peace and security. Integral development encompasses the economic, social, educational, cultural, scientific, and technological fields through which the goals that each country sets for accomplishing it should be achieved.

Article 30.

Inter-American cooperation for integral development is the common and joint responsibility of the Member States, within the framework of the democratic principles and the institutions of the inter-American system. It should include the economic, social, educational, cultural, scientific, and technological fields, support the achievements of national objectives of the Member States, and respect the priorities established by each country in its development plans, without political ties or conditions.

Article 31.

Inter-American cooperation for integral development should be continuous and preferably channeled through multilateral organizations, without prejudice to bilateral cooperation between Member States.

The Member States shall contribute in inter-American cooperation for integral development in accordance with their resources and capabilities and in conformity with their laws.

Article 32. "Development is a primary responsibility of each country and should constitute an integral and continuous process for the establishment of a more just economic and social order that will make possible and contribute to the fulfillment of the individual."

Articles 33–51.

Article 33 is now the old Article 31, with one small modification, as follows:
d. "Modernization of rural life and reforms leading to equitable and efficient land-tenure systems, increased agricultural productivity, expanded use of land [, . . . and] the means to attain these ends."

Article 34 is new and reads as follows: "The Member States should refrain from practicing policies and adopting actions or measures that have serious adverse effects on the development of other Member States."

Article 35 is also new, and the text reads as follows:

Transnational enterprises and foreign private investment shall be subject to the legislation of the host countries and to the jurisdiction of their competent courts and to the international treaties and agreements to which said countries are parties, and should conform to the development policies of the recipient countries.

Articles 36 and 37 are the old Articles 35 and 36, respectively.

Article 38 is the old Article 37 with modifications in subdivisions (a) and (b). In (b), (iii) was changed and (iv) was added, as follows:

The Member States, recognizing the close interdependence between foreign trade and economic and social development, should make individual and united efforts to bring about the following:
a. Favorable conditions of access to world markets for the products of the developing countries of the region, particularly through the reduction or elimination, by importing countries, of tariff and nontariff barriers that affect the exports of the Member States of the Organization, except when such barriers are applied in order to diversify the economic structure, to speed up the development of the less-developed Member States, and intensify their process of economic integration, or when they are related to national security or to the needs of economic balance;
b. Continuity in their economic and social development by means of:
　　[(i) and (ii) have not been changed;]
　　iii. Diversification of exports and expansion of export opportunities for manufactured and semimanufactured products from the developing countries; and

iv. Conditions conducive to increasing the real export earnings of the Member States, particularly the developing countries of the region, and to increasing their participation in international trade.

Articles 39, 40, 41, 42, 43, 44, and 45 represent the former Articles 38, 39, 40, 41, 42, 43, and 44, respectively.

Article 46 is basically the same as former Article 45. The word "technology" was added, as follows:

The Member States will give primary importance within their development plans to the encouragement of education, science, technology, and culture, oriented toward the overall improvement of the individual, and as a foundation for democracy, social justice, and progress.

Article 47 is almost the same as former Article 46. The words "for their integral development" were added, as follows:

The Member States will cooperate with one another to meet their educational needs, to promote scientific research, and to encourage technological progress for their integral development. They will consider themselves individually and jointly bound to preserve and enrich the cultural heritage of the American peoples.

Articles 48, 49, 50, and 51 have the same text as the old Articles 47, 48, 49, and 50.

Part Two: Chapters VIII-XIX

Chapter VIII (former Chapter X)

Article 52, the former Article 51, remained unchanged.

Chapter IX (former Chapter XI)

Article 53 also remained unchanged except for a new subdivision (f) which reads as follows:

f. To consider the reports of the Meeting of Consultation of Ministers of Foreign Affairs and the observations and recommendations presented by the Permanent Council with regard to the reports that should be presented by the other organs and entities, in accordance with the provisions of paragraph f) of Article 90, as well as the reports of any organ which may be required by the General Assembly itself.

Articles 54, 55, 56, 57, 58, and 59 have the same text as the former Articles 53, 54, 55, 56, 57, and 58, respectively.

Chapter X (former Chapter XII)

Articles 60, 61, 62, and 63, the former Articles 59, 60, 61, and 62, remained unchanged.

Article 64 has been modified and now reads as follows:

In case of an armed attack on the territory of an American State or within the region of security delimited by the treaty in force, the Chairman of the Permanent Council shall without delay call a meeting of the Council to decide on the convocation of the Meeting of Consultation, without prejudice to the provisions of the Inter-American Treaty of Reciprocal Assistance with regard to the States Parties to that instrument.

Articles 65, 66, 67, and 68 have not been changed. They follow the texts of the former Articles 64, 65, 66, and 67.

Chapter XI (former Chapter XIII)

Articles 69, 70, 71, and 72 are the same as the old Articles 68, 69, 70 and 71.

Article 73 contains a small change, as follows: "Each Council may, in urgent cases, convoke Specialized Conferences on matters within its competence, after consulting with the Member States and without having to resort to the procedure provided for in Article 127."

Articles 74, 75, 76, 77, and 78, the former Articles 73, 74, 75, 76, and 77, remained unchanged.

Chapter XII (former Chapter XIV)

Articles 79, 80, and 81 were not modified. Their texts are identical to the old Articles 78, 79, and 80.

Article 82 has a new text, as follows: "The Permanent Council shall serve provisionally as the Organ of Consultation in conformity with the provisions of the special treaty on the subject."

Article 83 is identical to the former Article 82.

Articles 84, 85, 86, and 87 have been changed in the sense that the Inter-American Committee on Peaceful Settlement, the successor to the Inter-American Peace Committee, was eliminated as an institution—it no longer served a useful purpose. This situation is reflected in the new texts.

Article 88 is identical to the former Article 89.

Article 89 eliminated the Inter-American Committee on Peaceful Settlement.

Article 90 follows the old Article 91 with two modifications, as follows:

c. Act as the Preparatory Committee of the General Assembly, in accordance with the terms of Article 59 of the Charter, unless the General Assembly should decide otherwise. . . .

f. Consider the reports of the other Councils, of the Inter-American Juridical Committee, of the Inter-American Commission on Human Rights, of the General Secretariat, of specialized agencies and conferences, and of other bodies and agencies, and present to the General Assembly any observations and recommendations it deems necessary.

Article 91 is identical to former Article 92.

Chapter XIII (former Chapter XV)

Article 92 is the same as former Article 93.

Article 93 has a new text as follows: "The purpose of the Inter-American Economic and Social Council is to promote cooperation among the American countries in order to attain accelerated economic and social development, in accordance with the standards set forth in Chapter VII."

Article 94 has a slight change in paragraph (e), as follows: "e. Promote the solution of the cases contemplated in Article 36 of the Charter, establishing the appropriate procedure."

Article 95 has the identical change: "or for the cases contemplated in Article 36 of the Charter."

Articles 96 and 97 are identical to former Articles 97 and 98.

Chapter XIV (former Chapter XVI)

Articles 98 and 99 are unchanged and follow the text of former Articles 99 and 100.

Article 100 is basically the same. However, paragraph (b) now reads: "b. Adopt or recommend pertinent measures to give effect to the standards contained in Chapter VII of the Charter."

Articles 101, 102, and 103 remained unchanged.

Chapter XV (former Chapter XVII)

Article 104 and 105 also remained unchanged.

Article 106 now has a second paragraph, as follows:

Vacancies that occur for reasons other than normal expiration of the terms of office of the members of the Committee shall be filled by the Permanent Council of the Organization in accordance with the criteria set forth in the preceding paragraph.

Articles 107, 108, 109, and 110 remained unchanged.

Chapter XVI (former Chapter XVIII)

There is no change in this chapter, which has only one provision: Article 111.

Chapter XVII (former Chapter XIX)

Articles 112 and 113 were not modified.

Article 114, former Article 115, has a slight change, as follows: "and, notwithstanding the provisions of Article 90.b."

Article 115, former Article 116, has been changed with two additions and now reads:

The Secretary General, or his representatives, may participate with voice but without vote in all meetings of the Organization.

The Secretary General may bring to the attention of the General Assembly or the Permanent Council any matter which in his opinion might threaten the peace and security of the Hemisphere or the development of Member States.

The authority to which the preceding paragraph refers shall be exercised in accordance with the present Charter.

This new provision gives the secretary general, or a representative, a stronger position, more like the position of the secretary general of the United Nations. Until that time, the secretary general's position in the OAS resembled more the position of the secretary general of the League of Nations.

Articles 116, 117, 118, 119, 120, 121, 122, 123, 124, 125, and 126 were not modified and are identical to the former Articles 117–127.

Chapter XVIII (former Chapter X)

The two provisions of this chapter, Articles 127 and 128, the former Articles 128 and 129, were kept unchanged.

Chapter XIX (former Chapter XXI)

There were no changes in this chapter. Thus, the new Articles 129, 130, 131, 132, 133, 134, and 135, reflect the identical texts of former Articles 130–136.

Part Three: Chapters XX-XXIII

Chapter XX (former Chapter XXII)

Article 136 was not modified.

Chapter XXI (former Chapter XXIII)

There was no change in Articles 137, 138, 139, 140, 141, and 142, which are identical to the former Articles 138–143.

A new Article 143 was added, as follows: "Within the provisions of this Charter, the competent organs shall endeavor to obtain greater collaboration from countries not members of the Organization in the area of cooperation for development."

Chapter XXII (former Chapter XXIV)

Articles 144, 145, 146, and 147 remained unchanged. A slight grammatical modification was introduced in Article 148, as follows: "the present Charter shall cease to be in force with respect to the denouncing State."

Chapter XXIII (former Chapter XXV)

Article 149 was kept unchanged.

Article 150 has only a slight change in the sense that it now refers to chapter XVI, whereas in the former article the reference was to chapter XVIII.

Article 151 was introduced as an additional provision in regard to membership but elapsed on December 10, 1990.

In summary, the elimination of the Inter-American Committee on Peaceful Settlement, the strengthening of the position of the secretary general, the new focus on integral development, a greater emphasis on the principle of nonintervention and continental cooperation, and a final decision on membership in the organization, with the green light for Belize and Guyana, represent the main points of the Protocol of Cartagena de Indias.

THE NEWEST ACTIVITY: MONITORING NATIONAL ELECTIONS

One of the most recent new activities of the OAS is the monitoring of national elections in order to forestall any possible electoral fraud and to eliminate international conflicts. This represents a difficult and complex task for which the organization was not really prepared, and in the case of the Nicaraguan elections in 1989–1990 it meant a displacement of hundreds of staff members from the general secretariat in order to do an effective and positive job. There is obviously another question involved, and quite a delicate one: Monitoring elections in member states represents an intervention in the affairs of a sovereign country, and the organization assumes the role of umpire and judge, a situation that could become worse if, in the process of monitoring, it has to disqualify a certain party or parties for wrongdoing. The international observers of the OAS, and the same would apply to the United Nations, thus walk a very thin line, especially since election results not only have national, but also international, consequences. In any case, by 1991 the OAS had accumulated much experience in this new area of activities, since it had monitored elections in El Salvador, Guatemala, Haiti, Nicaragua, Panama, Paraguay, and Suriname. It is true that in the 1960s the OAS had engaged in sending observers to presidential elections— Dominican Republic, 1961; Costa Rica, 1962; Honduras and Nicaragua, 1963; Bolivia, Costa Rica and Dominican Republic, 1966—but those activities were never as involved as the cases of monitoring elections in 1989–1991.

1. In the case of Central America, with its problems in the 1980s (especially El Salvador, Honduras, and Nicaragua), the Agreements of Esquipulas II (1987) had already established the firm obligation for all Central American states without exception to carry out national elections in the presence of international observers, with equal guarantees for elections contemplated

for a Central American Parliament.[13] There were two Esquipulas agreements, though Esquipulas II was the more important one. Held in that Guatemalan town in 1987, Esquipulas II was the site of an important meeting of the five Central American presidents, who despite profound ideological and political differences accepted Costa Rican President Oscar Arias Sánchez's Peace Plan as a basis for a Central American peace. Despite the fact that the United States never really warmed up to the Arias Plan, all five Central American governments went ahead with Esquipulas II. In the case of Nicaragua, the above-mentioned Agreements of Esquipulas II "hastened the Sandinista revolution's inevitable arrival at the ideological divide between a pluralistic democracy and one-party totalitarianism."[14] It should also be borne in mind that the difficult task of the Central Americans was to come to solutions which, while not quite sympathetic to the Sandinistas, would invalidate any justification for open U.S. intervention, which was already in place with the U.S. support of the Contra mercenaries, who were called the new "freedom fighters" by President Reagan. The acceptance of these national elections by the Sandinistas led, three years later, to the Sandinista defeat on February 25, 1990, and with it a liberal-democratic Nicaragua under Violeta Chamorro, which ended the Central American crisis in a very different manner than imagined by the U.S. Department of State. On the other hand, a Central American Parliament has not been set up so far.

The new OAS activity began in Nicaragua when Nicaraguan Foreign Minister Miguel d'Escoto Brockmann requested the OAS on March 3, 1989, to send observers for the national elections, to be held on February 25, 1990. The secretary general accepted this invitation on March 10, 1989, within the framework of article 138 of the charter (i.e., that the OAS shall enjoy for each of its members "all the privileges and immunities necessary for the fulfillment of its functions and for the realization of its objectives."[15] The OAS then proceeded to organize a team of international observers, and concluded two agreements: one with the government of Nicaragua in regard to privileges and immunities for the international observers, and the second with the Supreme Electoral Council of Nicaragua within the framework of Nicaraguan electoral legislation.[16]

At the beginning the OAS international observer corps included some sixty staff members who were recruited from all sorts of offices of the general secretariat and from the OAS National Office in Managua, but by the time of the elections, it had reached the impressive number of two hundred. During the electoral process, the OAS visited 3,084 of the 4,394 electoral sites throughout the country.[17] Without going into further detail, suffice it to say that the international observers from the OAS had full freedom to conduct their work and that they succeeded in this delicate and complex task which covered all kinds of activities including the means of social communication (television, radio, and the press); the financing of the political parties (state financing, domestic donations, and foreign financial aid); the conditions of electoral proselytism (violence in the realization of public acts, intimidations, and the use of a state's properties, like transportation), and the prevention of violence (regional political agreements, measures of the Supreme Electoral Council, and the behavior of the national authorities and the political parties).[18]

2. At the request of the Haitian Government, the OAS monitored the election of Jean-Bertrand Aristide on December 16, 1990. A team of some 200 international observers from twenty-two countries of the OAS traveled to Haiti to monitor the election in that country, which began in October 1990, when voter registration was started. As in other cases, at first a small number of international observers (some 35), arrived in that country, but at the height of the electoral campaign the OAS had close to 200 civil servants monitoring the elections. They were distributed in the nine regional capitals that functioned as departmental electoral offices. The OAS was very pleased with the work of its team since it is estimated that 65 percent of the registered voters, an extraordinary high percentage for a country like Haiti, participated in the election. It testified to the success of the OAS and its new monitoring activities, and Secretary General João Clemente Baena Soares concluded that the Haitian elections had been free and democratic, and he also acknowledged the excellent cooperation given by CARICOM.[19]

3. At the same time, the OAS was also engaged in a similar activity in Guatemala. At the request of that government, another team of international observers went to Guatemala to monitor that country's elections on November 11, 1990, and in January 1991 a new team arrived to monitor the second round of the presidential elections in which Jorge Serrano emerged as the winner.[20]

4. In the case of Suriname, the same procedure was used. At the request of the Suriname government, and in accordance with the initiative of the OAS, the organization sent a team of international observers to monitor the elections in that country. The team was headed, as in the case of Nicaragua, by the secretary general of the OAS himself, and worked in Suriname starting in February 1991. The mission's activity included observers in all electoral districts of the country, and it specifically involved the public inspection of the registered electoral lists and the registration of candidates and their respective political parties. Moreover, members of the OAS team held continuous meetings with electoral officials, government civil servants, opposition leaders, and members of the Suriname media.

On May 25, 1991, the day of the election, some forty members of the team of international observers from some sixteen countries, members of the OAS, monitored the national elections, which were held to renew fifty-one seats in the National Assembly, and in which some 160,000 of the 250,000 Suriname citizens who were entitled to vote participated. In June, the president and vice president were to be elected, and the OAS was to remain in the country until the inauguration of the new executive officers.[21]

5. Interestingly, at the same time that these OAS activities took place in Suriname, another team of international observers traveled to Paraguay, where municipal elections were being held on May 26, 1991. After the long regime of Alfredo Stroessner, Paraguay apparently had a great interest in showing the world and its neighbors that political life in the country had changed. The Alternate Representative of Paraguay on the Permanent Council of the OAS stated that "the OAS was present in an electoral process by the express wish of both our people and our Government," adding that "the presence of the OAS is a concrete testimony of the desire of my Government to build a solid democracy."[22]

6. In two other instances, in Panama and El Salvador, the OAS played a minor role compared to the cases mentioned earlier. In Panama, the OAS was already heavily involved in 1989 when Venezuela requested a Meeting of Consultation in view of the rising tension between the United States and Panama. The Twenty-first Meeting of Consultation, in Washington, D.C., 1989, appointed an Ad-Hoc Committee of Three (Ecuador, Guatemala, and Trinidad and Tobago) to negotiate a National Accord as a face-saving device to encourage General Manuel Noriega to leave the political scene. In the elections that Noriega permitted in that same year, the OAS was only present with members of its national office in Panama. Noriega's party lost the elections, which were then annulled by the general. Since the OAS apparently was unsuccessful at solving the problem, the United States took unilateral action which led to the Panama invasion of December, 1989.

7. Also in the case of El Salvador, the OAS presence was minimal and limited itself to staff members of the local OAS National Office in San Salvador. In the elections of March 19, 1989, which were easily won by ARENA, a member of the rightist party of Roberto d'Aubuisson, the aforementioned Alfredo Cristiani, became president. Consequently, U.S. policy collapsed.

10

Related Organizations: Latin America and the Caribbean Connection

Several intergovernmental organizations in both Latin America and the Caribbean must be mentioned. They are not part of the inter-American system, but in some indirect ways, they are related to the OAS as a kind of expanded family. Some of the Latin American organizations were set up as a prelude to future economic integration of the entire Latin American area, while others were created as an alternative to the OAS at a time when its prestige had gone down, and also as a demonstration of a Latin American will to decide the region's own future. Most of these organizations were disappointing, which, in turn, gave the OAS new strength as the only real option. The Caribbean also articulated its own process of regional integration.

LATIN AMERICA

Asociación Latinoamericana de Libre Comercio (Latin American Free Trade Association—ALALC)—Asociación Latinoamericana de Integracion (Latin American Association for Integration—ALADI)

The Latin American Free Trade Association was set up in Montevideo. It was here that the ALALC treaty was signed on February 18, 1960, and its permanent secretariat was established. ALALC became effective January 1, 1961. Its membership covered eleven countries: Argentina, Bolivia, Brazil, Chile, Colombia, Ecuador, Mexico, Paraguay, Peru, Uruguay, and Venezuela (1966). ALALC was sponsored by the United Nations Economic Commission for Latin America (CEPAL/UN–ECLA), and its purpose was to establish a free economic area among its members simply by eliminating trade barriers in stages over a period of twelve years (thus following European examples). In 1969, in a meeting in Venezuela, it was decided to postpone the target date of a future Latin American Common Market to 1980, but Colombia and Uruguay refused to ratify the Caracas Agreement. Although no state openly acknowledged the failure of ALALC, both the Andean Group and the River Plate Basin (which are discussed later in this chapter) were attempts to find a solution through smaller integration areas.

At the Nineteenth Extraordinary Conference of ALALC in Acapulco (June 16–27, 1980), a constitution was drafted for the establishment of a new organization, ALADI, which replaced the now defunct ALALC. The latter was officially ended on December 31, 1980, and the new organization modernized the concept of integration by aiming at an integrated Latin America and no longer at the establishment of a free trade area.

Comisión Especial de Coordinación Latinoamericana (Special Committee on Latin American Coordination—CECLA)

This Special Committee is an organization set up by the OAS and the United Nations jointly; it is a special UN agency. CECLA represents an important vehicle for the integration of Latin America, attempting in the 1960s to establish a united Latin American position in regard to foreign interests. Thus, CECLA succeeded in achieving this aim prior to the UNCTAD meetings in New Delhi (1968) and Santiago de Chile (1972). In 1969 it approved the Latin American Consensus in Viña del Mar, by which a common Latin American policy was established in regard to the United States. Finally, in 1970, the Declaration of Buenos Aires set Latin American policy concerning the European Community.[1]

Organización Para la Prohibición de Armas Nucleares en América Latina (Organization for the Prohibition of Nuclear Weapons in Latin America—OPANAL)

The Organization for the Prohibition of Nuclear Weapons in Latin America was set up in 1967 by the Treaty of Tlaltelolco, and its first meeting took place in 1969. Besides the Latin American countries, Barbados, Jamaica, and Trinidad and Tobago are also members. The Treaty for the Prohibition of Nuclear Weapons in Latin America was designed to make Latin America a nuclear free zone, and its agency is to oversee the good observance of the treaty. Thus, its main objective is to ensure the absence of nuclear weapons in Latin America and, at the same time, to encourage the peaceful uses of nuclear energy. Argentina and Brazil have not ratified the treaty, but they recently issued the "Joint Declaration of the Presidents of Argentina and Brazil, February 14, 1992, on the 25th Anniversary of Tlaltelolco," which states that "both countries will shortly submit to OPANAL some amendments of a technical nature to the text of the Treaty so that both countries can sign and ratify the Treaty, and thus make Latin America and the Caribbean a nuclear-free zone."

Sistema Económico Latinoamericano (Latin American Economic System—SELA)

This relatively new Latin American organization was launched by the presidents of Mexico and Venezuela who, in the early 1970s, proposed a new mechanism for Latin American economic and political cooperation. Symbolically meeting in Panama, the Latin American countries, including Caribbean states, as in the case of OPANAL, signed the Constitutional Agreement of SELA on November 25, 1975. By 1976, this was ratified by an absolute majority. It represented an impressive unity of twenty-five Latin American and Caribbean countries seeking a common policy. The purpose of SELA was to establish a mechanism for regional cooperation with the ultimate aim of setting up a full Latin American and Caribbean integration. Thus, its main objective was

To promote a permanent system of consultation and coordination, in order to adopt common strategies and positions on economic and social matters in the international institutions and assemblies, as well as in their relations with other countries or groups of countries.[2]

Thus, in the Extraordinary Meeting in Caracas (January 5, 1976), SELA achieved a united front for the next UNCTAD meeting in Nairobi (May 1976).

SELA has functioned since its inception to generate initiatives for integration, such as infrastructure investments benefiting two or more countries, and giving priority to so-called *multilatina* enterprises,[3] that is, where two or more Latin American enterprises would join forces, as did Brazil's VW corporation and Argentina's Ford.

Grupo Andino (Andean Group)

In the Agreement of Cartagena (May 26, 1969), the five countries of Bolivia, Chile, Colombia, Ecuador, and Peru established the Andean Group with the purpose of promoting a harmonious development of the signatory parties and accelerating their economic integration through the dismantling of tariffs and other trade barriers. Venezuela became a member of the group in 1973, and Mexico has considered itself a "working partner" since October 1972.

Since ALALC, the Latin American Free Trade Association, had not produced the expected results, the Andean Group was another attempt at achieving a common market within a smaller and more compatible area. The targets for a greater integration were 1986 for Chile, Colombia, and Peru, and 1991 for Bolivia and Ecuador. The most controversial tool was the Andean Foreign Investment Code (Decision 24)—foreign-owned enterprises must become mixed companies. The Cartagena Agreement of 1975 established an integrated petrochemical industry in each of the member states as a step toward the desired common market. The Andean Group did not fulfil the expectations in view of mounting economic and political problems, however. Chile left the group after the Allende regime was overthrown in 1973.

Cuenca del Río de la Plata (River Plate Basin)

A somewhat different regional understanding, though much less modest in scope, was accomplished by the River Plate Basin Agreements, which were signed by Argentina, Bolivia, Brazil, Paraguay, and Uruguay. These agreements, which began to function in the early 1970s, attempted the utilization and exploitation of the rivers in the River Plate Basin for common electric purposes benefiting both agriculture and industry. Several dams, such as Itaipú and Yaciretá, were built in the area for the benefit of the member states. The River Plate Basin was also a consequence of the increasing failure of ALALC and the Latin American attempt to arrive at a future common market and full integration via subregions and more modest targets.

Organización de los Estados Centroamericanos (Organization of Central American States—ODECA)

The Organization of Central American States was set up in 1951 through the adoption of its charter on October 14, 1951. It was the latest attempt to achieve the unity of Central America, which had been disrupted ever since the Captaincy-General of Guatemala collapsed in 1822 and the Federation of the United Provinces of Central America dissolved in 1838. To some extent, ODECA worked during the 1950s, but the difficult and increasing political, ideological, and economic problems made this regional international organization (a sort of mini-OAS), another victim of Latin American realities. Since the Soccer War between Honduras and El Salvador, it has remained inactive. One of its earlier successes was its active promotion of the Central American Common Market.

Mercado Común Centroamericano (Central American Common Market—MCCA)

Established·by treaty in 1960 in Managua, the Central American Common Market became effective in 1961. The treaty was originally signed by Guatemala, El Salvador, Honduras and Nicaragua; Costa Rica agreed much later. Its aim was to establish a Central American economic union—a common market—in less than five years. It was also believed that a united Central American region would have a better chance to integrate into the future Latin American Common Market than the five Central American republics as individual states. However, Costa Rica was never too enthusiastic, and the mounting difficulties made it impossible to advance. Honduras left the MCCA in 1969 as a result of the Soccer War with El Salvador. Peace talks between the two countries broke down in 1974, and the later complications in Central America, with the fall of Nicaragua's Somoza regime and the revolutionary spirit gaining ground in Nicaragua as well as in El Salvador, destroyed any chance to advance toward full integration. Thus, the issue of the MCCA died; however, it is now being reactivated.

Contadora Group

Another example of Latin American solidarity, though of more of an ad hoc character, is the Contadora Group, which functioned between 1983 and 1986. In early 1983, the four countries of Mexico, Colombia, Panama, and Venezuela met in La Contadora Island, off the coast of Panama, in order to elaborate a peace plan for Central America, thus dealing with the situation in El Salvador and Honduras and Nicaragua and trying to satisfy the different internal and external factors. The peace plan included the removal of foreign military advisors, the reduction of troops and weapons, the closing of foreign military bases, the end of all kinds of subversion and intervention, and the guarantee for democratic elections.

President Belisario Betancur of Colombia officially linked the Contadora Group to the spirit of Bolívar and the Congress of Panama when he said, on the occasion of the 200th anniversary of the *Libertador*'s birthday (July 24, 1983):

As President of Colombia, which together with Venezuela, Mexico and Panama has established the Contadora Group, I have to say that our mandate consists in reviving the Bolivarian spirit for the creation of a supraregional order that guarantees the selfdetermination of peoples, nonintervention, and the peaceful solution of conflicts among the nations.[4]

To give additional weight to the original Contadora Group, four other governments joined: Argentina, Brazil, Peru, and Uruguay, in the so-called Contadora Support Group. In their Declaration of Cartagena, the eight nations warned that "If a peaceful and negotiated solution is not found for the Central American conflict, this will affect the political and social stability of all Latin America."[5] The United States ignored the Contadora Group and its peace plan. Thus, when the Contadora Group failed to reach a treaty by its self-imposed deadline of June 6, 1986, it dissolved.

Cartagena Group

This group was similar to the Contadora Group. It was also an ad hoc group and was set up on the basis of Latin American solidarity and of common problems that plagued all of Latin America, in this case, the increasing debt problem. A group of eleven Latin American countries, which included the ten South American nations and Mexico, met in the mid-1980s in order to establish a joint front in regard to foreign creditors, private banks, and governments. They held several meetings but achieved little since the United States again paid no attention to them and preferred the usual path of individual negotiation. The Baker Plan, and the later Brady Plan, represented the somewhat more positive reactions from the United States. Like the Contadora Group, the Cartagena Group gradually disappeared from the political scene.

Ibero-American Summit Conferences

The First Ibero-American Summit Conference was held in Guadalajara, Mexico, July 18–20, 1991. It is not a new concept since it had been aired in the past and there have been earlier gatherings of this type, but what is new is the fact that for the first time it is being implemented, and on a regular, annual basis. It thus is not an irrelevant political action. These Ibero-American Summit Conferences are very much like the gatherings of the British Commonwealth of Nations. The Fifth Centennial of the Discovery of America, the so-called Encounter of Two Worlds is the launching pad for this type of summit meeting. It brings together the leaders of the twenty-one Spanish- and Portuguese-speaking nations of America and Europe. In the First Ibero-American Summit Meeting, King Juan Carlos of Spain, Fidel Castro of Cuba, Violeta Barrios de Chamorro of Nicaragua, and Alberto Fujimori of Peru were among the many chiefs of state and chiefs of government in attendance. It has been called an important new vehicle for regional cooperation and economic integration, and, obviously, also attempts to build a solid bridge to Europe and the European Community through Spain and Portugal and to deepen and strengthen political, economic, and cultural ties of a region in the world where only the powerful seem to have a voice. There is no question that this new instrument that bridges the Atlantic could be important, and it represents one of the four dimensions of Latin America, the other three being membership in the Non-Aligned Nations (especially the Group of 77, which is almost totally defunct); the Western world, of which Latin America is a part, although the United States and Europe interpret Latin America purely in economic terms and thus lump it into the lap of the Third World; and the inter-American system.

A Second Ibero-American Summit Conference was scheduled for 1992 in

Madrid as part of the festivities for the Fifth Centennial, a Third Ibero-American Summit Conference is planned in 1993 in Brazil, and finally, Venezuela has offered to be the site for the Fifth Ibero-American Summit Conference in Caracas.

Alianza Ecologica Latinoamericana (Latin American Ecological Alliance)

A Latin American Ecological Alliance has been proposed at the First Ibero-American Summit Conference in Guadalajara (1991), in a proposal delivered to the nineteen Latin American presidents by Colombian Gabriel García Márquez, Nobel Prize recipient in literature, and Mexican novelist and poet Homero Aridjis on the occasion of this important gathering on July 19, 1991. This alliance is a proposal that stands a good chance of being approved and will signal an important message to the world.

THE CARIBBEAN CONNECTION

The Caribbean Movements

The growing solidarity between Latin America and the Caribbean justifies the inclusion of the Caribbean movements in this section. In a wider sense, the Caribbean also looks to Simon Bolívar and the Congress of Panama as its idealistic foundation for union, even though different traditions play a great role here. Four different groups have to be distinguished, as follows:

Confederación Antillana (Antillean Confederation)

In view of the extraordinary variety of the area, with its distinct Spanish, French, English, and Dutch components, and its overall black, and in some cases East Indian, character and varied ethnic and cultural background, the possibility of achieving some type of union had to be more difficult in the Caribbean than elsewhere. The first attempt for some political union was in the Spanish-speaking Caribbean through the Spanish Constitution of 1812, which allowed political representation in both the Spanish components in the Caribbean and their representation in the Metropolis. The Constitution of Cadiz of 1812 was valid in the Spanish Caribbean in the years 1812–1814, 1820–1823, and 1836.

When Spain lost its empire in 1825, it retained Cuba and Puerto Rico. In 1861, when Santo Domingo—which had been handed over by Spain to France and joined to French St. Domingue in 1795 and later occupied by independent Haiti for over a quarter of a century, and which had been independent from Haiti since 1844—asked Spain to return, there was a possibility for a loose confederation of the Spanish Caribbean. It was then that the notion of Confederación Antillana was launched. Even when Spain lost control in Santo Domingo in 1865, the idea did not die. It was revived at the time of the September coup of 1868 in Spain, which coincided with the Grito de Lares in Puerto Rico, a failed attempt for Puerto Rican independence, and the Grito de Yara in Cuba, which set the stage for the ten-year war with Spain (1868–1878). The main proponents for a Confederación Antillana at that time were the Puerto Ricans Ramón Emeterio Betances and Eugenio María de Hostos. The latter had aired the concept publicly in the Ateneo of Madrid in December 1868, and later included it in his *La peregrinación de Bayoán*. However, even if the republic, and then the government of King Amadeo I, tried to improve the political situation, both the end of the short-lived First Republic and the ten-year war in Cuba nullified any prospect for such a Confederación Antillana. José Martí, the Cuban martyr, and the Dominican hero Gregorio Luperón also embraced the idea, but U.S. imperialism shattered these dreams at the time of Cuban independence. Finally, a last attempt in the direction of a Confederación Antillana was undertaken by José de Diego, the *caballero de la raza* ("the knight of the Hispanic peoples," as he was admiringly called), when he founded the Unión Antillana in 1915. It was as unrealistic as the idealism of Betances and Hostos or Martí and Luperón.

The Pan African Movement and Négritude

In the English- and French-speaking areas of the Caribbean, a very different concept developed. The Commonwealth Caribbean became the birthplace of Pan-Africanism. Like Zionism, Pan-Africanism was born in the diaspora. Pan-Africanism as a term had been coined by John Chilembwe, an African, who took it from Joseph Booth, an English farmer who had gone to New Zealand and in 1892 arrived in Nyassaland (today's Malawi) as a Baptist missionary. It was Booth who, between 1895 and 1898, authored the book *Africa for the Africans*. In 1897 he formed the African Christian Union in Blantyre with the aim of establishing a united Christian nation in Africa. During World War I, Chilembwe led a revolt in Nyassaland. He had previously studied in the United States during the years 1897–1900.

The Pan African movement began in earnest with William Edward Burghardt Du Bois of Great Barrington, Massachusetts. He introduced Pan-Africanism in London in 1900 at the first Pan African Congress, which was sponsored by the Trinidadian H. Sylvester Williams. The early stages of Pan-Africanism were marked by Du Bois and Marcus Aurelius Garvey, a Jamaican activist. The former cooperated in setting up the National Association for the Advancement of Colored Peoples (NAACP) in the United States, and the latter, who never set foot in Africa, founded the Universal Negro Improvement Association (UNIA).

The Pan African movement was from the beginning a Caribbean affair, and it was always in the hands of West Indians: George Padmore, C. L. R. James, Peter Milliard, and Otto Mackonnen, who were later joined by Africans like Azikiwe, Chief Akintole, and Jomo Kenyatta. Pan-African conferences followed each other in Europe. The last one was held in Manchester, England, in 1945 and asked for African autonomy. All these endeavors also benefited the Caribbean area after World War II, since the English-speaking Caribbean also began to move toward both self-government and federation.

In the 1930s a shift took place in the Caribbean toward Europe: London became the political center for Pan-Africanism, a clear echo of West Indian influence, while Paris turned into the literary headquarters, again the result of the Caribbean impact. The shift also showed the growing division between French-speaking and English-speaking blacks in both Africa and the West Indies. This division of political and literary Pan-Africanism, with its two European centers, further widened the abyss between the two groups. The ideas of the Paris-based groups developed into what later became known as *Négritude*: the sum total of black cultural values, which actually were to affect much more the French-speaking areas than the English-speaking regions. *Négritude* was promoted by two famous journals: *Légitime Défense* and *Présence Africaine*. Again, the Caribbean nations played a significant role, especially Martinique and Haiti. The Martinican poet Etienne Léro, together with Jules Monnerot and René Mesnil, were the guiding collaborators in *Légitime Défense*.

The heir to Léro was another Martinican: Aimé Césaire, who joined the group in Paris in 1931 at the time of the Colonial Exhibition. He represented Martinique in the French National Assembly and later became the mayor of Fort-de-France. It was he who coined the word *Négritude*, which later found its greatest echo in Africa, on the part of Léopold Sédar Senghor of Senegal and Félix Houphouët-Boigny of the Ivory Coast. However, the concept of *Négritude* was never really accepted in the English-speaking Caribbean. It expressed in an ambiguous way the contradictory situation of Martinique and Guadeloupe: through geography, history, ethnicity, it was a part of the West Indies, but politically it was part of France.

In 1956 *Présence Africaine* organized at the Sorbonne the First Congress of Negro Writers and Artists, with a second congress following in Rome in 1959, where Aimé Césaire and the Haitian Price Mars were the leading personalities. They called for a new synthesis between Africa and Europe, and thus echoed the special situation in the West Indies. The congress also showed the increasing gulf of the two linguistic and cultural groups that divided the black world. Actually, again West Indians led the discussion: Aimé Césaire for the French-speaking area and George Lamming, for the British West Indies.[6]

The West Indian Federation and the Tripartite Kingdom of the Netherlands

Both the Pan African movement and *Négritude*, although related to the political struggle in Africa, were obviously more closely linked to the Caribbean. They represented a political pressure for autonomy and federation in the Commonwealth Caribbean, whereas the French-speaking area in the West Indies opted for autonomy within the French Community in view of the historical legacy of Haitian independence (1789–1804). Thus, while the French-speaking area (Martinique, Guadeloupe, and French Guiana) remained politically French—as overseas departments—the English-speaking area choose a different path. Prepared by labor trouble in the 1930s and the establishment of labor unions during World War II, after 1945 the British government accepted the principle of both autonomy and federation for the British West Indies. The only exceptions were British Honduras and British Guiana. A report of 1950 concluded that federation was the best path for achieving political emancipation. In 1953 a West Indian Conference in London elaborated a Federal West Indian Draft Constitution which was approved in 1955. A year later a common currency was introduced, and finally, in the same year (1956), the last West Indian Conference accepted the constitution, so that the West Indian Federation saw the light of day in 1958. This Federation was based on a Parliament with two Houses: a Senate with regional representation and a House of Representatives, whose delegates were elected by general and secret ballot.[7]

At the same time the Dutch area also considered changes. Both Suriname and the Netherlands Antilles (Curaçao, Aruba, Bonaire, St. Maarten, and Saba) became in 1954 part of the Tripartite Kingdom of the Netherlands. This meant that both Suriname and the Netherlands West Indies became fully self-governing areas, almost on the same level as the Metropolis. However, riots that broke out in Willemstad in 1969 led to new changes aiming at emancipation for both Caribbean areas within a period of transition. Indeed, Suriname became independent in 1976, while the Netherlands West Indies kept loose ties with the Metropolis.[8]

The Caribbean Free Trade Association (CARIFTA) and the Caribbean Community (CARICOM)

The high hopes that had been raised in 1958 with the British West Indian Federation did not last. Internal problems between the more developed bigger partners Trinidad and Tobago, Barbados, Jamaica and Guyana, and the smaller islands finally broke the federation. However, this situation was unsatisfactory, and thus, new negotiations led to the establishment of the Caribbean Free Trade Association (CARIFTA). The original agreement was signed on December 15, 1965, between Antigua, Barbados, and Guyana, but new amendments led to the final treaty, which was signed on February 28, 1868, in Georgetown, Guyana. CARIFTA, which tried to do better than the defunct West Indian Federation, linked the newly independent areas of Barbados, Jamaica, Guyana, and Trinidad and Tobago with the East Caribbean Common Market (ECCM): Antigua, Dominica, Montserrat, St. Kitts-Nevis-Anguilla, St. Lucia, and St. Vincent. CARIFTA thus represented the Caribbean version of both the European Free Trade Association (EFTA) and the Latin American Free Trade Association (ALALC), or LAFTA in its English acronym.

Despite all the good intentions to overcome the difficulties that had destroyed the West Indian Federation, the old problems between the bigger and the smaller states reemerged, even though the smaller islands had organized themselves in the ECCM in order to present a united front in regard to their more powerful neighbors. Before the new problems could explode again, however, the entry of Great Britain into the European Community in 1973 changed the rules of the game. New negotiations had already begun in 1972 for a new Caribbean structure, a Caribbean Common Market. The Treaty of Chaguaramas (July 4, 1973) led to the establishment of the Caribbean Community—CARICOM, which included the Caribbean Common Market with its Common External Tariff. The treaty entered into force on August 1, 1973. Six less developed countries, the members of ECCM, signed the treaty on April 17, 1974. Hence, the membership of CARICOM in the late 1980s included: Antigua, Bahamas, Barbados, Belize, Dominica, Grenada, Guyana, Jamaica, Montserrat, St. Kitts-Nevis-Anguilla, St. Lucia, St. Vincent and the Grenadines, and Trinidad and Tobago. CARICOM, which thus superseded CARIFTA, addresses three basic problems: economic integration of the Commonwealth Caribbean; cooperation in noneconomic areas; and operation of certain common services as well as coordination of foreign policies of the component parts in regard to foreign countries, international groups, and international organizations.

The new Caribbean organization had similar problems as its predecessors and its Latin American counterparts. Thus it has not yet achieved the much desired goals and is struggling to keep above water. Echoes of the integration process in Europe (EFTA and EC) joined here with the Latin American experience, and can thus be linked, *in latu senso*, to the Bolivarian ideals of unity and confederation, since increasingly the Caribbean and Latin America are taking common positions in todays' world politics.

An important and interesting characteristic of CARICOM is the fact that it attempted to overcome the narrow Commonwealth Caribbean framework by inviting non-Commonwealth Caribbean areas to participate. As a matter of fact, Suriname became a member of CARICOM, and at one point Puerto Rico, under Governor Rafael Hernández Colón, tried to establish some kind of link with CARICOM but was promptly reminded by the United States that its political status did not allow such dangerous endeavors.

11

The OAS and International Law, Human Rights, and Democracy

The record of the many activities of the OAS over a century has demonstrated that it has achieved very many positive results, although it should be borne in mind that an intergovernmental agency like the OAS can only succeed if it continually receives the full support of its members. As membership has grown (now to thirty-five states), its work has become even more complex and difficult as in those decades when it was an organization limited to twenty-one. It is also obvious that the less the issues or items are politicized the more success is guaranteed, and this is particularly true of the so-called silent or nonpolitical activities of the organization.

In the wide area of legal and political affairs, the organization was able over decades, with various degrees of success, to solve a number of problems. From the very beginning the organization was very much engaged in the codification of international law, in which it was most successful; it was also engaged in the protection of human rights, the effective exercise of representative democracy, the pacific settlement of disputes, and collective security; in the area of economic and social affairs, it attempted to accelerate economic and social development and to encourage Latin American integration. Moreover, lately it is making great efforts in the field of drug abuse and drug trafficking, and also in monitoring, whenever desired, national elections.

CODIFICATION OF INTERNATIONAL LAW

The codification of international law, both private and public, was less a political issue and thus there is no question that the organization succeeded in this field to a large extent. The codification of international law has a long history and dates back to the earlier mentioned Juridical Congress of Lima (1877–1879) and the South American Congress of Private International Law of Montevideo (1888–1889). Though the results were limited at that stage, the endeavors continued and at the Third International Conference of American States in Rio de Janeiro (1906) a Convention of International Law was signed and ratified by seventeen states. This convention set up an International Commission of Jurists with the purpose of preparing two drafts: a draft Code of Private International Law, and a draft Code of Public International Law. The two projects were delayed in view of World War I, but a Second Meeting of the International Commission of Jurists in 1927, again in Rio de Janeiro, produced several drafts, including those of the Brazilian jurist Epitacio Pessoa and the Chilean Alejandro Alvarez, in the field of public international law, and by Lafayette Rodrigues Pereira and Antonio Sánchez de Bustamante in the field of private international law. The drafts were submitted to the Sixth International Conference of American States in Havana, 1928, where they served as a basis for several treaties and conventions. The conference also approved the continuation of the International Commission of Jurists and the organization of three commissions: the first, in Rio de Janeiro, for public international law; the second, in Montevideo, for private international law; and the third, in Havana, for comparative law and the uniformity of legislation.[1]

This International Commission of Jurists was the only official agency in the field of codification; it was obviously also the forerunner of the future Inter-American Council of Jurists. Despite its ups and downs and its lack of substantial achievement in the 1930s it survived, and in 1938 was replaced by the International Conference of American Jurists, at that time numbering about 225.[2]

A Committee of Experts had been set up at the Seventh International Conference of American States in Montevideo, in 1933, for the purpose of codification of international law. It was this committee that did most of the important work; originally with seven members, it was later enlarged to nine (Resolution XVII, Eighth International Conference of American States, Lima, 1938), and dealt with a variety of subjects, such as the definition of aggression—which the League of Nations had done with little success in the 1920s—sanctions, and prevention of war; investigation, conciliation, and arbitration; nationality; the peace code; immunity of state-owned vessels; and pecuniary claims.[3]

World War II accelerated the work of codification. Thus, already in 1939, at the First MCFMA, the Inter-American Neutrality Committee, was established. It was the committee, which three years later changed its name to Inter-American Juridical Committee and submitted an important draft to the Ninth ICAS at Bogotá, 1948, that constituted the basis for the Pact of Bogotá. It also was responsible for two more drafts: the draft Declaration of the International Charter of Rights and Duties of Man and a draft Inter-

American Charter of Social Guarantees, both accepted as such by the conference. Finally, the IAJC, like the Inter-American Council of Jurists, were incorporated in the original charter of the OAS. The Inter-American Council of Jurists held several meetings: first meeting, Rio de Janeiro, 1950; second meeting, Buenos Aires, 1953; third meeting, Mexico City, 1956; fourth meeting, Santiago de Chile, 1959; and fifth meeting, San Salvador, 1965. All kinds of problems were aired and researched: recognition of de facto governments, possible elimination of passports, an Inter-American Court to Protect Human Rights, the right of resistance; and the scope of the powers of the Council of the OAS. Other issues studied by the council included the effective exercise of representative democracy; political asylum, exiles, and refugees; revision of the Bustamante Code; international sale of personal property; international cooperation in judicial procedures; and territorial waters, nationality, and status of stateless persons.[4]

With the new emphasis on economic and social development in the 1950s and especially with the Alliance for Progress of 1961, the COAS requested the two judicial bodies to undertake the necessary legal studies. This was reflected in the topic, "Programming of Studies in the International Aspect of Legal and Institutional Problems of the Economic and Social Development of Latin America," which the COAS included in the Fifth Meeting of the Inter-American Council of Jurists in San Salvador in 1965. The two bodies were also responsible for studies in regard to the legal aspects of the Alliance for Progress, the new Special Development Assistance Fund, and both the Central American Common Market (MCCA) and the Latin American Free Trade Association (ALALC).

With the revision of the Charter of the OAS, the Inter-American Council of Jurists disappeared and the Inter-American Juridical Committee was upgraded and brought into a more direct relationship with the highest organ, the General Assembly. Thus it was put on the same level as the MCMFA, the three councils, the Specialized Conferences and Organizations, the IACHR, and the Inter-American Court of Human Rights.

In the last two decades, the IAJC continued its earlier impressive achievements with the elaboration of a variety of legal instruments. Suffice it to mention the following: Strengthening of the Inter-American System of Peace (1971); Strengthening of the Principle of Non-Intervention and Self-Determination and Strengthening of the Cultural Heritage of America as a Means of Strengthening Regional Integration (1972); Draft Legal Instrument Regarding the Definition of Cases where the Principle of Non-Intervention Was Violated, draft Convention on Extradition, Principles Regarding Relations among American States, and Inter-American Convention on Human Rights [Pact of San José de Costa Rica] (1973); Convention for the Protection of Flora, Fauna and the Natural Scenic Beauties of America (1976); draft Convention That Defines Torture as an International Crime (1980); Declaration on the Strengthening of Inter-American Relations in the Field of

Finance and Trade, draft Inter-American Convention on the Jurisdictional Immunity of States, and Inter-American Declaration on the Rights of the Family (1983); Legal Status of Asylees, Refugees, and Displaced Persons in the American Hemisphere, draft Additional Protocol to the American Convention on Human Rights [Pact of San José de Costa Rica], and Inter-American Convention to Prevent and Punish Torture (1985); New American Treaty of Pacific Settlement and draft of the Inter-American Convention on Judicial Assistance on Criminal Matters (1986); Additional Protocol to the American Convention on Human Rights to Abolish the Death Penalty (1987); Additional Protocol to the American Convention on Human Rights in the Area of Economic, Social and Cultural Rights [Protocol of San Salvador] (1988); Integration and Development of Inter-American Law; Revision of the Statutes, Rules of Procedure, and Other Instruments Governing the Organs, Agencies, and Entities of the Organization; Draft Inter-American Convention on the Forced Disappearance of Persons; and Creation of an Inter-American System for Nature Conservation (1989). Finally, in a special session of the General Assembly—the Third Special Session, Washington, D.C., 1971, the Convention to Prevent and Punish the Acts of Terrorism Taking the Form of Crimes against Persons and Related Extortion That Are of International Significance was approved.

THE PROTECTION OF HUMAN RIGHTS

The American Declaration of Rights and Duties of Man

The question of human rights had not arisen in 1959 when the Fifth MCMFA in Santiago de Chile created the Inter-American Commission on Human Rights (IACHR). As stated earlier, already at the Inter-American Conference for the Consolidation of Peace in Buenos Aires in 1936 and at the Eighth ICAS in Lima in 1938, the question had been dealt with. In 1938, in Lima, the conference adopted several resolutions on the topic, such as "Freedom of Association and Freedom of Expression of Workers," the Lima Declaration in Favor of Womens' Rights, Resolution XXXVI in which the American Republics declared that "any persecution on account of racial or religious motives . . . is contrary to the political and juridical system of America," and, especially, the "Declaration for the Defense of Human Rights," in which the American States expressed their concern over the increasing tensions in Europe and mentioned that "respect be given to those human rights not necessarily involved in the conflict, to humanitarian sentiments and to the spirit and material inheritance of civilization."[5]

The internationalization of human rights by the end of World War II was echoed in the inter-American system. Thus, the Chapultepec Conference in Mexico City—the Inter-American Conference on Problems of War and Peace, 1945—approved two resolutions that prepared the ground for the later protection of human rights: Resolution XXVII, entitled "Free Access to Information," and Resolution XL on "International Protection of the Essential Rights of Man." It was the latter resolution that proclaimed the adherence of the American Republics to the principles established by international law for safeguarding "the essential rights of man" and favored an international system for their protection. In order to make such protection feasible, it was necessary to define them, and thus the conference requested the IAJC to prepare such a draft declaration. Two years later, when the Rio Treaty was signed, the Preamble to the Inter-American Treaty of Reciprocal Assistance stated that "peace is founded on justice and moral order and, consequently, on the international recognition and protection of human rights and freedom."

It was the ninth ICAS in Bogotá (1948), that accepted the American Declaration of Rights and Duties of Man (Resolution XXX) mentioned earlier, and no doubt, it represented the first international instrument of its type adopted by governments, but it was not approved as a convention, as had been hoped. Also, it was not successful in creating an Inter-American Court of Human Rights. The declaration consisted of thirty-eight articles, and the preamble stated that "the essential rights of man are not derived from the fact that he is a national of a certain state, but are based upon attributes of his human personality." The American states thus acknowledged that human rights were not created by the governments, but existed prior to the formation of a state. The preamble also mentioned that "the affirmation given by the internal regimes of the States establish the initial system of protection considered by the American States as being suited to the present social and juridical conditions," and that "they should increasingly strengthen that system in the international field as conditions become more favorable."[6] Human rights were thus included in Article 5(j), in the original Charter of the OAS of 1948.

The Inter-American Commission on Human Rights (IACHR)

The legal instruments of the OAS—the IACJ and the IAJC—worked hard to perfect the system of human rights, especially since so far no enforcement agency had been set up and the entire subject matter was purely declamatory. Thus, new efforts had to be made, and much progress was achieved in the next decades. Both the fourth MCMFA in Washington, 1951, and the tenth ICAS in Caracas (1954), continued the debate, and the Declaration of Caracas of 1954 established a historical link between human rights, representative democracy, and economic development when it renewed the conviction of the American states that one of most effective means of strengthening their democratic institutions was to increase respect for the individual and social rights of humanity, without any discrimination, and to maintain and to promote an effective policy of economic well-being and social justice in order to raise the standard of living of their peoples.

Tensions in the Caribbean in the 1950s, which culminated in the Cuban Revolution, gave an extraordinary boost to the principles of human rights and representative democracy. As stated earlier, these increased tensions led to the convocation of the fifth MCMFA in Santiago de Chile (1959), where, among other items, the Inter-American Commission on Human Rights (IACHR) was created as one of the enforcement agencies. It also entrusted the Inter-American Council of Jurists to study the prevailing juridical relationship between the respect for human rights and the effective exercise of representative democracy.[7] The fifth MCMFA also requested from the legal bodies of the OAS a draft Convention on Human Rights which would include an Inter-American Court of Human Rights.

The commission was officially set up on September 10, 1959, when the COAS approved its statutes. Its powers, valid until 1965, were at that time rather weak. This, however, did not deter the commission, which went right ahead and looked into a variety of human rights problems: Dominican Republic (1960–1965), Cuba (1960–1965), Haiti (1963–1964), Ecuador (1964), Guatemala (1963), Honduras (1963), and Nicaragua (1962). With the exception of the Cuban case, all these human rights problems were satisfactorily solved, which in turn gave the OAS and the IACHR an increase in prestige. Many political problems remained, however, which were why the commission remained rather ineffective, and an Inter-American Court of Human Rights was not set up at the time. The Eighth MCMFA in Punta del Este, Uruguay (1962), observed that the commission's powers were too weak to be of any real use. Thus the ice was broken for a revision of its original statutes. A few years later, in 1965 and 1966, the powers of the IACHR were revised and broadened, and approved by the Second Special ICAS in Rio de Janeiro. These extended powers authorized the IACHR to examine communications submitted to it and any other available information, so that it may address to the governments of any American state a request for information deemed pertinent to the commission. It could also make recommendations when it deemed this appropriate, with the purpose of respecting human rights.

The Inter-American Convention on Human Rights

A further change came about with the Protocol of Buenos Aires of 1967 since it upgraded the IACHR to the extent that it was put on the same level as the other three councils of the OAS. It was also specifically mentioned in two articles of the new charter: Article 112 (now 111) stated that the IACHR has the function "to promote the observance and protection of human rights and to serve as a consultative Organ of the Organization in these matters," and stated further that "a convention on human rights shall determine the structure, competence and procedure of this commission, as well as those of other organs responsible for those matters." Article 150 charged the IACHR to keep "vigilance over the observance of human rights until the aforementioned convention on human rights enters into force."[8] Two years later, in 1969, in San José de Costa Rica, the organization finally fulfilled the goals expressed in 1945 at the Chapultepec Conference: it adopted the Inter-American Convention on Human Rights, which entered into force in 1978. The Convention not only strengthened the IACHR but the entire mechanism and it marked the culmination of a movement that had begun in the 1930s. The purpose of the convention was to consolidate a system of personal liberty and social justice based on respect for the essential rights of man. The broadened powers are especially visible in Article 43 of the Convention where it is stated that "The States parties undertake to provide the Commission with such information as it may request of them as to the manner in which their domestic law ensures the effective application of any provision of this Convention," which is different from the former statutes that only empowered the commission "to urge" the governments to supply it with information on the measures adopted by them in matters of human rights. The new statutes also gave the states parties the right to present petitions, although the provisions of Article 45 said that the right was conditioned upon state recognition of the jurisdiction of the commission to receive and examine an interstate communication by both the states exercising the right and the states against which the petition was lodged.[9] So far, only a few states have recognized the commission's jurisdiction to consider interstate complaints: Argentina, Costa Rica, Ecuador, Jamaica, Peru, and Venezuela.[10]

The IACHR, since 1967 a permanent organ of the OAS, was given a jurisdiction that extended beyond those states that were parties to the American convention and thus incorporated all the member states of the organization. The convention, which entered into force on July 18, 1978, was followed by Resolution 253 of the Permanent Council (September 20, 1978), which provided that the IACHR would continue to exercise its functions until the new commission, to be elected by the General Assembly, was duly installed. The commission's statutes give functions and powers with respect to all the member states of the OAS, but at the same time there are also some provisions that are only applicable to those member states that are parties to the Inter-American Convention on Human Rights.

At the Ninth Regular Session of the General Assembly the new statutes of the IACHR were adopted and the above-mentioned distinction was thus upheld. Later, at the forty-ninth session of the IACHR, new regulations were adopted which, in four titles, set forth the procedures to be followed: Title I regulates the nature and the membership of the commission; Title II, the different procedures to be applied to States parties to the convention and to those states that are not parties to the convention; Title III refers to the relations of the commission to the Inter-American Court of Human Rights; and Title IV contains the final provisions that regulate the interpretation of the regulations and any amendments.[11]

The Inter-American Court of Human Rights

Originally, the idea of an Inter-American Court of Human Rights came up at the Ninth ICAS in Bogotá (1948), although its intellectual roots go back to 1908 (as stated earlier). Resolution XXXI—"Inter-American Court to Protect the Rights of Man"—of the Ninth ICAS recommended that IAJC make a study of such an institution. In its report of September 26, 1949, to the IACJ, the latter stated that before proceeding with the court it would be advisable to prepare a draft convention containing rules of this nature, which the IACJ would submit to the next ICAS. Indeed, the tenth ICAS received the report and sidestepped the issue instructing the eleventh ICAS to take care of the matter. Of course, this eleventh ICAS never took place, but it was the fifth MCMFA, Santiago de Chile, 1959, which not only established the IACHR but also requested the IACJ to prepare two drafts: one on "Human Rights" and the other on an "Inter-American Court of Human Rights." As stated earlier, the IACJ carried out this request in its fourth meeting (Santiago, 1959), thus preparing a draft convention on human rights which included the creation of an Inter-American Court of Human Rights.

It was this draft, which was submitted to the Second Special ICAS in Rio de Janeiro (1965), that passed the subject matter over to the COAS to update and complete it. A Specialized Inter-American Conference would do the rest.[12] The IACHR presented its opinions to the COAS on April 1, 1967, and, as stated earlier, the Inter-American Convention on Human Rights was then adopted on November 22, 1969, in San José, Costa Rica. Chapter VII of Part II of the convention created the Inter-American Court of Human Rights.

The Inter-American Court of Human Rights has both adjudicating and advisory jurisdiction. In the former, only the commission and the states parties to the convention are empowered to submit cases concerning the interpretation and application of the convention. However, the respective procedures (Articles 48–50) must have been previously exhausted and the states against which a case is being brought before the court must recognize the jurisdiction of the Inter-American Court. In the latter case, the advisory function, Article 64 of the statutes of the convention, provides that any member state of the organization may consult the court on the interpretation of human rights in the member states. This right of consultation also extends to the organs listed in Chapter X of the revised OAS Charter. The court, on the request of a member state, can also "issue an opinion on the compatibility between any of its domestic laws and the aforementioned international instrument."

The seven judges of the court were elected by the General Assembly of the OAS at its Seventh Special Session (May 1979). Officially, the Inter-American Court of Human Rights was established in San José, Costa Rica, where it has its seat, on September 3, 1979. Finally, the General Assembly in its Ninth Regular Session in La Paz, Bolivia (October 1979), in its Resolution 448, approved the statutes of the court, which, in the first article is defined as "an autonomous judicial institution whose purpose is the application and interpretatiion of the American Convention on Human Rights."[13] Moreover, in its Third Regular Session, July 30–August 9, 1980, the court approved its rules of procedure.

After a record of more than half a century, when the problem of human rights was first aired, the organization can show positive results with its four instruments: the American Declaration of the Rights and Duties of Man, the IACHR, the Inter-American Convention on Human Rights, and the Inter-American Court of Human Rights. The organization dealt with the entire subject matter in a very careful manner, since it did not want to encroach on the principle of nonintervention. Although it would be difficult to say that everything related to human rights has been solved, the very fact of the existence of these four instruments has heightened the awareness of the entire problem, and it is a fact that both commission and court have played an increasingly important role. It may be mentioned that so far the United States has not ratified the Inter-American Convention on Human Rights.

DE FACTO GOVERNMENTS AND REPRESENTATIVE DEMOCRACY

The Recognition of De Facto Regimes

Recognition of de facto governments has always played a substantial role in Latin America, like nonintervention, diplomatic and territorial asylum, and the peaceful settlement of disputes. On top of the rather normal and objective difficulties in applying recognition to a de facto regime, which for one reason or another has achieved power in a given state, came the subjectivity of U.S. foreign policy with its double standard concerning when and how to apply nonrecognition—Wilsonianism versus pragmatism. The United States has always used the weapon of nonrecognition of de facto governments whenever it suited its interests, whereas the Latin Americans have always been more pragmatic on the issue. As idealists, Latin Americans wanted representative democracy, and thus we find the principle anchored in all major OAS treaties and conventions, especially the Charter of the OAS; as realists, Latin Americans know from experience that very often representative government has not worked in their midst, especially when economic and social conditions contradicted a rational system like democracy. The United States has often intervened on behalf of representative democracy, but these interventions were never hailed by Latin Americans who saw in them just another case of the United States imposing its views on weaker neighbors and always pursuing its selfish interests. On the other hand—in the notorious double standard—it was also the United States which, as long as it was possible, not only recognized but even protected Latin American governments which had come to power by force (some with and others without popular support), as the cases of Rafael Leónidas Trujillo in the Dominican Republic, Anastasio Somoza Debayle in Nicaragua, and others, testify.

It was thus obvious that the question of representative democracy and de facto regimes and their recognition would be important topics for discussion in a region where democracy had, to say the least, a difficult time. As time advanced and both liberalization and democratization achieved greater respectability, more and more pressure would be applied so that representative democracy became the only acceptable authority in Latin America, but the principle of nonintervention often complicated matters. There were those who wanted to pursue a policy of nonrecognition of any de facto government; there were others who wanted to use the multilateral approach in order to obtain democratic results. President Woodrow Wilson is, of course, the best example of how not to do things: Witness his intervention in Mexico in 1914 against Victoriano Huerta in order to teach Mexicans a lesson in democracy and how to elect honest citizens.

Until Wilson, the usual policy had been one that recognized a given de facto regime whenever it showed that it controlled the situation and was willing to acknowledge its responsibilities, which was in accordance with international law. Wilsonianism represented an attempt at legitimizing intervention for the sake of democracy, a very dubious undertaking. Already, the Calvo Clause and the Drago Doctrine were Argentina and Latin America's replies to the increasing distortions of the Monroe Doctrine (Dollar diplomacy, the Roosevelt Corollary, etc.) at the turn of the century. Later on, Mexico's Estrada Doctrine (1930) represented a new protest against unilateral North American intervention; in this case using recognition of a given government as a means of gaining privileges from the government to be recognized. The doctrine, however, did not prosper, for the simple reason that it went too far in that it threatened to abolish recognition altogether. It called for immediate and automatic recognition.

During World War II the links among representative democracy, recognition, and intervention became more evident than ever. The First MCMFA in Panama, 1939, in its Resolution XI recommended to the governments "that they take the necessary measures to eradicate from the Americas the spread of doctrines that tend to place in jeopardy the common inter-American democratic ideal." In the second MCMFA in Havana, 1940, the Union of American Republics went a step further when it summarized its agenda under the title "Exchange of information on activities which may develop within the territory and jurisdiction of any American republic that tend to endanger the common American democratic ideal," and the third MCMFA led to the creation of the Emergency Advisory Committee for Political Defense.[14] This committee recommended, on December 24, 1943, that as long as the war was going on, new governments established by force ought not to be recognized until the other governments had an opportunity to exchange views and determined the probable adherence to the continental security arrangements, an idea that, although under different circumstances, was reawakened recently—at the twenty-first GARS, Santiago de Chile, 1991. There was always in the minds of the Latin Americans the belief that a different course of action would constitute intervention.

The Chapultepec Conference in Mexico City (1945), produced two proposals on the subject of recognition of de facto regimes: one, a Guatemalan project—after all, General Jorge Ubico's regime (1931–1944) had just been replaced by Juan José Arévalo's reformist administration that was based on a humanistic socialism of Krausean vintage—that denied recognition of any regime established by force until free elections were held. It was overwhelmingly defeated. Arévalo, it may be recalled, had lived for more than a decade in Argentina where he was influenced by *krausista* philosophy— the philosophy of Karl Christian Friedrich Krause (1781–1832), mostly unknown in Germany but with enormous influence in Spain, where the First Republic (1873–1874) was a Krausean experiment, and in Latin America, where in many places his philosophy fell on fertile ground, since his democratic ideas idealistically proclaimed the rather mystic Krausean ideal of universal solidarity based on the rational knowledge of the common dependency of all humanity and on the idea of the moral perfection of nations. In the days of Napoleon I, and later of the Holy Alliance, Krause defended not only the rights of women but also of children, animals and plants, and stones and crystals. He also advocated that a state was an association within which many social groups existed for a variety of interests; the state had no right to interfere but had considerable restrictions and had the duty to care for all elements of society, especially the weak, the poor and the sick, the young and the old. He was obviously ahead of his time.

The other proposal, submitted by Ecuador, would have eliminated the recognition of de facto governments in the interest of the continuity of diplomatic relations. Both projects were referred to the IAJC for study and report to the next ICAS.[15]

At the ninth ICAS in Bogotá (1948), several drafts on the subject were submitted by Ecuador, Mexico, the United States, Peru, and Brazil. However, in view of increased revolutionary activities, a subcommittee considered these drafts and came up with a formula that satisfied all parties, except

Mexico. Its first part stated that the establishment of diplomatic relations was not to be used as a means of securing unjustified advantages—obviously an echo of the Estrada doctrine—and did not imply approval; the second part recommended consultation among the different governments. The final result was Resolution XXXV which stated:

a. Desirability of the continuation of diplomatic relations;

b. The right of establishing, maintaining or suspending diplomatic relations shall not be exercised as a means of obtaining unwarranted benefits;

c. The establishment or maintenance of diplomatic relations with a government did not imply any judgment on the domestic policies of the respective government.[16]

Another resolution—Resolution XXXVI—requested from the IACJ the preparation of a draft on recognition for the next ICAS. This draft stated that new governments had a right to be recognized provided they were in control of the country and were able and willing to fulfill all international obligations—again in total agreement with international law. The IAJC was just as divided as the governments, however, and thus, just as with the question of an Inter-American Court of Human Rights, the committee declared that the time was not ripe yet for a convention of this type and passed the matter to the tenth ICAS.

The tenth ICAS tried to ignore the subject, but Uruguay presented a proposal with the title "Resolution on the Prevention of the Intervention of Totalitarian Powers in the Establishment of Governments" which listed three rules: one, de facto regimes should not be recognized if they came into power through foreign intervention; second, there were certain conditions under which de facto regimes could be recognized; and third, consultation among American states should be carried out in order to see whether the above conditions had been met. This draft proposal was rejected and thus did not reach the IAJC for study.

The problem was thus not solved in 1954, and in the following years, with the Cuban Revolution and the succeeding military regimes that came into power in Brazil (1964), Argentina (1966), and Peru (1968), the question became even more thorny. On July 30, 1962, the COAS held a special meeting to consider a request from the Dominican Republic, Venezuela, Honduras, and Costa Rica, to hold a Meeting of Consultation under Article 39 of the charter in order to decide what action to take toward governments that arose by coup d'état. The immediate concern was a coup in Peru that had followed the ouster of President Arturo Frondizi in Argentina. The four governments felt that this situation even imperiled the OAS itself. Despite the seriousness, however, the COAS voted on August 10, 1962 not to convoke the MCMFA—seven countries favored it; eight were against; and five abstained.[17]

The subject matter of de facto governments was not closed here. The question was reopened at the second special ICAS in Rio de Janeiro, 1965, and here the American states were in favor of informal consultation. Resolution XXVI of the second special ICAS, after stating that nondemocratic governments represented a political threat to peace and recalling the earlier request to the IAJC under Resolution XXXVI of the ninth ICAS, recommended that until the time that a convention on recognition was ready for signature, the governments should consult immediately among themselves after the overthrow of any American government. Among the conditions for recognition would be the intent of holding free elections in the foreseeable future, and the prospect of respect for human rights with the implementation of the commitments included in the Declaration of the Peoples of the Americas and the Charter of Punta del Este. The resolution also made it clear that every government retained the right, after consultation, to determine its own course of action.[18]

The resolution of this second special ICAS represented the culmination in the solution of this difficult problem, and the novelty of 1965 was simply the fact that recognition was linked to two factors that would become increasingly more important in the next decades: the support of representative democracy and the protection of human rights.[19]

However, the Latin American reality of the 1970s and 1980s put a damper on a definitive solution of this problem. On one side, there was the establishment of military governments of the right in Argentina (1966, 1976), Brazil (1964), and Uruguay (1973) to combat internal subversion, corruption, and economic and social chaos; on the other side, there was the fascinating military coup in Peru (1968) where young officers had been thoroughly indoctrinated by Jorge Bravo, the chief ideologist of the American Popular Revolutionary Alliance (APRA), who was the leading lecturer at the Centro de Altos Estudios Militares in Lima for some fifteen years.[20] Indeed, amazingly, the Peruvian Army, the historic foe of APRA, was influenced to such a degree by its political and ideological enemy that after 1968 it implemented the reformist policies that APRA's founder, Raúl Víctor Haya de la Torre, had already advocated in 1931. There was also the electoral victory of Salvador Allende in Chile in 1970 which produced a legal socialist-marxist government in that country, but with it also brought economic chaos. Thus, a few years later, in 1973, there arose a triumphant counterrevolution led by August Pinochet, representing the propertied classes and lasting some sixteen years (until 1989), and not devoid of some very positive economic and social consequences. Finally, there was the end of the Somoza dynasty in Nicaragua and the establishment of the socialist Sandinista government in that country, which gradually led to increasingly serious confrontations with the United States, and to the Contras, and to terrorism and guerrilla warfare in El Salvador and Guatemala.

Thus, the question of recognition of de facto regimes was indefinitely postponed, the time just not being ripe for a positive solution. The question was compounded by the pragmatic approach of the United States which, in 1965, simply made a deal with Brazil, trading recognition and approval for a leading Brazilian role in the Inter-American Force at the time of the invasion of the Dominican Republic in order to forestall a new Cuban-style revolutionary regime. Another fact that compounded the situation was the success of the military regimes, at least in the beginning, in regard to economic matters, which was especially true of the Brazilian case. Thus, in sum, the entire question of recognition of de facto regimes in those years became irrelevant. The question arose only after the military governments collapsed in the 1980s, beginning with Argentina after its defeat in the War of the South Atlantic in 1982. After the Argentine military fell from power, the movement for democracy could not be stopped and gained momentum all over the continent. The unpopularity of the armed forces and their inability to cope with the increasing economic and social problems led to the rise of democratic governments, from Argentina, Brazil, Uruguay, and Chile to Peru, Bolivia, Paraguay, and even Mexico, where the Institutional Revolutionary Party (PRI) had set up a virtual dictatorship for half a century. All these countries witnessed movements for change.

It was thus no surprise that the twenty-first GARS (Santiago de Chile, 1991) tackled the question anew with the proposal that immediate consultation should take place in the event of a coup and the establishment of a de facto regime. However, as in the past, nobody wanted to go further than consultation, again leaving the ultimate decision to the individual states and their national interests. It is doubtful that any other solution could be attained.

The Exercise of Representative Democracy

Representative democracy is one of the principles of the organization. As a matter of fact one of its most important ones, and as such it is incorporated in the charter—Article 3(d)—and is linked to two other issues, the problem of human rights, discussed earlier, and the principle of nonintervention, the latter of which is just as substantial but elusive as representative democracy.

The question of representative democracy is not an easy one, since it is part and parcel of the Germanic or Anglo-Saxon and Scandinavian traditions, but not so much a part of Hispanic civilization, where Roman law together with the *Lex regia* (Royal law) and the famous principle of Ulpian, *Quod Principi placet, legis vigorum habet* ("What pleases the Prince has the force of law"), played an overwhelming role. The Germanic traditions survived very much in northern Spain—the Visigothic elements—and found an echo in the Castillian *cabildos, Cortes, fueros* and freedoms—and as such they were brought to the Spanish and Portuguese empires overseas but not to the extent of replacing Roman-law traditions. Roman law in Latin America and common law in the United States mirror the opposing legal as well as intellectual and cultural foundations. It is a paradox of modern history, as Lord Acton showed, that medieval Catholic political thought with the establishment of a representative system—after all representative democracy has its origin in the elective system of the Dominican order (Stephen Langton and Simon de Montfort)—with its freedoms and privileges surviving in Protestant England while it decayed on the European continent.[21] It was from England that the concept of representative democracy was introduced in Colonial North America as part of the Puritan heritage. It should thus be obvious that, besides differences in other intellectual, cultural, and historical elements, the entire question of representative democracy cannot be identical in the Anglo-Saxon United States and Hispanic Latin America.

Constitutional government became an ideal in the nineteenth century, and Latin America followed this ideal, even if in most cases it did not really work. Brazil with its constitutional monarchy and Chile with its aristocratic republic were the two great exceptions during the entire Latin American nineteenth century. With the end of the empire in Brazil in 1889 and the final collapse of the aristocratic republic in Chile in 1890, both countries entered a period of turmoil, although eventually both overcame their respective crises. Basically, moreover, despite its ups and downs, both Brazil and Chile recaptured their democratic foundations, largely due to their nineteenth-century experience. To a lesser extent, this could also be said of Colombia.

In the twentieth century, representative democracy advanced, especially with and after World War I, and as it gradually permeated the entire globe it also echoed with increasing fury in the Latin American area. Here again, the ideal was one side of the coin, while the other side showed the extraordinary difficulties to implement it, when in many cases, if not most, the basic foundations for a sound democracy—literacy, education, history, and tradition—were lacking.

The inter-American system, obviously, followed the trend, and the more the century advanced, the more attention was being paid to this important principle which did not arise with the American Revolution and the French Revolution but goes as far back as the Magna Carta in England and the Laws of Leon in Spain, and even further, to St. Augustine and St. Isidore of Seville. It has been said earlier that the most important principles incorporated in the Charter of the OAS were representative democracy and nonintervention, and both have been violated time and again. Representative democracy is obviously also linked to problems discussed before: human rights, recognition of de facto government, and economic and social development.

From the very beginning of the inter-American system, representative democracy became one of the ideals to be followed, and even when Latin American military regimes were in power they never ignored the possibility of returning sooner or later to a representative democratic government.

Thus, the ideal of representative democracy was as strong a tradition in Latin America as in the United States, but in the former, in view of history and culture, it was much more difficult to implement and enforce it. Over half a century ago, Cecil Jane, in his *Liberty and Despotism in Spanish America*, stressed the existence in that part of Latin America (even though it would largely also apply to Brazil) of two opposing principles: the love of freedom of the individual and the love for a perfect and efficient government. As he said:

The Spaniard loves . . . that ideal liberty for which there is no place in an imperfect world. He would be free to the very fullest extent, free in a wider sense than is in fact compatible with the continued existence of organized society. . . . He is, indeed, a passionate individualist, aspiring to attain an ideal individualism. . . .

But side by side with this passion for liberty is found recognition of the fact that government is a necessity and a consequent desire that government also should be ideal. The function of the ruler is to rule . . . fully, absolutely, exerting his authority without restraint and upon all in every relationship of life. He must be a despot or nothing, for if he be less[,] . . . he is forthwith imperfect, mediocre. He fails, if he be not absolute, to perform in the most complete manner those functions . . . ; he falls short of the ideal. That very individualism which impels the Spaniard to resist control leads him also to welcome control when it is the result of a vigorous assertion of individuality by another; the more vigorous the assertion, the more ready his submission. And hence, there is a perpetual tendency to alternate between a degree of liberty which amounts almost to the negation of all government and a degree of government which amounts almost to a negation of all liberty. This alternation, and the conflict of which it is the result, is the inevitable product of the Spanish mind, of the combination of love of freedom with love of efficient government, of that ardent idealism by which the race has always been inspired. And it is to the nature of the temperament of the race that the apparent contradictions of the political life of Spanish America, the conflict which constitutes that life, must be ultimately traced.[22]

Latin America was well aware of this situation: Domestically it realized that weak executives would not work and that presidential power must be strong; at the same time, the possibility of presidential abuse existed. Hence, the solution was to avoid an immediate second presidential term. In the inter-American system, while Latin America always adhered and advanced the cause of representative democracy, it rejected the idea that the lack of it justified intervention. It was thus willing to incorporate the principle into the Charter of the OAS and other instruments of the inter-American system, but at the same time, and over the years and decades, it continuously strengthened the principle of nonintervention. Thus, Latin America maintained that it was up to the Latin American governments to determine their own form of government—a point that was incorporated in the revised charter through the Protocol of Cartagena de Indias in Article 3(e)—although they made it abundantly clear that totalitarian regimes of any kind were not part of their tradition.

As stated earlier, the Argentine Drago Doctrine and the Calvo Clause, as well as the Mexican Estrada Doctrine aimed at U.S. intervention before the inter-American system had been put on a treaty basis. The notion of representative democracy was first expressed at the Inter-American Conference for the Consolidation of Peace, held in Buenos Aires in 1936, when it was said that "the existence of a common democracy throughout America" was the basis of the American republics.[23] Later, the Preamble of the Rio Treaty, signed in Rio de Janeiro in 1947, stated that "the obligation of mutual assistance and common defense of the American Republics is essentially related to their democratic ideals" and that "peace is founded in justice and moral order, and consequently, . . . on the effectiveness of democracy."[24] When the OAS Charter was promulgated, the notion of representative democracy was introduced in Article 5(d)—now Article 3(d)—where "the effective exercise of representative democracy" was one of the principles which guided the OAS.

Other resolutions of the ninth ICAS (Bogotá, 1948) repeated the principle. Thus, Resolution XXX of the American Declaration of the Rights and Duties of Man also cited representative democracy as a necessary foundation, and so did Resolution XXXII—"The Preservation and Defense of Democracy in America," which declared that social justice should be achieved within the framework of democratic government. After the ninth ICAS, the COAS repeatedly took action to strengthen the notion of representative democracy. It did so in 1950 in regard to the situation in the Caribbean when it acted as Provisional Organ of Consultation. In one of the five resolutions adopted at that time, the COAS declared that one of the factors contributing to the tensions and threats to peace and security was the presence of political refugees and exiles in various countries and that, consequently, it was necessary to make the principle of representative democracy more effective.[25]

The fourth MCMFA, Washington, 1951, in its Resolution VII—"Strengthening and Effective Exercise of Democracy"—referred to the tenth ICAS the aforementioned Resolution XXX of the ninth ICAS for implementation. Both the IACJ and the IAJC were requested to prepare studies and drafts for the Tenth ICAS, but the matter was sidestepped. At the tenth ICAS (Caracas, 1954), the Latin Americans linked the question of representative democracy to the improvement of the economic and social conditions in Latin America; in other words, that any totalitarian threat could be effectively countered with an improved standard of living, a principle that in 1961 would be incorporated in the Alliance for Progress. Obviously, the background of this linkage was the CIA-inspired invasion of Guatemala. After plenty of debate, the tenth ICAS produced the Declaration of Caracas, which reaffirmed the American Declaration of the Rights and Duties of Man, the

Universal Declaration of Human Rights, and several OAS resolutions covering this problem. It then stated:

to choose freely its [the people's] own institutions in the effective exercise of representative democracy, as a means of preserving its political sovereignty, achieving its economic independence, and living its own social and cultural life, without intervention on the part of any state or group of states, either directly or indirectly, in its domestic or external affairs, and, particularly, without the intrusion of any form of totalitarianism.[26]

It continued that the best way to combat the penetration of alien and totalitarian ideas was the respect of human rights, the promotion of social justice, the raising of the standard of living, and the effective exercise of representative democracy.

The highlight of the movement to promote the effective exercise of representative democracy was the fifth MCMFA, which was held in Santiago de Chile in 1959, as a consequence of the increasing tensions in the Caribbean. It was here that the ideal became a practical reality. The result of the deliberations was the Declaration of Santiago, which, as is usually the case, after referring to previous resolutions on the topic declared that inter-American peace depended on the realization of the democratic ideal and that the existence of antidemocratic regimes violated the principle on which the organization was based. The declaration stressed representative democracy as a desirable goal that would not weaken the respect for the right of peoples to choose their own form of government and would thus avoid any kind of undesirable intervention. The declaration then mentioned eight points necessary to fulfil the effective exercise of representative democracy: separation of powers, free elections, elimination of the illegal perpetuation in power, respect for fundamental human rights, protection of these rights through effective juridical procedures, rejection of the systematic use of political proscription, freedom of information and expression, and inter-American cooperation to "strengthen and develop their economic structures, and achieve just and humane living conditions for their peoples."[27] The fifth MCMFA, in its historic Declaration of Santiago, linked the effective exercise of representative democracy to human rights and to humane living conditions. Two years later, the Alliance for Progress would be seen, together with the declaration, as the best available weapon to fight subversion, revolutionary activity, and the immense echo of the Cuban Revolution all over the continent.

It is also interesting to note that at this fifth MCMFA, Nicaragua submitted a proposal on the use of observers in national elections for study by the COAS, which at that time represented quite a novelty but has lately been implemented in a variety of cases. Nicaragua was thus very much ahead of the time, since observers in presidential elections became a new tool for the implementation of the effective exercise of representative democracy almost three decades later in the very same country which proposed it. The MCMFA also requested the COAS to prepare a draft convention on the "Effective Exercise of Representative Democracy," to be submitted to the eleventh ICAS. Finally, the IACJ was instructed to study "the possible juridical relationship" between "respect for human rights" and the effective exercise of representative democracy, and the right to set in motion the machinery of American international law in force.[28]

So far, the action had been declamatory, but in order to put teeth into the Declaration of Santiago, the fifth MCMFA also passed Resolution IX setting up a special committee of seven members—Argentina, Brazil, Mexico, Nicaragua, Peru, Uruguay, and Venezuela (chair)—to prepare such a draft Convention on the Effective Exercise of Representative Democracy. At the end of the year such a draft was indeed submitted to the governments. It provided that in case of the overthrow of a freely elected government the de facto regime would neither be recognized nor allowed a seat at the COAS. The latter was also empowered to look into alleged violations of the standards mentioned in the draft convention, and if the challenged government did not reply within three months, then the COAS would publicly debate the issue, and if peace and security were endangered a MCMFA could be convoked by an absolute majority. The draft convention needed a two-thirds majority for ratification. The reaction, however, was not encouraging and the topic was shelved until the eleventh ICAS.[29]

The IACJ passed the entire matter to the IAJC, but the latter, after exhaustingly researching the difficult topic, came up with a report that intervention in any country in such a case would violate other principles, and that the only exception to this rule would be cases where a possible corruption of democracy had been the consequence of foreign aggression, or an act of this sort which would lie outside the control of the organization (i.e., invoking Article 6 of the Rio Treaty). It meant essentially that the view of the Uruguayan Foreign Minister Alberto Rodríguez Larreta of 1945, that collective action by the community of American nations was both necessary and legitimate in support of democracy, had again been overwhelmingly rejected.[30]

The topic was again raised at the Seventh MCMFA in San José, Costa Rica, in 1960. It was Venezuela that had taken action against Trujillo's Dominican Republic when the latter had made an unsuccessful attempt on the life of the Venezuelan president, Rómulo Betancourt. It should also be noted that once Venezuela eliminated the military government of Marcos Pérez Jiménez, it has pursued ever since a foreign policy devoted to the democratic ideal. It was thus also Venezuela, after relations had soured with Castro's Cuba, which followed a similar course against Havana. Venezuela's point of view was simply that a declaration or treaty on the topic of representative democracy was necessary, in which it would specifically be stated that governments that were not freely elected should be ostracized. Several drafts were then presented on the topic of free elections, including from Argentina and the United States, as well as the one from Nicaragua mentioned earlier concerning observers at elections of the highest officials of a given country, but nothing came of it. This seventh MCMFA simply shelved the debate to the COAS.

The issue did not die, however. The eighth MCMFA again dealt with the subject. Thus, Resolution III—"Reiteration of the Principles of Non-Intervention and Self-Determination"—stated that both the charter and the Declaration of Santiago said that governments should arise from free elections. Moreover, Resolution IV dealt with the topic of free elections as the most effective means of consulting the sovereign people and of guaranteeing "the restoration of a legal order based on the authority of the law and the respect for the rights of the individual."[31] Finally, Resolution V, which also linked the topic to the Declaration of Santiago of 1959, repeated the theme of economic and social development as essential "for the stability of democracy and the safeguarding of human rights."[32]

Not having been resolved so far, the subject matter continued to be on the agenda. As a result of the conclusions reached, however, the governments began to favor two important tools: one, the idea of technical assistance, and two, to send observers to presidential elections. In 1961 the new government of the Dominican Republic; in 1962 the government of Costa Rica; and in 1963 those of Honduras and Nicaragua requested and obtained such assistance.[33] Later, in 1966, Bolivia, Costa Rica, and the Dominican Republic availed themselves of similar services.[34]

A further development was the famous Symposium on Democracy which the Dominican Republic proposed and which was held in Santo Domingo, December 17–22, 1962. This symposium covered eight subjects, as follows:

(1) democracy as a way of life in which the State exists for individuals and not individuals for the State; (2) the necessity of affirming human rights which, in a democracy, set limits to the powers of government; (3) "the consent of the governed as the sole source of political power and the only principle that renders the exercise of that power legitimate," and the consequent need to guarantee civil and political rights, broaden the electoral base, and secure wide access to communications; (4) subjection to the rule of law; (5) democracy as limited government; (6) governmental responsibility; (7) active participation by the governed; and (8) the importance of "the establishment of high standards of social justice and the creation of equal opportunities for all."[35]

The symposium concluded that the following actions cannot be described as intervention:

1. Examination of the conduct of governments, either privately or publicly carried out;

2. Acts of international cooperation that are accepted by a State and are inspired by a desire to achieve the principles and goals of regional organization; or

3. Action by the authorities of the regional organization in fulfillment of international standards freely consented to by the State toward which they are directed.[36]

The Alliance for Progress linked the concept of representative democracy to an improvement in economic and social matters. The United States, which for a long time had opposed this link now accepted it in view of the Cuban Revolution and its spread to the continent, and the Alliance for Progress was viewed as the best instrument to fight revolutionary movements like Castro's. Already the Act of Bogotá of 1960, passed at the third session of the CECE, connected economic development to the strengthening of democracy, and the Charter of Punta del Este (1961), which launched the Alliance for Progress, stated the purpose of accelerating the economic and social development so that the various Latin American countries would achieve maximum levels of well-being, "with equal opportunities for all, in democratic societies adapted to their own needs and desires."[37]

An interesting exercise in futility was the call for an MCMFA at the request of Costa Rica and Venezuela in 1963 in order to strengthen the concept of representative democracy. The COAS then appointed a preparatory committee to consider all the necessary questions for the forthcoming meeting. In the meantime a draft Convention on Representative Democracy had been prepared by the Special Committee (set up as a result of the Fifth MCMFA) to be submitted to the eleventh ICAS, which was continuously postponed until it was finally called off indefinitely on April 1, 1964. Thus the preparatory committee took its time, knowing that there was no easy solution. Its work was interrupted, however, by the convocation of a different MCMFA, the ninth. Thus, the preparatory committee reported back that a special ICAS should study the topic as well as other matters which had accumulated in the meantime because the eleventh ICAS never got off the ground. Finally, in 1965, the COAS canceled the MCMFA requested two years earlier by Costa Rica and Venezuela and transmitted all pertinent documents to the second special ICAS.

The second special ICAS was held in Rio de Janeiro in 1965 but sidestepped the issue of representative democracy. After all, there had been a military coup in 1964 in Brazil, which triggered others in Argentina in 1966 and Peru in 1968. Obviously the time was wrong to pursue such a topic. The only project to be discussed concerning the question of representative democracy was a draft resolution about the informal consultation prior to the recognition of de facto governments (Resolution XXVI mentioned earlier).

The years after the Brazilian coup and the entire decade of the 1970s with new military upheavals (Uruguay and Chile in 1973, Argentina in 1976) were not propitious. Moreover, the Reagan administration closed an eye to these developments, and, generally speaking, initiated the "Benign Neglect" policy. Only with the collapse of the Argentine military in 1982 did the topic of representative democracy arise again, and this time with greater fury than ever. The OAS, obviously, reflected the zeitgeist when it again emphasized the concept of representative democracy in the Protocol of Cartagena de Indias of 1985 and reactivated the monitoring of national elections, which had been started in the early 1960s but had been discontinued in view of realities.

The record of the OAS in the three interrelated subjects of representative democracy, recognition of de facto regimes, and promotion of human rights, is essentially good. Since the problems began to be raised, after World War II, much progress has been achieved. In contrast to the United Nations Charter, which provides that it is the function of the international organization to promote respect for those rights, with no obligation on the part of the member states to cooperate with the United Nations, the OAS explicitly imposes such an obligation on the different member states of its organization; in other words, the obligation of the member states to care for the protection of human rights has a solid foundation in the inter-American system. Moreover, it should be stressed that the IACHR, which was an important step in the process of representative democracy, is not composed of government officials but of persons who enjoy full autonomy. The commission now has broad powers and has made it possible that individuals have recourse to an international organization where they can protest violations of governments, even their own—there is no question that this is quite an accomplishment.

Two points should be raised here: one, the fact that representative democracy is part and parcel of the inter-American system, even if it was not always complied with, in contrast to the UN system, where all types of regimes are tolerated. Totalitarian regimes are by definition incompatible with the inter-American system, and as such it was recognized by the American republics even before the Charter of the OAS was accepted in 1948. It was also this fact that provided the primary basis for Cuba's exclusion from the OAS in 1962: Resolution VI stated that "adherence of any Member of the Organization of American States to Marxism-Leninism is incompatible with the Inter-American System" (VI.1.), and "that this incompatibility excludes the present government of Cuba from participation in the inter-American system" (VI.3.). Two, in determining the recognition of de facto regimes it was not so much the right to be recognized if it met the classical type of conditions—to be in control of the country and to be able and willing to assume international obligations—but, in the opinion of the IAJC (1949), further conditions must be met in order to obtain diplomatic recognition, such as its conduct with respect to human rights and fundamental freedoms. Furthermore, when a de facto regime is the product of a revolution, it may signify the overthrow of a falsely democratic regime and the reestablishment of a political order which guarantees the respect for fundamental human rights. Thus, it is difficult to generalize, and Latin America will probably gain even more experience in these interrelated fields. Assistant secretary general of the OAS Val T. McComie has recently argued—in the case of Grenada—that the principle of nonintervention should not and could not be applied to cases where fundamental human rights had been violated, a point Latin America is not ready to accept. Moreover, the previously mentioned Rodríguez Larreta proposal of 1945 is still rejected today because the result of collective intervention might be abused, resulting in a worse situation. What has never been accepted—and will not be accepted—is unilateral intervention by the strongest power, in the name of democracy, protection of American lives and interests, or drug abuse and trafficking control when it is really due to the pursuit of its own selfish interests, as in the cases of the U.S. interventions in Guatemala, the Dominican Republic, Central America (indirectly), Grenada, and Panama.

Hence, in sum, the inter-American system has demonstrated an impressive achievement in the field of the effective exercise of representative democracy and its interrelated areas of the recognition of de facto regimes and the protection of human rights. No longer are neither democracy or human rights the exclusive competence of the state; they have transcended the national arena, and neither sovereignty nor nonintervention are absolutely taboo in today's world. As García Amador stated, both can no longer "be opposed to a collective action, perfectly justifiable in the light of other equally established principles in the legal structure of the Inter-American System."[38]

Of course, many will not be satisfied with this statement and would like more results. However, again we should not forget the basic difference between a practical and pragmatic culture like that of the United States and an idealistic Latin America. In these interrelated problems of representative democracy, recognition of de facto regimes, and protection of human rights, the latter realm visualizes an ideal objective that often cannot be realized. Does it not echo the philosophy of the sixteenth-century Spanish School of Late Scholasticism—the Dominicans Francisco de Vitoria, Domingo de Soto, Melchor Cano, Domingo Báñez, and Diego de Covarrubias, and the Jesuits Francisco Suárez, Luis de Molina, and Juan de Mariana, whose ideal was a Christian state based on the Christian natural law, exalting the spiritual power of the Pope and the rights of the people against monarchical absolutism—a civil authority derived from God with the free consent of the governed against the Machiavellian raison d'état? These are theories that led to the protection of the Indians and to the establishment of our modern international law. They condemned conquest in international politics, defending the individual against the state. They stated unequivocally that (a) all peoples were free, independent, and sovereign; (b) they could freely choose the form of government they considered appropriate; (c) a political regime was legitimately established if constituted by the free will of the subjects; and (d) all peoples, regardless of race, culture, and religion, were equal. They even proclaimed the right of free people to intervene in the affairs of sovereign states to avenge crimes against humanity and to correct offenses against the fundamental rights of the people.[39]

12

The OAS and Peace and Security

THE PACIFIC SETTLEMENT OF DISPUTES

The inter-American system has a long tradition in both the pacific settlement of disputes and collective security which goes back to Simón Bolívar's Congress of Panama of 1826 and to the Spanish American Congresses of the nineteenth century. All of them dealt with these issues; in all of them the attempt was made to secure conciliation or mediation—witness Article 13 of the Treaty of Perpetual Union, League, and Confederation of 1826, while Articles 16, 17, 18 and 19 introduced the obligation of a peaceful settlement of any controversy among the parties to the treaty. In the other treaties, the principle of peaceful settlement of disputes was expanded with the obligation of only employing "exclusively pacific means to terminate those differences."[1] The nineteenth century showed other examples where arbitration was used. Argentina's borders were largely fixed by such methods: the Misiones area through U.S. President Rutherford B. Hayes in 1878, the Atacama border with Chile through William I. Buchanan, U.S. minister to the Buenos Aires government in 1899; and other Argentine-Chilean frontiers through His Britannic Majesty in 1902.[2] Brazil attained an extraordinary prestige when it succeeded to solve almost all border questions through the peaceful settlement of controversies thanks to its foreign minister, Baron de Rio Branco, when he headed the ministry between 1902 and 1912. Finally, there was also Secretary of State William Jennings Bryan with his "cooling-off treaties"—"Treaties for the Advancement of Peace"—who, by 1914, had negotiated and ratified some twenty-one such conventions.[3]

Thus, when the Pan American movement was initiated, there already existed a well-defined tradition for the pacific settlement of disputes, despite the fact that such idealistic juridical provisions had not prevented even much larger international conflicts, such as the war between the empire of Brazil and the United Provinces of the River Plate (1825–1828), the U.S.-Mexican War (1846–1848), the War of the Triple Alliance (1865–1870), and the Pacific War (1879–1883), not to mention the interminable quarrels in Central America after independence had been declared in 1823, and especially after the collapse of the United Provinces of Central America in 1838. Finally, in the twentieth century, the Chaco War, and again the conflicts in Central America, could be mentioned for failures in reaching a peaceful solution to a variety of international problems. On the other hand, it was just this Central American area which provided an interesting model, mentioned earlier: the Central American Court of Justice, created by treaty and signed by the five Central American republics which had gone their separate ways since 1838, in 1907. The court functioned for ten years in the Costa Rican town of Cartago and was well ahead of its times when it provided for the court to deal with cases where individuals of one Central American country could raise claims against individuals of another Central American government because of violation of treaties. The court lasted until 1917, when the Bryan-Chamorro Treaty between the United States and Nicaragua dealt a final blow to a worthy cause that already had encountered plenty of problems in survival.

The traditions in regard to the pacific settlement of disputes accumulated in the nineteenth century were continued by the Pan American movement. Thus, already at the Second ICAS in Mexico City, 1902, a Treaty on Compulsory Arbitration was signed that contemplated arbitration and recourse to the Permanent Court of Arbitration in The Hague, established procedures of good offices and mediation, and foresaw the establishment of an International Commission of Inquiry. The treaty was ratified by six countries and entered into force in 1903.

The biggest advance, however, on the pacific settlement of conflicts was achieved after World War I. The famous Gondra Treaty of 1923, signed at the fifth ICAS, led the list. It provided that all controversies were to be submitted to arbitration in cases where diplomacy had failed, and to investigation by a five-member commission. Actually the treaty provided for two permanent commissions: one in Washington and the other in Montevideo. The Gondra Treaty entered into force in 1924 after twenty countries had ratified it.

Still, in order to perfect the Gondra Treaty, the International Conference on Conciliation and Arbitration was held in Washington, D.C., 1928–1929. It produced three documents. First was a General Convention of American Conciliation, with the obligation to submit all disputes to the procedure of conciliation, using the Gondra Treaty's two commissions. It entered into force in 1929 after having been ratified by eighteen countries. The second document was the General Treaty of Inter-American Arbitration, which dealt with compulsory arbitration and stated that once a decision had been reached, there was no appeal. Sixteen countries ratified the treaty, but ten did so with reservations; it also entered into force in 1929.[4] The third document was entitled The Protocol of Progressive Arbitration, which proposed to eliminate the many reservations attached to the previous General Treaty of Inter-American Arbitration, thus extending the field of arbitration. Only ten countries ratified the protocol, and it entered into force on the date on which each respective instrument of ratification was deposited.[5]

Another important step in the perfection of the pacific settlement of disputes was the Anti-War Treaty of Non-Aggression and Conciliation of 1933, known as the "Saavedra Lamas Pact." Carlos Saavedra Lamas, foreign minister of Argentina, president of the Assembly of the League of Nations (to which the country had returned after a decade of absence), and Nobel Peace Prize recipient, had restored Argentina "to a position of influence in both Hemisphere and world councils."[6] To increase efficiency in the hemispheric peace machinery, Saavedra Lamas proposed his Anti-War Pact, which was approved by all participants to the seventh ICAS in Montevideo, as well as by eleven European countries.[7] The Saavedra Lamas Pact condemned aggression, disputes to be settled only by peaceful means, and a conciliation commission to be installed in case a permanent one did not exist. At the same conference an Additional Protocol to the General Convention of American Conciliation was signed: It gave a permanent character to the committees of investigation and conciliation foreseen in Article 2 of the convention. Moreover, in fulfillment of the Gondra Treaty, these commissions were to be called "Permanent Diplomatic Commissions of Investigation and Conciliation." The protocol was signed by thirteen countries and ratified by nine. It entered into force in 1935.[8]

At the Inter-American Conference for the Consolidation of Peace in Buenos Aires (1936), five more legal instruments in the field of peaceful settlement were signed. In the first place, there was the Convention for the Maintenance, Preservation and Reestablishment of Peace of 1936. This convention is the famous Consultative Pact, which inaugurated the procedure of consultation in case of a threat to peace and led to the three MCMFAs during World War II. It was later incorporated into the Charter of the OAS of 1948. The convention was ratified by seventeen countries and entered into force in 1937.

The second instrument of this special ICAS was an Additional Protocol Relative to Non Intervention, the Latin American counterpart to the first instrument on consultation, which had amounted to a continentalization of the Monroe Doctrine. It again repeated the principle that no state had the right to intervene in the affairs, internal or external, of another. Violation of this principle would lead to mutual consultation. The Additional Protocol was ratified by sixteen countries and also entered into force in 1937.

The third instrument was the Treaty on the Prevention of Controversies, a preventive system that thought to solve the problem through the creation of mixed, bilateral commissions. It was ratified by fourteen countries and also entered into force in 1937.

The fourth instrument was the Inter-American Treaty on Good Offices and Mediation, which dealt with other methods to achieve a peaceful settlement of disputes. In this case, eminent citizens of any American country could offer good offices, or even mediation, in a dispute. It was ratified by fifteen countries and entered into force in 1937.

Finally, the fifth and last instrument accepted at the Buenos Aires Conference was the Convention to Coordinate, Extend and Assure the Fulfillment of the Existing Treaties between the American States, which reaffirmed the obligation to settle by pacific means all controversies of an international character. It was ratified by fourteen countries and entered into force in 1938.

Despite the achievements so far obtained, the eighth ICAS expressed the view that all these scattered efforts be coordinated in one legal instrument. For this purpose the Pan American Union was entrusted with the preparation of an International Conference of American Jurists that in turn should elaborate a "Peace Code," to be submitted to the next ICAS. Furthermore, the governing board of the Union of American Republics requested a second draft from the IAJC, this time on a "Peace Convention."

The Inter-American Conference on War and Peace (the Chapultepec Conference of 1945) again dealt with the problem of peaceful settlement of disputes. Resolution XXXIX recommended that the IAJC undertake the study of an "Inter-American Peace System," which would follow the concepts expressed earlier at the Eighth ICAS. The committee then elaborated a third draft, which was duly submitted to the governing board in 1947. In it, the committee had accepted obligatory arbitration for controversies of any nature, a position that it had not held earlier. In the meantime, at the Inter-American Conference for the Maintenance of Peace and Continental Security in Rio de Janeiro, 1947, the Rio Treaty had been approved, and the IAJC recalled Resolution X of that conference, which had stated that the next ICAS should study a pacific system of security based on "obligatory arbitration of any dispute which may endanger peace and which is not of a judicial nature."[9]

This is the background for the Pact of Bogotá, the Inter-American Treaty on Pacific Settlement, which was approved at the ninth ICAS and represented the culmination of an experience of almost half a century in the field of peaceful settlement of disputes. The new system established obligatory judicial procedures as the final method for the solution of controversies to be achieved through the International Court of Justice. Arbitration would only be obligatory when the court declared to have no jurisdiction in the dispute.[10]

The Pact of Bogotá, one of the three pillars on which the OAS is based—the other two being the charter and the Rio Treaty, declared the International Court of Justice as having compulsory jurisdiction; it covers arbitration, good offices and mediation, and investigation procedures, and it establishes the compulsory nature of the new system of pacific settlement of disputes. It was the latter issue that made it difficult for acceptance by a majority of American states. By the early 1950s, only ten countries had ratified it: Brazil, Costa Rica, the Dominican Republic, El Salvador, Haiti, Honduras, Mexico, Nicaragua, Panama, and Uruguay. Amendments were supposed to be introduced by the time of the next ICAS—the tenth ICAS—in order to make it possible for all American states to ratify it. The difficulties were too great, however, thus, the COAS was instructed by the tenth ICAS to ask the governments whether they considered it appropriate to revise the Pact of Bogotá. The inquiry began in 1954, and by 1957 the COAS decided that in view of the reaction, it was not suitable to revise the pact. In the same year the COAS began an inquiry in regard to the establishment of an Inter-American Court of Justice. This complex problem took even more time. By 1964, only eight governments had expressed an opinion, and the OAS was informed that three governments had been in favor (Costa Rica, Ecuador, and El Salvador); six stated different objections; Argentina, Chile and the United States opposed it; Brazil made its support subject to the structure and its relation to the Pact of Bogotá; Mexico did not consider it urgent; Venezuela thought it was premature; and the other nations remained silent.[11]

If the major legal instrument remained for a long time the Pact of Bogotá, the instruments for the peaceful settlement of disputes were many: the IAPC, the IACHR, the IADB, and the SCCS (although most directly involved was the first one). The IAPC, although established in 1940, began its operations in 1948 with its first statutes, which were approved in 1950. Under these rather flexible rules, the IAPC was involved in a series of problems covering in most cases the Caribbean, and more precisely, revolutionary activity of exiles plotting in a neighboring country against the authorities in their own. In the years 1948–1956, in accordance with these first statutes, the IAPC dealt with nine cases: (1) and (5) were alleged organization of revolutionary forces in Cuba directed against the Trujillo regime in the Dominican Republic (both in 1948); (2) tensions between Haiti and the Dominican Republic (1949); (3) a Cuban-Peruvian dispute arising from the Cuban embassy in Lima having granted diplomatic asylum to two Peruvian citizens (1949); (4) regarding the general Caribbean situation was not applicable, and the General Committee of the PAU declined to take any action (1949); (6) a Cuban allegation that several Cubans had been seized on board of the Guatemalan vessel *Quetzal* and detained by Dominican authorities (1951); (7) a Colombian-Peruvian dispute, a cause célèbre at the time, in view of Haya de la Torre having obtained diplomatic asylum in the Colombian Embassy in Lima

(1954); (8) violation of Guatemala's sovereignty just prior to the CIA-led invasion that toppled the government of Jacobo Arbenz (1954); and (9) new tensions between Batista's Cuba and Trujillo's Dominican Republic (1956).

With the revised statutes of 1956 the IAPC had been limited in its activities, and hence it remained rather inactive in the next years—it was virtually mothballed. The increasing tensions in the Caribbean prompted the OAS to call the fifth MCMFA, in Santiago, 1959, which in turn requested the IAPC to examine the existing tensions in the Caribbean (1959). It also led to new statutes which the Fifth MCMFA granted the IAPC thus reversing its powers and functions and eliminating the restrictions of 1956. The IAPC then engaged with renewed vigor in a variety of disputes between 1959 and 1964: (10) a request by Haiti to study the invasion of Haiti by revolutionary groups coming from Cuba (1959); (11) anti-Venezuelan leaflets dropped mistakenly over Curaçao but aimed for Venezuela and calling on the people of Venezuela to rise up against President Rómulo Bétancourt (1959); (12) violation of human rights and more international tensions in the Caribbean which in turn led to the Seventh MCMFA (1959–1960); (13) an Ecuadorean-Dominican dispute arising from the Embassy of Ecuador in the Dominican Republic having granted diplomatic asylum to thirteen Dominican citizens (1960); (14) violation of human rights in the Dominican Republic in further confrontations between Venezuela and the decaying Trujillo regime in the Dominican Republic (1960); (15) a request by Nicaragua in regard to a new border dispute which had almost led to war in 1957, when the Rio Treaty was invoked concerning the area of Gracias a Dios and Teotecacinte-Mocorón which, on December 23, 1906, King Alfonso XIII of Spain had awarded to Honduras (1961); (16) dispute between Mexico and Guatemala in regard to Guatemalan allegations that "communist" troops were training on Mexican territory (1961); (17) communist subversion in Latin America and examination of various arbitrary acts by the revolutionary government of Cuba requested by Peru (1961); and finally, (18) a request by Panama after the Canal Zone riots, related to the flag controversy, which then led to a Mixed Committee on Cooperation and eventually to the solution of a long simmering problem between that country and the United States: the two Panama Canal Treaties that were signed in 1977 ending the Canal Zone and setting up a new regime for the Canal itself which, by the year 2000, would be fully Panamanian.

It can be said that the OAS has developed an intricate and complex system in the field of the pacific settlement of disputes based on an experience that looks back to the nineteenth-century Spanish American Congresses (1826–1865) and to the impressive record of the Pan American movement of the Union of American Republics (1902–1948). Both juridical instruments and institutions are in place since almost a century. The OAS is thus in a unique position to solve conflicts and controversies whenever the will to do so is evident. In cases where the United States wanted its own solution (Central America), favored extracontinental powers (Malvinas issue), or decided to turn the clock backwards (Panama), there is nothing that either the OAS, or the Latin American members through their own efforts, can do. Criticisms of this kind are thus misplaced and not justified.

The Pact of Bogotá did not fulfil its objectives since it was never ratified, although it always remained an important guideline, and attempts were made time and again to revise it in order to satisfy most of the OAS members. That attempt was unsuccessful until very recently when a New Pact of Bogotá, a New American Treaty on Pacific Settlement, was drafted and will surely fill the needed vacuum. The IAPC, no doubt, was also an important tool for this peaceful settlement of disputes; it may not always have worked but the least one can say is that it was an extremely inexpensive instrument for the promotion of better relations or for the settlement of controversies which otherwise may have gotten out of hand. It was not always successful and it admitted so, on several occasions, but it certainly proved its worth over the decades of its activities. This was particularly true when its statutes had given it wide powers, in 1948–1956 and after 1959. When the Charter of the OAS was revised, the IAPC was converted into the Inter-American Committee on Peaceful Settlement, and as such it was incorporated into the Protocol of Buenos Aires of 1967. In the revised charter, which went into effect in 1970, Article 83 stated that "to assist the Permanent Council in the exercise of these powers, an Inter-American Committee on Peaceful Settlement shall be established." However, the experience of the 1970s negated the high hopes placed in this new committee, and it was definitely eliminated in the latest revision of the charter, the Protocol of Cartagena de Indias of 1985, at a time when a new version of the Pact of Bogotá, the New American Treaty on Pacific Settlement, was gaining momentum.

COLLECTIVE SECURITY

Collective security is the other factor (besides the peaceful settlement of disputes) in the quest for peace and security. It also has deep roots that go back to the nineteenth century, and it would be wrong to link it exclusively to the Charter of the OAS or the Rio Treaty of 1947.

As a matter of fact, the forerunners of collective security are to be found in the Congress of Panama of 1826 and in the subsequent Spanish American Congresses of the nineteenth century mentioned earlier. However, the first real modern attempt to deal with the issue of collective security within the inter-American system took place at the sixth ICAS in Havana, 1928, and at the seventh ICAS in Montevideo, 1933; in the former, the Convention on Duties and Rights of States in the Event of Civil Strife outlawed the right of conquest; in the latter, the Convention on Rights and Duties of States outlawed intervention. A further step was taken at the Inter-American Conference for the Consolidation of Peace in Buenos Aires, in 1936 (attended by U.S. President Franklin D. Roosevelt), in which the Consultative Pact was signed, with the principle of immediate consultation in case of a threat to the peace of the continent. The Consultative Pact, as stated earlier, amounted to the continentalization, multilateralization, or Pan-Americanization of the Monroe Doctrine. The Convention for the Maintenance, Preservation and Reestablishment of Peace accelerated the process for the incorporation of collective security into the inter-American system.

At the eighth ICAS in Lima, 1938, the principle of consultation was turned into reality: the MCMFAs were established, which then were inaugurated during World War II. The first three MCMFAs extended inter-American cooperation; the second MCMFA extended the principle of solidarity to cover "any attempt on the part of a non-American state against the integrity or inviolability of the territory, the sovereignty or the political independence of any American State."[12] Similar resolutions were passed at the third MCMFA (in Rio de Janeiro, 1942). The Inter-American Conference on Problems of War and Peace in Mexico (1945), amplified further the meaning of collective security by considering an act of aggression not only from outside the continent but also from within. It was also at this Chapultepec Conference that the reorganization and modernization of the inter-American system was decided upon.

The first step in that direction was undertaken at the Inter-American Conference for the Maintenance of Continental Peace and Security, in Rio de Janeiro (1947). It resulted in the Inter-American Treaty of Reciprocal Assistance, better known as the Rio Treaty, which thereafter furnished the basis for NATO, SEATO, and CENTO. The Rio Treaty, together with the Charter of the OAS and the Pact of Bogotá (both of 1948), represents the foundation on which the entire building of the OAS is based.

The Rio Treaty does not mean an automatic response of every single member state to an act of aggression. Actually, it is based on the experience acquired during World War II—of Argentina and Chile—and is divided into two basic points: self-defense and collective action. Every state has the inherent right of self-defense, and the signatories state in Article 3 that

An armed attack by any State against an American State shall be considered as an attack against all the American States and, consequently, each one of the said Contracting Parties undertakes to assist in meeting the attack in the exercise of the inherent right of individual or collective self-defense recognized by Article 51 of the Charter of the United Nations.[13]

In case of an aggression that is neither "an armed attack" nor "an extra-continental or intra-continental conflict," or in case of "any other fact or situation that might endanger the peace of America," Article 6 calls for an immediate meeting of the Organ of Consultation. This can be the COAS, or, since 1967–1970, either the PC, acting provisionally as such, or, when the situation calls for it, the convocation of an MCMFA. The original Charter of the OAS, in its Chapter V, Articles 24–25 (now Chapter VI, Articles 27–28), spelled out the more general lines; the chapter does not spell out what kind of action should be taken—that is left in more detail to the Rio Treaty—it is more flexible and more general, and deals with all types of aggression, and thus more liable to be used than the more specific provisions of the Rio Treaty. Both the charter and the Rio Treaty endorsed a certain flexibility for the application of either the former or the latter when dealing with acts of aggression. Also, as stated earlier, the question of how collective security should work in each case is left to the individual states until the Organ of Consultation decides on the common action to be taken.

Concerning the procedure, the application is rather simple. In case of an armed attack, foreseen in Article 3, other states shall undertake any assistance they deem fit as part of the exercise of the inherent right of self-defense. The Organ of Consultation shall meet immediately and decide on the common measures to be taken; in case Article 6 applies, then the Organ of Consultation shall also be convoked, and in case of Article 7—a conflict between two American states—the meeting of the Organ of Consultation is automatic; in case a peaceful settlement is rejected by one or both of the parties, it will be considered an aggression, to be dealt with accordingly. Article 8 covers the applicable measures, which may comprise a variety of alternative actions, except for the one of armed force which cannot be used without its consent (Article 20). The decision to convoke the MCMFA is done by absolute majority, but the decisions of the Organ of Consultation is by a two-thirds majority (Articles 16 and 17).

Finally, two more points should be mentioned that establish a link between the Charter of the OAS and the Rio Treaty and between these two documents and the United Nations. The revised charter, in its Articles 18 and 20, makes it absolutely clear that nonintervention is upheld as well as the nonrecognition of any territory by force. The other point, Article 10 of the Rio Treaty, states that "none of the provisions of the Treaty shall be construed as impairing the rights and obligations of the High Contracting Parties under the Charter of the United Nations."[14]

A different type of menace, that of political subversion, has also been covered by the inter-American system. Already the Inter-American Conference for the Consolidation of Peace in Buenos Aires (1936) dealt with the subject when it talked of "the existence of a common democracy throughout America,"[15] and at the third MCMFA in Rio de Janeiro, 1942, Resolution XVII with its attached memorandum, defined "acts of political aggression" or "aggression of a non-military character," which included propaganda, espionage, sabotage, instigation of public disorder, or any other activity designed to disturb the public life of the country."[16] To cope with such situations, the inter-American system created the Emergency Advisory Committee for Political Defense of 1941. Later, a similar institution was incorporated into the Charter of the OAS: the Special Consultative Committee on Security (SCCS), in 1962.

The topic of subversive activities was taken up on several occasions: at the ninth ICAS in Bogotá (1948), when it referred to the activities of international communism; at the tenth ICAS in Caracas (1954), when it condemned such activities; by the IAPC, in its report to the eighth MCMFA, when it called the activities of the Cuban government and the Sino-Soviet bloc "acts of political aggression," and at the ninth MCMFA in Washington (1964), when Venezuela requested sanctions against Cuba in view of Cuban complicity in increased terrorist activities in that country. All these activities were designated as acts of aggression covered by the respective provisions in the Rio Treaty. As García Amador pointed out, the decisions taken by the ninth MCMFA revealed clearly that other aspects of the system of collective security against subversion were incorporated into the inter-American system.[17]

At first it was recognized that subversion could be addressed by measures recommended by MCMFAs or ICAS through some type of international cooperation. The result was the aforementioned Emergency Advisory Committee for Political Defense of 1941, which functioned in Montevideo from 1942 to 1948. However, the revolutionary activities emanating from Cuba after Castro came to power were more serious than anything seen earlier during World War II, and the OAS responded to that challenge by expanding countermeasures as taken at the eighth MCMFA. The new threat was subversive, and guerrilla activity was organized from abroad and of a paramilitary nature. The SCCS, set up at that MCMFA, stated at the time that these new subversive activities "constitute a situation of such gravity and urgency that it can be adequately and effectively dealt with only by adopting measures provided for in the [Rio] Treaty."[18] By 1962, the countermeasures taken by the OAS actually amounted to self-defense.

The ninth MCMFA (1964) broadened the concept of self-defense, which had already been stated two years earlier at the eighth MCMFA and again emphasized at the Informal Meeting of Foreign Ministers (Washington, D.C., October 2–3, 1962), during the Cuban Missile Crisis, when it was declared that the Soviet Union's intervention in Cuba threatened the unity of America and its democratic institutions. The ninth MCMFA simply equated subversion with aggression and with intervention against the territorial integrity of Venezuela. It then contributed to the definition and application of what must be called "indirect aggression," explicitly stating that any country so attacked could apply the right of self-defense and even resort to the use of armed force, individually or collectively, to preserve their essential rights of sovereign states.

Finally, there is another matter that is quite important and should not be confused: the question of political exiles and refugees and the issue of government-directed subversive activity. The former was codified in three basic instruments: the Convention on Duties and Rights of States in the Event of Civil Strife (Havana, 1928), the Protocol to this Convention (1957), and the Convention on Territorial Asylum (Caracas, 1954). Here we are dealing with measures that the American states were to take in order to prevent activities that were intended to instigate civil strife in other countries. These may be subversive, even with the aid of some governments, but they are carried out by private individuals. On the other hand, the system of political defense refers to activities organized and financed by governments for the specific overthrow of a legal government. It is thus a question of governments violating the normal rules of international behavior. Already, the seventh MCMFA, held in San José, Costa Rica, in 1960, which dealt with the Cuban problem, stated clearly that the OAS was facing a new type of subversion, which needed to be met squarely. A resolution adopted at that time condemned this type of belligerent intervention, rejected the conditions of poverty and misery in some Latin American countries as a pretext for such revolutionary activities, reaffirmed the principle of nonintervention as well as the incompatibility of the inter-American system with any form of totalitarianism, proclaimed that all members of the OAS were dutifully bound to submit to the discipline of the inter-American system, declared that all controversies between member states should be resolved peacefully, and reaffirmed its faith in the regional system.[19]

At that time, the source of all these troubles was the Cuban Revolution, and the OAS acted against it through various channels, especially with the fifth, seventh, eighth, and ninth MCMFAs, and did so quite successfully in the long run. On the other hand, when the United States organized and financed such illegal activities with the Contras against the legal authorities in Nicaragua, the OAS was powerless, and so were the Central American countries when they attempted a Central American solution through the Esquipulas Agreements, and the Latin Americans, when, in turn, they tried a Latin American solution through the Contadora Group and the Contadora Support Group. Both attempts failed and the OAS was paralyzed, as it was in the Malvinas case of 1982 when Argentina and the Latin Americans invoked the Rio Treaty, but neither the weak nations of Latin America nor the OAS could do anything when the United States sided openly with an extracontinental power.

The Inter-American Treaty of Reciprocal Assistance (Rio Treaty) has been involved over a dozen times since it entered into force in 1948. These cases, which were not necessarily linked to an MCMFA, included the following:

Costa Rica–Nicaragua Conflict, 1948–1949

The background of this conflict was the alleged invasion of Costa Rica by Nicaraguan forces in December 1948. Costa Rica invoked Article 6 of the

Rio Treaty, and, on December 14, 1948, the COAS decided to convoke an MCMFA and constituted itself as the Provisional Organ of Consultation. It then appointed a committee to get to the facts. Had the situation been more serious, an MCMFA would have followed. In view of the fact that the two countries were willing to find solutions, however, this application of the Rio Treaty did not lead to more serious consequences. An Inter-American Commission of Military Experts—five members—proceeded to the two countries and was able to come to a final solution. A Pact of Amity was signed between the two countries in 1949, in which Costa Rica and Nicaragua recognized the validity of the Pact of Bogotá and the Convention on Duties and Rights of States in the Event of Civil Strife.[20]

Caribbean Situation, 1950

In January 1950 the government of Haiti complained to the COAS about a series of incidents with the Dominican Republic that in its view constituted a threat to the peace. Haiti thus requested the immediate convocation of the Organ of Consultation invoking Articles 6 and 8 of the Rio Treaty. A few days later, the Dominican Republic also asked for such a meeting. The COAS then constituted itself as the Provisional Organ of Consultation and appointed a committee to gather the facts. This investigating committee went to both countries as well as to Cuba, Guatemala, and Mexico, and reported back. The Organ of Consultation then approved five resolutions that were adhered to by the governments of the Dominican Republic, Haiti, Cuba, and Guatemala. In Resolution I, the first two governments were requested to prevent any subversive activities against their neighbors, to avoid systematic hostile propaganda, and to live in accordance with the Havana Convention of 1928 on the Duties and Rights of States in the Event of Civil Strife; in Resolution II, the governments of Cuba and Guatemala were addressed, since in both there existed armed groups of various nationalities, not part of the armed forces of these two countries, which were working toward the overthrow of the Dominican government, and since officials of both countries were aiding these groups. The resolution asked these two governments to refrain from such activities and to control war matériel from falling into the hands of such groups. It also recommended the IAPC, which had been active in regard to the Caribbean situation since 1948 (Dominican Republic–Cuba, 1948; Haiti–Dominican Republic, 1949; General Caribbean situation, 1949; Cuba–Dominican Republic, 1949). Resolution III set up a special committee to see that the aforementioned resolutions were being implemented correctly. Resolution IV reaffirmed the principle of representative democracy and stated that it did not

in any way nor under any concept authorize any government or group of governments to violate inter-American commitments relative to the principle of non-intervention or to give the appearance of legitimacy to violations of the rules contained in Article 1 of the Havana Convention of 1928, on Duties and Rights of States in the Event of Civil Strife, the Protocol Relative to Non-Intervention (Buenos Aires, 1936), and Article 15 of the Charter of the Organization of American States."[21]

Finally, Resolution V recommended, as a solution to the turbulent situation in the Caribbean—taken up in a variety of cases by the IAPC, and later, in 1959, by the fifth MCMFA of Santiago de Chile, 1959—the stimulation and the development of the effective exercise of representative democracy, the strengthening and perfection of the Havana Convention of 1928 on the Duties and Rights of States in the Event of Civil Strife as well as that of political asylees, refugees, and exiles. These recommendations were entrusted to the Department of International Law and Organization of the PAU, which should also draft an Additional Protocol on all points relative to the aforementioned Havana Convention of 1928, and to the IACJ or the IAJC in regard to the effective exercise of representative democracy and the regime of political asylees, exiles, and refugees. When all these studies and reports were ready, they would be submitted to the tenth ICAS. The result of these decisions by the COAS, acting provisionally as Organ of Consultation, led to the Draft Protocol to the Havana Convention of 1928 on Civil Strife, opened for signature in 1957, and the Conventions on Territorial Asylum and Diplomatic Asylum, approved by the tenth ICAS of 1954.[22]

Guatemala, 1954

The country had been ruled from 1931 to 1944 by General Jorge Ubico, but reformist groups had forced him out of power in 1944. The new president, Juan José Arévalo Bermejo, who, for many years, had been a political exile in Argentina, was elected in December 1944. This reformist movement was rather moderate, being led by a philosopher who, in Argentina (and, to be more precise, at the University of Tucumán) had received the impact of the Spanish version of *Krausismo*. He called his reform movement "spiritual socialism." In the elections of 1950, a more radical socialist, Jacobo Arbenz, Arévalo's minister of defense, and member of the National Renovation party, went further to the left, although any allegation of communism must be rejected out of hand. The problem in Guatemala was simply the state within the state—the United Fruit Company—and Arbenz introduced further socialist legislation, including an agrarian reform which meant expropriation of the vast United Fruit landholdings. The ire of the United States was now directed against the Arbenz government, and John Foster Dulles rushed to Caracas, site of the tenth ICAS, to get a resolution passed which outlawed international communism. Arbenz appealed to the United Nations and the Eastern Bloc countries (certainly a mistake, since appealing to the OAS would have given him a better shield). In any case, some ten countries, on June

26, 1954, appealed to the chair of the COAS and invoked Article 6 of the Rio Treaty in view of what these countries alleged: "demonstrated intervention of the international Communist movement in the Republic of Guatemala."

The COAS, on June 28, 1954, convoked an MCMFA; however, before the meeting could take place, there had been a violent change of government in that country: A CIA-financed and -led armed intervention from Honduras toppled Arbenz because he chose not to fight and put Colonel Carlos Castillo Armas in power. In view of this fait accompli, the COAS decided to postpone the meeting sine die. Thus, in this case, as in others before it, no MCMFA took place.[23]

Costa Rica–Nicaragua Conflict, 1955–1956

In reality, the application of the Rio Treaty in this new conflict between Costa Rica and Nicaragua was a continuation of the 1948–1949 dispute. Costa Rica again requested the MCMFA and the COAS constituted itself as Provisional Organ of Consultation (Article 12, Rio Treaty). The investigating committee traveled to the border region and reported back. Despite a more serious situation than in the previous case between the two countries, the problems were solved. The COAS called on the parties to appoint their respective delegates, in accordance with Article XVII of the Pact of Bogotá, to the Commission of Investigation and Conciliation, and to sign the bilateral agreement mentioned in Article IV of the Pact of Amity. It also created a special committee to cooperate in the reestablishment of peace. The problem was satisfactorily solved when the governments deposited copies of their agreement at the PAU in 1956.

Border Dispute between Honduras and Nicaragua, 1957

At the request of Honduras, and thereafter also of Nicaragua, the COAS decided to convoke the Organ of Consultation. Once this was done, an Investigating Committee—Argentina, Ecuador, Mexico, Panama, and the United States—traveled to both countries to obtain a cease-fire. This was soon accomplished by agreements in Tegucigalpa between the OAS and Honduras, and later between the OAS and Nicaragua. The problem of the dispute went back to the Arbitral Award of King Alfonso XIII of Spain in 1906 which decided that the area of Cape Gracias a Dios belonged to Honduras, though Nicaragua had never complied with this award and there remained a variety of disagreements, which had to be solved.

After the return of the investigating committee, the COAS, acting provisionally as Organ of Consultation, expressed its satisfaction at the happy ending and attached the text of the agreement between the two countries. The main point of this agreement was that both parties recognized the Pact of Bogotá and the International Court of Justice. If one of the parties would fail to comply with the obligations imposed upon it by the International Court of Justice, the other party, before having recourse to the Security Council of the United Nations, should request an MCMFA. If the application of the aforementioned judicial procedure did not lead to an accord, then the parties should apply the Pact of Bogotá. The final settlement of the border problem was signed on July 21, 1957, thus eliminating one more problem from the list of unresolved frontier disputes.

Nicaraguan Situation, 1959

The year 1959 represented the climax in the turbulent situation of the Caribbean that also had brought Fidel Castro to power in Cuba. The Nicaraguan government complained that its country was the target of an armed invasion by sea and air. The COAS convoked the Organ of Consultation, and then, as was usual in such cases, appointed a committee to get the facts. This committee went to Costa Rica and Nicaragua and reported back that, indeed, there were groups of armed troops in Honduras who were intent on invading Nicaragua, and there were also other groups of armed men in Costa Rica who aimed at the same goals. The COAS noted that there were in existence a series of agreements between these countries, which had not been ratified, and this lack of ratification was one factor in the turbulent situation. Hence, the COAS acting provisionally as Organ of Consultation did not call for an MCMFA but instead terminated its own role as Organ of Consultation and recommended to the respective governments to strengthen the measures "designed to maintain peace, observing the principle of non-intervention."[24]

Since the situation did not improve, the fifth MCMFA was convoked shortly thereafter and took place in Santiago de Chile, August 12–18, 1959, to deal effectively with the April–June disturbances in the Caribbean. Its result was the Declaration of Santiago and the establishment of the IACHR.

Early Repercussions of the Cuban Revolution, 1959

Soon after Castro took power, armed invasions by revolutionaries took place in Nicaragua, Panama, Haiti, and the Dominican Republic, the most important being in Panama. The representative of Panama, based on Article 6 of the Rio Treaty, requested the convocation of the Organ of Consultation, which was quickly constituted in the usual manner. The COAS acting provisionally as the Organ of Consultation then appointed an investigating committee which went to Panama and reported back that the country had indeed been the victim of an invasion and that the case was covered by the Rio Treaty (Article 6). It also reported that the rapid action taken by the OAS had resulted in a happy solution and that the incident had proven the importance of the Havana Convention of 1928 on Duties and Rights of States in the Event of Civil Strife. The investigating committee then urged that the countries which had not yet ratified the convention should do so. The Organ of Consultation then terminated its role as such, since the reasons that motivated the convocation had ceased to exist. Thus, an MCMFA was not convoked, although very soon it became clear that nothing solid had been accomplished in regard to the tensions in the Caribbean.[25]

Problems in the Dominican Republic, 1960–1962

On July 8, 1960, the Venezuelan government requested the convocation of the Organ of Consultation in view of acts of intervention by the Dominican Republic against Venezuela that culminated in attempts against the life of President Betancourt. The COAS then constituted itself as Organ of Consultation and appointed an investigating committee. This committee went to Venezuela and reported back that the Venezuelan allegations were correct, which in turn led to the convocation of the Sixth MCMFA in San José de Costa Rica in 1960. That meeting decided on sanctions against the Dominican Republic—breaking off diplomatic and economic relations—and to authorize the COAS to discontinue same when the situation warranted it. They were only canceled by the COAS on January 2, 1962, when a new situation had arisen in that country.[26] As stated earlier, the decisions taken at this sixth MCMFA were questionable and more in line with the zeitgeist and with selective indignation: Suddenly the Rightist dictatorships, in existence since the 1930s (Batista's Cuba, Trujillo's Dominican Republic, and Somoza's Nicaragua), had now increasingly become the target of disgrace and opprobrium while Castro's Cuba was riding a wave of popularity all over the continent.

Cuban Situation, 1960

The continued tensions that were originating in Cuba led to the convocation of the seventh MCMFA, which followed immediately after the sixth MCMFA in the same place, San José de Costa Rica. The sixth MCMFA had dealt with Trujillo, and the seventh with Castro, although the revolutionary was treated here with real kindness by a continent still fascinated with his personality. The Declaration of San José simply reaffirmed the familiar inter-American principles. This seventh MCMFA was not called on the basis of the Rio Treaty but rather on the basis of Article 39 of the Charter of the OAS, while the sixth MCMFA was indeed convoked on the basis of the Rio Treaty.

Cuban Expulsion of the OAS and Partial Trade Suspension, 1961–1962

On October 16, 1961, the Peruvian government requested the immediate convocation of an MCMFA in view of the Cuban situation, alleging acts of force, executions, deportations by the Cuban government at home, and actions of international communism abroad, including infiltration and subversion. The COAS, however, decided to pass the problem to the general committee, which in turn suggested, in accordance with Resolution IV of the fifth MCMFA, to have the IAPC deal with the situation presented by Peru. This action was again very much marked by politics, since Peru at that time was governed by the conservative economics of Pedro Beltrán, who had rescued the unfortunate economic policies of his president, Manuel Prado. The IAPC took up the challenge, but then Colombia also wanted an MCMFA. This is the background of the eighth MCMFA, which took place in Punta del Este, Uruguay, January 22–31, 1962. In both cases—the Peruvian as well as the Colombian request, Article 6 of the Rio Treaty was invoked.

It was this eighth MCMFA that adopted several resolutions mentioned earlier, some almost unanimously such as Resolution VI—the incompatibility of adherence to Marxism-Leninism with membership in the OAS, twenty votes for, one against (Cuba); Resolution VII—immediate exclusion of Cuba from the IADB. Cuba was also excluded from the inter-American system as such, as a consequence of the incompatibility of its political system with the former. At the same time, the eighth MCMFA suspended all trade in arms with Cuba and authorized the COAS to extend this prohibition to other areas. With a two-third vote of its members, it moved to discontinue these measures when the Cuban government demonstrated its compatibility with the organization.[27]

The Cuban Missile Crisis, 1962

At the request of the United States, the COAS met on October 23, 1962, to discuss the information about "offensive weapons with nuclear capability provided by extracontinental powers," which Cuba had permitted on its territory. The COAS then held two meetings on October 24, 1962: in the first meeting it convoked the Organ of Consultation in accordance with the Rio Treaty and decided to constitute itself as Provisional Organ of Consultation. In its second meeting of the same day, the COAS, acting provisionally as the Organ of Consultation, called for the immediate dismantling and withdrawal from Cuba of all missiles and other weapons of offensive capability and also recommended member states, according to Articles 6 and 8 of the Rio Treaty, to take all necessary steps to ensure that the Cuban government would not continue receiving military matérial from the Soviet Union. Moreover, it informed the Secretary General of the United Nations and also declared that it would continue to function as Provisional Organ of Consultation. As we know, the crisis ended when the missiles were taken out of Cuba; this terminated the activity of the COAS as Provisional Organ of Consultation in this very special case.[28] It is worthwhile to note that several countries, like Argentina, Colombia, Costa Rica, the Dominican Republic, Guatemala, Haiti, Honduras, and Panama, informed the COAS about their willingness to cooperate fully in accordance with the second recommendation.

New Waves of Terrorism Organized from Cuba, 1963–1964

At the request of Venezuela, which was the target of increasing terrorism as a consequence of the falling out between Betancourt and Castro, the COAS set itself up as Provisional Organ of Consultation, and, in the familiar manner, appointed an investigating committee that went to Venezuela. The Venezuelan request had been based on Article 6 of the Rio Treaty. This investigating committee traveled to Venezuela and, upon its return, submitted a well-documented report proving without doubt that the Venezuelan allegations were correct. In view of these facts, the ninth MCMFA was called. It met in Washington, D.C., on July 21–26, 1964. The Cuban government was given an opportunity to present its side of the story; instead, it cabled that it did not recognize the authority of the OAS.

The ninth MCMFA declared the Cuban actions to be an aggression, condemned the present government of Cuba, and, in application of Articles 6 and 8 of the Rio Treaty, adopted the following measures:

a. Elimination of all diplomatic and consular relations with Cuba by the American States;

b. Suspension of all trade, except foodstuffs, medicines, and medical equipment; and

c. Suspension of all sea transportation, except for humanitarian reasons.

Furthermore, the COAS was authorized, by a two-thirds majority, to discontinue these measures if the Cuban government ceased to constitute a danger to peace and security. The Ninth MCMFA also warned Cuba that if it persisted in its aggressive policies, the American states might have to act in self-defense by resorting to armed force. The meeting also urged other states that were not members of the organization to show solidarity with the states of the inter-American system, and it instructed the secretary general of the OAS to inform the Security Council of the United Nations of the decisions taken by the ninth MCMFA.

The Dominican Republic–Haiti, 1963–1965

Although this controversy represented a continuation of the familiar conflicts concerning political exiles of each in the territory of the other, and going back at least to 1949, it was the government of Costa Rica that, on April 28, 1963, requested an MCMFA, based on Articles 39 and 40 of the charter. The COAS accepted this request, and in view of specific aspects—

the fact that members of the Haitian Public Force had broken into the diplomatic mission of the Dominican Republic—it invoked the Rio Treaty and constituted itself provisionally as such. The Provisional Organ of Consultation appointed a Special Committee of Inquiry, consisting of five members, to study the situation alleged by the Dominican Republic. During the meeting, the Representative of Haiti produced a cable from his government stating that the Dominican Republic was about to invade his country. On May 8, 1963, the COAS, acting provisionally as the Organ of Consultation, decided to appeal to the two governments not to resort to the use of force and to solve their differences in a peaceful manner. It also authorized the Special Committee of Inquiry to make an on-the-spot study of the situation existing between Haiti and the Dominican Republic.

After the return of the Special Committee, the Organ of Consultation met again on July 28, 1963, and resolved as follows: It renewed the plea to both governments to refrain from acts incompatible with the obligations established by the Charter of the OAS and to submit the dispute to the procedure of pacific settlement; it urged the government of Haiti to agree to grant the respective safe conducts to the asylees who were still in the premises of various diplomatic missions in Port au Prince; it took note of the statements of the Haitian government that diplomatic missions would be respected; it urged both governments to observe human rights and the applicable inter-American treaties: the 1954 Convention on Territorial Asylum and the Convention on the Duties and Rights of States in the Event of Civil Strife, with the Additional Protocol thereto; and finally, it urged the two governments to avoid acts of hostility. The Provisional Organ of Consultation was maintained.

The trouble between the two countries did not end here. On August 6, the Organ of Consultation met again when Haiti submitted new charges against the Dominican Republic in the sense that an invasion of Haitian exiles from the Dominican Republic had taken place. The Organ of Consultation instructed the Special Committee to study the new cases, and new meetings were held. On October 24, the Special Committee issued its third report, which confirmed the invasion but could not determine whether the Dominican Republic was involved in it. The Organ of Consultation did not meet again until November 30, 1964. During this long period the Special Committee continued its work, which also led to direct negotiations between the two parties. On December 2, 1964, Haiti informed the COAS acting provisionally as Organ of Consultation that all persons having found refuge in the Argentine and Colombian embassies had been granted permission to leave the country. This resolution pointed the way toward a solution: The two governments would analyze the causes of friction between them and would follow the recognized procedures. Formal negotiations between the two governments began on January 2, 1965, "under the auspices of the Special Committee, at the headquarters of the PAU."[29]

Panama–United States, 1964

A much more serious problem developed between Panama and the United States in regard to the Canal and the Canal Zone. In January 1964, serious riots had taken place in the Canal Zone relating to the flag controversy, which symbolized increased Panamanian nationalism and resistance to the continued occupation of the Canal Zone. The background to this controversy can be found in the establishment of the independent Republic of Panama for the purpose of building a transisthmian canal. When Colombia, to which Panama originally belonged, refused a U.S. proposal with this in mind, a revolution broke out in Panama City. The United States immediately intervened militarily and did not allow Colombian troops to land and suppress the rebellion. The then-proclaimed independent Republic of Panama was legally based on the Hay-Bunau Varilla Convention of November 18, 1903, which established an independent Panama divided into two parts, with a United States-controlled Canal Zone ceded to the United States in perpetuity through which the future canal would run. The canal was built and inaugurated on August 14, 1914. Ever since the conclusion of the above convention, there arose problems about its interpretation; the United States interpreted it to include jurisdiction in regard to judicial matters (court system), taxes, and customs with exclusion of any Panamanian authorities. Panama disputed this. Negotiations for changing the status of the Canal Zone in favor of Panama took place in the years 1936 (as part of the Good Neighbor policy), 1942, 1947, and 1955. Gradually U.S. rights were restricted. These included the prohibition to acquire more territory for the Canal Zone, to adhere strictly to the principle of nonintervention in Panamanian affairs, and especially the obligation to build a link between the two Panamanian parts that were separated in view of the Canal Zone and to grant a larger annual payment for the lease of the Canal Zone. Finally, this also included the question of equality in the position of Panamanians with Americans and/or Zonians in the Canal Zone. As time went on, Panamanian pressures increased and Panama insisted that its flag should fly over the canal area. After riots in the years 1959 and 1960, the United States, under President John F. Kennedy, and Panama, under President Roberto F. Chiari, came to an understanding in 1962 that allowed the Panamanian flag to fly jointly with the U.S. flag in certain areas of the Canal. Apparently this did not solve the problem in view of Panamanian nationalism; on January 9, 1964, the conflict escalated with rioting Panamanians breaking into the U.S. controlled Canal Zone to fly their flag on the Balboa High School, after Zonians had shown only the U.S. flag. This led to more anti-American demonstrations and finally to Panama breaking off diplomatic relations with the United States and appealing to both the OAS and the United Nations. Gradually this problem led to the two Panama treaties and the U.S. evacuation of the Canal Zone. The IAPC had taken care of the matter, and it seemed that by January 15,

1964, the problem had been solved. Actually it had not, since more was at stake than the simple raising of the Panamanian flag in several places of the Canal. The representative of Panama, on January 29, 1964, requested the convocation of the Organ of Consultation, invoking Articles 6 and 9 of the Rio Treaty, in view of alleged acts of aggression by the United States. It also wanted compensation for the damages sustained by Panama as a result of this aggression.

The COAS, acting provisionally as the Organ of Consultation, met two days later (January 31, 1964) and resolved the following: It urged both governments to abstain from any act that might violate the peace in Panama and established a general committee, composed of all members of the COAS except the two parties, which should do as follows:

a. Investigate the facts and submit a report;

b. Propose the procedures that would ensure that peace will not be violated while efforts are being made to find a final solution to the dispute;

c. Assist the parties in their search for a fair solution;

d. Create the special committees necessary for the task; and

e. Request all governments and the OAS to give full cooperation for this endeavor.

The general committee that was set up with the Resolution of February 7, 1964, went to Panama and returned to Washington, D.C., with a report which was then submitted to the Provisional Organ of Consultation and which produced a joint declaration. This joint declaration stated that both governments would reestablish diplomatic relations and that within thirty days, both parties would appoint special ambassadors with full powers to negotiate a final settlement.

The joint declaration did not enter into force in view of new problems that had arisen after its publication and that were related to different interpretations. After new negotiations, the general committee announced that the two governments were ready to sign the Joint Declaration. It was indeed signed that same day: April 3, 1964.

The COAS, acting provisionally as the Organ of Consultation, then ended its action in this case. It should also be mentioned that while the OAS took care of the dispute between Panama and the United States, the Panamanian government had also appealed to the Security Council of the United Nations.[30] Finally, it is important to note that the two governments began to negotiate seriously the thorny question that took a long time to be settled: In 1979 the Panama Canal Treaty and the Treaty Concerning the Permanent Neutrality of the Canal and the Operation of the Panama Canal went into force. It was a victory not only for Panama and Latin America but also for justice and the improvement of relations between the United States and the entire Latin American world. Unfortunately, the Reagan administration was determined to reverse this settlement, and the Bush administration, using the pretext of General Manuel Noriega's alleged involvement with drugs, not only destroyed Panama economically but finally invaded it, in violation of international morality and a series of international agreements, including the Charter of the OAS, the Rio Treaty, the Pact of Bogotá, the Canal treaties themselves, and the principle of nonintervention—the Havana Convention of 1928 on Duties and Rights of States in the Event of Civil Strife. It is difficult to know at this stage what the United States really wants to do in the long run and whether it intends to live up to the spirit and letter of the 1977 treaties with Panama.

The Dominican Situation, 1965

One of the most serious cases after the Cuban Missile Crisis of 1962 was the deteriorating situation in the Dominican Republic after General Trujillo was assassinated. After thirty years of a dictatorial regime, and then with the political floodgates wide open, the country veered increasingly toward revolution, being pushed in that direction by the echoes of the Cuban Revolution of 1959. In 1962 Juan Bosch was elected, but instead of calming the country this led to greater upheaval and finally to military intervention. These events culminated in the revolution that openly attacked the Dominican government, and finally led to a U.S. invasion on April 24, 1965.

The landing of U.S. marines was done in response to purely domestic policies: Lyndon B. Johnson could not afford another "Cuba in the Caribbean." The U.S. action was obviously illegal and was unanimously rejected by all Latin American countries.

The first OAS institution to be involved was the IAPC, but it could not solve the riddle. On April 29, 1965, the COAS intervened, appealing to the Papal Nuncio in Santo Domingo, which also failed to help. At the request of Chile, the COAS met on April 29–30 and convoked an MCMFA for May 1, 1965, on the basis of Article 39 of the charter. In view of a request of the Papal Nuncio that the secretary general of the OAS should come to the Dominican Republic and help directly with a solution, the COAS authorized the secretary general—José Antonio Mora Otero—to do so, the first time in the entire history of the Pan American movement and the OAS, that the secretary general was asked to play such an important political role.

On May 1, 1965, the tenth MCMFA took place in Washington. It decided to appoint a special committee—Argentina, Brazil, Colombia, Guatemala, and Panama—that went to the Dominican Republic to reestablish peace and security. Its powers were: (1) to offer its good offices to all political groups in the country; (2) to arrange a cease-fire; (3) to evacuate all persons who had found asylum in diplomatic missions, and (4) to investigate all aspects of the current situation in the Dominican Republic.

The result of the negotiations of the Special Committee led to the Act of

Santo Domingo, in which the parties accepted the establishment of a security zone in the capital, bound them to respect this zone, and committed them to give all necessary facilities to the International Red Cross or any other international organization for the distribution of food, medicine, and medical and hospital equipment, as well as providing all necessary safety measures for the evacuation of asylees. The parties committed themselves to respect the diplomatic missions and they declared that they accepted and recognized the full competence of the special committee appointed by the tenth MCMFA.

The committee submitted two reports, since it went a second time to the Dominican Republic, and after this second visit it considered that its goals had been achieved. It then requested that a representative of the tenth MCMFA be appointed to act in the Dominican Republic in accordance with the decisions of the meeting. This appointed representative was the secretary general, Mora, who by that time was still in Santo Domingo.

On May 6, 1965, the tenth MCMFA agreed to request the governments to set up an inter-American force, its sole purpose being to restore order in the Dominican Republic, and thus to make it easier for the United States to eventually withdraw from its unilateral approach. The tenth MCMFA resolved in a further meeting on May 22, 1965, to establish a unified command, and the government of Brazil was requested to designate the commander of the force, with the United States to appoint the deputy commander. As stated earlier, what had happened behind the scenes was simply a deal: The United States would be more amenable to recognize the military coup of 1964 in Brazil in return for this favor, which would turn the U.S. invasion force into an inter-American one. Brazil's role was particularly important in this entire problem.

On May 23, 1965, the secretary general and the chiefs of the national contingents signed the "Act Establishing the Inter-American Peace Force," as it became known by a further resolution of the tenth MCMFA on June 2, 1965. Since the situation did not improve, the OAS then set up an ad hoc committee (Brazil, El Salvador, and the United States) which would act on behalf of the Special Committee continuing the tasks begun by it and aided by the secretary general for the purpose of achieving peace, helping the Inter-American Peace Force and informing the tenth MCMFA. This ad hoc committee and the secretary general came to the conclusion that early elections would solve the riddle, and on June 18, 1965, they reported these findings to all parties as follows:

a. General elections for president, vice president, and municipal authorities;

b. The election carried out with the full cooperation of the OAS with a technical advisory commission of experts and with the IACHR to remain in the country in the preelectoral period;

c. Full amnesty for those involved in the civil war; and

d. Establishment of a provisional government.

Both parties—the "Constitutional Government" and the "Government of National Reconstruction"—replied to these proposals, and as a consequence of new findings, the ad hoc committee launched the "Act of Dominican Reconciliation" which contained the elements for a final settlement. One of these elements was the acceptance of a provisional government headed by Héctor García Godoy, and of an "institutional act," pursuant to which this provisional government would function until the results of the election. Both acts were signed on August 31, 1965. The OAS provided all the necessary aid and then the ad hoc committee submitted the following recommendation to the tenth MCMFA:

1. That the tenth MCMFA continue its work until the installation of the constitutional government;

2. That both the tenth MCMFA and the ad hoc committee continue to function until the withdrawal of the Inter-American Peace Force;

3. That the tenth MCMFA recommend to the governments technical and economic aid to the Dominican government in view of the difficult economic situation of the country;

4. That the tenth MCMFA designate an outstanding personality to be the Special Representative of the OAS in the Dominican Republic to supervise and coordinate the economic and technical aid;

5. That the secretary general make a study of the claims of Dominican citizens to the OAS for damages and injuries suffered as a result of the armed action that began on April 24, 1965; and finally,

6. That, as requested by the ad hoc committee, the tenth MCMFA adopt a resolution amending paragraph 5 of the resolution of May 6, 1965, to read "that the manner and date of the withdrawal of the Inter American Peace Force" be determined jointly by the Provisional Government and the Tenth MCMFA when advisable.[31]

Thus, in conclusion, a difficult situation made worse by U.S. intervention, was satisfactorily solved the same year it started.

Three more MCMFAs took place within the framework of the old charter of 1948: the eleventh MCMFA concerned the faltering Alliance for Progress; the twelfth MCMFA dealt again with Cuban subversion, and the thirteenth MCMFA concerned the so-called Soccer War between El Salvador and Honduras. The procedure in these cases was identical to that followed earlier, with some having better results than others. The OAS was able to pump new life into the Alliance for Progress, although it could not inject the idealistic features of the AP in the early 1960s; it succeeded in taking additional measures against Cuba, and in stopping the war between the two Central American countries.

The first revision of the charter, the Protocol of Buenos Aires of 1967, did not change the procedure for peace and security, nor did the next revision, the Protocol of Cartagena de Indias of 1985. There were serious issues, like the fishing problem between the United States and Ecuador—fourteenth MCMFA—in which the same procedures were used as in earlier cases: appeal to the parties to avoid aggravating the problems, to negotiate, and to observe the principles of the Charter of the OAS. As a matter of fact, it did accomplish this, although the fourteenth MCMFA has officially not yet been closed.

The fifteenth MCMFA (1974) dealt with Cuban readmission to the OAS but did not achieve its purpose, and the sixteenth MCMFA agreed that the various member states were free to normalize their relations with Cuba. In both cases, the issue went to the General Committee of the General Secretariat, where the decision was taken in order to avoid a public debate. The seventeenth MCMFA focused on the new turmoil in Central America with the increasing isolation of the Somoza regime in Nicaragua, a kind of Central American version of the earlier collapse of the Trujillo regime in the Dominican Republic. The sixth MCMFA helped the collapse of Trujillo and the seventeenth, no doubt, did likewise with the Somoza regime. The procedures were similar, as in earlier cases, and the resolutions amounted to collective intervention in the affairs of Nicaragua when the MCMFA called for a replacement of the Somoza regime by one that was freely elected. The eighteenth MCMFA, which dealt with Nicaraguan violations of Costa Rican sovereignty, was very brief and actually was not really convoked: The PC, acting provisionally as Organ of Consultation, took care of the matter since Nicaragua reacted positively to the exhortations of the OAS to obey the principles of the inter-American system, and, in a similar manner, the organization also succeeded in diffusing a Peruvian-Ecuadorean border conflict in the El Condor mountain range. In the latter case, the nineteenth MCMFA was able to arrange a cease-fire and to achieve the demobilization of both Peruvian and Ecuadorean forces in the region. An investigating committee made up of the 1942 guarantors (Argentina, Brazil, Chile, and the United States) traveled to the El Condor region and monitored the cease-fire.

A different story, however, were the Malvinas conflict of 1982 (twentieth MCMFA) and the Panama invasion of 1989 (twenty-first MCMFA). Although the OAS presented a united front in both cases, it was powerless to achieve a just solution. In the first issue, British policy ignored diplomatic niceties and Mrs. Thatcher sabotaged the Peruvian Peace Plan offered by Peruvian President Fernando Belaúnde Terry by giving orders to sink the Argentine cruiser *General Belgrano*, even though the warship constituted no danger to British forces and was sailing toward the continent and not the islands. A similar failure was the unfortunate invasion of Panama by the United States in December 1989, which was well prepared several months in advance by the Bush administration in case the OAS efforts to remove General

Noriega peacefully from power should fail, as indeed they did. It would be unrealistic to expect the OAS to succeed in such a venture as the Panamanian one, since it could not be compared with the Somoza or Trujillo regimes of the past. Latin Americans interpreted the entire matter, even though they had little sympathy for the general, as a bilateral dispute between Panama and the United States, with the usual bullying tactics by Uncle Sam. Hence, Latin America distanced itself from the venture and rejected the pretexts for the invasion.

There were many cases in which requests for an MCMFA were rejected by the COAS or the PC, simply because, in the view of the majority of states, the respective situation did not warrant the convocation of the Organ of Consultation. In the early history of the OAS, such cases included Haiti (1949), Ecuador (1955), the Dominican Republic (1959), Peru (1961), and Bolivia (1962). In the first case, the request by Haiti to convoke the Organ of Consultation in view of the activity of Haitian revolutionaries on Dominican soil was rejected by the COAS, since it appeared that the Haitian and the Dominican governments could work out a viable solution, and they did, thus avoiding an MCMFA. In the second case, Ecuador requested the convocation of the Organ of Consultation in view of a threatening situation on its border with Peru. Actually, it was a situation similar to that which would arise in the El Condor mountain region and would be dealt with by the nineteenth MCMFA. The earlier case of 1955 was less serious, and both Peru and Ecuador were able to settle the matter promptly before the Organ of Consultation was called to meet. The third case is part of the Caribbean tensions that led to the convocation of the fifth MCMFA in Santiago de Chile in 1959. The Dominican government requested the convocation of the Organ of Consultation in view of alleged Dominican accusations regarding Cuban and Venezuelan invasions of Dominican territory. Both Cuba and Venezuela rejected the accusations, but since the situation remained extremely tense the COAS, instead of convoking the Provisional Organ of Consultation, decided right away for an MCMFA—the fifth MCMFA in Santiago de Chile in 1959, in accordance with Articles 39 and 40 of the Charter. Thus they did not apply the Rio Treaty.

The fourth case involved Peru and Cuba, but the COAS thought that the IAPC was the appropriate organ, in accordance with Resolution IV of the fifth MCMFA.[32] Thus, the Peruvian request was not accepted, and no MCMFA was convoked for this case. The fifth case involved Bolivia and Chile in regard to the diversion of waters from the River Laura by the latter country, thus threatening Bolivia. The case was solved when the COAS appealed to the two governments to restore diplomatic relations and to avail themselves of the instruments of the inter-American system, especially the Pact of Bogotá, in order to solve their differences. Thus, the Laura River case never reached the level of an MCMFA.

In conclusion, there is no question that the OAS has been able, in principle and in general terms, to provide peace and security and to defend and protect both, but it can do nothing except show solidarity and vote accordingly when the "Colossus of the North" decides to pursue its own unilateral policies, including the support of extracontinental powers—such as the United Kingdom in the case of the South Atlantic conflict—when this suits its interests.

13

The Balance Sheet and the Future

The OAS has existed now for some forty-five years and the inter-American system for a little over a century. Like any other institution, the OAS has had its ups and downs and seen good times and bad. The United States initiated the Pan American movement to further its own political and economic goals. U.S. influence and control were greatest during the movement's first fifty years, when the inter-American system was sailing under the name Union of American Republics, and was especially symbolized by the long and venerable tenure of Leo Stanton Rowe. Already at that time (and from the very beginning) the inter-American system was seen as the appropriate forum in which problems and differences between the mighty North American republic and the weaker Latin American neighbors—and also among the various Latin American nations themselves—could be discussed and possibly resolved, and through which the entire Latin American region stood a better chance of addressing problems of mutual interest than on a purely bilateral basis.

In the course of its long history, the inter-American system has always pursued the same goals of peace and security "founded on moral order and on justice," although at different times it has also emphasized other targets.[1] Under the old Union of American Republics, the main emphasis, especially until World War I, was on the expansion of trade and the protection of trademarks and copyrights, while in the period of the 1920s the prevention of conflicts and the perfection of procedures for conciliation and arbitration were the main objectives. Nonintervention was the paramount concern of Latin America in the entire period from the first ICAS to World War II, and actually continued to be a deep preoccupation of the organization, which was always perfecting existing legal instruments, or adding new ones, and thus widening and deepening the juridical framework of its basic tenets in order to protect itself from the United States.

After World War II, and with increasing speed and emphasis, the organization concentrated on economic and social development, highlighted by the Alliance for Progress (AP) of 1961 that aimed at accelerating "economic progress and broader social justice within the framework of personal dignity and political liberty."[2] At the same time (and ever since the late 1950s), human rights and representative democracy, both long incorporated in the Charter of the OAS, were finding particular expression in the establishment of the IACHR, the Inter-American Convention on Human Rights, and the Inter-American Court of Human Rights. Finally, in the decades of the 1970s and 1980s, development and integration of Latin America—again in view of world realities—became the prime targets of the contemporary OAS.

Despite the fact that relations between the United States and Latin America had been particularly bad ever since the United States, with its victory over Spain in 1898, had moved into the Caribbean and Central America, the inter-American system continued to stabilize relations and to grow from one conference to the next. After World War I, when these relations became even worse, Latin America attempted to find refuge in the newly established League of Nations but was disappointed by the U.S. absence from Geneva. The result had a sobering effect in the sense that reality forced Latin America to look for improvements of the one institution where its interests could be defended. Thus, it was no surprise that despite worsening relations between the United States and Latin America in the 1920s, the inter-American system continued to expand and Latin American influence began to assert itself as early as the Fifth ICAS in Santiago in 1923.

The Good Neighbor policy of the 1930s was obviously the highlight of U.S.–Latin American relations and thus was echoed in the regional organization to the extent that the Monroe Doctrine was even continentalized with the Consultative Pact at the Inter-American Conference for the Maintenance of Peace in Buenos Aires (1936). Moreover, in World War II, inter-American cooperation and solidarity found its best test so far. However, the increasing global role of the United States led to a curious tendency in Washington, now that the war had been won, to ignore the extraordinary benefits the Good Neighbor policy had reaped in the 1930s and during World War II and to seriously consider scuttling the inter-American system in favor of the United Nations. Common sense and diplomacy averted such an incredible error in judgment, and the policymakers in both the United States and Latin America decided on an opposite course at the Inter-American Conference on Problems of War and Peace (the Chapultepec Conference) in Mexico City in 1945. The conference laid down the blueprint with the result that in the next years the regional organization was strengthened; the Rio Treaty was signed, and the OAS was set up. (So far the Pan American movement had been functioning without a treaty as a legal basis.)

When the OAS was established in 1948, it did not create anything radically new but simply codified and perfected existing principles, putting the entire regional organization on more solid ground—through the three pillars of the Charter of the OAS, the Rio Treaty, and the Pact of Bogotá. The OAS was thus modernized, streamlined, and adjusted to the realities of the world situation as it appeared in the immediate post–World War II period.

At the end of the 1950s, however, a malaise set in that developed into a grave crisis. Gone were the days of the Good Neighbor policy, and although the Fair Neighbor policy had taken its place the drastic changes in the world increasingly affected Latin America. The OAS itself soon realized that the adjustments introduced in 1948 had not increased the efficiency of the organization and had not measured up to expectations, especially at a time when turmoil and revolution (in view of the increasing economic and social problems due to the widening abyss between rich and poor) had become the order of the day. Indeed, Latin America was fast losing its traditional markets, had not yet found suitable alternatives, was slipping fast in the field of technology, and was often applying incorrect solutions to its grave problems, such as the implementation of industrialization projects at the expense of traditional agriculture. Latin America's rating in the world was decreasing, and both symbolically and practically. Moreover, the OAS was downgraded by the United States, whose interests had become more global and less regional and where the priorities had dramatically shifted from the hemisphere to Europe and Asia. Obviously, Latin America echoed the U.S. position, and this reflected itself in a powerful manner in the organization. If earlier the U.S. secretary of state had had time to come to the PAU, after 1948, no such visits ever took place, and even the U.S. representatives to the OAS were not of the highest level. In a way, this may have been unavoidable when viewing the situation more from a global point of view than from a regional standpoint. The United States, which had received great benefits from the inter-American system in terms of cooperation and solidarity during World War II, was reluctant to commit itself wholeheartedly to economic and financial aid to Latin America as a kind of quid pro quo, and gradually turned its back to its neighbors to the South, except when its interests were at stake, as in the case of Guatemala in 1954. A new low was reached in U.S.–Latin American relations, which could be seen clearly in the pathetic visit of Vice President Richard Nixon to Peru and Venezuela in 1958, with its hostile and emotion-laden demonstrations and riots.

The Cuban Revolution increased the tensions and forced the United States, rather belatedly, to come up with a more positive approach, which, in the early 1960s, found expression, rather dramatically, with the establishment of the IDB in 1960 (long sought after by Latin America), the AP of 1961, and the necessary adjustments in the economic areas of the organization through a more efficient and upgraded IA-ECOSOC. At one point the AP seemed to revitalize the organization and to recapture the spirit of the Good Neighbor policy (at a time when it needed it most), and there is no doubt that the OAS profited handsomely from the idealism of John F. Kennedy and his generally positive and generous outlook. Unfortunately, the AP, which obviously could not, in a few years or decades, solve all the economic and social problems enumerated in its Charter of Punta del Este, gradually lost its mystique and idealistic framework and became more or less just another financial operation.

By the time the United States invaded the Dominican Republic in 1965 in order to prevent a "second Cuba," new attempts were being launched to revitalize the organization and to overhaul again its machinery on the basis of both the experience gained since 1948 and the new realities of the 1960s, when Europe was totally rebuilt and Africa became an almost totally independent continent. As a tangible symbol of Europe's reconstruction, the Organization of European Economic Cooperation (OEEC), the instrument of European reconstruction, had become the Organization of Economic Cooperation and Development (OECD), with totally different objectives. In fifteen years of reconstruction, 1945–1960, Europe had regained its position in the world and Japan was rapidly becoming the Asian economic giant. Latin America was the loser, and thus new adjustments were called for.

The new blueprint for these organizational adjustments was the famous Protocol of Buenos Aires of 1967, which again introduced major changes and which, no doubt, represented extraordinary gains. Of particular importance was the elimination of the ICAS that, until 1954, had met every five years— a mechanism that was hardly efficient in a world that was changing so rapidly—and its replacement with the annual General Assembly. On the other hand, the downgrading of the old Council of the OAS, now called the Permanent Council, and its elevation to the rank of the two other councils— IA-ECOSOC and CIECC—did not seem prudent. The reduction of the secretary general's term of office from ten to five years, with the possibility of reelection, was another excellent provision.

In any case, the new organization based on the revised charter went into effect in 1970, but by that time new problems had arisen that again had to be faced. In addition to the challenge of the newly independent Caribbean states, the 1970s represented a period in which military governments had come to power or had consolidated their position, and they attempted to show the region authoritarian alternatives to socialist adventures, especially the Cuban Revolution. In view of its successes in the late 1960s and early 1970s, Brazil became a model for a certain time, while Allende's Chile went from one upheaval to another and was finally terminated with Pinochet's coup and some U.S. financial aid. When U.S. President Jimmy Carter came to power in the United States, an attempt was made in Washington to improve relations with Latin America. The greatest symbol of this change was the signing and ratification of the Panama treaties, not only correcting a grave injustice to that small nation by ending the Canal Zone and gradually terminating U.S. control of the Panama Canal, but also making a significant gesture toward the entire Latin American region. At one point, the ceremony of the Panama Canal treaties seemed, in practical terms, a return to the historic Good Neighbor policy, as during the time of President Kennedy in the early 1960s, but this was of short duration. The Reagan and Bush years hardened the U.S. position toward all international organizations in general, and the OAS in particular. It also undertook a series of actions that could only hurt U.S.–Latin American relations and that reverberated through the entire continent: the cynical use of mercenaries, called Freedom Fighters, in Nicaragua in order to destabilize a legal government, intervention in other parts of Central America, approval and support of the British reoccupation of the Malvinas, and, at the pinnacle, the insane U.S. invasions of Grenada and Panama in defiance of the most elementary notions of international morality and the law of nations.

The OAS reflected these reactionary policies and answered (what else could it do?) with new elaborations and perfections of the principle of non-intervention. It was also at this time that Latin Americans seriously looked for alternatives to the OAS by establishing their own organizations or by simply bypassing the OAS. Already in the 1960s such economic groups had been established outside the OAS, such as ALALC in 1960–1961, which in 1980 was terminated (since it had dismally failed) and replaced by ALADI. Now in 1975 it was the turn of the Latin American Economic System, or SELA, and in the 1980s we witness the Contadora Group (Colombia, Venezuela, Panama, and Mexico) and the Contadora Support Group (Argentina, Brazil, Peru, and Uruguay) in order to achieve a just and lasting peace in Central America. These groups operated totally outside the OAS but were unsuccessful since the United States opposed them as much as it opposed Spanish, French, and West German efforts to help the Nicaraguan economy. There was also the Cartagena Group, comprising the eleven members of ALALC/ALADI and attempting the establishment of a common front in regard to the debt problem. When Mexico refused to go along in view of its special relationship with the United States, the Cartagena Group also operated in a vacuum and gradually went down the drain. In a nutshell, these Latin American attempts represented failures and proved that in reality there was no alternative to the OAS, even at a time when the organization was not in the best of shape. With all its many shortcomings and serious weaknesses, the OAS remained the regional organization that provided the best forum for discussion and the possible solution of problems between all nations of the hemisphere, and the fact that Canada, after an absence of a century, has finally decided to take the plunge and "join the club" is ample evidence of the necessity and vitality of the inter-American system and its instrument, the OAS.

In the midst of the 1980s, the OAS again revised its charter, as amended earlier (in 1967) by the Protocol of Buenos Aires. The new changes introduced with the Protocol of Cartagena de Indias of 1985 were not as deep as those made eighteen years earlier, but still represented new adjustments. Perhaps the three most important items were the welcome mat extended to Guyana and Belize (and thus a gesture to the entire Caribbean), the strengthening of the secretary general, and the elimination of the Inter-American Committee on Peaceful Settlement. The upgrading of the secretary general represents quite a novelty, and again, the OAS followed in the footsteps of the United Nations, where the secretary general holds a powerful position, in contrast to the situation in the League of Nations. When the Colombian President Alberto Lleras Camargo became the first secretary general of the OAS in 1948, he was determined to take a strong position but was quickly reminded by Mexico's representative, Luis Quintanilla, that the position of secretary general of the OAS did not allow him to do so. As a matter of fact, no secretary general of the OAS has since used his high position for speaking out (the only exception being Mora during the Dominican crisis, when OAS members specifically called for a strong initiative). In any case, the new powers now conferred upon the secretary general with the Protocol of Cartagena de Indias is a move in the right direction. Another significant change is the final demise of the IAPC (since 1967, called the Inter-American Committee on Peaceful Settlement). This organization was obviously redundant in view of the fact that the New Pact of Bogotá hopefully will fill the vacuum that the older Pact of Bogotá was never able to fill, although it always remained a valid guide in the pursuit of the pacific settlement of disputes.

There is no question that the financial status of the organization, which was already quite a problem in the 1950s, did not improve in the following decades. It actually became an uphill battle for simple survival, since so many Latin American governments were unable to come up with their annual quotas. This was compounded in the Reagan years, with the United States not only turning a cold shoulder to the organization but even refusing to pay its full share. A notorious and especially petty case was the withholding of $43,000 that was in arrearages by the United States to the Pan American Institute of Geography and History at a time when the head of PAIGH (elected for the next four-year term) was an American, the dean of the University of Tennessee.[3]

The financial crunch was a problem that, in reality, was never solved, and in the 1980s it forced the OAS and its general secretariat to make drastic reductions with tremendous decreases in personnel and their corresponding activities. This was obviously triggered by the Reagan administration with its negative position toward all international organizations, and particularly the OAS, a policy that was not justified, even though there may indeed have been some abuses—it represented the usual method of overkill. Only lately, when it seemed to serve its interests, the United States has seen it appropriate to fulfil its obligations and take the international organizations with a greater sense of seriousness.

The OAS has served a useful purpose and has survived serious challenges in the last forty-five years. Despite all the criticisms and shortcomings, it will not only survive but will play an increasingly significant role at a time when the world is again witnessing extraordinary changes: Not only has international communism been as totally discredited as fascism some forty-five years ago, but the Cold War has ended. Trading blocs have arisen and are playing an increasingly significant role. As Europe and Asia are creating their respective economic spheres, the United States is also beginning to change course. The North American Free Trade Agreement (NAFTA) between the United States, Canada, and Mexico establishes a powerful North American Bloc. President Bush's Enterprise for the Americas is the cornerstone of this new economic movement. At the same time, the more progressive parts of South America are doing likewise, not only in order to integrate their respective economies, but also to be in a better position in regard to this North American Free Trade Market, which, in the future, they might join. Argentina, Brazil, Paraguay, and Uruguay established MERCOSUR, the Common Market of the Southern Cone, which was eventually to be joined by Chile and Bolivia. The United States has already signed economic agreements with Colombia, Ecuador, Bolivia, with others to follow—Costa Rica, Venezuela, and Chile, and, just recently, the "Rose Garden Agreement" with MERCOSUR. Four regional trading groups are emerging: the North American, with the United States, Canada, and Mexico; the Central American Common Market, which will be reactivated; the Andean Common Market, with Bolivia, Peru, Ecuador, Colombia, and Venezuela; and the Southern Cone Common Market. Recently the Regional Consultative Group for Central America, organized and financed by the IDB, has begun to encourage integration of Central America through the IDB-financed Program of Support for Development and Integration in Central America, which includes support for three regional integration institutions: the Permanent Secretariat of the General Treaty for Central American Economic Intergration, the Central American Monetary Council, and the Federation of Private Sector Entities of Central America and Panama. We are witnessing the beginnings of the establishment of a hemispheric free trade area (possibly a common market) from Alaska to Tierra del Fuego, as embodied in the Enterprise of the Americas, a comprehensive policy that had not been seen since the Alliance for Progress was launched thirty years ago.

A kind of revival or continuation of the defunct Contadora and Contadora Support Groups was set up a few years ago as the "Rio Group," so called because it was formally established in Rio de Janeiro. It was already functioning at the time of the twenty-first MCMFA (January 8, 1990), when it proposed its own draft resolution in lieu of the original Nicaraguan proposal regarding U.S. violation of Nicaraguan Embassy premises in Panama City on December 29, 1989. We thus witness within the OAS, at the present time, three definite blocs that intend, whenever possible, to come up with joint positions: the Rio Group (7); the Central American Group, which now also includes Panama (6); and the Caribbean Group (10).

It is obvious that within this new context, the OAS will play a significant role at a time when extraordinary changes are also taking place in Latin America. It is true that the 1980s appear to be a lost decade for that region, as was much of the nineteenth century, but no evil lasts forever, and the Latin American crisis of the 1980s, with debt and drugs topping the list of its serious issues, will not continue indefinitely. Already there are signs of change: ideology, statism, protectionism, and socialist adventurism of doubtful repute are giving way, under the impact of realism, to more positive solutions. In the long run, the OAS will profit from these fundamental changes, and if the United States takes the OAS more seriously, as it probably will do, the Latin Americans will respond positively and enthusiastically.

The United States will continue to play a pivotal role in the OAS, and the more it respects its neighbors and discontinues its "cowboy politics" (which are reminiscent of nineteenth-century gunboat policies), the better it will be for U.S.–Latin American relations in general, and for the OAS in particular. As Latin America becomes more important, the United States, with its practical and pragmatic orientation, will no doubt quickly shift course and get its priorities straight. In this context, it is expected that the United States will honor the letter and the spirit of the Panama treaties, will find definitive solutions for Puerto Rico, will normalize relations with Havana, will eventually give up and return Guantánamo Bay to its legitimate owners, and will avoid military expeditions or covert operations in the name of all kinds of alleged threats and cures.

The OAS cannot be a one-way street for U.S. policies in the hemisphere, and the sooner the United States acknowledges this fact the better it will be for everybody (for U.S.–Latin American relations, inter-American affairs, and the OAS itself). The recent decision by the U.S. Supreme Court (passed by a six-to-three vote) justifying kidnapping operations abroad in regard to individuals indicted in this country represents an incredible and unfortunate development, since it is in opposition to the most elementary notions of the law of nations and has had quite a detrimental effect all over the world. One hopes that, besides the Mexican case that was the target of the decision, it will not be implemented as the Bush Administration has promised Latin American nations.

The military coup that deposed the freely elected Haitian President Jean-Bertrand Aristide in September 1991 put the OAS on the spot. As will be recalled, the Twenty-First Regular General Assembly (Santiago de Chile, June 2–8, 1991), unanimously passed a resolution that called for the immediate convocation of an MCMFA in cases where a freely elected government was eliminated by a coup, in order to discuss such a serious threat to political liberties and adopt the necessary measures for the reestablishment of a democratic government. This is (as stated earlier) a clear and dramatic departure from traditional Latin American viewpoints regarding the principle of nonintervention, and thus it signals a weakening of the concept of national sovereignty. However, it also means the revival of Alberto Rodríguez Larreta's Uruguayan proposal of the 1940s. It is, of course, debatable whether the Latin American delegates, meeting in Santiago and displaying their characteristic idealistic zeal, acted wisely. Sooner than expected, the military coup in Haiti posed an extraordinary challenge to the organization. This was further compounded by two military revolts in Venezuela in January and November 1992, which almost succeeded.

Since September 1992, the OAS has coped with the Haitian problem. It is besides the point that democracy never worked in Haiti and is not part of Haitian tradition. Moreover, 90 percent of the population is illiterate—and, as K. Chr. F. Krause said in the early part of the nineteenth century, an uneducated person has hardly any chance of freedom. The OAS met, as required by the Santiago resolution, and adopted measures. These were the usual economic sanctions but did not topple the military forces—which have some support, especially from the wealthier sections of the country—but rather created economic turmoil and mass migrations to the United States. The sanctions have hurt Haiti, but it is doubtful that they will achieve their aims. A military invasion and occupation have been discussed but nobody wants to become involved in that kind of action, and certainly not the United States, which once occupied the country for almost two decades and whose immediate interests are not involved. Thus, the situation has remained in an impasse, with all sorts of negotiations, open and hidden, to find a face-saving solution for all parties concerned.

Moreover, in April 1992, President Alberto Fujimori of Peru made what is now called an *autogolpe* (usurping his presidential powers), by dissolving the Peruvian Congress, suspending several articles of the constitution, imposing censorship, and prohibiting political activity. He then announced, as reported by the media, the establishment of a "government of emergency and national reconstruction" in order to cope with terrorism, drug trafficking, and corruption. Eventually, political reforms will be put before voters in a plebiscite. Thus, after the Haitian coup, which is nowhere near a solution, the OAS faces a new challenge that seems to signal that democracy, which only a few years ago was heralded by some as being almost permanently established, is in trouble. If the Haitian problem could so far not be solved, the Peruvian case will be even more difficult to remedy, and it will be interesting to watch how the OAS is going to face reality. It is clear that the Santiago Resolution has put the OAS in an extraordinary situation from which it must extricate itself if it does not want to look ridiculous. Recently, a suggestion was made that a Military Force of the Americas be set up (a concept similar to the one that was pushed by the United States in 1965, at the time that President Lyndon Johnson sent U.S. marines to the Dominican

Republic in order to forestall a repetition of the Cuban Revolution). At that time it was unanimously rejected by the Latin American nations, but times have changed, although the recent sequence of events—Haiti, Venezuela, Peru, and perhaps others—may put a damper on such lofty thoughts. In any case, the Resolution of Santiago will haunt the OAS because it is not realistic and exemplifies once more the idealistic character of Hispanic civilization.

Thus, despite the new challenges of the Santiago Resolution, the future of the OAS looks bright and imposing, with its membership of thirty-five countries. Clearly, its role in inter-American affairs will increase in proportion to the growing importance of Latin America and the Caribbean as the Americas draw closer.

APPENDIXES

Appendix 1
Charter of the Organization of American States*

IN THE NAME OF THEIR PEOPLES, THE STATES REPRESENTED AT THE NINTH INTERNATIONAL CONFERENCE OF AMERICAN STATES,

Convinced that the historic mission of America is to offer to man a land of liberty and a favorable environment for the development of his personality and the realization of his just aspirations;

Conscious that that mission has already inspired numerous agreements, whose essential value lies in the desire of the American peoples to live together in peace and, through their mutual understanding and respect for the sovereignty of each one, to provide for the betterment of all, in independence, in equality and under law;

Convinced that representative democracy is an indispensable condition for the stability, peace and development of the region;

Confident that the true significance of American solidarity and good neighborliness can only mean the consolidation on this continent, within the framework of democratic institutions, of a system of individual liberty and social justice based on respect for the essential rights of man;

Persuaded that their welfare and their contribution to the progress and the civilization of the world will increasingly require intensive continental cooperation;

Resolved to persevere in the noble undertaking that humanity has conferred upon the United Nations, whose principles and purposes they solemnly reaffirm;

Convinced that juridical organization is a necessary condition for security and peace founded on moral order and on justice; and

In accordance with Resolution IX of the Inter-American Conference on Problems of War and Peace, held in Mexico City,

HAVE AGREED
upon the following

---

*Signed in Bogotá in 1948 and amended by the Protocol of Buenos Aires in 1967 and by the Protocol of Cartagena de Indias in 1985. In force as of November 16, 1988.

CHARTER
OF THE ORGANIZATION OF AMERICAN STATES

PART ONE

Chapter I

NATURE AND PURPOSES

Article 1

The American States establish by this Charter the international organization that they have developed to achieve an order of peace and justice, to promote their solidarity, to strengthen their collaboration, and to defend their sovereignty, their territorial integrity, and their independence. Within the United Nations, the Organization of American States is a regional agency.

The Organization of American States has no powers other than those expressly conferred upon it by this Charter, none of whose provisions authorizes it to intervene in matters that are within the internal jurisdiction of the Member States.

Article 2

The Organization of American States, in order to put into practice the principles on which it is founded and to fulfill its regional obligations under the Charter of the United Nations, proclaims the following essential purposes:

a)   To strengthen the peace and security of the continent;

b)   To promote and consolidate representative democracy, with due respect for the principle of nonintervention;

c)   To prevent possible causes of difficulties and to ensure the pacific settlement of disputes that may arise among the Member States;

d)   To provide for common action on the part of those States in the event of aggression;

e)   To seek the solution of political, juridical, and economic problems that may arise among them;

f)   To promote, by cooperative action, their economic, social, and cultural development; and

g)   To achieve an effective limitation of conventional weapons that will make it possible to devote the largest amount of resources to the economic and social development of the Member States.

Chapter II

PRINCIPLES

Article 3

The American States reaffirm the following principles:

a) International law is the standard of conduct of States in their reciprocal relations;

b) International order consists essentially of respect for the personality, sovereignty, and independence of States, and the faithful fulfillment of obligations derived from treaties and other sources of international law;

c) Good faith shall govern the relations between States;

d) The solidarity of the American States and the high aims which are sought through it require the political organization of those States on the basis of the effective exercise of representative democracy;

e) Every State has the right to choose, without external interference, its political, economic, and social system and to organize itself in the way best suited to it, and has the duty to abstain from intervening in the affairs of another State. Subject to the foregoing, the American States shall cooperate fully among themselves, independently of the nature of their political, economic, and social systems;

f) The American States condemn war of aggression: victory does not give rights;

g) An act of aggression against one American State is an act of aggression against all the other American States;

h) Controversies of an international character arising between two or more American States shall be settled by peaceful procedures;

i) Social justice and social security are bases of lasting peace;

j) Economic cooperation is essential to the common welfare and prosperity of the peoples of the continent;

k) The American States proclaim the fundamental rights of the individual without distinction as to race, nationality, creed, or sex;

l) The spiritual unity of the continent is based on respect for the cultural values of the American countries and requires their close cooperation for the high purposes of civilization;

m) The education of peoples should be directed toward justice, freedom, and peace.

Chapter III

MEMBERS

Article 4

All American States that ratify the present Charter are Members of the Organization.

Article 5

Any new political entity that arises from the union of several Member States and that, as such, ratifies the present Charter, shall become a Member of the Organzation. The entry of the new political entity into the Organization shall result in the loss of membership of each one of the States which constitute it.

Article 6

Any other independent American State that desires to become a Member of the Organization should so indicate by means of a note addressed to the Secretary General, in which it declares that it is willing to sign and ratify the Charter of the Organization and to accept all the obligations inherent in membership, especially those relating to collective security expressly set forth in Articles 27 and 28 of the Charter.

Article 7

The General Assembly, upon the recommendation of the Permanent Council of the Organization, shall determine whether it is appropriate that the Secretary General be authorized to permit the applicant State to sign the Charter and to accept the deposit of the corresponding instrument of ratification. Both the recommendation of the Permanent Council and the decision of the General Assembly shall require the affirmative vote of two thirds of the Member States.

Article 8

Membership in the Organization shall be confined to independent States of the Hemisphere that were members of the United Nations as of December 10, 1985, and the nonautonomous territories mentioned in document OEA/Ser. P, AG/doc.1939/85, of November 5, 1985, when they become independent.

Chapter IV

FUNDAMENTAL RIGHTS AND DUTIES OF STATES

Article 9

States are juridically equal, enjoy equal rights and equal capacity to exercise these rights, and have equal duties. The rights of each State depend not upon its power to ensure the exercise thereof, but upon the mere fact of its existence as a person under international law.

Article 10

Every American State has the duty to respect the rights enjoyed by every other State in accordance with international law.

Article 11

The fundamental rights of States may not be impaired in any manner whatsoever.

Article 12

The political existence of the State is independent of recognition by other States. Even before being recognized, the State has the right to defend its integrity and independence, to provide for its preservation and prosperity, and consequently to organize itself as it sees fit, to legislate concerning its interests, to administer its services, and to determine the jurisdiction and competence of its courts. The exercise of these rights is limited only by the exercise of the rights of other States in accordance with international law.

Article 13

Recognition implies that the State granting it accepts the personality of the new State, with all the rights and duties that international law prescribes for the two States.

Article 14

The right of each State to protect itself and to live its own life does not authorize it to commit unjust acts against another State.

Article 15

The jurisdiction of States within the limits of their national territory is exercised equally over all the inhabitants, whether nationals or aliens.

Article 16

Each State has the right to develop its cultural, political, and economic life freely and naturally. In this free development, the State shall respect the rights of the individual and the principles of universal morality.

Article 17

Respect for and the faithful observance of treaties constitute standards for the development of peaceful relations among States. International treaties and agreements should be public.

Article 18

No State or group of States has the right to intervene, directly or indirectly, for any reason whatever, in the internal or external affairs of any other State. The foregoing principle prohibits not only armed force but also any other form of interference or attempted threat against the personality of the State or against its political, economic, and cultural elements.

Article 19

No State may use or encourage the use of coercive measures of an economic or political character in order to force the sovereign will of another State and obtain from it advantages of any kind.

Article 20

The territory of a State is inviolable; it may not be the object, even temporarily, of military occupation or of other measures of force taken by another State, directly or indirectly, on any grounds whatever. No territorial acquisitions or special advantages obtained either by force or by other means of coercion shall be recognized.

Article 21

The American States bind themselves in their international relations not to have recourse to the use of force, except in the case of self-defense in accordance with existing treaties or in fulfillment thereof.

Article 22

Measures adopted for the maintenance of peace and security in accordance with existing treaties do not constitute a violation of the principles set forth in Articles 18 and 20.

Chapter V

PACIFIC SETTLEMENT OF DISPUTES

Article 23

International disputes between Member States shall be submitted to the peaceful procedures set forth in this Charter.

This provision shall not be interpreted as an impairment of the rights and obligations of the Member States under Articles 34 and 35 of the Charter of the United Nations.

Article 24

The following are peaceful procedures: direct negotiation, good offices, mediation, investigation and conciliation, judicial settlement, arbitration, and those which the parties to the dispute may especially agree upon at any time.

Article 25

In the event that a dispute arises between two or more American States which, in the opinion of one of them, cannot be settled through the usual diplomatic channels, the parties shall agree on some other peaceful procedure that will enable them to reach a solution.

Article 26

A special treaty will establish adequate means for the settlement of disputes and will determine pertinent procedures for each peaceful means such that no dispute between American States may remain without definitive settlement within a reasonable period of time.

Chapter VI

COLLECTIVE SECURITY

Article 27

Every act of aggression by a State against the territorial integrity or the inviolability of the territory or against the sovereignty or political independence of an American State shall be considered an act of aggression against the other American States.

Article 28

If the inviolability or the integrity of the territory or the sovereignty or political independence of any American State should be affected by an armed attack or by an act of aggression that is not an armed attack, or by an extracontinental conflict, or by a conflict between two or more American States, or by any other fact or situation that might endanger the peace of America, the American States, in furtherance of the principles of continental solidarity or collective self-defense, shall apply the measures and procedures established in the special treaties on the subject.

Chapter VII

INTEGRAL DEVELOPMENT

Article 29

The Member States, inspired by the principles of inter-American solidarity and cooperation, pledge themselves to a united effort to ensure international social justice in their relations and integral development for their peoples, as conditions essential to peace and security. Integral development encompasses the economic, social, educational, cultural, scientific, and technological fields through which the goals that each country sets for accomplishing it should be achieved.

Article 30

Inter-American cooperation for integral development is the common and joint responsibility of the Member States, within the framework of the democratic principles and the institutions of the inter-American system. It should include the economic, social, educational, cultural, scientific, and technological fields, support the achievement of national objectives of the Member States, and respect the priorities established by each country in its development plans, without political ties or conditions.

Article 31

Inter-American cooperation for integral development should be continuous and preferably channeled through multilateral organizations, without prejudice to bilateral cooperation between Member States.

The Member States shall contribute to inter-American cooperation for integral development in accordance with their resources and capabilities and in conformity with their laws.

Article 32

Development is a primary responsibility of each country and should constitute an integral and continuous process for the establishment of a more just economic and social order that will make possible and contribute to the fulfillment of the individual.

Article 33

The Member States agree that equality of opportunity, equitable distribution of wealth and income, and the full participation of their peoples in decisions relating to their own development are, among others, basic objectives of integral development. To achieve them, they likewise agree to devote their utmost efforts to accomplishing the following basic goals:

a) Substantial and self-sustained increase of per capita national product;

b) Equitable distribution of national income;

c) Adequate and equitable systems of taxation;

d) Modernization of rural life and reforms leading to equitable and efficient land-tenure systems, increased agricultural productivity, expanded use of land, diversification of production and improved processing and marketing systems for agricultural products; and the strengthening and expansion of the means to attain these ends;

e) Accelerated and diversified industrialization, especially of capital and intermediate goods;

f) Stability of domestic price levels, compatible with sustained economic development and the attainment of social justice;

g) Fair wages, employment opportunities, and acceptable working conditions for all;

h) Rapid eradication of illiteracy and expansion of educational opportunities for all;

i) Protection of man's potential through the extension and application of modern medical science;

j) Proper nutrition, especially through the acceleration of national efforts to increase the production and availability of food;

k) Adequate housing for all sectors of the population;

l) Urban conditions that offer the opportunity for a healthful, productive, and full life;

m) Promotion of private initiative and investment in harmony with action in the public sector; and

n) Expansion and diversification of exports.

Article 34

The Member States should refrain from practicing policies and adopting actions or measures that have serious adverse effects on the development of other Member States.

Article 35

Transnational enterprises and foreign private investment shall be subject to the legislation of the host countries and to the jurisdiction of their competent courts and to the international treaties and agreements to which said countries are parties, and should conform to the development policies of the recipient countries.

Article 36

The Member States agree to join together in seeking a solution to urgent or critical problems that may arise whenever the economic development or stability of any Member State is seriously affected by conditions that cannot be remedied through the efforts of that State.

Article 37

The Member States shall extend among themselves the benefits of science and technology by encouraging the exchange and utilization of scientific and technical knowledge in accordance with existing treaties and national laws.

Article 38

The Member States, recognizing the close interdependence between foreign trade and economic and social development, should make individual and united efforts to bring about the following:

a) Favorable conditions of access to world markets for the products of the developing countries of the region, particularly through the reduction or elimination, by importing countries, of tariff and nontariff barriers that affect the exports of the Member States of the Organization, except when such barriers are applied in order to diversify the economic structure, to speed up the development of the less-developed Member States, and intensify their process of economic integration, or when they are related to national security or to the needs of economic balance;

b) Continuity in their economic and social development by means of:

i. Improved conditions for trade in basic commodities through international agreements, where appropriate; orderly marketing procedures that avoid the disruption of markets, and other measures designed to promote the expansion of markets and to obtain dependable incomes for producers, adequate and dependable supplies for consumers, and stable prices that are both remunerative to producers and fair to consumers;

ii. Improved international financial cooperation and the adoption of other means for lessening the adverse impact of sharp fluctuations in export earnings experienced by the countries exporting basic commodities;

iii. Diversification of exports and expansion of export opportunities for manufactured and semimanufactured products from the developing countries; and

iv. Conditions conducive to increasing the real export earnings of the Member States, particularly the developing countries of the region, and to increasing their participation in international trade.

Article 39

The Member States reaffirm the principle that when the more developed countries grant concessions in international trade agreements that lower or eliminate tariffs or other barriers to foreign trade so that they benefit the less-developed countries, they should not expect reciprocal concessions from those countries that are incompatible with their economic development, financial, and trade needs.

Article 40

The Member States, in order to accelerate their economic development, regional integration, and the expansion and improvement of the conditions of their commerce, shall promote improvement and coordination of transportation and communication in the developing countries and among the Member States.

Article 41

The Member States recognize that integration of the developing countries of the Hemisphere is one of the objectives of the inter-American system and, therefore, shall orient their efforts and take the necessary measures to accelerate the integration process, with a view to establishing a Latin American common market in the shortest possible time.

Article 42

In order to strengthen and accelerate integration in all its aspects, the Member States agree to give adequate priority to the preparation and carrying out of multinational projects and to their financing, as well as to encourage economic and financial institutions of the inter-American system to continue giving their broadest support to regional integration institutions and programs.

Article 43

The Member States agree that technical and financial cooperation that seeks to promote regional economic integration should be based on the principle of harmonious, balanced, and efficient development, with particular attention to the relatively less-developed countries, so that it may be a decisive factor that will enable them to promote, with their own efforts, the improved development of their infrastructure programs, new lines of production, and export diversification.

Article 44

The Member States, convinced that man can only achieve the full realization of his aspirations within a just social order, along with economic development and true peace, agree to dedicate every effort to the application of the following principles and mechanisms:

a) All human beings, without distinction as to race, sex, nationality, creed, or social condition, have a right to material well-being and to their spiritual development, under circumstances of liberty, dignity, equality of opportunity, and economic security;

b) Work is a right and a social duty, it gives dignity to the one who performs it, and it should be performed under conditions, including a system of fair wages, that ensure life, health, and a decent standard of living for the worker and his family, both during his working years and in his old age, or when any circumstance deprives him of the possibility of working;

c) Employers and workers, both rural and urban, have the right to associate themselves freely for the defense and promotion of their interests, including the right to collective bargaining and the workers' right to strike, and recognition of the juridical personality of associations and the protection of their freedom and independence, all in accordance with applicable laws;

d) Fair and efficient systems and procedures for consultation and collaboration among the sectors of production, with due regard for safeguarding the interests of the entire society;

e) The operation of systems of public administration, banking and credit, enterprise, and distribution and sales, in such a way, in harmony with the private sector, as to meet the requirements and interests of the community;

f) The incorporation and increasing participation of the marginal sectors of the population, in both rural and urban areas, in the economic, social, civic, cultural, and political life of the nation, in order to achieve the full integration of the national community, acceleration of the process of social mobility, and the consolidation of the democratic system. The encouragement of all efforts of popular promotion and cooperation that have as their purpose the development and progress of the community;

g) Recognition of the importance of the contribution of organizations such as labor unions, cooperatives, and cultural, professional, business, neighborhood, and community associations to the life of the society and to the development process;

h) Development of an efficient social security policy; and

i) Adequate provision for all persons to have due legal aid in order to secure their rights.

Article 45

The Member States recognize that, in order to facilitate the process of Latin American regional integration, it is necessary to harmonize the social legislation of the developing countries, especially in the labor and social security fields, so that the rights of the workers shall be equally protected, and they agree to make the greatest efforts possible to achieve this goal.

Article 46

The Member States will give primary importance within their development plans to the encouragement of education, science, technology, and culture, oriented toward the overall improvement of the individual, and as a foundation for democracy, social justice, and progress.

Article 47

The Member States will cooperate with one another to meet their educational needs, to promote scientific research, and to encourage technological progress for their integral development. They will consider themselves individually and jointly bound to preserve and enrich the cultural heritage of the American peoples.

Article 48

The Member States will exert the greatest efforts, in accordance with their constitutional processes, to ensure the effective exercise of the right to education, on the following bases:

a) Elementary education, compulsory for children of school age, shall also be offered to all others who can benefit from it. When provided by the State it shall be without charge;

b) Middle-level education shall be extended progressively to as much of the population as possible, with a view to social improvement. It shall be diversified in such a way that it meets the development needs of each country without prejudice to providing a general education; and

c) Higher education shall be available to all, provided that, in order to maintain its high level, the corresponding regulatory or academic standards are met.

Article 49

The Member States will give special attention to the eradication of illiteracy, will strengthen adult and vocational education systems, and will ensure that the benefits of culture will be available to the entire population. They will promote the use of all information media to fulfill these aims.

Article 50

The Member States will develop science and technology through educational, research, and technological development activities and information and dissemination programs. They will stimulate activities in the field of technology for the purpose of adapting it to the needs of their integral development. They will organize their cooperation in these fields efficiently and will substantially increase exchange of knowledge, in accordance with national objectives and laws and with treaties in force.

Article 51

The Member States, with due respect for the individuality of each of them, agree to promote cultural exchange as an effective means of consolidating inter-American understanding; and they recognize that regional integration programs should be strengthened by close ties in the fields of education, science, and culture.

PART TWO

Chapter VIII

THE ORGANS

Article 52

The Organization of American States accomplishes its purposes by means of:

a)   The General Assembly;

b)   The Meeting of Consultation of Ministers of Foreign Affairs;

c)   The Councils;

d)   The Inter-American Juridical Committee;

e)   The Inter-American Commission on Human Rights;

f)   The General Secretariat;

g)   The Specialized Conferences; and

h)   The Specialized Organizations.

There may be established, in addition to those provided for in the Charter and in accordance with the provisions thereof, such subsidiary organs, agencies, and other entities as are considered necessary.

Chapter IX

THE GENERAL ASSEMBLY

Article 53

The General Assembly is the supreme organ of the Organization of American States. It has as its principal powers, in addition to such others as are assigned to it by the Charter, the following:

a)   To decide the general action and policy of the Organization, determine the structure and functions of its organs, and consider any matter relating to friendly relations among the American States;

b)   To establish measures for coordinating the activities of the organs, agencies, and entities of the Organization among themselves, and such activities with those of the other institutions of the inter-American system;

c)   To strengthen and coordinate cooperation with the United Nations and its specialized agencies;

d)   To promote collaboration, especially in the economic, social, and cultural fields, with other international organizations whose purposes are similar to those of the Organization of American States;

e)   To approve the program-budget of the Organization and determine the quotas of the Member States;

f)   To consider the reports of the Meeting of Consultation of Ministers of Foreign Affairs and the observations and recommendations presented by the Permanent Council with regard to the reports that should be presented by the other organs and entities, in accordance with the provisions of paragraph f) of Article 90, as well as the reports of any organ which may be required by the General Assembly itself;

g)   To adopt general standards to govern the operations of the General Secretariat; and

h)   To adopt its own rules of procedure and, by a two-thirds vote, its agenda.

The General Assembly shall exercise its powers in accordance with the provisions of the Charter and of other inter-American treaties.

Article 54

The General Assembly shall establish the bases for fixing the quota that each Government is to contribute to the maintenance of the Organization, taking into account the ability to pay of the respective countries and their determination to contribute in an equitable manner. Decisions on budgetary matters require the approval of two thirds of the Member States.

Article 55

All member States have the right to be represented in the General Assembly. Each State has the right to one vote.

Article 56

The General Assembly shall convene annually during the period determined by the rules of procedure and at a place selected in accordance with the principle of rotation. At each regular session the date and place of the next regular session shall be determined, in accordance with the rules of procedure.

If for any reason the General Assembly cannot be held at the place chosen, it shall meet at the General Secretariat, unless one of the Member States should make a timely offer of a site in its territory, in which case the Permanent Council of the Organization may agree that the General Assembly will meet in that place.

Article 57

In special circumstances and with the approval of two thirds of the Member States, the Permanent Council shall convoke a special session of the General Assembly.

Article 58

Decisions of the General Assembly shall be adopted by the affirmative vote of an absolute majority of the Member States, except in those cases that require a two-thirds vote as provided in the Charter or as may be provided by the General Assembly in its rules of procedure.

Article 59

There shall be a Preparatory Committee of the General Assembly, composed of representatives of all the Member States, which shall:

a) Prepare the draft agenda of each session of the General Assembly;

b) Review the proposed program-budget and the draft resolution on quotas, and present to the General Assembly a report thereon containing the recommendations it considers appropriate; and

c) Carry out such other functions as the General Assembly may assign to it.

The draft agenda and the report shall, in due course, be transmitted to the Governments of the Member States.

Chapter X

THE MEETING OF CONSULTATION OF
MINISTERS OF FOREIGN AFFAIRS

Article 60

The Meeting of Consultation of Ministers of Foreign Affairs shall be held in order to consider problems of an urgent nature and of common interest to the American States, and to serve as the Organ of Consultation.

Article 61

Any Member State may request that a Meeting of Consultation be called. The request shall be addressed to the Permanent Council of the Organization, which shall decide by an absolute majority whether a meeting should be held.

Article 62

The agenda and regulations of the Meeting of Consultation shall be prepared by the Permanent Council of the Organization and submitted to the Member States for consideration.

Article 63

If, for exceptional reasons, a Minister of Foreign Affairs is unable to attend the meeting, he shall be represented by a special delegate.

Article 64

In case of an armed attack on the territory of an American State or within the region of security delimited by the treaty in force, the Chairman of the Permanent Council shall without delay call a meeting of the Council to decide on the convocation of the Meeting of Consultation, without prejudice to the provisions of the Inter-American Treaty of Reciprocal Assistance with regard to the States Parties to that instrument.

Article 65

An Advisory Defense Committee shall be established to advise the Organ of Consultation on problems of military cooperation that may arise in connection with the application of existing special treaties on collective security.

Article 66

The Advisory Defense Committee shall be composed of the highest military authorities of the American States participating in the Meeting of Consultation. Under exceptional circumstances the Governments may appoint substitutes. Each State shall be entitled to one vote.

Article 67

The Advisory Defense Committee shall be convoked under the same conditions as the Organ of Consultation, when the latter deals with matters relating to defense against aggression.

Article 68

The Committee shall also meet when the General Assembly or the Meeting of Consultation or the Governments, by a two-thirds majority of the Member States, assign to it technical studies or reports on specific subjects.

Chapter XI

THE COUNCILS OF THE ORGANIZATION

Common Provisions

Article 69

The Permanent Council of the Organization, the Inter-American Economic and Social Council, and the Inter-American Council for Education, Science, and Culture are directly responsible to the General Assembly and each has the authority granted to it in the Charter and other inter-American instruments, as well as the functions assigned to it by the General Assembly and the Meeting of Consultation of Ministers of Foreign Affairs.

Article 70

All Member States have the right to be represented on each of the Councils. Each State has the right to one vote.

Article 71

The Councils may, within the limits of the Charter and other inter-American instruments, make recommendations on matters within their authority.

Article 72

The Councils, on matters within their respective competence, may present to the General Assembly studies and proposals, drafts of international instruments, and proposals on the holding of specialized conferences, on the creation, modification, or elimination of specialized organizations and other inter-American agencies, as well as on the coordination of their activities. The Councils may also present studies, proposals, and drafts of international instruments to the Specialized Conferences.

Article 73

Each Council may, in urgent cases, convoke Specialized Conferences on matters within its competence, after consulting with the Member States and without having to resort to the procedure provided for in Article 127.

Article 74

The Councils, to the extent of their ability, and with the cooperation of the General Secretariat, shall render to the Governments such specialized services as the latter may request.

Article 75

Each Council has the authority to require the other Councils, as well as the subsidiary organs and agencies responsible to them, to provide it with information and advisory services on matters within their respective spheres of competence. The Councils may also request the same services from the other agencies of the inter-American system.

Article 76

With the prior approval of the General Assembly, the Councils may establish the subsidiary organs and the agencies that they consider advisable for the better performance of their duties. When the General Assembly is not in session, the aforesaid organs or agencies may be established provisionally by the corresponding Council. In constituting the membership of these bodies, the Councils, insofar as possible, shall follow the criteria of rotation and equitable geographic representation.

Article 77

The Councils may hold meetings in any Member State, when they find it advisable and with the prior consent of the Government concerned.

Article 78

Each Council shall prepare its own statutes and submit them to the General Assembly for approval. It shall approve its own rules of procedure and those of its subsidiary organs, agencies, and committees.

Chapter XII

THE PERMANENT COUNCIL OF THE ORGANIZATION

Article 79

The Permanent Council of the Organization is composed of one representative of each Member State, especially appointed by the respective Government, with the rank of ambassador. Each Government may accredit an acting representative, as well as such alternates and advisers as it considers necessary.

Article 80

The office of Chairman of the Permanent Council shall be held by each of the representatives, in turn, following the alphabetic order in Spanish of the names of their respective countries. The office of Vice Chairman shall be filled in the same way, following reverse alphabetic order.

The Chairman and the Vice Chairman shall hold office for a term of not more than six months, which shall be determined by the statutes.

Article 81

Within the limits of the Charter and of inter-American treaties and agreements, the Permanent Council takes cognizance of any matter referred to it by the General Assembly or the Meeting of Consultation of Ministers of Foreign Affairs.

Article 82

The Permanent Council shall serve provisionally as the Organ of Consultation in conformity with the provisions of the special treaty on the subject.

Article 83

The Permanent Council shall keep vigilance over the maintenance of friendly relations among the Member States, and for that purpose shall effectively assist them in the peaceful settlement of their disputes, in accordance with the following provisions.

Article 84

In accordance with the provisions of this Charter, any party to a dispute in which none of the peaceful procedures provided for in the Charter is under way may resort to the Permanent Council to obtain its good offices. The Council, following the provisions of the preceding article, shall assist the parties and recommend the procedures it considers suitable for peaceful settlement of the dispute.

Article 85

In the exercise of its functions and with the consent of the parties to the dispute, the Permanent Council may establish ad hoc committees.

The ad hoc committees shall have the membership and the mandate that the Permanent Council agrees upon in each individual case, with the consent of the parties to the dispute.

Article 86

The Permanent Council may also, by such means as it deems advisable, investigate the facts in the dispute, and may do so in the territory of any of the parties, with the consent of the Government concerned.

Article 87

If the procedure for peaceful settlement of disputes recommended by the Permanent Council or suggested by the pertinent ad hoc committee under the terms of its mandate is not accepted by one of the parties, or one of the parties declares that the procedure has not settled the dispute, the Permanent Council shall so inform the General Assembly, without prejudice to its taking steps to secure agreement between the parties or to restore relations between them.

Article 88

The Permanent Council, in the exercise of these functions, shall take its decisions by an affirmative vote of two thirds of its members, excluding the parties to the dispute, except for such decisions as the rules of procedure provide shall be adopted by a simple majority.

Article 89

In performing their functions with respect to the peaceful settlement of disputes, the Permanent Council and the respective ad hoc committee shall observe the provisions of the Charter and the principles and standards of international law, as well as take into account the existence of treaties in force between the parties.

Article 90

The Permanent Council shall also:

a) Carry out those decisions of the General Assembly or of the Meeting of Consultation of Ministers of Foreign Affairs the implementation of which has not been assigned to any other body;

b) Watch over the observance of the standards governing the operation of the General Secretariat and, when the General Assembly is not in session, adopt provisions of a regulatory nature that enable the General Secretariat to carry out its administrative functions;

c) Act as the Preparatory Committee of the General Assembly, in accordance with the terms of Article 59 of the Charter, unless the General Assembly should decide otherwise;

d) Prepare, at the request of the Member States and with the cooperation of the appropriate organs of the Organization, draft agreements to promote and facilitate cooperation between the Organization of American States and the United Nations or between the Organization and other American agencies of recognized international standing. These draft agreements shall be submitted to the General Assembly for approval;

e) Submit recommendations to the General Assembly with regard to the functioning of the Organization and the coordination of its subsidiary organs, agencies, and committees;

f) Consider the reports of the other Councils, of the Inter-American Juridical Committee, of the Inter-American Commission on Human Rights, of the General Secretariat, of specialized agencies and conferences, and of other bodies and agencies, and present to the General Assembly any observations and recommendations it deems necessary; and

g) Perform the other functions assigned to it in the Charter.

Article 91

The Permanent Council and the General Secretariat shall have the same seat.

Chapter XIII

THE INTER-AMERICAN ECONOMIC AND SOCIAL COUNCIL

Article 92

The Inter-American Economic and Social Council is composed of one principal representative, of the highest rank, of each Member State, especially appointed by the respective Government.

Article 93

The purpose of the Inter-American Economic and Social Council is to promote cooperation among the American countries in order to attain accelerated economic and social development, in accordance with the standards set forth in Chapter VII.

Article 94

To achieve its purpose the Inter-American Economic and Social Council shall:

a) Recommend programs and courses of action and periodically study and evaluate the efforts undertaken by the Member States;

b) Promote and coordinate all economic and social activities of the Organization;

c) Coordinate its activities with those of the other Councils of the Organization;

d) Establish cooperative relations with the corresponding organs of the United Nations and with other national and international agencies, especially with regard to coordination of inter-American technical assistance programs; and

e) Promote the solution of the cases contemplated in Article 36 of the Charter, establishing the appropriate procedure.

Article 95

The Inter-American Economic and Social Council shall hold at least one meeting each year at the ministerial level. It shall also meet when convoked by the General Assembly, the Meeting of Consultation of Ministers of Foreign Affairs, at its own initiative, or for the cases contemplated in Article 36 of the Charter.

Article 96

The Inter-American Economic and Social Council shall have a Permanent Executive Committee, composed of a Chairman and no less than seven other members, elected by the Council for terms to be established in the statutes of the Council. Each member shall have the right to one vote. The principles of equitable geographic representation and of rotation shall be taken into account, insofar as possible, in the election of members. The Permanent Executive Committee represents all of the Member States of the Organization.

Article 97

The Permanent Executive Committee shall perform the tasks assigned to it by the Inter-American Economic and Social Council, in accordance with the general standards established by the Council.

Chapter XIV

THE INTER-AMERICAN COUNCIL FOR
EDUCATION, SCIENCE, AND CULTURE

Article 98

The Inter-American Council for Education, Science, and Culture is composed of one principal representative, of the highest rank, of each Member State, especially appointed by the respective Government.

Article 99

The purpose of the Inter-American Council for Education, Science, and Culture is to promote friendly relations and mutual understanding between the peoples of the Americas through educational, scientific, and cultural cooperation and exchange between Member States, in order to raise the cultural level of the peoples, reaffirm their dignity as individuals, prepare them fully for the tasks of progress, and strengthen the devotion to peace, democracy, and social justice that has characterized their evolution.

Article 100

To accomplish its purpose the Inter-American Council for Education, Science, and Culture shall:

a) Promote and coordinate the educational, scientific, and cultural activities of the Organization;

b) Adopt or recommend pertinent measures to give effect to the standards contained in Chapter VII of the Charter;

c) Support individual or collective efforts of the Member States to improve and extend education at all levels, giving special attention to efforts directed toward community development;

d) Recommend and encourage the adoption of special educational programs directed toward integrating all sectors of the population into their respective national cultures;

e) Stimulate and support scientific and technological education and research, especially when these relate to national development plans;

f) Foster the exchange of professors, research workers, technicians, and students, as well as of study materials; and encourage the conclusion of bilateral or multilateral agreements on the progressive coordination of curricula at all educational levels and on the validity and equivalence of certificates and degrees;

g) Promote the education of the American peoples with a view to harmonious international relations and a better understanding of the historical and cultural origins of the Americas, in order to stress and preserve their common values and destiny;

h) Systematically encourage intellectual and artistic creativity, the exchange of cultural works and folklore, as well as the interrelationships of the different cultural regions of the Americas;

i) Foster cooperation and technical assistance for protecting, preserving, and increasing the cultural heritage of the Hemisphere;

j) Coordinate its activities with those of the other Councils. In harmony with the Inter-American Economic and Social Council, encourage the interrelationship of programs for promoting education, science, and culture with national development and regional integration programs;

k) Establish cooperative relations with the corresponding organs of the United Nations and with other national and international bodies;

l) Strengthen the civic conscience of the American peoples, as one of the bases for the effective exercise of democracy and for the observance of the rights and duties of man;

m) Recommend appropriate procedures for intensifying integration of the developing countries of the Hemisphere by means of efforts and programs in the fields of education, science, and culture; and

n) Study and evaluate periodically the efforts made by the Member States in the fields of education, science, and culture.

Article 101

The Inter-American Council for Education, Science, and Culture shall hold at least one meeting each year at the ministerial level. It shall also meet when convoked by the General Assembly, by the Meeting of Consultation of Ministers of Foreign Affairs, or at its own initiative.

Article 102

The Inter-American Council for Education, Science, and Culture shall have a Permanent Executive Committee, composed of a Chairman and no less than seven other members, elected by the Council for terms to be established in the statutes of the Council. Each member shall have the right to one vote. The principles of equitable geographic representation and of rotation shall be taken into account, insofar as possible, in the election of members. The Permanent Executive Committee represents all of the Member States of the Organization.

Article 103

The Permanent Executive Committee shall perform the tasks assigned to it by the Inter-American Council for Education, Science, and Culture, in accordance with the general standards established by the Council.

Chapter XV

THE INTER-AMERICAN JURIDICAL COMMITTEE

Article 104

The purpose of the Inter-American Juridical Committee is to serve the Organization as an advisory body on juridical matters; to promote the progressive development and the codification of international law; and to study juridical problems related to the integration of the developing countries of the Hemisphere and, insofar as may appear desirable, the possibility of attaining uniformity in their legislation.

Article 105

The Inter-American Juridical Committee shall undertake the studies and preparatory work assigned to it by the General Assembly, the Meeting of Consultation of Ministers of Foreign Affairs, or the Councils of the Organization. It may also, on its own initiative, undertake such studies and preparatory work as it considers advisable, and suggest the holding of specialized juridical conferences.

Article 106

The Inter-American Juridical Committee shall be composed of eleven jurists, nationals of Member States, elected by the General Assembly for a period of four years from panels of three candidates presented by Member States. In the election, a system shall be used that takes into account partial replacement of membership and, insofar as possible, equitable geographic representation. No two members of the Committee may be nationals of the same State.

Vacancies that occur for reasons other than normal expiration of the terms of office of the members of the Committee shall be filled by the Permanent Council of the Organization in accordance with the criteria set forth in the preceding paragraph.

Article 107

The Inter-American Juridical Committee represents all of the Member States of the Organization, and has the broadest possible technical autonomy.

Article 108

The Inter-American Juridical Committee shall establish cooperative relations with universities, institutes, and other teaching centers, as well as with national and international committees and entities devoted to study, research, teaching, or dissemination of information on juridical matters of international interest.

Article 109

The Inter-American Juridical Committee shall draft its statutes, which shall be submitted to the General Assembly for approval.

The Committee shall adopt its own rules of procedure.

Article 110

The seat of the Inter-American Juridical Committee shall be the city of Rio de Janeiro, but in special cases the Committee may meet at any other place that may be designated, after consultation with the Member State concerned.

Chapter XVI

THE INTER-AMERICAN COMMISSION ON HUMAN RIGHTS

Article 111

There shall be an Inter-American Commission on Human Rights, whose principal function shall be to promote the observance and protection of human rights and to serve as a consultative organ of the Organization in these matters.

An inter-American convention on human rights shall determine the structure, competence, and procedure of this Commission, as well as those of other organs responsible for these matters.

Chapter XVII

THE GENERAL SECRETARIAT

Article 112

The General Secretariat is the central and permanent organ of the Organization of American States. It shall perform the functions assigned to it in the Charter, in other inter-American treaties and agreements, and by the General Assembly, and shall carry out the duties entrusted to it by the General Assembly, the Meeting of Consultation of Ministers of Foreign Affairs, or the Councils.

Article 113

The Secretary General of the Organization shall be elected by the General Assembly for a five-year term and may not be reelected more than once or succeeded by a person of the same nationality. In the event that the office of Secretary General becomes vacant, the Assistant Secretary General shall assume his duties until the General Assembly shall elect a new Secretary General for a full term.

Article 114

The Secretary General shall direct the General Secretariat, be the legal representative thereof, and, notwithstanding the provisions of Article 90.b, be responsible to the General Assembly for the proper fulfillment of the obligations and functions of the General Secretariat.

Article 115

The Secretary General, or his representative, may participate with voice but without vote in all meetings of the Organization.

The Secretary General may bring to the attention of the General Assembly or the Permanent Council any matter which in his opinion might threaten the peace and security of the Hemisphere or the development of the Member States.

The authority to which the preceding paragraph refers shall be exercised in accordance with the present Charter.

Article 116

The General Secretariat shall promote economic, social, juridical, educational, scientific, and cultural relations among all the Member States of the Organization, in keeping with the actions and policies decided upon by the General Assembly and with the pertinent decisions of the Councils.

Article 117

The General Secretariat shall also perform the following functions:

a) Transmit ex officio to the Member States notice of the convocation of the General Assembly, the Meeting of Consultation of Ministers of Foreign Affairs, the Inter-American Economic and Social Council, the Inter-American Council for Education, Science, and Culture, and the Specialized Conferences;

b) Advise the other organs, when appropriate, in the preparation of agenda and rules of procedure;

c) Prepare the proposed program-budget of the Organization on the basis of programs adopted by the Councils, agencies, and entities whose expenses should be included in the program-budget and, after consultation with the Councils or their permanent committees, submit it to the Preparatory Committee of the General Assembly and then to the Assembly itself;

d) Provide, on a permanent basis, adequate secretariat services for the General Assembly and the other organs, and carry out their directives and assignments. To the extent of its ability, provide services for the other meetings of the Organization;

e) Serve as custodian of the documents and archives of the Inter-American Conferences, the General Assembly, the Meetings of Consultation of Ministers of Foreign Affairs, the Councils, and the Specialized Conferences;

f) Serve as depository of inter-American treaties and agreements, as well as of the instruments of ratification thereof;

g) Submit to the General Assembly at each regular session an annual report on the activities of the Organization and its financial condition; and

h) Establish relations of cooperation, in accordance with decisions reached by the General Assembly or the Councils, with the Specialized Organizations as well as other national and international organizations.

Article 118

The Secretary General shall:

a) Establish such offices of the General Secretariat as are necessary to accomplish its purposes; and

b) Determine the number of officers and employees of the General Secretariat, appoint them, regulate their powers and duties, and fix their remuneration.

The Secretary General shall exercise this authority in accordance with such general standards and budgetary provisions as may be established by the General Assembly.

Article 119

The Assistant Secretary General shall be elected by the General Assembly for a five-year term and may not be reelected more than once or succeeded by a person of the same nationality. In the event that the office of Assistant Secretary General becomes vacant, the Permanent Council shall elect a substitute to hold that office until the General Assembly shall elect a new Assistant Secretary General for a full term.

Article 120

The Assistant Secretary General shall be the Secretary of the Permanent Council. He shall serve as advisory officer to the Secretary General and shall act as his delegate in all matters that the Secretary General may entrust to him. During the temporary absence or disability of the Secretary General, the Assistant Secretary General shall perform his functions.

The Secretary General and the Assistant Secretary General shall be of different nationalities.

Article 121

The General Assembly, by a two-thirds vote of the Member States, may remove the Secretary General or the Assistant Secretary General, or both, whenever the proper functioning of the Organization so demands.

Article 122

The Secretary General shall appoint, with the approval of the respective Council, the Executive Secretary for Economic and Social Affairs and the Executive Secretary for Education, Science, and Culture, who shall also be the secretaries of the respective Councils.

Article 123

In the performance of their duties, the Secretary General and the personnel of the Secretariat shall not seek or receive instructions from any Government or from any authority outside the Organization, and shall refrain from any action that may be incompatible with their position as international officers responsible only to the Organization.

Article 124

The Member States pledge themselves to respect the exclusively international character of the responsibilities of the Secretary General and the personnel of the General Secretariat, and not to seek to influence them in the discharge of their duties.

Article 125

In selecting the personnel of the General Secretariat, first consideration shall be given to efficiency, competence, and integrity; but at the same time, in the recruitment of personnel of all ranks, importance shall be given to the necessity of obtaining as wide a geographic representation as possible.

Article 126

The seat of the General Secretariat is the city of Washington, D.C.

Chapter XVIII

THE SPECIALIZED CONFERENCES

Article 127

The Specialized Conferences are intergovernmental meetings to deal with special technical matters or to develop specific aspects of inter-American cooperation. They shall be held when either the General Assembly or the Meeting of Consultation of Ministers of Foreign Affairs so decides, on its own initiative or at the request of one of the Councils or Specialized Organizations.

Article 128

The agenda and rules of procedure of the Specialized Conferences shall be prepared by the Councils or Specialized Organizations concerned and shall be submitted to the Governments of the Member States for consideration.

Chapter XIX

THE SPECIALIZED ORGANIZATIONS

Article 129

For the purposes of the present Charter, Inter-American Specialized Organizations are the intergovernmental organizations established by multilateral agreements and having specific functions with respect to technical matters of common interest to the American States.

Article 130

The General Secretariat shall maintain a register of the organizations that fulfill the conditions set forth in the foregoing Article, as determined by the General Assembly after a report from the Council concerned.

Article 131

The Specialized Organizations shall enjoy the fullest technical autonomy, but they shall take into account the recommendations of the General Assembly and of the Councils, in accordance with the provisions of the Charter.

Article 132

The Specialized Organizations shall transmit to the General Assembly annual reports on the progress of their work and on their annual budgets and expenses.

Article 133

Relations that should exist between the Specialized Organizations and the Organization shall be defined by means of agreements concluded between each organization and the Secretary General, with the authorization of the General Assembly.

Article 134

The Specialized Organizations shall establish cooperative relations with world agencies of the same character in order to coordinate their activities. In concluding agreements with international agencies of a worldwide character, the Inter-American Specialized Organizations shall preserve their identity and their status as integral parts of the Organization of American States, even when they perform regional functions of international agencies.

Article 135

In determining the location of the Specialized Organizations consideration shall be given to the interest of all of the Member States and to the desirability of selecting the seats of these organizations on the basis of a geographic representation as equitable as possible.

PART THREE

Chapter XX

THE UNITED NATIONS

Article 136

None of the provisions of this Charter shall be construed as impairing the rights and obligations of the Member States under the Charter of the United Nations.

Chapter XXI

MISCELLANEOUS PROVISIONS

Article 137

Attendance at meetings of the permanent organs of the Organization of American States or at the conferences and meetings provided for in the Charter, or held under the auspices of the Organization, shall be in accordance with the multilateral character of the aforesaid organs, conferences, and meetings and shall not depend on the bilateral relations between the Government of any Member State and the Government of the host country.

Article 138

The Organization of American States shall enjoy in the territory of each Member such legal capacity, privileges, and immunities as are necessary for the exercise of its functions and the accomplishment of its purposes.

Article 139

The representatives of the Member States on the organs of the Organization, the personnel of their delegations, as well as the Secretary General and the Assistant Secretary General shall enjoy the privileges and immunities corresponding to their positions and necessary for the independent performance of their duties.

Article 140

The juridical status of the Specialized Organizations and the privileges and immunities that should be granted to them and to their personnel, as well as to the officials of the General Secretariat, shall be determined in a multilateral agreement. The foregoing shall not preclude, when it is considered necessary, the concluding of bilateral agreements.

Article 141

Correspondence of the Organization of American States, including printed matter and parcels, bearing the frank thereof, shall be carried free of charge in the mails of the Member States.

Article 142

The Organization of American States does not allow any restriction based on race, creed, or sex, with respect to eligibility to participate in the activities of the Organization and to hold positions therein.

Article 143

Within the provisions of this Charter, the competent organs shall endeavor to obtain greater collaboration from countries not members of the Organization in the area of cooperation for development.

Chapter XXII

RATIFICATION AND ENTRY INTO FORCE

Article 144

The present Charter shall remain open for signature by the American States and shall be ratified in accordance with their respective constitutional procedures. The original instrument, the Spanish, English, Portuguese, and French texts of which are equally authentic, shall be deposited with the General Secretariat, which shall transmit certified copies thereof to the Governments for purposes of ratification. The instruments of ratification shall be deposited with the General Secretariat, which shall notify the signatory States of such deposit.

Article 145

The present Charter shall enter into force among the ratifying States when two thirds of the signatory States have deposited their ratifications. It shall enter into force with respect to the remaining States in the order in which they deposit their ratifications.

Article 146

The present Charter shall be registered with the Secretariat of the United Nations through the General Secretariat.

Article 147

Amendments to the present Charter may be adopted only at a General Assembly convened for that purpose. Amendments shall enter into force in accordance with the terms and the procedure set forth in Article 145.

Article 148

The present Charter shall remain in force indefinitely, but may be denounced by any Member State upon written notification to the General Secretariat, which shall communicate to all the others each notice of denunciation received. After two years from the date on which the General Secretariat receives a notice of denunciation, the present Charter shall cease to be in force with respect to the denouncing State, which shall cease to belong to the Organization after it has fulfilled the obligations arising from the present Charter.

Chapter XXIII

TRANSITORY PROVISIONS

Article 149

The Inter-American Committee on the Alliance for Progress shall act as the permanent executive committee of the Inter-American Economic and Social Council as long as the Alliance is in operation.

Article 150

Until the inter-American convention on human rights, referred to in Chapter XVI, enters into force, the present Inter-American Commission on Human Rights shall keep vigilance over the observance of human rights.

Article 151

The Permanent Council shall not make any recommendation nor shall the General Assembly take any decision with respect to a request for admission on the part of a political entity whose territory became subject, in whole or in part, prior to December 18, 1964, the date set by the First Special Inter-American Conference, to litigation or claim between an extracontinental country and one or more Member States of the Organization, until the dispute has been ended by some peaceful procedure. This article shall remain in effect until December 10, 1990.

A-41. CHARTER OF THE ORGANIZATION OF AMERICAN STATES

Signed at Bogotá, April 30, 1948, at the
Ninth International Conference of American States

ENTRY INTO FORCE: 13 December 1951, in accordance with Article 145 of
                     the Charter.
DEPOSITORY: OAS General Secretariat (Original instrument and
                     ratifications).
TEXT: OAS, Treaty Series, Nos. 1-C and 61.
UN REGISTRATION: 16 January 1952, No. 1609, UN Treaty Series, Vol. 119.

SIGNATORY COUNTRIES	DEPOSIT OF RATIFICATION		
1/ Antigua and Barbuda	3 December	1981	
Argentina	10 April	1956	
2/ Bahamas, C.	3 March	1982	
3/ Barbados	15 November	1967	
Bolivia	18 October	1950	a/
Brazil	13 March	1950	
Chile	5 June	1953	
Colombia	13 December	1951	
Costa Rica	16 November	1948	
Cuba	16 July	1952	
4/ Dominica, C..	22 May	1979	
Dominican Republic	22 April	1949	
Ecuador	28 December	1950	
El Salvador	11 September	1950	
5/ Grenada	13 May	1975	
Guatemala	6 April	1955	b/
Haiti	28 March	1951	
Honduras	7 February	1950	
6/ Jamaica	20 August	1969	
Mexico	23 November	1948	
Nicaragua	26 July	1950	
Panama	22 March	1951	
Paraguay	3 May	1950	
Peru	12 February	1954	c/
8/ Saint Lucia	22 May	1979	
1/ Saint Vincent and the			
Grenadines	3 December	1981	
7/ St. Kitts and Nevis	12 March	1984	
9/ Suriname	8 June	1977	
10/ Trinidad and Tobago	17 March	1967	
United States	19 June	1951	d/
Uruguay	1 September	1955	
Venezuela	29 December	1951	

All States listed herein signed the Charter on 30 April 1948, with
exception of those indicated in the notes.

1. Signed 3 December 1981 at the Eleventh Regular Session of the General Assembly in Saint Lucia.
2. Signed 3 March 1982 at the Ninth Special Session of the General Assembly in Washington, D.C.
3. Signed 9 October 1967 at the OAS General Secretariat.
4. Signed 22 May 1979 at the OAS General Secretariat.
5. Signed 13 May 1975 at the OAS General Secretariat.
6. Signed 27 June 1969 at the OAS General Secretariat.
7. Signed 12 March 1984 at the Eleventh Special Session of the General Assembly in Washington, D.C.
8. Signed 22 May 1979 at the OAS General Secretariat.
9. Signed 22 February 1977 at the OAS General Secretariat.
10. Signed 13 March 1967 at the OAS General Secretariat.

a. Bolivia:

   (Declaration made at the time of ratification)

   The Honorable National Congress

   Resolves:

   That the Executive Power, at the time of depositing in the Pan American Union the ratification of the Charter of the Organization of American States, signed in Bogotá on April 30, 1948, should make the following declaration:

   The Government of Bolivia maintains, in agreement with the context of the Bogotá Charter, that "the respect for and the faithful observance of treaties" which is upheld in Articles 5 and 14 as a standard of international relations, does not exclude the revision of those articles by the peaceful procedures which are referred to in Articles 21, 22, and 23 of that Charter, when they affect the fundamental rights of States.

b. Guatemala:

(Reservation made at the time of ratification)

None of the stipulations of the present Charter of the Organization of American States may be considered as an impediment to Guatemala's assertion of its rights over the territory of Belize by such means as at anytime it may deem advisable.*/

c. Peru:

(Reservation made at the time of ratification)

With the reservation that the principles of inter-American solidarity and cooperation and essentially those set forth in the preamble and declarations of the Act of Chapultepec constitute standards for the mutual relations between the American States and juridical bases of the Inter-American system.

d. United States:

(Reservation made at the time of ratification)

That the Senate give its advice and consent to ratification of the Charter with the reservation that none of its provisions shall be considered as enlarging the powers of the Federal Government of the United States or limiting the powers of the several states of the Federal Union with respect to any matters recognized under the Constitution as being within the reserved powers of the several states.

---

*/ With respect to this reservation, the General Secretariat consulted the signatory governments, in accordance with the procedure established by paragraph 2 of Resolution XXIX of the Eighth International Conference of American States, to ascertain whether they found it acceptable or not. At the request of the Government of Guatemala, this consultation was accompanied by a formal declaration of that Government to the effect that its reservation did not imply any alteration in the Charter of the Organization of American States, and that Guatemala is ready to act at all times within the bounds of international agreements to which it is a party. In view of this declaration, the States that previously did not find the reservation acceptable expressed their acceptance.

PROTOCOL OF AMENDMENT TO THE CHARTER OF THE
ORGANIZATION OF AMERICAN STATES
"PROTOCOL OF BUENOS AIRES"

Signed at Buenos Aires on February 27, 1967, at the
Third Special Inter-American Conference

ENTRY INTO FORCE: 27 February 1970, in accordance with Article XXVI of the Protocol.
DEPOSITORY: OAS General Secretariat (Original instrument and ratifications).
TEXT: OAS, Treaty Series, No. 1-A.
UN REGISTRATION: 12 March 1970, Vol. 1609.

SIGNATORY COUNTRIES	DEPOSIT OF RATIFICATION
1/ Antigua and Barbuda	3 December 1981
2/ Argentina	21 July 1967
3/ Bahamas, C.	3 March 1982
4/ Barbados	16 March 1970
Bolivia	27 February 1970
Brazil	11 December 1968
Chile.	15 April 1971
Colombia	27 February 1970
Costa Rica	5 June 1968
5/ Dominica, C..	22 May 1979
Dominican Republic	26 July 1968
6/ Ecuador	30 September 1970 a/
El Salvador	11 July 1968
Grenada	13 May 1975
Guatemala	26 January 1968
Haiti.	19 June 1970
Honduras	27 February 1970
7/ Jamaica	27 February 1970
Mexico	22 April 1968
Nicaragua	23 September 1968
8/ Panama	29 April 1969
Paraguay	23 January 1968
Peru.	27 February 1970
9/ Saint Lucia	22 May 1979
10/ Saint Vincent and the Grenadines	3 December 1981
11/ St. Kitts and Nevis	12 March 1984
12/ Suriname	8 June 1977
13/ Trinidad and Tobago	20 May 1968
United States	26 April 1968
Uruguay	16 April 1974
Venezuela	10 October 1968

All States listed herein signed the Protocol on 27 February 1967, with exception of those indicated in the notes.

1. Signed 3 December 1981 in Saint Lucia (Eleventh Regular Session of the General Assembly).

2. Argentina:

   (Declaration made at the time of signature)

   On signing the present Protocol, the Argentine Republic reiterates its firm conviction that the amendments introduced in the Charter of the OAS do not duly cover the requirements of the Organization, inasmuch as its basic instrument should contain, in addition to the organic, economic, social, and cultural standards, the essential provisions that would make the security system of the Hemisphere effective.

3. Signed 3 March 1982 at Washington, D.C. (Ninth Special Session of the General Assembly).
4. Signed 16 March 1970 at the OAS General Secretariat.
5. Signed 22 May 1979 at the OAS General Secretariat.

6. Ecuador:

   (Declaration made at the time of signature)

   The Delegation of Ecuador, drawing its inspiration from the devotion of the people and the Government of Ecuador to peace and law, states for the record that the provisions approved with respect to peaceful settlement of disputes do not carry out the purpose of Resolution XIII of the Second Special Inter-American Conference, and that the Permanent Council has not been given sufficient powers to aid the Member States effectively in the peaceful settlement of their disputes.

   The Delegation of Ecuador signs this Protocol of Amendment to the Charter of the Organization of American States in the understanding that none of its provisions in any way limits the right of the Member States to take their disputes, whatever their nature and the subject they deal with, to the Organization, so that it may assist the parties and recommend the suitable procedures for peaceful settlement thereof.

7. Signed 27 February 1970 at the OAS General Secretariat.

8. Panama:

   (Declaration made at the time of signature)

   The Delegation of Panama, upon signing the Protocol of Amendment to the Charter of the Organization of American States, states that it does so in the understanding that none of its provisions limits or in any way impedes the right of Panama to bring before the Organization any conflict or dispute that may have arisen with another Member State to which a just solution has not been given within a reasonable period after applying, without positive results, any of the procedures for peaceful settlement set forth in Article 21 of the present Charter.

9. Signed 22 May 1979 at the OAS General Secretariat.
10. Signed 3 December 1981 at Washington, D.C. (Eleventh Special Session of the General Assembly).
11. Signed 12 March 1984 at the OAS General Secretariat.
12. Signed 22 February 1977 at the OAS General Secretariat.
13. Signed 20 May 1968 at the OAS General Secretariat.

a. Ecuador:

(Declaration made at the time of ratification)

I have the honor to advise Your Excellency that the Government of Ecuador has ratified the Protocol of Buenos Aires by means of Decree No. 252 of August 17, 1970, without reservation, but putting on the record the following Declaration: In ratifying the Protocol of Amendment to the Charter of the OAS, the Government of Ecuador declares that it is not satisfied with the provisions approved on the peaceful settlement of disputes, which do not respond to the intent of Resolution XIII of the Second Special Inter-American Conference, as the Permanent Council has not been assigned the necessary powers to give the member states effective aid in the peaceful settlement of their disputes. The Government of Ecuador formally states that it ratifies this Protocol of Amendment to the Charter of the OAS in the understanding that none of its provisions in any way limits the rights of the member states to bring their disputes, of whatever kind and on whatever matter, before the regional body so that it may recommend to them the appropriate procedures for the peaceful solution of those disputes, or the right to air them directly before the world organization for appropriate application of the relevant rules established in the United Nations Charter.

A-50. PROTOCOL OF AMENDMENT TO THE CHARTER
OF THE ORGANIZATION OF AMERICAN STATES
"PROTOCOL OF CARTAGENA DE INDIAS"

Signed at Cartagena de Indias, Colombia, on December 5, 1985, at
the Fourteenth Special Session of the General Assembly

ENTRY INTO FORCE: 16 November 1988, in accordance with Article IX of the
Protocol.
DEPOSITORY: OAS General Secretariat (Original instrument and
ratifications).
TEXT: OAS, Treaty Series, No. 66.
UN REGISTRATION:

SIGNATORY COUNTRIES	DEPOSIT OF RATIFICATION		
1/ Antigua and Barbuda	24	November	1986
Argentina	7	November	1988
Bahamas, C.	7	November	1986
Barbados	2	December	1986
Bolivia	16	November	1988
Brazil	3	October	1988
Chile			
Colombia	12	March	1987
Costa Rica			
Dominica, C..	18	November	1986
Dominican Republic	3	December	1986
2/ Ecuador			
El Salvador	16	November	1988
3/ Grenada	12	November	1986
Guatemala			
Haiti			
Honduras	15	April	1987
Jamaica	7	November	1986
Mexico	11	October	1988 a/
Nicaragua	16	November	1988
4/ Panama			
Paraguay	27	March	1987
5/ Peru			
Saint Lucia	6	February	1987
9/ Saint Vincent and the			
Grenadines	28	September	1987
6/ St. Kitts and Nevis	4	December	1986
Suriname	12	November	1987
7/ Trinidad and Tobago	7	November	1986
8/ United States			
Uruguay			
Venezuela			

All States listed herein signed the Protocol on December 5, 1985,
with exception of those indicated in the notes.

1.   Signed 14 February 1986 at the OAS General Secretariat.

2.   Ecuador:

(Statement made at the time of signature)

With regard to the Permanent Council's functions vis-à-vis the peaceful settlement of disputes, the Delegation of Ecuador believes that unilateral recourse by any of the parties to a dispute to obtain the Council's good offices is governed by the obligation that the Permanent Council has, in application of the Charter's principles and lofty purposes for peace, "to assist the parties and to recommend the procedures it considers suitable for the peaceful settlement of the dispute." All of this is now a broad mandate to the Permanent Council to watch over the maintenance of friendly relations among the member states and to assist them effectively in the peaceful settlement of their disputes. Even if the procedure is not accepted by one of the parties, the Council may take steps to achieve an agreement.

3.   Signed 10 June 1986 at the OAS General Secretariat.
4.   Signed 13 June 1986 at the OAS General Secretariat.

5.   Peru:

(Statement made at the time of signature)

Upon signing this Protocol of Amendment, the Delegation of Peru states that it is only an initial, albeit significant, step in the process of restructuring the inter-American system, as provided for in resolution AG/RES. 745 (XIV-0/84). In order to be complete, this restructuring calls for, among other amendments, the inclusion of collective economic security in the Charter of the Organization. This goes hand in hand with the preservation of peace and security in the hemisphere and also with overall development, which has been included in this amendment. The Delegation of Peru states by way of a reservation that the powers conferred upon the Secretary General in Article 116 may not be exercised for matters that have already been resolved through settlement by the parties or through the decision of an arbitrator or a judgment handed down by an international court, or that are governed by agreements or treaties in force. Also, in accordance with international law, good offices are a means of peaceful settlement whose scope has been specified in international treaties, including the Pact of Bogotá. This procedure assumes the consent of the parties, and it is in this sense that the Delegation of Peru understands the powers conferred upon the Permanent Council in the new Article 84 of this Protocol.

6.   Signed 16 April 1986 at the OAS General Secretariat.
7.   Signed 15 April 1986 at the OAS General Secretariat.

8. United States:

    (Statement made at the time of signature)

Signed 7 November 1986 at the OAS General Secretariat with the following statement:

    The United States, upon signing the Protocol of Amendment to the Charter of the Organization of American States, states that it does so subject to the following understandings and that the provisions of the Protocol shall be effective with respect to the United States only insofar as they are interpreted and applied in a manner consistent with such understandings:

    Article 1 of the Charter, as amended by the Protocol, does not limit the existing powers and functions of the Organization of American States (OAS) as practiced over the last forty years and any action taken by the OAS under the Charter or the Inter-American Treaty of Reciprocal Assistance (Rio Treaty), such as actions in furtherance of democracy or security, will not be considered to be inconsistent with this article.

    Article 3 of the Charter, as amended by the Protocol, paragraph (e), must be interpreted consistent with, and does not derogate from, the democratic principles embodied in paragraph (d) of this same article. Accordingly, it neither bars the promotion under the Charter and Rio Treaty of democracy and security by the Organization and its member states, nor requires the OAS or its member states to accept regimes that are undemocratic or otherwise hostile to inter-American values, nor is it intended in any way to change the fundamental character of the OAS as an organization of democratic states.

    Article 23 of the Charter, as amended by the Protocol, does not affect the obligation of member states to continue to submit disputes with other American states to the peaceful procedures set forth in the Charter of the Organization of American States before referring such disputes to the United Nations Security Council, consistent with Article 52(2) of the United Nations Charter and with the purpose of the Protocol to strengthen the Organization.

    Articles 29, 30 and 31 of the Charter, as amended by the Protocol, do not create enforceable legal obligations and do not affect the sovereign rights and discretion of donor and recipient states with respect to the provision and receipt of assistance, including the terms, conditions and mechanisms under and through which such assistance may be provided. The pledge to ensure international social justice continues the requirements that member states mobilize their own national human and material resources through suitable programs and recognize the importance of operating within an efficient domestic structure as fundamental conditions for their economic and social progress and for assuring effective inter-American cooperation. In this regard, the United States will continue to help member states fulfill their goals of social justice through assistance it considers appropriate to support democracy, human rights, and the poor of the region.

Article 35 of the Charter, as amended by the Protocol, does not derogate in any way from the obligation of states reflected in Article 3 faithfully to fulfill their international obligations with respect to transnational enterprises whether derived from treaties and agreements or other sources of international law, nor does it derogate from the jurisdiction other states may have with regard to such enterprises.

Article 38 of the Charter, as amended by the Protocol, establishes nonbinding goals, including the important goal of reducing or eliminating tariff and nontariff barriers to exports of all member states, and does not affect the competence or scope of the General Agreement and Tariffs and Trade (GATT), as the principal rulemaking body for the international trading system, to address negotiable issues such as special and differential treatment for developing country exports.

9. Saint Vincent and the Grenadines:

Signed 28 September 1987 at the OAS General Secretariat.

a. Mexico:

(Statement made at the time of ratification)

"The Government of Mexico states that it hereby ratifies the Protocol of Amendment to the Charter of the Organization of American States, Protocol of Cartagena de Indias, especially pleased by the inclusion within the Charter of guiding principles that renew our faith in the Organization, and reaffirms that:

1. The second paragraph of Article 1 of the Protocol specifically establishes that the Organization of American States has no implicit or residual powers, rejects the legal possibility of extensive interpretations of its governing precepts, and subordinates the Organization itself to the principle set forth in Article 18 of the Charter whereby no State or group of States has the right to intervene, directly or indirectly, for any reason whatever, in the internal or external affairs of any other State.

2. Article 3 e) introduces political pluralism into the Charter as the guiding principle of inter-American coexistence and stresses the inalienable right of every State to choose, without external interference, the political, economic and social organization best suited to it, establishes the obligation of the American States to cooperate fully among themselves, independently of their political, economic and social systems, and aspires to a plural and democratic Organization composed of all the American States.

3.   Article 23 of the Charter, amended by the Protocol of Cartagena, definitively eliminates the supposed conflict of competition between regional and universal forums by stating that the obligation to submit international disputes among the Member States to the peaceful procedures indicated in the Charter does not impair the rights and obligations of the Member States, pursuant to Article 35 of the Charter of the United Nations, thus reaffirming the sovereign faculty of the States to have recourse to the forum best suited to their interests as soon as they deem it necessary.

4.   Articles 29 and 30, which regulate the principle enuciated in Article 3 j), commit the Member States to a united effort to ensure international social justice in their relations and to attain integral development for their peoples through free and unconditional cooperation, in accordance with the goals and priorities set by each country.

5.   Article 35 of the Protocol, which supplements and develops Article 15 of the Charter with reference to transnational enterprises and private investment, stipulates that such enterprises and investments shall adapt to the development policy of the recipient countries and are subject to their legislation, to the jurisdiction of their competent courts, and to any international treaties and agreements to which they are parties."

Appendix 2
The Organization of American States

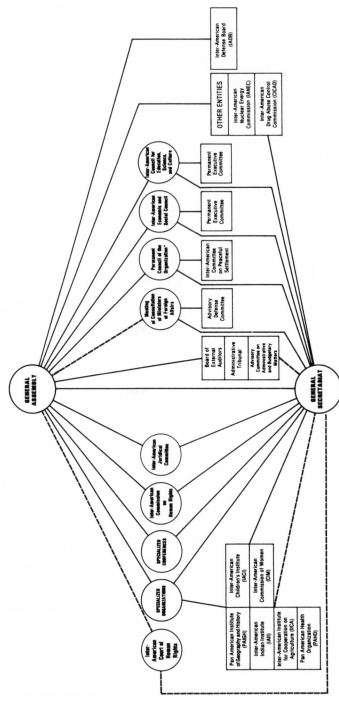

July 1987

*Acts as Preparatory Committee of the
General Assembly until the Assembly
decides otherwise.

348

Appendix 3
General Secretariat of the Organization of American States

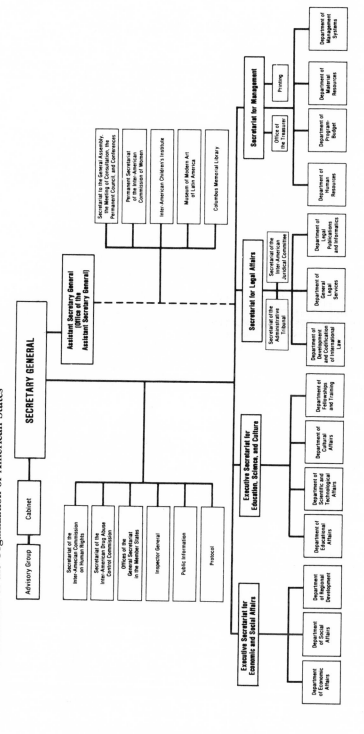

Appendix 4
Permanent Observer Countries to the OAS (April 1992)

Country	*Entry Date*
Algeria	June 10, 1987
Austria	April 5, 1978
Belgium	December 20, 1972
Cyprus	April 17, 1985
Egypt	March 16, 1977
Equatorial Guinea	March 4, 1987
European Community	November 18, 1989
Finland	January 6, 1988
France	September 20, 1972
Germany	December 6, 1972
Greece	September 27, 1979
Holy See	July 1, 1978
Hungary	September 12, 1990
India	May 9, 1991
Israel	February 2, 1972
Italy	May 17, 1972
Japan	December 12, 1973
Korea (Republic of)	June 3, 1981
Morocco	November 18, 1981
Netherlands	March 15, 1972
Pakistan	January 6, 1988
Portugal	March 26, 1975
Romania	October 31, 1990
Saudi Arabia	October 22, 1980
Spain	February 2, 1972
Switzerland	September 13, 1978
Tunisia	September 12, 1990

Appendix 5
Countries at the First International Conference of American States, 1889-1890

Argentina	Haiti
Bolivia	Honduras
Brazil	Mexico
Chile	Nicaragua
Colombia	Paraguay
Costa Rica	Peru
Ecuador	United States of America
El Salvador	Uruguay
Guatemala	Venezuela

Appendix 6
OAS Secretaries General

Alberto Lleras Camargo	Colombia	1948-1954
Carlos Dávila	Chile	1954-1955
José A. Mora	Uruguay	1956-1968
Galo Plaza	Ecuador	1968-1975
Alejandro Orfila	Argentina	1975-1984
João Clemente Baena Soares	Brazil	1984-

Appendix 7
Organization of American States, 1948-1967/1970

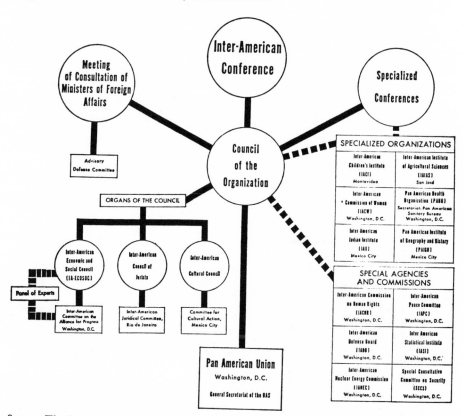

Source: The Pan American Union, Washington, D.C., 1964.

Appendix 8
Pan American Union, 1948-1967/1970

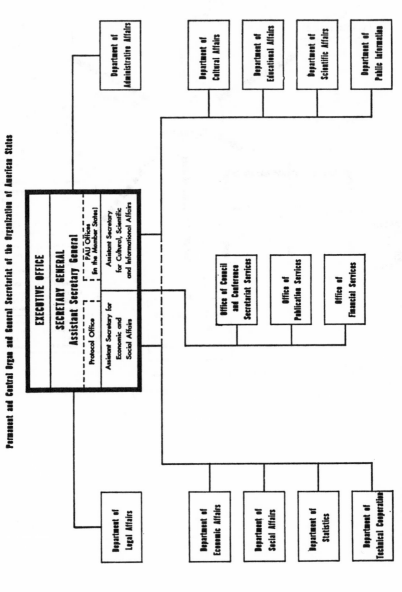

Permanent and Central Organ and General Secretariat of the Organization of American States

EXECUTIVE OFFICE

SECRETARY GENERAL

Assistant Secretary General

Protocol Office

PAU Offices (in the Member States)

Assistant Secretary for Economic and Social Affairs

Assistant Secretary for Cultural, Scientific and Informational Affairs

Department of Administrative Affairs

Department of Cultural Affairs

Department of Educational Affairs

Department of Scientific Affairs

Department of Public Information

Office of Council and Conference Secretariat Services

Office of Publication Services

Office of Financial Services

Department of Legal Affairs

Department of Economic Affairs

Department of Social Affairs

Department of Statistics

Department of Technical Cooperation

Source: The Pan American Union, Washington, D.C., 1964.

354

Appendix 9
Spanish-American Congresses, 1826-1888*

Name	Date	Location	Countries Attending	Major Agenda Items	Outcome
Panama Congress	1826	Panama City, Panama	Central America, Gran Colombia, Mexico, Peru	Peace and security; federal union for Latin America; suppression of slavery.	Several agreements signed; none ratified by all signatories.
Congress of Lima (or "American Congress")	1847–48	Lima, Peru	Bolivia, Chile, Ecuador, New Granada (Colombia), Peru	Consideration of defensive measures to be taken to prevent Spanish reconquest of west coast states of South America.	Three treaties signed; none ratified.
Continental Congress	1856	Santiago, Chile	Chile, Ecuador, Peru	Consideration of collective measures to be taken in event of U.S. incursions.	A treaty of mutual assistance, stating that if signatories were attacked by the U.S., all would unite against the U.S.
Congress of Lima	1864–65	Lima, Peru	Bolivia, Colombia, Chile, Ecuador, Guatemala, Peru, Venezuela	Consideration of possible responses to presence of Spanish in Santo Domingo and French in Mexico.	Treaty of "Union and Alliance" signed; not ratified.

* Forerunners of Pan American Conferences.

Source: U.S. Senate, Committee on Foreign Relations, *United States–Latin American Relations. The Organization of American States* (Washington, D.C.: Government Printing Office, 1959). p. 16.

Pan American Conferences, 1889-1967

Name	Date	Location	Countries Attending	Major Agenda Items	Outcome
First International Conference of American States	October 2, 1889–April 19, 1890	Washington, D.C., United States	All the American republics then in existence, except the Dominican Republic (18)	Discussion of problems of mutual interest, principally questions of peace, trade, and communications.	Formation of the International Union of American Republics and the "Bureau of American Republics."
Second International Conference of American States	October 22, 1901–January 22, 1902	Mexico City, Mexico	All the American republics then in existence (19)	Discussion of international legal questions; procedures for arbitration of disputes; problems of hemispheric peace.	Protocol of adherence to Hague Convention for Pacific Settlement of International Disputes. Treaty of Arbitration for Pecuniary Claims.
Third International Conference of American States	July 21–August 26, 1906	Rio de Janeiro, Brazil	All the American republics except Haiti and Venezuela (19)	Consideration of problem of forcible collection of debts; discussion of Drago and Calvo doctrines.	Conference decided to take question of forcible collection of debts to Second Hague Conference. Convention on International Law.
Fourth International Conference of American States	July 12–August 30, 1910	Buenos Aires, Argentina	All the American republics except Bolivia (20)	Consideration of various economic and cultural matters.	Decision to change name of International Bureau of American Republics to Pan American Union.

Conference	Date	Place	Participants	Purpose	Results
Fifth International Conference of American States	March 25–May 3, 1923	Santiago, Chile	All the American republics except Bolivia, Mexico, and Peru (18)	Discussion of reorganization of Pan American Union (PAU) for purpose of reducing U.S. dominance; discussion of possible modification of Monroe Doctrine.	Treaty To Avoid or Prevent Conflicts Between American States (Gondra Treaty). Decision to make chairmanship of PAU elective.
Sixth International Conference of American States	January 16–February 29, 1928	Havana, Cuba	All the American republics (21)	Latin American delegates anxious to secure condemnation of U.S. intervention in the Caribbean.	Convention on Duties and Rights of States in the Event of Civil Strife (designed to prevent use of other American countries as bases for launching revolutionary activity).
International Conference of American States on Conciliation and Arbitration	December 10, 1928–January 5, 1929	Washington, D.C., United States	All the American republics except Argentina (20)	Problem of arbitration and conciliation of disputes.	General Convention of Inter-American Conciliation. General Treaty of Inter-American Arbitration.
Seventh International Conference of American States	December 3–26, 1933	Montevideo, Uruguay	All the American republics except Costa Rica (20)	Problem of U.S. dominance and intervention.	Convention on Rights and Duties of States; concerned with the principle of nonintervention.

Name	Date	Location	Countries Attending	Major Agenda Items	Outcome
Inter-American Conference for the Maintenance of Peace	December 1–23, 1936	Buenos Aires, Argentina	All the American republics (21)	Security of hemisphere in event of war in Europe or Far East; principle of nonintervention.	Declaration of Principles of Inter-American Solidarity and Cooperation; additional protocol relative to nonintervention.
Eighth International Conference of American States	December 9–27, 1938	Lima, Peru	All the American republics (21)	Consideration of the relation of American republics to Europe and possible German and Italian penetration of the hemisphere.	Declaration of the Principles of the Solidarity of America; established the Meeting of Consultation of Foreign Ministers.
Inter-American Conference on Problems of War and Peace	February 21–March 8, 1945	Mexico City, Mexico	All the American republics except Argentina (20)	Consideration of possible postwar problems. Hemispheric relations of Argentina.	Act of Chapultepec; dealt with acts or threats of aggression against any American republic; recommended consideration of a treaty to deal with such acts and measures to take when they occurred.
Inter-American Conference for the Maintenance of Continental Peace and Security	August 15–September 2, 1947	Rio de Janeiro, Brazil	All the American republics except Nicaragua (20)	Consideration of proposals for a treaty of mutual defense of the hemisphere.	Inter-American Treaty of Reciprocal Assistance (Rio Treaty).

Conference	Date	Place	Participants	Purpose	Results
Ninth International Conference of American States	March 30–May 2, 1948	Bogotá, Colombia	All the American republics (21)	Discussion of means to strengthen the inter-American system and to promote inter-American economic co-operation; consideration of juridical and political matters, including recognition of governments and colonies.	Charter of the OAS; American Treaty on Pacific Settlement (Pact of Bogotá); American Declaration of the Rights and Duties of Man; Economic Agreement of Bogotá.
Tenth International Conference of American States	March 1–28, 1954	Caracas, Venezuela	All the American republics except Costa Rica (20)	Consideration of hemispheric policy respecting the intervention of Communism in the Americas; discussion of possible economic assistance to Latin America.	Declaration of Solidarity for the Preservation of the Political Integrity of the Americas against the Intervention of International Communism.
First Special International Conference of American States	December 16–18, 1964	Washington, D.C., United States	All the American republics except Cuba (20)	Consideration of the procedures for admitting new members.	Act of Washington, setting forth procedure for admitting new members (two-thirds vote of the Council), but excluding territories which are subject to claim by an American state.

Appendix 10 – Continued

Name	Date	Location	Countries Attending	Major Agenda Items	Outcome
Second Special International Conference of American States	November 17-30, 1965	Rio de Janeiro, Brazil	All the American Republics except Cuba (20)	Recognition of urgent need to reform the Charter. Also discussion of IACHR.	Gave go-ahead for the revision of the Charter and broadened the Statutes of IACHR.
Third Special International Conference of States	February 27, 1967	Buenos Aires, Argentina	All the American Republics except Cuba (20)	Continuation of the First and Second Special Conferences.	Protocol of Buenos Aires which substantially revised the original Charter and entered into force on February 27, 1970.

Source: U.S. Senate, Committee on Foreign Relations, *United States–Latin American Relations. The Organization of American States* (Washington, D.C.: Government Printing Office, 1959), pp. 8-9; author's own data.

Appendix 11
Meetings of Consultation of Ministers of Foreign Affairs, 1939-1990

Meeting	Location	Date	Major Agenda Items	Outcome
First	Panama City, Panama	September 23–October 3, 1939 (after start of World War II)	Consideration of means for maintenance of the neutrality of the hemisphere.	Declaration of Panama, establishing a hemispheric zone embracing the American republics within which the belligerent nations were to commit no hostile acts; general declaration of neutrality.
Second	Havana, Cuba	July 21–30, 1940 (after fall of France)	Discussion of European possessions in the Americas and the danger of their possible transfer to other non-American powers.	Act of Havana and Convention of Havana, concerning the provisional administration of European colonies and possessions in the Americas. (Resolution XV: Any attempt by a non-American state against sovereignty or independence of an American state to be considered an attack on all.)
Third	Rio de Janeiro, Brazil	January 15–28, 1942 (after Pearl Harbor)	Determination of attitude to be adopted by American republics in face of attack by a non-American power upon an American state and subsequent declaration of war by Germany and Italy.	Resolution: "The American Republics . . . recommend the breaking of their diplomatic relations with Japan, Germany and Italy." Establishment of the Inter-American Defense Board; establishment of the Emergency Advisory Committee for Political Defense.

* Each meeting was attended by representatives of all twenty-one American republics, except the Ninth Meeting, which was held without representation from Cuba.

Appendix 11 – Continued

Meeting	Location	Date	Major Agenda Items	Outcome
Fourth	Washington, D.C., United States	March 26–April 7, 1951 (after Korea)	Consideration of problems of Communism and hemispheric security.	Recommendation that each republic examine its resources to determine what steps it could take to contribute to collective defense of continent; recommendation that governments examine their laws with view to adopting changes considered necessary for prevention of subversive activities of Communists.
Fifth	Santiago, Chile	August 12–18, 1959 (after April–June disturbances in Caribbean)	Consideration of problems of unrest in the Caribbean; discussion of problems of democracy and human rights in Latin America.	Declaration of Santiago, concerning principles of democracy and respect for human rights; special temporary power assigned to Inter-American Peace Committee to investigate and conciliate in cases of invasion by foreign-based rebels.
Sixth	San José, Costa Rica	August 16–21, 1960 (after attempt on life of Venezuelan President Betancourt)	Request of Venezuelan Government regarding policy of intervention of the Dominican Republic (attempt to kill President Betancourt).	Breaking of diplomatic relations and partial interruption of economic relations with the Dominican Republic.
Seventh	San José, Costa Rica	August 22–29, 1960 (Cuban question)	Continental solidarity; defense of the inter-American system and of democratic principles.	Declaration of San José de Costa Rica regarding restatement of inter-American principles; establishment of a Committee of Good Offices.

362

Eighth	Punta del Este, Uruguay	January 22–31, 1962 (after increased Cuban tension)	Cuban, Soviet, and Communist Chinese subversive activities; general threat to continental unity and to democratic institutions.	Exclusion of the present Cuban Government from the inter-American system; exclusion of Cuba from the Inter-American Defense Board; prohibition of any armament trade with Cuba and request to the Council of the OAS to extend this prohibition possibly also to other commercial goods; establishment of the Special Consultative Committee on Security (SCCS) against Communist subversion; recommendation for amendment of the Statutes to the Inter-American Commission on Human Rights.
Ninth	Washington, D.C., United States	July 21–26, 1964	Venezuelan request for sanctions against Cuba in view of Cuban complicity in terrorist activities in Venezuela.	Breaking of diplomatic and consular relations with Cuba; interruption of commercial and maritime relations with Cuba; expression of sympathy for the Cuban people; regional and international economic cooperation within the framework of the Charter of Alta Gracia.

Appendix 11 – Continued

Meeting	Location	Date	Major Agenda Items	Outcome
Tenth	Washington, D.C.	*First Period of Sessions:* May 1, 1965-June 2, 1965. *Second Period of Sessions:* August 9, 1965-November 2, 1965-1970.	United States invasion of the Dominican Republic. Strong Latin American protest. U.S. landing in violation of Arts. 15 and 17 of the Charter.	Established Investigating Committee of five members. Sets up Inter-American Armed Force; resolution passed: 16 *in favor;* 1 *against;* and 4 *abstentions.*
Eleventh	Washington, D.C. Buenos Aires, Argentina Punta del Este, Uruguay	*First Period of Sessions:* Jan. 24-Feb. 1, 1967; *Second Period of Sessions:* Feb. 5-28, 1967; *Third Period of Sessions:* April 8-14, 1967 (Meeting of American Chiefs of State).	Alliance for Progress. Latin American Economic Integration	Strengthening and Consolidation of the Alliance for Progress. Intensificaiton of inter-American cooperation in order to accelerate the economic and social development of Latin American and reaffirmation of the Charter of Punta del Este.
Twelfth	Washington, D.C.	June 19-September 24, 1968	Subversive activities of Cuba in Venezuela denounced by the Venezuelan Government	Established Committee to go to Venezuela to gather information and informed UN Security Council. Condemned Cuba for repeated violations in Venezuela and other Latin American countries. Recommended OAS members to take the matter to the UN Security Council. Set up Committee of Eight to report on the Afro-Asian Latin American People's Solidarity Conference.

364

Thirteenth	Washington, D.C.	*First Period of Sessions*: July 26-July 30, 1969; *Second Period of Sessions*: August 1969-November 17, 1980 (a total of 21 plenary sessions).	Honduras requested a Meeting in regard to the war between this country and El Salvador ("Soccer War").	Ordered immediate withdrawal of Salvadorean troops and monitored said withdrawal through an Ad Hoc Committee. The second period of session dealt with the reestablishment of friendly relations between the two countries.
Fourteenth	Washington, D.C.	January 30-31, 1971-	Convoked on the request of Ecuador in regard to "Coercive Measures Affecting the Sovereignty of States and their Economic and Social Development." Dispute between Ecuador, supported by Peru and Chile, regarding territorial waters (Ecuador had seized, tried and levied fines on foreign fishing boats within 200 miles; the United States suspended military sales to Ecuador. Peru and Chile had a similar problem with the United States).	Urged parties to avoid aggravation of their differences and to observe the principles of the Charter of the OAS.

365

Appendix 11 – Continued

Meeting	Location	Date	Major Agenda Items	Outcome
Fifteenth	Quito, Ecuador	November 8-12, 1974	Request by Colombia, Costa Rica and Venezuela to discontinue the application of Res. I of the Ninth Meeting of Consultation (1964) in regard to Cuba.	Based on a Statement of the governments of Argentina, Colombia, Costa Rica, Domincan Republic, Ecuador, El Salvador, Honduras, Mexico, Panama, Peru, Trinidad and Tobago, and Venezuela, recommended to discontinue the measures taken against Cuba in 1964. The proposal was not successful since it did not obtain the required two-thirds majority. Draft Resolution was submitted by Colombia, Costa Rica, and Venezuela, and the voting in the General Committee prior the meeting was as follows: *In favor:* 12 (the above); *Against:* Chile, Paraguay, Uruguay; *Abstention:* United States, Guatemala, Brazil, Bolivia, Haiti, Nicaragua.

Sixteenth	San José, Costa Rica	July 29, 1975	"Freedom of Action of the States parties to the Inter-American Treaty of Reciprocal Assistance to normalize or conduct their relations with the Government of Cuba at the level and in the manner that each State deems advisable."	Reaffirmed the principle of non-intervention and left "the States Parties to the Rio Treaty free to normalize or conduct their relations with the Republic of Cuba at the level and in the manner that each State deems advisable, in accordance with each one's national policy and interests." The voting results in the General Committee prior to the Meeting on this Resolution was as follows: *In favor*: Argentina, Bolivia, Colombia, Costa Rica, Dom. Rep., Ecuador, El Salvador, Guatemala, Haiti, Honduras, Mexico, Panama, Peru, Trinidad and Tobago, United States, Venezuela; *Against*: Chile, Paraguay, Uruguay (3); *Abstentions*: Brazil, Nicaragua (2).

Appendix 11 – Continued

Meeting	Location	Date	Major Agenda Items	Outcome
Seventeenth	Washington, D.C.	*First Period of Sessions:* September 21-23, 1978; *Second Period of Sessions:* June 23, 1979.	Incidents in Central America brought to the attention of the OAS Council by Costa Rica and Nicaragua	In the first period of sessions the governments directly involved were urged to refrain from aggravating the present situation. In the second period, "the inhuman conduct of the dictatorial regime governing" Nicaragua, led to the Meetings' declaration that the Somoza regime be replaced by one that represented the free will of the people with "the holding of free elections as soon as possible" so that "a truly democratic government that guarantees peace, freedom and justice" be set up. *In favor:* Jamaica, Haiti, Venezuela, Peru, Ecuador, Barbados, Grenada, U.S., Bolivia, Brazil, Panama, Colombia, Mexico, Argentina, Surinam, Dom. Rep., Costa Rica (17); *Against:* Nicaragua, Paraguay (2); *Abstention:* Guatemala, Honduras, El Salvador, Uruguay, and Chile (5); (Trinidad and Tobago did not participate in the voting).

Eighteenth	Washington, D.C.	December 30, 1978	Request by Costa Rica concerning threat to its sovereignty and territorial integrity by Nicaragua.	Did not result in the convocation of this Meeting of Consultation. The Permanent Council of the OAS reaffirmed the principle proscribing the threats and use of force in international relations (Art. 1, Rio Treaty; Art. 21, Charter; Arts. 2 and 4, UN Charter), and requested Nicaragua to refrain from any threat against Costa Rica.
Nineteenth	Washington, D.C.	February 2-4, 1981	Requested by Ecuador and relating to military operations in the El Condor mountain range by Peru.	Urged Ecuador and Peru to demobilize and disperse their forces and took note of the four guarantor countries of 1942 (Argentina, Brazil, Chile, United States) that a team would be sent to the border area to monitor observance of cease-fire.
Twentieth	Washington, D.C.	*First Period of Sessions:* April 26-28, 1982; *Second Period of Sessions:* May 27, 1982-	South Atlantic conflict between United Kingdom and Argentina over the Malvinas/Falkland Islands.	In the first period of sessions urged the government of the United Kingdom to cease hostilities within the security zone of the Rio Treaty, and likewise the government of Argentina not to exacerbate the situation; also urged the parties to agree to a truce "taking into account the rights of sovereignty of the Republic of Argentina over the Malvinas Islands and the interests of the islanders. Deplored the coercive measures of the European Community and other states which constitute a serious

Appendix 11 – Continued

Meeting	Location	Date	Major Agenda Items	Outcome
				precedent not covered by Resolution 502 (1982) of the UN Security Council and incompatible with the charter of the OAS and GATT (Resolution I). *In favor*: 17; *Against*: 0; *Abstentions*: Colombia, Chile, Trinidad and Tobago, U.S. (4).
				In the second period of sessions, Res. II condemned the United Kingdom, deplored British actions frustrating peace efforts and demanded that Britain immediately cease all hostilities. It also requested the United States and the European Community to cease immediately all sanctions against Argentina. It also asked all members of the OAS to apply the Rio Treaty and help Argentina. The meeting considered all coercive measures against Argentina a violation of international law, including the blockade of the Argentine coast by Britain. This resolution had the following result: *In favor*: 17; *Against*: 0; *Abstentions*: Colombia, Chile, Trinidad and Tobago, U.S. (4).

Twenty-first Washington, D.C.	*First Period of Sessions:* May 17, 1988;	Panama and General Manuel Noriega. Request by the Government of Venezuela.	In the first period of sessions urged all authorities and political forces in Panama to abstain from taking any measure or executing any action that may aggravate the situation. Ecuador, Guatemala and Trinidad and Tobago were appointed to negotiate a National Accord in Panama for a quick transfer of political power through democratic means.
	Second Period of Sessions: December 20, 21, and 22, 1989.	United States invasion of Panama. Request by the Government of Panama.	In the second period of sessions the United States was declared to be in violation of international law and condemned for the invasion of Panama. The voting results were as follows: *In favor:* 20; *Against:* 1 (United States); *Abstentions:* 6 (Antigua/Barbuda, Costa Rica, El Salvador, Guatemala, Honduras, Venezuela).
	January 8, 1990.	Violation of the Nicaraguan Embassy in Panama City by U.S. troops on December 29, 1990. Request by the Government of Nicaragua.	The United States was condemned for violating the Convention of Havana of 1928 and the Convention of Vienna of 1961. Voting results were as follows: *In favor:* 19; *Against:* 0; *Abstentions:* 7 (United States, Jamaica, Grenada, Panama, El Salvador, Honduras, Canada).

Source: U.S. Senate, Committee on Foreign Relations, *United States–Latin American Relations. The Organization of American States* (Washington, D.C.: Government Printing Office, 1959), p. 11; author's own data.

Appendix 12
Activities of the Inter-American Peace Committee, 1948-1964

Situation	Date Request for Action Received	Date Action Terminated	Charges by Country Initiating Action or Reasons for Requesting Action	Outcome	Countries Involved in the Situation
1. Dominican Republic–Cuba situation	August 13, 1948	September 9, 1948	Dominican Republic alleged organization of revolutionary forces in Cuba directed against Dominican Republic.	Both sides agreed to continue negotiations.	Dominican Republic, Cuba
2. Haiti-Dominican Republic situation	March 21, 1949	June 9, 1949	Haiti requested Committee's good offices in a dispute with the Dominican Republic. Haiti cited certain acts it claimed could create situation between both countries endangering the peace.	Both governments signed a joint declaration of friendly relations on June 9, 1949.	Haiti, Dominican Republic
3. Cuba-Peru situation	August 3, 1949	(Not applicable)	Cuban Embassy in Lima gave asylum to two Peruvian citizens; on August 14, asylees left embassy and incident was closed.	Cuba withdrew its request that the Committee meet.	Cuba, Peru
4. General Caribbean situation	(Not applicable)	September 14, 1949	U.S. requested the Committee study the general situation in the Caribbean.	Committee declined to take action; said jurisdiction limited to specific matters of controversy.	

Situation					
5. Cuba–Dominican Republic situation	December 6, 1949	(Not applicable)	Cuba invited the Committee to investigate charges by Dominican Republic that Cuba was permitting movement to exist in its borders directed at Dominican Republic.	Committee declined the invitation; no situation calling for specific measures.	Cuba, Dominican Republic
6. Cuba–Dominican Republic situation	November 26, 1951	December 25, 1951	Cuba alleged that five Cuban sailors on a Guatemalan vessel were seized and imprisoned by the Dominican Republic.	Dominican Republic and Cuba signed a joint declaration of peacefulness and nonintervention.	Cuba, Dominican Republic
7. Colombia-Peru situation	November 18, 1953	January 21, 1954	Colombia called attention to the dispute over presence of Raúl Haya de la Torre, a Peruvian, in Colombian Embassy in Lima.	Committee recommended the resumption of bilateral negotiations.	Colombia, Peru
8. Guatemalan situation	June 19, 1954	June 30, 1954	Guatemala requested Committee meet to consider acts violating her sovereignty. Withdrew request, renewed it on June 26.	Committee sent subcommittee to make study; however, before it reached scene, new government in Guatemala.	Guatemala, Honduras, Nicaragua

Situation	Date Request for Action Received	Date Action Terminated	Charges by Country Initiating Action or Reasons for Requesting Action	Outcome	Countries Involved in the Situation
9. Cuba–Dominican Republic situation	February 27, 1956	April 20, 1956	Cuba requested Committee meet to study certain difficulties existing between it and the Dominican Republic.	Committee expressed its hope that parties arrive at solution through regular diplomatic channels.	Cuba, Dominican Republic
10. Request by Haiti	August 17, 1959	There was no formal termination. Case was settled in October, 1959.	Haiti asked the Foreign Ministers of the OAS to study invasion of Haiti by group coming from Cuba.	Matter was studied by Committee operating under the new *ad hoc* powers granted at Santiago. Since the Cuban invasion was unsuccessful and Haiti did not accuse Cuba directly, the matter had no consequences.	Haiti, Cuba
11. Anti-Venezuelan leaflets over Curaçao	November 25, 1959	There was no formal termination of the case, since further charges were leveled against the Dominican regime by Venezuela and Ecuador.	A U.S. plane with Cuban pilots threw leaflets on Curaçao calling on the Venezuelan Army to rise up against the Betancourt regime. The leaflets were supposed to come down on Venezuelan territory. The plane, however, made a forced landing in Aruba.	The Committee found that the Dominican Government was implicated in the matter (stopover of plane in Santo Domingo).	Venezuela, Dominican Republic

374

12. Ecuador–Dominican Republic situation	February 16, 1960	April 12, 1960	Controversy between Ecuador and the Dominican Republic regarding thirteen Dominican citizens who had been granted asylum in the Embassy of Ecuador in Santo Domingo. Dominican measures which affected this right of asylum.	The attempt of direct negotiations between Ecuador and the Dominican Republic failed, since the Dominican Government refused to accept the "bases of agreement." The Committee then expressed the hope that the matter might find a bilateral solution.	Ecuador, Dominican Republic
13. Violation of human rights in the Dominican Republic	February 17, 1960	June 6, 1960	Venezuela requested the Committee "to examine the flagrant violation of human rights in the Dominican Republic," since it increased the tension in the Caribbean area. However, the Dominican Government did not authorize a visit of the Committee.	The Committee came to the conclusion that the tensions in the Caribbean area had increased through the violation of human rights by the Dominican Republic (Report of the Committee dated June 6, 1960).	Venezuela, Dominican Republic

375

Appendix 12 – Continued

Situation	Date Request for Action Received	Date Action Terminated	Charges by Country Initiating Action or Reasons for Requesting Action	Outcome	Countries Involved in the Situation
14. Violation of human rights and international tensions in the Caribbean area	August, 1959	August 16, 1960 (Seventh Meeting of Consultation, August 22–29, 1960, San José, Costa Rica)	The Fifth Meeting of Consultation in Santiago, Chile, August, 1959, instructed the Inter-American Peace Committee to examine the reason for the existing tensions in the Caribbean area, apart from specific individual cases, and to report about it to the next IA Conference or Meeting of Consultation.	The Committee came to the conclusion that there existed on the American continent a serious crisis which made itself felt most acutely in the Caribbean area. It had economic and social causes—the peoples were dissatisfied with their lot—and was directed against any kind of dictatorial tutelage (Special Report dated April 14, 1960, and condensed Final Report of August 5, 1960).*	Latin America in general, with special reference to the Caribbean area.
15. Request by Nicaragua	February 16, 1961	December, 1962	Guarantee of the execution of the decision of the International Court of Justice of November 18, 1960, regarding the validity of the arbitration award of the King of Spain (December 23, 1906).	The case was terminated in 1962 after the requested assistance was given. (The final solution of this controversy had been made at The Hague in favor of Honduras.)	Honduras, Nicaragua

* This more general activity of the IAPC on the basis of the mandate of the Fifth Meeting of Consultation of Ministers of Foreign Affairs is closely linked to cases 10–13.

376

16. Request by Mexico	June 2, 1961	June 5, 1961	Charges by Guatemala regarding the alleged training of Communist agents on Mexican territory were to be examined by the Committee.	The case needed no examination, since the IAPC came to the conclusion that a visit to Mexico was not required because Mexico was keeping its international obligations.	Mexico, Guatemala
17. Request by Peru	November 27, 1961	January 22, 1962	Examination of various arbitrary acts in Cuba; Communist subversion in Latin America.	The IAPC reported to the Eighth Meeting of Consultation in Punta del Este as follows: The ideological and political links of the Cuban Government were in contradiction to the principles of the Charter of the OAS; there was systematic violation of human rights by Cuba; subversive activities of the Soviets and of Cuba were equivalent to political aggression.	Peru, Cuba

Appendix 12 – Continued

Situation	Date Request for Action Received	Date Action Terminated	Charges by Country Initiating Action or Reasons for Requesting Action	Outcome	Countries Involved in the Situation
18. Request by Panama	January 10, 1964	January 15, 1964	Panama requested the assistance of the IAPC after the Canal Zone riots, which were related to the flag controversy.	On January 15, 1964, after arriving in Panama City, the IAPC announced that the immediate crisis had terminated and that it was therefore possible to begin negotiations regarding a revision of U.S. control rights.	Panama, the United States

Source: U.S. Senate, Committee on Foreign Relations, *United States–Latin American Relations. The Organization of American States* (Washington, D.C.: Government Printing Office, 1959), p. 28; author's own data.

Appendix 13
Inter-American Treaty of Reciprocal Assistance (Rio de Janeiro, 1947)

In the name of their Peoples, the Governments represented at the Inter-American Conference for the Maintenance of Continental Peace and Security, desirous of consolidating and strengthening their relations of friendship and good neighborliness, and

CONSIDERING: That Resolution VIII of the Inter-American Conference on Problems of War and Peace, which met in Mexico City, recommended the conclusion of a treaty to prevent and repel threats and acts of aggression against any of the countries of America;

That the High Contracting Parties reiterate their will to remain united in an inter-American system consistent with the purposes and principles of the United Nations, and reaffirm the existence of the agreement which they have concluded concerning those matters relating to the maintenance of international peace and security which are appropriate for regional action;

That the High Contracting Parties reaffirm their adherence to the principles of inter-American solidarity and cooperation, and especially to those set forth in the preamble and declarations of the Act of Chapultepec, all of which should be understood to be accepted as standards of their mutual relations and as the juridical basis of the Inter-American System;

That the American States propose, in order to improve the procedures for the pacific settlement of their controversies, to conclude the treaty concerning the "Inter-American Peace System" envisaged in Resolution IX and XXXIX of the Inter-American Conference on Problems of War and Peace;

That the obligation of mutual assistance and common defense of the American Republics is essentially related to their democratic ideals and to their will to cooperate permanently in the fulfillment of the principles and purposes of a policy of peace;

That the American regional community affirms as a manifest truth that juridical organization is a necessary prerequisite of security and peace, and that peace is founded on justice and moral order and, consequently, on the international recognition and protection of human rights and freedoms, on the indispensable well-being of the people, and on the effectiveness of democracy for the international realization of justice and security,

Have resolved, in conformity with the objectives stated above, to conclude the following Treaty, in order to assure peace, through adequate means, to provide for effective reciprocal assistance to meet armed attacks against any American State, and in order to deal with threats of aggression against any of them:

ARTICLE 1
The High Contracting Parties formally condemn war and undertake in their international relations not to resort to the threat or the use of force in any manner inconsistent with the provisions of the Charter of the United Nations or of this Treaty.

ARTICLE 2
As a consequence of the principle set forth in the preceding Article, the High Contracting Parties undertake to submit every controversy which may arise between them to methods of peaceful settlement and to endeavor

to settle any such controversy among themselves by means of the procedures in force in the Inter-American System before referring it to the General Assembly or the Security Council of the United Nations.

ARTICLE 3

1. The High Contracting Parties agree that an armed attack by any State against an American State shall be considered as an attack against all the American States and, consequently, each one of the said Contracting Parties undertakes to assist in meeting the attack in the exercise of the inherent right of individual or collective self-defense recognized by Article 51 of the Charter of the United Nations.

2. On the request of the State or States directly attacked and until the decision of the Organ of Consultation of the Inter-American System, each one of the Contracting Parties may determine the immediate measures which it may individually take in fulfillment of the obligation contained in the preceding paragraph and in accordance with the principle of continental solidarity. The Organ of Consultation shall meet without delay for the purpose of examining those measures and agreeing upon the measures of a collective character that should be taken.

3. The provisions of this Article shall be applied in case of any armed attack which takes place within the region described in Article 4 or within the territory of an American State. When the attack takes place outside of the said areas, the provisions of Article 6 shall be applied.

4. Measures of self-defense provided for under this Article may be taken until the Security Council of the United Nations has taken the measures necessary to maintain international peace and security.

ARTICLE 4

The region to which this Treaty refers is bounded as follows: beginning at the North Pole; thence due south to a point 74 degrees north latitude, 10 degrees west longitude; thence by a rhumb line to a point 47 degrees 30 minutes north latitude, 50 degrees west longitude; thence by a rhumb line to a point 35 degrees north latitude, 60 degrees west longitude; thence due south to a point in 20 degrees north latitude; thence by a rhumb line to a point 5 degrees north latitude, 24 degrees west longitude; thence due south to the South Pole; thence due north to a point 30 degrees south latitude, 90 degrees west longitude; thence by a rhumb line to a point on the Equator at 97 degrees west longitude; thence by a rhumb line to a point 15 degrees north latitude, 120 degrees west longitude; thence by a rhumb line to a point 50 degrees north latitude, 170 degrees east longitude; thence due north to a point in 54 degrees north latitude; thence by a rhumb line to a point 65 degrees 30 minutes north latitude, 168 degrees 58 minutes 5 seconds west longitude; thence due north to the North Pole.

ARTICLE 5

The High Contracting Parties shall immediately send to the Security Council of the United Nations, in conformity with Articles 51 and 54 of the Charter of the United Nations, complete information concerning the activities undertaken or in contemplation in the exercise of the right of self-defense or for the purpose of maintaining inter-American peace and security.

ARTICLE 6

If the inviolability or the integrity of the territory or the sovereignty or political independence of any American State should be affected by an aggression which is not an armed attack or by an extra-continental or intra-continental conflict, or by any other fact or situation that might endanger the peace of America, the Organ of Consultation shall meet immediately in order to agree on the measures which must be taken in case of aggression to assist the victim of the aggression or, in any case, the measures which should be taken for the common defense and for the maintenance of the peace and security of the Continent.

ARTICLE 7

In the case of a conflict between two or more American States, without prejudice to the right of self-defense in conformity with Article 51 of the Charter of the United Nations, the High Contracting Parties, meeting in consultation shall call upon the contending States to suspend hostilities and restore matters to the *statu quo ante bellum,* and shall take in addition all other necessary measures to reestablish or maintain inter-American peace and security and for the solution of the conflict by peaceful means. The rejection of the pacifying action will be considered in the determination of the aggressor and in the application of the measures which the consultative meeting may agree upon.

ARTICLE 8

For the purposes of this Treaty, the measures on which the Organ of Consultation may agree will comprise one or more of the following: recall of chiefs of diplomatic missions; breaking of diplomatic relations; breaking of consular relations; partial or complete interruption of economic relations or of rail, sea, air, postal, telegraphic, telephonic, and radiotelephonic or radiotelegraphic communications; and use of armed force.

ARTICLE 9

In addition to other acts which the Organ of Consultation may characterize as aggression, the following shall be considered as such:

a. Unprovoked armed attack by a State against the territory, the people or the land, sea or air forces of another State;

b. Invasion, by the armed forces of a State, of the territory of an American State, through the trespassing of boundaries demarcated in accordance with a treaty, judicial decision, or arbitral award, or, in the absence of frontiers thus demarcated, invasion affecting a region which is under the effective jurisdiction of another State.

ARTICLE 10

None of the provisions of this Treaty shall be construed as impairing the rights and obligations of the High Contracting Parties under the Charter of the United Nations.

ARTICLE 11

The consultations to which this Treaty refers shall be carried out by means of the Meetings of Ministers of Foreign Affairs of the American Republics which have ratified the Treaty, or in the manner or by the organ which in the future may be agreed upon.

ARTICLE 12

The Governing Board of the Pan American Union may act provisionally as an organ of consultation until the meeting of the Organ of Consultation referred to in the preceding Article takes place.

ARTICLE 13

The consultations shall be initiated at the request addressed to the Governing Board of the Pan American Union by any of the Signatory States which has ratified the Treaty.

ARTICLE 14

In the voting referred to in this Treaty only the representatives of the Signatory States which have ratified the Treaty may take part.

ARTICLE 15

The Governing Board of the Pan American Union shall act in all matters concerning this Treaty as an organ of liaison among the Signatory States which have ratified this Treaty and between these States and the United Nations.

ARTICLE 16

The decisions of the Governing Board of the Pan American Union referred to in Articles 13 and 15 above shall be taken by an absolute majority of the Members entitled to vote.

ARTICLE 17

The Organ of Consultation shall take its decisions by a vote of two-thirds of the Signatory States which have ratified the Treaty.

ARTICLE 18

In the case of a situation or dispute between American States, the parties directly interested shall be excluded from the voting referred to in the two preceding Articles.

ARTICLE 19

To constitute a quorum in all the meetings referred to in the previous Articles, it shall be necessary that the number of States represented shall be at least equal to the number of votes necessary for the taking of the decision.

ARTICLE 20

Decisions which require the application of the measures specified in Article 8 shall be binding upon all the Signatory States which have ratified this Treaty, with the sole exception that no State shall be required to use armed force without its consent.

ARTICLE 21

The measures agreed upon by the Organ of Consultation shall be executed through the procedures and agencies now existing or those which may in the future be established.

ARTICLE 22

This Treaty shall come into effect between the States which ratify it as soon as the ratifications of two-thirds of the Signatory States have been deposited.

ARTICLE 23

This Treaty is open for signature by the American States at the city of Rio de Janeiro, and shall be ratified by the Signatory States as soon as possible in accordance with their respective constitutional processes. The ratifications shall be deposited with the Pan American Union, which shall notify the Signatory States of each deposit. Such notification shall be considered as an exchange of ratifications.

ARTICLE 24

The present Treaty shall be registered with the Secretariat of the United Nations through the Pan American Union, when two-thirds of the Signatory States have deposited their ratifications.

ARTICLE 25

This Treaty shall remain in force indefinitely, but may be denounced by any High Contracting Party by a notification in writing to the Pan American Union, which shall inform all the other High Contracting Parties of each notification of denunciation received. After the expiration of two years from the date of the receipt by the Pan American Union of a notification of denunciation by any High Contracting Party, the present Treaty shall cease to be in force with respect to such State, but shall remain in full force and effect with respect to all the other High Contracting Parties.

ARTICLE 26

The principles and fundamental provisions of this Treaty shall be incorporated in the Organic Pact of the Inter-American System.

IN WITNESS WHEREOF, the undersigned Plenipotentiaries, having deposited their full powers found to be in due and proper form, sign this Treaty on behalf of their respective Governments, on the dates appearing opposite their signatures.

Done in the city of Rio de Janeiro, in four texts respectively in the English, French, Portuguese and Spanish languages, on the second of September nineteen hundred forty-seven.

RESERVATIONS MADE AT THE TIME OF SIGNING

Honduras

The Delegation of Honduras, in signing the present Treaty and in connection with Article 9, section (b), does so with the reservation that the boundary between Honduras and Nicaragua is definitively demarcated by the Joint Boundary Commission of nineteen hundred and nineteen hundred and one, starting from a point in the Gulf of Fonseca, in the Pacific Ocean, to Portillo de Teotecacinte and, from this point to the Atlantic, by the line that His Majesty the King of Spain's arbitral award established on the twenty-third of December of nineteen hundred and six.

Nicaragua

The Delegate of Nicaragua, in signing the present Treaty, and with respect to the reservation made by the Delegation of Honduras on signing it and to the provisions of Article 9 (b), does so with the reservation that the boundary between Nicaragua and Honduras from the point known by the name of Portillo de Teotecacinte to the Atlantic Ocean has not been definitively drawn, by virtue of the fact that the royal Award rendered by His Majesty the King of Spain on December twenty-third, nineteen hundred six, has been impugned and protested by Nicaragua as nonexistent, null, and void. Consequently, the signing of this Treaty by Nicaragua may not be alleged as acceptance of arbitral awards that Nicaragua has impugned or whose validity is not definite.

Ecuador

The Republic of Ecuador signs the present Inter-American Treaty of Reciprocal Assistance without reservations, because it understands that other instruments and the principles of international law do not bar the revision of treaties, either by agreement between the Parties or by the other pacific means consecrated by international law itself.

RESERVATIONS MADE AT THE TIME OF RATIFYING

Guatemala

The present Treaty poses no impediment whatever to Guatemala's assertion of its rights over the Guatemalan territory of Belize by whatever means it considers most appropriate; a Treaty that may at any time be invoked by the Republic with respect to the aforesaid territory.[1]

Honduras

With the reservation made at the time of signing.

Nicaragua

With the reservation made at the time of signing.

Ecuador

With the statement made on signing the Treaty.

---

[1] With respect to this reservation, the Pan American Union consulted the signatory governments, in accordance with the procedure established by paragraph 2 of Resolution XXIX of the Eighth International Conference of American States, to ascertain whether they found it acceptable or not. A number of replies being unfavorable, a second consultation was made accompanied, at the request of the Government of Guatemala, by a formal declaration of that Government to the effect that its reservation did not imply any alteration in the Inter-American Treaty of Reciprocal Assistance, and that Guatemala was ready to act at all times within the bounds of international agreements to which it was a party. In view of this declaration, the States that previously had not found the reservation acceptable now expressed their acceptance.

INTER-AMERICAN TREATY OF RECIPROCAL ASSISTANCE

Signed at the Inter-American Conference for the
Maintenance of Continental Peace and Security, held
in Rio de Janeiro from August 15 to September 2, 1947

SIGNATORY COUNTRIES	DATE OF INSTRUMENT OF RATIFICATION	DATE OF DEPOSIT OF THE INSTRUMENT OF RATIFICATION
Argentina	July 19, 1950	August 21, 1950
Bolivia	September 18, 1950	September 26, 1950
Brazil	March 5, 1948	March 25, 1948
Colombia	January 10, 1948	February 3, 1948
Costa Rica	November 20, 1948	December 3, 1948
Cuba	December 4, 1948	December 9, 1948
Chile	January 28, 1949	February 9, 1949
Dominican Republic	November 7, 1947	November 21, 1947
Ecuador	October 30, 1950	November 7, 1950
El Salvador	February 19, 1948	March 15, 1948
Guatemala	March 18, 1955*	April 6, 1955*
Haiti	October 30, 1947	March 25, 1948
Honduras	January 15, 1948*	February 5, 1948*
Mexico	November 23, 1948	November 23, 1948
Nicaragua	November 1, 1948*	November 12, 1948*
Panama	December 31, 1947	January 12, 1948
Paraguay	July 7, 1948	July 28, 1948
Peru	October 9, 1950	October 25, 1950
United States	December 12, 1947	December 30, 1947
Uruguay	September 7, 1948	September 28, 1948
Venezuela	September 9, 1948	October 4, 1948

* With a reservation.

In the name of their peoples, the Governments represented at the Ninth International Conference of American States have resolved, in fulfillment of Article XXIII of the Charter of the Organization of American States, to conclude the following Treaty:

CHAPTER ONE

GENERAL OBLIGATION TO SETTLE DISPUTES BY PACIFIC MEANS

ARTICLE I

The High Contracting Parties, solemnly reaffirming their commitments made in earlier international conventions and declarations, as well as in the Charter of the United Nations, agree to refrain from the threat or the use of force, or from any other means of coercion for the settlement of their controversies, and to have recourse at all times to pacific procedures.

ARTICLE II

The High Contracting Parties recognize the obligation to settle international controversies by regional pacific procedures before referring them to the Security Council of the United Nations.

Consequently, in the event that a controversy arises between two or more signatory states which, in the opinion of the parties, cannot be settled by direct negotiations through the usual diplomatic channels, the parties bind themselves to use the procedures established in the present Treaty, in the manner and under the conditions provided for in the following articles, or, alternatively, such special procedures as, in their opinion, will permit them to arrive at a solution.

ARTICLE III

The order of the pacific procedures established in the present Treaty does not signify that the parties may not have recourse to the procedure which they consider most appropriate in each case, or that they should use all these procedures, or that any of them have preference over others except as expressly provided.

ARTICLE IV

Once any pacific procedure has been initiated, whether by agreement between the parties or in fulfillment of the present Treaty or a previous pact, no other procedure may be commenced until that procedure is concluded.

ARTICLE V

The aforesaid procedures may not be applied to matters which, by their nature, are within the domestic jurisdiction of the state. If the parties are not in agreement as to whether the controversy concerns a matter of domestic jurisdiction, this preliminary question shall be submitted to decision by the International Court of Justice, at the request of any of the parties.

ARTICLE VI

The aforesaid procedures, furthermore, may not be applied to matters already settled by arrangements between the parties, or by arbitral award or by decision of an international court, or which are governed by agreements or treaties in force on the date of the conclusion of the present Treaty.

ARTICLE VII

The High Contracting Parties bind themselves not to make diplomatic representations in order to protect their nationals, or to refer a controversy to a court of international jurisdiction for that purpose, when the said nationals have had available the means to place their case before competent domestic courts of the respective state.

ARTICLE VIII

Neither recourse to pacific means for the solution of controversies, nor the recommendation of their use, shall, in the case of an armed attack, be ground for delaying the exercise of the right of individual or collective self-defense, as provided for in the Charter of the United Nations.

CHAPTER TWO

PROCEDURES OF GOOD OFFICES AND MEDIATION

ARTICLE IX

The procedure of good offices consists in the attempt by one or more American Governments not parties to the controversy, or by one or more eminent citizens of any American State which is not a party to the controversy, to bring the parties together, so as to make it possible for them to reach an adequate solution between themselves.

ARTICLE X

Once the parties have been brought together and have resumed direct negotiations, no further action is to be taken by the states or citizens that have offered their good offices or have accepted an invitation to offer them; they may, however, by agreement between the parties, be present at the negotiations.

ARTICLE XI

The procedure of mediation consists in the submission of the controversy to one or more American Governments not parties to the controversy, or to one or more eminent citizens of any American State not a party to the controversy. In either case the mediator or mediators shall be chosen by mutual agreement between the parties.

ARTICLE XII

The functions of the mediator or mediators shall be to assist the parties in the settlement of controversies in the simplest and most direct manner, avoiding formalities and seeking an acceptable solution. No report shall be made by the mediator and, so far as he is concerned, the proceedings shall be wholly confidential.

ARTICLE XIII

In the event that the High Contracting Parties have agreed to the procedure of mediation but are unable to reach an agreement within two months on the selection of the mediator or mediators, or no solution to the controversy has been reached within five months after mediation has begun, the parties shall have recourse without delay to any one of the other procedures of peaceful settlement established in the present Treaty.

ARTICLE XIV

The High Contracting Parties may offer their mediation, either individually or jointly, but they agree not to do so while the controversy is in process of settlement by any of the other procedures established in the present Treaty.

CHAPTER THREE

PROCEDURE OF INVESTIGATION AND CONCILIATION

ARTICLE XV

The procedure of investigation and conciliation consists in the submission of the controversy to a Commission of Investigation and Conciliation, which shall be established in accordance with the provisions established in subsequent articles of the present Treaty, and which shall function within the limitations prescribed therein.

ARTICLE XVI

The party initiating the procedure of investigation and conciliation shall request the Council of the Organization of American States to convoke the Commission of Investigation and Conciliation. The Council for its part shall take immediate steps to convoke it.

Once the request to convoke the Commission has been received, the controversy between the parties shall immediately be suspended, and the parties shall refrain from any act that might make conciliation more difficult. To that end, at the request of one of the parties, the Council of the Organization of American States may, pending the convocation of the Commission, make appropriate recommendations to the parties.

ARTICLE XVII

Each of the High Contracting Parties may appoint, by means of a bilateral agreement consisting of a simple exchange of notes with each of the other signatories, two members of the Commission of Investigation and Conciliation, only one of whom may be of its own nationality. The fifth member, who shall perform the functions of chairman, shall be selected immediately by common agreement of the members thus appointed.

Any one of the contracting parties may remove members whom it has appointed, whether nationals or aliens; at the same time it shall appoint the successor. If this is not done, the removal shall be considered as not having been made. The appointments and substitutions shall be registered with the Pan American Union, which shall endeavor to ensure that the commissions maintain their full complement of five members.

ARTICLE XVIII

Without prejudice to the provisions of the foregoing article, the Pan American Union shall draw up a permanent panel of American conciliators, to be made up as follows:

a) Each of the High Contracting Parties shall appoint, for three-year periods, two of their nationals who enjoy the highest reputation for fairness, competence and integrity;

b) The Pan American Union shall request of the candidates notice of their formal acceptance, and it shall place on the panel of conciliators the names of the persons who so notify it;

c) The governments may, at any time, fill vacancies occurring among their appointees; and they may reappoint their members.

ARTICLE XIX

In the event that a controversy should arise between two or more American States that have not appointed the Commission referred to in Article XVII, the following procedure shall be observed:

a) Each party shall designate two members from the permanent panel of American conciliators, who are not of the same nationality as the appointing party.

b) These four members shall in turn choose a fifth member, from the permanent panel, not of the nationality of either party.

c) If, within a period of thirty days following the notification of their selection, the four members are unable to agree upon a fifth member, they shall each separately list the conciliators composing the permanent panel, in order of their preference, and upon comparison of the lists so prepared, the one who first receives a majority of votes shall be declared elected. The person so elected shall perform the duties of chairman of the Commission.

ARTICLE XX

In convening the Commission of Investigation and Conciliation, the Council of the Organization of American States shall determine the place where the Commission shall meet. Thereafter, the Commission may determine the place or places in which it is to function, taking into account the best facilities for the performance of its work.

ARTICLE XXI

When more than two states are involved in the same controversy, the states that hold similar points of view shall be considered as a single party. If they have different interests they shall be entitled to increase the number of conciliators in order that all parties may have equal representation. The chairman shall be elected in the manner set forth in Article XIX.

ARTICLE XXII

It shall be the duty of the Commission of Investigation and Conciliation to clarify the points in dispute between the parties and to endeavor to bring about an agreement between them upon mutually acceptable terms. The Commission shall institute such investigations of the facts involved in the controversy as it may deem necessary for the purpose of proposing acceptable bases of settlement.

ARTICLE XXIII

It shall be the duty of the parties to facilitate the work of the Commission and to supply it, to the fullest extent possible, with all useful documents and information, and also to use the means at their disposal to enable the Commission to summon and hear witnesses or experts and perform other tasks in the territories of the parties, in conformity with their laws.

ARTICLE XXIV

During the proceedings before the Commission, the parties shall be represented by plenipotentiary delegates or by agents, who shall serve as intermediaries between them and the Commission. The parties and the Commission may use the services of technical advisers and experts.

ARTICLE XXV

The Commission shall conclude its work within a period of six months from the date of its installation; but the parties may, by mutual agreement, extend the period.

ARTICLE XXVI

If, in the opinion of the parties, the controversy relates exclusively to questions of fact, the Commission shall limit itself to investigating such questions, and shall conclude its activities with an appropriate report.

ARTICLE XXVII

If an agreement is reached by conciliation, the final report of the Commission shall be limited to the text of the agreement and shall be published after its transmittal to the parties, unless the parties decide otherwise. If no agreement is reached, the final report shall contain a summary of the work of the Commission; it shall be delivered to the parties, and shall be published after the expiration of six months unless the parties decide otherwise. In both cases, the final report shall be adopted by a majority vote.

ARTICLE XXVIII

The reports and conclusions of the Commission of Investigation and Conciliation shall not be binding upon the parties, either with respect to the statement of facts or in regard to questions of law, and they shall have no other character than that of recommendations submitted for the consideration of the parties in order to facilitate a friendly settlement of the controversy.

ARTICLE XXIX

The Commission of Investigation and Conciliation shall transmit to each of the parties, as well as to the Pan American Union, certified copies of the minutes of its proceedings. These minutes shall not be published unless the parties so decide.

ARTICLE XXX

Each member of the Commission shall receive financial remuneration, the amount of which shall be fixed by agreement between the parties. If the parties do not agree thereon, the Council of the Organization shall determine the remuneration. Each government shall pay its own expenses and an equal share of the common expenses of the Commission, including the aforementioned remunerations.

CHAPTER FOUR
JUDICIAL PROCEDURE
ARTICLE XXXI

In conformity with Article 36, paragraph 2, of the Statute of the International Court of Justice, the High Contracting Parties declare that they recognize, in relation to any other American State, the jurisdiction of the Court as compulsory *ipso facto*, without the necessity of any special agreement so long as the present Treaty is in force, in all disputes of a juridical nature that arise among them concerning:

    a) The interpretation of a treaty;

    b) Any question of international law;

    c) The existence of any fact which, if established, would constitute the breach of an international obligation;

    d) The nature or extent of the reparation to be made for the breach of an international obligation.

ARTICLE XXXII

When the conciliation procedure previously established in the present Treaty or by agreement of the parties does not lead to a solution, and the said parties have not agreed upon an arbitral procedure, either of them shall be entitled to have recourse to the International Court of Justice in the manner prescribed in Article 40 of the Statute thereof. The Court shall have compulsory jurisdiction in accordance with Article 36, paragraph 1, of the said Statute.

Article XXXIII

If the parties fail to agree as to whether the Court has jurisdiction over the controversy, the Court itself shall first decide that question.

Article XXXIV

If the Court, for the reasons set forth in Articles V, VI and VII of this Treaty, declares itself to be without jurisdiction to hear the controversy, such controversy shall be declared ended.

Article XXXV

If the Court for any other reason declares itself to be without jurisdiction to hear and adjudge the controversy, the High Contracting Parties obligate themselves to submit it to arbitration, in accordance with the provisions of Chapter Five of this Treaty.

Article XXXVI

In the case of controversies submitted to the judicial procedure to which this Treaty refers, the decision shall devolve upon the full Court, or, if the parties so request, upon a special chamber in conformity with Article 26 of the Statute of the Court. The parties may agree, moreover, to have the controversy decided *ex aequo et bono*.

Article XXXVII

The procedure to be followed by the Court shall be that established in the Statute thereof.

CHAPTER FIVE

PROCEDURE OF ARBITRATION

Article XXXVIII

Notwithstanding the provisions of Chapter Four of this Treaty, the High Contracting Parties may, if they so agree, submit to arbitration differences of any kind, whether juridical or not, that have arisen or may arise in the future between them.

Article XXXIX

The Arbitral Tribunal to which a controversy is to be submitted shall, in the cases contemplated in Articles XXXV and XXXVIII of the present Treaty, be constituted in the following manner, unless there exists an agreement to the contrary.

Article XL

(1) Within a period of two months after notification of the decision of the Court in the case provided for in Article XXXV, each party shall name one arbiter of recognized competence in questions of international law and of the highest integrity, and shall transmit the designation to the Council of the Organization. At the same time, each party shall present to the Council a list of ten jurists chosen from among those on the general panel of members of the Permanent Court of Arbitration of The Hague who do not belong to its national group and who are willing to be members of the Arbitral Tribunal.

(2) The Council of the Organization shall, within the month following the presentation of the lists, proceed to establish the Arbitral Tribunal in the following manner:

a) If the lists presented by the parties contain three names in common, such persons, together with the two directly named by the parties, shall constitute the Arbitral Tribunal;

b) In case these lists contain more than three names in common, the three arbiters needed to complete the Tribunal shall be selected by lot;

c) In the circumstances envisaged in the two preceding clauses, the five arbiters designated shall choose one of their number as presiding officer;

d) If the lists contain only two names in common, such candidates and the two arbiters directly selected by the parties shall by common agreement choose the fifth arbiter, who shall preside over the Tribunal. The choice shall devolve upon a jurist on the aforesaid general panel of the Permanent Court of Arbitration of The Hague who has not been included in the lists drawn up by the parties;

e) If the lists contain only one name in common, that person shall be a member of the Tribunal, and another name shall be chosen by lot from among the eighteen jurists remaining on the above-mentioned lists. The presiding officer shall be elected in accordance with the procedure established in the preceding clause;

f) If the lists contain no names in common, one arbiter shall be chosen by lot from each of the lists; and the fifth arbiter, who shall act as presiding officer, shall be chosen in the manner previously indicated;

g) If the four arbiters cannot agree upon a fifth arbiter within one month after the Council of the Organization has notified them of their appointment, each of them shall separately arrange the list of jurists in the order of their preference and, after comparison of the lists so formed, the person who first obtains a majority vote shall be declared elected.

Article XLI

The parties may by mutual agreement establish the Tribunal in the manner they deem most appropriate; they may even select a single arbiter, designating in such case a chief of state, an eminent jurist, or any court of justice in which the parties have mutual confidence.

Article XLII

When more than two states are involved in the same controversy, the states defending the same interests shall be considered as a single party. If they have opposing interests they shall have the right to increase the number of arbiters so that all parties may have equal representation. The presiding officer shall be selected by the method established in Article XL.

Article XLIII

The parties shall in each case draw up a special agreement clearly defining the specific matter that is the subject of the controversy, the seat of the Tribunal, the rules of procedure to be observed, the period within which the award is to be handed down, and such other conditions as they may agree upon among themselves.

If the special agreement cannot be drawn up within three months after the date of the installation of the Tribunal, it shall be drawn up by the International Court of Justice through summary procedure, and shall be binding upon the parties.

Article XLIV

The parties may be represented before the Arbitral Tribunal by such persons as they may designate.

ARTICLE XLV

If one of the parties fails to designate its arbiter and present its list of candidates within the period provided for in Article XL, the other party shall have the right to request the Council of the Organization to establish the Arbitral Tribunal. The Council shall immediately urge the delinquent party to fulfill its obligations within an additional period of fifteen days, after which time the Council itself shall establish the Tribunal in the following manner:

a) It shall select a name by lot from the list presented by the petitioning party.

b) It shall choose, by absolute majority vote, two jurists from the general panel of the Permanent Court of Arbitration of The Hague who do not belong to the national group of any of the parties.

c) The three persons so designated, together with the one directly chosen by the petitioning party, shall select the fifth arbiter, who shall act as presiding officer, in the manner provided for in Article XL.

d) Once the Tribunal is installed, the procedure established in Article XLIII shall be followed.

ARTICLE XLVI

The award shall be accompanied by a supporting opinion, shall be adopted by a majority vote, and shall be published after notification thereof has been given to the parties. The dissenting arbiter or arbiters shall have the right to state the grounds for their dissent.

The award, once it is duly handed down and made known to the parties, shall settle the controversy definitively, shall not be subject to appeal, and shall be carried out immediately.

ARTICLE XLVII

Any differences that arise in regard to the interpretation or execution of the award shall be submitted to the decision of the Arbitral Tribunal that rendered the award.

ARTICLE XLVIII

Within a year after notification thereof, the award shall be subject to review by the same Tribunal at the request of one of the parties, provided a previously existing fact is discovered unknown to the Tribunal and to the party requesting the review, and provided the Tribunal is of the opinion that such fact might have a decisive influence on the award.

ARTICLE XLIX

Every member of the Tribunal shall receive financial remuneration, the amount of which shall be fixed by agreement between the parties. If the parties do not agree on the amount, the Council of the Organization shall determine the remuneration. Each Government shall pay its own expenses and an equal share of the common expenses of the Tribunal, including the aforementioned remunerations.

CHAPTER SIX
FULFILLMENT OF DECISIONS
ARTICLE L

If one of the High Contracting Parties should fail to carry out the obligations imposed upon it by a decision of the International Court of Justice or by an arbitral award, the other party or parties concerned shall, before resorting to the Security Council of the United Nations, propose a Meeting of Consultation of Ministers of Foreign Affairs to agree upon appropriate measures to ensure the fulfillment of the judicial decision or arbitral award.

CHAPTER SEVEN
ADVISORY OPINIONS
ARTICLE LI

The parties concerned in the solution of a controversy may, by agreement, petition the General Assembly or the Security Council of the United Nations to request an advisory opinion of the International Court of Justice on any juridical question.

The petition shall be made through the Council of the Organization of American States.

CHAPTER EIGHT
FINAL PROVISIONS
ARTICLE LII

The present Treaty shall be ratified by the High Contracting Parties in accordance with their constitutional procedures. The original instrument shall be deposited in the Pan American Union, which shall transmit an authentic certified copy to each Government for the purpose of ratification. The instruments of ratification shall be deposited in the archives of the Pan American Union, which shall notify the signatory governments of the deposit. Such notification shall be considered as an exchange of ratifications.

ARTICLE LIII

This Treaty shall come into effect between the High Contracting Parties in the order in which they deposit their respective ratifications.

ARTICLE LIV

Any American State which is not a signatory to the present Treaty, or which has made reservations thereto, may adhere to it, or may withdraw its reservations in whole or in part, by transmitting an official instrument to the Pan American Union, which shall notify the other High Contracting Parties in the manner herein established.

ARTICLE LV

Should any of the High Contracting Parties make reservations concerning the present Treaty, such reservations shall, with respect to the state that makes them, apply to all signatory states on the basis of reciprocity.

ARTICLE LVI

The present Treaty shall remain in force indefinitely, but may be denounced upon one year's notice, at the end of which period it shall cease to be in force with respect to the state denouncing it, but shall continue in force for the remaining signatories. The denunciation shall be addressed to the Pan American Union, which shall transmit it to the other Contracting Parties.

The denunciation shall have no effect with respect to pending procedures initiated prior to the transmission of the particular notification.

ARTICLE LVII

The present Treaty shall be registered with the Secretariat of the United Nations through the Pan American Union.

Article LVIII

As this Treaty comes into effect through the successive ratifications of the High Contracting Parties, the following treaties, conventions and protocols shall cease to be in force with respect to such parties:

Treaty to Avoid or Prevent Conflicts between the American States, of May 3, 1923;

General Convention of Inter-American Conciliation, of January 5, 1929;

General Treaty of Inter-American Arbitration and Additional Protocol of Progressive Arbitration, of January 5, 1929;

Additional Protocol to the General Convention of Inter-American Conciliation, of December 26, 1933;

Anti-War Treaty of Non-Aggression and Conciliation, of October 10, 1933;

Convention to Coordinate, Extend and Assure the Fulfillment of the Existing Treaties between the American States, of December 23, 1936;

Inter-American Treaty on Good Offices and Mediation, of December 23, 1936;

Treaty on the Prevention of Controversies, of December 23, 1936.

Article LIX

The provisions of the foregoing Article shall not apply to procedures already initiated or agreed upon in accordance with any of the above-mentioned international instruments.

Article LX

The present Treaty shall be called the "PACT OF BOGOTÁ."

IN WITNESS WHEREOF, the undersigned Plenipotentiaries, having deposited their full powers, found to be in good and due form, sign the present Treaty, in the name of their respective Governments, on the dates appearing below their signatures.

Done at the City of Bogotá, in four texts, in the English, French, Portuguese and Spanish languages respectively, on the thirtieth day of April, nineteen hundred forty-eight.

RESERVATIONS

Argentina

"The Delegation of the Argentine Republic, on signing the American Treaty on Pacific Settlement (Pact of Bogotá), makes reservations in regard to the following articles, to which it does not adhere:

1) VII, concerning the protection of aliens;

2) Chapter Four (Articles XXXI to XXXVII), Judicial Procedure;

3) Chapter Five (Articles XXXVIII to XLIX), Procedure of Arbitration;

4) Chapter Six (Article L), Fulfillment of Decisions.

Arbitration and judicial procedure have, as institutions, the firm adherence of the Argentine Republic, but the Delegation cannot accept the form in which the procedures for their application have been regulated, since, in its opinion, they should have been established only for controversies arising in the future and not originating in or having any relation to causes, situations or facts existing before the signing of this instrument. The compulsory execution of arbitral or judicial decisions and the limitation which prevents the states from judging for themselves in regard to matters that pertain to their domestic jurisdiction in accordance with Article V are contrary to Argentine tradition. The protection of aliens, who in the Argentine Republic are protected by its Supreme Law to the same extent as the nationals, is also contrary to that tradition."

Bolivia

"The Delegation of Bolivia makes a reservation with regard to Article VI, inasmuch as it considers that pacific procedures may also be applied to controversies arising from matters settled by arrangement between the Parties, when the said arrangement affects the vital interests of a state."

Ecuador

"The Delegation of Ecuador, upon signing this Pact, makes an express reservation with regard to Article VI and also every provision that contradicts or is not in harmony with the principles proclaimed by or the stipulations contained in the Charter of the United Nations, the Charter of the Organization of American States, or the Constitution of the Republic of Ecuador."

United States of America

"1. The United States does not undertake as the complainant State to submit to the International Court of Justice any controversy which is not considered to be properly within the jurisdiction of the Court.

2. The submission on the part of the United States of any controversy to arbitration, as distinguished from judicial settlement, shall be dependent upon the conclusion of a special agreement between the parties to the case.

3. The acceptance by the United States of the jurisdiction of the International Court of Justice as compulsory *ipso facto* and without special agreement, as provided in this Treaty, is limited by any jurisdictional or other limitations contained in any Declaration deposited by the United States under Article 36, paragraph 4, of the Statute of the Court, and in force at the time of the submission of any case.

4. The Government of the United States cannot accept Article VII relating to diplomatic protection and the exhaustion of remedies. For its part, the Government of the United States maintains the rules of diplomatic protection, including the rule of exhaustion of local remedies by aliens, as provided by international law."

Paraguay

"The Delegation of Paraguay makes the following reservation:

Paraguay stipulates the prior agreement of the parties as a prerequisite to the arbitration procedure established in this Treaty for every question of a non-juridical nature affecting national sovereignty and not specifically agreed upon in treaties now in force."

Peru

"The Delegation of Peru makes the following reservations:

1. Reservation with regard to the second part of Article V, because it considers that domestic jurisdiction should be defined by the state itself.

2. Reservation with regard to Article XXXIII and the pertinent part of Article XXXIV, inasmuch as it considers that the exceptions of *res judicata*, resolved by settlement between the parties or governed by agreements and

treaties in force, determine, in virtue of their objective and peremptory nature, the exclusion of these cases from the application of every procedure.

3. Reservation with regard to Article XXXV, in the sense that, before arbitration is resorted to, there may be, at the request of one of the parties, a meeting of the Organ of Consultation, as established in the Charter of the Organization of American States.

4. Reservation with regard to Article LXV, because it believes that arbitration set up without the participation of one of the parties is in contradiction with its constitutional provisions."

Nicaragua

"The Nicaraguan Delegation, on giving its approval to the American Treaty on Pacific Settlement (Pact of Bogotá) wishes to record expressly that no provisions contained in the said Treaty may prejudice any position assumed by the Government of Nicaragua with respect to arbitral decisions the validity of which it has contested on the basis of the principles of international law, which clearly permit arbitral decisions to be attacked when they are adjudged to be null or invalidated. Consequently, the signature of the Nicaraguan Delegation to the Treaty in question cannot be alleged as an acceptance of any arbitral decisions that Nicaragua has contested and the validity of which is not certain.

Hence the Nicaraguan Delegation reiterates the statement made on the 28th of the current month on approving the text of the abovementioned Treaty in Committee III."

Notes

CHAPTER 1

1. Indalecio Liévano Aguirre, *Bolivarismo y Monroísmo* (2d ed.; Bogotá, Colombia: Tercer Mundo Editores, 1988).

2. Antonio José Rivadeneira Vargas, *El bogotano J. M. Torres Caicedo (1830–1889)—La multipatria latinoamericana* (Bogotá, Colombia: Academia Colombiana de Historia, Alcaldía Mayor de Bogotá, Instituto Distrital de Cultura y Turismo, 1989), 73.

3. Organization of American States, *The OAS and the Evolution of the Inter-American System* (Washington, D.C.: OAS, General Secretariat, Department of Public Information, January 1988), 2.

4. "Simón Bolívar: Carta de Jamaica (1815)," in José Luis Romero, *Pensamiento político de la Emancipación*, prólogo de José Luis Romero, selección, notas y cronología de José Luis Romero y Luis Alberto Romero (2 vol. Barcelona: Biblioteca Ayacucho no. 24, 1985), 2:89.

5. "Documento convocatorio del Congreso de Panamá," in Rivadeneira Vargas, *Torres Caicedo*, 244.

6. Inter-American Institute of International Legal Studies, *The Inter-American System: Its Development and Strengthening*. Explanatory note by F.V. García Amador, Secretary General (Dobbs Ferry, N.Y.: Oceana Publications, 1966), xvii–xix.

7. Ibid., xix.

8. In ibid.

9. Ibid.

10. Ibid., xix–xx.

CHAPTER 2

1. Harold F. Peterson, *Argentina and the United States, 1810–1960* (Albany: State University of New York, 1964), 326.

2. Ibid., 328.
3. Ibid., 367.
4. Cf. Julius W. Pratt, *A History of United States Foreign Policy* (Englewood Cliffs, N.J.: Prentice-Hall, 1961), 608; Samuel Flagg Bemis, *A Short History of American Foreign Policy and Diplomacy* (New York: Henry Holt, 1959), 501.
5. Dotación Carnegie para la Paz Internacional, *Conferencias Internacionales Americanas, 1889–1936*; preface, Leo S. Rowe; Introd., James Brown Scott (Washington, D.C.: Dotación Carnegie para la Paz Internacional, 1938), 468–69.
6. J. Lloyd Mecham, *A Survey of United States–Latin American Relations* (Boston: Houghton Mifflin Company, 1965), 386.

CHAPTER 3

1. This is specifically mentioned in Book II, Title 1, Law 4 of the *Recopilación de leyes de los Reynos de las Indias* of 1680 (Spain, Consejo de la Hispanidad, [3 vols.; Madrid: Gráficas Ultra, 1943], I:218).
2. J. M. Ots Capdequí, *El estado español en las Indias* (3d ed.; Mexico: Fondo de Cultura Económica, 1957), 12–15, especially p. 14. Andrés Angulo y Pérez, "Instituciones de gobierno en América. Epoca carolingia," vol. 3. Congreso de Cooperación intelectual. (Madrid: Instituto de Cultura Hispánica, October, 1958), 3.

CHAPTER 4

1. R. R. Palmer and Joel Colton, *A History of the Modern World* (3d ed.; New York: Alfred A. Knopf, 1968), 450.
2. Tom J. Farer (ed.), *The Future of the Inter-American System* (New York: Praeger, 1979), 124.
3. Organization of American States [OAS], *Annual Report of the Secretary General, 1960*, (Washington, D.C.: Pan American Union, 1960), 17.
4. Organización de los Estados Americanos, *Aplicaciones del Tratado Interamericano de Asistencia Recíproca, 1948–1960* (3d. ed.: Washington, D.C.: Pan American Union, Department of Legal Affairs, 1960), 15–16.
5. M. Margaret Ball, *The OAS in Transition* (Durham, N.C.: Duke University Press, 1969), 463–64.
6. Ibid., p. 464 n. 190.
7. Ibid., nn. 190–91.
8. Organización de los Estados Americanos, *Octava Reunión de Consulta de Ministros de Relaciones Exteriores para servir de órgano de consulta en aplicación del Tratado Interamericano de Asistencia Recíproca* (Eighth Meeting of Consultation of Ministers of Foreign Affairs), Punta del Este, Uruguay, January 22–31, 1962, *Actas y documentos (Final Act)*, Doc. 68, Rev. (January 31, 1962).
9. Article V, "Organización de la Unión Panamericana," Quinta Conferencia Internacional Americana (Fifth International Conference of American States), in Dotación Carnegie para la Paz Internacional, *Conferencias Internacionales Americanas, 1889–1936* (Washington, D.C.: Dotación Carnegie para la Paz Internacional, 1938), 269.
10. Ball, *OAS in Transition*, 469.

11. Tenth Meeting of Consultation of Ministers of Foreign Affairs, Doc. 78, Rev., 6 Corr. (July 21, 1966), 3–4.

12. Ibid., 9.

13. Ball, *OAS in Transition*, 477.

14. Ibid.

15. Ibid., 477–78.

16. Ibid., 478–79.

17. Ibid., 480.

18. Ibid.

CHAPTER 5

1. Ball, *OAS in Transition*, 277.

2. Ibid.

3. Ibid., 290.

4. Ibid., 303.

5. OAS, *Annual Report, 1960*, 106–7; see also OAS, Secretary General, *The Organization of American States, 1954–1959* (Washington, D.C.: Pan American Union, 1959), 142–43.

6. Ball, *OAS in Transition*, 293.

7. Ibid., 294–95.

8. Ibid., 296–97.

9. Organización de los Estados Americanos, *Informe Anual del Secretario General, 1962* (Washington, D.C.: Pan American Union, 1962), 88.

10. Ball, *OAS in Transition*, 285.

11. Reference should be made here to the *Catalogue of Publications* of the PAU as well as the *Lista trimestral de publicaciones en circulación de la Unión Panamericana*. These catalogues convey an idea of the numerous publications of the organization at that time.

12. The reader is also referred to two booklets, *The Alliance for Progress: Its First Year, 1961–1962* (Washington, D.C.: Pan American Union, 1963) and *The Alliance for Progress: The Second Year, 1962–1963* (Washington, D.C.: Pan American Union, 1964).

CHAPTER 6

1. Ball, *OAS in Transition*, 127–28.

2. Ibid., 128–29.

3. Ibid., 129.

4. Ibid., 129–30.

5. Ibid., p. 130 n. 138.

6. Ibid., 130–31.

7. Ibid., 131.

8. Inter-American Institute of International Legal Studies, *Inter-American System*, 16.

9. Ibid.

10. Ibid., 17.

11. Ibid.
12. Ibid., 18.
13. Ball, *OAS in Transition*, 314–15.
14. Ibid., 314.
15. Ibid.
16. Ibid., 322.
17. Ibid., 326.
18. Ibid., 327.
19. Ibid., 328.
20. Ibid., 347.
21. Ibid.
22. OAS, *Chronicle*, 1, no. 5, p. 12.
23. Ball, *OAS in Transition*, 348.
24. Ibid.
25. Ibid.
26. Arturo Ardao, Jorge Basadre, Daniel F. Rubín de la Borbolla, Ricardo Caillet-Bois, Alfonso Caso, José María Chacón y Calvo, Howard F. Cline, João Cruz Costa, Juan E. Pivel Devoto, Ricardo Donoso, Juan Friede, Pedro Grases, Lewis Hanke, Guillermo Lohmann-Villena, Augusto Mijares, Catts Pressoir, Jean Price-Mars, Antonio Gómez Robledo, Mariano Picón Salas, Luis E. Valcárcel, Rafael Heliodoro Valle, Arthur P. Whitaker, Silvio Zavala, and Leopoldo Zea, to name a few.
27. Ball, *OAS in Transition*, 355.
28. Ibid.
29. Ibid., 356.
30. See Appendix: Charter of the OAS.
31. Hernán Montealegre, "Cuatro Perspectivas de los Derechos Humanos en el Sistema Interamericano," Organización de los Estados Americanos, Comisión Interamericana de Derechos Humanos, *Derechos Humanos en las Américas: Homenaje a la Memoria de Carlos A. Dunshee de Abranches* (Washington, D.C.: Secretaría General, 1984), 54.
32. Inter-American Institute of International Legal Studies, *Inter-American System*, 42.
33. Ibid., 44.
34. Ibid.
35. John C. Dreier, *The Organization of American States and the Hemisphere Crisis* (New York: Harper and Row, for the Council on Foreign Relations, 1962), 104.
36. Organization of American States, *Annual Report of the Secretary General, Fiscal Year 1964–1965* (Washington, D.C.: Pan American Union, n.d.), 24.
37. Ball, *OAS in Transition*, 377.
38. Second Special Inter-American Conference, *Actas y Documentos* 4:259–61.
39. Ibid., 4:480–83.
40. Second Special Inter-American Conference, *Final Act*, 32–34; and Organization of American States, *Annual Report of the Secretary General, Fiscal Year 1965–1966* (Washington, D.C.: Pan American Union, n.d.), 8.
41. Ball, *OAS in Transition*, 378.
42. Organization of American States, *The OAS and the Inter-American System*, 25.

43. Inter-American Institute of International Legal Studies, *The Inter-American System*, 45–55.

44. Ball, *OAS in Transition*, 367.

45. Ibid., 368.

46. Ibid., 369.

47. See the discussion of the peaceful settlement of disputes and of the activities of the Inter-American Peace Committee in chapter 12.

48. Ball, *OAS in Transition*, 371–72.

49. Third Special Inter-American Conference, *Documentos*, 4 vols. (Washington, D.C.: Pan American Union, November 15, 1966), 1:282.

50. Ball, *OAS in Transition*, 384–85.

51. OAS, *Annual Report, 1964–1965*, 10.

52. OAS, *Annual Report, 1965–1966*, 5.

53. Ball, *OAS in Transition*, 388.

54. Organization of American States, *Annual Report of the Secretary General, Fiscal Year 1962* (Washington, D.C.: Pan American Union, 1962).

55. Ball, *OAS in Transition*, 484.

56. Inter-American Development Bank, *Social Progress Trust Fund Agreement* (Washington, D.C.: IDB, 1964), sec. 1.04.

57. Ibid., art. 8, secs. 1, 2.

58. Ball, *OAS in Transition*, 398–99.

59. Ibid., 401–402.

CHAPTER 7

1. William Manger, *Pan America in Crisis* (Washington, D.C.: Public Affairs Press, 1961), 69.

2. Second Special Inter-American Conference, *Actas y documentos* (4 vols.: Washington, D.C.: Pan American Union, 1965), I:55–56, reprinted in Organization of American States, Secretary General, *Annual Report of the Secretary General, Fiscal Year 1964–1965* (Washington, D.C.: Pan American Union, n.d.), 21.

3. Ball, *OAS in Transition*, 33.

4. Second Special Inter-American Conference, *Actas y documentos* 2:161, 228.

5. Second Special Inter-American Conference, *Final Act*, 38–39.

6. Ball, *OAS in Transition*, 35–36.

7. Ibid., 36.

8. Ibid., 38–39.

9. Ibid., 40.

CHAPTER 8

1. *Proceedings: Volume I*, AG/RES.748 (XV–0/85)—AG/RES.794 (XV–0/85). *Fifteenth Regular Session, Cartagena de Indias, Colombia, December 5–9, 1985*, Certified Texts of the Resolutions (Washington, D.C.: OAS, General Assembly, 1986).

2. *Proceedings: Volume I*, AG/RES.852 (XVII–0/87)—AG/RES.905 (XVII–0/87). *Seventeenth Regular Session, Washington, D.C., November 9–14, 1987*, Certified Texts of the Resolutions (Washington, D.C.: OAS, General Assembly, 1988).

3. *Proceedings: Volume I,* AG/RES.906 (XVIII–0/88)—AG/RES.962 (XVIII–0/88). *Eighteenth Regular Session, San Salvador, El Salvador, November 14–19, 1988,* Certified Texts of the Resolutions (Washington, D.C.: OAS, General Assembly, 1989).

4. *Proceedings: Volume I,* AG/RES.963 (XIX–0/89)—AG/RES.1024 (XIX–0/89). *Nineteenth Regular Session, Washington, D.C., November 13–18, 1989,* Certified Texts of the Resolutions (Washington, D.C.: OAS, General Assembly, 1989).

5. *La Nación* (Buenos Aires), June 5, 1990, 5.

6. *Charter of the Organization of American States. As Amended by the Protocol of Buenos Aires in 1967 and by the Protocol of Cartagena de Indias in 1985.* (OEA/Ser. A/2 [English] Rev. 2. Treaty Series No. 1-D; Washington, D.C.: OAS, General Secretariat, 1989), 44.

7. Organization of American States, "Final Act. Sixteenth Meeting of Consultation of Ministers of Foreign Affairs, Serving as Organ of Consultation in Application of the Inter-American Treaty of Reciprocal Assistance," in *Meeting of Consultation of Ministers of Foreign Affairs. Collection of Final Acts (The Eleventh through the Twentieth),* vol. 2 (Washington, D.C.: OAS, General Secretariat, 1989), 355.

8. Unión Panamericana, *Conferencias Internacionales Americanas. Segundo Suplemento, 1945–1954* (Washington, D.C.: Secretaría General de la Décima Conferencia Interamericana, 1956), 203–208.

9. See Appendix: Revised Charter of the OAS (Protocol of Buenos Aires), art. 71.

10. Ninth International American Conference, *Actas y documentos* (7 vols.; Bogotá: Ministerio de Relaciones Exteriores, 1953), 6:297–302.

11. Ibid., 208–9. The quotation within the quotation refers to Article XXXVIII, the last of the "Duties."

12. Ball, *OAS in Transition,* 508–9.

13. Ibid., 509–10.

14. Ibid., 511.

15. Thomas L. Karnes, *The Failure of Union: Central America, 1824–1960* (Chapel Hill: University of North Carolina Press, 1961), 183–87.

16. Ibid., 187–90.

17. Ibid., 190.

18. Ibid., 190–203.

19. OAS, *Inter-American Program of Action of Rio de Janeiro against the Illicit Use and Production of Narcotic Drugs and Psychotropic Substances and Traffic Therein* (Washington, D.C.: OAS, General Secretariat, 1986), 3–4.

20. Ibid., 4–9.

21. See the work by Irving G. Tragen, Executive Secretary, Inter-American Drug Abuse Control Commission (CICAD), *Overview of the Drug Problem in the Americas* (Washington, D.C.: OAS, Inter-American Drug Abuse Control Commission, July 1989), 5.

22. Ibid., 7.

CHAPTER 9

1. Cf. Ralph Lee Woodward, Jr., *Central America: A Nation Divided* (2d ed.; New York: Oxford University Press, 1985), 255–56, 274–79, 302.

2. For two different Argentine views, cf. Osiris G. Villegas, *El conflicto con Chile en la región austral* (2d ed.; Buenos Aires: Editorial Pleamar, 1978), and Bonifacio del Carril, "El mar para los argentinos; las islas para los chilenos," *La Nación* (Buenos Aires), August 22, 1984, 9.

3. Woodward, *Central America*, 259–67.

4. Laurio H. Destefani, *Malvinas, Georgias y Sandwich del Sur, ante el conflicto con Gran Bretaña* (Buenos Aires: Edipress, 1982), 53–72, 133–35.

5. Ibid., 77–79.

6. Ibid., 90–110. For a discussion of the entire Malvinas/Falkland question, cf. Julius Goebel, *The Struggle for the Falkland Islands: A Study in Legal and Diplomatic History* (1927: repr. New Haven: Yale University Press, 1982).

7. Wayne S. Smith, "Britain Bases Claim to Falklands on Force," *New York Times*, June 17, 1991.

8. Val T. McComie, Secretario General Adjunto de la Organización de los Estados Americanos, *La reforma de la OEA desde la perspectiva del Caribe de habla inglesa* (Washington, D.C.: Secretaría General de la Organización de los Estados Americanos, Oficina de Información Pública, October 1985).

9. Ibid., 7.

10. Ibid., 20.

11. *Charter of the Organization of American States*, p. 38 (B-31/2).

12. OAS, *The OAS and the Inter-American System*, 44.

13. Sergio Ferrari, "Elecciones y verificacíon: Un nuevo modelo para resolver algunos conflictos internacionales?" *El Nuevo Diario* (Managua, Nicaragua), February 25, 1990.

14. Clifford Krauss, *Inside Central America: Its People, Politics and History* (New York: Summit Books, Simon and Schuster, 1991), 167.

15. OEA, Consejo Permanente, *Segundo Informe sobre la Observación del Proceso Electoral de Nicaragua (13 de julio a 3 de noviembre de 1989)* (OEA/Ser. G; CP/INF.2850/89 add. 1, 7 diciembre 1989; Washington, D.C.: Secretaría General de la Organización de los Estados Americanos, 1989), 29.

16. Ibid.

17. "Elections in Nicaragua," *Americas* (Washington, D.C.), 42, no. 1 (1990): 52.

18. Cf. the four reports of the OAS on the Monitoring of National Elections in Nicaragua: OAS, Consejo Permanente, *Primer Informe sobre la Observación del Proceso Electoral de Nicaragua, Segundo Informe, Tercer Informe, Cuarto Informe,* and as well as the *Informe del Secretario General sobre la Observación de la Aprobación de las Leyes Electoral y de Medios de Comunicación de Nicaragua y Acuerdo Relativo a Privilegios e Inmunidades de Observadores del Proceso Electoral Nicaraguense* (OEA/Ser. G; CP/INF.2850/89; Washington, D.C.: OEA, Secretaría General, August 2, 1989).

19. "Observación de elecciones," *Américas* (Washington, D.C.), 42, no. 6 (1990–1991): 53.

20. Ibid.

21. "Últimas noticias sobre las elecciones," *Américas* (Washington, D.C.), 43, no. 2 (1991); 57.

22. Ibid.

CHAPTER 10

1. Javier Ocampo López, *Historia de las ideas de integración de América Latina*, Publicaciones del Instituto de Estudios para el Desarrollo y la Integración de América Latina, Serie Fundamentos y doctrina, vol. 1 (Tunja-Boyacá, Colombia: Editorial Bolivariana Internacional, 1981), 233.

2. Joseph Grunwald (ed.), *Latin America and World Economy: A Changing International Order*, Latin American International Affairs Series, vol. 2 (Beverly Hills, Calif.: Sage Publications, 1978), 235.

3. Ibid., 234.

4. "Ansprache von Herrn Dr. Luis González Barros, Botschafter von Kolumbien— Im Namen der Botschafter der iberoamerikanischen Länder," *Mitteilungen* (Hamburg: Ibero-Amerika Verein, October 12, 1983), 7.

5. E. Bradford Burns, *Latin America: A Concise Interpretive History* (5th ed.; Englewood Cliffs, N.J.: Prentice Hall, 1990), 238.

6. O. Carlos Stoetzer, "Dreams of Integration: The Antilles Confederation, Pan Africanism, and Other Movements Promoting Caribbean Integration," *Caribbean Review*, 7, no. 2 (April/May/June 1978): 28–32.

7. Cf. Elisabeth Wallace, *The British Caribbean: From the Decline of Colonialism to the End of Federation* (Toronto: University of Toronto Press, 1977).

8. Cf. Cornelius Ch. Goslinga, *A Short History of the Netherlands Antilles and Surinam* (The Hague: Martinus Nijhoff, 1979).

CHAPTER 11

1. Inter-American Institute of International Legal Studies, *Inter-American System*, 26–30.

2. Ibid., 31.

3. Ibid.

4. Ibid., 35–36.

5. Organization of American States, General Secretariat, *Handbook of Existing Rules Pertaining to Human Rights in the Inter-American System (updated to July 1st, 1985)* (Washington, D.C.: OAS, General Secretariat, 1985), 6.

6. Ibid., 8, 7.

7. Ibid., 8.

8. Ibid., 9–10.

9. Ibid., 10–11.

10. Ibid., p. 12 n. 19.

11. Ibid., 13–14.

12. Ibid., 14–15.

13. Ibid., 15–16.

14. Ball, *OAS in Transition*, pp. 437–38.

15. Ibid., 498–99.

16. Ibid., 499–500.

17. Ibid., 501–502.

18. Ibid., 502.

19. Ibid.

20. Burkhard Wittek, *Der Staatsstreich von 1968 in Peru—Seine Ursachen und seine Konsequenzen* (Hamburg: Deutsche Ibero-Amerika Stiftung, 1972), 19.

21. Joseph F. Costanzo, "Catholic Politeia II," *Fordham Law Review* 21 (1952), 276, quoting Frank Edward Lally, *As Lord Acton Says* (Newport, R.I.: R. Ward, 1942), 55.

22. Cecil Jane, *Liberty and Despotism in Spanish America* (New York: Cooper Square Publishers, 1966), 26–27.

23. Inter-American Institute of International Legal Studies, *Inter-American System*, 56.

24. Ibid., 56–57.

25. Ibid., 57.

26. Ball, *OAS in Transition*, 487.

27. Ibid., 488.

28. Ibid.

29. Ibid., 489.

30. Ibid., 490–91.

31. Inter-American Institute of International Legal Studies, *Inter-American System*, 58.

32. Ball, *OAS in Transition*, 495.

33. Inter-American Institute of International Legal Studies, *Inter-American System*, 60–61.

34. Ball, *OAS in Transition*, 495.

35. Ibid., 495–96.

36. Ibid., 496.

37. Ibid., 496–97.

38. Inter-American Institute of International Legal Studies, *Inter-American System*, 68.

39. Luciano Pereña Vicente, *Misión de España en América, 1540–1560* (Madrid: Consejo Superior de Investigaciones Científicas, Instituto Francisco de Vitoria, 1956), 309, 310.

CHAPTER 12

1. Inter-American Institute of International Legal Studies, *Inter-American System*, 69–70.

2. Osiris G. Villegas, *El conflicto con Chile*, 189, Anexo 11-A; 191–96; Anexos 11-B, 12-A, 12-B.

3. Samuel Flagg Bemis, *A Short History of American Foreign Policy and Diplomacy* (New York: Henry Holt and Company, 1959), 258–59.

4. Inter-American Institute of International Legal Studies, *Inter-American System*, 72–73.

5. Ibid., 73.

6. Peterson, *Argentina*, 390.

7. Inter-American Institute of International Legal Studies, *Inter-American System*, 74. The European countries were Bulgaria, Czechoslovakia, Finland, Greece, Italy, Norway, Portugal, Rumania, Spain, Turkey, and Yugoslavia (ibid).

8. Ibid., 74–75.

9. Ibid., 77–78.

10. Ibid., 78.

11. Ibid., 78–82.

12. Inter-American Institute of International Legal Studies, *Inter-American System*, 107.

13. See Appendix: Rio Treaty.

14. See Appendix: Rio Treaty.

15. Inter-American Institute of International Legal Studies, *Inter-American System*, 114.

16. Ibid.

17. Ibid., 115.

18. Ibid., 115–17.

19. Ibid., 120–21, Resolution of the Seventh MCMFA: OEA/Ser. C/II.7, August 29, 1960.

20. Inter-American Institute of International Legal Studies, *Inter-American System*, 122–24.

21. Ibid., 129.

22. Ibid., 131.

23. Ibid., 131–32.

24. Ibid., 139.

25. Ibid., 154–57.

26. Ibid., 139–42.

27. Ibid., 157–62.

28. Ibid., 162–66.

29. Ibid., 146.

30. Ibid., 146–50.

31. Ibid., 178.

32. Ibid., 150–53.

CHAPTER 13

1. Charter of the OAS, "Preamble," Appendix.

2. Charter of Punta del Este, "Preamble."

3. U.S. Congress, House of Representatives, *The Role of the Organization of American States in the 1990s. (Vol. 2)*, Hearing before the Subcommittees on Human Rights and International Organizations, and on Western Hemisphere Affairs of the Committee on Foreign Affairs, 101st Congress, 2 sess., May 1, 1990 (Washington, D.C.: U.S. Government Printing Office, 1990), 28–29.

Bibliography

Acevedo, Domingo E. "The Right of Members of the Organization of American States to Refer Their 'Local' Disputes Directly to the United Nations Security Council." *The American University Journal of International Law and Policy* (Washington, D.C.), 4, 1 (Winter 1969): 25–66.

Américas [entire issue], 42, 6 (1990–1991).

———, 43, 2 (1991).

Aspen Institute for Humanistic Studies. *The Americas in 1988: A Time for Choices. A Report of the Inter-American Dialogue.* Lanham, Md.: University Press of America, 1988.

Ball, Mary Margaret. *The Problem of Inter-American Organizations.* Stanford, Calif.: Stanford University Press, 1947.

———. *The OAS in Transition.* Durham, N.C.: Duke University Press, 1969.

Barber, William Foster, and Ronning, C. Neale. *Internal Security and Military Power: Counter-insurgency and Civic Action in Latin America.* Columbus: Ohio State University Press, 1966.

Bernstein, Harry. *Making an Inter-American Mind.* Gainesville: University of Florida Press, 1961.

Burns, E. Bradford. *Latin America: A Concise Interpretive History*, 5th ed. Englewood Cliffs, N.J.: Prentice Hall, 1990.

Canyes, Manuel. *El sistema interamericano y la organización de las Naciones Unidas.* Washington, D.C.: Pan American Union, 1945.

Chalmers, Douglas A. (ed.). *Changing Latin America: New Interpretations of Its Politics and Society.* New York: Academy of Political Science, 1972.

Comisión Interamericana de Paz. *Informe de la Comisión Interamericana de Paz a la Séptima Reunión de Consulta de Ministros de Relaciones Exteriores, San José, Costa Rica, Agosto de 1960.* Washington, D.C.: Pan American Union, 1960.

————. *Informe de la Comisión Interamericana de Paz a la Octava Reunión de Consulta de Ministros de Relaciones Exteriores, 1962.* Washington, D.C.: Pan American Union, 1962.

Connell-Smith, Gordon. *The Inter American System* [Issued under the auspices of the Royal Institute of International Affairs]. London: Oxford University Press, 1966.

Cordero Torres, José María. *Textos básicos de América.* Madrid: Instituto de Estudios Políticos, 1955.

Costanzo, Joseph F. "Catholic Politeia II," *Fordham Law Review* 21 (1952).

Cotler, Julio, and Fagen, Richard R. (eds.). *Latin America and the United States: The Changing Political Realities.* Stanford, Calif.: Stanford University Press, 1974.

Council on Hemispheric Affairs. *Washington Report on the Hemisphere.* Washington, D.C.: COHA, 1980.

Del Carril, Bonifacio. "El mar para los argentinos; las islas para los chilenos," *La Nación* (Buenos Aires), August 22, 1984, p. 9.

Destefani, Laurio H. *Malvinas, Georgias y Sandwich del Sur, ante el conflicto con Gran Bretāna.* Buenos Aires: Edipress, 1982.

Dreier, John C. *The Organization of American States and the Hemisphere Crisis.* New York: Harper and Row, 1962.

Dunker, Hans-Joachim. *Die interamerikanischen Beziehungen und der Gedanke der gleichberechtigten Partnerschaft.* Hamburg: Publication Series of the Institut für Auswärtige Politik, no. 1, 1957.

Dupuy, René-Jean. *Le Nouveau Panaméricanisme: L'évolution du système interaméricain vers le fédéralisme.* Paris: Editions A. Pedone, 1956.

Eisenhower, Milton Stover. *The Wine Is Bitter: The United States and Latin America.* Garden City, N.J.: Doubleday, 1963.

Farer, Toni J. *The Future of the Inter-American System.* New York: Praeger Publishers, 1988.

Fenwick, Charles G. *The Organization of American States: The Inter-American Regional System.* 2d ed. Washington, D.C.: Kaufman Printing Co., 1963.

Fernández-Shaw, Félix G. *La Organización de los Estados Americanos (OEA).* 2d. ed. Madrid: Cultura Hispánica, 1963.

Ferrari, Sergio. "Elecciones y verificación: Un nuevo modelo para resolver algunos conflictos internacionales?" *El nuevo diario* (Managua, Nicaragua), February, 1990.

————. *El nuevo diario* (Managua, Nicaragua), February 1990.

————. "Experiencia sin precedente: Observación electoral: Un nuevo modelo para la paz?" *El nuevo diario* (Managua, Nicaragua), February 1990.

Flagg Bemis, Samuel. *A Short History of American Foreign Policy and Diplomacy.* New York: Henry Holt and Co., 1959.

Goebel, Julius. *The Struggle for the Falkland Islands: A Study in Legal and Diplomatic History.* 1927. Reprint, with an introduction by C.J.C. Metford. New Haven, Conn.: Yale University Press, 1982.

Goldenberg, Boris. "Lateinamerika—Reform oder Revolution?" Supplement to *Das Parlament*, 33, 63 (Hamburg: August 14, 1963).

Goslinga, Cornelius Ch. *A Short History of the Netherlands Antilles and Surinam.* The Hague: Martinus Nijhoff, 1979.

Grunwald, Joseph. (ed.). *Latin America and World Economy: A Changing International Order.* Latin American International Affairs Series, vol. 2. Beverly Hills, Calif.: Sage Publications, 1978.

Herring, Hubert. "Inter-American Relations: The Balance Sheet." In *A History of Latin America from the Beginning to the Present,* pp. 810–18. 2d. rev. ed. New York: Alfred A. Knopf, 1961. See also 3d. ed., rev. and enl., 1968.

Instituto Panamericano de Geografía e Historía. *XII Asamblea General: Informe del Secretario General, 1977–1982.* Mexico: IPGH, 1982.

———. *XIII Asamblea General: Informe Quadrienal del Secretario General.* Mexico: IPGH, 1985.

Inter-American Commission of Human Rights. *Human Rights in the Americas: Homage to the Memory of Carlos A. Dunshee de Abranches.* Washington, D.C.: Organization of American States, General Secretariat, 1984.

Inter-American Development Bank. *Social Progress Trust Fund Agreement.* Washington, D.C.: IDB, 1964.

Inter-American Institute for Cooperation on Agriculture. *Annual Report 1988.* San José, Costa Rica: IICA, 1988.

Inter-American Institute of International Legal Studies. *The Inter American System: Its Development and Strengthening.* Explanatory Note by F. V. García Amador, Secretary General of Inter-American Institute of International Legal Studies. Dobbs Ferry, N.Y.: Oceana Publications, 1966.

Inter-American Review of Bibliography. *El primer siglo del sistema interamericano: The First Century of the Inter-American System.* Washington, D.C.: Organization of American States, General Secretariat, 1989 [vol. 39, no. 4].

Jane, Cecil. *Liberty and Despotism in Spanish America.* New York: Cooper Square Publishers, 1966.

Karen, Ruth. *Neighbors in a New World: The Organization of American States.* Cleveland: World Publishing Co., 1966.

Karnes, Thomas L. *The Failure of Union: Central America, 1824–1960.* Chapel Hill: The University of North Carolina Press, 1961.

Krauss, Clifford. *Inside Central America: Its People, Politics, and History.* New York: Summit Books, Simon and Schuster, 1991.

Langley, Lester D. *America and the Americas: The United States in the Western Hemisphere.* Athens: University of Georgia Press, 1989.

Liévano Aguirre, Indalecio. *Bolivarismo y Monroísmo.* 2d. ed. Bogotá: Tercer Mundo Editores, 1988.

Lieuwen, Edwin. *The United States and the Challenge to Security in Latin America.* Columbus: Ohio State University Press, 1966.

McClellan, Grant S. (ed.). *U.S. Policy in Latin America.* New York: H. W. Wilson, 1963.

McComie, Val T. *La reforma de la OEA desde la perspectiva del Caribe de habla inglesa.* Washington, D.C.: Secretaría General de la Organización de los Estados Americanos, Oficina de Información Pública, October 1985.

McGann, Thomas F. *Argentina, the United States and the Inter-American System, 1880–1914.* Cambridge, Mass.: Harvard University Press, 1957.

Madariaga, Salvador de. *Latin America between the Eagle and the Bear.* New York: Praeger, 1962.

Manger, William. *Pan America in Crisis.* Washington, D.C.: Public Affairs Press,

1961. (With an Introduction by Alberto Lleras Camargo, President of Colombia, and Foreword by Heĉtor David Castro, former Chairman of the OAS.)

————. *The Two Americas: Dialogue on Progress and Problems.* Foreword by Eduardo Frei Montalva, President of Chile. New York: P. J. Kennedy and Sons, 1965.

Marinho, Ilmar Penna. *O funcionamento do sistema interamericano dentro do sistema mundial.* Rio de Janeiro: Livraria Freitas Bastos, 1959.

Mattfeldt, Rudolf. "Monroe-Doktrin, Kuba und OAS," *Aussenpolitik* (Stuttgart), 11, 10 (October 1960): 619–99.

Mecham, J. Lloyd. *The United States and Inter American Security, 1889–1960.* Austin: University of Texas Press, 1961.

————. *A Survey of United States–Latin American Relations.* Boston: Houghton Mifflin Company, 1965.

Mitteilungen. Hamburg: Ibero-Amerika Verein, October 12, 1983.

Mundo Nuevo: Revista de Estudios Latinoamericanos Special issue: *La OEA en la encrucijada.* [Caracas: Instituto de Altos Estudios de America Latina, Universidad Simón Bolívar], 9, 32/34 (April–December 1986).

Ocampo Lopez, Javier. *Historia de las ideas de integración de América Latina.* Publicaciones del Instituto de Estudios para el Desarrollo y la Integración de América Latina. Serie Fundamentos y doctrina. Vol. 1 Tunja-Boyacá, Colombia: Editorial Bolivariana Internacional, 1981.

Organización de los Estados Americanos (OEA). *Aplicaciones del Tratado Interamericano de Asistencia Recíproca, 1948–1960.* 3d. ed. Washington, D.C.: Pan American Union, 1960.

————. *Informe Anual del Secretario General, 1961.* Washington, D.C.: Pan American Union, 1961.

————. *Aplicaciones del Tratado Interamericano de Asistencia Recíproca, Suplemento 1960–1961.* Washington, D.C.: Pan American Union, 1962.

————. *Informe Anual del Secretario General, 1962.* Washington, D.C.: Pan American Union, 1962.

————. *Tratados y Convenciones Interamericanos: Firmas, ratificaciones y depósitos con notas explicativas.* Washington, D.C.: Secretaría General, OEA, Subsecretaría de Asuntos Jurídicos: Serie sobre Tratados, no. 9, 1985.

————. *Informe Anual del Secretario General, 1988–1989.* Washington, D.C.: OEA, Secretaría General, 1989.

————. Asamblea General. Décimonoveno Período Ordinario de Sesiones. Washington, D.C.: Del 13 al 18 de noviembre de 1989. *Actas y Documentos,* vol. 1. Washington, D.C.: OEA, Secretaría General, 1989.

————. Asamblea General. Décimonoveno Período Ordinario de Sesiones. *Informe Anual del Consejo Permanente a la Asamblea General (Del 27 de julio al 10 de noviembre de 1989).* Washington, D.C.: OEA, Secretaría General, 1989.

————. Asamblea General. Décimonoveno Período Ordinario de Sesiones. *Informe Anual del Consejo Permanente a la Asamblea General (Del 30 de noviembre de 1988 al 26 de julio de 1989).* Washington, D.C.: OEA, Secretaría General, 1989.

————. Consejo Permanente. *Informe del Secretario General sobre la Observación de la Aprobación de las Leyes Electoral y de Medios de Comunicación de Nicaragua y Acuerdo Relativo a Privilegios e Inmunidades de Observadores del*

Proceso Electoral Nicaragüense. Washington, D.C.: OEA, Secretaría General, 1989.

————. Consejo Permanente. *Segundo Informe sobre la Observación del Proceso Electoral de Nicaragua (13 de julio a 3 de noviembre de 1989).* Washington, D.C.: OEA, Secretaría General, 1989.

————. Consejo Permanente. *Tercer Informe sobre la Observación del Proceso Electoral de Nicaragua, 4 de noviembre al 31 de diciembre de 1989.* Washington, D.C.: OEA, Secretaría General, 1989.

————. Consejo Permanente. *Cuarto Informe sobre la Observación del Proceso Electoral de Nicaragua, período del 1 de enero al 15 de febrero de 1990.* Washington, D.C.: OEA, Secretaría General, 1990.

————. Quinta Reunión de Consulta de Ministros de Relaciones Exteriores. Santiago de Chile, August 12–18, 1959. *Actas y documentos.* Washington, D.C.: Pan American Union, 1961.

————. Sexta Reunión de Consulta de Ministros de Relaciones Exteriores para servir de órgano de consulta en aplicación del Tratado Interamericano de Asistencia Recíproca. San José, Costa Rica, August 12–21, 1960. *Actas y documentos.* Washington, D.C.: Pan American Union, 1961.

————. Séptima Reunión de Consulta de Ministros de Relaciones Exteriores. San José, Costa Rica, August 22–29, 1960. *Actas y documentos.* Washington, D.C.: Pan American Union, 1961.

————. Octava Reunión de Consulta de Ministros de Relaciones Exteriores para servir de órgano de consulta en aplicación del Tratado Interamericano de Asistencia Recíproca. Punta del Este, Uruguay, January 22–31, 1962. *Actas y documentos.* Washington, D.C.: Pan American Union, 1963.

————. Novena Reunión de Consulta de Ministros de Relaciones Exteriores para servir de órgano de consulta en aplicación del Tratado Interamericano de Asistencia Recíproca. Unión Panamericana. Washington, D.C.: July 21–26, 1964. *Documentos de la Reunión.* Washington, D.C.: Pan American Union, 1964.

Organization of American States (OAS). *Annual Report of the Secretary General, 1960.* Washington, D.C.: Pan American Union, 1960.

————. *Annual Report of the Secretary General, 1962.* Washington, D.C.: Pan American Union, 1962.

————. *Annual Report of the Secretary General, Fiscal Year 1964–1965.* Washington, D.C.: Pan American Union, n.d.

————. *Annual Report of the Secretary General, Fiscal Year 1965–1966.* Washington, D.C.: Pan American Union, n.d.

————. *Handbook of Existing Rules Pertaining to Human Rights in the Inter-American System (updated to July 1st, 1985).* Washington, D.C.: OAS, General Secretariat, 1985.

————. *Inter-American Program of Action of Rio de Janeiro against the Illicit Use and Production of Narcotic Drugs and Psychotropic Substances and Traffic Therein.* Washington, D.C.: OAS, General Secretariat, 1986.

————. *The OAS and the Evolution of the Inter-American System.* Washington, D.C.: OAS, General Secretariat, Department of Public Information, January 1988.

————. *Charter of the Organization of American States: As Amended by the Protocol* of *Buenos Aires* in 1967 and by the Protocol of *Cartagena de Indias* in 1985. Treaty Series no. 1-D. Washington, D.C.: OAS, General Secretariat, 1989.

————. *Meetings of Consultation of Ministers of Foreign Affairs. Collection of Final Acts (The Eleventh through the Twentieth).* Vol. 2. Washington, D.C.: OAS, General Secretariat, 1989.

————. General Assembly. Fifteenth Regular Session. Cartagena de Indias, December 5–9, 1985. *Proceedings.* Vol. 1. Washington, D.C.: OAS, General Secretariat, 1986.

————. General Assembly. Seventeenth Regular Session. Washington, D.C., November 9–14, 1987. *Proceedings.* Vol. 1. Washington, D.C.: OAS, General Secretariat, 1988.

————. General Assembly. Eighteenth Regular Session. San Salvador, El Salvador, November 14–19, 1988. *Proceedings.* Vol. 1. Washington, D.C.: OAS, General Secretariat, 1989.

————. General Assembly. Nineteenth Regular Session. Washington, D.C., November 13–18, 1989. *Proceedings.* Vol. 1. Washington, D.C.: OAS, General Secretariat, 1989.

————. International Conferences of American States (ICAS). Ninth ICAS, *Actas y documentos.* 7 vols. Bogotá, Colombia: Ministerio de Relaciones Exteriores, 1953.

————. Second Special ICAS. *Actas y documentos.* Washington, D.C.: Pan American Union, 1965.

————. Second Special ICAS. *Final Act.* Washington, D.C.: Pan American Union, 1965.

————. Third Special ICAS. *Documentos.* 4 vols. Washington, D.C.: Pan American Union, 1966.

————. Secretary General. *The Organization of American States, 1954–1959.* Washington, D.C.: Pan American Union, 1959.

Ots Capdequí, J. M. *El estado español en las Indias.* 3d. ed. Mexico: Fondo de Cultura Económica, 1957.

Palmer, R. R., and Colton, Joel. *A History of the Modern World.* 3d. ed. New York: Alfred A. Knopf, 1968.

Pan American Union. *Conferencias Internacionales Americanas, 1889–1936.* Pref. Leo S. Rowe, introd. James Brown Scott. Washington, D.C.: Dotación Carnegie para la Paz Internacional, 1938.

————. *Conferencias Internacionales Americanas: Primer Suplemento, 1938–1942.* Washington, D.C.: Dotación Carnegie para la Paz Internacional, 1943.

————. *Anuario Jurídico Interamericano, 1948.* Washington, D.C.: Pan American Union, 1949.

————. *Anuario Jurídico Interamericano, 1949.* Washington, D.C.: Pan American Union, 1950.

————. *Conferencias Internacionales Americanas: Segundo Suplemento, 1945–1954.* Washington, D.C.: Secretaría General de la Décima Conferencia Interamericana, 1956.

————. *La Organización de los Estados Americanos: Informe presentado por la Unión Panamericana a la Undécima Conferencia Interamericana.* Washington, D.C.: Pan American Union, 1959.

Pereña Vucente, Luciano. *Misión de España en América, 1540–1560.* Madrid: Instituto Francisco de Vitoria, Consejo Superior de Investigaciones Científicas, 1956.

Peterson, Harold F. *Argentina and the United States, 1810–1960.* Albany: State University of New York, 1964.

Petras, James F. *Latin America: Bankers, Generals, and the Struggle for Social Justice.* Totowa, N.J.: Rowman and Littlefield, 1986.

Pratt, Julius W. *A History of United States Foreign Policy.* Englewood Cliffs, N.J.: Prentice-Hall, 1961.

Prellwitz, Jürgen V. "Das Prinzip der Nichteinmischung als Grundlage der interamerikanischen Beziehungen." *Zeitschrift für Politik,* 7 (1960): 110–33.

Rivadeneira Vargas, Antonio José. *El bogotano J. M. Torres Caicedo (1830–1889)— La multipatria latinoamericana.* Bogotá, Colombia: Academia Colombiana de Historia, Alcaldía Mayor de Bogotá, Instituto Distrital de Cultura y Turismo, 1989.

Rogers, William D. *The Twilight Struggle: The Alliance for Progress and the Politics of Development in Latin America.* Introd. Robert F. Kennedy. New York: Random House, 1967.

Romero, José Luis. (ed.). *Pensamiento político de la Emancipación.* Preface, José Luis Romero; selección, notas y cronología, José Luis Romero and Luis Alberto Romero. 2 vols. Barcelona: Biblioteca Ayacucho (no. 24), 1985.

Ronning, C. Neale. (ed.). *Intervention in Latin America.* Introd. C. Neale Ronning. New York: Alfred A. Knopf, 1970.

Rubio García, Leandro. "Méjico, la no intervención y el sistema interamericano," *Cuadernos Hispanoamericanos* (Madrid), 169 (January 1964): 71–85.

Sansón Terrán, José. *El interamericanismo en marcha.* Washington, D.C.: University Press, 1949.

Scheman, L. Ronald. *The Inter-American Dilemma: The Search for Inter-American Cooperation at the Centennial of the Inter-American System.* New York: Praeger Publishers, 1988.

———. (ed.). *The Alliance for Progress. A Retrospective.* New York: Praeger, 1988.

Slater, Jerome. *The OAS and United States Foreign Policy.* Kent: Ohio State University Press, 1967.

Smith, Wayne S. "Britain Bases Claim to Falklands on Force," *New York Times,* June 17, 1991.

Soward, Frederick Hubert, and Macauley, A. M. *Canada and the Pan American System.* Toronto: Ryerson Press, 1948.

Spain. Consejo de la Hispanidad. *Recopilación de leyes de los Reynos de las Indias.* 3 vols. Madrid: Gráficas Ultra, 1943.

Stoetzer, O. Carlos. "La Unión Panamericana," *Jornal* (Madrid), 76 (September–October 1959): 441–44.

———. "Geschichte der panamerikanischen Bewegung." In *Ibero-Amerika: Ein Handbuch,* edited by Friedrich Wehner, 5th ed. Hamburg: Übersee-Verlag, 1964.

———. "Dreams of Integration: The Antilles Confederation, Pan Africanism, and other movements promoting Caribbean integration," *Caribbean Review,* 7, 2 (April–June 1978): 28–32.

———. "Die Organisation der Amerikanischen Staaten." *Aussenpolitik* (Stuttgart), 9, 2 February 1958), 105–15.

Thomas, Ann van Wynen, and Thomas, A. J., Jr. *The Organization of American States.* Dallas, Texas: Southern Methodist University Press, 1960.

Tragen, Irving G. *Overview of the Drug Problem in the Americas.* Washington, D.C.: OAS, Inter American Drug Abuse Control Commission (CICAD), July 1989.

United States. Congress. House of Representatives. *The Role of the Organization of American States in the 1990s.* (Vol. 1), Hearing before the Subcommittees on Human Rights and International Organizations, and Western Hemisphere Affairs of the Committee on Foreign Affairs. 101st Congress. 1st sess. July 12, 1989. Washington, D.C.: U.S. Government Printing Office, 1989.

———. *The Role of the Organization of American States in the 1990s.* Vol. 2. Hearing before the Subcommittees on Human Rights and International Organizations, and on Western Hemisphere Affairs of the Committee on Foreign Affairs. House of Representatives. 101st Congress. 2d sess. May 1, 1990. Washington, D.C.: U.S. Government Printing Office, 1990.

United States. Congress. Senate. Committee on Foreign Relations. *United States–Latin American Relations.* Compilation of studies under the direction of the Subcommittee on American Republics Affairs of the Committee on Foreign Relations, U.S. Senate, pursuant to S. Res. 330, 85th Congress, S. Res. 31 and S. Res. 250, 86th Congress. Washington, D.C.: U.S. Government Printing Office, 1960. (See especially study no. 3, "The Organization of American States," prepared by Northwestern University, December 27, 1959, pp. 183–275).

Villegas, Osiris G. *El conflicto con Chile en la región austral.* 2d ed. Buenos Aires: Editorial Pleamar, 1978.

Wallace, Elisabeth. *The British Caribbean: From the Decline of Colonialism to the End of Federation.* Toronto: University of Toronto Press, 1977.

Whitaker, Arthur P. *The Western Hemisphere Idea: Its Rise and Decline.* Ithaca, N.Y.: Cornell University Press, 1954.

Williams, Mary Wilhelmine, Bartlett, Ruhl J., and Miller, Russell E. *The People and Politics of Latin America.* 4th ed. Boston, Mass.: Ginn and Co., 1955.

Wittek, Burkhard. *Der Staatsstreich von 1968 in Peru—Seine Ursachen und seine Konsequenzen.* Hamburg: Deutsche Ibero-Amerika Stiftung, 1972.

Wood, Bryce. *The Dismantling of the Good Neighbor Policy.* Austin: University of Texas Press, 1985.

Woodward, Ralph Lee, Jr. *Central America: A Nation Divided.* 2d ed. New York: Oxford University Press, 1985.

Index

ABC countries, 17
Acapulco, 3, 230
Acre Territory, 215
Act Establishing the Inter-American Force, 287
Act of Bogotá, 81, 140, 261
Act of Chapultepec, 28, 29, 185
Act of Dominican Reconciliation, 55, 288
Act of Havana Concerning the Provisional Administration of European Colonies and Possessions in America, 24
Act of Rio de Janeiro, 124, 144
Act of Santo Domingo, 54, 55, 286–87
Act of Washington, 43, 143, 144, 149, 167, 208, 209, 210
Action Program of Rio. *See* Inter-American Program of Action of Rio De Janeiro against the Illicit Use and Production of Narcotic Drugs and Psychotropic Substances and Traffic Therein
Acton, Lord, 255
Adams, John Quincy, 14
Additional and Explanatory Protocol of 1893, 203
Additional Protocol to the Convention on Duties and Rights of States in the Event of Civil Strife, 277, 283, 286
Additional Convention to the General Convention of Inter-American Conciliation, 21
Additional Protocol Relative to Non-Intervention, 41, 267
Admission of new members, 207
Africa, 236, 237, 296

Africa for the Africans, 236
African Christian Union, 236
Afro-Asian-Latin American Peoples' Solidarity Conference, First, 57, 127
Afro-Asian-Latin American Peoples' Solidarity Organization (AALAPSO), 58
Aggression, 136, 145, 149, 242, 259, 267, 272, 273, 274, 282, 285
Agrarian Reform, 86, 114, 140
Agreement of Cartagena (Andean Group), 231, 232
Agreement of Esquipulas II, 224
Agreement on Privileges and Immunities and Headquarters Agreement, 162
Agricultural Research Institute of the Uruguayan Government, 113
Agricultural University La Molina (Peru), 113
Agriculture, 98, 111–14, 131, 150
Aguilar, Andrés, 159
Akintole, Chief, 236
Alalc Treaty. *See* Latin American Free Trade Association (LAFTA) (ALALC)
Alaska, 299
Alberdi, Juan Bautista, 5
Alessandri, Jorge, 137
Alfonsín, Raúl, 202
Alfonso XIII, king of Spain, 270, 278
Algunos aspectos de la situación de las escuelas de servicio social en América Latina, 88
Alianza Popular Revolucionaria Americana (APRA) (Peru), 253
Allende, Salvador, 232, 253, 296

Alliance of the Americas against Drug
    Trafficking, 216
Alliance Newsletters, 96
Alliance for Progress, xi, 36, 48, 49, 56, 57,
    61, 68, 69, 70, 74, 80, 82, 83, 84, 86, 87,
    88, 89, 90, 91, 94, 95, 96, 100, 107, 111,
    114, 118, 130, 139, 140, 141, 142, 145,
    150, 153, 178, 184, 215, 243, 257, 258,
    261, 288, 294, 295, 296, 299; First Annual
    Assembly on, 92; Special Fund, 74
Allied Cause, 27
Alvarez, Alejandro, 242
Amadeo I, king of Spain, 236
Amazon, 21
Amazonian area, 203
America/Americas, ix, xi, 6, 22, 28, 49, 70,
    93, 95, 102, 107, 117, 126, 155, 158, 159,
    160, 179, 234, 250, 257, 272, 273, 274,
    301
América en cifras, 89
América indígena (IAII), 111
American community, 27, 99, 193
"American Congress" (Lima). *See* Congress
    of Lima, First
American continent, 1, 2, 14, 136, 156, 158,
    261
American Convention on Extradition and
    Preventive Measures in Drug Trafficking,
    161
American Convention on Human Rights,
    118, 155, 156, 184, 189, 190, 191, 214,
    243, 246–48, 249, 294; Additional
    Protocol, 159, 161, 215, 244; Additional
    Protocol to the American Convention on
    Human Rights in the Area of Economic,
    Social and Cultural Rights, 215, 244
American Convention on Human Rights to
    Abolish the Death Penalty, 161, 162;
    Additional Protocol, 215, 244
American countries/nations/peoples, 5, 95,
    106, 107, 108, 119, 120, 125, 130, 145,
    153, 178, 212, 213, 221, 222, 259, 268
American Declaration of the Rights and
    Duties of Man, 30, 115, 116, 117, 187,
    188, 242, 244, 249, 257
American governments (OAS Member
    States), 42, 63, 105, 106, 108, 117, 118,
    119, 121, 122, 130, 144, 146, 147, 154,
    167, 170, 172, 175, 176, 177, 178, 179,
    188, 189, 190, 192, 193, 194, 195, 196,
    197, 199, 203, 213, 217, 218, 219, 220,
    221, 222, 223, 225, 247, 253, 269, 271,
    275
American Indians, 24, 36, 109–11, 263
American Institute for Free Labor
    Development (AIFLD) (United States), 87
American International Association, 114
American International Institute for the
    Protection of Childhood, 104

American international law, 5, 259
Americanist, 5
American monuments, 157
American presidents, 141
American republics, 39, 59, 62, 64, 95, 102,
    128, 244, 245, 257, 262
American Revolution (United States), 255
American Revolutionary Popular Alliance
    (APRA) (Peru), 253
American Scientific Congress (United
    States), 111
American states, 1, 18, 19, 22, 32, 33, 34,
    35, 39, 40, 41, 43, 44, 45, 47, 51, 52, 58,
    62, 100, 101, 107, 112, 113, 114, 117,
    120, 125, 143, 151, 154, 155, 156, 158,
    165, 167, 175, 176, 180, 181, 182, 183,
    184, 185, 244, 245, 246, 247, 252, 253,
    262, 269, 272, 275, 282
American Treaty on Pacific Settlement. *See*
    Pact of Bogotá
American Union, 1
American Zone of Security, 136
Américas, 93, 94
Amoroso Lima, Alceo, 71
Anarchism, 15–16
Ancient Greece, 115
Andean Common Market, 299
Andean countries. *See* Andean states
Andean Federation, 6
Andean Foreign Investment Code, 232
Andean Group, 4, 62, 230, 231
Andean states, 9, 164
Andean Zone (IICA), 113
Anglo-Saxon tradition, 8, 254
*Annals of the Organization of American
    States*, 96
Anschluss, 23
Antarctic, 172
Antigua and Barbuda, 1, 157, 162, 172, 195,
    209, 238, 239
Anti-war Treaty of Non-aggression and
    Conciliation (Saavedra Lamas Treaty), 267
*Antología de los cronistas de las culturas
    precolombinas*, 93
Anuario indigenista (IAII), 111
Aranda, count of, 4
Arbenz Guzmán, Jacobo, 40, 201, 270, 277
Arbitral Award of 1906 (Alfonso XIII, king of
    Spain), 278
Arbitration, 9, 10, 13, 15, 16, 20, 21, 35,
    41, 136, 138, 242, 266, 267, 268, 269, 293
Ardito-Barletta, Nicolás, 173
ARENA. *See* National Republican Alliance
    (El Salvador)
Arevalo Bermejo, Juan Jose, 251, 277
Argentina/Argentines, 1, 2, 4, 7, 10, 11, 16,
    17, 20, 22, 24, 26, 27, 32, 34, 36, 41, 49,
    50, 52, 53, 54, 81, 89, 91, 93, 97, 104,

109, 110, 112, 113, 120, 122, 124, 130,
144, 163, 169, 170, 171, 172, 185, 190,
195, 196, 200, 202, 203, 204, 205, 207,
216, 229, 230, 231, 232, 233, 247, 250,
251, 252, 253, 254, 257, 259, 260, 261,
262, 265, 267, 269, 272, 275, 277, 278,
282, 283, 286, 289, 297, 299
Argentina-Uruguay Binational Prevention
  Program, 196
Argentine-Chilean Accord of 1984 on the
  Beagle, 202
Argentine Scientific Society, 97
Arias Peace Plan, 225
Arias Sánchez, Oscar, 225
Aridjis, Homero, 235
Aristide, Jean-Bertrad, 226, 300
Aristocratic Republic (Chile), 255
Aruba, 238
Asia, 29, 295, 299
Asian rim, 163
Assembly of Planning Experts and Planning
  Officials (Santiago de Chile, 1962), 83
Assistance. *See* Reciprocal assistance
Assistant Secretary General of the
  Organization of American States, 60, 71,
  72, 75, 76, 79, 137, 144, 146, 166, 181,
  182, 186, 206, 207, 209, 210, 211, 262–63
Association, xi
Asunción, 163, 206
Asylum: diplomatic, 11, 21, 243, 249, 269,
  270, 283, 286; territorial, 21, 188, 243,
  249, 275
Atacama, 265
Ateneo (Madrid), 236
Atlanta, Georgia, 156
Atlantic, 21, 23, 44, 202, 234
Atlantic Community Development Group
  for Latin America (ADELA), 141
Atlas de América (PAIGH), 108
Atomic energy, 114
Austria, 7, 23, 127
Autogolpe (Peru), 301
Axis powers, 24
Ayacucho, 6, 7
Azikiwe, 236

Baena Soares, João Clemente, 166, 207, 226
Bahamas, Commonwealth of, 1, 158, 166,
  172, 195, 209, 239
Bajan, 211
Baker Plan, 234
Balaguer, Joaquín, 55, 201
Ball, Margaret, 55, 75, 127
Báñez, Domingo, 263
Barbados, 1, 59, 166, 170, 172, 207, 209,
  211, 230, 238, 239
Barrios de Chamorro, Violeta, 226, 234
Basadre, Jorge, 71

Batista y Zaldívar, Fulgencio, 45, 270 280
Bay of Pigs, 48, 201
Beagle Channel, 158, 202
Belaúnde Terry, Fernando, 203, 289
Belgium, 23, 90, 207
Belgrano, Manuel, 6
Belize, 1, 43, 142, 157, 162, 167, 185, 208,
  209, 210, 212, 213, 217, 224, 239, 298
Belo Horizonte, 88
Beltrán, Pedro, 281
Benign Neglect policy, 200, 261–62
Berlin Wall, 206
Betances, Ramón Emeterio, 236
Betancourt, Rómulo, 46, 259, 270, 280, 282
Betancur, Belisario, 233
Bibliografía antropológica (IAII), 111
Biblioteca popular latinoamericana (PAU),
  95
Bidlack-Mallarino Treaty, 3
Bioceanic principle, 202
Blaine, James G., 2, 13
Blantyre, 236
Bogotá, 8, 29, 30, 31, 40, 62, 63, 65, 71, 81,
  84, 87, 93, 94, 98, 100, 101, 113, 115,
  123, 124, 128, 129, 130, 139, 187, 209,
  242, 245, 248, 251, 257, 274
Bogotá Conference. *See* International
  Conference of American States, Ninth
Boletín (IICI), 105
Boletín de noticias (PAU), 96
*Boletín intercambio de personas, becas y
  préstamos de la Organización de los
  Estados Americanos y sus Organismos
  Especializados para estudios en el
  extranjero* (OAS), 92
Bolívar, Simón, 1, 2, 4, 6, 7, 8, 9, 10, 13,
  36, 123, 233, 235, 239, 265
Bolivarian Congress (1826), 60
Bolivarian Constitution. *See* Bolivian
  Constitution of 1826
Bolivarismo y Monroísmo, 2
Bolivia/Bolivians, 1, 4, 7, 9, 10, 20, 21, 22,
  36, 49, 50, 52, 57, 80, 83, 84, 89, 93, 104,
  107, 109, 110, 112, 124, 144, 157, 158,
  159, 160, 161, 162, 163, 164, 169, 170,
  195, 204, 215, 224, 229, 231, 232, 249,
  254, 260, 290, 299
Bolivian access to the Pacific, 157, 158, 159,
  160, 161, 162, 163, 204, 215
Bolivian-Brazilian Agreement on the Acre
  Territory, 215
Bolivian Constitution of 1826, 7, 36
Bonaire, 238
Bonn, 86
Booth, Joseph, 236
Border Treaty of 1881 (Argentina, Chile),
  203
Bosch, Juan, 52, 286

Boston, 96
Brady Plan, 234
Brasilia, 158
Bravo, Jorge, 253
Brazil/Brazilians, x, 1, 4, 7, 10, 11, 12, 16,
    17, 36, 49, 50, 52, 53, 54, 60, 61, 75, 80,
    81, 85, 86, 91, 95, 96, 104, 109, 110, 112,
    113, 120, 124, 130, 139, 143, 144, 163,
    166, 169, 170, 171, 189, 193, 195, 200,
    205, 207, 229, 230, 231, 232, 233, 235,
    251, 252, 253, 254, 255, 256, 259, 261,
    265, 266, 269, 286, 287, 289, 296, 297,
    299
Brazilian Careers and Social Structure: A
    Case History and Model (PAU), 85
Brazilian Careers and Social Structure, with
    Implications for Planning and Actions
    Programs (PAU), 85
Briand, Aristide, 34
Britain. *See* United Kingdom
British, 2, 3, 171, 172, 203, 204, 212, 218,
    235, 236, 289, 297
British Arbitral Award of 1971, 203
British Commonwealth of Nations, 212, 234
British Empire, 212
British Guiana, 238
British Honduras, 238
British Royal Navy, 14
British tradition, 211
British West Indies, 237, 238
Bromsen, Maury S., 93
Brussels, 141
Bryan, William Jennings, 265
Bryan-Chamorro Treaty, 192, 266
Buchanan, William I., 265
Buenos Aires, 6–7, 16, 19, 21, 23, 27, 37,
    44, 56, 71, 83, 100, 104, 108, 124, 128,
    129, 130, 139, 144, 146, 171, 187, 243,
    244, 257, 265, 267, 268, 271, 273, 294
Bunker, Ellsworth, 55
Bush, George, 164, 169, 174, 200, 206, 286,
    289, 297, 299, 300

Cabildo, 254
Cadogan, Sir Alexander, 25
California, 14
Calvo Clause, 14, 250, 257
Canada/Canadians, xii, 1, 23, 32, 89, 103,
    108, 126, 130, 157, 162, 163, 200, 207,
    210, 212, 213, 299
Canal Zone. *See* Panama Canal Zone
Cano, Melchor, 263
Capitalism, 115
Caracas, 40, 43, 47, 75, 78, 98, 99, 106,
    109, 115, 121, 129, 137, 139, 188, 231,
    235, 245, 257, 274, 275, 277
Caracas Agreement (LAFTA), 230

Características da estructura demográfica
    dos países americanos (PAU), 89
Caribbean, xi xii, 2, 4, 13, 24, 42, 43, 45,
    46, 47, 116, 118, 122, 123, 136, 142, 157,
    159, 162, 172, 189, 191, 200, 201, 206,
    207, 208, 209, 210, 211, 212, 213, 215,
    216, 229, 231, 235, 236, 237, 239, 246,
    257, 258, 269, 270, 276–77, 279, 280, 286,
    290, 294, 296, 298, 302
Caribbean Common Market, 239
Caribbean Community (CARICOM), 4, 195,
    196, 226, 238, 239
Caribbean Connection, 235–39
Caribbean Corn Islands, 192
Caribbean Free Trade Association
    (CARIFTA), 4, 238–39
Caribbean Group, 300
Caribbean movements for union, 235–39
Caribbean Regional Drug Abuse Abatement
    Programme, 196
Caribbean situation (1950), 276–77
Caribbean Subregion, 156
Carnegie, Andrew, 18
Carta aérea (PAU), 96
Cartagena de Indias, 159, 166, 205, 209,
    214, 217
Cartagena Group, 4, 209, 234, 297
Cartago (Costa Rica), 192, 266
Carta de Jamaica, 6
Carter, Jimmy, 20, 173, 200, 296
Castelli, Juan José, 5
Castillian, 254
Castillo Armas, Carlos, 278
Castries (St. Lucia), 157, 213, 214
Castro, Fidel, 45, 46, 47, 48, 50, 52, 164,
    173, 201, 234, 259, 261, 274, 279, 280,
    282
Castro forces, 136
Castro Revolution. *See* Cuban Revolution
Catholic political thought (medieval), 255
CECE (OAS). *See* Special Committee to
    Study the Formulation of New Measures
    of Economic Cooperation (OAS)
CEIFI (OAS). *See* Special Committee for an
    Inter-American Financial Institution
    (CEIFI) (OSA)
CEMLA. *See* Center of Latin American
    Monetary Studies (CEMLA)
Censo de América, 89
Centennial Declaration, 163
Center of Colombian Studies (Bogotá,
    Colombia), 209
Center of Latin American Monetary Studies
    (CEMLA), 92, 114
Central America, xi, 2, 3, 4, 5, 7, 9, 17, 40,
    47, 49, 50, 62, 85, 91, 93, 103, 110, 158,
    159, 160, 161, 163, 164, 169, 170, 191,
    192, 193, 200, 201, 204, 205, 206, 207,

216, 225, 226, 232, 233, 263, 266, 270, 275, 288, 289, 294, 297

Central American Bank for Economic Integration, 133

Central American Common Market (MCCA), 58, 83, 84, 232–33, 299

Central American Court of Justice (1908–1917), 192–93, 213, 243, 266

Central American Defense Council, 125

Central American Group, 299

Central American Monetary Council, 299

Central American Parliament, 225

Central American Peace: 1907, 191; 1990, 225, 233

Central American Peace efforts (1985–1990), 204, 205, 206, 233, 297

Central American refugees, 158, 159, 161, 162, 163, 205

Central American School of Industrial Chemistry, 91

Central Intelligence Agency (CIA) (United States), 43, 53, 173, 257, 270, 278

Central Treaty Organization (CENTO), 29, 272

Centro de Altos Estudios Militares (Peru), 253

Centro de Desarrollo de la Universidad Central de Venezuela (CENDES). *See* Development Center of the Central University of Venezuela (CENDES)

Cervantes, Miguel de, 36

Césaire, Aimé, 237

Chaco, 22

Chaco War, 21, 22, 41, 215, 266

Chamorro, General Emiliano, 192

Chamorro, Violeta, 225

Chamorro-Bryan Treaty. *See* Bryan-Chamorro Treaty

Chapultepec, 41, 64, 65, 115, 139

Chapultepec Conference. *See* Inter-American Conference on Problems of War and Peace (Chapultepec Conference, 1945)

Charles III, king of Spain, 4, 5

Charter of Punta del Este, 56, 62, 85, 253, 261, 296

Charter of the Organization of American States (original), 29, 30, 31, 32–38, 41, 42, 44, 53, 55, 56, 59, 61, 62, 67, 71, 72, 98, 100, 101, 116, 117, 118, 123, 124, 129, 135, 139, 143, 144, 149, 167, 176, 181, 183, 184, 188, 199, 209, 216, 217, 243, 245, 249, 252, 254, 255, 256, 257, 260, 262, 267, 269, 271, 272, 273, 274, 277, 280, 282, 283, 286, 290, 294, 295; revised charter (1967), 143, 144, 146, 147–87, 199, 208, 209, 211, 216, 243, 248, 271, 273, 289, 296; revised charter (1985), 165, 212, 215–24, 226, 256, 286

Chase, Gilbert, 93

Chiari, Roberto F., 284

Chicago, 92

Chile, 1, 4, 5, 6, 7, 9, 10, 11, 17, 24, 26, 36, 49, 50, 52, 53, 54, 60, 62, 78, 84, 86, 87, 90, 91, 104, 106, 109, 110, 113, 121, 124, 137, 142, 143, 144, 145, 163, 168, 169, 170, 171, 172, 187, 189, 190, 195, 200, 202, 203, 206, 209, 229, 231, 232, 253, 254, 255, 265, 269, 272, 286, 289, 290, 296, 299

Chilembve, John, 236

China, 22, 45, 47, 48, 200

China, Republic of (Taiwan), 90, 163

Christian Democracy (El Salvador), 206

Christian Natural Law, 263

Chronology of the Pan American Highway (PAU), 84

Ciencia interamericana (PAU), 95

CIME. *See* Intergovernmental Committee for European Migrations

Clark Memorandum, 15, 20

Clayton-Bulwer Treaty, 3

Clulow, Carlos, 81

Code of Private International Law, 242

Code of Public International Law, 242

Codification of International Law, 241–44

Cold Shoulder policy, 200

Cold War. *See* East-West conflict

Collective action, 51, 149, 259, 272

Collective security, 6, 9, 10, 24, 28, 29, 31, 32, 33, 34, 35, 40, 41, 43, 45, 46, 47, 48, 52, 57, 64, 120, 124, 127, 133, 136, 137, 139, 143, 144, 145, 149, 157, 163, 167, 201, 211, 212, 216, 219, 223, 241, 257, 259, 265, 271–91, 293

Colombia, 1, 2, 3, 4, 7, 10, 30, 32, 36, 48, 49, 53, 60, 61, 62, 74, 78, 83, 84, 87, 91, 104, 107, 109, 110, 122, 124, 145, 159, 164, 166, 168–69, 170, 172, 189, 195, 205, 206, 209, 229, 230, 231, 232, 233, 235, 255, 269, 281, 282, 283, 284, 286, 297, 298, 299

Colombian Institute for Technical Research Abroad (ICETEX), 92

Colonial Exhibition (Paris, 1931), 237

Colonial territories in the American hemisphere. *See* Non-Autonomous territories located on the American continent

Colossus of the North. *See* United States

Columbus, xii

Comisión Especial Coordinadora para la América Latina (CECLA). *See* Special Coordinating Committee for Latin America (CECLA)

Comité Interamericano de Educación (CIE). *See* Inter-American Education Committee (CIE)

Commemorative Meeting of the Presidents of the American Republics, 60, 100, 112–13, 129, 139

Commercial Bureau of the American Republics, 15, 63, 70–71, 73

Commission of Investigation and Conciliation (Costa Rica–Nicaragua), 278

Commodity series (PAU), 96

Common action. *See* Collective action

Common law, 254

Common Market of the Southern Cone. *See* MERCOSUR

Commonwealth Caribbean, 42, 103, 142, 143, 208, 209, 210, 212, 236, 238, 239

Communism/Communists (International), 29, 40, 41, 45, 47, 49, 53, 56, 127, 128, 205, 206, 270, 277, 278, 281, 299

Comparative law, 242

Conciliation, 7, 41, 53, 266, 267

Confederación Antillana, 235–36

Confederation, 6, 7, 8, 9, 11, 13

Conference on Education and Economic and Social Development in Latin America (Santiago de Chile, 1962), 94

Congress of Jurists (Lima, 1877–1879). *See* Juridical Congress of Lima

Congress of Lima: First (1848), 9; Second (1865), 10

Congress of Panama (1826), 4, 6, 7, 8, 9, 11, 13, 123, 233, 235, 265, 271

Congresses of Negro Writers and Artists, 237

Constitutional Agreement of Sela (Latin American Economic System), 231

"Constitutional Government" (Dominican Republic), 288

Constitutional law, 115

Constitutional monarch (Brazil), 255

Constitution of 1826. *See* Bolivian Constitution of 1826

Constitutions Series (PAU), 82

Consultative Emergency Committee on Political Defense, 127

Consultative Pact. *See* Convention for the Maintenance, Preservation and Reestablishment of Peace

Contadora Group, 4, 159, 160, 161, 205, 209, 233, 234, 275, 297, 299

Contadora Support Group, 160, 161, 205, 209, 233, 275, 297, 299

Continental Congress of Santiago (1856), 3, 9

Continentalization. *See* Latin-Americanization

Continental solidarity, 1, 6, 8, 10, 23, 24, 34, 41, 45, 47, 49, 64, 116, 145, 212, 218, 219

Contras (Nicaragua), 205, 225, 253, 275

Convention for the Maintenance, Preservation and Reestablishment of Peace (1936), 22, 267, 271, 272, 294

Convention for the Protection of Flora, Fauna and the Natural Scenic Beauties of America (1976), 156, 214, 243

Convention of International Law, 242

Convention on Diplomatic Asylum, 247

Convention on Duties and Rights of States in the Event of Civil Strife, 19, 33, 271, 275, 276, 277, 280, 283; Additional Protocol, 277, 283, 286; Protocol to the Convention, 275

Convention on Naturalized Citizens, 16

Convention on Pecuniary Claims (1906), 16

Convention on Rights and Duties of States, 21, 33

Convention on Territorial Asylum (Caracas, 1954), 275, 277, 283

Convention on the Inter-American Institute of Agricultural Sciences, 112, 113

Convention that Defines Torture as an International Crime (1980), 157, 243

Convention to Coordinate, Extend and Assure the Fulfillment of the Existing Treaties Between the American States, 268

Cooling-off treaties, 265

Cooperative movement, 86

Copenhagen, 85

Corinth, 6

Corinto Pact (Costa Rica), 191

Cortes (Spain), 254

Costa Rica, 1, 3, 4, 10, 17, 30, 36, 46, 54, 79, 82, 86, 91, 106, 109, 110, 112, 113, 114, 124, 139, 155, 156, 168, 169, 170, 171, 191, 192, 203, 207, 213, 224, 233, 247, 248, 249, 252, 259, 260, 261, 266, 269, 275, 276, 278, 279, 280, 282, 289, 299; Nicaragua (1955–1956), 278; Nicaraguan conflict (1948–1949), 275–76

Council of Europe, 189

Council of the Organization of American States (COAS), 37, 39, 44–45, 46, 49, 50, 51, 52, 53, 58, 59, 60, 61, 62, 63, 64, 65, 67, 68, 69, 70, 71, 72, 74, 75, 76, 77, 78, 80, 81, 89, 90, 95, 97, 98, 99, 100, 101, 104, 106, 107, 112, 115, 116, 117, 118, 119, 120, 121, 122, 123, 124, 125, 127, 129, 138, 143, 144, 146, 167, 176, 177, 181, 182, 189, 190–91, 243, 246, 248, 252, 257, 258, 259, 260, 261, 269, 272, 276, 277, 278, 279, 280, 281, 282, 283, 285, 286, 290, 296

Countries not members of the organization. *See* Non-American Governments/States

Covarrubias, Diego de, 263

CREFAL. *See* Regional Center of

Fundamental Education for Latin America (CREFAL)
Cristiani, Alfredo, 206, 227
Cuba, Cubans, 1, 3, 7, 15, 16, 19, 20, 40, 41, 45, 46, 47, 48, 49, 50, 51, 52, 55, 57, 58, 63, 80, 82, 103, 108, 120, 121, 127, 136, 137, 144, 163, 164, 165, 168, 169, 172, 173, 187, 201, 216, 235, 236, 246, 259, 262, 269, 270, 274, 275, 276, 279, 280, 281, 282, 286, 288, 289, 290, 296
Cuban expulsion from the OAS (1961–1962), 280–81
Cuban Missile Crisis (1962), 51, 59, 137, 201, 274, 281–82, 286
Cuban Revolution, 46, 118, 123, 136, 140, 201, 246, 252, 254, 258, 261, 275, 279–80, 286, 295, 296, 302
Cuban situation (1960), 280
Cultural heritage of America, 155, 159
Cultural standards (OAS), 35, 153, 179, 185, 210, 216, 219, 223
Curaçao, 238, 270
Cyprus, 72
Czechoslovakia, 23

Darien gap. 74
D'Aubuisson, Roberto, 206, 227
Dávila, Carlos, 78, 206
De facto governments, 145, 243, 249, 250–54, 259, 262
Debt. *See* International Debt
Declaración del Centenario. *See* Centennial Declaration
Declaration for the Defense of Human Rights, 244
Declaration of Bogotá (1966), 62
Declaration of Bogotá of CIECC (1980), 157, 215
Declaration of Brasilia, 158, 215
Declaration of Buenos Aires, 4, 230
Declaration of Caracas, 245, 257
Declaration of Cartagena, 233
Declaration on Extradition and Preventive Measures in Drug Trafficking, 161
Declaration of Guatemala, 160, 215
Declaration of the International Charter of Rights and Duties of Man. *See* American Declaration of the Rights and Duties of Man
Declaration of the International Rights and Duties of Man. *See* American Declaration of the Rights and Duties of Man
Declaration of La Paz, 157, 204
Declaration of Lima, 23
Declaration of Mexico, 27
Declaration of Panama, 23
Declaration of the Peoples of the Americas, 253

Declaration on the Principles of Representative Democracy and Human Rights, 45, 46
Declaration on "The Question of the Malvinas Islands," 216
Declaration of San José, 47, 280
Declaration of Santiago, 258, 259, 260, 279
Declaration of Satisfaction on the Beagle, 158
Declaration of Solidarity for the Preservation of the Political Integrity of the Americas against the Intervention of International Communism, 40
Declaration on Strengthening the Inter-American Relations in the Field of Finance and Trade, 158, 215, 243–44
Declaration of the United Nations, 25
Declaration of Washington, 45
Delvalle, Eric, 174
Del Valle, José Cecilio, 5
Democracy. *See* Representative Democracy
Denmark, 87, 89, 90
D'Escoto Brockmann, Miguel, 226
Development Center of the Central University of Venezuela (CENDES), 104
Díaz, Porfirio, 191, 192
Diccionario de la literatura latinoamericana (PAU), 93
Diego, José de, 236
Discovery of America, xii
District of Columbia. *See* Washington, D.C.
"Dollar Diplomacy," 14, 250
Dominica, 1, 157, 162, 166, 209, 238, 239
Dominican Order, 255
Dominican problems (1960–1962), 280
Dominican Republic/Dominicans, 1, 14, 15, 17, 44, 46, 47, 48, 49, 51, 52, 53, 54, 55, 56, 59, 78, 82, 83, 91, 103, 106, 112, 120, 121, 122, 124, 127, 136, 137, 143, 164, 169, 170, 201, 203, 216, 224, 236, 246, 250, 252, 254, 259, 260, 263, 269, 270, 276, 279, 280, 282, 283, 286, 287, 288, 289, 290, 296, 298, 301; Haiti controversy (1963–1965), 282–83
Dominican situation (1965), 286–88
Draft Convention on the Effective Exercise of Representative Democracy, 259, 261
Drago, Luis María (Drago Doctrine), 14, 250, 257
Dreier, John C., 117
Drug Abuse and trafficking, xii, 158, 159, 160, 161, 162, 163, 164, 173, 174, 193, 194, 195, 196, 197, 212, 216, 241, 263, 286, 299, 301
Drug Enforcement Agency (United States), 173
Duarte, Inés, 206
Duarte, José Napoleón, 206

Du Bois, W.E.B., 236
Dulles, John Foster, 40, 123, 277
Dumbarton Oaks Proposals, 25
Dutch area in the Caribbean. See
    Netherlands Antilles
Dutch-speaking, 1, 42

East, 168
East Caribbean Common Market (ECCM),
    238, 239
Eastern Block, 277
Eastern Europe, 163, 206
East Indian, 235
East-West conflict, 135, 137, 299
Economic Agreement of Bogotá. See
    General Economic Pact of Bogotá
Economic Charter of the Americas, 28
Economic Commission for Latin America
    (ECLA) (CEPAL) (United Nations), 62,
    70, 83, 89, 114, 129, 139, 229
Economic Conference of the OAS, 100, 129,
    139
Economic integration. See Latin-American
    Economic Integration
Economic and Social Act of Rio de Janeiro
    (1965), 145
Economic Society of the Friends of the
    Country (Bogotá, Colombia), 209
Economic standards (OAS), 149–52, 185,
    216, 219, 223
Ecuador, 1, 4, 9, 10, 36, 41, 49, 50, 52, 53,
    54, 60, 62, 78, 83, 84, 91, 93, 104, 109,
    110, 120, 122, 124, 157, 164, 168, 169,
    170, 171, 174, 185, 189, 202, 203, 207,
    228, 229, 231, 232, 246, 247, 251, 269,
    270, 278, 289, 290, 299
Educational, scientific and cultural standards
    (OAS), 153, 210
Egaña, Juan, 5, 6
Eisenhower, Dwight D., 130, 139
Ejército de Libración Nacional (ELN)
    (Argentina), 57
El Condor mountain range, 171, 203, 289,
    290
El cooperativismo agrario en América
    Latina (PAU), 86
El desarrollo industrial y el financiamiento
    del sector privado (PAU), 83
Elections. See Monitoring national elections
El movimiento cooperativo en América
    Latina (PAU), 86
El Paso, Texas, 103
El Salvador, 1, 2, 4, 10, 36, 54, 58, 79, 91,
    109, 112, 124, 143, 157, 160, 161, 162,
    169, 170, 173, 189, 191, 192, 202, 205,
    206, 207, 224, 227, 232, 233, 253, 269,
    287, 288

Emancipation. See Spanish American
    Revolution
Emergency Advisory Committee for Political
    Defense (1941), 251, 273–74
Encounter of Two Worlds. See Fifth
    Centennial of Columbus' Discovery of
    America
Encuesta anual sobre el intercambio
    interamericano de personas (PAU), 92
England. See United Kingdom
English. See British
English colony, 211
English-speaking, 1, 42, 237
English-speaking Caribbean, 196, 237
English tradition. See British tradition
English Translations of Latin American
    Literature (PAU), 93
Enlace (IACW), 106
Enlightenment, 115
Enterprise for the Americas, 164, 299
Escuela Nacional de Antropología e Historia
    (Mexico), 88
Escuela Técnica Superior de Ingenieros de
    Montes (Spain), 90
Esequibo area (Guyana), 142
Esquipulas Agreements, 225, 275
Estadística (IASI), 89
Estrada, Genaro (Estrada Doctrine), 250,
    252, 257
Estrada, Juan, 192
Estrada Cabrera, Manuel, 191
Ethiopia, 22
Euratom, 95, 127, 189
European Coal and Steel Community
    (ECSC), 127, 189
European Common Market (EEC), 80–81,
    84, 127, 138, 189
European Community (EC), 2, 4, 81, 127,
    162, 163, 171, 172, 230, 234, 239
European Convention on Human Rights,
    189
European Declaration of the Rights of Man,
    116
European Free Trade Area (EFTA), 81, 238,
    239
European governments, 81
Europe/Europeans, ix, 2, 8, 14, 22, 26, 27,
    28, 40, 47, 80, 81, 85, 105, 127, 129, 130,
    137, 138, 140, 141, 142, 163, 189, 200,
    230, 234, 237, 239, 244, 255, 267, 295,
    296, 299
Extra-continental conflict, 272
Extra-continental peoples/powers/states,
    211, 270, 275, 281, 291
Extraordinary International American
    Conference on Conciliation and
    Arbitration, 20, 266

Fair Neighbor policy, xi, 200, 295
Falkland Islands. See Malvinas Islands

Far East, 28
Farabundo Martí National Liberation Front (FLNFM) (El Salvador), 206
Fascism, 299
Federal West Indian Constitution, 238
Federation of the Andes, 7
Federation of Private Sector Entities of Central America and Panama, 299
Fifth Centennial of Columbus' Discovery of America, xii, 158, 159, 161, 162, 235
Finland, 90
First Conference on the Law of the Sea, 100
First Decade of Regional Programs in Education, Science and Culture (OAS), 157, 215
First Inter-American Conference of Experts on Indian Life in the Americas, 109
First International American Scientific Congress, 97
First Latin American Workshop on Narcotics Public Awareness, 196
First Republic, 1873–1874 (Spain), 236, 251
First South American Congress on Private International Law (1888–1889), 11, 12, 242
Florence, 90
Flores, Juan José, 10
Florida, 3
Food and Agriculture Organization (FAO) (United Nations), 83, 88, 105, 114; Seventh Regional Conference of FAO for Latin America (Rio de Janeiro, 1962), 86
Ford, Gerald, 200
Ford (in Argentina), 231
Ford Foundation, 113
Fordney Tariff Act (United States), 27
Fort-de-France, 237
Fort McNair, 125
France, 7, 10, 23, 26, 90, 102, 141, 162, 207, 235, 237
Free access to information, 245
Freedom of Action of the States Parties to the Inter-American Treaty of Reciprocal Assistance to Normalize or Conduct Their Relations with the Government of Cuba at the Level and in the Manner Each State Deems Advisable, 169
Freedom of association and freedom of expression of workers, 244
Frei Montalva, Eduardo, 142
French, 10, 14, 96, 235, 238, 297
French Antilles, 24, 103, 237, 238
French Community, 238
French Guiana, 24, 103, 238
French National Assembly, 237
French Revolution, 7, 162, 255
French St. Domingue, 235
French-speaking, 1, 208, 237

French West Indies. *See* French Antilles
Frondizi, Arturo, 252
Fueros (Spain, Spanish America), 254
Fujimori, Alberto, 234, 301
Fundamental rights and duties of states, 149
Fund for Special Operations (IDB), 130, 131, 132, 133

García Amador, F. V., 11, 100, 263, 274
García Godoy, Héctor, 55, 288
García Márquez, Gabriel, 235
Garvey, Marcus Aurelius, 236
General Agreement on Tariffs and Trade (GATT), 81, 164, 172
General Assembly, 44, 144, 146, 153, 154–67, 175–76, 177, 178, 180, 181, 182, 183, 184, 186, 193, 195, 201, 207, 209, 221, 222, 223, 243, 247, 296; First Regular Session, 155, 207, 213; Second Regular Session, 155; Third Regular Session, 155, 216; Fourth Regular Session, 156, 217; Fifth Regular Session, 156; Sixth Regular Session, 156, 214, 216; Seventh Regular Session, 156, 216, 249; Eighth Regular Session, 156, 213, 214; Ninth Regular Session, 157, 204, 215, 247, 249; Tenth Regular Session, 157, 204, 214, 215; Eleventh Regular Session, 157, 213, 214; Twelfth Regular Session, 157–58, 204, 213; Thirteenth Regular Session, 158, 204, 214, 215; Fourteenth Regular Session, 158, 193, 204, 215; Fifteenth Regular Session, 159, 204, 205, 214; Sixteenth Regular Session, 159–60, 195, 204, 205, 215; Seventeenth Regular Session, 160–61, 204, 205, 214–15; Eighteenth Regular Session, 161–62, 204, 205, 213, 215; Nineteenth Regular Session, 162–63, 204, 205, 215; Twentieth Regular Session, 163–64, 204, 205, 209; Twenty-first Regular Session, 164–65, 251, 254, 300; First Special Session, 165; Second Special Session, 166; Third Special Session, 166, 214, 244; Fourth Special Session, 166; Fifth Special Session, 166; Sixth Special Session, 166; Seventh Special Session, 166; Eighth Special Session, 166; Ninth Special Session, 166; Tenth Special Session, 166; Eleventh Special Session, 166; Twelfth Special Session, 166; Thirteenth Special Session, 166; Fourteenth Special Session, 166–67, 216; Fifteenth Special Session, 167
General Belgrano (Argentine cruiser), 203, 289
General Convention of Inter-American

Conciliation, 20, 266; Additional Protocol, 267

General Declaration of Neutrality of the American Republics, 23

General Economic Pact of Bogotá (1948), 30, 139

General Secretariat, 32, 37, 39, 67, 68, 72, 73, 78, 80, 104, 138, 141, 144, 146, 147, 153, 156, 159, 161, 177, 178, 181–82, 183, 184, 186, 195, 202, 212, 213, 222, 225, 289, 298; Administrative Tribunal, 186, 187, 213; Advisory Committee on Administrative and Budgetary Matters, 186; Advisory Group, 186; Cabinet, 186; Department of Development and Codification of International Law, 186; Department of Educational Affairs, 186; Department of Fellowship and Training, 186; Department of Human Resources, 187; Department of General Legal Services, 186; Department of Legal Publications and Information, 186; Department of Management Systems, 187; Department of Material Resources, 187; Department of Program-Budget, 187; Department of Regional Development, 186; Department of Scientific and Technological Affairs, 186; Executive Office, 75–76, 77, 78; Executive Secretary for Economic and Social Affairs, 166, 182, 186; Executive Secretary for Education, Science and Culture, 166, 182, 186; Inspector General, 186; Museum of Modern Art of Latin America, 186; Office of the Treasurer, 187; (OAS) Offices abroad (see Offices of the General Secretariat in the Member States and Europe); Offices of the General Secretariat in the Member States and Europe, 75, 79–81, 141, 157, 158, 166, 186, 226, 228

General Treaty for Central American Economic Integration, 299

General Treaty of Inter-American Arbitration, 20, 266, 267

Geneva, 81, 87, 294

Georgetown (Guyana), 238

Georgia, 156

German Foundation for Development Aid (Deutsche Stiftung für Entwicklungshilfe), 86

Germanic tradition, 254

Germany, 23, 24, 26, 27, 87, 90, 141, 207, 251, 297

Getulio Vargas Foundation (Brazil), 89

Godoy, Manuel, 5

Gondra, Manuel, 19

Gondra Treaty, 19, 266, 267

Good Neighbor policy, xi, 2, 15, 20, 21, 22, 24, 25, 27, 43, 199, 200, 284, 294, 295, 296, 297

Goulart, João, 54

"Government of National Reconstruction" (Dominican Rep.), 288

Gracias a Dios (Honduras), 270, 278

Greater Colombia, 6, 7, 10

Greece/Greeks, 6, 86, 115

Grenada, 1, 53, 156, 170, 172, 209, 211, 215, 239, 263, 297

Grinnell College, 92

Grito de Lares (Puerto Rico), 236

Grito de Yaya (Cuba), 236

Gromyko, Andrei, 25

Group of 77, 234

Guadalajara (Mexico), 100, 234, 235

Guadeloupe, 237, 238

Guantánamo Bay, 300

Guatemala, 1, 4, 7, 10, 11, 15, 36, 40, 42, 43, 47, 53, 83, 88, 89, 91, 100, 103, 109, 110, 112, 113, 120, 124, 137, 142, 143, 159, 161, 169, 170, 174, 185, 191, 193, 195, 201, 205, 212, 216, 224, 226, 227, 232–33, 246, 251, 253, 257, 263, 269, 270, 276, 277–78, 282, 286, 295

Guatemala, Captaincy-General of, 232

Guatemala invasion (1954), 277–78

Guerrilla/guerrilla warfare, 125, 169, 206, 274

Guevara, Ernesto (Ché), 57

Gulf of Fonseca (Honduras), 192

A Guide to Latin American Music, 93

Guyana, 1, 43, 142, 167, 207, 208, 209, 210, 212, 213, 217, 224, 238, 239, 298

Hague, 266

Hague Court of Arbitration, 192

Hague Peace Conference: First (1899), 16; Second (1907), 192

Haiti, x, 1, 7, 14, 17, 20, 46, 49, 50, 83, 85, 96, 103, 107, 109, 120, 121, 124, 136, 144, 169, 170, 224, 226, 227, 235, 237, 238, 246, 269, 270, 276, 279, 282, 283, 290, 300, 301, 302

Hamburg (Germany), ix

Havana, 18, 19, 23, 47, 51, 52, 57, 64, 105, 107, 111, 120, 242, 251, 259, 271, 275, 276, 300

Havana Convention of 1928. See Convention on Duties and Rights of States in the Event of Civil Strife

Hawaiian Islands, 44

Haya de la Torre, Víctor Raúl, 253, 269

Hay-Buneau Varilla Convention (1903), 284

Hayes, Rutherford B., 265

Hernández Colón, Rafael, 239

Herter, Christian, 47

His Britannic Majesty. *See* United Kingdom
Hise-Silva Treaty, 3
Hispanic America, x, 8, 36, 37
Hispanic American solidarity, 8
Hispanic civilization. *See* Hispanic tradition
Hispanic tradition, 8, 34, 36, 37, 77, 254, 302
Holy Alliance, 7, 9, 14, 40, 251
Honduras, 1, 3, 4, 15, 36, 54, 58, 60, 82, 83, 84, 91, 107, 109, 110, 112, 120, 124, 139, 157, 161, 169, 170, 191, 192, 202, 224, 232, 233, 246, 252, 260, 269, 270, 278, 279, 282, 288
Honduras–Nicaragua border dispute (1957), 278–79
Hong Kong, 163
Hostos, Eugenio Maria de, 236
Houphouet-Boigny, Felix, 237
House of the Americas, 18
Huerta, Victoriano, 17, 250
Human rights, xii, 28, 45, 46, 49, 53, 115, 116, 117, 118, 119, 120, 142, 144, 156, 162, 163, 164, 174, 180, 184, 187, 188, 189, 193, 201, 206, 210, 212, 217, 241, 244, 245, 246, 247, 248, 249, 253, 254, 255, 258, 259, 260, 262, 263, 270, 283, 294
Human Rights (Draft), 248

Iberian countries, xii
Iberian heritage. *See* Hispanic tradition
Iberian peninsula, 8
Ibero-American Summit Conference, 234–35
ICEM. *See* Intergovernmental Committee for European Migration (United Nations)
Inca Garcilaso de la Vega, 93
Independence (Latin American), xi, 3, 4–5, 6, 14, 17
Indian/Indians/Indian affairs. *See* American Indians
Indian legislation, 110
Indices de precios al consumidor (costo de la vida) de las naciones americanas (PAU), 89
Infantes (Spain), 5
Informal Meetings of Ministers of Foreign Affairs (MCMFA), 59, 274
Informe técnico (IAIAS/IICA), 114
Institute of Ibero-American Studies (Institut für Iberoamerika-Kunde, Hamburg), ix
Institutional Act (Dominican Republic), 288
Institutional Revolutionary Party (PRI) (Mexico), 254
Instituto Caro y Cuervo (Colombia), 93
Instituto de Crédito Territorial (Colombia), 84
Instituto de Relaciones Laborales (Colombia), 87

Institutos de investigación tecnológica— informe preliminar (PAU), 84
Integral development (OAS), 219, 220, 221, 224
Integration. *See* Latin American economic integration
Integration and development of Inter American law, 162, 244
Inter-American Action Program of Rio de Janeiro. *See* Inter-American Program of Action of Rio de Janeiro against the Illicit Use and Production of Narcotic Drugs and Psychotropic Substances and Traffic Therein
Inter-American affairs. *See* Inter American relations
Inter-American Agreements, 69, 203
Inter-American Alliance to Combat Illicit Drug Trafficking, 193
Inter-American assemblies/gatherings, 15, 18, 26, 28, 46, 53, 56
Inter-American Assemblies of Ministers of Education: Second, 99; Third, 94
Inter-American Association for Economic and Cultural Development, 112
Inter-American Bank (IDB), 15, 114, 128, 129, 140
Inter-American Board of Agricultural Defense, 111
Inter-American Center for Advanced Studies in Journalism for Latin America (CIESPAL), 96
Inter-American Center of Capacitation in Business Administration (CICAP), 157
Inter-American Center of Rural Education (CIER) (Venezuela), 94
Inter-American Center for Teaching in the Field of Statistics (CIENES) (PAU–IASI), 89–90
Inter-American character, 73
Inter-American Charter of Social Guarantees, 30, 242–43
Inter-American Childrens' Congresses, 105. *See also* Pan American Child Congresses
Inter-American Childrens' Institute, 20, 74, 101, 104–5, 160, 183, 186, 195; Forty-third Meeting (Montevideo), 104; Thirty-eighth Meeting (Lima), 104
Inter-American Cocoa Agency, 112
Inter-American Commission for the Protection of Human Rights, 190
Inter-American Commission of Women (UACW), 20, 30, 69, 74, 98, 101, 104, 105–7, 127, 160, 183, 186, 195; First Conference (Havana, 1930), 105
Inter-American Commission on Agriculture, 111
Inter-American Commission on Human

Rights (IACHR), 37, 44, 58, 82, 114, 115–
20, 123, 146, 153, 156, 157, 158, 159,
160, 163, 166, 178, 179, 180, 184, 186,
187, 189, 190, 191, 222, 243, 244, 245–46,
247, 248, 249, 262, 269, 279, 287, 294;
Thirteenth Period of Sessions, 119;
Fourteenth Period of Sessions, 119;
Forty-ninth Period of Sessions (new
regulations), 247
Inter-American Committee for Cultural
Action, 61, 62, 93, 147, 179
Inter-American Committee of Personal
Representatives of the Presidents (CIRP),
90, 113, 126, 129, 139
Inter-American Committee on Methods for
the Special Solution of Conflicts. *See*
Inter-American Peace Committee
Inter-American Committee on Peaceful
Settlement, 176, 177, 183, 221, 224, 271,
298
Inter-American Committee on the Alliance
for Progress (ICAP), ix, 61, 62, 83, 84, 89,
147, 184; Ninth Meeting (Bogotá, 1966),
62
Inter-American Community/Family, 168,
169
Inter-American Conference for the
Consolidation of Peace (1936), 21, 22, 23,
27, 41, 128, 187, 244, 257, 267, 268, 271,
273
Inter-American Conference for the
Maintenance of Continental Peace and
Security (1947), 28, 29, 42, 268, 272
Inter-American Conference of Ministers of
Agriculture, Ninth Conference, 160
Inter-American Conference of Ministers of
Labor (1963), 87
Inter-American Conference of Ministers of
Labor regarding the Alliance for Progress,
100
Inter-American Conference on Problems of
War and Peace (Chapultepec Conference,
1945), 26, 27, 28, 29, 30, 41, 50, 64, 115,
123, 128, 139, 187, 244, 247, 251, 268,
272, 294
Inter-American Congresses of Public
Health, 98
Inter-American controversies, 136
Inter-American Convention which Defines
Torture as an International Crime, 214,
215
Inter-American Convention on Extradition,
155, 156, 157, 214, 243
Inter-American Convention on the Forced
Disappearance of Persons, 162, 244
Inter-American Convention on the Granting
of Civil Rights to Women, 30, 107
Inter-American Convention on the Granting
of Political Rights to Women, 30, 107

Inter-American Convention on Human
Rights. *See* American Convention on
Human Rights
Inter-American Convention on Immunities
of Jurisdiction of the States. *See* Inter-
American Convention on the
Jurisdictional Immunity of States
Inter-American Convention of Judicial
Assistance on Criminal Matters. *See* Inter-
American Convention on Judicial
Assistance in Penal Matters
Inter-American Convention on Judicial
Assistance in Penal Matters, 160, 161,
215, 244
Inter-American Convention on the
Jurisdictional Immunity of States, 158,
159, 214, 244
Inter-American Convention to Prevent and
Punish Acts of Terrorism Taking the Form
of Crimes Against Persons and Related
Extortion that are of International
Significance, 166, 213–14, 244
Inter-American Convention to Prevent and
Punish Torture, 159, 244
Inter-American cooperation, 41, 97, 99, 149,
150, 151, 153, 156, 159, 160, 231
Inter-American Council for Education,
Science and Culture (CIECC), 144, 153,
155, 156, 157, 159, 160, 161, 162, 165,
175, 176, 179, 181, 183, 222, 243, 246,
248, 296; Eleventh Ordinary Session, 157,
215; FEMCIECC, 161, 162; Permanent
Executive Commission, 179
Inter-American Council of Jurists (IACJ), 17,
61, 62, 82, 98, 115, 116, 123, 144, 145,
176, 179, 180, 190, 190, 242, 243, 245,
246, 248, 252, 257, 259, 277; First
Meeting (1950), 188, 243; Second Meeting
(1953), 243; Third Meeting(1956), 243;
Fourth Meeting (1959), 189, 243, 248;
Fifth Meeting (1965), 243
Inter-American Council of Music (CIDEM),
93
Inter-American Course of Administration of
Programs of Social Welfare, 89
Inter-American Court, 115, 213
Inter-American Court for the Protection of
Human Rights, 116, 189, 243
Inter-American Court of Human Rights,
154, 156, 157, 159, 160, 166, 186, 187–93,
213, 214, 243, 245, 246, 248–49, 252, 294;
Third Regular Session (1980), 249
Inter-American Court of Justice, 269
"Inter-American Court to Protect the Rights
of Man," 248
Inter-American Cultural Committee. *See*
Inter-American Committee for Cultural
Action

Inter-American Cultural Council (ICC), 61, 62, 98, 123, 147, 179

Inter-American Data Bank (CICAD), 196–97

Inter-American Declaration on the Rights of the Family, 158, 215, 244

Inter-American Defense Board (IADB), 37, 50, 74, 114, 123–25, 183, 186, 269, 281

Inter-American Defense College (IADB), 125

Inter-American Development Bank (IDB), 70, 83, 85, 128–33; 295

Inter-American Documentation Center (CICAD), 196–97

Inter-American Drug Abuse and Control Commission (CICAD), 160, 186, 187, 193–97, 213, 215; Inter-American Information Center (CICAD), 195

Inter-American Economic Conferences, 98, 129

Inter-American Economic and Social Council (IA-ECOSOC), ix, 17, 61, 62, 68, 69, 82, 83, 84, 87, 98, 110, 123, 126, 128, 129, 139, 140, 141, 144, 146, 147, 153, 156, 159, 160, 161, 162, 165, 175, 176, 178, 179, 181, 183, 222, 243, 246, 248, 295, 296; Extraordinary Meeting at the Ministerial Level (1954), 128; First Annual Meeting (Mexico City, 1962), 83; Fourth Special Ministerial Meeting, 146; Permanent Executive Commission (CEPCIES), 161, 178, 184

Inter-American Education Committee (CIE), 105

Inter-American Financial and Economic Advisory Committee (FEAC), 128

Inter-American Financial Fund for Haiti, 160

Inter-American Force, 53–55, 125, 145, 201, 254, 287, 288

Inter-American Fund for Emergency Situations (FONDEM), 157

Inter-American Harbor Conferences, 99; First (San José/Costa Rica), 99; Second (Mar del Plata, Argentina), 100

Inter-American High Commission, 17

Inter-American Indian Action, 156, 158, 159

Inter-American Indian Conferences and Congresses, 98; First Inter-American Conference of Experts on Indian Life in the Americas, 109; Third Congress, 99; Fourth Congress, 100

Inter-American Indian Institute (IAII), 24, 89, 101, 109–11, 160, 183, 195

Inter-American Information System (CICAC), 196

Inter-American Institute for Cooperation in Agriculture (IICA), 160, 183

Inter-American Institute for Housing and Planning (CINVA), 84, 85

Inter-American Institute for the Financing of Cooperatives, 107

Inter-American Institute of Agricultural Sciences, now Inter-American Institute for Cooperation in Agriculture (IICA), 30, 79, 101, 111–14

Inter-American Institute of International Legal Studies, 11

Inter-American Institute of Tropical Agriculture, 111

Inter-American Juridical Committee (IAJC), 61, 62, 82, 115, 121, 122, 144, 145, 146, 153, 156, 157, 159, 160, 163, 166, 178, 179–80, 184, 187, 188, 189, 195, 222, 242, 243, 245, 248, 251, 252, 253, 257, 259, 262, 268, 277

Inter-American Meetings of Ministers of Education, 98; First Inter-American Assembly of Ministers of Education (Lima, 1956), 99

Inter-American Milestone of 1961, 96

Inter-American multilateral treaties, 161

Inter-American Music Bulletin, 93

Inter-American Neutrality Committee, 242

Inter-American Nuclear Energy Commission (IANEC), 37, 95, 114, 126–27, 160, 183, 186

Inter-American organizations, 70, 101

Inter-American Peace Committee (IAPC), 37, 45, 46, 48, 82, 114, 116, 120–23, 144, 145, 176, 183, 184, 221, 269, 270, 271, 274, 276, 277, 281, 284, 286, 290, 298

Inter-American Peace System, 268

Inter-American Policy for Cooperation on Sugar, 161

Inter-American Port and Harbor Conferences. *See* Inter-American Harbor Conferences

Inter-American principles, 53

Inter-American procedures, 34

Inter-American Program for Urban and Regional Planning (PIAPUR), 88, 89

Inter-American Program for the Training of Personnel for the Development of Indigenous Communities, 88

Inter-American Program for the Training of Post-Graduates in the Field of Applied Social Sciences (PICSA), 88

Inter-American Program of Action of Rio de Janeiro against the Illicit Use and Production of Narcotic Drugs and Psychotropic Substances and Traffic Therein, 160, 193, 194, 195

Inter-American Program of Basic Statistics, 89

Inter-American Program of Higher Learning of the Social Sciences in the Caribbean Area (PICSES), 88

Inter-American relations, 18, 27, 29, 30, 53, 64, 65, 155, 185, 300, 302
Inter-American Review of Bibliography (RIB) (OAS), 93
Inter-American Seminar on Educational Matters (Bogota, 1962), 92
Inter-American solidarity, 45, 47, 64, 145, 185, 218, 294, 295
Inter-American Special Agencies and Commission, 114–28
Inter-American Specialized Agencies and Commission, other entities, 80, 100, 102, 124, 127, 130, 146, 154, 159, 175, 182, 183–84, 207, 222
Inter-American Specialized Conference on Conservation of Natural Resources, 98
Inter-American Specialized Conference on Drug Trafficking. *See* Inter-American Specialized Conference on Trafficking in Narcotic Drugs
Inter-American Specialized Conference on Private International Law (CIDIP), Fourth, 159, 162
Inter-American Specialized Conference on Trafficking in Narcotic Drugs, 159, 193, 194, 195
Inter-American Specialized Conferences, 19, 37, 60, 68, 97–100, 153, 155, 175, 181, 182–83, 184, 207, 222, 243, 248
Inter-American specialized organizations, 37, 60, 65, 74, 97, 99, 100–102, 103, 104, 105, 106, 107, 109, 110, 111, 124, 126, 127, 130, 153, 155, 158, 159–60, 161, 175, 181, 183, 184, 243
Inter-American Statistical Congresses, 98; Third (Quitandinha, 1955), 99
Inter-American Statistical Institute (IASI), 37, 69, 89, 90, 114, 126, 127, 183, 212–13
Inter-American Statistical Systems (CICAD), 196
Inter-American System (IAS), xi, xii, 1, 2, 6, 13, 15, 16, 17, 18, 19, 20, 22, 23, 24, 25, 28, 29, 31, 32, 36, 38, 40, 42, 43, 44, 47, 48, 49, 50, 61, 64, 65, 69, 77, 78, 79, 80, 95, 97, 101, 102, 103, 104, 106, 107, 108, 110, 111, 115, 116, 117, 120, 123, 124, 125, 128, 130, 139, 142, 143, 145, 152, 154, 155, 156, 159, 163, 168, 185, 187, 199, 207, 208, 212, 216, 217, 219, 229, 234, 244, 255, 256, 257, 262, 263, 265, 271, 272, 273, 274, 275, 281, 282, 289, 290, 293, 294, 297
Inter-American System for Nature Conservation, 162, 213, 244
Inter-American Telecommunications Commission (CITEL), 157, 160, 213
Inter-American Tourist (Travel) Congress, 98, 155; Fifth (Panama, 1954), 99; Sixth

(San José/Costa Rica, 1956), 99; Seventh (Montevideo, 1958), 100; Eighth (Guadalajara/Mexico, 1962), 100
Inter-American Treaty on Good Offices and Mediation, 268
Inter-American Treaty of Reciprocal Assistance. *See* Rio Treaty
Interdepartmental Committee on Cooperation with the American Republics (United States), 111
Interdepartmental Committee of Nutrition for National Defense (ICNND) (United States), 105
Intergovernmental, ix, xi, 124, 125, 228, 241
Inter-Governmental Committee for European Migration (ICEM) (United Nations), 83
Inter-Governmental Regional Agencies of the Americas, 99
Inter-Institutional Committee of CREFAL, Eighth Regular Assembly (Mexico, 1963), 88
International Agency for Atomic Energy, 95
International Association of Schools of Social Service, 88
International Association of Students of Economics (AIESEC), 82
International Bank for Reconstruction and Development (IBRD), 129
International Bureau of the American Republics, 15, 62, 63, 71
International Center for Advanced Studies in Journalism for Latin America (CIESPAL) (Quito), 96
International Commission of Inquiry, 266
International Commission of Jurists, 242
International Committee of the Red Cross, 157
International Conference of American Jurists, 242, 268
International Conferences of American States (ICAS), ix, 15–16, 18–20, 21–23, 26–30, 36, 39–44, 50, 59, 60, 62, 63, 65, 68, 69, 71, 74, 76, 77, 97, 98, 105, 106, 124, 128, 137, 138, 143, 144, 146, 155, 167, 184, 186, 248, 251, 252, 261, 274, 296; First (1889–1890), 2, 13, 15, 63, 128, 293; Second (1902), 13, 15, 63, 64, 97, 102, 128, 266; Third (1906), 13, 16, 79, 97, 128, 242; Fourth (1910), 13, 16, 19, 71, 97; Fifth (1923), 18–19, 63, 71, 102, 105, 111, 184, 294; Sixth (1928), 16, 18, 19, 105, 107, 111, 242, 266, 271; Seventh (1933), 21, 24, 27, 109, 128, 242, 267, 271; Eighth (1938), 23, 41, 44, 106, 109, 115, 128, 187, 242, 244, 268, 272; Ninth (1948), 29–30, 31, 32, 40, 97, 98, 101, 106, 115, 121, 123, 128, 129, 187, 188,

242, 245, 248, 251, 253, 257, 268, 274;
Tenth (1954), 40–41, 43, 47, 75, 78, 98,
106, 115, 121, 129, 137, 139, 188, 189,
245, 248, 252, 257, 269, 274, 277;
Eleventh (1959), 41, 42, 116, 122, 137,
138, 142, 189, 190, 248, 259, 261; First
Special (1964), 42–43, 44, 142–43; Second
Special (1965), 43–44, 118, 119, 123, 124,
143–46, 190, 246, 248, 253, 261; Third
Special (1967), 37, 44, 57, 123, 124, 143,
144, 145, 146–47
International Conference on Central
American Refugees, 163
International Conference on Conciliation
and Arbitration. *See* Extraordinary
International American Conference on
Conciliation and Arbitration
International Congress of Americanists,
Thirty-fifth, 111
International Cooperation Administration
(ICA) (United States), 112
International Court of Justice, 268, 269, 279
International Debt, xi, 4, 14, 163, 164, 209,
212, 299
International economics, 84
International Finance Corporation (IFC)
(United Nations), 129
International Group of Labor Leaders, 87
International Health Conference (1946), 102
International Institute for Trade Unions
Studies (Geneva), 87
International Labor Organization (ILO), 81,
83, 88, 107
International law, 33, 34, 115, 172, 174,
177, 180, 204, 210, 212, 214, 241, 245,
250, 252, 263, 297, 300
International Law Commission, 17, 81, 100
International Monetary Fund (IMF), 129
International morality, 174, 297
International organizations, ix
International politics, ix
International private law, 11, 16, 19, 21, 62,
159, 242; Fourth Inter-American
Specialized Conference on Private
International Law (CIDIP), 159, 162
"International Protection of the Essential
Rights of Man," 245
International public law, 16, 21, 62, 158,
242
International recognition, 145
International Red Cross, 287
International Sanitary Bureau, 102
International Sanitary Conferences, 102
International terrorism, 166, 282, 301
International trade, 13, 15
International Union for the Education of the
Public in Questions of Health, Fifth
Conference (Philadelphia, 1962), 88

Interoceanic Route. *See* Transisthmian Canal
Intervention, xi, xii, 10, 14, 18, 20, 21, 25,
35, 36, 43, 47, 49, 56, 117, 118, 119, 123,
163, 192, 203, 204, 205, 208, 210, 214,
217, 218, 225, 250, 251, 256, 257, 258,
259, 263, 267, 271, 274, 275, 278, 286,
289, 297
Intra-continental conflict, 272
Invasion, xi
Iran-Contra affair, 173
Israel, 86, 87, 90, 207
Isthmian Canal. *See* Transisthmian Canal
Istituto Agronomico per l'Oltremare
(Florence), 90
Istituto di Studi per lo Sviluppo Economico
(Naples), 90
Itaipú (Paraguay), 232
Italy, 22, 24, 26, 86, 87, 90, 141, 207
Ius Uti Possidetis/Ita Possedeatis, 171, 204
Ivory Coast, 237

Jamaica, 1, 42, 143, 162, 170, 172, 195, 209,
230, 238, 239, 247
James, C.L.R., 236
Jane, Cecil, 256
Japan, 2, 22, 24, 27, 130, 140, 141, 163,
200, 207, 296
Jewett, David, 204
Johnson, Lyndon B., 52, 141, 286, 301
Joint Declaration (Panama–United States),
285
Joint Declaration of the Presidents of
Argentina and Brazil (1992), 230
Juan Carlos, king of Spain, 234
Junín, 6
Juridical Congress of Lima (1877–1879), 10,
11, 12, 242
Justice. *See* Social justice

Kellogg, Frank B., 34
Kellogg-Briand Pact of Paris, 34
Kellogg Foundation, 112
Kelpers, 171
Kennedy, John F., x, 20, 284, 296, 297
Kenyatta, Yomo, 236
Krause, Karl Christian Friedrich, 251, 301
Krausismo, 251, 277
Kubitschek Oliveira, Juscelino, 59, 61, 130,
139

La Contadora Island (Panama), 233
La educación (PAU), 94
La educación cooperativa en América Latina
(PAU), 86
La Estanzuela (Uruguay), 113
La estructura agropecuaria de las naciones
americanas (PAU), 89
La experiencia cooperativa como método de

desarrollo de regiones y comunidades (PAU), 86
La Lola (Costa Rica), 114
La Paz, 40, 80, 88, 99, 157, 215, 249
La peregrinación de Bayoán, 236
La situación de la vivienda: Análisis estadístico-censal de los resultados obtenidos bajo el Programa del Censo de las Américas de 1950 (PAU), 89
La televisión educativa (PAU), 94
La voz de la OEA, 96
Laborers, 115
Labor relations, 86–87
Lacalle, Luis, 163
Lake Nicaragua, 192
Lamming, George, 237
Langley, Virginia, 173
Langton, Stephen, 255
"Las Dos América," 2
Late scholasticism. *See* Sixteenth-century late scholastic philosophy
Latin America/Latin Americans, ix, x, xi, xii, 1, 2, 3, 4, 8, 11, 12, 14, 15, 16, 17, 18, 19, 20, 21, 22, 24, 25, 26, 27, 28, 30, 34, 36, 37, 40, 41, 42–43, 46, 47, 48, 53, 54, 56, 58, 59, 62, 63, 64, 65, 67, 69, 71, 72, 75, 77, 79, 81, 83, 84, 85, 86, 87, 88, 91, 92, 93, 94, 95, 96, 105, 111, 113, 118, 123, 125, 127, 128, 129, 132, 135, 136, 137, 138, 139, 140, 141, 142, 143, 144, 145, 151, 152, 155, 157, 162, 163, 164, 165, 168, 169, 172, 173, 196, 199, 200, 201, 202, 204, 205, 206, 207, 208, 209, 210, 211, 212, 213, 214, 217, 229, 230, 231, 233, 234, 235, 239, 249, 250, 251, 253, 254, 255, 256, 257, 261, 262, 263, 267, 270, 271, 275, 285, 286, 290, 293, 294, 295, 296, 297, 298, 299, 300, 301, 302
Latin American affairs, ix, 19, 20, 23, 27, 69
Latin American Association for Integration (ALADI), 3, 229–30, 297
Latin American Common Market, 57, 152, 230, 232, 233
Latin American Consensus (Viña del Mar, Chile), 4, 230
Latin American Ecological Alliance, 235
Latin American Economic Integration, xii, 4, 8, 56, 84, 129, 133, 142, 144, 151, 152, 155, 158, 163, 220, 221, 230, 231, 232, 234, 241, 294
Latin American Economic System (SELA), 4, 172, 231, 297; Extraordinary Meeting (Caracas, 1976), 231
Latin American Free Trade Association (LAFTA) (ALALC), 3, 83, 84, 85, 133, 229–30, 231, 232, 238, 239; 243; 297; Nineteenth Extraordinary Conference of ALALC (Acapulco, 1980), 3, 230

Latin American governments/states, 8, 12, 14, 37, 42, 48, 50, 77, 88, 129, 208, 209
Latin American Institute for Economic and Social Planning (ILPES), 133
Latin Americanism, 26
Latin American Iron and Steel Institute (ILAFA), 133
Latin Americanization, 71, 77, 79, 135, 267, 272, 294
Latin American ministries of labor, 87
Latin American Seminar on Housing Statistics and Housing Programs (Copenhagen, 1962), 85
Latin American Seminar on Planning (Santiago de Chile, 1962), 85
Latin American Studies Association (LASA), 209
Latin American union/unity, 3, 4, 172, 233, 234
Latin American Workshop on Narcotics Public Awareness, First (Santo Domingo, 1989), 196
Law of Nations. *See* International Law
Law of the Sea, First Conference on the Law of the Sea (Geneva, Switzerland, 1958), 100
Laws of León, 255
League Health Organization, 102
League of Nations, 17, 22, 25, 76, 223, 242, 267, 294, 298
Lebanon, 72
Lee, Ralph, 113
Legal Instrument Regarding the Definition of Cases Where the Principle of Nonintervention was Violated (1973), 214, 243
Legal series (PAU), 82
Legal Status of Asylees, Refugees, and Displaced Persons in the American Hemisphere, 244
Légitime Défense, 237
Lennox, 202
León (Nicaragua), 170
Leo S. Rowe Memorial Fund (PAU), 90
Léro, Etienne, 237
Lex Regia, 254
Libertador de Venezuela. *See* Bolivar, Simon
Liberty and Despotism in Spanish America, 256
Library of Congress (United States), 93
Liévana Aguirre, Indalecio, 2
Lima, 23, 41, 44, 80, 88, 99, 104, 106, 113, 128, 167, 187, 242, 244, 253, 269, 272
Lima Declaration in Favor of Womens' Rights, 244
Lippmann, Walter, 137
Lleras Camargo, Alberto, 43, 61, 71, 77, 78, 93, 206, 298

London, 171, 236, 237, 238
Los Angeles, California, 85
Lower California, 2
Loyola University (Chicago), 92
Luperón, Gregorio, 236

Machiavelli, Niccolò, 263
McComie, Valerie Theodore, 166, 207, 209–12, 263
Mackonnen, Otto, 236
Madeira-Mamoré Railroad (1903), 21–22, 215
Madrid, 234, 236
Magna Carta, 255
Malvinas (Falkland Islands), 2, 158, 159, 160, 161, 162, 163, 171–73, 204, 212, 215, 217, 270, 275, 289, 297
Managua, 169, 225, 232
Manchester (United Kingdom), 237
Manger, William, 71, 79, 137, 206
Manifest Destiny, 3
Manual de educación cooperativa (PAU), 86
Manual de organización y administración de empresas cooperativas (PAU), 86
Maracay, 160
"Marblehead" Talks, 191, 192
Mar del Plata (Argentina), 100
Mariana, Juan de, 263
Marín, Juan, 71
Mars, Price, 237
Martí, José, 236
Martínez de Rozas, 5
Martinique, 237, 238
Marxism, 16, 253
Marxism-Leninism, 49, 262, 281
May Revolution (Argentina), 16
Medieval political thought. See Catholic political thought (medieval)
Meeting of American Chiefs of State (Punta del Este, 1967), 56, 57, 118
Meeting of Consultation of Ministers of Foreign Affairs (MCMFA), ix, 23, 36, 39, 40, 41, 44–59, 60, 64, 65, 68, 69, 76, 97, 118, 120, 123, 124, 144, 153, 154, 164, 165, 167–75, 177, 178, 181, 182, 184, 186, 201, 207, 221, 227, 243, 259, 261, 272, 273, 274, 275, 276, 278, 279, 280, 281, 282, 286, 288, 290, 300; First (1939), 23, 128, 242, 250, 252, 267, 272; Second (1940), 23–24; 120, 251, 267, 272; Third (1942), 24, 123, 125, 128, 251, 267, 272, 273; Fourth (1951), 45, 188, 245, 257; Fifth !959), 45–46, 48, 50, 116, 122, 123, 136, 189, 244, 246, 248, 258, 259, 261, 270, 275, 277, 279, 281, 290; Sixth (1960), 46, 47, 48, 51, 52, 137, 280, 289; Seventh (1960), 46–48, 136, 137, 259, 260, 270, 275, 280; Eighth (1962), 48–51, 52, 118,

127, 167, 246, 260, 274, 275, 281; Ninth (1964), ix, 51–52, 136, 137, 168, 261, 274, 275, 282; Tenth (1965–1970), 52–56, 58, 59, 78, 286, 287, 288; Eleventh (1967), 56–57, 58, 288; Twelfth (1968), 57–58, 201, 288; Thirteenth (1969–1980), 58, 202, 288; Fourteenth (1971), 168, 202, 289; Fifteenth (1974), 168–69, 201, 289; Sixteenth (1975), 169, 201, 289; Seventeenth (1978–1979), 169–70, 203, 289; Eighteenth (1978–), 170–71, 203, 289; Nineteenth (1981), 171, 203, 289, 290; Twentieth (1982–), 171–73, 203, 289; Twenty-first (1989–), 173–75, 227, 289, 299
Meeting of Copyright Experts of the American Republics, 98
Member states. *See* American states
Memorandum on the Monroe Doctrine, 20
Memoria Sobre la Conveniencia y Objetos de un Congreso General Americano, 5
Mercado Comun Centroamericano. *See* Central American Common Market (MCCA)
MERCOSUR (Mercado Común del Cono Sur—Southern Cone Common Market), 299
Mesnil, René, 237
Mestizo, 36
Mexican, 2, 18, 107, 250
Mexican Conference (1945). *See* Inter-American Conference on Problems of War and Peace (Chapultepec Conference)
Mexican Revolution, 192
Mexican War (1846–1848). *See* United States–Mexican War
Mexico, 1, 2, 3, 4, 7, 10, 17, 20, 36, 43, 49, 50, 52, 53, 54, 63, 83, 94, 95, 100, 103, 109, 110, 111, 118, 120, 121, 123, 124, 130, 144, 157, 159, 163, 165, 166, 169, 170, 187, 188, 190, 191, 195, 205, 229, 231, 233, 234, 235, 250, 251, 252, 254, 257, 259, 269, 270, 272, 276, 278, 297, 298, 299, 300
Mexico City, 8, 15, 20, 24, 29, 45, 50, 61, 62, 63, 64, 83, 88, 93, 95, 102, 103, 107, 108, 109, 110, 111, 113, 128, 243, 244, 251, 266, 268, 294
Miami, Florida, 80, 173, 174
Middle Ages, 115
Middle East, 200
Migone, Raúl C., 81
Military Force of the Americas, 301
Military regimes, 252–54, 255, 259, 261, 262, 296
Milliard, Peter, 236
Miranda, Francisco de, 5
Misiones (Argentina), 265

Mixed Committee on Cooperation (United States–Panama), 270
Molas, Mariano Antonio, 5
Molina, Luis de, 263
Monitoring national elections, 224–27, 241, 258, 260, 262; Bolivia, 260; Costa Rica, 260; Dominican Republic, 260; El Salvador, 228; Guatemala, 227; Haiti, 226–27; Honduras, 260; Nicaragua, 225–26, 260; Panama, 227–28; Paraguay, 227; Suriname, 227
Monnerot, Jules, 237
Monroe, James, 14
Monroe Doctrine, 14, 15, 17, 18, 20, 22, 173, 204, 250, 267, 294
Monteagudo, Bernardo, 5
Montealegre, Hernán, 116
Montevideo, 3, 11, 12, 20, 21, 23, 24, 27, 40, 48, 86, 100, 104, 105, 109, 113, 128, 229, 242, 266, 267, 271, 274
Montfort, Simon de, 255
Montserrat, 238, 239
Morality. *See* International morality
Mora Otero, José Antonio, 44, 72, 78, 206, 286, 287, 298
Mora Porras, Juan Rafael, 3
Morquió, Luis, 104
Morrow, Dwight D., 20
Motoring to Mexico (PAU), 84
Muller, Lauro, 17
Multilaterialization. *See* Latin Americanization
Multilatina enterprises, 231
Munich, 23

Nairobi, 231
Naón, Rómulo S., 17
Naples (Italy), 90
Napoleon/Napoleonic, 7, 251
Nashville, Tennessee, 2
National Association for the Advancement of Colored Peoples (NAACP) (United States), 236
National Association of Foreign Student Advisors (NAFSA) (United States), 92
Nationalism, 7
National Renovation Party (Guatemala), 277
National Republican Alliance (ARENA) (El Salvador), 206, 228
National Science Foundation (United States), 95
Negritude, 236, 237
Netherlands, 7, 23, 90, 102, 141, 207, 238
Netherlands Antilles, 24, 103, 143, 235, 238
Netherlands West Indies. *See* Netherlands Antilles
Neutrality, 41

New American Treaty of Pacific Settlement, 160, 214, 244, 271, 298
New Delhi, 230
New Granada, 3, 9, 10
New Pact of Bogotá. *See* New American Treaty of Pacific Settlement
News Bulletin (IACW), 106
New Spain, 5
The New World will be a Better Place, 96
New York, 81
New Zealand, 236
Nicaragua, 1, 2, 3, 4, 9, 36, 46, 54, 82, 107, 109, 110, 112, 120, 124, 136, 143, 162, 164, 169, 170, 171, 173, 174, 191, 195, 200, 203, 206, 224–25, 226, 233, 246, 250, 253, 258, 259, 260, 266, 269, 270, 275, 276, 278, 279, 280, 289, 297, 299
Nicaraguan Civil War, 204
Nicaraguan Embassy in Panama City, 174, 175, 299
Nicaraguan Revolution, 200, 203
Nicaraguan situation, 1959, 279
Nicaraguan Supreme Electoral Council, 225
"Nine Wise Men," 62, 83, 84
Nixon, Richard Milhous, 140, 200, 295
Nobel Peace Prize, 267
Non-Aligned nations, 234
Non-American governments/states, 92, 156, 159, 224, 272
Non-Autonomous territories located on the American continent, 156, 159, 162
Non-Governmental Organizations (NGO), 196
Non-Hispanic Caribbean, 208, 209
Non-recognition of any territory by force, 273
Non-recognition of governments, 250
Nootka Sound Convention of 1790, 204
Noriega, Manuel, 173, 174, 227, 286, 289–90
North America, xii, 2, 250, 255
North American Free Trade Area (NAFTA), 163, 299
North Atlantic Treaty Organization (NATO), 29, 123, 125, 272
North Korea, 45
North Pole, 44
Norway, 90
Noticiario (IICI), 105
Noticias (IACW), 106
Nuclear Free Zone, 230
Nueva, 202
Nyassaland (today's Malawi), 236

OAS Chronicle (PAU), 96
Obligatory Consultation, 41
Observer countries, 166, 207
October Revolution, 115

O'Higgins, Bernardo, 6
Operation Just Cause, 174
Operation Pan America, 59, 70, 130, 139
Oregon, 14
Orfila, Alejandro, 207
Organization and Structure of Latin American Universities (PAU), 94
Organization for Economic Cooperation and Development (OECD), 81, 83, 296
Organization for European Economic Cooperation (OEEC), 296
Organization for the Prohibition, of Nuclear Weapons in Latin America (OPANAL), 4, 210, 230–31
Organization of American Cooperatives (Montevideo), 86
Organization of American States (OAS), ix, xi, xii, 1, 2, 3, 4, 6, 13, 26, 29, 30, 31, 32, 33, 34, 36, 37, 38, 39, 40, 41, 42, 43, 44, 46, 47, 48, 49, 50, 51, 53, 54, 55, 56, 57, 58, 59, 60, 62, 63, 64, 65, 67, 69, 70, 71, 72, 73, 74, 75, 76, 77, 78, 79, 80, 81, 83, 85, 86, 88, 89, 90, 91, 92, 93, 94, 95, 96, 97, 99, 101, 103, 104, 105, 106, 107, 110, 111, 113, 115, 117, 118, 120, 121, 122, 123, 124, 125, 126, 127, 130, 133, 135, 136, 137, 138, 139, 140, 141, 142, 143, 144, 145, 146, 147, 149, 154, 155, 156, 157, 158, 160, 161, 162, 163, 164, 165, 166, 172, 176, 177, 178, 180, 181, 182, 183, 184, 185, 186, 187, 191, 193, 195, 199, 200, 201, 202, 203, 204, 205, 206, 207, 208, 209, 210, 211, 212, 213, 214, 215, 216, 217, 218, 220, 223, 224, 225, 226, 227, 228, 229, 230, 232, 241, 245, 246, 247, 249, 252, 254, 258, 259, 261, 262, 265, 269, 270, 271, 274, 275, 277, 278, 279, 281, 282, 284, 285, 286, 287, 288, 289, 290, 293, 294, 295, 296, 297, 298, 299, 300, 301; Advisory Defense Board, 45; Advisory Defense Committee, 124, 167; Board of External Auditors, 159, 186; Order of Precedence for OAS delegations and permanent observers, 166; Printing, 187; Program budget, 166, 207; Provisional Organ of Consultation, 276; Public Information, 186; Secretariat for Special Political Affairs, 161; Secretariat of Legal Affairs, 186; Special Development Assistance Fund, 73, 92; Under Secretariat of Cooperation and Development, 213; Under Secretary of Administration and Common Services, 166; Womens' Offices, 213; Youth Office, 207. *See also* Assistant Secretary General of the OAS; Charter of the OAS; Council of the OAS; General Assembly of the OAS; General Secretariat of the OAS;

Organ of Consultation of the OAS; Organs of the OAS; Permanent Council of the OAS; Secretary General of the OAS
Organization of Central American States (ODECA), 4, 232
Organization of Latin American Solidarity (OLAS), 57
Organ of Consultation of the Organization of American States, 45, 51, 58, 167, 222, 246, 272, 273, 276, 278, 279, 280, 281, 282, 283, 285, 289, 290
Organs of the Organization of American States, 69, 99, 100, 153, 159, 160, 161, 162, 166
Ostende Manifesto, 3

Pacificador de Colombia. *See* Bolivar, Simon
Pacific Confederation, 6
Pacific Ocean, 13, 23, 44, 157, 192, 202, 204
Pacific settlement of disputes, 7, 10, 11, 15, 19, 28, 32, 33, 34, 35, 142, 143, 144, 145, 149, 158, 176, 177, 184, 185, 204, 211, 233, 241, 249, 265–71, 273, 275, 283, 298
Pacific War, 10, 21, 163, 204, 215, 266
Pact of Amity (Costa Rica–Nicaragua), 276, 278
Pact of Bogotá, 30, 31, 32, 33, 121, 135, 136, 144, 161–62, 211, 214, 242, 268, 269, 271, 272, 276, 278, 278–79, 286, 290, 295, 298
Pact of San Jose de Costa Rica. *See* American Convention on Human Rights
Pactos de Mayo (1902) (Argentina–Chile), 203
Padmore, George, 236
Palerm, Angel, 75
Pan African Congress: First (1900), 236; Last (1945), 237
Pan African Movement/Pan Africanism, 236–37
Panama, xi, 1, 2, 3, 4, 6, 7, 15, 16, 17, 20, 23, 46, 53, 60, 74, 83, 91, 106, 109, 110, 113, 124, 126, 128, 136, 139, 143, 144, 145, 159, 162, 169, 170, 173, 174, 175, 185, 192, 195, 205, 216, 224, 227, 231, 233, 250, 263, 269, 270, 271, 278, 279, 282, 284, 285, 286, 289, 290, 297, 299, 300; United States problem in, 1964, 284–86
Panama Canal, 284, 285, 297
Panama Canal Commission, 173
Panama Canal Dues, 157, 158, 159, 160, 161, 162
Panama Canal Treaties. *See* Panama Treaties on Permanent Neutrality and Functioning of the Canal
Panama Canal Zone, 185, 270, 284, 296

Panama City, 60, 99, 100, 113, 174, 175, 284, 299
Panama National Accord, 228
Panamanian Defense Forces, 173
Panamanian Revolution, 173
Panama Railroad, 3
Panama Treaties on Permanent Neutrality and Functioning of the Canal, 156, 157, 173, 174, 200, 214, 215, 270, 284, 285, 286, 296, 300
Panama Treaty (1903), 20, 284
Pan America in Crisis, 137
Pan American affairs, 64
Pan American Building (PAU palace), 18, 60, 106, 212
Pan American Child Congress, 98, 104; Second, 104; Fourth, 104; Tenth, 99; Eleventh, 100. *See also* Inter-American Childrens' Congresses
Pan American conferences. *See* International Conferences of American States
Pan American Day, 15, 80
Pan American Development Fund, 156, 159
Pan American Health Conferences: Fourteenth, 99; Fifteenth, 100
Pan American Health Organization (PAHO), 101, 102–4, 160, 183, 195
Pan American Highway, 22, 74
Pan American Highway Congresses, 155; Sixth, 99; Seventh, 99; Ninth, 100
Pan American Institute of Geography and History (PAIGH), 20, 98, 101, 107–9, 126, 160, 183, 298; Fourth General Assembly (Caracas, 1946), 107, 109; Fifth General Assembly (Mexico City, 1960), 107; Seventh General Assembly (Buenos Aires), 107
Panamericanism. *See* Pan American Movement
Pan American Movement, 1, 2, 6, 8, 13, 17, 18, 20, 21, 25, 26, 27, 28, 29, 41, 50, 65, 78, 199, 208, 212, 265, 266, 270, 286, 293, 294
Pan American Party, 96
Pan American Peace Pact (Saavedra Lamas), 17
Pan American Rhapsody, 96
Pan American Sanitary Bureau (PASB), 17, 97, 102, 103, 183
Pan American Sanitary Code of Havana, 103
Pan American Sanitary Conferences, 98, 102, 103; Fifteenth, 102
Pan American Training Center for the Evaluation of Natural Resources (CEPERN), 107
Pan American Union (PAU), ix, 1, 16, 18, 19, 24, 31, 32, 37, 50, 60, 63, 64, 67, 68, 69, 70, 71, 72, 73, 74, 75, 76, 77, 78, 79, 80, 84, 89, 90, 93, 94, 96, 104, 106, 109, 111, 114, 115, 119, 124, 125, 126, 127, 128, 138, 139, 144, 181, 183, 184, 189, 213, 268, 269, 277, 278, 283, 294; Assistant Secretary for Cultural, Scientific and Information Affairs, 68, 73, 76, 92; Assistant Secretary for Economic and Social Affairs, 68, 73, 76, 82–83, 92; Columbus Memorial Library, 93, 186; Department of Administrative Affairs, 68, 72, 75, 76, 81; Department of Cultural Affairs, 68, 71, 75, 76, 92–94; Department of Economic Affairs, 68, 75, 76, 82, 83–84, 186; Department of Economic and Social Affairs, 75, 82; Department of Education, 68, 76, 92, 94–95; Department of Information and Public Affairs, 76, 95–96; Department of International Law and Organization, 277; Department of Legal Affairs, 68, 75, 76, 79, 82, 119, 277; Department of Public Information, 68, 69, 70, 75, 76, 92, 94; Department of Scientific Affairs, 68, 95; Department of Social Affairs, 68, 75, 76, 82, 84–89, 186; Department of Statistics, 68, 75, 76, 82, 89–90, 126, 213; Department of Technical Cooperation, 68, 74, 76, 82, 88, 90–92, 108, 111, 112, 114, 162; Director/Director General, 15, 16, 63; Finance Committee, 74; Governing Board, 15, 16, 18, 62–63, 64, 65, 71, 102, 106, 111, 112, 120, 268; Office of Council and Conferences Secretariat Services, 68, 75, 76; Office of Financial Services, 68, 76; Office of Publication Services, 68, 76; Protocol Office, 75, 79, 186; Retirement and Pensions Fund, 74; Technical Unit for Latin American Economic Integration, 83
Pan American Union Bulletin (PAU), 94
Pan American Unity, 41
Pan American Week, 64, 80, 96
Papacy, 263
Papal Arbitration Award, 203
Papal Nuncio (Santo Domingo), 286
Paraguay, 1, 4, 5, 7, 10, 11, 19, 21, 22, 36, 49, 54, 85, 104, 109, 112, 113, 114, 120, 124, 163, 169, 170, 195, 200, 206, 224, 227, 229, 232, 254, 299
Paris, 81, 141, 237
Partido Revolucionario Institucional (PRI) (Mexico), 254
Patria chica, 209
Patria grande, 209
Patzcuaro (Mexico), 24, 94, 109
Peace in Central America, 158, 159, 160, 161, 162, 163, 164, 205, 233
Peace Code, 268
Peace Convention, 268

Peace Corps (United States), 92
Peaceful settlement of Controversies. *See* Pacific settlement of disputes
Peace Treaty Between El Salvador and Honduras, 157
Pearl Harbor, 24
Peninsular War, 77
Pérez Jiménez, Marcos, 259
Permanent Council of the Organization of American States (PC), 123, 146, 153, 156, 160, 161, 162, 165, 166, 167, 170, 175, 176–78, 179, 181, 182, 183, 184, 185, 186, 193, 207, 221, 222, 223, 227, 243, 246, 247, 248, 271, 272, 289, 290, 296; Committee of Program and Budget, 74, 124; General Committee, 48, 168, 169, 269, 281, 285, 289
Permanent Court of Arbitration (The Hague), 192, 266
Permanent Diplomatic Commission of Investigation and Conciliation, 267
Permanent Observer Status, 162
Permanent Tribunal at the Hague. *See* Permanent Court of Arbitration
Perón, Juan Domingo, 32
Pershing, John, 17
Peru, 1, 4, 5, 6, 7, 9, 10, 11, 36, 41, 46, 48, 49, 53, 54, 62, 83, 95, 104, 107, 109, 110, 112, 113, 120, 121, 124, 144, 164, 166, 168, 169, 170, 171, 185, 195, 196, 200, 202, 203, 205, 229, 231, 232, 233, 247, 251, 252, 253, 254, 259, 261, 269, 270, 280, 281, 289, 290, 295, 297, 299, 301, 302
Peruvian Peace Plan (Malvinas), 289
Pessoa, Epitácio, 242
Philadelphia, 88
PIAPUR, 88–89
PICSA, 88
PICSES, 88
Picton, 202
Pierce, Franklin, 3
Pinochet, Augusto, 253, 296
Planning Institute (Lima), 88, 89
Planning Seminar (Guatemala, 1962), 83
Platt Amendment, 20
Plaza Lasso, Galo, 78, 207
Poland, 23
Political freedoms, 254, 262
Political stability, 48
Polk, James K., 14
Polk Corollary, 14
Port-au-Prince, 283
Portugal/Portuguese, 8, 36, 234
Portuguese Empire/Portuguese rule, 8, 209, 254
Portuguese-speaking, 1, 96, 208, 234
Positive law, 115

Potosí, 152
Power politics, xii
Prado, Miguel, 281
Pragmatism, 249
Prébisch, Raúl, 129, 139
Preinvestment Fund for Latin American Integration (IDB), 131
Présence Africaine, 237
The Preservation and Defense of Democracy in America, 257
Prince of Peace. *See* Godoy, Manuel
Principle of Consultation, 22, 23, 267, 271, 272
Principle of Nonintervention, 21, 22, 35, 36, 41, 43, 47, 48, 49, 117, 118, 119, 145, 155, 159, 163, 165, 169, 188, 199, 207, 210, 211, 212, 216, 217, 224, 233, 249, 250, 254, 255, 256, 260, 263, 273, 275, 276, 279, 284, 286, 293, 297, 300
Principle of Solidarity, 272
Principles Regarding Relations among American States (1973), 214, 243
Private international law. *See* International private law
Procedure for Establishing a Firm and Lasting Peace in Central America, 161, 162, 205
Procedure of Consultation, 22, 267
"Programming of Studies in the International Aspect of Legal and Institutional Problems of the Economic and Social Development of Latin America," 243
Protocol of Amendments of Buenos Aires (1967), xi, 37, 44, 57, 58, 65, 67, 71, 72, 76, 79, 120, 133, 147, 149, 154, 176, 180, 183, 184, 187, 199, 209, 210, 216, 217, 218, 246, 271, 289, 296, 297
Protocol of Amendments of Cartagena de Indias (1985), xi, 160, 165, 167, 199, 208, 212, 215–24, 256, 262, 271, 289, 298
Protocol of Amendments to the Convention of the IAIAS (IICA), 113
Protocol of Progressive Arbitration, 267
Protocol Relative to Nonintervention (Buenos Aires, 1936), 277
Protocol of San Salvador, 161, 215
Protocol of Troppau, 40
Provisional Organ of Consultation, 59, 60, 64, 65, 167, 170, 257, 277, 278, 279, 281, 282, 283, 285, 289, 290
Prussia, 7
Public international law. *See* International public law
The Public Philosophy, 137
Puerto Casado, 22
Puerto Rico, 7, 103, 235, 236, 239, 300
Pueyrredón, Juan Martín de, 6

Punta del Este (Uruguay), xi, 48, 52, 56, 63, 69, 83, 246, 281
Puritanism, 8, 34, 255
Pyrrhic victories, 48

Quagliotti de Bellis, Bernardo, 202
Québec, 92
"Quetzal," 269
Quincentennial of the Discovery of America. *See* Fifth Centennial of Columbus' Discovery of America
Quintanilla, Luis, 298
Quitandinha (Brazil), 28, 99
Quitandinha Conference. *See* Inter-American Conference for the Maintenance of Continental Peace and Security
Quito, 10, 40, 41, 189
Quod Principi placet, Legis vigorum habet, 254

Reagan, Ronald, 60, 74, 75, 169, 173, 174, 200, 206, 225, 261, 285, 297, 298
Real Barreras, Eduardo, 55
Reciprocal Assistance, 6, 24, 28, 29, 42
Recognition of De Facto Regimes, 249–54, 255, 262, 263
Recopilacion de las Leyes de los Reynos de Indias (Indian Legislation), 36
Regional action, 1, 4, 28, 231
Regional Center of Fundamental Education for Latin America (CREFAL), 94, 111, 114
Regional Consultative Group for Central America, 299
Regional Fund for Economic Cooperation, 157
Regionalism, 26, 37
Regional Program of Cultural Development (PRDC), 157
Reiteration of the Principles of Nonintervention and Self-Determination, 260
Renaissance, 115
Report on Standards for Inter-American Conferences, 99
Representative democracy, xii, 30, 34, 36, 43, 45, 46, 48, 49, 55, 69, 115, 116, 117, 119, 128, 142, 144, 158, 162, 163, 164, 165, 170, 179, 193, 201, 210, 211, 212, 217, 220, 225, 227, 241, 243, 245, 246, 249, 250, 251, 253, 254–63, 273, 274, 276, 277, 294, 300, 301; First Meeting on Representative Democracy (Dominican Republic, 1962), 82, 260
Republicanism, 7
Republics, x, xi
Resolution of La Paz, 157, 215
Resolution of Maracay (Venezuela), 161, 162

Resolution of Santiago de Chile, 164, 302
Resolution on the Prevention of the Intervention of Totalitarian Powers in the Establishments of Governments, 252
Revision of the Statutes, Rules of Procedure, and Other Instruments Governing the Organs, Agencies, and Entities of the Organization, 244
Revista de Historia de America (PAIGH), 109
Revista Interamericana de Ciencias Sociales (PAU), 86
Riobamba, 10
Rio Branco, Baron de, 265
Rio Group (Argentina, Brazil, Colombia, Mexico, Peru, Uruguay, Venezuela), 299–300
Rio de Janeiro, 16, 24, 28, 31, 42, 43, 61, 62, 64–65, 77, 79, 80, 104, 108, 109, 115, 123, 128, 143, 180, 190, 193, 242, 243, 246, 248, 253, 257, 261, 268, 272, 273, 299
Rio Piedras (Puerto Rico), 88, 93
Rio Treaty, 26, 29, 31, 32, 33, 44, 48, 51, 53, 55, 59, 64, 65, 135, 136, 137, 139, 167, 169, 170, 171, 172, 199, 208, 209, 221, 245, 257, 259, 268, 269, 270, 271, 272–73, 274, 275, 276, 278, 279, 280, 281, 282, 283, 285, 286, 290, 294, 295
Rivadavia, Bernardino, 6
River Laura, 290
River Plate area, 5, 6, 7, 22, 23
River Plate Basin Agreements (Cuenca del Río de la Plata), 4, 230, 231
Rockefeller Foundation, 112, 113, 114
Rodrigues Pereira, Lafayette, 242
Rodríguez de Francia, Gaspar, 5
Rodríguez Larrata, Alberto (Rodríguez Larreta proposal), 259, 263, 300
Rodríguez Larreta, Daniel, 81, 301
Roman Empire, 6
Roman law, 254
Rome, 115
Roosevelt, Franklin Delano, 20, 22, 27, 271
Roosevelt, Theodore, 14, 191
Roosevelt Corollary, 14, 250
Rose Garden Agreement, 299
Row, Leo Stanton, 71, 73, 78, 293
Royal Commentaries (Inca Garcilaso de la Vega), 93
Rubio (Venezuela), 94
Russia, 7

Saavedra Lamas Treaty (Carlos Saavedra Lamas), 267
Saba, 238
St. Augustine, Bishop of Hippo, 255

St. Christopher and Nevis, 1, 158, 162, 166, 209, 238
St. George's (Grenada), 156
St. Isidore of Seville, 255
St. Kitts and Nevis. *See* St. Christopher and Nevis
St. Kitts-Nevis-Anguilla, 238, 239
St. Lucia, 1, 157, 166, 209, 213, 214, 238, 239
St. Maarten, 238
St. Vincent and the Grenadines, 1, 157, 209, 238, 239
Sánchez de Bustamante, Antonio, 19, 242
Sanders, William, 79, 206
Sandinistas, 169, 170, 173, 205, 206, 225, 253
Sandino, César Augusto, 169
San Francisco (California), 28, 41
San José (Costa Rica), 46, 47, 99, 111, 113, 136, 137, 155, 156, 169, 191, 207, 213, 247, 248, 249, 259, 275, 280
San Juan (Puerto Rico), 100
San Juan River (Nicaragua), 152
San Lorenzo (Paraguay), 114
San Martín, José de, 5, 6
San Salvador (El Salvador), 161, 215, 227, 243
Santander, Francisco Paula de, 6
Santiago, Congress of (1856), 9–10
Santiago de Chile, 18, 19, 40, 45, 46, 50, 63, 71, 77, 80, 90, 94, 99, 104, 105–6, 111, 116, 122, 129, 136, 146, 156, 184, 189, 214, 217, 230, 243, 244, 246, 248, 251, 254, 258, 270, 277, 279, 290, 294, 300, 301
Santo Domingo, 10, 52, 53, 55, 59, 78, 84, 99, 196, 235, 260, 286, 287
São Paulo, 61, 88, 89, 141
Saporé, Cardenal, 202
Sarmiento, Domingo Faustino, 93
Scandinavian Tradition, 254
School of Labor and Industrial Relations of the State of New York (United States), 87
"Se acata, pero no se cumple," 36
SEATO. *See* South East Asia Treaty Organization
Secretary General of the Organization of American States, 43, 44, 55, 60, 62, 69, 71, 72, 74, 75, 76–79, 80, 88, 92, 105, 106, 125, 126, 138, 141, 142, 143, 144, 146, 181, 182, 183, 186, 206, 207, 223, 224, 226, 227, 282, 286, 287, 296, 298
Security. *See* Collective security
Sédar Senghor, Léopold, 237
Self-determination, 47, 49, 155, 207, 212, 233, 258, 260
Seminar on Social Structure, Social Strata and Mobility (Rio de Janeiro), 85

Senegal, 237
September coup (Spain, 1868), 236
Serie de las Repúblicas Americanas (PAU), 96
Serrano, Jorge, 226
Settlement of conflicts, 136
Singapore, 163
Sino-Soviet Block, 47, 48, 274
Síntesis de la seguridad social (PAU), 87
Sixteenth-century late scholastic philosophy, 263
Smith, Wayne S., 204
Smoot-Hawley Tariff Act (1930) (United States), 27
Soccer War (El Salvador–Honduras), 58, 202, 232, 233, 288
Socialism, 115, 251, 253
Social justice, 48, 116, 150, 179, 219, 220, 246, 247, 257, 258, 294
Social Program Trust Fund (IDB), 130, 131
Social Standards (OAS), 152–53, 185, 210, 216, 219, 223
Sociedad Latinoamericana de Estudios Sobre América Latina y el Caribe (SOLAR), 208
Solidarity. *See* Continental solidarity
Somoza Debayle, Anastasio, Jr., 170, 250
Somoza García, Anastasio, Sr., 164, 169, 170
Somoza, Luis, 170
Somoza regime, 169, 170, 200, 203, 233, 253, 280, 289, 290
Sonora, 2
Sorbonne, 237
Soto, Domingo de, 263
South America/South American, xii, 4, 6, 9, 24, 27, 81, 116, 118, 123, 133, 163, 189, 196, 200, 201, 234, 299
South American Accord on Narcotic Drugs and Psychotropic Substances (ASEP), 95
South American Congress of Private International Law. *See* First South American Congress of Private International Law
South Atlantic, 22, 27, 171, 172, 216
South Atlantic Conflict (Malvinas/Falklands), xi, 171–73, 200, 203, 204, 209, 254
South East Asia Treaty Organization (SEATO), 29, 272
Southern Cone, 30
Southern Cone Common Market. *See* MERCOSUR
Southern Zones (IAIAS/IICA), 113
South Korea, 45, 163
South Pole, 44
Soviet Block, 47, 200, 205
Soviet Union, 25, 47, 48, 50, 51, 115, 201, 206, 274, 281
Spain/Spaniards, 2, 3, 5, 8, 26, 36, 77, 90,

171, 207, 234, 235, 251, 254, 255, 256, 270, 294
Spanish, 8, 9, 10, 96, 204, 235, 256, 297
Spanish-America, x, 2, 5, 6, 9, 10, 11, 12, 13, 256
Spanish-American countries, 7, 40
Spanish-American Congresses, 6–10, 265, 270, 271
Spanish-American Federation, 6
Spanish-American kingdoms, 5
Spanish-American Revolution, 5, 6
Spanish-American solidarity, 8, 10, 11
Spanish-American union, 2, 4, 11
Spanish-American War, 17, 26, 191
Spanish Caribbean, 235
Spanish Civil War, 22
Spanish Constitution of 1812 (Cádiz), 235
Spanish Crown, 5
Spanish Empire, 2, 5, 6, 8, 209, 254
Spanish king, 2, 5,
Spanish-Portuguese speaking nations, 234
Spanish-speaking, x, 1, 42, 208, 234, 235
Special Agencies and Commissions (OAS), 183, 184
Special Commission for Consultation and Negotiation (CECON), 156
Special Committee for an Inter-American Financial Institution (CEIFI) (OAS), 130, 139
Special Committee for Planning and Program Formulation (Buenos Aires), 83
Special Committee to Study the Formulation of New Measures of Economic Cooperation (OAS), 81, 130, 139, 140, 261
Special Consultative Committee on Security (SCCS) (OAS), 37, 82, 114–15, 127–28, 183, 269, 274
Special Consultative Committee on Security against the Subversive Actions of International Communism, 49
Special Coordinating Committee for Latin America (CECLA), 3, 230
Special Development Assistance Fund, 243
Special Fund (United Nations), 114
Specialized Conference on External Financing, 158
Specialized Inter-American Conference on the Preservation of Natural Resources: Continental Shelf and Waters (OAS), 99
Special Multilateral Fund of the Inter-American Council for Education, Science and Culture (FEMCIECC), 160
Spiritual socialism, 277
Stability. *See* Political stability
Station WRUL, 96
Stettinius, Edward, 25
Stimson, Frederic Jessup, 17

Strengthening and Effective Exercise of Democracy, 257
Strengthening of the Cultural Heritage of America as a Means of Strengthening Regional Integration, 243
Strengthening of the Inter-American System of Peace, 243
Stroessner, Alfredo, 227
Study in Latin America (PAU), 94
Suárez, Francisco, 263
Sucre, Antonio José de, 6
Sucre (Bolivia), 157
Suplemento bibliográfico (IAIAS/IICA), 114
Suriname, 1, 24, 42, 160, 163, 166, 170, 172, 209, 224, 226, 227, 238, 239
Sweden, 90
Switzerland, 90
Symposium on Representative Democracy (Dominican Republic), 82, 260

Tacubaya, 8, 9
Taft, William H., 14, 192
Taiwan, 163
Tampa, 174
Tampico, 17
Teaching Opportunities in Latin America for U.S. Citizens, 94
Technical Assembly on the Formation of Capital for Housing in the Latin American Economy (Los Angeles, California) (CINVA), 85
Tegucigalpa, 278
Tennessee, 2, 9
Tenth International Student Conference (Quebec), 92
Ten-Year War (1868–1878) (Cuba), 236
Teotecacinte–Mocorón (Honduras–Nicaragua), 270
Territorial waters, 168, 202, 243
Texas, 14
Thatcher, Margaret, 172, 203, 289
Third World, 57, 234
Thomas, Christopher R., 207
Tierra del Fuego, 299
Tierra Firme, 5
Tlaltelolco, 230
Torres Caicedo, José María, 2
Torrijos, Omar, 173
Totalitarianism, 47, 225, 257, 258, 262, 275
Transandean Railroad, 5
Transisthmian Canal, 3, 9, 192, 294
Travel in . . . Series (PAU), 84
Travels (Domingo Faustino Sarmiento), 93
Treaties for the Advancement of Peace, 265
Treaties on Literary and Artistic Copyright (1888–1889), 11
Treaties on Merchants' and Manufacturers' Trademarks (1888–1889), 11

Treaty Concerning the Permanent
Neutrality of the Canal and the Operation
of the Panama Canal. *See* Panama Treaties
on Permanent Neutrality and Functioning
of the Canal
Treaty of Chaguaramas, 239
Treaty of Lima (1848), 9
Treaty of Mutual Assistance, Union and
Confederation (1856), 9
Treaty of Perpetual Union, League, and
Confederation (1826), 6, 8–9, 265
Treaty of Tlaltelolco, 4, 230, 231
Treaty of Union and Alliance (1864), 10
Treaty of Union, League, and Perpetual
Confederation. *See* Treaty of Perpetual
Union, League, and Confederation
Treaty of Washington (1856), 10
Treaty on Compulsory Arbitration, 266
Treaty on International Civil Law (1888–
1889), 11
Treaty on International Penal Law (1888–
1889), 11
Treaty on Patents of Invention (1888–1889),
11
Treaty on Procedural Law (1888–1889), 11
Treaty on the Prevention of Controversies,
267
Treaty series (PAU), 82
Treaty to Avoid or Prevent Conflicts
Between American States (Gondra
Treaty), 19
Tribunal of Central American Arbitration,
191
Tricontinental Conference, 57
Trifinio Plan, 161
Trinidad and Tobago, 1, 42, 56, 59, 143,
157, 169, 170, 172, 174, 207, 209, 228,
230, 236, 238, 239
Tripartite Kingdom of the Netherlands, 238
Tripartite Powers, 24, 26
Triple Alliance (1865–1870), 10, 266
Tropical Research and Teaching Center for
Graduates (IAIAS/IICA), 114
Troppau, 40
Trujillo Molina, Rafael Leónidas, 46, 47, 48,
52, 137, 164, 201, 250, 259, 269, 270,
280, 286, 289, 290
Tucumán (Argentina), 277
Tuna fish embargo, 157, 158
Turkey, 72
Turrialba (Costa Rica), 30, 111, 112, 113,
114
Turrialba (IAIAS/IICA), 114

Ubico, General Jorge, 251, 277
Ulpian (Domitius Ulpianus), 254
Ungo, Guillermo, 206
Unión Antillana, 236

*Unión Latinoamericana: Pensamiento de
Bolívar para formar una Liga Americana;
su orígen y su desarrollo,* 2
Union of American Republics, 13, 16, 18,
29, 30, 31, 67, 78, 79, 102, 138, 208, 212,
251, 268, 270, 293
Union of Central America, 191
United Fruit Company, 114, 277
United Kingdom, 2, 3, 7, 9, 26, 27, 90, 102,
105, 171, 172, 204, 207, 237, 239, 255,
291
United Nations, 3, 25, 27, 28, 30, 31, 33,
35, 37, 41, 43, 45, 50, 54, 55, 57, 58, 60,
64, 69, 73, 74, 76, 77, 80, 81, 88, 89, 99,
115, 125, 138, 143, 154, 155, 157, 160,
161, 170, 171, 172, 177, 178, 179, 184,
195, 201, 208, 210, 212, 218, 223, 224,
230, 262, 272, 273, 277, 279, 281, 282,
284, 285, 294, 298
United Nations Atomic Energy Agency, 127
United Nations Charter, 28, 171, 262, 272,
273
United Nations Childrens' Fund (UNICEF),
105
United Nations Commission of Women, 106
United Nations Conference on Trade and
Development (UNCTAD), 230, 231
United Nations Educational, Scientific and
Cultural Organization (UNESCO), 83, 88,
93, 94, 105; Regional Seminar of
UNESCO for Social Research and Rural
Problems in Mexico, Central America,
and the Caribbean Area (Mexico City), 86
United Nations European Headquarters, 81
United Nations Fund for Drug Abuse
Control, 196
United Nations High Commissioner for
Refugees, 159
United Nations Special Fund. *See* Special
Fund (United Nations)
United Provinces of Central America, 232,
266
United Provinces of the River Plate, 6, 204,
266
United States, ix, xi, xii, 1, 2, 3, 4, 5, 6, 7,
8, 9, 10, 13, 14, 15, 17, 18, 19, 20, 21,
22, 23, 24, 25, 26, 27, 29, 30, 36, 40, 41,
42, 43, 44, 46, 47, 48, 49, 50, 51, 52, 53,
54, 55, 56, 57, 59, 60, 61, 62, 63, 64, 65,
69, 71, 72, 74, 75, 77, 78, 79, 85, 87, 91,
93, 95, 96, 103, 105, 106, 107, 109, 110,
111, 112, 117, 118, 120, 121, 122, 124,
125, 128, 129, 130, 131, 132, 133, 135,
136, 137, 138, 139, 140, 141, 144, 145,
146, 157, 159, 163, 168, 169, 170, 171,
172, 173, 174, 175, 185, 190, 191, 192,
193, 195, 196, 199, 200, 201, 202, 203,
204, 205, 206, 207, 208, 209, 210, 213,

214, 216, 225, 227, 228, 230, 233, 234,
236, 239, 249, 250, 251, 253, 254, 255,
256, 257, 260, 261, 263, 266, 269, 270,
275, 277, 278, 281, 284, 285, 286, 287,
288, 289, 290, 291, 293, 294, 295, 296,
297, 298, 299, 300, 301
United States Atomic Energy Commission,
112
United States Department of State, 17, 22,
40, 63
United States General System of Trade
Preferences, 157, 158, 160, 161
United States invasion of Panama, 174
United States–Latin American relations, 41,
43, 45, 46, 48, 65, 129, 135, 137, 138,
171, 172, 173, 174, 214, 293, 294, 295,
296, 297, 299, 300
United States Law of International Trade.
See United States General System of
Trade Preferences
United States–Mexican War, 3, 266
United States Senate, 192
United States Supreme Court, 300
United States Virgin Islands, 103
Universal Declaration of Human Rights,
116, 258
Universalism, 26
Universal morality, 47
Universal Negro Improvement Association
(UNIA) (United States), 236
Universal solidarity, 251
Universidad Catolica de Lima, 92
Universidad de Puerto Rico, 88, 93
Universidad Nacional de Ingenieria (Lima),
88
University of Bogotá, 87
University of Chile, 87
University of Los Angeles (UCLA), 85
University of Santo Domingo, 84
University of Tennessee, 298
University of Tucuman, 277
Upper Peru, 5
Urquia, Miguel Rafael, 207
Uruguay, xi, 1, 2, 3, 4, 10, 11, 36, 48, 49,
52, 53, 56, 69, 78, 81, 85, 91, 104, 105,
112, 113, 115, 121, 124, 143, 144, 163,
169, 170, 187, 189, 190, 195, 202, 205,
206, 229, 230, 232, 233, 246, 252, 253,
259, 269, 281, 297, 299, 300
Uti Possidetis, Ita Possideatis Ius, 204

Vandenberg, Arthur, 28
Vanderbilt, Cornelius, 3
Vatican, 174
Venezuela, 1, 2, 4, 5, 10, 36, 42, 43, 46, 49,
50–51, 53, 54, 57, 62, 94, 103, 104, 109,
110, 120, 122, 124, 130, 136, 137, 142,
157, 159, 160, 164–65, 168, 169, 170, 174,

189, 195, 205, 212, 227, 229, 230, 231,
233, 235, 247, 252, 259, 261, 269, 270,
274, 280, 282, 290, 295, 297, 299, 301,
302
Veracruz, 17
Verissimo, Erico, 71
Vernet, Luis, 171, 204
Veto right, 37, 208
Viceroyalty/viceroyalties, 5
Vienna, 127
Villa, Pancho, 17
Viña del Mar (Chile), 4, 230
Virginia, 211
Visigothic, 254
Vitoria, Francisco de, 34, 263
Voice of the OAS (*La Voz de la OEA*), 96
VW in Brazil, 231

Walker, William, 2, 3, 9
War of the Pacific. *See* Pacific War
War of the South Atlantic. *See* South
Atlantic Conflict
War of the Triple Alliance. See Triple
Alliance
Washington, D.C., 2, 15, 18, 20, 25, 26, 27,
40, 41, 42, 43, 45, 47, 51, 52, 56, 57, 58,
59, 61, 62, 67, 72, 78, 79, 86, 94, 96, 100,
102, 103, 105, 106, 112, 115, 119, 128,
130, 136, 138, 142, 154, 155, 156, 157,
158, 165, 166, 167, 168, 169, 170, 171,
172, 173, 174, 182, 188, 191, 192, 197,
201, 202, 203, 205, 214, 216, 228, 245,
257, 266, 274, 282, 285, 286, 296
Washington Conference (1907), 192
Wellington, duke of, 77
West, 57, 141, 168, 234
Western Europe. *See* Europe
Western Hemisphere, xi, 7, 13, 18, 21, 22,
24, 25, 26, 43, 45, 47, 49, 56, 69, 70, 149,
150, 151, 155, 159, 161, 162, 165, 167,
179, 180, 185, 196, 201, 207, 208, 211,
212, 213, 216, 217, 218, 223, 267, 295,
297, 299, 300
Western World. *See* West
West Indian Conference (London), 238
West Indian Constitution, 238
West Indian Federation, 4, 237–38, 239
West Indians, 236, 237
West Indies, 237
White House, 59, 63, 176
Willemstad, 238
Williams, H. Sylvester, 236
Wilson, Woodrow, 17, 25, 250
Wilsonianism, 17, 249, 250
Women, 115, 158, 159, 161, 251
World Health Organization (WHO), 81, 88,
102, 103, 105, 183

World War I, 16, 17, 18, 25, 27, 115, 128, 212, 236, 242, 255, 266, 293, 294
World War II, 20, 23, 25, 26, 27, 28, 30, 41, 44, 45, 49, 64, 73, 86, 102, 107, 112, 113, 115, 123, 127, 128, 138, 140, 211, 212, 237, 238, 242, 244, 250, 262, 267, 272, 274, 293, 294, 295; after the war, 28

Yaciretá, 232
Yale University, 84, 88
Yrigoyen, Hipólito, 17

Zamora, Rubén, 206
Zeitgeist, 164, 262, 280
Zelaya, José Santos, 191, 192
Zelaya Coronado, Jorge Luis, 207
Zionism, 236
Zone of Peace (Caribbean, 1979), 157, 215
Zonians (U.S. Canal Zone, Panama), 284

About the Author

O. CARLOS STOETZER is Professor Emeritus of History at Fordham University in New York City. From 1950 to 1961 he served as a staff member of the OAS in Washington, D.C. He is the author of several books in German and English, including *The Scholastic Roots of the Spanish American Revolution* (1979).